Grand-Ole Fishwrapper Stories

Volume II

The Best Fishwrapper Stories from 2004-2008

Printed By

LITTLE MOUNTAIN PRINTING

Home Of The Fishwrapper

First Printing, June 2012,

Printed by Little Mountain Printing, Inc.,

234 E. Rosebud Road, Myerstown, PA 17067

—ISBN 780984 817016—

Printed in the United States of America

Foreword

Over the years, readers of all ages have enjoyed The Fishwrapper. They have cried along with us when stories were heart wrenching, and laughed if they were funny. They have been challenged, encouraged, educated, and strengthened for what lies ahead on the road of life. Many have saved their copies and given them to relatives and friends. Some have helped distribute them in homes for the elderly, in hospitals, and in doctors' offices. Most of our efforts have been focused on simply bringing together what others have contributed. We are deeply humbled by the expressions of appreciation we have received over the years. Thank You! It is our utmost desire that God would receive the glory, for He alone is worthy of our thanks and our praise.

This second volume is another 5-year compilation of inspirational stories, quotes, and humor, contributed by people from many places and diverse backgrounds. Some of the stories are true happenings, others are fiction, but all have a lesson to teach. We have been blessed to be the recipients of newspaper clippings that people found when emptying their kitchen drawers. Some of these were torn, ragged, and yellowed with age. They simply put them in an envelope and forwarded them to us. Others arrived by e-mail or fax. Some were retrieved from old magazines and books that are no longer in print. Still others came from folks who wanted to share some of their creative writings or poetry. Because of the diverse, hand-me-down way we receive material, it is impossible to give individual credit to all who have contributed, without missing someone. Effort has been given to obtain permission for the use of articles and to give credit where possible. In the event we have omitted a reference or printed something without permission, we ask that you contact us so we can correct it for future printings.
The Staff of The Fishwrapper

The vision and realization for a volume set of Grand Ole Fishwrapper Stories, would never have been possible without the efforts of many people. I would like to express my appreciation to each person for the many hours that went into typesetting, editing, organizing, proofreading, and design. This book is truly a combined effort to produce a book that is filled with some witty humor along with functional wisdom in a format that is easy to read.

I was surprised again, how quickly tears could surface while reading over stories where I already knew the outcome. Or produce a burst of laughter when I already knew the punch-line. I invite you to get a cup of tea, a warm blanket, and then snuggle up by the fireplace and enjoy a relaxing time of reading. I trust you will enjoy The Fishwrapper, Volume II, as much as our staff has enjoyed putting it together. Thank You!

Merle Gingrich, editor

Table of Contents

Animals •1

Attitudes •11

Beauty •21

Business •23

Christmas •33

Church •39

Discipline •47

Faith •49

Fathers •67

Friendship •71

Giving •81

God's Word •83

Growth •93

History •109

Humor •117

Influence •233

Integrity •271

Life •277

Love • 285

Miracles • 295

Miscellaneous • 303

Mothers •321

Prayer •327

Puzzlers •335

Quotations •339

Time •353

Trivia •367

Values •381

Animals

Animal Football

One day the big animals and the little animals decided to have a football game. As the first half went along, the big animals were scoring at will. Every time they got the ball they would run it in for a touchdown.

Then came the second half…

First play: The elephant ran the ball up the middle. WAP!! Tackled for a five yard loss.

The little animals went back to the huddle cheering and congratulating each other.

"Who made that tackle?" asked the ant.

"I did," said the centipede.

Second play: The rhinoceros ran the ball up the middle. WHOMP!! Tackled for another five yard loss.

Back in the huddle the flea asked, "Who made that great stop?"

"I did," said the centipede.

Third play: The gorilla tried an end sweep, led by the hippo throwing the lead blocks. SMACK!!

The centipede tackled him for a ten yard loss.

Back in the huddle, the gnat asked the centipede, "Where were you in the first half?"

The centipede replied, "Puttin' on my shoes!"

A Rattlesnake Is A Rattlesnake

A young girl was trudging along a mountain path, trying to reach her grandmother's home. It was bitterly cold and the wind cut like a knife. When she was within sight of her destination, she heard a rustle at her feet. Looking down, she saw a snake. Before she could move, the snake spoke to her. He said, "I am about to die. It is too cold for me up here and I am freezing. There is no food in these mountains and I am starving. Please put me under your coat and take me with you."

"No," replied the girl, " I know you. You are a rattlesnake. If I pick you up, you will bite me and your bite is poisonous."

"No, no," said the snake. "If you help me, you will be my best friend. I will treat you differently."

The little girl sat down on a rock for a moment to think things over. She looked at the beautiful markings on the snake and had to admit that it was the most beautiful snake she had ever seen. Suddenly she said," I believe you. I will save you. All living things deserve to be treated with kindness." The little girl reached over, put the snake gently in her pocket and proceeded toward her grandmother's house.

But suddenly, she felt a sharp pain in her side. After only a few moments in her warm pocket, the snake had bitten her. "How could you do this to me she cried? You promised you would not bite me if I would protect you from the bitter cold."

"You knew what I was when you picked me up," the snake hissed, and slithered away.

The lesson of this story is clear. If we give in to the voice of temptation and take sin into our coat pockets, we will surely be bitten. No matter how enticing and convincing the snake's words, a rattlesnake will always remain a rattlesnake.

Barking

One morning at 2:00 A.M. a dog at the end of the block began to bark. It started a chain reaction!! Soon all the dogs on the block were barking. Only the first dog knew why he was barking. He was barking at the moon. This is similar to repeating stories or gossip. Before you bark, know why you are barking!!

Brushing The Dog's Teeth

A father found his four year old daughter outside brushing their dog's teeth using his toothbrush.

Dad asked, "What are you doing with my toothbrush?"

The daughter replied, "I'm brushing the dog's teeth. But don't worry dad, I'll rinse it out when I'm done just like I always do."

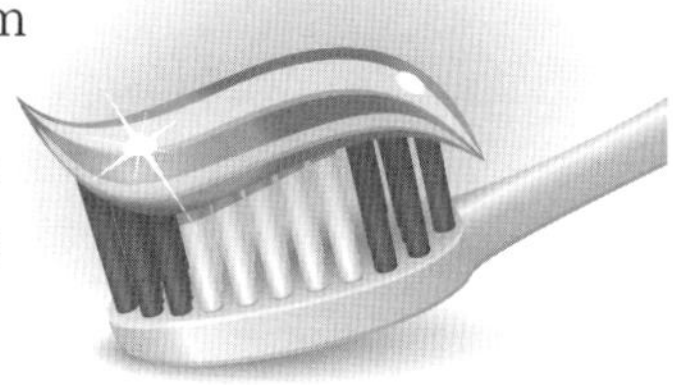

Cat Sitting

One night while I was cat-sitting my daughter's indoor feline, it escaped outside. When it failed to return the following morning, I found the beast clinging to a branch about thirty feet up in a spindly tree. Unable to lure it down, I called the fire department.

"We don't do that anymore," the woman dispatcher said. When I persisted, she was polite but firm. "The cat will come down when it gets hungry enough."

"How do you know that?" I asked.

"Have you ever seen a cat skeleton in a tree?" she said. Two hours later the cat was back, looking for breakfast.

Deer Crossing

A man in West Virginia called the local police department and asked for a favor. The desk sergeant said he might be able to help, depending on the request. The caller asked if he could take down the deer-crossing sign that was on the road in front of his house. He went on to explain that too many people hit deer on that stretch of road, and it was just not a good place to tell deer to cross the road.

Deer-Hunting

It was Saturday morning as Jake, an avid hunter, woke up raring to go bag the first deer of the season. He walked down to the kitchen to get a cup of coffee and to his surprise he found his wife, Alice, sitting there fully dressed in camouflage. Jake asked her, "What are you up to?" Alice smiled and said, "I'm going hunting with you!"

Jake, though he had many reservations about this, reluctantly decided to take her along. Three hours later they arrived at a game preserve just outside of San Marcos, Texas.

Jake set his wife safely up in the tree stand and told her, "If you see a deer, take careful aim on it and I'll come running back as soon as I hear the shot!"

Jake walked away with a smile on his face knowing that Alice couldn't bag an elephant—much less a deer. Not ten minutes passed when he was startled to hear an array of gunshots. Quickly, Jake started running back. As he got closer to her stand, he heard Alice screaming, "Get away from my deer."

Confused and frightened, Jake raced faster towards his screaming wife. And again he heard her yell, "Get away from my deer now!" followed by another volley of gunfire!

Now within sight of where he had left his wife, Jake was surprised to see a Texas cowboy, with his hands high in the air. The cowboy, obviously distraught, said, "Okay, lady! You can have your deer. Just let me get my saddle!"

Dog Bites

A man answered his doorbell, and a friend walked in followed by a very large dog. As they began talking the dog knocked over a lamp, jumped on the sofa with muddy paws, and started chewing on a pillow. The outraged man yelled at his house guest, "Can't you control your dog better?"

"My dog?" exclaimed the friend. "I thought it was your dog!"

Dog Mind Games

- After your owner gives you a bath, don't let them towel dry you! Instead, run to their bed, jump up, and dry yourself off on the sheets. This is especially good if it's right before your owner's bedtime.
- Let them teach you a brand new trick. Learn it perfectly. When they try to demonstrate it to someone else, stare blankly back at them. Pretend you have no idea what they're talking about.

- Make them be patient. When you go outside to go "Potty" sniff around the entire yard as they wait. Act as if the spot you choose to go potty will ultimately decide the fate of the earth.
- When they call you to come back in, always take your time. Walk as slowly as possible back to the door.
- Make your own rules. Don't always bring back the sticks when playing fetch. Make them go and chase it for awhile.
- Wake up twenty minutes before the alarm clock is set to go off, and make them take you outside. As soon as you get back inside, fall asleep. (Since humans can rarely fall back asleep after going outside, this will drive them nuts!)

Dogs Already Know How To Do That

I had been called to examine a ten-year-old Irish Wolfhound named Belker. The dog's owners, Ron, his wife, Lisa, and their little boy, Shane, were all very attached to Belker and they were hoping for a miracle. I examined Belker and found he was dying of cancer. I told the family there were no miracles left for Belker, and offered to perform the euthanAsia procedure for the old dog in their home. As we made arrangements, Ron and Lisa told me they thought it would be good for four-year-old Shane to observe the procedure. They felt as though Shane might learn something from the experience. The next day, I felt the familiar catch in my throat as Belker's family surrounded him. Shane seemed so calm, petting the old dog for the last time, that I wondered if he understood what was going on. Within a few minutes, Belker slipped peacefully away. The little boy seemed to accept Belker's transition without any difficulty or confusion.

We sat together for a while after Belker's death, wondering aloud about the sad fact that animal lives are shorter than human lives. Shane, who had been listening quietly, piped up, "I know why."

Startled, we all turned to him. What came out of his mouth next stunned me. I'd never heard a more comforting explanation. He said, "People are born so that they can learn how to live a good life—like loving everybody all the time and being nice, right?" The four-year-old continued, "Well, dogs already know how to do that, so they don't have to stay as long."

Dog Talk

- Can we sit on the couch? Or is it the same old story?
- Why are cars named for the eagle, the cougar, the mustang, the colt, the stingray, the rabbit, etc., but not ONE named for a dog? Would it be so hard to rename the 'Chrysler Eagle' the 'Chrysler Beagle'?
- If a dog barks his head off in the forest and no human hears him, is he still a bad dog?
- Are there dogs on other planets or are we alone?
- I have been howling at the moon and stars for a long time, but all I ever hear back is the Schnauzer across the street.
- Do I need to apologize to mailmen?
- Dogs can understand human verbal instructions, hand signals, whistles, horns, clickers, beepers, scent IDs, electromagnetic energy fields and Frisbee flight paths. What do humans understand?

Things I must remember (in order to keep my present living arrangements):

- The garbage collector is not stealing our stuff.
- I do not need to suddenly stand straight up when I'm lying under the coffee table.
- I will not roll my toys behind the fridge, behind the sofa or under the bed.
- I must shake the rainwater out of my fur before entering the house.
- I will not eat the cats' food before they eat it.
- I will stop trying to find the few remaining pieces of clean carpet in the house when I am about to get sick.
- When in the car, I will not insist on having the window rolled down when it's raining outside.
- The sofa is not a face towel; neither are Mom's nor Dad's laps.
- My head does not belong in the refrigerator.
- I will not bite the officer's hand when he reaches in for Mom's driver's license and registration.
- I will not roll around in the dirt right after getting a bath.
- The cat is not a squeaky toy; so when I play with him and he makes that noise, it's usually not a good thing.

Dog Weather

To tell the weather, go to your back door and look for the dog. If the dog is at the door and he is wet, it's probably raining. But if the dog is standing there really soaking wet, it is probably raining really hard. If the dog's fur looks like it's been rubbed the wrong way, it's probably windy. If the dog has snow on his back, it's probably snowing.

Of course, to be able to tell the weather like this, you have to leave the dog outside all the time, especially if you expect bad weather.

Sincerely,
The Cat

Donkeys, Goats, & Sheep

An African Parable

There was a mountainous region through which wound a very narrow and dangerous path. There was not room for passing on this trail and when two people met it created quite a problem.

One day two donkeys met on this path. They looked at one another and then began a conversation that went something like this:

"Listen," said the first one, "I'm going to the place you've just left so get out of the way and let me pass."

"Not on your life," said the second donkey. "You get out of my way or I'll knock you flat!"

Soon their argument turned into a fight, with the result that both fell over the cliff and died.

Another day two goats met at the same spot. They too looked at one another, surveyed the possibilities of passing, then sat down to think it over.

"Say, I've got an idea," said one goat to the other.

"Yes? What is it?" asked the second goat.

"Let's just turn around and go back where we came from. That way we won't fight and end up in trouble."

And that is just what they did.

Still another day two sheep met. They exchanged looks and greetings and then they too sat down to figure a way out of their predicament.

"I have it," said one finally.

"Oh, what?" asked the other.

"I'll lie down on the path. Then you step up on me and pass over. Then I'll get up and we can both be on our way again."

This pleased the sheep very much, and that is the way they passed on that narrow path.

Now, I ask you, which of the three groups was the smartest?

How often we as Christians fail to get the blessing God has for us because we are like the donkeys. Or like goats—just plain indifferent and unwilling even to try. Many difficulties could be turned into rich blessing if one of us were willing to lie down and let the other tramp on him.

—Rev. Gerald E. McGarvey

Fascinating Feline Facts

1. Egyptians worshipped cats as gods and shaved their eyebrows as a sign of mourning when their cats died. In ancient Egypt, killing a cat was punishable by death.

2. Cats have been domesticated for only half as long as dogs.
3. Cats are the only animals that purr. They purr at about 26 cycles per second, the same frequency as an idling diesel engine.
4. Cat nose pads are unique like fingerprints.
5. Cat hearts beat twice as fast as human hearts...110 to 140 beats per minute.
6. The domestic cat is the only type of cat that can hold its tail upright when walking. Wild cats tuck their tails between their legs or hold them horizontally when walking.
7. Cats' ears pivot 180 degrees and contain 30 muscles. It takes a minimum of 12 muscles to control a cat's ear movement.
8. Cats have some of the sharpest hearing in the animal kingdom.
9. A falling cat takes 1.8 seconds to right itself and land on its feet. First it rotates its head. Second it twists its spine. Third, it aligns its rear legs and finally, it arches its back to lessen the impact of landing.
10. A cat walks by moving both left feet then both right feet. This promotes speed, agility and silence. The only other animals that walk this way are giraffes and camels.
11. Cats can see up to 120 feet away. Their peripheral vision is about 185 degrees.
12. In relation to their body size, cats have the largest eyes of any mammal. Their eyes come in three shapes: round, slanted, and almond.
13. A cat born with one blue eye is usually deaf in the ear closest to the blue eye.

14. Cats have three eyelids. The third eyelid is called the "haw" or nictating membrane. It's the tiny triable of pink tissue that you see in the corner of a cat's eye.
15. If a cat becomes so fat that its sides stick out farther than its whiskers, it will lose its sense of perception and stability.
16. An average cat's meal is equivalent to five mice.
17. In cats and humans, the same region of the brain is responsible for emotion.
18. A cat can't see directly under its nose—that's why they have trouble finding treats on the floor.
19. A cat can jump five to seven times its height.
20. A domestic cat can run up to 30 mph.
21. Cats do not have a true collarbone—that's why they can squeeze into any opening big enough for their head.
22. Cats walk on their toes.
23. The life expectancy for a neutered, well-cared for, indoor male cat is 15-17 years; for a female it's 17-19 years. For an outdoor cat it's three to five years.
24. There are 600 million domestic cats in the world.
25. Ailurophilia is the love of cats. It comes from the Greek and means "tail wavers."
26. Ailurophobia is the fear or hatred of cats.
27. Cats almost never meow at another cat. They use this sound to communicate with humans.
28. More than 35,000 kittens are born in the United States each year.
29. Cats sleep an average of 16 hours a day. That means a seven year old cat has been asleep for five years of its life!
30. Americans spend $4 billion a year on cat food. They spend $3 billion a year on baby food.
31. There is about one cat for every four people in the U.S.
32. In 1987, cats reached the number one spot in popularity, replacing dogs as America's favorite pet.
33. Cats spend about 30% of their time grooming and don't ordinarily need to be bathed.
34. Cat bites are more likely to become infected than dog bites—but human bites are the most dangerous of all, containing much more bacteria.
35. A group of kittens is called a kindle. A group of grown cats is called a clowder.

Fear Of Flying

I was flying from San Francisco to Los Angeles. By the time we took off, there had been a 45-minute delay and everybody on board was upset.

Unexpectedly, we stopped in Sacramento on the way. The flight attendant explained that there would be another 45-minute delay, and if we wanted to get off the aircraft, we would reboard in 30 minutes.

Everybody got off the plane except one gentleman who was blind. I noticed him as I walked by and could tell he had flown before because his Seeing Eye dog lay quietly underneath the seats in front of him throughout the entire flight. I could also tell he had flown this very flight before because the pilot approached him and, calling him by name, said, "Keith, we're in Sacramento for almost an hour. Would you like to get off and stretch your legs?"

Keith replied, "No thanks, but maybe my dog would like to stretch his legs."

Alas, all the people in the gate area came to a completely quiet standstill when they looked up and saw the pilot walk off the plane with the Seeing Eye dog! The pilot was even wearing sunglasses. People scattered. They not only tried to change planes, they were also trying to change airlines!

Fitness Program

You've seen those ads promising amazing results from all sorts of contraptions. Well, there's no need to invest in fancy equipment. If you have (or can borrow) a dog, you have everything you need to get in shape now!!!

The following exercises can be done anywhere, anytime.

- Upper Body Strength: Lift the dog—off the couch, off the bed, out of the flower bed. Repeat, repeat, repeat. As the dog ages, this exercise is reversed—onto the couch, onto the bed, into the car, and so on.
- Balance and Coordination, Exercise 1: Remove your puppy from unsuitable tight places. If they're too small for him, they're certainly too small for you. Do it anyway!
- Balance and Coordination, Exercise 2: Practice not falling when your dog bounds across the full length of the room, sails through the air, and slams both front paws into the back of your knees.
- Balance and Coordination, Exercise 3: (for use with multiple dogs) Remove all dogs from lap and answer the phone before it stops ringing.
- Balance and Coordination, Exercise 4: (alternate) For older dogs, I attempt to cross a room without tripping

over the dog. Get off your couch without crushing any part of a sleeping elderly dog.

- Upper Arms: Throw the ball. Throw the squeaky toy. Throw the Frisbee. Repeat until nauseous.
- Upper Arms: (alternate) Tug the rope. Tug the pull toy. Tug the sock. Repeat until your shoulder is dislocated or the dog gives up (we all know which comes first).
- Hand Coordination: Remove foreign object from dog's locked jaw. This exercise is especially popular with puppy owners. Repeat. Repeat. Repeat. Remember, this is a timed exercise. Movements must be quick and precise to prevent trips to the vet.
- Calves: After the dog has worn out the rest of your body, hang a circular toy on your ankle and let the dog tug while you tug back. WARNING: This is feasible only for those with strong bones and small dogs. Have you taken your calcium supplement today?
- Calves: (alternate) Run after dog—pick any reason, there are plenty. Dogs of any size can be used for this exercise. Greyhounds are inadvisable.
- Neck Muscles: Attempt to outmaneuver the canine tongue headed for your ear, mouth, or eyeball. This is a lifelong fitness program. A dog is never too old or too feeble to kiss you when you least expect it.

Grin And Bear It

It is the first day of bear season in Pennsylvania and hunters of all shapes and sizes take to the woods in anticipation of taking a prized trophy. Visions aplenty kept you awake past midnight but here it is "bearly" 3 a.m. and you are ready to go. Some of them huff and puff and "bearly" make it to the top of the ridge. (Before being too critical, remember it's been a whole year since they were last here.)

As the first rays of dawn begin to light the horizon you can sense the excitement. Suddenly, a few shots ring out just over the ridge. Immediately you are on high alert for a black ball of fur. The leaves rustle and sure enough the opportunity of a lifetime is yours. In almost no time you empty the gun and in disbelief you watch the bear disappear into the brush. "Bearly" able to get down off of your stand because of the violent shaking that has now set in, you begin to search for some sign of a hit even though you already know the un"bear"able truth.

Now you face the task of relating the events in a way that others will hopefully understand. It happened so fast you "bearly" had time to think, and it was pretty thick brush and the scope was fogged, and you had bumped it slightly when you slipped that morning. You quickly realize it would have been easier if you had not seen a bear at all than to put up with the ribbing of your hunting buddies.

As you retire for the night the visions of a trophy hunt are all gone. All you can think of is the almost that wasn't. You are so tired you can "bearly" stay awake another minute. In the final moments before you enter into a night's hibernation you recall seeing the sign that said, "bear left", on your way into camp. You wondered what it meant and now you know.

The sign theory is really a cop out for those who don't hunt. For those who do hunt don't give up so easily. I suggest you get some exercise and take your gun for a walk. Not every hunt ends in success, but hopefully enough of them do to make it worth your while. There is no need for excuses. It's all a part of hunting. There is a lot of room out around those animals and a lot of obstacles in between them and you. As for the ribbing when you miss, you might as well just grin and bear it!

—M. Gingrich

Helpful Honks

Each fall we are visited by flocks of migrating geese that stop off at a meadow near our home. For several weeks those birds fly in long, wavy V-formations over our house, honking as they go. But then, as winter approaches, they are off again on their long flight south.

A student of mine increased my appreciation for these visitors from the north. He told me that geese fly at speeds of 40 to 50 miles per hour. They travel in formation because as each bird flaps its wings an updraft is created for the bird behind it. They can go 70 percent farther in a group than they could if they flew alone.

Followers of Christ are like that, in a way. As we work together to move toward a common goal, we strengthen and help one another (Acts 18:23-27). We can accomplish more together than we can alone.

Geese also honk at one another. They are not critics but encouragers. Those in the rear sound off to exhort those up front to stay on course and maintain their speed.

We too can make greater progress if there is someone behind us encouraging us to stay on track and keep going. Is someone flying in formation with you today to whom you might give some "helpful honks"?

How To Photograph A New Puppy

1. Remove film from box and load camera.
2. Remove film box from puppy's mouth and throw in trash.
3. Remove puppy from trash and brush coffee grounds from muzzle.
4. Choose a suitable background for photo.
5. Mount camera on tripod and focus on puppy and take dirty sock from mouth.
6. Place puppy in prefocused spot and return to camera.
7. Forget about spot and crawl after puppy on knees.
8. Focus with one hand and fend off puppy with other hand.
9. Get tissue and clean nose print from lens.
10. Put cat outside and put peroxide on the scratch on puppy's nose.
11. Put magazines back on coffee table.
12. Try to get puppy's attention by squeaking toy over your head.
13. Replace your glasses and check camera for damage.
14. Jump up in time to grab puppy by scruff of neck and say, "No, outside! No, outside!"
15. Clean up mess.
16. Sit back in chair with lemonade and resolve to teach puppy "sit" and "stay" the first thing in the morning.

How To Prepare For A New Cat

1. Take cold chicken and stars soup straight from the can and splash it across the carpet and the foot of the bed and then walk in it in the dark with your socks on.
2. Set up a mouse trap at the foot of the bed each night so that if you move a toe one inch while you are sleeping, you are sure to get snapped.
3. Cover all your best suits with cat hair. Dark suits must use white hair, and light suits must use dark hair. Also, float some hair in your first cup of coffee in the morning.
4. Put everything cat-toy sized into a water bowl to marinate.
5. Practice cutting your chicken into teeny tiny bites so that when they steal, it won't be the whole breast.
6. Tip over a basket of clean laundry, and scatter clothing all over the floor.
7. Leave your clothing on the living room floor, because that's where the cat will drag it anyway (especially when you have company).
8. Gouge the surface of the dining room table several times with an exacto knife. It's going to get scratched anyway.
9. Practice searching every closet and open cabinet door before you shut it.
10. Knock all small items off your kitchen counter.
11. Chew the eraser off every pencil in the house.
12. Take a fork and shred the roll of toilet paper while it's still hanging up. Pull a few sheets off and scatter them around the bathroom.
13. Take a staple remover and punch two holes in every scrap of paper around the house.
14. Get a litter tray without a lid and fill it with cat litter and then tip it over right before the company comes. Make sure your guests get to find this before you do.
15. Buy a mixed bag of cat toys and stuff them under the refrigerator. Practice getting up at 2:00 am and fishing them out with a ruler or broom stick.
16. Take a warm cuddly blanket out of the dryer and immediately wrap it around yourself. This is the feeling you will get when your new cat falls asleep on your lap.

There now, once you've done all these, you've passed the test, and are ready to take on that little furry critter!

How Wise The Eagle

Do you know how an eagle knows when the storm is approaching long before it breaks? The eagle will fly to some high spot and wait for the winds to come.

When the storm hits, it sets its wings so that the wind will pick it up and lift it high above the storm.

While the storm rages below, the eagle is soaring high above it, gliding with ease.

The eagle does not escape the storm, it just simply uses the storm to lift it higher. It rises on the winds that bring the storm into the world.

When the storms of life come upon us, and all of us will experience them, we can rise above them by setting our minds and hearts toward God! The storms do not have to overcome us.

We can allow God to lift us above them. God enables us to ride the winds of the storm that bring sickness, pain, tragedy, failure, hurts, and disappointments in our lives, and make something good come from it. We can soar above the storm. Remember, it is not the burdens of life which weigh us down, but it is how we handle them that counts, and Jesus is always there to help us handle them.

—*Unknown*

Investigation

A woman had a beautiful black cat with white feet, named Socks. Socks spent his days outside and came indoors only at night. One cool October evening, he disappeared.

She searched for him high and low, for several days, but all in vain. The following spring, however, Socks reappeared, looking healthy and clean.

Everything was back to normal until that autumn, when Socks once again disappeared. The next spring, just as the prior year, he returned. When it happened for the third year in a row, she became very perplexed, and decided to investigate. She started by asking her neighbors to see what, if any, information they might have.

She was down to the last house on the block, the home of an older couple. If they didn't have the answer, she wasn't sure where she would turn. So she went up and knocked on the door. The lady of the house answered, and she asked her, "By any chance, have you ever seen a black cat with four white feet around here?"

"A black cat?" the woman said. "With four white feet? Oh my, yes! He's the sweetest thing. My husband and I kept seeing him outside every fall. We hated it that the poor thing had to be out in the cold, so we decided that when we go south for the winter, we'd take him with us. He's been going to Florida with us every winter for the last few years."

No Pets Allowed

There's a guy with a Doberman Pinscher and a guy with a Chihuahua. The guy with the Doberman Pinscher says to the guy with a Chihuahua, 'Let's go over to that restaurant and get something to eat.'

The guy with the Chihuahua says, 'We can't go in there. We've got dogs with us.'

The guy with the Doberman Pinscher says, 'Just follow my lead.'

They walk over to the restaurant, and the guy with the Doberman Pinscher puts on a pair of dark glasses, and he starts to walk in.

A guy at the door says, 'Sorry, Mac, no pets allowed.'

The guy with the Doberman Pinscher says, 'You don't understand. This is my seeing-eye dog.'

The guy at the door says, 'A Doberman Pinscher?'

He says, 'Yes, they're using them now, they're very good.'

The guy at the door says, 'Come on in.'

The guy with the Chihuahua figures, 'Why not,' so he puts on a pair of dark glasses and starts to walk in.

The guy at the door says, 'Sorry, pal, no pets allowed.

The guy with the Chihuahua says, 'You don't understand. This is my seeing-eye dog.'

The guy at the door says, 'A Chihuahua?'

The guy with the Chihuahua says, 'You mean they gave me a Chihuahua?"

Not All Heroes Are People

James Crane worked on the 101st floor of Tower One of the World Trade Center. He is blind so he has a golden retriever named Daisy. After the plane hit 20 stories below, James knew that he was doomed, so he let Daisy go, out of an act of love. She darted away into the darkened hallway. Choking on the fumes of the jet fuel and the smoke James was just waiting to die. About 30 minutes later, Daisy came back along with James' boss, who Daisy just happened to pick up on floor 112.

On her first run of the building, she led James, James' boss, and about 300 more people out of the doomed building. But she wasn't through yet, as she knew there were others who were trapped. So, against James' wishes she ran back into the building.

On her second run, she saved 392 lives. Again, she went back in. During this run, the building collapsed.

James heard about this and fell on his knees in tears.

Against all known odds, Daisy made it out alive, but this time she was carried by a firefighter. "She led us right to the people before she got injured," the fireman explained.

Her final run saved another 273 lives. She suffered acute smoke inhalation, severe burns on all four paws, and a broken leg, but she saved 967 lives. The next week, Mayor Guiliani rewarded Daisy with the Canine Medal of Honor of New York. Daisy is the first civilian Canine to win such an honor.

Pet Gift

In an upscale pet-supply store, a customer wanted to buy a red sweater for her dog. The clerk suggested that she bring in her dog for a proper fit.

"I can't do that!" the lady said. "The sweater is a surprise!"

Rattlesnakes

Felix, my husband, was playing golf with our town's fire chief when he hit a ball into the rough. As Felix headed for the brush to find his ball, the chief warned him, "Be careful, the rattlesnakes are out."

The chief explained that calls had been coming in all week requesting assistance with removing the snakes.

"You've got to be kidding," Felix replied in astonishment. "People actually call the fire department to help them with rattlesnakes? What do you say to them?"

"Well," said the chief, "the first thing I ask is, 'Is it on fire?'"

The Cat's New Year Resolutions

- My masters will never let me eat their pet hamster, and I am at peace with that.
- I will not slurp fish food from the aquarium surface.
- I will not eat large numbers of assorted bugs, then come home and throw them up so that people can see that I'm getting plenty of roughage.
- I will not lean way over to drink out of the tub, fall in, and then pelt right for the box of clumping cat litter. (It took forever to get the stuff out of my fur).
- I will not use the bathtub to store live mice for late-night snacks.
- I cannot leap through closed windows to catch birds outside. If I forget this and bonk my head on the window and fall behind the couch in my attempt, I will not get up and do the same thing again.
- I will not assume the patio door is open when I race outside to chase leaves.
- I will not stick my paw into any container to see if there is something in it. If I do, I will not hiss and scratch when my master has to shave me to get the rubber cement out of my fur.
- I will not bite the cactus because it will bite back.
- When it rains, it will be raining on all sides of the house. It is not necessary to check every door.
- I will not play "Dead cat on the stairs" while people are trying to bring in groceries or laundry, or else one of these days, it will really come true.
- When the people play darts, I will not leap into the air and attempt to catch them.
- I will not swat at people's head repeatedly when they are on the family room floor trying to do sit ups.
- When people are typing at the computer, I will not try to use their forearms as a hammock.
- I will not drag dirty socks onto the bed at night and then yell at the top of my lungs so that my master can admire my "kill."
- I will not perch on my people's chest in the middle of the night and stare until they wake up.
- If I must give a present to my human guests, my toy mouse is much more socially acceptable than a big live bug, even if it isn't as tasty.

The Trapper And His Dog

Peter Dobley was a young trapper who lived alone in the wilderness away out back of beyond. He lived alone, that is, except for Prince, his huge sled dog, an animal more wolf than malamute. Each fall Pete and his intelligent, grey coated companion came out of the bush for their winter supplies, then vanished again; each spring they reappeared with their season's catch of furs.

Prince was truly a silent partner for he shared every hardship, every danger of his master. As long as the object of his devotion was nearby it mattered not to the big wolf dog whether they slept under the cold stars or in the snug comfort of their cabin; in his yellow eyes smoldered an amber glow of adoration. It burned as steadily as an altar light and only when danger threatened his idol did the wolf in him reveal itself; then he bristled savagely and bared his fangs and into his eyes came the glare of the killer.

Some dogs can take room in their affections for only one person but Prince's heart was as big as his frame—big enough to include Margaret, when Pete married her. The next spring when small Peter arrived and there were three to watch over instead of two, Prince took the job and shared the happiness that radiated from the cabin.

But the North Woods was about to witness a tragedy. Margaret didn't regain her strength, and the first snows of autumn fell upon a fresh mound beneath the pines where a heartbroken man and a huge grey wolf dog kept silent vigil.

Somehow Pete made Prince understand that the dog could no longer help tend the trap lines and share the excitement of the outdoors. One partner must stay at home to guard the baby while the other made the rounds and brought in food.

Thereafter from the window Prince would watch Pete disappear into the woods then with a mighty sigh he would lie down near little Peter. When the child awoke or whimpered there was always soft fur for him to burrow into and the quick caress of a warm tongue to comfort him.

One day a blizzard struck while Pete was far from home. In no time the forest was hidden in a milk-white smother. Compass in hand he set out for home. It was slow going, and night overtook him. However, Prince would surely keep the child warm, he reflected.

The gale stopped as dawn came and soon after he staggered into the clearing. He whistled. Always that signal had brought Prince to the window in hysterical antics of welcome, but this time there was neither sight nor sound of the dog. Pete's heart grew cold: shouting hoarsely he broke into a run and flung himself against the door which, he saw now, stood half open.

The baby's crib was empty. The blankets were red with blood and there were great smears of blood on the floor. As the father stood rooted in horror, Prince crept from under the bed; his muzzle, too, was red and the fur of his neck was matted. He did not look at the man or try to approach him, but lay there, silent, head down, eyes averted.

In a flash Pete understood. Once wolf, always wolf! Hunger had aroused the primitive instinct of his kind. With a cry the man raised his axe, ready to strike with all his strength, when suddenly there came a whimper from somewhere back of Prince. The father stooped and with trembling hands drew the baby from beneath the bed. Peter's clothing was torn and bloodstained but he was unhurt. In a daze the father stared around the cabin, and for the first time he saw in a dark corner the carcass of a gaunt timber wolf. In its teeth was still clenched a piece of Prince's bloody fur.

Watch Dogs

A girl was visiting her friend who had acquired two new dogs, and asked her what their names were. Her friend responded by saying that one was named Rolex and the other named Timex. Her friend said, "Whoever heard of someone naming dogs like that?" "Oh," she said, "they're watchdogs!"

Attitudes

Are You Ever?

One evening I was driving my eight-year-old daughter to her grandparent's home for an overnight stay. It was late, there was very little traffic, and we were enjoying a peaceful ride. It was a far cry from the usual chaos surrounding us when I drive her to various activities during rush hour.

My daughter seemed deep in thought when she said, "I have a question."

"What do you want to know?" I responded.

"Mom, when you're driving," she asked, "are YOU ever the idiot?"

Be Thankful

Every day be thankful for what you have and who you are.

Even though I clutch my blanket and growl when the alarm rings, thank you, Lord, that I can hear. There are many who are deaf.

Even though I keep my eyes closed against the morning light as long as possible, thank you, Lord, that I can see. Many are blind.

Even though I huddle in my bed and put off rising, thank you, Lord, that I have the strength to rise. There are many who are bedridden.

Even though the first hour of my day is hectic, when socks are lost, toast is burned, tempers are short, and my children are so loud, thank you, Lord, for my family. There are many who are lonely.

Even though our breakfast table never looks like the picture in magazines and the menu is at times unbalanced, thank you, Lord, for the food we have. There are many who are hungry. Even though the routine of my job often is monotonous, thank you, Lord, for the opportunity to work. There are many who have no job.

Even though I grumble and bemoan my fate from day to day and wish my circumstances were different, thank you, Lord, for life.

Be Thankful For Work

Thank God every morning when you get up that you have something to do which must be done, whether you like it or not. Being forced to work, and forced to do your best, will breed in you temperance and self-control, diligence and strength of will, cheerfulness and contentment, and a hundred virtues which the idle never know.

—Charles Kingsley

Bodies

Somebody, Everybody, Anybody, and Nobody were neighbors. Odd people, they were hard to understand. The way some of them lived was a shame, and Everybody knew it. For example, Somebody was gossiping about his neighbors, and Everybody knew it was wrong. Anybody might have refused to listen, but Nobody did. Anybody knew that Everybody was talking about Somebody.

All four belonged to the same Church. Anybody wanted to worship, but wouldn't go to Church because he wasn't speaking to Somebody. Nobody was faithful to Church. Nobody tithed. Nobody sang is the choir. Nobody did visitation. Nobody would do work in the Church. When they needed a Sunday School teacher, Everybody thought that Anybody would do, and Somebody thought Everybody could do it better than he. Guess who was the one who finally did it? Nobody.

A fifth neighbor (an unbeliever) moved into the neighborhood. Everybody thought Somebody will visit him. Anybody could have made the effort, but didn't. Do you know who finally won him to the Lord? Nobody!

—Selected

Burden to Blessing

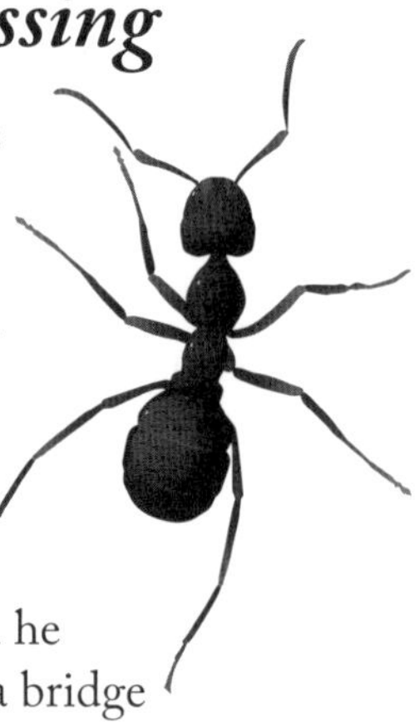

A small ant was carrying a piece of straw twice his weight. As he was traveling toward his home, he became discouraged with carrying it. He was ready to give up.

Then he came to a crack in the sidewalk. He thought, "The straw is too heavy and there's a crack in the sidewalk. I can't get across." Then he thought, "Why not use the straw as a bridge to cross the crack?"

This he did, walking to the other side. His burden became a blessing. Often our burdens, troubles, trials, and sickness may be a blessing in disguise.

Dealing With "Sandpaper" People

Sandpaper is a wonderful substance for working with wood. It removes all the rough spots, making wood as smooth as glass and just as nice to touch. But sandpaper is not nice if it is woven into the fabric of a person's personality.

"Sandpaper" people are those who rub us the wrong way. It could be anything from the way they wear their hair to the way they talk. Most of us can probably identify at least one person like this who taxes our patience and Christian spirit.

Perhaps it would help if we try to take a different view of these people. We should pray for such people and ask God to love them through us. This will help us to be more tolerant and forgiving in our attitude.

Counting Your Blessings

If you woke up this morning with more health than illness, You are more blessed than the million that won't survive the week.

If you have never experienced the danger of battle, the loneliness of imprisonment, the agony of torture, or the pangs of starvation, You are ahead of twenty million people around the world.

If you attend a church meeting without the fear of harassment, arrest, torture, or death, You are more blessed than almost three billion people in the world.

If you have food in the refrigerator, clothes on your back, a roof over your head, and a place to sleep, You are richer than 75% of the entire world.

If you have money in the bank, in your wallet, or spare change in a jar, You are among the top 8% of the world's wealthy.

If your parents are both alive and still married, You are very rare, especially in the United States.

If you hold up your head and smile, and are truly thankful, You are blessed because the majority can, but most do not.

If you can hold someone's hand, hug them, or even touch them on the shoulder, You are blessed because you can offer them God's healing touch.

If you can read this message, You are more blessed than two billion people who cannot read anything at all.

You are so blessed in so many ways you may never know. Praise God for all your gifts and feel the blessings.

Donkey Story

One day a farmer's donkey fell down into a well. The animal cried piteously for hours as the farmer tried to figure out what to do. Finally, he decided the animal was old and the well needed to be covered up anyway; it just wasn't worth it to retrieve the donkey.

He invited all his neighbors to come over and help him. They all grabbed a shovel and began to shovel dirt into the well. At first,the donkey realized what was happening and cried horribly. Then, to everyone's amazement, he quieted down. A few shovel loads later, the farmer finally looked down the well and was astonished at what he saw. With every shovel of dirt that hit his back, the donkey was doing something amazing. He would shake it off and take a step up. As the farmer's neighbors continued to shovel dirt on top of the animal, he would shake it off and take a step up. Pretty soon, everyone was amazed as the donkey stepped up over the edge of the well and trotted off!

Life is going to shovel dirt on you—all kinds of dirt. The trick to getting out of the well is to shake it off and take a step up. Each of our troubles is a stepping-stone. We can get out of the deepest wells just by not stopping, never giving up! Shake it off and take a step up.

Don't Be Disappointed

Whenever I'm disappointed with my spot in life, I stop and think about little Jamie Scott. Jamie was trying out for a part in a school play.

His mother told me that he'd set his heart on being in it, though she feared he would not be chosen.

On the day the parts were awarded, I went with her to collect him after school.

Jamie rushed up to her, eyes shining with excitement. "Guess what mom," he shouted, and then said those words that will remain a lesson to me: "I've been chosen to clap and cheer."

—Contributed by John M. Drescher

Guilt Trip

I had not really planned on taking a trip this time of year, and yet I found myself packing rather hurriedly. This trip was going to be unpleasant, and I knew in advance that no real good would come of it. I'm talking about my annual "Guilt Trip."

I got tickets to fly there on "Wish I Had" airlines. It was an extremely short flight. I got my not check baggage, which I could not check. I chose to carry it myself all the way. It was weighted down with a thousand memories of what might have been. No one greeted me as I entered the terminal to the "Regret City International Airport." I say international because people from all over the world come to this dismal town.

As I checked into the "Last Resort Hotel", I noticed that they would be hosting the year's most important event, the "Annual Pity Party". I wasn't going to miss that great social occasion. Many of the town's leading citizens would be there. First, there would be the "Done family," you know, "Should Have,Would Have and Could Have". Then came the "I Had family". You probably know of "Wish Man" and his clan. Of course, the "Opportunities" would be present, "Missed and Lost". The biggest family would be the "Yesterday's". There are far too many of them to count, but each one would have a very sad story to share. Then "Shattered Dreams" would surely make an appearance. And "It's Their Fault" would regale us with stories (excuses) about how things had failed in his life, and each story would be loudly applauded by "Don't Blame Me" and "I Couldn't Help It".

Well, to make a long story short, I went to this depressing party knowing that there would be no real benefit in doing so, and, as usual became very depressed. But as I thought about all of the stories of failures brought back from the past, it occurred to me that all of this trip and subsequent "pity party" could be cancelled by ME! I started to truly realize that I did not have to be there. I didn't have to be depressed. One thing kept going through my mind, I CAN'T CHANGE YESTERDAY, BUT I DO HAVE THE POWER TO MAKE TODAY A WONDERFUL DAY. I can be happy, joyous, fulfilled, encouraged, as well as encouraging.

Knowing this, I left the "City of Regret" immediately and left no forwarding address. Am I sorry for mistakes I've made in the past? YES! But there is no physical way to undo them. So, if you're planning a trip back to the "City of Regret", please cancel all your reservations now. Instead, take a trip to a place called, "Starting Again". I liked it so much that I have now taken up permanent residence there. My neighbors, the "I Forgive Myself" and the "New Starts" are so very helpful. By the way, you don't have to carry around heavy baggage because the load is lifted from your shoulders upon arrival. God bless you in finding this great town. If you can find it, it's in your own heart. Please look me up. I live on "I CAN DO IT" street.

—Larry Harp

Half Price

He was a good man but a bit stingy. He would bargain and haggle on a price, never paying the price asked. He especially hated paying his medical fees.

One day, while eating fish, a bone became lodged in his throat and within minutes he could scarcely breathe. His wife frantically called the family doctor, who arrived just as the patient's face was turning blue. The physician quickly removed the bone with a pair of forceps.

After he was breathing normally again, although overwhelmed with gratitude to the doctor for saving his life, he began to worry about the medical fees.

Trying his best to keep his costs down, he turned to the good doctor and asked, "How much do I owe you for this small two-minute job?"

The doctor, who knew his patient's miserly habit all too well, replied, "Just pay me half of what you would have when the bone was still stuck in your throat!"

I Am Thankful For...

...The taxes I pay because it means that I am employed;
...The clothes that fit a little too snug because it means that I have enough to eat;
...My shadow who watches me work because it means that I am out in the sunshine;
...A lawn that needs mowing, windows that need clean ing, and gutters that need fixing, because it means that I have a home;
...The spot I find at the far end of the parking lot because it means that I am capable of walking;
...My huge heating bill because it means that I am warm;
...The lady behind me in church who sings off key be cause it means I can hear;
...The alarm that goes off in the early morning hours because it means that I am alive.

Mud Slinging

One day while listening to yet another news story involving political mud slinging I was reminded of the quote, "he who throws mud loses ground." I wondered to myself what would happen if that effort were channeled into positive and innovative ideas for solving issues rather than finding fault with everything the opposition does. I am not suggesting for a moment that we close our eyes or turn our backs, but I am suggesting that perhaps we would make better use of our time if we focused on ways to improve instead of tearing each other apart. Neither am I taking sides. There is enough blame to go around.

Mud slinging can happen in government, business, home, church, school, and every area of life. Character assignation and exploiting another person's weaknesses for personal advantage is wrong. It shows that a person is unable to build reputation on personal character and innovative ideas. I came across a saying by Friedrich Hebbel that goes like this, "There are persons who always find a hair in their plate of soup for the simple reason that, when they sit down before it, they shake their heads until one falls in." Society has nurtured a "looking over the shoulder" mentality that is ready to pounce at any given moment.

No one likes to find hair in their soup. When we have the misfortune of finding a hair, the soup no longer tastes as good as before no matter how hard you try to forget about it. It can happen easily enough without shaking our heads and trying it. Whether it be government, church, home, or business it is time we clean our shoes, remove the hair, and be honest and forthright. It is of little surprise that many folks have a bad taste in their mouth.

—M. Gingrich

Recipe For A Happy Home

Take three cups of love and two cups of understanding, add four teaspoons of courage and two teaspoons each of thoughtfulness and helpfulness, sift together thoroughly, then stir in an equal amount of work and play. Add three teaspoons responsibility. Season to taste with study and culture, then fold in a generous amount of worship. Place in a pan well-greased with security and lined with respect for personality. Sprinkle lightly with a sense of humor. Allow to set in an atmosphere of mutual sharing. Bake in a moderate oven. When well done, remove and top with a thick coating of Christian teachings. Serve on a platter of friendliness garnished with smiles.

Reflections On Happiness

Even the foundational beliefs in America see the "pursuit of happiness" as a basic right of all individuals. Yet with all our pursuit, happiness seems to elude many of us for much of our lives.

Nathaniel Hawthorne said, "Happiness is a butterfly, which, when pursued, is always just beyond your grasp, but which, if you will sit down quietly, may alight upon you."

Reverend Ray Inman said, "Happiness, like an old friend, is inclined to drop in unexpectedly—when you're working hard on something else."

"Joy in Christ requires a commitment to working at the Christian lifestyle. Salvation comes as a gift, but the joy of Salvation demands disciplined action. Most Christians I know have just enough of the Gospel to make them miserable, but not enough to make them joyful. They know enough about the biblical message to keep them from doing the things which the world tempts them to do; but they do not have enough of a commitment to God to do those things through which they might experience the fullness of his joy" (Tony Campolo, "Seven Deadly Sins").

"Without exception, I have found that every person who was sincerely happy, radiantly alive, was living for a purpose or a cause beyond himself" (Abraham Maslow).

Fanny Crosby was the great hymn writer in the last half of the 19th Century. Even though she had been blind since she was six weeks old, she used to describe herself as "the happiest woman on earth." She experienced gusto through godliness.

Dr. Victor Frankl was imprisoned by the Nazis because he was a Jew. The Nazis killed his wife, his children, and his parents, stripped him of his clothes, and cut off his wedding band. Frankl's response: "You can take away my wife. You can take away my children. You can strip me of my clothes and my freedom but there is one thing that no person can ever take away from me—and that is my freedom to choose how I will react to what happens to me!"

Joni Eareckson Tada, who was paralyzed from the neck down while still a teenager, wrote, "You don't have to be alone in your hurt! Comfort is yours. Joy is an option. And it's all been made possible by your Savior. He went without comfort so you might have it. He postponed joy so you might share in it. He willingly chose isolation so you might never be alone in your hurt and sorrow" (Joni Eareckson Tada, Christian Reader, Vol. 32, No. 2).

"Dependent people need others to get what they want. Independent people can get what they want through their own effort. Interdependent people combine their own efforts with the efforts of others to achieve the greatest success" (Stephen Covey, "The Seven Habits of Highly Effective People").

In a book that literally sings with "Con Brio," called "Finally Comes the Poet" the author recalls that the great G. K. Chesterton once argued that because we are sinners, when it comes to ultimate joy, God alone is thoroughly childlike in Spirit. Chesterton asks us to consider how God might have created daisies. Did He create them all at once, with one swoop of His mighty hand? Or did He create them one-by-one, experiencing childlike delight in each new flower? If you throw your toddler up in the air or bounce the child off your knee, the likelihood is that the child will shout, "Do it again!" and they don't even notice the cringing mother! And if you do it again, you probably will get the same response. I think probably that, each time you toss the child in the air, the laughter will become more uncontrolled. Twenty times later, the child, never tiring of the fun, can be counted on to be overwhelmed with hysteria while still shouting, "Do it again"! So I think it might be that way with God. In the beginning, God may have created one daisy, and something within Him spontaneously whispered, "Do it again!" And daisy number two came into being. And once again God said, "Do it again!" And there was a third, and then a fourth, and then a fifth daisy. And so He went on creating daisies. Until after a hundred billion trillion daisies, the great Almighty Creator who spun the galaxies into space and created all the animals, that same God is still creating daisies, and with childlike glee, still saying, "Do it again!"

Mother Teresa said, "A person filled with joy preaches without preaching."

Rules To Be Happy

Remember these Five Simple Rules to Be Happy:

1. Free your heart from hatred.
2. Free your mind from worries.
3. Live simply.
4. Give more.
5. Expect less.

No one can go back and make a brand new start. Anyone can start from now and make a brand new ending. God didn't promise days without pain, laughter without sorrow, sun without rain, but he did promise strength for the day, comfort for the tears, and light for the way.

Disappointments are like road humps, they slow you down a bit but you enjoy the smooth road afterwards. Don't stay on the humps too long. Move on! When you feel down because you didn't get what you want, just sit tight and be happy, because God has thought of something better to give you.

When something happens to you, good or bad, consider what it means. There's a purpose to life's events, to teach you how to laugh more or not to cry too hard.

It's better to lose your pride to the one you love, than to lose the one you love because of pride.

We spend too much time looking for the right person to love or finding fault with those we already love, when instead we should be perfecting the love we give.

Never abandon an old friend. You will never find one who can take his place.

Sacrifice Or Greed?

Bank failures and mergers, avaricious CEO's, political bailouts, extravagant lifestyles, and reckless hedging or gambling against the odds are the news headlines today. What has happened to the financial system? It used to be that a handshake was all that was needed to seal the deal. Now it takes a file full of legal documents to protect against lawsuits and insurance fraud and whatever else. Rarely a day goes by without a new case of corruption charges. Men and women of high degree lay aside principles of integrity in their quest for position and prestige. Need we wonder then why there is a lack of trust?

Once, I was engaged in a conversation where it was suggested that greed was the culprit of the financial woes we are facing in this country. I've thought much about that since and I agree. It is an issue that confronts us from the youngest to the oldest and the richest to the poorest. We all tend to like ourselves and find convenient ways to make sure we are taken care of if at all possible. We tune in to the station, WIIFM, What's In It For Me? Let us consider several of the greed mentalities that abound in society.

"I want it now" mentality! Selling tactics are geared to try and make us feel dissatisfied or cheated if we don't have the latest and greatest. Promotions feast on the ego and offer "buy it now, pay later" options, to make them attractive. Easy credit has caught many in the snare of uncontrolled spending and excessive debt. A swipe with plastic and the tangible feeling of having an ipod, a laptop, a BMW, or even a house is more than some can resist. But payday comes and the initial excitement quickly evaporates.

"If I can get away with it, it is okay" mentality! "Shoplifters will be prosecuted" signs are posted in the supermarket. Stealing is wrong! Some people have the mentality that if I cheat a little bit it won't hurt anyone. If I take advantage of someone because they weren't intelligent enough that is their problem. My employer is making a killing so it's okay if I reap a little bit of the profits. Wrong! Shoplifting has gone high tech! Corporate style! It is still wrong! It is not mine unless it is rightfully given to me or I pay for it. Stealing in any form will have its consequences.

"The world owes it to me" mentality! Many are duped into thinking that they ought to be handed the world on a silver platter. They want a smorgasbord of benefits wrapped into their compensation package along with a top dollar salary. All of that can work if there is a performance on the part of the employee that merits it. Otherwise, it is destined to fail, especially if there is writing in the contract that makes it difficult to dismiss an employee who does not perform. A society whose people look for ways to contribute will be far better than one with open hands looking for handouts.

"It is mine" mentality! Really? How much will you take with you when you die? How much did you bring with you when you came? But I earned it! I worked hard! It is mine! Of course you did, but think about this. Do you pay for the air you breath? Did you earn a healthy body? Did you have anything to do with your body's ability to digest food and pump nutrients into the blood stream so that you have energy to work. Where will your next heartbeat come from? It is a gift! So then, is anything I have really mine?

"A life of luxury" mentality! A woman lamented the fact that she and her husband stayed home and had spaghetti every Friday night instead of going out to eat because of the troubled economic conditions. To her it seemed a real sacrifice. Well, maybe it is in this day and age, but a generation ago most folks would have considered it a luxury to eat out once or twice a year much less every week. Every society develops it's set of so called "normals", that are eventually viewed as necessities. Then when those necessities elude our reach we feel cheated. Perhaps the luxury mentality has clouded our reasoning.

Today's generation has a lot to learn about sacrifice if their definition of it is not being able to eat out. Webster tells us that sacrifice is something of value that is surrendered or destroyed for the sake of something having a higher or more pressing claim. We need then to ask ourselves, what is important to me? Do I want people to take me at my word? Do I want them to trust me? Am I willing to give up things I may deem important and do without for the greater cause of my integrity. Do I value honesty and trustworthiness? Is my life centered around what I can accumulate for myself or how I can help others?

When we lose ourselves in serving the needs of others we will find the true meaning of the words, "It is more blessed to give than to receive". The joy of sacrifice will far surpass any gratification extricated from greed.

—M. Gingrich

Thankfulness!

Thanksgiving is a time of family get-togethers, a time of reflecting on the bounties of the earth, a time of pausing to consider how blessed we really are. Truly, we ought to be grateful each and every day, but Thanksgiving

Day is a day set aside to remind us anew that the blessings we enjoy are really a gift. They are gifts we should not take lightly, or assume that they are rightfully ours, for in one moment any one of them can be taken away.

If we can get out of bed, if we can walk down the street, if we can bend down and tie our shoes, then, we ought to be thankful. If we can see the morning sunrise, the fall foliage, or the rolling waves of the ocean, then, we ought to be thankful. If we can hear the sound of laughter, the rippling of a brook, or the relaxing strains of music as they waft across the air waves, then, we ought to be thankful. If we can feel the breeze as it blows through our hair, a loving hand on our shoulder that says I care, or the warmth of a fire burning in the fireplace, then, we ought to be thankful. If we can smell the aroma of freshly baked bread, enjoy the scent of fresh cut flowers, or the room filled essence of a candle burning, then, we ought to be thankful. If we can taste the flavor of pumpkin pie and enjoy the variety of delicacies that grandma prepares, then, we ought to be thankful. If we can think clearly, if we can process our thoughts and make wise choices, then, we ought to be thankful. If we have a place to sleep, food to eat, a family to call our own, and friends, then, we ought to be thankful. There are many who can't claim these blessings that many of us have been given the privilege to enjoy. We are blessed far greater than we deserve!

Thankfulness is a choice that we make. We can choose to be grateful, or we can choose to be unappreciative. We can choose to assume that we deserve these things. They are really a gift that God has given to us. We can taste, see, smell, feel, hear, think, walk, talk, etc., because God has so designed us. We are a wonderful masterpiece of God's creation. We are creatures of choice. We can choose to withhold our thanksgiving. We can choose to withhold our praise. We can choose to spurn or turn up our noses at the blessings we receive. To do so, however, is tragic indeed, for it shows a heart that is cold, indifferent, proud, and arrogant. It shows a heart that has a void because love is absent. Yes, thankfulness is a choice, an attitude, that indicates who and what we are.

Abraham Lincoln wrote in his Thanksgiving proclamation, "The year that is drawing towards its close, has been filled with the blessings of fruitful fields and healthful skies. To these bounties, which are so constantly enjoyed that we are prone to forget the source from which they come, others have been added, which are of so extraordinary a nature, that they cannot fail to penetrate and soften even the heart which is habitually insensible to the ever watchful providence of Almighty God." He writes further, "No human counsel hath devised nor hath any mortal hand worked out these great things. They are the gracious gifts of the Most High God, who, while dealing with us in anger for our sins, hath nevertheless remembered mercy. It has seemed to me fit and proper that they should be solemnly, reverently, and gratefully acknowledged as with one heart and voice by the whole American people. I do therefore invite my fellow citizens in every part of the United States, and also those who are at sea and those who are sojourning in foreign lands, to set apart and observe the last Thursday of November next, as a day of Thanksgiving and Praise to our beneficent Father who dwelleth in the Heavens." Abraham Lincoln recognized the source of his blessings. He invited the nation to join in praise to Almighty God.

Can those we meet feel our appreciation? Does our thankfulness cause them to wonder about its source? Can we direct their eyes toward heaven and God who is the giver of every perfect gift. Yes, there are those who refuse to accept that God exists. They choose to live in denial of His blessings. They choose to disregard the one who knows their every thought, who fashioned them in their mother's womb, who gives them every breath of air they breathe. Their refusal to give God His due honor, robs them of joy and peace and happiness. I trust that we, with Abraham Lincoln, will recognize the source of our blessings and give Him the glory due unto His name. He is worthy of our praise, our adoration, and our thanksgiving!

Thanks For What?

It's not an easy task to find yourself heading into the holidays when there's little joy in your life. It had been a bad year, one that would be remembered for the loss of two loved ones, a year that saw financial despair and job loss. Then there were the health issues. Not everyday concerns, but life-threatening attacks. Nothing, but nothing went right.

Still, the family gathered as always for the thanksgiving day feast. They came from all around the country to share once more in what was always a beautiful family tradition.

The setting was the same as always at grandma's house. Aunt Esther would bring her famous sweet potatoes. Uncle Joe would play the piano in the great room.

Mom would set the table while dad...Well, dad would listen to football.

Aunts and uncles, brothers and sisters would hug that warm loving embrace that says it's been much too long.

Or would they?

"It's really not the same without her here," someone said. Uncle Peter pretended not to hear it and continued on with an almost believable smile on his face.

"Do you remember when George would tell that funny story about his first Thanksgiving turkey?"

"It was really not that funny, but to hear George tell it. You laughed because of him!"

There was an uneasy silence in the room.

"Time for dinner!" Grandma announced.

One by one, they all took their places at the table. There was an awkward moment when they discovered the two empty seats where they always sat.

"Maybe it's time for Sissy and Jack to move up to the big table," someone said.

"Yes, come sit here next to me," Uncle Peter motioned. "I could use some company right now."

"Okay, everyone bow your heads for grace," grandma told them.

"Lord, we are gathered here once again in thanks for all your blessings. We are grateful to you for the bounty of this feast and for the family we share it with. Amen."

It was now the tradition of this family to take the time to share one thing they were each thankful for from the past year.

"Who would like to go first?" Grandma asked.

There was silence—an uncomfortable moment that most everyone dreaded this year.

"Come, now. Who will start?"

Jack, now the youngest one there at the grown-up table, rose to his feet and tried to slip away.

Jack had lost his mother just a few weeks earlier after a long struggle with cancer.

"Jack, you have not asked to be excused," grandma said sharply. "Perhaps you would like to begin?"

"Thanks? For what?" He said sharply. "Thanks for taking my mom? Thanks for Uncle Dan losing his job and having to sell his house? Thanks for the cancer that has taken all too many lives?" He said with anger in his voice. "Thanks for what?"

Most of the adults sat quietly with their heads lowered. Some struggled to hold back tears. It was a difficult time, and no one there went unaffected by the loss and tragedies of this past year.

Then suddenly a small voice could be heard: "Thanks for the love."

Heads raised slowly. Looking around the room to see who had spoken, you could hear the rattle of the dishes and the scraping of the chairs against the floor as some repositioned themselves to get a better look.

"Who said that?" Grandma said softly.

Nervously the young child raised his hand and could barely be seen in the far corner of the room.

It was the children's table, occupied this year by only two. The others had been promoted to fill the vacancies at the adult table.

"Jacob, please stand up," grandma urged. "Tell us again. What are you thankful for this Thanksgiving?"

"I am thankful for the love. You can lose a job. God can call all of us home. What will always remain is the love. The love. I'm thankful for the love."

The stillness in the room was unsettling.

"I'm thankful for you, Jacob," someone said.

"Well, I'm thankful for...Ever having your mom in my life. Even if only for such a brief time," Jack's father said.

"I'm thankful for the memories," someone else added.

"I'm thankful for the chance to start over with a new career," Uncle Dan said.

"I'm thankful for cranberry sauce!" the little child yelled out.

Everyone was laughing. Jack returned to his seat as he listened to the others announce what they were thankful for.

"My golf score!"

"My new dress."

"My trip to the Grand Canyon last summer with our neighbors. It was awesome!"

Finally it went full circle right back to Jack.

There was a sudden hush in the room as everyone waited to see if he would join in.

Then looking up with tears in his eyes, Jack said, "Thanks for being my mom!"

Family rushed to his side, and surrounding him, they hugged, kissed, and held his hands.

"Let's eat!" Grandma said.

The young man in the corner whispered, "See, God? Thanks for the love."

Thanksgiving Is A Heart Condition

November is a time we reflect on the bountiful harvest of the past growing season. We remember the first ripe strawberries with their succulent taste. We remember preparing the ground and planting and hoeing and weeding and watering all in the anticipation of a harvest. As each crop produced its fruit we were rewarded with the tasty treats. There was the usual variety of peas and corn, tomatoes and zucchini, beans and squash, lettuce and potatoes, cauliflower and cabbage, cantaloupes and melons. There were fruits aplenty from the orchard too, including cherries and peaches, pears and apples. Each fruit and each vegetable had its own unique taste and texture. Each had its own season where it slowly ripened to its peak flavor and then tapered off. Some of the seasons overlapped each other providing an array of fresh goodies at the same time. The harvest is a time of reaping the rewards of our efforts in caring for the crops. There is nothing more gratifying then to reap a bumper crop.

But what if the harvest is poor? What if the rains are insufficient or too frequent? What if the crops just don't produce? What if they get a disease or fail to pollinate well? What if a thunderstorm or hailstorm comes along and ruins the crop just as things are beginning to ripen? What if? Are we still thankful? Is thanksgiving to be offered only when we are on the receiving end of overflowing blessings? Is that the only time we stop to give thanks? Certainly a bountiful harvest should produce within us even more thanks but it should not be the determining factor of our thanks. Our thanks should come from a heart that sees life in a much larger perspective. Each breath we take, each family member, every friend, every opportunity is a gift we should cherish. It is not something we have earned but something we have been gifted. In a moment it can slip from our grasp. Our thanks then is derived from a much broader perspective than just the everyday circumstances. It is expressed from a heart that has learned to appreciate the many things of life that are often taken for granted. The air we breathe, the freedom we enjoy, our heritage, our ability to think and reason, our ability to communicate, healthy bodies, and the beauty of nature are just a few of the things we could mention.

We understand that not everything about life is pleasant. There is sickness, there is death, there is hatred, there is envy and strife, and there are trials we need to face. But in the overall perspective we can choose to show kindness in the midst of strife, love in the face of hatred and compassion in the hour of death. We need not be overwhelmed by tragedy as difficult as it may be. We can allow it to make us better or we can become bitter. That choice will reflect the condition of our heart.

It is important for each of us to ask ourselves the questions, "Am I a person who wallows in selfishness and pity, or am I a person who recognizes the sovereignty of God? Do I appreciate the fact that I have already received far more than I deserve?"

When we come then to this time set aside to reflect and express our thanks it should really be nothing new or different. It is simply what we do each and every day if our heart is where it ought to be. May we ever strive to be more grateful on a daily basis for all the blessings that are ours and may we express that gratitude from the very depth of our heart. A well conditioned heart will receive more blessings in return than it can give. Try as we might, we cannot out-give God!

—*M. Gingrich*

The Application

A soap manufacturer who was a non-churchgoer walked down the street with a minister.

"The gospel you preach hasn't done much good," he said. "The world is still filled with wickedness."

They passed a little girl making mud pies, and very much involved in her work. "Soap hasn't done much good, would you say?" asked the minister, pointing to the child.

"It's useful only when applied," said the manufacturer.

"Precisely," said the minister.

The Best Day Of My Life

Today, when I awoke, I suddenly realized that this is the best day of my life, ever. There were times when I wondered if I would make it to today; but I did! And because I did, I'm going to celebrate! Today, I'm going to celebrate what an unbelievable life I have had so far: the accomplishments, the many blessings, and, yes, even the hardships because they have served to make me stronger. I will go through this day with my head held high and a happy heart. I will marvel at God's seemingly simple gifts: the morning dew, the sun, the clouds, the trees, the flowers, the birds.

Today, none of these miraculous creations will escape my notice.

Today, I will share my excitement for life with other people. I'll make someone smile. I'll go out of my way to perform an unexpected act of kindness for someone I don't even know.

Today, I'll give a sincere compliment to someone who seems down. I'll tell a child how special he is, and I'll tell someone I love just how deeply I care for them and how much they mean to me.

Today is the day I quit worrying about what I don't have and start being grateful for all the wonderful things God has already given me. I'll remember that to worry is just a waste of time because my faith in God and His divine plan ensures everything will be just fine.

And tonight, before I go to bed, I'll go outside and raise my eyes to the heavens. I will stand in awe at the beauty of the stars and the moon, and I will praise God for these magnificent treasures. As the day ends and I lay my head down on my pillow, I will thank the Almighty for the best day of my life. And I will sleep the sleep of a contented child, excited with expectation because I know tomorrow is going to be the best day of my life, ever!

The Difference Between Winners And Losers

1. A winner says, "Let's find out." A loser says, "Nobody knows."
2. When a winner makes a mistake, he says, "I was wrong." When a loser makes a mistake, he says, "It wasn't my fault."
3. A winner isn't nearly as afraid of losing, as a loser is secretly afraid of winning.
4. A winner works harder than a loser and has more time; a loser is always "too busy" to do what is necessary.
5. A winner goes through a problem; a loser goes around it, and never gets past it.
6. A winner makes commitments; a loser makes promises.
7. A winner says, "I'm good, but not as good as I ought to be." A loser says, "I'm not as bad as a lot of other people."
8. A winner listens; a loser just waits until it's his turn to talk.
9. A winner respects those who are superior to him and tries to learn from them; a loser resents those who are superior to him, and tries to find chinks in their armor.
10. A winner explains; a loser explains away.
11. A winner feels responsible for more than his job; a loser says, "I only work here."
12. A winner says, "There ought to be a better way to do it." A loser says, "That is the way it's always been done here."
13. A winner paces himself; a loser has only two speeds—hysterical and lethargic.

—Author Unknown

The Ego Cure

Sometime, when you're feeling important
Sometime, when your ego's in bloom,
Sometime, when you take it for granted
You're the best qualified man in the room.

Sometime when you feel that your going
Would leave an unfillable hole,
Just follow these simple instructions
And see how it humbles your soul.

Take a bucket and fill it with water
Put your hand in it up to the wrist.
Pull it out and the hole that remains
Is a measure of how much you'll be missed.

You may splash all you please when you enter
You can stir up the water galore,
But stop and you'll find in a moment
That it looks quite the same as before.

The moral in this quaint example
Is just do the best that you can,
Be yourself but always remember
There is no indispensable man.

—Anonymous, based on an ancient French Proverb

Beauty

Lightning Storm

A little girl walked to and from school daily.

Though the weather that morning was questionable and clouds were forming, she made her daily trek to the elementary school. As the afternoon progressed, the winds whipped up, along with thunder and lightning. The mother of the little girl felt concerned that her daughter would be frightened as she walked home from school and she herself feared that the electrical storm might harm her child. Following the roar of thunder, like a flaming sword, lightning would cut through the sky.

Full of concern, the mother quickly got into her car and drove along the route to her child's school. As she did so, she saw the little girl walking along, but at each flash of lightning, the child would stop, look up and smile. Another and another were to follow quickly and with each the little girl would look at the streak of lightning and smile. When the mother's car drew up beside the child she lowered the window and called to her, "What are you doing? Why do you keep stopping?" The child answered, "I am trying to look pretty. God keeps taking my picture."

Moral of the story: May you be blessed today as you face the storms that come your way.

Man & Woman

When I created the heavens and the earth, I spoke them into being. When I created man, I formed him and breathed life into his nostrils. I allowed a deep sleep to come over him so I could patiently and perfectly fashion the woman. I chose the bone that protects man's life. I chose the rib, which protects his heart and lungs and supports him, as you the woman are meant to do. Around this one bone I shaped her. I created her perfectly and beautifully. Her characteristics are as the rib, strong yet delicate and fragile. She provides protection for the most delicate organ in man, his heart. His heart is the center of his being; his lungs hold the breathe of life. The rib cage will allow itself to be broken before it will allow damage to the heart.

Dear woman, support man as the rib cage supports the body. You were not taken from his feet, to be under him, nor were you taken from his head, to be above him. You are my beautiful creation. You have grown to be a splendid woman of excellence and my eyes fill when I see the virtues of your heart. Your eyes—don't change them. Your lips—how lovely when they part in prayer. Your nose, so perfect in form, your hands so gentle to touch. I've caressed your face in your deepest sleep; I've held your heart close to mine. Of all that lives and breathes, you are the most like me. Adam walked with me in the cool of the day and yet he was lonely. He could not see me or touch me. He could only feel me. So everything I wanted Adam to share and experience with me, I fashioned in you: my holiness, my strength, my purity, my love, my protection, and support. You are special because you are the extension of me. Man represents my image—woman my emotion. Together, you represent the totality of God.

So man—treat woman well. Love her, respect her, for she is fragile. In hurting her you hurt me. What you do to her you do to me. In crushing her, you only damage your own heart, the heart of your Father, and the heart of her Father.

Woman support man. In humility, show him the power of emotion I have given you. In gentle quietness show your strength. In love, show him that you are the rib that protects his inner self.

—Your Heavenly Father

The Marvels Of Creation

Have you ever wondered how a robin can hear a worm? Or why geese form a v-shape when they fly? Why do some birds migrate while others do not? And how do they know where to go? Why do some creatures look awkward and strange while others are cuddly and cute? Why are some ferocious while others are timid and shy?

Why do some plants bloom early and others late? Why does one tree bear apples, another peaches and another cherries? Why do some trees lose their foliage while others stay green all winter? Why do peas grow on a stalk while potatoes grow underground? How do the kernels end up in neat little rows on an ear of corn? How does a walnut form its unique shape and package it inside a hard brittle shell? How can their be such intricate detail in a single flower?

How does a snowflake form, and how can every flake be different? How do the rain drops get up in the clouds only to fall back down again? Again and again! Where does the wind go when it blows? Where does it get its strength? How does the sun know when to rise and when to set? How do winter, spring, summer, and fall know when to take their place in the rotation?

How can every human being have a different appearance? Even the sound of their voice and how they walk is unique! Consider the marvels of the human body! How does it take food and process it by pulling out the nutrients and distributing it into the blood stream? How is it that we can see? Or hear? Or talk? Taste? Feel? How does the human brain process millions of signals daily, deciphering and shouting instructions to other members of the body so that we function properly?

Every single thing has a purpose! A skunk releases its putrid odor to ward off enemies. The finch nests much later than other birds, waiting until the thistles bloom so it can use the blossoms to form its nest. A wood chuck burrows underground for protection. A bee uses its sting for self defense. A monkey is suited for climbing while an elephant wouldn't get off the ground. A cat has the stealth and quickness to catch a mouse while a dog would simply bark.

Each part of creation has its own uniqueness in how it looks, functions and reproduces. I marvel at all the differences and yet they all fulfill a purpose. They provide a variety and balance to all of nature. As we step back and observe this masterpiece, we can't help but marvel at the Creator who designed it all!

—M. Gingrich

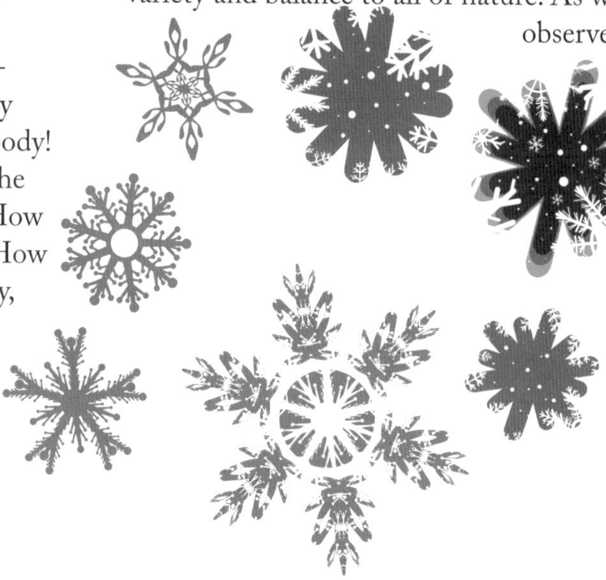

Business

Blah, Blah, Blah

The CEO was scheduled to speak at an important convention, so he asked one of his employees to write him a punchy, 20-minute speech.

When the CEO returned from the big event, he was furious. "What's the idea of writing me an hour long speech?" he demanded to know. "Half the audience walked out before I finished."

The employee was baffled. "I wrote you a 20-minute speech," he replied. "I also gave you the two extra copies you asked for."

Fast Food—Slow!

My latest run in with incompetent employees happened when my wife and I stopped at a fast food establishment on our way home one evening. We both wanted milkshakes to sip on. As I pulled into the parking lot the first thing I noticed was the absence of vehicles. There were two to be exact. I pulled along side one of them and as I walked toward the entrance I noticed that they had a play area for children but it was dark even though it was only eight o'clock in the evening. As I opened the door and stepped inside there was no one around. No customers and no employees. My first thought was trouble, but then out of the back recesses of the kitchen there arrived a face to inquire of my desires. I said we would each like a milkshake to which he responded, the machine has already been cleaned. Well, no wonder the parking lot was empty and I now realized that I had parked next to the employees' vehicles. This was along a well traveled route and at a chain restaurant that has considerable name recognition.

Since I like this particular restaurant's milkshakes we decided to try another one a bit further along. This place had more customers. I placed my order and waited. They were finishing up several other orders so I stepped back from the counter. When the manager went to make our milkshakes he discovered they needed more syrup. So off to the back room one of the employees trudged, sipping on what was to be my milkshake, to get some more syrup. While he was gone several other employees were carousing around, including the girl who took our order. As the fellow who went to get the syrup came sauntering back the girl spoke into the microphone so everyone present could hear. "Hurry up with that syrup, my customers are tired of waiting for their order." She was right, but her comments were totally out of place. If she was concerned about her customers she would have apologized for the delay instead of making them part of her snide comments. Finally, after almost fifteen to twenty minutes our order was complete. During the whole episode there was not one apology for the delay or inconvenience. When my fast food slow order was finally placed on the counter it was done as though everything had been completed in a timely manner. I was totally disgusted with the manner in which everything was handled but especially so with the manager who was more interested in hearing a friend blow his car horn when he left then he was in serving his customers and making sure his employees were courteous and polite. All this had taken place in his presence.

I shall not be at all surprised when the "out of business" shingle goes in the window at those two restaurants. Neither shall I feel any remorse for they shall have readily earned their demise. But do they even care? Given their attitude, probably not. My milkshake was good but incompetent employees made the experience frustrating. Two questions employees should ask themselves are, "What is my attitude toward customers?" and "Is my level of service producing satisfied customers for my employer?" Your answer to those questions can spell the difference between "in business" or "out of business".

—*M. Gingrich*

Good Help

The story is told of a man who was looking for a boy to start working in his hardware store and learn the business. He picked three boys for a tryout, Ed Marble, Jack Morris and Tom Beech. Taking them one at a time and on separate days, he handed each boy a parcel containing an aluminum pie pan with instructions to deliver it to Mrs. J.B. Peterson of 789 Chestnut Street.

Ed telephoned back to the hardware store to ask whether the number was possibly 798 or 897, as he could not find a residence at 789, and finally he returned with the pan saying there was no such number on Chestnut Street.

Jack returned in due time bringing his pie pan and reporting that 789 Chestnut Street was a church, but that a Mrs. J.B. Peterson had lived at 789 ½ and had recently moved away.

Tom Beech took longer than the other boys to do the errand, but he returned without the pie pan. He had learned the same thing as Jack had learned but he didn't stop there. He sought out Mrs. Peterson's new address and went to see her. She informed him that she had not ordered a pie pan (which of course was true) but Tom unwrapped it, told her the price that had been mentioned to him and persuaded her to buy it. Tom Beech got the job.

I hear many business people complain about not being able to get good help and quite frequently there is sufficient evidence to support their claims. Good work ethics, loyalty, and commitment are indeed becoming a rare find. Nonetheless, they do exist. While I have experienced my fair share of mediocre, indifferent, and "who cares" kind of people when doing business, I have also experienced a goodly share of people who have shown a diligent and commendable effort. There are good employees to be had. There are people who are committed. Recently I read an article about a very successful company. They recognized that their competitors could replicate the products they sell but they couldn't replicate its employees. New employees at this company received 240 hours of training in their first year compared to the industry average of seven. Employees were paid two to three times more than industry standard and were given a generous discount of 40% for personal purchases. Their theory is this, "If we astonish our employees they will in turn astonish our customers." Successful businesses not only hire good prospects, but they train and reward them as well.

Sometimes we get in a rut and it helps to look at things from a fresh and different perspective. We live in a world of mega companies that can make it tough to compete if all we are doing is selling the same products. We must learn to focus on what we can do better than the big giants and then do it. It is no longer a business of selling a product, it is a business of selling your services. A client who is sold on your services is a good client to have. Seek them out. They are there. Delivering a product is your duty, but selling your services while you are doing it is your privilege and an opportunity to astonish your client. The rewards will be forthcoming!

—M. Gingrich

Honesty In Business

There was a farmer who sold a pound of butter to the baker. One day the baker decided to weigh the butter to see if he was getting a pound and he found that he was not. This angered him and he took the farmer to court.

The judge asked the farmer if he was using any measure. The farmer replied, "Your Honor, I am primitive. I don't have a proper measure, but I do have a scale."

The judge asked, "Then how do you weigh the butter?"

The farmer replied "Your Honor, long before the baker started buying butter from me, I have been buying a pound loaf of bread from him. Every day when the baker brings the bread, I put it on the scale and give him the same weight in butter. If anyone is to be blamed, it is the baker."

How To Place New Employees

Take the prospective employees you are trying to place and put them in a room with only a table and two chairs. Leave them alone for two hours, without any instruction. At the end of that time, go back and see what they are doing.

- If they have taken the table apart, put them in Engineering.
- If they are counting the individual flowers on the wallpaper, assign them to Finance.
- If they are waving their arms and talking out loud, send them to Consulting.
- If they are talking to the chairs, Personnel is a good spot for them.
- If they are wearing green sunglasses and need a haircut, Computer Information Systems is their niche.
- If they mention what a good price we got for the table and chairs, put them into Purchasing.
- If they mention that hardwood furniture DOES NOT come from rain forests, Public Relations would suit them well.
- If they are writing up the experience, send them to the Technical Documents team.
- If they don't even look up when you enter the room, assign them to Security.
- If they try to tell you it's not as bad as it looks, send them to Marketing.
- If they are sleeping, they are management material.

Job Search Jargon

Whether you are a student looking for that first time summer job or a long-time veteran looking for a change of pace, this Job Search Jargon should help you get on your way...

- Competitive Salary: We remain competitive by paying less than our competitors.
- Flexible Hours: Work 55 hours; get paid for 37.5.
- Good Communication Skills: Management communicates, you listen and figure out what they want you to do.
- Ability to Handle a Heavy Workload: You whine, you're fired.
- Career-Minded: We expect that you will want to flip hamburgers until you are 70.
- Self-Motivated: Management won't answer questions.
- Some Overtime Required: Some time each night and some time each weekend.
- Duties Will Vary: Anyone in the office can boss you around.
- Competitive Environment: We have a lot of turnover.
- Sales Position Requiring Motivated Self-Starter: We're not going to supply you with leads (there's no base salary; you'll wait thirty days for your first commission check).
- Casual Work Atmosphere: We don't pay enough to expect that you'll dress up.
- Seeking Candidates With a Wide Variety of Experience: You'll need it to replace three people who just left.
- Problem-Solving Skills A Must: You're walking into a company in perpetual chaos.

Knowing And Selling Your Product And Services!

How well do you know the product you are selling? Are you acquainted with the services your company offers? If you don't know the answer to a customers question do you seek to find the answer? If you were on the purchasing side of the equation, would you buy the product or products you represent from someone with as little knowledge about the product as you? Do you point your finger at other departments when mistakes occur? Do you leave the customer hanging out on a limb when their expectations are not met?

Many times the difference between a sale or no sale is the knowledge and service level of the employees. Knowledgeable and service-oriented employees will achieve a higher percentage of sales then those who are unwilling to take the extra steps to satisfy a customers demands or who seem uncertain about a products capability. I, personally, have gone into a store with the full intent of making a purchase and have left without doing so, because the salesperson was unable to answer questions to my satisfaction. I either made my purchase elsewhere or returned at a time when a different sales person was on duty.

A thorough understanding of how your product works, what it is made of, why it is better than its competitor, and why it will service the customer are all keys to making a sale. Your company's willingness to stand behind the products offer an additional guarantee and expresses confidence in the products they represent.

Another key ingredient in selling your services is listening to the customers' needs. It doesn't really matter how good your product is or how well it performs, if it doesn't meet the needs and expectations of what the customer wants they are going to be dissatisfied.

I believe this short account of a businessman who was forced to close shop during the depression demonstrates that service is meeting the needs of the customer. The sign in the store window read, "John is closing shop on the first. The following services we have rendered for the past twenty years will be found at these places: Stamps at the post office, free ice water at the soda fountain next door, telephone at the hotel, baseball scores at Western Union, railroad information at the depot, magazines at the drug store, and loafing on the courthouse lawn."

—Poor John

—M. Gingrich

Knowing Where To Peck

Perhaps we have forgotten the value of trained and experienced employees in our places of business. Competition has forced many businesses to find ways of cutting costs. Longtime employees, who obviously get paid more because of experience and longevity, will often be let go by businesses attempting to cut payroll.

They have helped the business grow to where it is. They also bring to the table a knowledgeable relationship with long time customers. It seems that perhaps we have placed too little emphasis on these virtues. Employees' wages and benefits are one issue. Keeping a company profitable is another. In today's business climate of mass merchandising and technological advances there is ever increasing demand to get more for less. In an effort to meet this demand the service level in many companies has declined. Is this healthy for the economy in the long term?

I have heard instances of people buying auto parts on-line or at the auto parts store and taking them to the local garage to get them installed. They do this to try and save a few dollars. What they forget is that part of the mechanic's overall income is supplemented by the profits he makes on selling that same part. It is likely that you can buy a part cheaper where it is mass marketed but is it ethical to expect the mechanic to do your work when you have just eliminated a portion of his income? He has no choice but to raise his labor rate to cover that loss. Furthermore when he puts a part on your vehicle that you purchase from him, part of the price reflects a guarantee or a commitment on his part that it will fix the problem. You don't have that when you buy at a megastore. Is saving a few dollars worth the risk of jeopardizing a good business relationship between you and your mechanic?

In yet another example, an intricate machine broke down halting production in a busy factory. All the company's best machinists were called in to diagnose the trouble, but to no avail. It was suggested that a specialist, a master mechanic, be brought in. He came, looked the apparatus over, and asked for the smallest hammer on hand. He then pecked on a critical area and said, "Now turn on the power. It ought to work." It did. Later, when he sent a bill for $100, the top brass were astounded at the exorbitant fee. They wrote, asking him to send an itemized statement, which he did, without reducing the amount. The itemized version read: $1 for pecking, $99 for knowing where to peck.

There is a dollar value attached to knowledge. The person that has that knowledge deserves to be reimbursed for it. In the case of the example just given we fail to consider how little it costs as compared to the whole factory being shut down for hours and hours. Let us not forget that peace of mind comes with a price and we get it by dealing with someone who knows where to peck. The alternative is to endure the pain as is illustrated by the following account: a patient complained bitterly, "Fifty dollars is a lot of money for pulling a tooth—just a couple of seconds work."

"Well," replied the dentist, "If you wish, I can pull it slowly."

—M. Gingrich

Late Fees & Bank Charges

My aunt died this past January. The bank billed her for February and March for their monthly service charge on her credit card, and then added late fees and interest on the monthly charge. The balance, which had been $0.00, now was somewhere around $60.00). I placed the following phone call to the bank:

Me: "I am calling to tell you that she died in January."
Bank: "The account was never closed and the late fees and charges still apply."
Me: "Maybe, you should turn it over to collections…"
Bank: "Since it is 2 months past due, it already has been."
Me: "So, what will they do when they find out she is dead?"
Bank: "Either report her account to the frauds division, or report her to the credit bureau…maybe both!"
Me: "Did you just get what I was telling you…the part about her being dead?"
Bank: "Sir, you'll have to speak to my supervisor!" (Super visor gets on the phone)
Me: "I'm calling to tell you, she died in January."
Bank: "The account was never closed and the late fees and charges still apply."
Me: "You mean you want to collect from her estate?"
Bank: "…(stammer) Are you her lawyer?"
Me: "No, I'm her great nephew." (Lawyer info given…)
Bank: "Could you fax us a certificate of death?"
Me: "Sure." (Fax number is given)
Bank: (After they get the fax) "Our system just isn't set up for death"
Me: "Oh…"
Bank: "Sir: I don't know what more I can do to help…"
Me: "Well…if you figure it out, great! If not, you could just keep billing her. I suppose…don't really think she will care…"
Bank: "Well…the late fees and charges do still apply."
Me: "Would you like her new billing address?"
Bank: "That might help."
Me: "Odessa Memorial Cemetery Hwy 129" (and plot number given).
Bank: "Sir, that's a cemetery!"
Me: "What do you do with dead people on your planet?!!"

New Windows

Last year I replaced all the windows in my house with those expensive double-pane energy-efficient kind. But this week I got a call from the contractor who installed them, complaining that his work had been completed a whole year ago, and I had yet to pay for them. Boy oh boy, did we go around!! I proceeded to tell him just what his fast talking sales guy had told me last year: namely, that in one year the windows would pay for themselves. There was silence on the other end of the line, so I just hung up…and I have not heard back. Guess I won that argument!

Office Answering Message

"Hello, you have reached an office that thought it was so smart getting all it's employees cordless phones. The person you are trying to reach is here right now, staring at me as I answer this call and searching desperately for their cordless phone in the mess on their desk.

"It won't matter if they find it since they didn't leave it on the charger last night and the battery is dead. So you might as well leave a message with me and I'll have them call you after the four hour handset recharge period is completed."

Office Vocabulary

Latest terms to add to your vocabulary at the office:

- Blamestorming—Sitting around in a group discussing why a deadline was missed or a project failed and who was responsible.
- Seagull Manager—A manager who flies in, makes a lot of noise, messes up everything, and then leaves.
- Blowing Your Buffer—Losing your train of thought.
- Chainsaw Consultant—An outside expert brought in to reduce the employee headcount, leaving the brass with clean hands.
- CLM (Career-Limiting Move)—Used among microserfs to describe ill-advised activity, e.g., trashing your boss while he or she is within earshot is a serious CLM.
- Depotphobia—Fear associated with entering a Costco or Kmart because of how much money one might spend. Electronics geeks experience Shackophobia, Tandyagonia, or Circuit Cityatosis.
- Adminisphere—The rarefied organizational layers beginning just above the rank and file. Decisions that fall from the Adminisphere are often profoundly inappropriate or irrelevant to the problems they were designed to solve.
- Flight Risk—Used to describe employees who are suspected of planning to leave the company or department soon.
- 404—Someone who's clueless. From the World Wide Web error message "404 Not Found," meaning that the requested document could not be located. "Don't bother asking him—he's 404, man."
- Generica—Features of the American landscape that are exactly the same no matter where one is, such as fast food joints, strip malls, or housing development subdivisions. Used as in "We were so lost in Generica that I forgot what city we were in."
- GOOD ("Get-Out-Of-Debt") Job—A well-paying job people will take to pay off their debts, which they will quit as soon as they are solvent again.
- Keyboard Plaque—The disgusting buildup of dirt and crud found on computer keyboards.
- Oh no second—That minuscule fraction of time in which you realize that you've just made a BIG mistake.
- Percussive Maintenance—The fine art of whacking the daylights out of an electronic device to get it to work again.
- Prairie Dogging—When someone yells or drops something loudly in a "cube farm" (an office full of cubicles) and all the coworkers' heads pop up over the walls to see what's going on.
- Telephone Number Salary—A salary (or project budget) that has seven digits.

Selling Extras

An old rancher went to town to buy a pickup truck that he saw advertised in the paper for a certain price. After telling the salesman which truck he wanted, they sat down to do the paperwork.

The salesman handed the rancher the bill, and the rancher declared, "This isn't the price I saw!" The salesman went on to tell the old rancher how he was getting extras such as power brakes, power windows, special tires etc. and that was what took the price up. The rancher needed the truck badly, paid the price and went home.

A few months later, the salesman called up the rancher and said, "My son is in 4-H and he needs a cow for a project. Do you have any cows for sale?" The rancher said, "Yes, I have a few cows, and I would sell one for $500.00. Come look at them and take your pick."

The salesman said he and his son would be right out. After spending a few hours in the field checking out all the rancher's cows, the two decided on one and the salesman proceeded to write out a check for $500.00.

The rancher said, "Now, wait a minute, that's not the final price of the cow. You're getting extras with it and you have to pay for the extras, too."

"What extras?" asked the salesman.

Below is the list the rancher gave the salesman for the final price of the cow:

BASIC COW	$500.00
Two tone exterior	$45.00
Extra stomachs	$75.00
Product storing equipment	$60.00
Straw compartment	$120.00
4 Spigots @$10 ea	$40.00
Leather upholstery	$125.00
Dual horns	$45.00
Automatic fly swatter	$38.00
GRAND TOTAL	$1,048.00

The Big Sale

"How many customers did you serve today?" the manager asked.

"One."

"Only one? How much was the sale?"

"$58,334.00," was the reply.

Flabbergasted, the manager asked him to explain. The salesman said, "First I sold the man a fishhook. Then I sold him a rod and a reel. Then I asked him where he was planning to fish, and he replied down the coast. So I suggested he'd need a boat. He bought that six-meter motor boat. When he said his car might not be able to pull it, I took him to the auto department and sold him a big vehicle."

The amazed boss asked, "You sold all that to a guy who came in for a fishhook?"

"No," the salesman replied.

"He actually came in for a bottle of aspirin for his wife's migraine." I told him, "Your weekend's shot, you should probably go fishing."

Unused Potential!

"The average person puts only twenty—five percent of his energy and ability into his work. The world takes off its hat to those who put in more than fifty percent of their capacity, and stands on its head for those few and far between souls who devote one hundred percent" (Andrew Carnegie).

This observation by Andrew Carnegie portrays a scenario depicted by many employers; it is hard to find good, dependable help. Employee's that are hard-working, honest, and dependable are in demand. They have little trouble finding a decent paying job. Obviously, the economic condition and availability of jobs in a given area are determining factors as well.

It has, however, always puzzled me how you can have a five or six percent unemployment rate and "Help Wanted" signs hanging in the windows at the same time. I recognize that those help wanted signs may represent lower paying, entry level positions, and may not be sufficient to support a family.

To me "Help Wanted" represents two things. First, there is an unfulfilled need, and second, there is a willingness to pay the wages. Unemployment also represents two things. First, there is an unfulfilled need, namely, food on the table, and secondly, the need must be met by an alternative source, namely, unemployment compensation. Considering these factors I would assume that there could be some value in a compromise between the two. Taking a job at the place that has "Help Wanted" signs would fulfill that company's need and would in turn provide a savings to unemployment compensation by contributing a portion of the proceeds via wages. Unemployment would then pick up the remainder of the tab, rather than foot the entire bill. It would seem to me that it would be a win-win situation.

All too common as well is the mentality of "the company owes it to me." That mentality is foreign to those who learned to work hard. I especially think of those folks who went through the great depression era.

They were glad for work of any kind, even if it provided only a meager income.

Hannah Whitall Smith writes, "The mother eagle teaches her little ones to fly by making their nest so uncomfortable that they are forced to leave it and commit themselves to the unknown world of air outside." Perhaps the nest has become too comfortable for many. In a land of ease and wealth and plenty, there is a tendency to grow accustomed to giving little and receiving plenty. The end result is under developed wings that will never reach their full potential.

While this scenario is evidenced in the workplace, we can also draw an analogy in relation to church work and our spiritual lives. Sitting on the sidelines and giving little, produces stagnation. When people feel needed, when they become part of the work, they develop their potential and they blossom. They reach out into unfamiliar territory strengthening their wings. They expand their horizons. They grow excited. They feel rewarded as they see the results of their contributions. The more they give the more they receive in return. Eventually the average become the extraordinary as they soar to new and greater heights in developing their full potential. They find a sense of worth and usefulness as they become a part of the solution rather than a part of the problem.

Updated Timesheet Codes

Memo From Accounting Department

It has come to our attention recently that many of you have been turning in timesheets that specify large amounts of "Miscellaneous Unproductive Time" (Code 5309). However, we need to know exactly what you are doing during your unproductive time.

Attached below is a sheet specifying a tentative extended job code list based on our observations of employee activities. The list will allow you to specify with a fair amount of precision what you are doing during your unproductive time. Please begin using this job-code list immediately and let us know about any difficulties you encounter.

Thank you, Accounting

Extended Job-Code List Code & Description

5316 Useless Meeting
5317 Obstructing Communications at Meeting
5318 Trying to Sound Knowledgeable While in Meeting
5319 Waiting for Break
5320 Waiting for Lunch
5321 Waiting for End of Day
5322 Vicious Verbal Attacks Directed at Coworker
5393 Covering for Incompetence of Coworker Friend
5400 Trying to Explain Concept to Coworker Who is Not Interested in Learning
5481 Buying Snack
5482 Eating Snack
5500 Filling Out Timesheet
5501 Inventing Timesheet Entries
5502 Waiting for Something to Happen
5503 Wishing Something Would Happen
5504 Sleeping
5510 Feeling Bored
5511 Feeling Sleepy
5600 Complaining About Lousy Job
5601 Complaining About Low Pay
5602 Complaining About Long Hours
5603 Complaining About Coworker (See Codes #5322 & #5323)
5604 Complaining About Boss
5605 Complaining About Personal Problems

5701 Not Actually Present At Job
5702 Suffering from Eight-Hour Flu
6103 Waiting for Food Delivery to Arrive
6104 Taking It Easy While Digesting Food
6202 Making Excuses After Accidentally Destroying Company Goods
6203 Using Company Phone to Make Long-Distance Personal Calls
6205 Hiding from Boss
6206 Gossip
6207 Planning a Social Event (e.g. vacation, wedding, etc.)
6210 Feeling Sorry For Yourself
6211 Updating Resume
6212 Faxing Resume to Another Employer/Headhunter
6213 Out of Office on Interview
6221 Pretending to Work While Boss Is Watching
6222 Pretending to Enjoy Your Job
6238 Miscellaneous Unproductive Pretending
6350 Playing Pranks on the New Guy/Girl
6601 Running your own Business on Company Time (See Code #6603)
6602 Complaining
6603 Writing a Book on Company Time
6611 Staring Into Space
6612 Staring At Computer Screen

7281 Extended Visit to the Bathroom (at least ten minutes)
7401 Talking With Plumber on Phone
7402 Talking With Dentist on Phone
7403 Talking With Doctor on Phone
7425 Talking With Boy/Girlfriend on Phone
8100 Reading e-mail
8102 Laughing while reading e-mail

Vacation Offer

A newspaper writer, after working for 17 long years, was finally granted two months leave, during which time he would be fully paid. However, he turned down his boss' kind offer.

The boss asked, "Why would you turn down such a generous offer?"

The newspaper writer said there were two reasons.

"Well, what are they?" asked the boss.

"The first," he said, "Is that I thought that my taking such a long leave might affect the newspaper's circulation."

The boss asked him what the other reason was.

"The other reason," replied the writer, "Is that I thought my taking such a long leave might not affect the newspaper's circulation."

Work Ethics

Earning Your Wages!

Did you know that a ten minute coffee break five days a week amounts to 43 ⅓ hours during a year—over a full week's vacation in time? A break, like many other things in life, is something many folks take for granted. There is nothing wrong with a short break to refresh oneself for the task at hand, however it is one of those things that I have seen violated many times. It comes on gradually, first just a minute over, than two, and soon five or more. I have observed folks check their watch and announce that break time is over then proceed to use the restroom or take care of other personal needs.

Break time is not the only area where time is misused. I have also observed folks arriving for work at the last minute, running to punch in on time and then hang up their coat, use the restroom, comb their hair and finally show up for actual work ten minutes later. These things can run rampant in a company if they are not kept in check. Employees grow accustomed to thinking that the company owes it to them, but an employee needs to remember they also owe the *f* a good day's work. Employees want commitment from a company but it is vital to a company as well that the employees are committed to them. A good employer/employee relationship is one that benefits both parties.

Misuse of company time at today's wages can put a company in dire straits rather quickly. Breaks are not the only area of time wasting. Other areas could include visiting with friends, making personal phone calls, or simply goofing off. We are creatures of habit and unfortunately some habits we form are not always the best and may need to be broken.

Questions that we can all ask ourselves are this: Am I giving my best? Am I being fair to my employer? Have I become lax in keeping track of my time on the clock? Am I willing to give a few minutes extra even when I'm not on the clock? Am I really earning my wages, or as they used to say years ago, am I worth my salt?

Common Courtesy

We've all been there! As a cashier is ringing up your order she is also engaged in a conversation with another employee about her plans for the weekend. She is almost oblivious to your presence other than the fact that there is merchandise on the counter to be rung up. Finally as the last item is rung up she looks your direction and in rather sarcastic fashion says for all the world to hear, "One hundred, twenty four dollars and twenty three cents." There is no "courtesy in her voice", not a "thank you", no "please", no "have a good day", no "smile". It is just a nonchalant blank stare transaction.

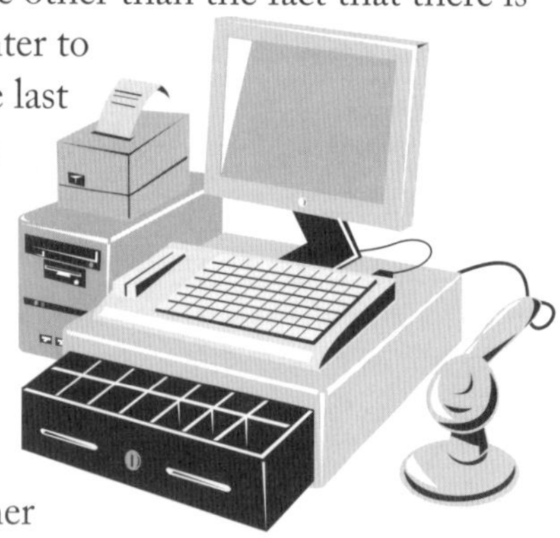

All of us can probably attest to the flip side of that scenario as well, where a cashier as been very courteous and made us feel much better about parting with our money. Perhaps we could chalk off the first scenario to having a bad day if it were only an occasional occurrence. But how many bad days can a person have? Do employees sometimes forget that without the customer they don't have a job? Common courtesy should be part of the transaction whether its fifty cents or several hundred dollars.

Customers can be quite demanding. They want to be heard. They want recognition. They want to be treated fairly and respectfully. If your place of employment can't provide service with a smile, customers will find one that does. It doesn't take a lot to tip the scales in the wrong direction. The success of a company depends on customer relations. The attitude of an employee towards a customer is often the bond that holds the business relationship together or the knife that severs it.

The waitress that is friendly, cheerful and does her best to serve, gets my tip. The service person behind the counter who answers my questions or finds someone who can answer them if he is unable to, gets my business. The clerk who smiles, knows my name, and is interested in my day, rings up my purchases. The banker who cares about me even if I'm just a blip on his customer list, gets my checking account.

It all comes down to quality product, fair price, and exceptional customer service. That combination will make any business a tough competitor and provide job security. A smile, a thank you, and a listening ear go a long way toward customer satisfaction. Satisfied customers bring more customers and more customers mean you have a job.

Integrity & Honesty

Some time ago I had the pleasant experience of having a work project finished for less than what the original estimate was. It made me feel good about the person who performed the work. The work was done neatly and efficiently. While there was not a written contract in place I had been given a verbal estimate of what the project could run. I made a special effort to let that person know I was a satisfied customer.

Underbidding to get the job is a far too common practice. It is unfortunate. In fact, if it is done intentionally, it is dishonest. It is of utmost importance that there is a clear understanding between the customer and the bidder as to what work is to be performed. The customer must understand then that any changes made could affect the quoted price. That is only fair. If there are no changes however, then the work ought to be performed at the price that was quoted even if the person quoting the job quoted too low. Any changes ought to be documented and signed. There are some jobs that contain unknowns until the work is in progress. Portions of a job that contain unknown variables need to be itemized as such.

Another way of beating the system is to cut corners. A newly installed door may look good and work great but its functionality is only recognized two or three years down the road. Using a lower insulating R-value is not something that is readily seen but certainly it is felt over the years. If that is what the customer orders, okay, but when item #1 is ordered it is wrong to sub item #2 of lesser quality.

The lowest price isn't always the cheapest price in the long run. A rate of $50 an hour may cost you more than a rate of $100 an hour for the complete job. Some things to consider are the type of equipment being used and also the operators experience.

Most business people are honest. Most business people want you, the consumer, satisfied and will treat you fairly and with respect. Unfortunately, there are always those who care more about themselves. Your best protection as a consumer is to be as educated and as well informed as possible about the work you want done. Do research. Ask questions. Deal with local reputable people that you've seen working for others in your neighborhood. A business person who is honest will treat you with dignity and respect and will have a good rapport with his clients.

Relationships In The Workplace!

In this series we have been dealing with different aspects of the workplace and how we can improve. The workplace is of vital importance when we consider that somewhere between ¼ to ⅓ of our lives is spent at work: 42 hours a week is ¼, 56 hours is ⅓ and 84 hours is ½ of your time. When we consider the amount of time we are at work, nothing is more significant than our relationships. When I hear people say, "I hate my job!", I feel sorry that they spend so much of their lives in misery. Some folks simply don't have the courage to make a change while others happen to be the victim of circumstances, such as a good paying job went away and they were forced to get something else, or what they would like to do just doesn't pay enough to support their family. Sometimes people are caught in between, having worked up through the ranks at their job and are not willing or able to start all over again. Like many things in life some of it comes down to what we are willing to make of it.

For starters we do well to ask ourselves some questions and do a personal evaluation (or, if you are real brave, you could ask a co-worker to evaluate you). If we are honest with ourselves this evaluation will probably cause some anxiety and deflate our ego. That aside, here goes. Ask yourself, how well do I relate to my fellow employees, my boss, customers etc.? Do I insist on my way or am I willing to consider other people's suggestions? Am I willing to admit when I make a mistake and take proper measures so it doesn't happen again? Am I considerate of the fact that each of us look at things through different eyes? Do I respect others feelings? Do I exercise patience and forbearance? Am I cheerful and kind? The fact is, all of us have areas that we can improve. No one is perfect. The real question is, am I willing to try?

Employers find it increasingly difficult to find and keep good, dependable, and dedicated employees. As a boss or a person in a supervisory position a personal performance evaluation can be beneficial as well. Ask yourself, am I willing to roll up my sleeves and pitch in to help get the work done? Am I a dictator? Do I have an ear open for suggestions? Do I admit a mistake? Do I carry a chip on my shoulder? Is my attitude one of throwing my weight around? Do I express appreciation for good work? Do I offer a pat on the back or a word of thanks? Do I care about the personal needs of my employees?

People have feelings. They are not robots. They are not a piece of machinery. They have needs that require consideration. They must be handled with kindness and respect. People are the main ingredient in any business transaction. People give a personal touch to a business that an answering machine or voice mail cannot. People are the backbone of a business. People can be the difference between success and failure. A smiling face, a kind deed, and a cheerful spirit can make a customer want to buy. Performance in the workplace is improved when people feel needed and are treated with respect and customers are more likely to patronize a business where employees are kind and courteous.

How you relate to others, whether you are the boss, an employee or a customer, will have an effect on your outlook on life in general. Good relationships will lessen stress and cultivate good health. Good relationships are a benefit to all parties involved. The boss is elated, the employee is content, and the customer is pleased. That type of relationship produces long term results. The boss knows he has a good customer and will do his best to please them. The employee knows he has long term employment and the customer has an unwritten insurance policy on his purchases. It's a "win-win" situation!

Personal Hygiene In The Workplace!

Personal hygiene is of vital importance in the workplace. Cleanliness is often ranked at the top of the list in surveys of what is most important to customers. This is especially true in places where food is prepared or handled, such as restaurants and grocery stores. Bad breath, body odor, unkempt hair, and dirty hands are all detriments to business. No one likes to hold their breath for extended periods of time because of foul odors emitting from someone who doesn't bathe or who has alligator breath.

Neatness about oneself carries over into tidiness in the workplace, paying attention to detail, and promptness to do neat work. Wearing gloves when handling food is a positive sanitary step, but it is an effort in futility if they are left on when you blow your nose or scratch your scalp. Restrooms tell a lot about an establishment and its employees. Taking the time to maintain restrooms and using them properly shows customers you care.

Those signs that say, "Employees must wash their hands before returning to work", should really say, "Please wash your hands!" It applies to everyone! Washing your hands is important but sometimes getting out of the room without becoming recontaminated is a challenging task. You wash your hands and grab the door knob, the same door knob that the last three guys grabbed who didn't wash their hands. That's the reason I keep a paper towel in my hand until I pull the door open and then toss it into the waste basket.

Even better is the type of door that pushes out with your foot so you don't need to touch anything.

Good personal hygiene is nothing scientific. It's as simple as soap, water, toothpaste, a comb, and good habits. Good hygiene presents a positive image and will result in being hired for a job more quickly. It will allow you to be a candidate for a promotion within your company. It will make you a more pleasant person to be around and will be most appreciated by your coworkers. It only makes sense. Real good scents!

—M. Gingrich

Work Problems

The boss ordered one of his men to dig a hole eight feet deep. After the job was completed the boss returned and explained an error had been made and the hole wouldn't be needed. "Fill 'er up," he ordered. The worker did as he'd been told. But he ran into a problem. He couldn't get all the dirt packed back into the hole without leaving a mound on top. He went to the office and explained his problem.

The boss snorted, "Honestly! The kind of help you get these days! There's obviously only one thing to do. You'll have to dig that hole deeper!"

Christmas

A Brother Like That

A friend of mine named Paul, received an automobile from his brother as a Christmas present. On Christmas Eve when Paul came out of his office, a street urchin was walking around the shiny new car, admiring it.

"Is that your car, Mister?" he asked.

Paul nodded. "My brother gave it to me for Christmas."

The boy was astounded. "You mean your brother gave it to you? Boy, I wish…" he hesitated.

Of course Paul knew what he was going to wish for. He was gong to wish for a brother like that. But what the lad said jarred Paul all the way down to his heels.

"I wish," the boy went on, "that I could be a brother like that."

Paul looked at the boy in astonishment, then impulsively added, "Would you like to take a ride in my automobile?"

"Oh yes, I'd love that."

After a short ride, the boy turned and with his eyes aglow, said, "Mister, would you mind driving in front of my house?"

Paul smiled a little. He thought he knew what the lad wanted. He wanted to show his neighbors that he could ride home in a big automobile. But Paul was wrong again. "Will you stop where those two steps are?" the boy asked.

He ran up the steps. Then in a little while Paul heard him coming back, but he was not coming fast. He was carrying his little crippled brother. He sat him down on the bottom step, then sort of squeezed up against him and pointed to the car. "There she is, buddy, just like I told you upstairs. His brother gave it to him for Christmas and it didn't cost him a cent. And some day I'm gonna give you one just like it. Then you can see for yourself all the pretty things I've been trying to tell you about."

Paul got out and lifted the lad to the front seat of his car. The three of them began a memorable holiday ride.

That Christmas eve, Paul learned what Jesus meant when he said, "It's more blessed to give…"

—Dan Clark

A Remarkable Story

We begin each year with renewed vigor and enthusiasm, having in place lofty goals and high aspirations. As we reach the end of the year many of the goals have been surpassed, but others still lie beyond our grasp. And so it is, as we reflect upon the year so quickly passed, that we again recognize our limitations. Everything we have accomplished is nothing unless it is done for the glory of God. Without him giving us life and breath, health and strength, the pages would be left unturned and the wheels would grind to a halt. We owe him our thanksgiving, our praise, our adoration, and our worship.

In the Christmas season we are reminded of the miraculous birth of Jesus Christ as a babe, with a manger for his bed in a lowly stable room. It is hardly the setting for a king. A remarkable story indeed and one that must be told from beginning to end. It began long before man came into existence. God created the world, the sun, the moon, the stars, and all the earth. He created the animals and the plants. Of the dust he formed man in his likeness, a creature of choice, and breathed into his nostrils and man became a living soul, an eternal being. Adam and Eve, the first human beings God created, sinned by a choice of disobedience and all generations of humanity have suffered the consequences of that one choice. As a result, we are born into this world with a sinful Adamic nature. But God in His love had formed a plan even before Adam and Eve disobeyed. He would send his son, his only son as a babe to earth, to live a sinless life, to minister and teach, to show by example, to give his life on Calvary, to shed his blood as an atonement for the sins of mankind. He would die, but then he would rise again triumphant over death and the grave. History records the events as they unfolded. We today, like Adam and Eve, have a choice. Believe, accept, obey—eternal life. Doubt, reject, disobey—eternal doom.

It is so much more than just a story. It is real! It is alive! It affects each person not only for time but for all eternity. It affects how we live today, what we say, what we do, our personality, our attitude, and our focus for life. The excitement and joy of becoming a part of the story is such that it compels us to repeat it again and again. It stirs a passion of wanting others to experience the freedom we have found. It is a rescue from the depths of despair and hopelessness to the realms of joy and gladness. It transcends all generations, all cultures, and all people.

The story continues to unfold. "I go to prepare a place for you and if I go and prepare a place for you, I will come again and receive you unto myself that where I am you may be also." Mansions, streets of gold, pure water, no night, no sadness, no death, no bickering, no fighting, no stealing, no hatred, but all will be joy and peace. While God had it all planned, man sees the future with limited understanding. By reading the scriptures and then observing things taking place in the world we see his promises unfolding before our eyes. "When you see these things come to pass, look up for your redemption draweth nigh!"

The story encompasses why we are here in the first place: to bring honor and glory to God, our Creator. Will you honor Him? If you accept Him, and obey His word, you will find the true meaning of why Christmas really exists. King of Kings and Lord of Lords.

—M. Gingrich

Christmas by the Cupful

- A heaping cup of happiness,
- 2 of love and caring,
- 1 of understanding,
- 1 of joyful sharing.
- A level cup of wisdom,
- 1 of artful living,
- 1 of thoughtful insight,
- 1 of selfless giving.
- Mix ingredients together,
- Toss in a little flair,
- Serve to everyone you know
- Topped with a tiny prayer.

May every measure of happiness be yours this Christmas time!

Christmas Shopping

It was Christmas and the judge was in a merry mood as he asked the prisoner, "What are you charged with?"

"Doing my Christmas shopping early," replied the defendant.

"That's no offense," said the judge. "How early were you doing this shopping?"

"Before the store opened," countered the prisoner.

Christ's Christmas Wish List

If you want to give Me a present in remembrance of My birth, here is My wish list. Choose something from it.

1. Instead of writing protest letters objecting to the way My birthday is being celebrated, write letters of love and hope to those who are away from home and lonely.
2. Visit someone in a nursing home. You don't have to know them personally. They just need to know that someone cares about them.
3. Instead of writing George complaining about the wording on the cards his staff sent out this year, why don't you write and tell him that you'll be praying for him and his family this year? Then follow up. It will be nice hearing from you again.
4. Instead of giving your children a lot of gifts you can't afford and they don't need, spend time with them. Tell them the story of My birth, and why I came to live with you down here. Hold them in your arms and remind them that I love them.
5. Pick someone who has hurt you in the past and forgive him or her.
6. Did you know that someone in your town will attempt to take their own life this season because they feel so alone and hopeless? Since you don't know who that person is, try giving everyone you meet a warm smile; it could make the difference. Also, you might consider supporting the local Hot Line; they talk with people like that every day.
7. Instead of nitpicking about what the retailer in your town calls the holiday, be patient with the people who work there. Give them a warm smile and a kind word. Even if they aren't allowed to wish you a "Merry Christmas", that doesn't keep you from wishing them one.
8. If you really want to make a difference, support a missionary, especially one who takes My love and Good News to those who have never heard My name. You may already know someone like that.

9. There are individuals and whole families in your town who will have no presents to give or receive. If you don't know them (and I suspect you don't), buy some food and a few gifts, and give them to a charity that believes in Me. They will make the delivery for you.
10. Finally, if you want to make a statement about your belief in and loyalty to Me, then support it with your actions. Don't do things in secret that you wouldn't do in My presence. Words are cheap. Your actions will reveal your level of commitment.

P.S. Don't forget; My Father and I can take care of Ourselves. Just love Us and do what I have asked you to do. I'll take care of all the rest. Check out the list and get to work. And do have a most blessed Christmas with all those whom you love. And remember, I LOVE YOU.

Family Togetherness

The Christmas holiday is noted for family get togethers, a kind of once-a-year reunion of sorts. It is a time of catching up on the news and happenings of the past year. We take time out to reminisce, share friendships, and simply reacquaint ourselves. Family is, and always has been, an important factor in the social fabric of humanity. It gives us a sense of belonging.

Most of us can trace our character traits and mannerisms (whether that is good or bad) back to our formative years of growing up surrounded by father and mother and siblings. Those childhood years were instrumental in shaping our future. Part of that growing up probably included going to grandma's house for Christmas and being together with family and friends around a table laden with food. That same togetherness draws us back year after year.

The retail industry and social peer pressure have largely commercialized Christmas. Together, they have pushed consumer debt to an all time high. Why? Consumers are spending money they do not have to buy gifts for people who have no need. Is that what Christmas is really about? Should it not be a time of clearing rather than incurring debt?

Jesus came to earth to erase a debt mankind could not pay. He gave to the poor and needy, the halt and the lame, the blind and the beggar and all who would surrender their hearts to Him. His gift was not one of monetary value but rather it was one of eternal value. Eternal life in place of death so that we could be together with Him in heaven. Jesus Christ as a babe in the manger was God's gift to all the world. His only son would grow up and walk the earth, teaching and preaching and then giving His own life so that others could be debt free—free from the curse of sin and death. Therein lies the real reason for the season! Won't you accept God's gift and make it your reason, too?

—M. Gingrich

Good Intentions For Christmas

A kindly 90-year-old grandmother found buying presents for family and friends a bit much one Christmas. She decided to write out checks for all of them to put in their Christmas cards. In each card she carefully wrote, "Buy your own present" and then sent them off. After the Christmas festivities were over, she found the checks under a pile of papers on her desk! Everyone on her gift list had received a beautiful Christmas card from her with "Buy your own present" written inside—without the check!

Great Gift Responses

What do you say when you get a gift you "Really Don't Like"?

9. "Well, well, well—now, there's a gift!"
8. "Hey, as long as I don't have to feed it, or clean up after it, or put batteries in it, I'm happy!"
7. "No, really, I didn't know that there was a ChiaPettie! Oh, wow! It's a clip-on too!"
6. "You know, I always wanted one of these! Jog my memory—what's it called again?"
5. "You know what?—I'm going to find a special place to put this!"
4. "Boy, you don't see craftsmanship like that every day!"
3. "And it's such an interesting color, too!"
2. "You say that was the last one? Am I ever glad that you snapped that baby up!"

And the number one thing to say about the Christmas gifts you didn't like is:

1. "You shouldn't have! I mean it—you really shouldn't have!"

Packing Up Christmas

John was tasked with taking the Christmas decorations up to the attic for another year's storage. During one trek up the stairs, heavily laden with boxes, he slipped and fortunately only fell about two steps before landing on his side.

His wife heard the noise and yelled, "What was that thump?"

"I just fell down the stairs," he explained.

She rushed into the room, "Anything broken?!"

"No, no, I'm fine." There was just a slight pause before his loving wife said, "No, I meant my decorations? Are any of them broken?"

The Christmas Card List

There is a list of folks I know
All written in a book,
And every year at Christmas time
I go and take a look,

And that is when I realize
Those names are all a part
Not of the book they're written in,
But deep inside my heart.

For each name stands for someone
Who has touched my life sometime,
And in that meeting they've become
A special friend of mine.

I really feel that I'm composed
Of each remembered name,
And my life is so much better
Than it was before they came.

Once you've known that "someone"
All the years cannot erase
The memory of a pleasant word
Or of a friendly face.

So never think my Christmas cards
Are just a mere routine
Of names upon a list that are
Forgotten in between.

For when I send a Christmas card
That is addressed to you,
It is because you're on that list
Of folks I'm indebted to.

And whether I have known you
For many years or few,
The greatest gift that God can give
Is having friends like you!

The Christmas Invitation

It was the biggest night of the year in a little town called Cornwall. It was the night of the annual Christmas pageant. It was an especially big deal for the children in town—they get to try out for the roles in the Christmas story. Everybody wants a part.

Which leads us to the problem of Harold. Harold really wanted to be in the play, too, but he was—well, he was kind of a slow and simple boy. The directors were ambivalent—I mean, they knew Harold would be crushed if he didn't have a part, but they were afraid he might mess up the town's magic moment. Finally, they decided to cast Harold as the innkeeper—the one who turns Mary and Joseph away the night Jesus is to be born. He had only one line—"I'm sorry, we have no room." Well, no one could imagine what that one line was going to do to everyone's Christmas...

The night of the pageant the church was packed, as usual. The Christmas story unfolded according to plan—angels singing, Joseph's dream, and the trip to Bethlehem. Finally, Joseph and Mary arrived at the door of the Bethlehem Inn, looking appropriately tired. Joseph knocked on the inn door, and Harold was there to open the door.

Joseph asked his question on cue—"Do you have a room for the night?" Harold froze. After a long pause, Harold mumbled his line, "I'm sorry—we have no room." And, with a little coaching, he shut the door. The directors heaved a sigh of relief—prematurely. As Mary and Joseph disappeared into the night, the set suddenly started shaking again—and the door opened. Harold was back! And then, in an unrehearsed moment that folks would not soon forget, Harold went running after the young couple, shouting as loud as he could—"Wait! Don't go Joseph. Bring Mary back! You can have my room!"

I think little Harold may have understood the real issue of Christmas better than anyone else there that night. How could he leave Jesus outside? He had to make room for Jesus. And that may be the issue for you this

Christmas. What will you do with this Son of God who came to earth to find you?

Jesus is the one who trades a throne room for a stable, and the praise of angels for human mockery. This is the Creator who gives himself on a cross! The Bible gives us the only appropriate response: "The life I now live I live by faith in the Son of God who loved me and gave himself for me" (Gal. 2:20). You look at what Jesus did to pay for your sin on that cross, and you say those life-changing words—"For me."

Jesus is at your door this Christmas. Maybe he's been knocking for a long time. He may not keep knocking much longer. All your life—even the events of the last few months—have been to prepare you for this cross-roads moment with Jesus your Savior. Don't leave him outside any longer. Open the door this Christmas day. Allow Jesus to have your room…your life.

The Christmas Stranger

There was a man at Christmas time
Who looked so out of place,
As people rushed about him
At a hurried sort or pace.

He stared at all the Christmas lights
The tinsel everywhere.
The shopping center Santa Claus
With children gathered near.

The music from a stereo
Was playing loud and clear,
Of Santa Claus and snowmen
And a funny-nosed reindeer.

He heard the people talk about the
Good times on the way,
Of parties, fun, and food galore and
Gifts exchanged that day.

"I'd like to know what's going on,"
The man was heard to say,
"There seems to be some sort
Of celebration on the way.

"And would you tell me who this is
All dressed in red and white?
And why are children asking him
About a special night?"

The answer came in disbelief,
"I can't believe my ears!
I can't believe you do not know
That Christmas time is here!

"The time when Santa comes around
With gifts for girls and boys.
When they're asleep on Christmas eve
He brings them books and toys!

"The man you see in red and white
Is Santa Claus so sly.
The children love his joyful laugh
And the twinkle in his eye.

"They learn to love this jolly man while
They are still quite small.
When Christmas comes, he is
The most important one of all!"

The stranger hung His head in shame,
He looked at nail-pierced hands.
His body shook in disbelief,
T'was not as He had planned.

A shadow crossed His stricken face,
His voice was low but clear.
"After all these years they still don't know."
And Jesus shed a tear.

The Shopping Frenzy!

The shop 'til you drop gift buying frenzy is on. One week left to get all those remaining gifts. Gloves for Uncle Joe, a scarf for Aunt Suzy, a toy for each of the grandchildren, a gift certificate for the grandparents, and still undecided on school teachers, friends, and even my spouse. Time is running out! I just have to get something! It wouldn't be right if I didn't! It's expected even though none of it is really needed! Hopefully, I've remembered everyone! Wouldn't that be just awful if I forgot someone?

Do you feel stressed out and caught in the rut of buying gifts because it's the thing to do? Do you sense a tinge of guilt because the gift you got for someone was much less than what they got for you? Are you going to be paying off your holiday spending for the next half year? Why do Americans put themselves through this cycle? Is it a tradition that it out of control? Are we afraid we might offend someone if we break the cycle?

This frenzy has some disastrous results. Folks are bombarded with advertising gimmicks and are easily talked into purchasing things they normally would not, because they need to fill out their gift list. People put themselves in dire financial straits because of overspending. There is also the status quo to be reckoned with. Keeping up with the Joneses next door is important to some people even if they can't afford it.

How can we get out of this rut? A few suggestions! Set a predetermined conservative amount of what you are going to spend. Never put it on credit. If you don't have the money then don't buy gifts. Volunteer some time rather than give a gift. Make sure that gifts you do give are useful and practical. Spread your gift giving: throughout the year. It will be more meaningful, and better appreciated. A small token that is given with heartfelt appreciation will resonate with the recipient more than a large gift that is given with a feeling of obligation.

In this land of plenty we have fallen prey to the deceit that things bring happiness. That is false! Those things are displayed in mass quantity on the sidewalk waiting for the garbage man a few weeks after Christmas. The sooner we remove ourselves from the frenzy, the sooner we will enjoy the true meaning of Christmas. Christmas is a time to reflect on the greatest gift of all time, the Christ Child.

This Christmas, Give Gifts That Keep On Giving

To a friend…Your heart.
To your child…A good example.
To your parents…Respect.
To someone who has wronged you…Forgiveness.
To all men…Love.
God's gift to us: Luke 2:11, John 3:16

Top Ten Things To Say About A Christmas Gift You Don't Like

10. "Hey! There's a gift!"
9. "Well, well, well…"
8. "Boy, if I had not recently shot up four sizes that would've fit."
7. "This is perfect for wearing around the basement."
6. "Wow! I hope this never catches fire! It is fire season though. There are lots of unexplained fires."
5. "If the dog buries it, I'll be furious!"
4. "I love it—but I fear the jealousy it will inspire."
3. "Sadly, tomorrow I enter the Federal Witness Protection Program."
2. "To think—I got this the year I vowed to give all my gifts to charity."
1. "I really don't deserve this."

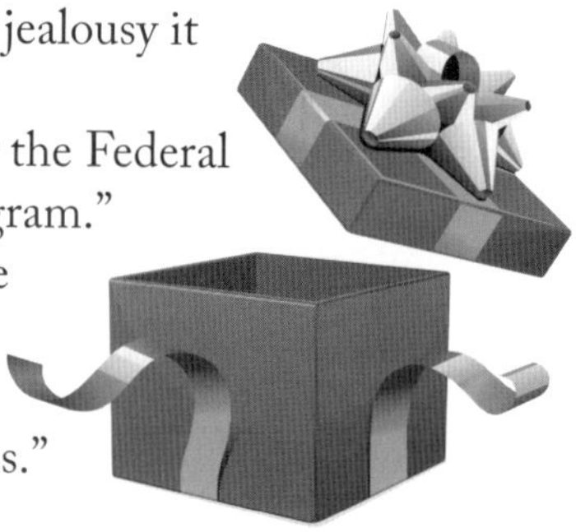

Wouldn't It Be Nice?

Wouldn't it be nice, on Christmas day,
If we would take the time,
To just sit down, and close our eyes,
And picture in our mind.

The little town of Bethlehem,
Though far away it be,
In a manger, in a stable,
A newborn child, we see.

This new born child is heaven-sent,
Christ Jesus is his name,
Born to redeem mankind from sin,
And not to garner fame.

This holy Son, of holy God,
Born here on planet earth,
Has power to, forgive our sins,
And give us second birth.

So if it be, on Christmas day,
That we have found the time,
Let us whisper…"Thank you, Father,
For Jesus, Lord divine.

And if it be, Thy will, we ask,
As we, with closed eyes, pray,
May more of mankind, by thy grace,
Turn to Jesus, every day."

—*Robert K. Phillips*

Church

Attend Church When It Rains

Strange, but some people won't attend church Sunday morning when it rains, but don't miss work Monday when it rains.

If I miss church because it rains, I may miss a sermon that was especially for me.

I expect the pastor to be in the church, and his wife and his family to be present. If I don't excuse them from missing church, why should I excuse myself?

Just imagine. If the rapture happens on a rainy day would some say, "Wait Lord, until the rain is over, I can't go out in the rain."

Poor example. Parents require their children to attend school when it rains, but don't require them to attend church when it rains.

Shopping. The malls are busy when it rains, but why does church attendance drop 15% and sometimes more when it rains Sunday morning?

Blood Of Jesus

One night in a church service a young woman felt the tug of God at her heart. She responded to God's call and accepted Jesus as her Lord and Savior. The young woman had a very rough past, involving alcohol, drugs, and prostitution. But, the change in her was evident.

As time went on she became a faithful member of the church. She eventually became involved in the ministry, teaching young children. It was not very long until this faithful young woman had caught the eye and heart of the pastor's son. The relationship grew and they began to make wedding plans. This is when the problems began.

You see, about one half of the church did not think that a woman with a past such as hers was suitable for a pastor's son. The church began to argue and fight about the matter. So they decided to have a meeting. As the people made their arguments, the tensions increased. The meeting was getting completely out of hand. The young woman became very upset about all the things being brought up about her past. As she began to cry the pastor's son stood to speak. He could not bear the pain it was causing his wife-to-be. He began to speak and his statement was this: "My fiancée's past is not what is on trial here. What you are questioning is the ability of the blood of Jesus to wash away sin. Today you have put the blood of Jesus on trial. So, does it wash away sin or not?" The whole church began to weep as they realized that they had been slandering the blood of the Lord Jesus Christ.

Too often, even as Christians, we bring up the past and use it as a weapon against our brothers and sisters. Forgiveness is a very foundational part of the Gospel of our Lord Jesus Christ. If the blood of Jesus does not cleanse the other person completely then it cannot cleanse us completely. If that is the case, then we are all in a lot of trouble.

What can wash away my sins? Nothing but the blood of Jesus! End of case!!!

"Cast your burden upon the Lord, and He shall sustain you. He shall never suffer the righteous to be moved" (Psalm 55:23).

Building Or Demolition?

The house was over a hundred years old. Much of the work, interior and exterior, was hand carved wood. It took almost a year to build.

A demolition crew of two trucks and a bulldozer came at 7:30 a.m., and by 3:30 p.m. the house was completely razed, the foundation removed and filled with ground. It appeared there was never a house at this location.

It takes years to build a strong Church. Lies, gossip, criticism, and rebellion can weaken and destroy it. It takes a lifetime to build strong Christian character, but it can be quickly destroyed by accusations and rumors.

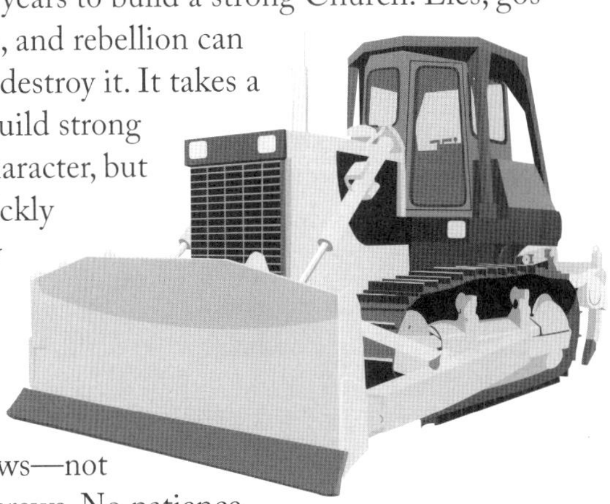

God is seeking for building crews—not demolition crews. No patience, skill, or work is required to destroy. Allow God to use you to build—not to destroy!

Cardboard

A young minister was filling in for Norman Vincent Peale at Marblegate Cathedral. Ascending the pulpit he looked at the magnificent colored glass windows and told the congregation: "You know, these beautiful windows remind me of your pastor and his sermons. I'm afraid that I will be like that piece of cardboard in that broken window over there by comparison." After finishing a marvelous sermon, he said farewell to the people leaving.

One little old lady warmly shook his hand and gazing fondly up at him gushed: "Oh, Pastor, you weren't just a piece of cardboard, you were a real pane!"

Church Attendance

I have been amazed at how many people seem to have developed the idea that summers are not for attending church services. Summers are for taking long extended times away from church. Is church attendance necessary? Does the Lord really expect us to be faithful in attendance at regular church services? The answer is found from Hebrews 10:25, "Not forsaking the assembling of ourselves together, as the manner of some is; but exhorting one another: and so much the more as ye see the day approaching."

Now, please consider the following from an Ann Landers column. "Dear Church Member: Don't wait until the hearse hauls you to church. If you do, you will go regardless of the weather. There will be beautiful flowers there, but you won't enjoy them. The pastor may say some good things about you, but you won't be able to hear them. There will be beautiful music, but you won't be enjoying it. There will be heartfelt prayers, but they will not touch your heart. There will be friends and relatives there, but you will not worship with them. You will go, no matter how many hypocrites are there. You will go, no matter how much you are needed at home. You won't be concerned about whether you're dressed right. After that final trip you will never have to decide whether to attend church or not. You'll never get another chance. Aren't you glad to be alive and well and have the choice of whether or not to go to church?"

Church Building Or Wrecking Crew

Ten little church members came to worship all the time.
One fell out with the pastor, and then there were nine.

Nine little members stayed up late.
One overslept and then there were eight.

Eight church members praying to heaven.
One took the low road and now there are seven.

Seven church members all chirping like chicks.
One didn't like the music, now there are six.

Six church members seemed very much alive,
But one got 'travelitis'; this left five.

Five church members pulling for glory's shore.
One tired and got disgruntled, and this left four.

Four church members, busy as can be;
But one got his feelings hurt, and now there are three.

Three church members and the story's almost done,
For two of them got weary and this left one.

Now everybody knows that one can't do much,
But one brought a friend last month
and then there were two.

Two church members each won one more.
Now don't you see? 2+2=4!

Four church members worked early and late.
Each one brought one and now there are eight.

Have you got the message, pointed and true?
Come on folks, we've got a job to do.

For you see, these eight church members,
If they double as before,
In just seven weeks, would have 1,024!

In this little jingle there is a lesson true.
You belong to one of the two—
Either the building or the wrecking crew.

Dear Pastor, I liked your sermon on Sunday. Especially when it was finished.

Church Lesson

One Sunday morning when my son was about five, we were attending church in our community. It was common for the preacher to invite the children to the front of the church and have a small lesson before the beginning of the sermon. He would bring in an item they could find around the house and relate it to a teaching from the Bible.

This particular morning, the visual aid for his lesson was a smoke detector. He asked the children if anyone knew what it meant when an alarm sounded from the smoke detector.

My child immediately raised his hand and said, "It means daddy's cooking dinner."

Dear Pastor

Letters From Children

Dear Pastor, Please say in your sermon that Peter Peterson has been a good boy all week. I am Peter Peterson.

Dear Pastor, My father should be a minister. Every day he gives us a sermon about something.

Dear Pastor, I'm sorry I can't leave more money in the plate, but my father didn't give me a raise in my allowance. Could you have a sermon about a raise in my allowance?

Dear Pastor, Please pray for all the airline pilots. I am flying to California tomorrow.

Dear Pastor, Please say a prayer for our Little League team. We need God's help or a new pitcher. Thank you.

Dear Pastor, My father says I should learn the Ten Commandments. But I don't think I want to because we have enough rules already in my house.

If I Were Your…

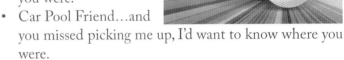

- Wife…and you missed supper, I'd want to know where you were.
- Boss…and you missed work, I'd want to know where you were.

- Coach…and you missed practice, I'd want to know where you were.
- Golf Partner…and you missed our tee-off, I'd want to know where you were.
- Car Pool Friend…and you missed picking me up, I'd want to know where you were.
- Teacher…and you missed class, I'd want to know where you were.

But I am your Pastor, and you missed Church on Sunday, but I'm not supposed to be nosey?

—*Source Unknown*

Just Like Me?

What would the Church be like, if everyone attended the Sunday morning service as often as me?

What would the Church be like, if everyone attended the Sunday night services as often as me?

What would the Church be like, if everyone attended the Wednesday night services as often as me?

What would the Church be like, if everyone gave of their finances just like me?

What would the Church be like, if everyone prayed for the Church just like me?

What would the Church be like, if everyone witnessed to others as often as me?

New Church

A rich man went to his minister and said, "I want you and your wife to take a three-month trip to the Holy Land at my expense. When you come back, I'll have a surprise for you".

The minister accepted the offer, and he and his wife went off to the Middle East. Three months later they returned home and were met by the wealthy parishioner.

He told them that while they were gone, he had a new church built. "It's the finest building money can buy," said the man. "No expense was spared."

And he was right. It was a magnificent edifice both inside and out. But there was one striking difference. There was only one pew, and it was at the very back.

"A church with only one pew?" asked the minister.

"You just wait until Sunday," the rich man said.

When the time came for the Sunday service, the early arrivals entered the church, filed onto the one pew and sat down. When the pew was full, a switch clicked silently, a circuit closed, the gears meshed, a belt moved and, automatically, the rear pew began to move forward. When it reached the front of the church, it came to a stop. At the same time, another empty pew came up from below at the back and more people sat down.

And so it continued, pews filling and moving forward until finally the church was full, from front to back. "Wonderful!" said the minister, "Marvelous!"

The service began, and the minister started to preach his sermon. He launched into his text and, when 12 o'clock came, he was still going strong, with no end in sight. Suddenly a bell rang, and a trap door in the floor behind the pulpit dropped open.

"Wonderful!" said the congregation, "Marvelous!"

No Excuses

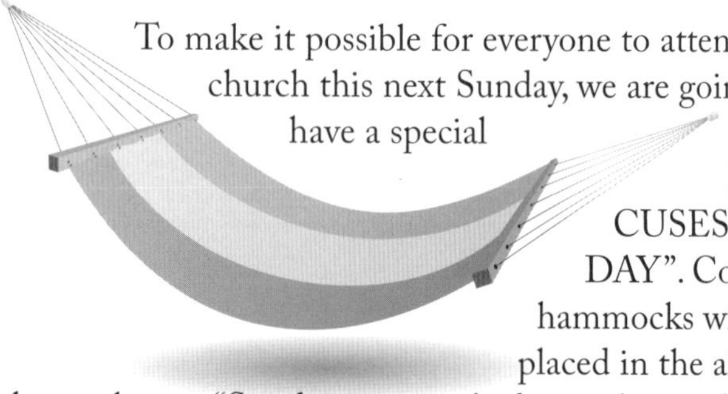

To make it possible for everyone to attend church this next Sunday, we are going to have a special "NO EXCUSES SUNDAY". Cots and hammocks will be placed in the aisles for those who say "Sunday is my only day to sleep in."

Eye drops and extra coffee will be provided for those with tired eyes from being out too late Saturday night.

There will be a special section with padded recliner chairs for those who feel that our pews are too hard.

Doctors and nurses will be in attendance for those who plan to be sick on Sunday.

We will have steel hard hats available for those who say. "the roof would cave in if I ever came to church."

One section will be decorated with trees and grass for those who like to seek God in nature.

Scorecards and pens will be provided for those who wish to list the hypocrites present.

Blankets will be furnished for at those who say the church is too cold and portable fans for those who say it is too hot.

And finally, the sanctuary will be decorated with both Christmas wreaths and Easter lilies for those who have never seen the church without them.

See you on Sunday. No excuses!

Real Church Signs

- "Worry is the darkroom in which negatives develop."
- "The best vitamin for a Christian is B1."
- "Under same management for over 2000 years."
- "Tithe if you love Jesus! Anyone can honk!"
- "You can give without loving, but you cannot love without giving."
- "Beat the Christmas rush, come to church this Sunday!"
- "Don't wait for the hearse to take you to church."
- "We should be more concerned with the Rock Of Ages, instead of the age of rocks."
- "Reputation is what people think about you. Character is what people know you are."
- "Seven days without prayer makes one weak."
- "No Jesus—no peace, Know Jesus—know peace!"
- "Worry is interest paid on trouble before it is due."
- "A man's character is like a fence. It cannot be strengthened by whitewash."
- "Preach the gospel at all times. Use words if necessary."
- "Delay is preferable to error."
- "Prevent truth decay. Brush up on your Bible."
- "Repent before payday."
- "Can't sleep? Try counting your blessings."
- "Forbidden fruit creates many jams."
- "Christians, keep the faith. But not from others!"
- "Satan subtracts and divides. God multiplies and multiplies."

- "To belittle is to be little."
- "God answers knee mail."
- "It's hard to stumble when you're down on your knees."
- "A clear conscience makes a soft pillow."
- "The wages of sin is death."

Service For One

On Sunday, the new young pastor arrived at church and found only an old farmer had shown up. After waiting a while, the disappointed pastor remarked to the old farmer, "Well, it appears no one else is coming, so we should probably cancel service today."

The farmer, dressed in his Sunday best, looked at the young preacher and said, "Well pastor, I don't know much 'bout preachin', but I do know something 'bout farmin' and if I went out in the field and found only one cow, I'd still feed 'em."

This excited the young preacher who preached for the next forty-five minutes a fierce fire and brimstone sermon. Afterwards, the pastor asked the old farmer what he thought.

The old farmer remarked, "Well pastor, I don't know much 'bout preachin', but I do know somethin' 'bout farmin' and if I went out in the field and found only one cow, I wouldn't give 'em the whole bale."

Shoes In Church

I showered and shaved,
I adjusted my tie.
I got there and sat,
In a pew just in time.

Bowing my head in prayer,
As I closed my eyes.
I saw the shoe of the man next to me
Touching my own. I sighed.

With plenty of room on either side,
I thought, "Why must our soles touch?"
It bothered me, his shoe touching mine,
But it didn't bother him much.

A prayer began: "Our Father"
I thought, "This man with the shoes has no pride.
They're dusty, worn, and scratched.
Even worse, there are holes on the side!"

"Thank You for blessings," the prayer went on.
The shoe man said a quiet "Amen."
I tried to focus on the prayer,
But my thoughts were on his shoes again.

"Aren't we supposed to look our best
When walking through that door?"
"Well, this certainly isn't it,"
I thought, glancing toward the floor.

Then the prayer was ended
And the songs of praise began.
The shoe man was certainly loud,
Sounding proud as he sang.

His voice lifted the rafters,
His hands were raised high.
The Lord could surely hear
The shoe man's voice from the sky.

It was time for the offering,
And what I threw in was steep.
I watched as the shoe man
Reached into his pockets so deep.

I saw what was pulled out,
What the shoe man put in.
Then I heard a soft "clink",
As when silver hits tin.

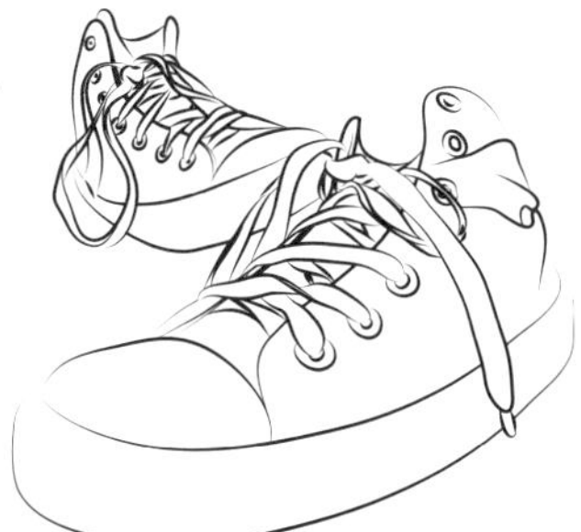

The sermon really bored me,
To tears, and that's no lie.
It was the same for the shoe man,
For tears fell from his eyes.

At the end of the service,
As is the custom here.
We must greet new visitors,
And show them all good cheer.

But I felt moved somehow,
And wanted to meet the shoe man.
So after the closing prayer,
I reached over and shook his hand.

He was old and his skin was dark,
And his hair was truly a mess.
But I thanked him for coming,
For being our guest.

He said, "My name's Charlie,
I'm glad to meet you, my friend."
There were tears in his eyes,
But he had a large, wide grin.

"Let me explain," he said,
Wiping tears from his eyes.
"I've been coming here for months,
And you're the first to say 'Hi.'"

"I know that my appearance
Is not like all the rest."
"But I really do try
To always look my best."

"I always clean and polish my shoes
Before my very long walk.
"But by the time I get here,
They're dirty and dusty, like chalk."

My heart filled with pain,
And I swallowed to hide my tears.
As he continued to apologize
For daring to sit so near.

He said, "When I get here,
I know I must look a sight."
"But I thought if I could touch you,
Then maybe our souls might unite."

I was silent for a moment,
Knowing whatever was said,
Would pale in comparison,
I spoke from my heart, not my head.

"Oh, you've touched me" I said,
"And taught me, in part;"
"That the best of any man
Is what is found in his heart."

The rest, I thought,
This shoe man will never know.
Like just how thankful I really am,
That his dirty old shoe touched my soul.

Stern Announcement

During a sermon one Sunday, the pastor heard two teenage girls in the back giggling and disturbing people. He interrupted his sermon and announced sternly, "There are two of you here who have not heard a word I've said." That quieted them down again.

When the service was over, he went to greet people at the front door. Three different adults apologized for going to sleep in church, promising it would never happen again.

The Art Of Meddling

Smith and Jones were on the outs over a trivial matter. Both attended the same church but were not on speaking terms. This worried Deacon Brown and he determined to heal the breach.

He called on Smith and said, "What do you think of Jones?"

"Oh, he is the meanest crank in town!"

"But," said the deacon, "you must admit he is very kind to his family."

"Oh sure, he is very kind to his family."

Next day Deacon Brown went to Jones and said, "Do you know what Smith says about you?"

"I can imagine what he says about me."

"Well, he says that you are very kind to your family."

"What! Did Smith say that?"

"Yes, What do you think of Smith?" asked the Deacon.

"He's a low-down scalawag."

"But" said the deacon, "you will have to admit that he is very honest."

"Yes, he is honest, but what has that to do with it?"

The next day the deacon called Smith again and said, "Do you know what Jones says about you? He says you are very honest."

"You don't mean it!"

"I do. I heard it with my own ears."

The next Sunday in church, Smith and Jones were seen in friendly conversation.

The Church—A Lighthouse

The archbishop of Canterbury asked Thomas Betterton, a famous actor, why it seemed actors had no difficulty making an impression on their audiences. His reply was, actors speak of things imaginary as if they were real, while you preachers too often speak of things real as if they were imaginary.

A young minister having some difficulty in his congregation sought some advice. J. Vernon Mcgee told the young preacher of his experience as a boy on the farm. "When I would go to the barn at night to feed the horse or the cow, I would light a lantern and carry it with me. As I opened the barn door two things would happen. The rats would scurry for cover, and the birds roosting in the rafters would begin to sing. Light had those two very different effects." He advised the young preacher to go back home and preach the word of God, and the rats will run for cover and the birds will begin to sing.

Has the light of the church grown dim and misguided so that the rats no longer run scared? Have too many preachers become politicians and actors? Have churches today become social centers of entertainment more interested in catering to pleasure seekers than preaching gospel truth? Has the church forgotten her call? Has she caved in to the whims and wishes of a carefree society? Is it possible that the church has overstepped its bounds in trying to orchestrate the roles of government? Has she forgotten the power of God in setting up kings and rulers? Has she forgotten the power of prayer? Has she forgotten that God is sovereign? Has she forgotten that her mission is to meet the spiritual needs of mankind?

Her call is not to make people feel good about living in sinful bondage but to show them the joy of deliverance from sin. Her mission is to bring sinners to repentance and salvation. Her call is a call of spiritual dimensions that guide our choices in life, our thoughts, and our actions. It is founded on Jesus Christ who not only taught, but lived by example, a life of sacrifice and submission. The call of the church is to show that same type of love and compassion. It spans the gulf of race and government. It is a love that hates sin but loves the sinner.

The church is called to lead people from earth to eternal glory. It is a calling that is superior to any earthly government. Thrones and kingdoms cease, men pass off the scene, but the church is eternal. Jesus, the one who conquered death and the grave is still building his church and he has promised that the gates of hell shall not prevail against it. Generation after generation there are those who heed his call to lay down their lives and follow him. When the light of the gospel penetrates the darkness of sin in their lives and they repent and seek the forgiveness of God, they experience a joy of deliverance that makes them want to sing from the rafters. Those who refuse God's hand of mercy, scurry for cover when they are exposed to the gospel, ashamed of their sinful deeds. There is nothing imaginary about it. It is real!

Could we say then, that the church is like a lighthouse that shines through the darkness, warning of danger, and guiding weary pilgrims safely home?

—M. Gingrich

The Dollar Bill

They were burning the old paper money at the U.S. Mint in Washington, D.C. A hundred dollar bill and a fifty dollar bill were telling all the resorts and vacation places they had attended. They asked the one dollar bill where he had been. His reply, "The only place I've been is church."

The Front Pew

An elderly woman walked into the local country church. The friendly usher greeted her at the door and helped her up the flight of steps.

"Where would you like to sit?" he asked politely.

"The front row please," she answered.

"You really don't want to do that," the usher said. "The pastor is really boring."

"Do you happen to know who I am?" the woman inquired.

"No," he said.

"I'm the pastor's mother," she replied indignantly.
"Do you know who I am?" he asked.
"No," she said.
"Good," he answered, "Let me show you the front pew."

Where Were You?

You invited a coworker to visit your church. You spoke how you loved to attend your church. However, your coworker visited on a Sunday night and you were absent. Where were you?

Who Will Do The Work?

The following letter, which speaks for itself, was circulated in a large congregation.

Dear Friend:
Our Church membership......................1400
Nonresident members...............................75
Balance left to do the work..................1325

Elderly who have done their share...........25
Balance left to do the work..................1275

Sick and shut-in.......................................25
Balance left to do the work..................1275

Members who do not give......................350
Christmas and Easter members..............300
Balance left to do the work.....................625

Members who are overworked................300
Balance left to do the work.....................325

Members with alibis...............................200
Balance left to do the work....................125

Members too busy with other things......123
Balance left to do the work........................2

Just you and me, friend, and you had better get busy, busy, because it's too much for me!

—*Our Daily Bread*

You Took My Place

One day, a man went to visit a church. He arrived early, parked his car, and got out. Another car pulled up near him, and the driver told him, "I always park there. You took my place!"

The visitor went inside for Sunday school, found an empty seat, and sat down.

A young lady from the church approached him and stated, "That's my seat! You took my place!"

The visitor was somewhat distressed by this rude welcome, but said nothing.

After Sunday school, the visitor went into the church sanctuary and sat down.

Another member walked up to him and said, "That's where I always sit. You took my place!"

The visitor was even more troubled by this treatment, but still said nothing.

Later, as the congregation was praying for Christ to dwell among them, the visitor stood, and his appearance began to change. Horrible scars became visible on his hands and on his sandaled feet.

Someone from the congregation noticed him and called out, "What happened to you?"

The visitor replied, "I took your place."

Discipline

As A Man Thinketh

Does our thought life have an impact on our actions? Can we alter a pattern of wrong behavior by changing our thinking? The answer to these questions is a resounding yes! Our thinking is developed and characterized by the things we read, the things we hear, the things we see; and it is reinforced through our actions. You may argue that wrong actions are the result of a lack of thinking. It may be true that not much thought was given to the possible consequences; however, I believe that wrong actions are fueled by feeding our thoughts with garbage. Wrong thinking leads to deceptive characteristics that produce inappropriate conduct. Right thinking leads to a character of integrity and results in honorable actions.

There is a lot of publicity on how harmful spanking is to our children. I agree, if it is done in anger. There is, however, many a person who was set straight in life because of a spanking that was properly administered in a kind and loving way by his or her parents. A child must be taught right and wrong at a very young age. They need to know that wrong actions bring undesirable consequences and right actions bring positive and pleasant rewards. Discipline administered properly will instill into a child the desire to do what is right. Far too often we want to throw away these time proven principles that work, for ideas that sound more pleasant, but prove otherwise. The pain of a rebellious and unrestrained child is far greater than the few meetings it takes back at the old woodshed. Discipline must never be carried out in anger. Holding your child on your lap after the discipline is administered will demonstrate to the child that you love them but not their actions. That is positive reinforcement. The child will soon forget the pain of the moment and will find joy in the fact that my parent loves me and a peace that my parent forgives me.

Technology today is such that we are bombarded on every side with garbage that is unfit for human consumption and yet society is consuming it. The old adage that says input = output is visibly relevant around us. Will we as a society alter the course in our homes and communities? It begins with right thinking that is developed by a proper diet of wholesome literature. It will require turning off the television and spending time together with our children. It will require weeding out the magazines and videos that are inappropriate. It will take effort but you can alter the course in your home. It begins with you thinking wholesome thoughts and taking the needed actions to teach your children, so they in turn will grow into men and women of integrity. We have a choice to make a difference. To default is unacceptable. We will reap the rewards. As a man thinketh in his heart so is he.

—M. Gingrich

At The Bakery

A customer in a bakery was observed carefully examining all the rich-looking pastries displayed on trays in the glass cases.

When a clerk approached him and asked, "What would you like?" he answered, "I'd like that chocolate-covered, cream-filled doughnut, that jelly-filled doughnut, and that cheese danish."

Then with a sigh he added. "But, I'll take an oat-bran muffin."

Classroom Disorder

It was the first day of school. The previous principal had just retired and a new principal just started. As the principal made his rounds, he heard a terrible commotion coming from one of the classrooms.

He rushed in and spotted one boy, taller than the others, who seemed to be making the most noise. He seized the lad, dragged him to the hall, and told him to wait there until he was excused.

Returning to the classroom, the principal restored order and lectured the class for half an hour about the importance of good behavior.

"Now," he said, "are there any questions?"

One girl stood up timidly. "Please sir," she asked, "May we have our teacher back?"

Tent Caterpillars

On a drive through the Blue Marsh Recreation area I noticed a proliferation of tent caterpillar nests. Certain trees were totally stripped of their leaves and were covered with nests leaving a very unsightly appearance. It was a panorama of devastation. Another time while traveling I saw some large areas of trees completely stripped of their foliage by gypsy moths. It too, was an unpleasant sight. Both situations were caused by an over saturation of a destructive predator and failure to combat it. The result was clearly undesirable. If those trees continue to be neglected and receive that kind of onslaught they will eventually succumb to the elements and die. Both of these situations could have been avoided with the proper treatment. Sometimes that treatment is not given because of the cost involved. It may be considered to be too expensive. Other times it may go untreated because no one wants to take responsibility, and at other times it may simply be caused by neglect.

As I observed the results of these two scenarios, I concluded that doing nothing is even more costly. Those trees are going to die. Those predators are going to continue their rampage and move on to other trees. Untreated the devastation will continue to spread.

I thought about how this compares to disciplining and training children. When we allow tent caterpillars like rebellion, slothfulness, selfishness, and disobedience to go unchecked and untreated it produces ugly and devastating results. The cost to treat them escalates and the damage caused is irreversible. Disciplining children is viewed by many in our society as being harsh and harmful. Our society, in general, refuses to tackle issues at their core. They try approaches that appear less harsh and seem less intimidating, but the fact remains that a heart untreated will bear ugly fruit. Preventive treatment is far more effective and less costly than picking up the pieces afterwards. Proper discipline gently applied with love will break the rebellious spirit, it will teach the joy of sharing and will guide the heart to willing obedience. Disrespect for authority does not begin in the teens. It begins in early childhood. Disobedience does not begin in adolescence. It begins when mom and dad say no and the child chooses to disobey, because they want their own way. I have observed parents yelling and screaming at their children with little or no results. The child has learned that if they hold out, the storm will pass and they will get their own way. A child whose will is broken is teachable and will respect authority. Certainly a small dosage of discipline at an early age is less taxing on parents and their children.

Children want to know where the boundaries lie. They want clear cut directions. Then they can grow and mature into healthy teenagers and mature responsible adults without a lot of ugly scars. For that to happen we need to address the core issues. Anything else is too little, too late.

—M. Gingrich

Ten Ways To Raise A Juvenile Delinquent

1. Begin at infancy to give a child everything he wants. In this way he will grow up to believe the world owes him a living.
2. When he picks up bad words, laugh at him. This will make him think he's cute.
3. Never give him any spiritual training. Wait until he is 21 and then let him decide for himself.
4. Pick up everything he leaves lying around—books, shoes, clothes. Do everything for him so that he will be experienced in throwing all responsibility on others.
5. Quarrel frequently in his presence. In this way, he will not be too shocked when the home is broken up later.
6. Give a child all the spending money he wants. Never let him earn his own. Why should he have things as tough as you had them?
7. Satisfy his every craving for food, drink, and comfort. Denial may lead to harmful frustration.
8. Take his part against neighbors, teachers, policemen. They are all prejudiced against your child.
9. When he gets into trouble, apologize for yourself by saying "I never could do anything with him."
10. Prepare for a life of grief. You are bound to have it!

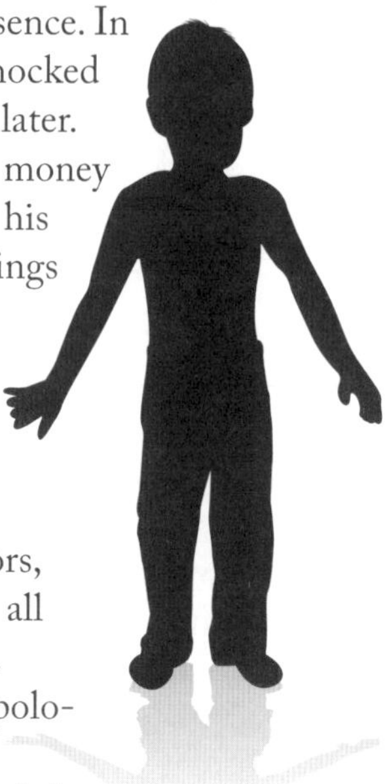

Faith

A Backslider's Prayer

LORD! If you can find it in your heart to just forgive, I'll come back and live the way you wanted me to live. All I want is just to be your child. Please come and get me and take me to your world. Take me to your world away from all of this sin. Where I won't have to be afraid or ever sin again. A place where love is found and there is plenty to go around. A place of beauty and great peace, and GOD meets every need.

LORD! Take me to your world and make me forget the way I used to live. Where people say I love you, and love is not a sin. A place you can start a new life again. A place of beauty and splendor and all you have to do is surrender. Surrender to the LOVE of GOD.

Worship HIM, Praise HIM, make HIM number ONE in all you say and do, and GOD will always come through. HE loves you so very much, so PLEASE stay in touch. Remember HE died for you. So the least you can do, is love HIM too.

LORD! Forgive me when I whine. Help me to remember when YOU were not mine. LORD, have mercy on me, and thanks for setting me free. Help me make it through each and every day, to live a GODLY way. Let me be a blessing to someone in need and lead them to JESUS!

About Those New Year's Resolutions

New Year's resolutions, although they have become a joke to many people, can be of real value, don't you think? Your resolutions may take the form of goals for the year ahead; or you may wish to establish rules for day by day living. Here are seven rules for daily living which were practiced by the late F. B. Meyer:

1. Make a daily definite consecration of yourself audibly to God.
2. Tell God that you are willing to be made willing about everything.
3. Reckon on Christ to do his part perfectly.
4. Confess sin instantly.
5. Hand over to Christ every temptation and every care.
6. Keep in touch with Christ. Read the Bible and good books, pray, and seek places and people where He is.
7. Expect the Holy Spirit to work in, with, and for you.

How wonderful it is to know that God is the Lord of time, and that He will be until the stream of time is swallowed up in the ocean of eternity!

—Copied

A Christian's Uniform

A policeman in his uniform receives more respect than when not in uniform. The same applies to a nurse, airplane pilot, and others who are required to wear a special uniform.

Paul tells us to put on Christ (Col. 3:8-9). In simple words, live like Christ lived. This is the Christian uniform.

An Anchor In The Midst Of Change!

For a whole year we heard the winds of change. The president elect promised change in the way government operates. He promised change Americans can believe in. Less than a month after his election and prior to his taking office, we heard grumbling and discrepancies that he was not following up on his promises. There are those on one side of the aisle who say, "We supported you, now support our cause." On the other side of the aisle are more outstretched hands, clamoring for their place in line. Therein lies the dilemma for the president elect. How can I satisfy the majority on both sides of the aisle and still maintain the promises that I have made?

Change there will be. America has experienced a change of presidents many times in the past, and along with those changes have come many challenges. Some presidents have served well and the country has prospered. Some have inherited difficult situations while others have served in periods of relative ease. Each president brought new ideas, a list of goals, and an agenda of how to accomplish them. Change is really nothing new, sometimes it is just old ideas resurrected by a new generation. Change can be good but it must be founded on principles of integrity and honesty or it will not bring lasting satisfaction. Change for the sake of change will be short-lived.

In the midst of all this change there are two things that haven't changed. The first is that all mankind is born of a sinful nature. Every man and woman since the fall of Adam and Eve is subject to a nature that pursues pride, selfishness, and greed. It is an arrogant nature that destroys others in its pursuit of self-esteem and tramples underfoot the prompting of the conscience. It desires for itself a life of ease and pleasure and cares little how it is secured. Man in this state becomes an unpredictable and atrocious being.

The second thing that remains unchanged is God. He promised Noah he would never send a flood to cover the earth again. He placed a symbol of that promise in the form of a rainbow. He promised Abraham he would make him the father of many nations. Not a day goes by that his descendants are not in the forefront of the news. He promised to send a Savior to atone for the sins of all mankind. He sent his only Son to give His life a ransom for all who will accept. He promised that as long as the earth remains there will be seed time and harvest. He promised the sun by day and the moon by night. He promised to bless those who love Him and obey His commands. He promised to prepare an eternal place for those who live their lives for Him. He also promised eternal judgement on those who curse His name and reject is merciful plan of redemption.

For 6000 years God's promises have not failed even once. His track record is precise and flawless. Not one sparrow falls to the ground without notice under His watchful eye. Every promise He makes is sure because He is a God of truth. He cannot back down on His word nor does He need to, because all that He does is true and right. His promises extend to all generations, across all cultural barriers and to the ends of the earth. He does not discriminate. His promises are ours to claim whether we be rich or poor, halt or lame, young or old, whatever race, whatever locale, and whatever heritage.

As each new year unfolds there are bound to be many changes. Will the new leadership adhere to the time tested principles outlined by a sovereign God? Will they follow them to their blessing or will they reject them to their hurt? Will the inscription on our currency, "In God we trust" continue to be our motto? Time will tell.

As these changes come, may we find strength in the fact that God makes no mistakes. His promises are sure. Regardless of the struggles and trials that come our way we can hold on to the anchor that is grounded in God's love for all mankind. It will hold regardless of the fury of the storms. It has held for generations past, it will hold for us today, and it will be there for future generations as well. An anchor in the midst of change!

—M. Gingrich

A Prayer For The New Year

Our dear God of love and care,
Another year of our lives has passed.
Please take from our hearts the burden we bear
Of the "luggage" we held so fast.

Resentment, envy, self-pity, and pride,
Help us forget all our fear.
Help us to put away things that abide
To hinder the joys of this year.

May we put behind us all of the old
To make room for the new ahead.
The new year is filled with days of gold,
If we look for the good instead.

No more of the luggage of the past;
A new year beckons us on.
Please help us to make it a better one
Than the old year that is gone.

We pray for your guidance and care
In all that we undertake.
Please help us to follow you everywhere
Through this bright new year,
For Christ's sake.

—Lucille Calhoun Stewart

Are You Jesus?

A group of salesmen went to a regional sales convention in Chicago. They had assured their wives that they would be home in plenty of time for Friday night's dinner. Well, as such things go, one thing led to another. The sales manager went longer than anticipated and the meeting ran overtime.

Their flights were scheduled to leave out of Chicago's O'Hare Airport, and they had to race pell-mell to the airport. With tickets in hand, they barged through the terminal to catch their flight back home. In their rush, with tickets and briefcases, one of these salesmen inadvertently kicked over a table which held a display of baskets of apples. Apples flew everywhere.

Without stopping or looking back, they all managed to reach the plane in time for their nearly missed boarding. All but one. He paused, took a deep breath, got in touch with his feelings, and experienced a twinge of compassion for the girl whose apple stand had been overturned.

He told his buddies to go on without him, waved goodbye, told one of them to call his wife when they arrived at their home destination and explain his taking a later flight. Then he returned to the terminal where the apples were all over the terminal floor. He was glad he did.

The 16 year old girl was totally blind! She was softly crying, tears running down her cheeks in frustration, and at the same time helplessly groping for her spilled produce as the crowd swirled about her, no one stopping, and no one to care for her plight.

The salesman knelt on the floor with her, gathered up the apples, put them into the baskets, and helped set the display up once more. As he did this, he noticed that many of them had become battered and bruised; these he set aside in another basket. When he had finished, he pulled out his wallet and said to the girl, "Here, please take this $20 for the damage we did. Are you okay?"

She nodded through her tears. He continued on with, "I hope we didn't spoil your day too badly."

As the salesman started to walk away, the bewildered blind girl called out to him, "Mister…". He paused and turned to look back into those blind eyes. She continued, "Are you Jesus?"

He stopped in mid-stride, and he wondered. Then slowly he made his way to catch the later flight with that question burning in his mind: "Are you Jesus?"

Do people mistake you for Jesus? That's our destiny, is it not? To be so much like Jesus that people cannot tell the difference as we live and interact with a world that is blind to His love, life and grace.

If we claim to know Him, we should live, walk, and act as He would. Knowing Him is more than simply quoting scripture and going to church. It's actually living the Word as life unfolds day to day.

You are the apple of His eye even though we, too, have been bruised by a fall. He stopped what He was doing and picked you and me up on a hill called Calvary and paid in full for our damaged fruit.

—K. Fritz

A Voice

One evening while I cried in pain
I realized my life was all in vain;
I had no hope, nothing I shared
Alone, I felt like no one cared.

There was no reason to continue on
My days were spent wishing them gone;
What reason I yelled, why am I here?
I heard His voice and shed a tear.

My child your birth was no mistake,
You see, I give, for you to take;
I've watched your every day and night
Waiting for you to see my light.

Just know you never are alone,
I watch the world from on my throne,
When needed most, then I am there
To wash away your every care.

Just hear my voice and you will know
What you must do and where to go;
My instruction will guide you in your walk
Just listen and you wilt hear Me talk.

No one is here for fun and play,
There's work to do along the way;
Just do your best while in my land
And know I hold you in my hand.

Barbershop

A man went to a barbershop to have his hair cut and his beard trimmed as always. He started to have a good conversation with the barber who attended him. They talked about so many things and various subjects.

Soon, they touched the subject of God. The barber said: "Look man, I don't believe that God exists."

"Why do you say that?" asked the client.

"Well, it's so easy, you just have to go out in the street to realize that God does not exist. Oh, tell me, if God existed, would there be so many sick people? Would there be abandoned children? If God existed, there would be no suffering nor pain. I can't think of loving a God who permits all of these things."

The client stopped for a moment thinking, but he didn't want to respond so as to cause an argument. The barber finished his job and the client went out of the shop. Just after he left the barber shop he saw a man in the street with long hair and a beard (it seems that it had been a long time since he had his hair cut and he looked so untidy).

Then the client again entered the barber shop and he said to the barber: "You know what? Barbers do not exist."

"How can you say they don't exist?" asked the barber. "I am here and I am a barber."

"No!" the client exclaimed. "They don't exist because if they did there would be no people with long hair and a beard like that man who walks in the street."

"Ah, barbers do exist, what happens is that people do not come to me."

"Exactly!" affirmed the client. "That's the point. God does exist, what happens is people don't go to Him and do not look for Him. That's why there's so much pain and suffering in the world."

Cell Phone Vs. Bible

Do you ever wonder what would happen if we treated our Bible like we treat our cell phones?

- What if we carried it around in our purses or pockets?
- What if we turned back to get it if we forgot it?
- What if we flipped through it several times a day?
- What if we used it to receive messages from the text?
- What if we treated it like we couldn't live without it?
- What if we gave it to our children as gifts?
- What if we used it as we traveled?
- What if we used it in case of an emergency?

Oh, and one more thing, unlike our cell phones, we don't ever have to worry about our Bible being disconnected because Jesus already paid the bill!

Facing The New Year

Today, I gently close the well-worn door
Of this, another year-so soon gone by.
Like some bright ember lying on the hearth,
I see the glowing face and watch it die.

Old memories stir; it was a precious year,
Each day was overshaded by His wings,
Each step was with the guidance of His eye
Each desert place was watered by His springs.

Sometimes the way was rough, but there 'twas marked
With blood that showed He's passed that way before.
Sometimes my weakness sank beneath His cross;
Then He my strength and courage did restore.

There were some heavy burdens, but I found
The load was never greater than His grace;
There were dark clouds, but all of them did rift,
Revealing brighter glimpses of His face.

And best of all, I learned to harder lean,
To trust Him when I could not understand,
To know that nothing in my life was chance,
But that each part was ordered by His hand.

I close the old year's door without regret,
And stand upon the threshold of the new
With courage high, by faith in Him alone,
Glad for another year to dare and do.

Glad that I face it in His matchless strength,
Glad for the glorious hope that I shall be
Faith become sight, each longing realized
At last at home with Christ eternally.

—Gracia L. Fero

Give Up

Boy scouts from the city were on a camping trip. The mosquitoes were so fierce, the boys had to hide under their blankets to avoid being bitten.

One of them saw some lightning bugs and said to his friend, "We might as well give up. They are coming after us with flashlights."

God Holds The Key

Is there some problem in your heart to solve,
Some passage seeming full of mystery?
God knows who brings the hidden things to light
He holds the key.

Is there some door closed by the Father's hand,
Which widely open you have hoped to see?
Trust God and wait—for when He shuts the door.
He holds the key.

Is there some earnest prayer unanswered yet,
Or answered not as you had thought t'would be?
God will make clear His purpose by and by.
He holds the key.

Unfailing comfort, sweet and blessed rest.
To know that to every door God holds the key.
That He at last when He sees 'tis best
Will give it unto thee.

—Author Unknown

God In Providence

There is a story told of an old lady who was praying for bread in a time of great distress. Some rude boys heard her prayer, and thinking they would fool her, they brought a loaf of bread. Ringing her doorbell, they slipped away and left it there. The old lady got the loaf of bread and immediately got down on her knees and thanked God for answering her prayer.

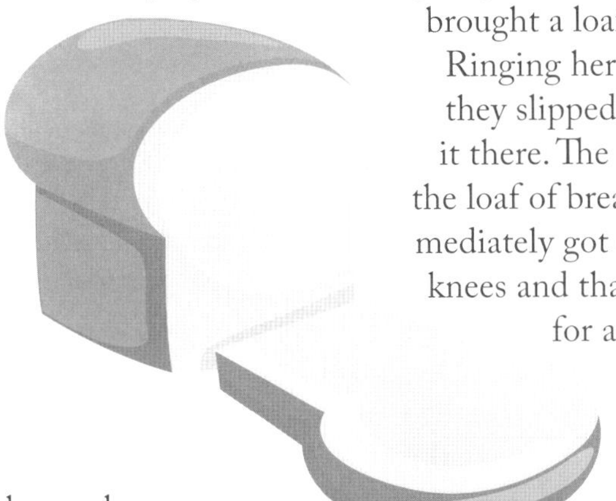

This was too much for the boys who were near and listening, so they broke in on her and told her that she was only fooling herself; God had not sent the bread at all; they had just brought it.

"Ah," she said, "Boys, I know better. It was the Lord that sent it even if it was some boys that brought it."

There are many things which the devil brings, but the child of God can see that God sent it.

God's Strength

- No Weakness is beyond God's Strength
- No Sorrow is beyond God's Comfort
- No Worry is beyond God's Assurance
- No Question is beyond God's Answer
- No Problem is beyond God's Solution
- No Sin is beyond God's Forgiveness
- No Anxiety is beyond God's Peace
- No Sickness is beyond God's Healing
- Even if in death and then it's Eternal
- No Need is beyond God's Grace

Settle it therefore in your heart.

Heaven

A man may go to heaven

- Without health,
- Without wealth,
- Without fame,
- Without a great name,
- Without learning,
- Without culture,
- Without friends,
- Without ten thousand other things.

But he can never go to heaven without Christ.

His Yoke Is Easy

A man was carrying a heavy basket. His son asked to help him. The father cut a stick and placed it through the handle of the basket so that the end toward himself was very short, while the end toward the boy was three or four times as long. Each took hold of his end of the stick, and the basket was lifted and easily carried. The son was bearing the burden with the father, but he found his work easy and light because his father assumed the heavy end of the stick. Just so it is when we bear the yoke with Christ; He sees to it that the burden laid on us is light; He carries the heavy end!

—John T. Faris

If Jesus Came To Your House

If Jesus came to your house
To spend a day or two,
If He came unexpectedly,
I wonder what you'd do.

Oh, I know you'd give your nicest room
To such an honored Guest,
And all the food you'd serve to Him
Would be the very best,

And you would keep assuring Him
You're glad to have Him there—
That serving Him in your own home
Is joy beyond compare.

But—when you saw Him coming, would
You meet Him at the door
With arms outstretched in welcome
To your Heav'nly Visitor?

Or would you have to change your clothes
Before you let Him in,
Or hide some magazines and put
The Bible where they'd been?

Would you turn off the radio
And hope He hadn't heard
And wish you hadn't uttered
That last loud, hasty word?

Would you hide your worldly music
And put some hymn books out?
Could you let Jesus walk right in,
Or would you rush about?

And I wonder—if the Saviour
Spent a day or two with you,
Would you go right on doing
The things you always do?

Would you keep right on saying
The things you always say?
Would life for you continue
As it does from day to day?

Would your family conversation
Keep up its usual pace,
And would you find it hard each meal
To say a table grace?

Would you sing the songs you always sing
And read the books you read,
And let Him know the things on which
Your mind and spirit feed?

Would you take Jesus with you
Everywhere you'd planned to go,
Or would you maybe change your plans
For just a day or so?

Would you be glad to have Him meet
Your very closest friends,
Or would you hope they'd stay away
Until His visit ends?

Would you be glad to have Him stay
Forever on and on,
Or would you sigh with great relief
When He at last was gone?

It might be interesting to know
The things that you would do
If Jesus Christ in person came
To spend some time with you.

—Lois Blanchard

I Looked For You Today

I looked for you today as the morning sun crept slowly, high into the eastern sky. Golden rays trumpeting thru the darkness, announcing a brand new day. I spoke the dawn into being, a promise just for you. I will never leave you or forsake you. I am always close to you. I looked for you at noontime full of love and concern. Anxiously I waited but the need was not returned. I listened for a prayer or petition in your defense. Instead, you chose to walk alone with dread and torment. Eagerly I waited for even just a glance, for greater is He who is in you, a fact, not by chance. I looked for you at sunset, a truly breathless sight. I spoke it into being for reflection at twilight. Peaceful, quiet moments to diffuse your scrambled soul. There are powers at work that would harm you but let Me make you whole. Choose not to embrace the darkness nor take it to your bed. It's peace, perfect peace, I desire for you instead.

I Needed the Quiet

I needed the quiet
So He drew me aside.
Into the shadows
Where we could confide.

Away from the bustle
Where all the day long
I hurried and worried
When active and strong.

I needed the quiet,
Tho' at first I rebelled
But gently, so gently,
My cross He upheld

And whispered so sweetly
Of spiritual things
Tho weakened in body,
My spirit took wings

To heights never dreamed of
When active all day.
He loved me so greatly
He drew me away.

I needed the quiet.
No prison my bed,
But a beautiful valley
Of blessings instead.

A place to grow richer
In Jesus to hide.
I needed the quiet
So He drew me aside.

—Alice Hansche Mortenson

It Didn't Just Happen

Things don't just happen
to the children of God.
They're part of a wonderful plan;
The troubles, reserves, the sorrows, the rod.
Are strokes of the Great Sculptor's hand.

When some dread accident
strikes you a blow
And you worry and fret and demand;
Why try so hard the mystery to know?
It's not just an accident, it's planned.

Have you been dropped from a place of power?
Do you wonder and reprimand?
Don't rebel but look to Him in that hour;
This didn't just happen; it's planned.

Persecution, tribulation come down like a storm;
Friends disappoint and withstand;
At last, all alone, bewildered, forlorn,
You look, and He smiles: 'This is planned."

Do you wonder why God to affliction should call
And why you must suffer and moan?
"No man should be moved by affliction;" says Paul
"For you know it is part of the plan."

Did some dear one sicken and finally die?
Did your heart break with anguish and woe?
Did you question your Lord, and cry; "My God why?"
Don't question, He planned it just so.

Things don't just happen to children of God.
The blue print was made by His hand;
He designed all details to conform to His Son
So all things that happen are planned.

No matter what happens to those called "His own"
Events that are awful or grand;
Every trial of your life He sends from His throne;
Things just don't happen, they're planned.

—Unknown

Joys Of Heaven

We have the choice, which we may take
Choose our destination and the path it will make
Or choose our path, we wish to take
And accept the destiny that it will make.

Jesus said I go to prepare for you a place
For us to enjoy and look on his face;
To enjoy what God has for us there
We must fellowship with him here.

There we shall know no sorrow
It will surely disappear on the morrow;
There all things will be made new
And will be blessed with heavenly dew.

The streets of pure gold will be
And we will be able to eat of life's tree;
The city foundation is full of precious stones
The singing will all be in perfect tones.

There we shall not have night
For Jesus himself will be the light;
Joy will be ours for Jesus is there,
We'll all sing hallulejah, I do declare.

To God's glory can no one compare
His glory will be seen everywhere;
The greatest of our joy that we'll know
We'll always be with Jesus, His face aglow

We'll forever worship
Before His throne
And praise Him eternally
For our heavenly home.

—Warren Clugston

Judgment Day

When we stand before God on the judgment day
What, oh, what will we ever say?
Who else will we declare
Is responsible for my own welfare?

We cannot for our wrong blame another,
We'll stand alone without a brother.
What are we doing for God's kingdom?
Are we burying a talent for lack of wisdom?

What does our life show in the record?
Does it reveal that I'm lead by the Word?
Do I live believing the Word is able,
To build my life and keep me stable?

Do I live and work with God,
Or work only for Him on life's road?
Is God's word enough for me,
His word established for eternity?

May we live so our accountability
Will welcome us His face to see.
Even though we stand alone,
May his blood our sin atone.

When on that day we see His face,
We'll sing, He saved us by His grace.

—Warren Clugston

Longevity

Mankind has long pursued the "fountain of youth". We have an inborn desire to stay young and to live as long as possible. We are intrigued when we meet someone who is a hundred years old. We consider them as having defied the odds. Most people don't live to be that old and so when someone reaches that plateau we are fascinated. We wonder about their lifestyle, what they ate, how they maintained their fitness, etc., wondering if we, too, can somehow live to be that old.

When we buy a car we hope it lasts for a long time. We want it to run for years and years and so we do regular maintenance to keep it in top running condition. We boast about how many miles-per-gallon of gas we get. We like to see how many miles we can get out of a set of tires before having to replace them. It is all part of economics.

When we look at a tree we wonder how long it has been there. It stands majestically, towering above the rooftops, shading the grass below and providing nesting place among its branches. We are awed by its beauty and magnificence. The scars and gnarled branches give silent witness to the storms it has endured. We are gently reminded of the sheer volume of leaves it grows each year when it comes time to rake. Trees have provided a natural playground for many youngsters whether it was by means of a tree house or a rope swing or simply an object to climb. The decision to cut a tree down is made more difficult because we know it takes years to replace it.

The laws of nature are a witness to the process of aging. From the time something is born or takes root it begins a cycle. Eventually it will die. It will succumb to the very elements that provide the sustenance of life in its prime. While it lives or while it lasts, whether it be a person, a tree or even a car, its longevity is something to be appreciated. A person who is aged carries with them the tales of "the good old days". A tree is respected for the shade it gives on a hot summer day. A car that performs its duty for many years is spoken kindly of.

We look at longevity from a finite viewpoint. We have difficulty in understanding infinite because everything we relate to is finite. It has a beginning and an ending. When we consider God, however, we see one who always was and always will be. Therefore He speaks of one day as a thousand and a thousand as one day because He sees it from an infinite or eternal perspective. A lifespan then is but a few days and is compared to grass springing up and soon withering away.

It is in the perspective of eternity then that a life-span of a hundred years pales in comparison. At the time of creation God did something to man that he didn't do to any other creature. He breathed into his nostrils the breath of life and man became a living soul. Man is unique from the rest of creation. God made man in His likeness. He wanted man to worship Him. Through disobedience man brought the curse of death upon himself. But God again reached down and in love provided the gift of eternal life to all mankind through the blood of Jesus Christ, if we believe in Him. If we confess our sins He is faithful and just to forgive us our sins. If we reject Him we will spend eternity in hell. The choice is ours. Yes, this body will still age and decay, but our soul will inherit a new body that will not decay. Eternity is a long time. Where will you spend it?

—M. Gingrich

No Reason To Worry

A pastor had been on a long flight between church conferences. The first warning of the approaching problems came when the sign on the airplane flashed on: "Fasten your seat belts."

Then, after a while, a calm voice said, "We will not be serving the beverages at this time as we are expecting a little turbulence. Please be sure your seat belt is fastened."

As the pastor looked around the aircraft, it became obvious that many of the passengers were becoming apprehensive.

Later, the voice on the intercom said, "We are so sorry that we are unable to serve the meal at this time. The turbulence is still ahead of us."

And then the storm broke...

The ominous cracks of thunder could be heard even above the roar of the engines. Lightning lit up the darkening skies, and within moments that great plane was like a cork tossed around on a celestial ocean. One moment the airplane was lifted on terrific currents of air; the next, it dropped as if it were about to crash.

The pastor confessed that he shared the discomfort and fear of those around him. He said, "As I looked around the plane, I could see that nearly all the passengers were upset and alarmed. Some were praying. The future seemed ominous and many were wondering if they would make it through the storm.

"Then, I suddenly saw a little girl. Apparently the storm meant nothing to her. She had tucked her feet beneath her as she sat on her seat; she was reading a book and everything within her small world was calm and orderly.

"Sometimes she closed her eyes, then she would read again; then she would straighten her legs, but worry and fear were not in her world.

"When the plane was being buffeted by the terrible storm when it lurched this way and that, as it rose and fell with frightening severity, when all the adults were scared half to death, that marvelous child was completely composed and unafraid." The minister could hardly believe his eyes.

It was not surprising therefore, that when the plane finally reached its destination and all the passengers were hurrying to disembark, our pastor lingered to speak to the girl whom he had watched for such a long time.

Having commented about the storm and the behavior of the plane, he asked why she had not been afraid.

The child replied, " 'Cause my daddy's the pilot, and he's taking me home."

Physical, mental, financial, domestic, and many other storms can easily and quickly darken our skies and throw our plane into apparently uncontrollable movement. We have all known such times, and let us be honest and confess, it is much easier to be at rest when our feet are on the ground than when we are being tossed about a darkened sky.

Let us remember that our Father is the Pilot. He is in control. There is no reason to worry!

No Time For God

You've time to build houses, and in them dwell
And time to do business—to buy and to sell;
But none for repentance, or deep earnest prayer;
To seek your salvation you've no time to spare.

You've time for earth's pleasures, for frolic and fun,
For her glittering treasures, how quickly you run;
But care not to seek that fair mansion above,
The favor of God or the gift of His love.

You've time to take voyages over the sea,
And time to take in the world's jubilee;
But soon your bright hopes will be lost in the gloom
Of the cold, dark river of death and the tomb.

You've time to resort to the mountain and glen,
And time to gain knowledge from books and from men;
Yet no time to search for the wisdom of God,
But what of your soul when you're under the sod?

For time will not linger when helpless you lie,
Staring death in the face you will take time to die.
Then what of your judgement—pause, think, I implore
For time will be lost on eternity's shore.

—*Author Unknown*

P.U.S.H.

A man was sleeping one night in his cabin when he had a dream. His room suddenly filled with light, and the Lord appeared.

The Lord told the man he had work for him to do, and showed him a large rock in front of his cabin. The Lord explained that the man was to push against the rock with all his might. So, this the man did, day after day.

For many years he toiled from sun up to sun down, his shoulders set squarely against the cold massive surface of the unmoving rock, pushing with all of his might. Each night the man returned to his cabin sore and worn out, feeling that his whole day had been spent in vain.

Since the man was showing discouragement, the Adversary (Satan) decided to enter the picture by placing thoughts into his weary mind: "You have been pushing against that rock for a long time, and it hasn't moved." Thus, he gave the man the impression that the task was impossible and that he was a failure. These thoughts discouraged and disheartened the man. Satan said, "Why kill yourself over this? Just put in your time, giving just the minimum effort and that will be good enough."

That's what the weary man planned to do, but decided to make it a matter of prayer and to take his troubled thoughts to the Lord.

"Lord," he said, "I have labored long and hard in your service, putting all my strength to do that which you have asked. Yet, after all this time, I have not even budged that rock by half a millimeter. What is wrong? Why am I failing?"

The Lord responded compassionately, "My friend, when I asked you to serve Me and you accepted, I told you that your task was to push against the rock with all of your strength, which you have done. Never once did I mention to you that I expected you to move it. Your task was to push. And now you come to Me with your strength spent, thinking that you have failed. But, is that really so? Look at yourself. Your arms are strong and muscled, your back sinewy and brown; your hands are calloused from constant pressure, your legs have become massive and hard. Through opposition you have grown much, and your abilities now surpass that which you used to have. True, you haven't moved the rock. But your calling was to be obedient and to push and to exercise your faith and trust in My wisdom. That you have done. Now I, my friend, will move the rock."

At times, when we hear a word from God, we tend to use our own intellect to decipher what He wants, when actually what God wants is just simple obedience and faith in Him. By all means, exercise the faith that moves mountains but know that it is still God who moves the mountains.

- When everything seems to go wrong…just P.U.S.H.!
- When the job gets you down…just P.U.S.H.!
- When people don't react the way you think they should…just P.U.S.H.!

- When your money is "gone" and the bills are due… just P.U.S.H.!
- When people just don't understand you…just P.U.S.H.!

P—PRAY
U—UNTIL
S—SOMETHING
H—HAPPENS

Redeemed

I stood before the judge one day.
"Condemned to death", I heard him say.
I hung my head in utter shame,
My sins so great, I was to blame.

So hopeless, lost and in despair
My sinful life had brought me there.
All the wrong that I had done
Was all against God's own dear Son.

Then all at once, "One" stood forth,
And in a gentle, loving voice
Said, "My life I'll give, hers to redeem,
And pay her sin's full penalty."

Oh, the love that drew salvation's plan
That "One" would condescend to man,
And on the cross would take my place
To bear my shame and sin's disgrace.

Oh, the love, and at what cost
For Jesus Christ to come and save the lost.
It was His loss that is my gain,
And true to Him I will remain!

—Patricia A. Large

Showing Through

A little girl on the way home from church turned to her mother and said, "Mommy, the preacher's sermon this morning confused me."

The mother said, "Oh! Why is that?"

The girl replied, "Well, he said that God is bigger than we are. Is that true?"

"Yes, that's true," the mother replied.

"He also said that God lives within us. Is that true, too?"

Again the mother replied, "Yes."

"Well," said the girl. "If God is bigger than us and he lives in us, wouldn't He show through?"

I like that little girl's way of putting it. If God lives in us, then there's no way of keeping Him from "showing through". That's the essence of Christian living—living in such a way that people around will see God in our lives. "Let your light so shine before men, that they may see your good works and glorify your Father in heaven" (Matthew 5:16).

Someone

There is Someone, that I talk to,
Time after time each day,
Someone that knows before I speak,
Each word that I will say.

Someone who knows, each single thought,
That comes into my mind,
Someone that I have come to know,
Only by grace divine.

Though this Someone, is far away,
Yet, He is always near,
His silent voice is heard by those,
Who lend a willing ear.

This Someone is as close to us,
As we desire He be,
And one day, we'll meet this Someone,
Our eyes have yet to see.

And so, I'll talk to this Someone,
Time after time each day,
Although He knows before I speak,
Each word that I will say.

To Do As He Would Have Me Do,
This is my daily aim,
For this Someone is my Master,
Lord Jesus is His name.

—Robert Phillips

Stop, Look, Listen

Stop! People, look all around you
Each and every day
And take a good look
At all the people going astray;

All your friends and loved ones
Living deep in sin,
Tell them about Jesus
And the way He wants them to live.

Sin abounds much more now
Than it's ever been,
People don't care anymore
What they say or how they live.

People are selfish, self-centered,
Mean and unkind,
It's about time we try
To change their mind.

Look! At what Jesus has done
To keep us from hell;
He hung on a cross at Calvary
Doing His Father's will.

Jesus gave His life
So we would be free of sin;
The least we can do
Is tell the world about Him.

Tell everyone about Jesus
And His saving grace,
How over 2000 years ago
He died in our place.

Surrender to Jesus,
Turn everything over to Him,
Make him your Savior
And He'll teach you how to live.

Listen! To what people are saying
Each and every day,
So much negative talk,
No wonder people are going astray.

Get to know Jesus
And He'll give you a new heart,
Believe in Him
And help someone make a new start.

Go to church
And hear the word preached,
Study the word
So someday you may teach;

Teach others about Jesus
And His love for all
And how Jesus will always be there
When you fall.

—Kenneth C. Showalter

The Answer Is Blowing In The Wind

Wind is one of those invisible elements of nature and yet it carries with it highly visible qualities. You can see the branches of the trees bend and bow. You can feel the gusts penetrate the cracks around windows and doors. You can hear the howling of the wind blowing around the corner of the house as you lie in bed at night. You can see the clouds float across the sky and disappear over the horizon. You pull your coat a little bit tighter around you as the night breeze brings a chill to the air. You hear the sound it makes, you feel it, you see what it does, you can smell the fragrance it brings and sometimes you can even taste it (ex., salt water), but you can't see the wind.

The birds don't seem to mind as they utilize the wind to their benefit, allowing the currents to lift them higher and higher into the air. The windmill spins faster and faster drawing water with every turn as it strains against the restraints holding it back from spinning out of control. The sail boat is literally useless without the wind to fill its sails and without the wind the wind chimes fail to resonate. Without the wind there would be nothing to move the clouds of precipitation we so desperately need.

When wind becomes powerful enough it wreaks havoc. Hurricanes and tornadoes bring destruction to whatever stands in their path. Even well built structures are no match for the tremendous force they exert. They lift and turn and toss the lighter objects and stack them on top of each other in disorderly fashion. Small objects have been found impaled in other objects following a severe storm. How it happens defies human reasoning.

Wind, then, is both a tool and a destroyer. It is useful as a tool when its energy is harnessed and channeled in the right direction. When it unleashes its fury we can only stand in awe and wonder and give due respect to its power

Jesus' disciples learned a valuable lesson regarding the wind as they found themselves in the midst of a powerful storm on the Sea of Galilee. They feared greatly that their boat was about to sink. Calling upon Jesus they found an answer to their predicament. He rebuked the storm and the wind relented and the waters calmed. In awe they whispered, "Even the winds and the waves obey his voice!"

The answer is blowing in the wind! The winds of change are upon us today as well. Life comes at you fast. Politics, warfare, the economy, relationships, financial straits, etc., can leave you feeling exhausted. You may find yourself bewildered, frustrated, miserable, and defeated. As did the disciples you, too, can turn to the Master of the universe and find calmness and peace. He is the same yesterday, today, and forever. The wind is not visible and neither is Jesus visible today as a person but the change that He brings to people's lives is unmistakable. In Him, Jesus Christ, the winds are suddenly manageable, the fears are calmed, the broken pieces are repaired and life takes on a new meaning. The nighttime breeze that brought a chill now brings a warm reassurance that all is well. All is well!

—*M. Gingrich*

The Buzzard, The Bat, & The Bumblebee

Buzzard

If you put a buzzard in a pen that is 6 feet by 8 feet and is entirely open at the top, the bird, in spite of its ability to fly, will be an absolute prisoner. The reason is that a buzzard always begins a flight from the ground with a run of 10 to 12 feet. Without space to run, as is its habit, it will not even attempt to fly, but will remain a prisoner for life in a small jail with no top.

Bat

The ordinary bat that flies around at night, a remarkably nimble creature in the air, cannot take off from a level place. If it is placed on the floor or flat ground, all it can do is shuffle about helplessly and, no doubt, painfully, until it reaches some slight elevation from which it can throw itself into the air. Then, at once, it takes off like a flash.

Bumblebee

A bumblebee, if dropped into an open tumbler, will be there until it dies, unless it is taken out. It never sees the means of escape at the top, but persists in trying to find some way out through the sides near the bottom. It will seek a way where none exists, until it completely destroys itself.

People

In many ways, we are like the buzzard, the bat, and the bumblebee. We struggle about with all our problems and frustrations, never realizing that all we have to do is look up. Sorrow looks back, worry looks around, but faith looks up.

The Lack Of Patience

The great preacher and songwriter Phillip Brooks said, "The hardest task in my life is to sit down and wait for God to catch up to me."

Years ago, if you missed a stagecoach, you waited several weeks for the next one to pass through. Today if we miss our turn in a revolving door, we get ulcers.

We order our breakfast from a drive-through window, take our clothes to a one-hour cleaner, then drive to the one-hour photo shop. We cook our meals in a microwave, have instant coffee and a cake made by an instant cake mix. Often, we need a quick relief to cure an upset stomach or headache.

We have been in such a rush that we haven't taken time to wait on God (Isa. 40:31). We have little if any time to meditate, allowing God to speak to us.

Someone said, "The hurrier I go, the behinder I get." Also note this "Beware of the bareness of a busy life."

Time waiting before God is never wasted time! Most of our problems are caused because we are so busy and have no time to listen to God!

The Passenger Got The Tip

"Someone left this Gospel of John on your back seat," I said, calling the taxi driver's attention to the little paperback which had a pamphlet tucked inside it.

"I put it there," he answered.

"I want you to know how much I appreciate finding it," I told him. "I'm a Christian and it means something to me."

"I'm a Christian too," the driver commented. "I've been driving a taxi in New York City for 20 years. This is how I witness."

The driver proceeded to tell me how the Gospel of John, which bore the emblem of the American Bible Society, and an accompanying tract, telling how to find Christ as Savior, always evoked conversation. "Some of my fares," he said, "you can tell are having some problems. They ask me to pray for them."

Not every rider reacts favorably. Once a colorful trial lawyer, whose name was in the headlines for defending a group of demonstrators, boarded his cab.

When the famous attorney saw the gospel and tract, he demanded with disgust, "What's this? Who put this here?"

"The spirit gave me the boldness to reply, 'I put it there,'" the driver recalled.

"Well, I'll have nothing to do with it," the passenger shot back. "I've always managed for myself and I always will."

"There'll come a time, no matter how famous a lawyer you are, when you won't be able to take care of yourself," I told him, "when you stand before the judgment bar of God without Jesus as your Savior."

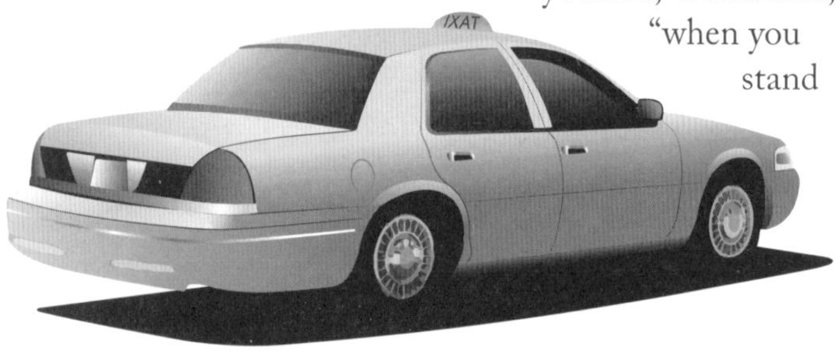

"Oh, don't give me any of that," the attorney retorted. When this disgusted passenger got out, he counted his fare carefully to the exact penny. "He didn't even give me a dime tip. But I gave him something, I gave him the Word."

"It's not my job to make Christians of them. It's only my job to witness to them; to sow the seed," he observed.

The driver said over the years he'd given out 25,000 copies of the Gospel of John and more than 40,000 tracts.

I started to get out as soon as we reached my destination. The driver stopped me. "Do you have time for us to pray together?" He clasped my hand and on Wall Street, involved me in a powerful moment of intercession.

After I'd left the taxi, I thought of the verse commanding us to be "witnesses in Jerusalem." Here was this taxi driver, in what I consider one of the most difficult locations to have an impact for Christ, witnessing effectively in a way that only a taxi driver could.

The Secret

A woman named Vicki once knew a young person at church named Susan. Susan always seemed effervescent and happy, although Vicki knew she had faced struggles in her life, but decided she would live it with utmost enjoyment and satisfaction. Susan was active in Sunday school, in the choir, and as a leader of the junior high girls' group. Vicki enjoyed knowing Susan. Susan's whole face seemed to smile.

One day Vicki asked Susan, "How is it that you are always so happy, you have so much energy, and you never seem to get down?"

With her eyes smiling, Susan said, "I know the secret!"

"What secret is that? What are you talking about?" Vicki asked.

Susan replied, "I'll tell you all about it, but you have to promise to share the secret with others."

Vicki agreed, "Okay, now what is it?"

The Secret is this: "I have learned there is little I can do in my life that will make me truly happy. I must depend on God to make me happy and meet my needs. When a need arises in my life, I have to trust God to supply according to His riches. I have learned most of the time I don't need half of what I think I do. He has never let me down. Since I learned that secret I am happy."

Vicki's first thought was, That's too simple! But upon reflecting over her own life she recalled how she thought a bigger house would make her happy—but it didn't! She thought a better-paying job would make her happy—but it hadn't. When did she realize her greatest happiness? Sitting on the floor with her grandchildren, playing games, eating pizza or reading a story, a simple gift from God. Susan knew the secret, Vicki learned the secret, and now you know it, too!

We can't depend on people to make us happy. Only God in His wisdom can do that. Trust Him! And now I pass the secret on to you! So once you get it, whatchya-gonna do? You have to tell someone the secret, too! That God in His wisdom will take care of You!

The Wisdom Of God's Plan

It is sometimes very difficult
For us to understand,
The wisdom and love behind
The things that God has planned.

But we wouldn't have the rainbow
If we didn't have the rain;
We wouldn't know of pleasure
If we never tasted pain.

We wouldn't love the sunrise
If we hadn't felt the night;
And we wouldn't know our weakness
If we hadn't sensed God's might.

We couldn't have the springtime
Or the yellow daffodil;
If we hadn't first experienced
The winter's frosty chill.

And though the brilliant sunshine
Is something God has made,
He knew too much could parch our souls
So He created shade.

So God's given us a balance:
Enough joys to keep us glad,
Enough tears to keep us humble
Enough good to balance bad.

And if you'll trust in Him you'll see
Though yesterday brought sorrow,
The clouds will part and dawn will bring
A happier tomorrow.

—Unknown

Things Don't Just Happen

Things don't just happen to us who love God,
They're planned by His own dear hand.
Then molded and shaped and timed by His clock,
Things don't just happen, they're planned.

We don't just guess on the issues of life,
We Christians just rest in our Lord
We are directed by His sovereign will
In the light of His Holy Word.

We who love Jesus are walking by faith
Not seeing one step that's ahead,
Not doubting one moment what our lot might be,
But looking to Jesus instead.

We praise our dear Saviour for loving us so,
for planning each card of our life.
Then giving us faith to trust Him for all,
The blessings, as well as the strife.

Things don't just happen to us who love God,
To us who have taken our stand,
No matter the lot, the course, or the price,
Things don't just happen, they're planned.

-Esther L. Fields

Tomorrow's Doubts

Tomorrow's doubts may cloud the skies
And hide the sun from view,
Then all you see is toil and strife
In the way ahead of you.

How dark and cold the future looks,
You wish to turn away;
No courage left within your heart
To face another day.

Yet somehow when your faith is low,
Your courage getting dim.
It's then you need your Father most
To turn your cares to Him.

His grace is all sufficient,
For every passing day
His love is sure to lead you
And cheer the weary way.

Why do we doubt or falter
Within our Father's hand?
Someday He'll tell the reason,
Then we'll understand.

Triumph Over Tragedy

In the town of Port Hope, Canada, there stands a monument, not for the leading citizen who just died, but for a poor, unselfish working man who gave most of his life and energy to help those who could not repay him.

Joseph Scriven was born in Dublin in 1820. In his youth, he had the prospect of a great citizen with high ideals and great aspirations. He was engaged to a beautiful young woman who had promised to share his dreams, but on the eve of their wedding her body was pulled from a pond into which she had accidentally fallen and drowned.

Young Scriven never overcame the shock. Although a college graduate and ready to embark on a brilliant career, he began to wander to try to forget his sorrow. His wanderings took him to Canada where he spent the last forty-one of his sixty-six years. He became a very devout Christian. His beliefs led him to do servile labor for poor widows and sick people. He often served for no wages.

It was not known that Mr. Scriven had any poetic gifts until a short time before his death. A friend, who was sitting with him during an illness, discovered a poem he had written to his mother in a time of sorrow, not intending that anyone should see it. His poem was later set to music and has become a much-loved gospel song. It is said to be the first song that many missionaries teach their converts. In polls taken to determine the popularity of hymns and gospel songs, his poem set to music is always near the top. What was his poem?

What a friend we have in Jesus,
All our sins and griefs to bear.
What a privilege to carry
Everything to God in prayer.
Oh, what peace we often forfeit,
Oh what needless pain we bear,
All because we do not carry,
Everything to God in prayer.

—*The Cross and the Crown*

Trusting What You Can't See

The eagle is a great bird, but it was created by someone. Who? And, who taught it to build its nest in the rocky ledges where it could have its babies and raise them without danger? From where does such wisdom come that makes mother eagle flop her powerful wings, forcing her babies out on the nothingness of air at the right time in life?

Who taught mother eagle to swoop under her struggling, scared babe in midair, so scared babe could land on her back and ride to safety? Who taught mother eagle and baby to do that over again and again until baby eagle learned to fly like her strong mother?

It had to be someone greater than mother eagle! It could only be the Living God who made mother eagle, the rocky cliff she made her nest on, the baby she hatched and cared for, and even the air that baby eagle could not see, but had to learn to trust!

The air that baby eagle couldn't see was able to save it from crashing to the ground in death. But, the baby eagle had to be kicked out of its comfortable nest. And, it had to learn to trust the air even though it could not see it! That's the only way it could mature—become a real adult eagle.

We cannot see God. We cannot see air, either. But we trust the air because it is life to us from the time we are born.

Now we must be as reasonable and sensible about God's spiritual truth. From the time of birth He makes Himself known to us—giving us air, food, water, etc., and without all of that we would crash to physical death.

He gave Himself in the person of Jesus Christ, to save our soul from its death-separation from His life in His Heaven. That's why we must be "kicked out" of the nest of our self-desire, self-comfort, self-religion, so we can and will learn to put our trust in Him! He will be there to save our soul, just as sure as mother eagle saved her babe!

Under the Bed

My brother Kevin thinks God lives under his bed. At least that's what I heard him say one night. He was praying out loud in his dark bedroom, and I stopped outside his closed door to listen. "Are you there, God?" he said. "Where are you? Oh, I see, under the bed."

I giggled softly and tiptoed off to my own room. Kevin's unique perspectives are often a source of amusement. But that night something else lingered long after the humor. I realized for the first time the very different world Kevin lives in.

He was born 30 years ago, mentally disabled as a result of difficulties during labor. Apart from his size (he's 6-foot-2), there are few ways in which he is an adult. He reasons and communicates with the capabilities of a seven-year-old, and he always will. He will probably always believe that God lives under his bed and that airplanes stay up in the sky because angels carry them. I remember wondering if Kevin realizes he is different. Is he ever dissatisfied with his monotonous life? Up before dawn each day, off to work at a workshop for the disabled, home to walk our cocker spaniel, return to eat his favorite macaroni-and-cheese for dinner, and later to bed.

The only variation in the entire scheme are laundry, when he hovers excitedly over the washing machine like a mother with her newborn child. He does not seem dissatisfied. He lopes out to the bus every morning at 7:05, eager for a day of simple work. He wrings his hands excitedly while the water boils on the stove before dinner, and he stays up late twice a week to gather our dirty laundry for his next day's laundry chores.

And Saturdays—oh, the bliss of Saturdays! That's the day my Dad takes Kevin to the airport to have a soft drink, watch the planes land, and speculate loudly on the destination of each passenger inside. "That one's goin' to Chi-car-go!" Kevin shouts as he claps his hands. His anticipation is so great he can hardly sleep on Friday nights. And so goes his world of daily rituals and weekend field trips.

He doesn't know what it means to be discontent. His life is simple. He will never know the entanglements of wealth or power, and he does not care what brand of clothing he wears or what kind of food he eats. His needs have always been met, and he never worries that one day they may not be. His hands are diligent. Kevin is never so happy as when he is working. When he unloads the dishwasher or vacuums the carpet, his heart is completely in it. He does not shrink from a job when it is begun, and he does not leave a job until it is finished. But when his tasks are done, Kevin knows how to relax.

He is not obsessed with his work or the work of others. His heart is pure. He still believes everyone tells the truth, promises must be kept, and when you are wrong, you apologize instead of argue. Free from pride and unconcerned with appearances, Kevin is not afraid to cry when he is hurt, angry, or sorry. He is always transparent, always sincere. And he trusts God.

Not confined by intellectual reasoning, when he comes to religion, he comes as a child. Kevin seems to know God…to really be friends with Him in a way that is difficult for an "educated" person to grasp. God seems like his closest companion. In my moments of doubt and frustration, I envy the security Kevin has in his simple faith. It is then that I am most willing to admit that he has some divine knowledge that rises above my mortal questions. It is then I realize that perhaps he is not the one with the handicap—I am. My obligations, my fear, my pride, my circumstances—they all become disabilities when I do not trust them to God's care.

Who knows if Kevin comprehends things I can never learn? After all, he has spent his whole life in that kind of innocence, praying after dark and soaking up the goodness and love of God. And, one day, when the mysteries of heaven are opened, and we are all amazed at how close God really is to our hearts, I'll realize that God heard the simple prayers of a boy who believed that God lived under his bed. Kevin won't be surprised at all!

We Can Say God Led

We can say,
God knows just what He's doing
When he sends a child so small,
That is filled with words of cooing
That is joy and fun for all.
We can say,
God knows just what He's doing
When He gives him strength and mind,
That makes a man of intellect
And yet so meek and kind,
We can say,
God knows just what He's doing
When He joins two different souls,
In marriage and in harmony
With deepening love, as years do roll.
We can say,
God knows just what He's doing
When the sun sends joyful rays,
And our life is what we wanted
And our wish, becomes our ways.
But, can we say,
God knows just what He's doing
When He takes before our eyes,
That dear soul, the one we love
To His abode, in yonder skies?
Yes, we can say,
God knows just what He's doing
When our plans lie crushed and dead.
He will lead tho' hopes are shattered.
And will give us grace instead.
Yes, we can say,
God knows just what He's doing,
Not because we have our way;
But we know that God is leading
For our best; we'll take His way.

What Did You Find?

The surgeon sat beside the boy's bed. The boy's parents sat across from him, "Tomorrow morning", the surgeon began, "I'll open up your heart".

"You'll find Jesus in there," the boy interrupted.

The surgeon looked up, annoyed, "I'll cut your heart open," he continued, "to see how much damage has been done…"

"But, when you open up my heart, you'll find Jesus in there."

The surgeon looked to the parents who sat quietly, "When I see how much damage has been done, I'll sew your heart and chest back up and I'll plan how much to do next."

"But you'll find Jesus in my heart. The Bible says He lives there, the hymns all say He lives there, you'll find Him in my heart."

The surgeon had had enough, "I'll tell you what I'll find in your heart. I'll find damaged muscle, low blood supply, and weakened vessels, and I'll find out if I can make you well."

"You'll find Jesus there, too. He lives there,"

The surgeon left, He sat in his office recording his notes from surgery, "damaged aorta, damaged pulmonary vein, widespread muscle degeneration, no hope for transplant, no hope for cure. Therapy: painkillers and bed rest. Prognosis…", here he paused, "death within one year."

He stopped the recorder, but there was more to be said.

"Why?" he asked aloud, "Why did You do this? You've put him here. You've put him in this pain and You've cursed him to an early death. Why?"

The Lord answered and said, "The boy, My lamb, was not meant for your flock for long, for he is a part of My flock, and will forever be. Here, in My flock, he will feel no pain, and will be comforted as you cannot imagine. His parents will one day join him here, and they will know peace, and My flock will continue to grow."

The surgeon's tears were hot, but his anger was hotter, "You created that boy, and You created that heart. He'll be dead in months. Why?"

The Lord again answered, "The boy, My lamb, shall return to My flock, for he has done his duty: I did not put My lamb with your flock to lose him, but to retrieve another lost lamb. You!" The surgeon wept.

The surgeon sat beside the boy's bed; the boy's parents sat across from him. The boy awoke and whispered, "Did you cut open my heart?"

"Yes," said the surgeon. "What did you find?" asked the boy.

"I found Jesus there," said the surgeon.

What's On The Other Side?

A sick man turned to his doctor as he was preparing to leave the examination room and said, "Doctor, I am afraid to die. Tell me what lies on the other side."

Very quietly, the doctor said, "I don't know."

"You don't know? You, a Christian man, do not know what is on the other side?"

The doctor was holding the handle of the door. On the other side of which came a sound of scratching and whining, and as he opened the door, a dog sprang into the room and leaped on him with an eager show of gladness. Turning to the patient, the doctor said, "Did you notice my dog? He's never been in this room before. He didn't know what was inside. He knew nothing except that his master was here, and when the door opened, he sprang in without fear. I know little of what is on the other side of death, but I do know one thing…I know my Master is there and that is enough."

Windshield Message From a Child

One rainy afternoon I was driving along one of the main streets of town, taking those extra precautions necessary when the roads are wet and slick. Suddenly, my son Matthew spoke up from his relaxed position in the front seat. "Mom, I'm thinking of something."

This announcement usually meant he had been pondering some fact for a while, and was now ready to expound all that his seven-year-old mind had discovered. I was eager to hear.

"What are you thinking?" I asked.

"The rain," he began, "is like sin, and the windshield wipers are like God wiping our sins away."

After the chill bumps raced up my arms I was able to respond.

"That's really good, Matthew."

Then my curiosity broke in. How far would this little boy take this revelation?

So I asked, "Do you notice how the rain keeps on coming? What does that tell you?"

Matthew didn't hesitate one moment with his answer: "Even though we may sin again and again, God just keeps on forgiving us."

I will always remember this whenever I turn my wipers on.

Fathers

Father

Mender of toys,
Leader of boys.

Changer of fuses,
Kisser of bruises.

Mover of couches,
Soother of ouches.

Pounder of nails,
Teller of tales.

Hanger of screens,
Counselor of teens.

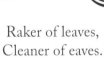

Fixer of bikes,
Partner on hikes.

Raker of leaves,
Cleaner of eaves.

Drier of dishes,
Catcher of fishes.

A Leader in prayers,
Bless him, O Lord!

Fathers Responsibility

Father is a name given to a male figure who engenders the birth of a child. While it is a title of respect, admiration, authority, and honor, it also demands responsibility and leadership. It is not a title that gives someone the authority to rule by force or with an iron hand but rather it gives authority to lead by example. A father who takes the lead role and leaves a good example for his family to follow will be honored and admired by them.

A father figure should be a role model for his children. It is his responsibility to provide for, to protect, to teach, to train, and to exemplify a character that his children can follow. A father who shoulders his responsibility is a blessing to his family and an asset to society. A father who loves his children, shows them how to love. A father who disciplines his children, teaches them that there are consequences for wrong actions. A father who instructs his children, shows them the value of learning. A father who takes the time and learns to listen to his children's needs, will develop a close knit relationship that will carry into adulthood. A father who provides encouragement, gives evidence to his children, that they have a dad who cares about them. A father who leads out in his home is setting an example for his children to follow. It is a blessing to a father to hear his child say, when I grow up I want to be just like my dad! The greatest hero for a child should be a loving caring father.

As I reflect on the many attributes of a good father, I realize that every father has faltered at some time, in at least one area. As fathers, we need to realize that failure is when we give up. There are times when we stumble, there are times when we trip, but we haven't failed if we pick up the pieces, ask for forgiveness and we try again. Failure comes when we quit trying. Being a good father is not once and done. It is a lifetime dedication to love and cherish our children.

To the many fathers who have tried diligently to shoulder their responsibility, I commend you. To those who have shunned their duties, it's never too late to change. To admit to your mistakes takes a real man and in most cases, children will appreciate your efforts to make a change. We can't change the past but we can alter our course for the future.

May every father be a leader and shoulder the burden of responsibility in his family. Collectively, let us take up the mantle for the betterment of our homes and the society in which we live.

—M. Gingrich

F.A.T.H.E.R.S.

F aithful.
A lways there.
T rustworthy.
H onoring.
E ver-loving.
R ighteous.
S upportive.

—*Unknown*

Flu Notes

(Notes pinned to the pillow of a mother who has the flu by a well-meaning husband who has inherited the house and children.)

Monday A.M.

Dearest: Sleep late. Everything under control. Lunches packed. Children off to school. Menu for dinner planned. Your lunch is on a tray in refrigerator: fruit cup, finger-sandwiches. Thermos of hot tea by bedside. See you around six.

Tuesday A.M.

Honey: Sorry about the egg rack in the refrigerator. Hope you got back to sleep. Did the children tell you about the coke I put in the thermoses? The school might call you on this. Dinner may be a little late. I'm doing your door-to-door canvas for liver research. Your lunch is in refrigerator. Hope you like leftover chili.

Wednesday A.M.

Dear Doris: Why would you put soap powder in the flour canister! If you have time, could you please come up with a likely spot for Chris's missing shoes? We've checked the clothes hamper, garage, back seat of the car, and wood box. Did you know the school has a ruling on bedroom slippers? There's some cold pizza for you on a napkin in the oven drawer. Will be late tonight. Driving eight girl scouts to tour meatpacking house.

Thursday A.M.

Doris: Don't panic over water in hallway. It crested last night at 9 p.m. Will finish laundry tonight. Please pencil in answers to following:

1. How do you turn on the garbage disposal?
2. How do you keep the milkman from leaving too much milk?
3. Why would a child leave his shoes in his boots?
4. How do you remove ink from the palm of a small boy's hand?
5. What do you do with leftovers when they begin to snap at you when you open the door?

I don't know what you're having for lunch! Surprise me!

Friday A.M.

Hey: don't drink from pitcher by the sink. I am trying to restore a pink dress shirt to original white. Take heart. Tonight, the ironing will be folded, the house cleaned and the dinner on time. I called your mother.

Only A Dad

Only a dad with a tired face
Coming home from the daily race,
Bringing little of gold or fame
To show how well he has played the game;
But glad in his heart that his own rejoice
To see him home and to hear his voice.

Only a dad with a brood of four,
One of ten million men or more
Plodding along in the daily strife
Bearing the whips and the scorns of life,
Will never whimper of pain or hate,
For the sake of those who at home await.

Only a dad neither rich nor proud,
Merely one of the surging crowd,
Toiling, striving from day to day,
Facing whatever may come his way,
Silent whenever the harsh condemn,
And bearing it all for the love of them.

Only a dad but he gives all
To smooth the way for his children small,
Doing with courage stern and grim
The deeds that his father did for him.
This is the line that for him I pen:
Only a dad, but the best of men.

—Edgar Guest

Penny Trick

After tucking their three-year-old child Sammy in for bed one night, his parents heard sobbing coming from his room. Rushing back in, they found him crying hysterically. He managed to tell them that he had swallowed a penny and he was sure he was going to die. No amount of talking seemed to help.

His father, in an attempt to calm him down, palmed a penny from his pocket and pretended to pull it from Sammy's ear. Sammy was delighted.

In a flash, he snatched it from his father's hand, swallowed, and then cheerfully said, "Do it again, Dad!"

Teach Him, World, But Gently, Please

This article was written years ago but still holds true today...proving, no doubt, that generation gaps may come and go but a father's love for his son never changes.

My young son starts going to school on Tuesday... it's all going to be strange and new to him for a while, and world, I wish you would sort of treat him gently.

You see, up to now, he's been king of the roost...he's been boss of the back yard...his mother has always been around to repair his wounds...and I've always been handy to soothe his feelings.

But now things are going to be different.

Tuesday morning he's going to walk down the front steps, wave his hand, and start out on the great adventure. It's an adventure that may take him across continents...it's an adventure that will likely include tragedy and sorrow.

Teach him to live his life as the world he has to live in will require faith and love and courage. So, world, I wish you would sort of take him by his young hand and teach him the things he will have to know.

Teach him...but gently, if you can.

He will have to learn, I know, that all men are not just, that all men are not true. But teach him, also, that for every scoundrel there is a hero...that for every crooked politician, there is a dedicated leader...teach him that for every enemy, there is a friend.

It will take time, world, I know, but teach him, if you can, that a nickel earned is of far more value than a dollar found...teach him to learn to lose...and enjoy winning.

Steer him away from envy, if you can, and teach him the secret of quiet laughter.

Let him learn early that the bullies are the easiest people to lick. Teach him, if you can, the wonder of books...but also give him quiet time to ponder the eternal mystery of birds in the sky, bees in the sun, and flowers on a green hill.

In school, world, teach him it is far more honorable to fail than to cheat. Teach him to have faith in his own ideas, even if everyone tells him they are wrong.

Teach him to be gentle with gentle people and tough with tough people.

Try to give my son the strength not to follow the crowd when everyone else is getting on the bandwagon... teach him to listen to all men...but teach him also to filter all he hears on a screen of truth and take only the good that comes through.

Teach him, if you can, how to laugh when he is sad...teach him there is no shame in tears...teach him there can be glory in failure and despair in success.

Teach him to scoff at cynics and to beware of too much sweetness. Teach him to sell his brawn and brains to the highest bidders but never to put a price tag on his heart and soul. Teach him to close his ears to a howling mob...and to stand and fight if he thinks he's right.

Treat him gently, world, but don't cuddle him, because only the test of fire makes fine steel. Let him have the courage to be impatient...let him have the patience to be brave. Teach him always to have sublime faith in himself. Because then he will have sublime faith in mankind. This is a big order, world, but see what you can do... he's such a nice little fellow...my son!

What Is A Dad?

A dad is a person
Who is loving and kind,
And often he knows
What you have on your mind.

He's someone who listens,
Suggests, and defends
A dad can be one
Of your very best friends!

He's proud of your triumphs,
But when things go wrong,
A dad can be patient
And helpful and strong.

In all that you do,
A dad's love plays a part
There's always a place for him
Deep in your heart

And each year that passes,
You're even more glad,
More grateful and proud
Just to call him your dad!

Thank you, Dad…
For listening and caring,
For giving and sharing,
But, especially, for just being you!

—Author Unknown

Friendship

A Hug

It's wondrous what a hug can do.
A hug can cheer you, when you're blue.
A hug can say, "I love you so."
Or, "I hate to see you go."

A hug is "Welcome back again,
And "Great to see you! Where've you been?"
A hug can soothe a small child's pain
And bring a rainbow after rain.

The hug, there's just no doubt about it—
We scarcely could survive without it!
A hug delights and warms and charms;
It must be why God gave us arms.

Hugs are great for fathers and mothers
Sweet for sisters, swell for brothers;
And chances are your favorite aunts
Love them more than potted plants.

Kittens crave them, puppies love them,
Heads of States are not above them.
A hug can break the language barrier
And make your travel so much merrier.

No need to fret about your store of 'em
The more you give, the more there's more of 'em.
So stretch those arms without delay
And give someone a hug today!

—Dean Walley

A Very Special Friend

What is a true friend you may ask?

Someone who will always be there for you,
No matter what you are going through.
Someone who will always say,
"Please don't worry, everything will turn out okay.
Someone who can take that frown from your face,
And put a smile in it's place.
Someone who can make it seem all right,
In spite of all the hurt inside.

Someone that is always caring,
And always ends up sharing.
Someone who will stand by you
Through thick and thin, but will never rub it in.

Someone who will cry with you when you are sad,
And laugh with you when you are glad.
Someone that will put it all on the line,
Because they are so very kind.

Someone that will stand by you,
No matter what others may say or do.
Someone you can trust within,
Because you know where they have been.

Someone that will humble himself,
And give credit to someone else.
Someone who will go out of their way,
Just so you have a wonderful day.

Someone with a heart so kind,
You want them around all the time.
Someone who never talks bad about his friends,
And keeps on forgiving over and over again.

Someone like this is so very hard to find,
But I have someone in mind.
If you don't know who I mean by now,
I'll tell you His name anyhow.

Only one person can do all of this, and
most people think He is a myth.

His Name Is Jesus Christ!!!!

—Kenneth C. Showalter

Be That Friend

The late J. Wilbur Chapman, famous evangelist, said that the New Testament records tell of forty people, each suffering from some disease, who have been healed by Jesus. Of this number, thirty-four were either brought to Jesus by friends or Jesus was taken to them. In only six cases out of forty did sufferers find their way to Christ without assistance.

One wonders whether the percentage would be any different today. Of the vast number of people who find their way to Jesus, most of them will reach Him because of the interest and cooperation of friends genuinely interested and concerned about their spiritual welfare.

—*Sword of the Lord*

Clay Balls

A man was exploring caves by the seashore. In one of the caves he found a canvas bag with a bunch of hardened clay balls. It was like someone had rolled clay balls and left them out in the sun to bake.

They didn't look like much, but they intrigued the man, so he took the bag out of the cave with him. As he strolled along the beach, he would throw the clay balls one at a time out into the ocean as far as he could.

He thought little about it, until he dropped one of the clay balls and it cracked open on a rock. Inside was a beautiful, precious stone!

Excited, the man started breaking open the remaining clay balls. Each contained a similar treasure. He found thousands of dollars worth of jewels in the 20 or so clay balls he had left. Then it struck him.

He had been on the beach a long time. He had thrown maybe 50 or 60 of the clay balls with their hidden treasure into the ocean waves. Instead of thousands of dollars in treasure, he could have taken home tens of thousands, but he had just thrown it away!

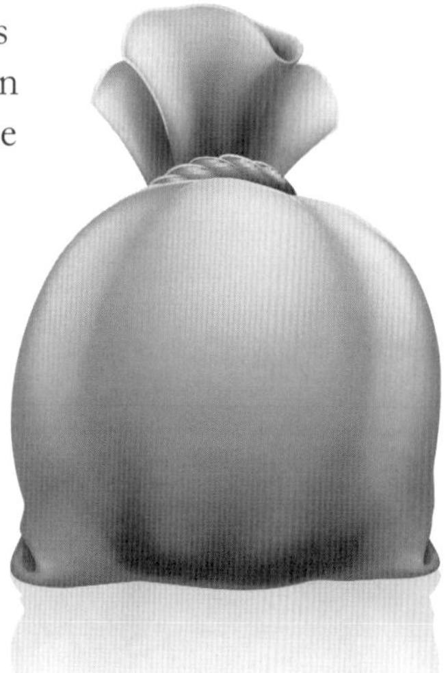

It's like that with people. We look at someone, maybe even ourselves, and we see the external clay vessel. It doesn't look like much from the outside. It isn't always beautiful or sparkling, so we discount it.

We see that person as less important than someone more beautiful or stylish or well known or wealthy; but we have not taken the time to find the treasure hidden inside that person.

There is a treasure in each and every one of us. If we take the time to get to know that person, and if we ask God to show us that person the way He sees them, then the clay begins to peel away and the brilliant gem begins to shine forth.

May we not come to the end of our lives and find out that we have thrown away a fortune in friendships because the gems were hidden in bits of clay. May we see the people in our world as God sees them.

I am so blessed by the gems of friendship I have with each of you.

Thank you for looking beyond my clay vessel.

Signed,
A Clay Ball!

Friends

A friend is somebody who has a close, personal relationship of mutual affection and trust with another. They are not enemies. When you are making friends, you are trying to get acquainted with them.

Try making friends soon. The next time a visitor comes to church, get acquainted with them. Tell them who you are, the name of your parents, your age, what school you go to, the names of your siblings, and so on. Give them a smile. Make them feel as if they are at their own church. Introduce your other friends to that person as well. Do not feel embarrassed. When you talk to a visitor one time, it will not be as hard to do it the next time.

Now, look at the types of friends that are around each of us, and see if you are like any of these types:

The Loving Friends**:** They have an intense feeling of tender affection and compassion for others. They sometimes enjoy putting little notes inside their friends' desks.

The Kind Friends**:** They let others go first. Pushing and shoving is not a problem for them. When at a water fountain, they absolutely do not spray water at the other person who is also taking a drink.

The Trusting Friends**:** They are the ones that have the responsibility of taking care of someone. You have to be around a friend before you know if they are trusting. Trusting friends are fair and truthful. If a friend asks you to go along shopping for the day, would you trust them?

The Caring Friends: They have compassion and concern for others. When little Johnny falls and hurts his knee, a caring friend will fix little Johnny up again. They ask you if you are okay when you fall or do something that hurts.

Were any of these types of friends like you? If not, perhaps you should change your attitude and become loving, kind, trusting, and caring.

—*D.J.G.*

Good Neighbors

Someone has defined good neighbors as someone who cares about me and I care about them. I feel fortunate to have good neighbors like that. The circle of people I call my close neighbors probably extends to at least a one mile radius. Even though they come from all walks of life there is a camaraderie that develops because of living in the same vicinity. We talk about what's happening in the community. We discuss how much rain we had, how the garden is doing and a host of other things including the property tax increases we don't think are necessary.

Most of my neighbors are the kind of people who will help if there is a tragedy. They are people who will stop and chat when you meet in the grocery store. They wave when you pass each other on the highway. Most of them know each other by name, know about their families, know their place of employment, and perhaps what some of their hobbies are.

Having good neighbors is nice, but being a good neighbor is important as well. We must respect each others property. We must be friendly if we expect it in return. We must show kindness when opportunity affords it. Things that may not seem important to us may be important to them. Good neighbors will develop a level of trust and appreciation for each other. They will mind their own business but when something doesn't seem quite right they will make it their business to make sure everything is okay.

In a technological age where so much of our correspondence is done via computers and email, face to face communication with good neighbors is of more importance than ever. A good neighbor relationship provides a backdrop of comfort and security in an otherwise unconcerned society. It provides a feeling of caring and belonging. It connects us with families and community in a place we call home.

—M. Gingrich

Lunch With God

There once was a little boy who wanted to meet God. He knew it was a long trip to where God lived, so he packed his suitcase with Twinkies® and some root beer, and started off.

When he had gone about three blocks, he met an old woman. She was sitting by herself in the park just staring at some pigeons. The boy sat down next to her and opened the suitcase. He was about to take a drink from his root beer when he noticed that the old lady looked hungry, so he offered her a Twinkie®. She gratefully accepted it and smiled at him. Her smile was so pretty that the boy wanted to see it again, so he offered her a root beer. Once again, she smiled at him. The boy was delighted! They sat there all afternoon eating and smiling,

but they never said a word. As it grew dark, the boy realized how tired he was and he got up to leave, but before he had gone more than a few steps, he turned around, ran back to the old woman, and gave her a hug. She gave him her biggest smile ever!

When the boy opened the door to his own house a short time later, his mother was surprised by the look of joy on his face. She asked "What did you do today that made you so happy?"

He replied, "I had lunch with God."

But before his mother could respond, he added, "You know what? She's got the most beautiful smile I've ever seen!"

Meanwhile, the old woman, also radiant with joy, returned to her home. Her son was stunned by the look of peace on her face and he asked, "Mother, what did you do today that made you so happy?" She replied, "I ate Twinkies® in the park with God." But before her son responded, she added, "You know, he's much younger than I expected!"

Too often we underestimate the power of a touch, a smile, a kind word, a listening ear, an honest compliment, or the smallest act of caring, all of which have the potential to turn a life around. People come into our lives for a reason, a season, or a lifetime.

Old Friends

There are no friends like the old friends
And none so good and true;
We greet them when we meet them
As roses greet the dew.

No other friends are dearer
Though born of kindred mold;
And while we prize the new ones,
We treasure more the old.

There are no friends like old friends,
Wherever we dwell or roam;
In lands beyond the ocean
Or near the bounds of home.

And when they smile to gladden
Or sometimes frown to guide,
We fondly wish those old friends
Were always by our side.

There are no friends like old friends,
To help us with the load,
That all must bear who journey
O'er life's uneven road.

And when unconquered sorrows
The weary hours invest,
The kindly words of old friends
Are always found the best.

There are no friends like old friends,
To calm our frequent fears;
When shadows fall and deepen
Through life's declining years.

And when our faltering footsteps
Approach the Great Divide
We'll long to meet the old friends
Who wait on the Other Side.

Old Friends Forget

Two elderly ladies had been friends for many decades. Over the years, they had shared all kinds of activities and adventures. Lately, their activities had been limited to meeting a few times a week to play games.

One day they were playing games when one looked at the other and said, "Now don't get mad at me. I know we've been friends for a long time, but I just can't think of your name! I've thought and thought, but I can't remember it. Please, tell me what your name is."

Her friend glared at her. For at least three minutes she just stared and glared at her. Finally, she said, "How soon do you need to know?"

Sharing the Pain

Susie was late coming home from school. When asked why she was late, she said, "Betty fell down and hurt herself. I sat down and helped her cry."

Some Things We Keep

I grew up in the fifties with practical parents; my mother, God love her, washed aluminum foil after she cooked in it and then reused it. She was the original recycle queen, before they had a name for it. My father was happier getting old shoes fixed than buying new ones.

Their marriage was good, their dreams focused.

Their best friends lived barely a wave away. I can see them now, dad in trousers, tee shirt, and a hat and mom in a house dress, lawn mower in one hand, dishtowel in the other.

It was the time for fixing things—a curtain rod, the kitchen radio, screen door, the oven door, the hem in a dress. Things we keep.

It was a way of life, and sometimes it made me crazy.

All that re-fixing, reheating, renewing, I wanted just once to be wasteful.

Waste meant affluence. Throwing things away meant there'd always be more.

But then my mother died, and on that clear summer's night, in the warmth of the hospital room, I was struck with the pain of learning that sometimes there isn't any 'more'.

Sometimes, what we care about most gets all used up and goes away…Never to return.

So while we have it, it's best we love it…and care for it…and fix it when it's broken…and heal it when it's sick.

This is true for marriage and old cars and children with bad report cards and dogs with bad hips and aging parents and grandparents.

We keep them because they are worth it, because we are worth it.

Some things we keep.

Like a best friend that moved away—or—a classmate we grew up with.

There are just some things that make life important, like people we know who are special…and so, we keep them close!

Surround Yourself With Friends!

One of the saddest things in life is to lose a friend. Even more sad is to not have friends in the first place. A friend is someone who cares. A friend is someone you like being with. It is someone you learn to trust. It is one in whom you learn to confide. Friends come in all sorts of different packages. Some friends are of general acquaintance, while others may be on a more intimate level. Some are friends because they enjoy the same hobbies or similar activities. Some are friends because they attend the same church or school. Some are friends because they have the same name or the same birthday. Some friendships develop through means of happenstance. An accident, a party, a customer at work, a hospital experience, a yard sale, or a chance meeting at the grocery store, all have the potential for developing friendships.

Friendships don't usually just happen. They develop and mature. A "just happened" friendship will not have very strong ties. The bond strengthens as the lives of people are intertwined. The level of maturity in a friendship will be a deciding factor in determining how easily a friendship is broken. Friendships can be very fragile. A lifetime friendship can be destroyed with one wrong move. All of us make mistakes. Sometimes we have a poor choice of words or actions and we may offend even our best friends. Sometimes we are the recipient of those actions. Whichever it may be, we have a choice. We can allow our friendship to dissolve and bitterness and anger to set in, or we can choose to forgive each other, resolve to improve, and move on. The latter is the ideal and will result in lasting friendship, however, it can also be the most difficult. It goes against human nature. A good friendship takes a lot of effort. It requires a willingness to make it work. It is a fact of life that hurts and differences will come. How we handle them is the difference. To have friends we need to be a friend.

To be without friends is lonely. Even misery loves company. A miserable grump likes someone else to be a grump with him. A criminal finds friendship with other criminals. Someone has said, "You get like the people you are around". This is very often the case. Therein lies the importance of not only having friends, but taking care to choose our friends wisely. This is especially important for young people who's lives are still being molded and shaped. Surrounding yourself with good company is a giant step in finding success and enjoyment in life. There is many a person who has found themselves in the wrong crowd because they wanted to feel accepted and reaped for themselves a life of bitter regrets.

There are many things we can do to develop friendships. We can give a listening ear to someone who has lost a loved one. We can share some fresh veggies from the garden. We can lend a hand with our neighbor's work project. We can send a note of encouragement to the sick. Even small deeds along the way like holding the door open, carrying a package, or picking up what fell are ways to build friendships. They are expressions of appreciation.

In case you haven't noticed, friendships happen by focusing on the needs of others. Constantly rambling about our needs and a focus that zooms in on self is counterproductive to developing friendships. Learn to zero in on others and talk to them about the things they enjoy and you will gain a wealth of knowledge. A smile and a wave are universal conversation in all languages. Learn to use them and you will surround yourself with something even the poorest can afford, the priceless possession of friendship!

—M. Gingrich

The Bricked Up Fireplace

Joe Henley sat alone on a park bench. This was his choice, although he was presented with no other. It was not quite four-thirty on a freezing Monday morning.

The sun was far from rising, but it was also far from dark; the city never progressed beyond dusk in that respect. He was an early riser and always the first to work, especially on Mondays. This was not because he loved his job or even because he wanted to please his boss, but rather because he simply loved Mondays. It was his favorite day, even more so than Fridays or the weekend that followed, and he greeted each with enthusiasm.

But it had not always been this way. Growing up, he hated Mondays like most, but changes were made. The intent was not to cultivate a love for the first day of the week; that was merely the road he happened to stay on, even after he got to where he was going. It had occurred to Joe as he approached the age of eleven that there was an inverse relationship, long before he knew what one was, between excitement and anticipation. The more he looked forward to something, the longer it took to arrive. Armed with this understanding, he set out to lengthen his weekends, and to accomplish this he cultivated a love for Monday mornings. He convinced himself that it was his favorite day of the week. He requested his favorite breakfast and made sure to wear his most favorite clothes. Over time, and not as much as one might think, he began to look forward to Monday mornings so much that his weekends began to drag. Only slightly at first, but soon he found his love for Mondays actually made his weekends seem to last twice as long as they once did. His plan had worked. Twenty-one years later, Joe still loved Monday mornings.

Four-thirty was when he normally started for the office, which easily had him sitting behind his desk by five. So it was at this time that he instinctively stood and began walking in that direction, but instead of turning left at the usual spot, he paused and then took a route that would lead him back home. He had no other place to go.

Joe's building was small and quiet. Only one resident occupied each of the Brownstone's six apartments, including the basement, which was home to the maintenance man. Mr. Laskowski was seventy-seven and his skills at repair were not nearly confined to leaky faucets and squeaky doors. As far as anyone knew, he had lived in the basement apartment for as long as there had been a basement apartment. Its door was tucked behind the stairway, hidden unless you knew it was there to begin with.

Joe's apartment occupied one-half of the top floor, three flights up. The building was without an elevator, but the stairs were welcomed as they kept the rent down. Their creaks also served to announce each move made on them. Joe had learned to identify his neighbors based solely on their respective creaks. Mrs. Lunderberg, well into her fifties and overweight, moved slowly; she was an easy one. Paul Thackery was easy, too, but for the opposite reason. He was a nervous man and moved quickly with a light foot, much as though everywhere he went he was on a bed of hot coals. Joe could quickly detect him flitting down the stairs and each time imagined that they were lined with smoldering embers, burning his feet at every step.

The apartments were small and each different. Joe's was a studio, the only one in the building, and therefore the smallest. As if to make up for the size, it was also the only one in which the fireplace remained exposed, though its use was forbidden. His lease, renewed each year without increase, listed eviction as the penalty. "The chimney's topped, your apartment would fill with smoke," he was told, "and it would cost a fortune to clean it." So he used the small space to store magazines and newspapers, but in the past, during winter months, he had made it to look as though it were one match away from a blaze. This proved to be a temptation he would rather live without, so the space became a far less decorative but much more functional storage bin for his magazines and newspapers.

At four forty-five on that cold Monday morning, Joe entered his building less than an hour after he had left it, and started up the stairs. He did not get far.

"What you doing back here? Forget something?" The voice was coarse and accented. Joe immediately recognized it as belonging to Mr. Laskowski, although it came slightly weaker than usual. He turned to see the old man emerge from the dark corner behind the stairs.

Joe smiled. They had formed a friendship that began the day Joe moved in. He felt immediately as though Mr. Laskowski knew him, understood him, and even cared for him, and Joe liked him as much as anyone in the city. Their interaction had leaned heavily toward the personal over the years, Joe having had few needs—the heater always worked when it was supposed to, the water was never cold, unless he wanted it to be. To Joe, Mr. Laskowski was more of a friend than a maintenance man, and a very good friend at that.

"Mr. Laskowski, I got fired," Joe said.

"This morning, already?" Mr. Laskowski asked, looking at his watch and seeing that it was not yet five o'clock.

"No," Joe replied. "On Friday. I got fired on Friday."

"Old habits die hard, yes?" Mr. Laskowski asked.

"I guess so," Joe said.

Mr. Laskowski looked deeply into Joe's eyes, into his soul. "Are you okay?" he asked. "Do you want to talk about it?"

"Yes," Joe answered, "I do."

And Mr. Laskowski listened.

"This wasn't part of the plan," Joe said. "I don't know what to do now. I feel so alone, so lost."

"These things, they happen for a reason," said Mr. Laskowski.

"A reason?" Joe asked. "I lost my job. Are you telling me there's a good reason for it? I just don't see it."

"Good reasons don't always seem that way in the beginning. You should take some time, take a trip. You have a car, yes? Start driving. One discovers many things about himself from behind the wheel of a car. I am old. I don't have a car and couldn't drive it even if I did. But when I was your age, I drove from ocean to ocean. I soaked up everything this country gave me. I learned many things during those travels, mostly about myself. Maybe this is what you need?"

"Maybe," Joe said. "And maybe I need to figure out how I'm going to pay rent next month." He forced a smile.

Mr. Laskowski coughed loudly. His eyes had become glassy and seemed to focus on nothing. "Yes," he said, "This is true. But you have been a good tenant for many years. The landlord will understand, I think. Don't you?"

"I don't know. Something will come up, it always does."

"Put forth the effort, Joe. Search for it. Don't wait for it to come to you or you might find you are waiting for a long time."

"But how? I don't even know where to look. Or what I'm looking for."

"Yes, this may be true, but life has a way of working with us," Mr. Laskowski said. "It rarely does the work for us, but it will work with us. Think about the trip. It would be good for you. And remember, money is needed to live, but it's not healthy to live for money. I have lived a happy life with few material pleasures. You can't buy happiness, but given the means, many people will try. Those with limited means will be forced to find happiness in the only place it truly exists."

Wondering where that place was, Joe promised to think about the trip. "Sure is cold out there," he said. "Wish I could go up and light a fire. When did they brick that thing up?" he asked, changing the subject.

Mr. Laskowski changed it back. "Joe, you do need to light a fire," he said, "But the place for it is in your heart. Once lit, it will burn just as brightly and just as hot as any other, but maybe that fireplace is bricked up too, yes?"

"Maybe so," Joe said. He then began his announcement to the rest of the building that he had returned home.

The days that followed were spent alone. Joe made no attempt to find a new job, even though the end of the month was nearly upon him, bringing with it a fresh round of bills he would be unable to pay.

It occurred to him that he should eat more, but he felt no hunger. His lack of appetite was partially influenced by a lack of food in his apartment, which was wholly influenced by a lack of motivation to buy any. After four days, he finally did, slipping out of the building unnoticed and back in a mere half hour later that same way. As he unlocked the door, his eye caught something not there when he had left. It was a white envelope. Upon inspection, he saw his name written across the front, followed by his apartment number, all in an unfamiliar handwriting.

He studied it cautiously, wondering what message was about to jump out. Eviction was his first thought. "Mr. Laskowski told them I got fired and they're kicking me out," he thought. He walked inside, laid the envelope on the mantle, and left it there unopened as he prepared his first full meal in four days.

He looked again toward the mantle and could see the top half of the white envelope. It had been lying quietly, as if waiting for the proper moment to pounce. Eviction was still the prevailing theory, but others had surfaced. Raised rent was currently running a close second.

Fear was eventually outweighed by curiosity. He stared for a final moment and then opened the letter. The typed note was brief. He read it twice. "This can't be happening," he said. He read it once more and then left his apartment. A moment later, a loud knock brought Mr. Laskowski to the door. It was opened slowly and the look on Mr. Laskowski's face immediately caused Joe to forget why he was there. "Mr. Laskowski, are you okay?" Joe asked.

His face was pale and his lips pasty. His hair was uncombed and he was without his teeth and glasses. Barely recognizable, he smiled warmly. "Oh yes, Joe, I'm fine," he said. "Just fine," he repeated, and though the spark in his eyes remained, the tone of his voice suggested otherwise.

"No, you're not," Joe said. "You're sick. Have you been to a doctor? We need to get you to a doctor!"

"I don't need a doctor," Mr. Laskowski said, coughing his way through the short sentence, "what I need is for you to calm down and come inside, sit with me and tell me what brings you. I haven't seen you in days."

Joe remembered the letter he was holding. He leaned forward. "Did you do this?" He asked.

"Did I do what?" Mr. Laskowski answered.

"This," Joe said, handing over the letter. Mr. Laskowski replaced his glasses and began reading.

Dear Mr. Henley:

Black mold has been detected in your apartment. As you may be aware, the potential destruction resulting from this is enormous, and it will require immediate attention to prevent it from spreading to the rest of the building. This process will take approximately one week and will require that you vacate the premises during that time. We sincerely apologize for any inconvenience and have waived your rent for the month of February.

The cleaning and repair process will begin on Monday, January 30 at 8:00 am. If you have any questions, please do not hesitate to contact us.

Regards,

The Manhattan Management Group

Mr. Laskowski smiled, broad and toothless. He coughed and then handed the letter back to Joe, asking, "Where will you go?"

"Don't you mean where will I stay?" Joe asked.

"No, Joe. I mean where will you go?"

"Why'd you do this?"

"Joe," Mr. Laskowski said, "Take this time and use it. A journey awaits you and although you may not know what you're searching for, that won't prevent it from being found."

Joe shook his head slowly and turned away. It was Friday afternoon. He had two days to pack.

"Mr. Laskowski!" Joe shouted. "You home?" This was followed by a second round of knocks, much louder than the first. It was six o'clock on Sunday morning. Joe was not anxious to go on a journey in search of something that quite possibly existed only in the mind of an old man.

After the third round of knocks, the door opened. Joe's eyes filled with tears.

"Joe, please do not worry for me. Please?" Mr. Laskowski asked.

"But Mr. Laskowski," his sentence was cut off. "Please?" His voice was weak. "Are you packed?" he asked.

"I am," Joe answered.

"But are you mentally packed?" Mr. Laskowski asked. "This journey, it will only be one if you treat it as such. Otherwise, you're just going for a drive. Understand?" His tone then became reflective, as if speaking from experience. He was. "Don't play the radio. Keep it off

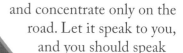

and concentrate only on the road. Let it speak to you, and you should speak back—don't be afraid. Stay away from the interstates and take your time through the small towns. Take time to talk to the people who live in them. You'll be surprised at how receptive they are. Listen to their stories, each one contains a lesson. Learn from them.

"Find a restaurant and talk with the locals—good, hard-working people. They'll recognize you as an outsider, but will welcome you just the same. When it becomes late, find a hotel, preferably one where the owner is also the attendant. And each morning, drive again just as you did the day before, listening to the road, to your heart. You will surely meet a hitchhiker along the way. Take a chance on him; he's on a journey, too. He's searching for answers just as you are. Your story may be part of his answer; his may be part of yours. When you let him off, look him in the eyes and thank him, and wish him well. He'll know what you mean, and he'll return the sentiments. You'll never see him again, but the meeting will not be in vain, I assure you.

"When you come to a town that agrees with you more than the others, stay for a few days. Settle in, get to know the people, and allow them to know you. Observe the way they live, observe the simple life that brings them so much pleasure. We all have this ability, few of us realize it, even fewer act on it—this city can spoil us for the rest of the world. Perform kind deeds. Help an elderly man change a flat, carry a women's groceries to her car. Give more than you could ever expect to receive, and through these acts, you will receive much more than you ever gave.

"Visit the local barber and have him cut your hair. Listen to his story, too. Observe the care and precision in which he performs his task. Notice the pride he takes in his work, however lowly you perceive it to be. This is his lesson, learn it.

"And when the time is right, slip away. Say no good-byes, leave without warning. You won't see them again, but you won't forget them. And they won't forget you. And as you drive home, again listen to the road. The message will be more clear, the words more easily forthcoming. They'll be your words, Joe, and you'll realize that it's not the road talking, it's your heart. Listen to it. The answers were there all along. And when you get back, come find me, because I'll want to hear all about it."

Twelve days later, Joe was back. "Mr. Laskowski!" He screamed, beating on the door. There was no answer. "Mr. Laskowski, I'm back. I just got back. You in there?" Nobody was. It was Friday afternoon. Mr. Laskowski played bingo every Friday afternoon.

Joe danced up the stairs. He had taken a backpack, which was thrown over his shoulders, but he floated up the stairs as if there were no extra weight at all. It had proved to be a journey indeed. The road had spoken to him, just as Mr. Laskowski said it would, and before the journey's end, Joe was fully aware of who was really doing the talking. The haze had lifted, leaving beneath a clear view of the world.

Joe unlocked his door and paused before opening it. "There was no black mold," he thought, and smiled. He walked in and found his apartment just as it had been left, confirming his thought. Nothing had been cleaned and from his first glance, it appeared no one had even entered. And then he sensed it. Something was different. He scanned the small space, and then again, and then his eyes came to rest in disbelief. He slowly walked to the fireplace and stared open-mouthed at what he saw. It was again made with kindling and logs, all neatly stacked and ready to be lit. There was a note on the mantle, folded neatly beneath a box of matches. The handwriting was barely legible.

Joe,

This is the last fireplace in the building. Please, use it as it was intended. There is nothing to stop you. I know you had a wonderful journey and I hope this fire will match the one now burning in your heart, and that both will burn brightly for many years to come.

Your friend,

Mr. Laskowski

"There's nothing to stop you?" Joe said as he re-read the words, "what does that mean?" He would soon find out.

"Joe, this is Ed Crawford," cracked the voice on the answering machine. It was the only message that had been left. "I'm with Crawford & Simpson. Please return my call as soon as you get this message." He went on to say it was a most urgent matter and then ended with his phone number, which he repeated. Joe listened to the message again and then once more. "What's going on?" He then wondered if Mr. Laskowski had something to do with this, too.

"Hi. My name's Joe Henley and I'm—

"Just one moment please, Mr. Henley," Joe was cut off before he could finish his sentence. "I'll connect you with Mr. Crawford. He's been waiting for your call."

The phone fell silent. There was no music, no recorded voice speaking about the firm. He had looked up Crawford & Simpson in the phone book and could find no trace of them. "Joe, hi. Ed Crawford." He spoke quickly without giving Joe the chance to respond. "I'm an attorney."

A lump formed. "Have I done something wrong?" Joe asked.

"Joe, would it be possible for you to drop by my office? I'd rather have this conversation in person." It was possible, though not enticing. He agreed anyway.

Soon, Joe was introducing himself to the receptionist, who immediately pressed a button that connected her with Ed Crawford's office. Joe took this time to study the lobby. The office was unpretentious, in a very pretentious location. The furnishings were modest, the wall hangings mass-produced, the receptionist just as plain as her surroundings. Joe would not have the chance to test the couch, but it looked hard and uncomfortable. There were no bookshelves against the walls or magazines on the coffee table. No sculpture in the corner. No grand chandelier hanging from above.

"Joe, hi," Ed Crawford said to him, just as he had on the phone. "Please, come back, and thanks for coming."

"Please, sit down." Ed said once they had entered his office, which was just as unimposing as the lobby.

"What have I done?" Joe asked.

"Joe, please relax. You've done nothing wrong, but I'm afraid I have some difficult news." Joe braced himself. "Mr. Laskowski passed away. He died three days ago." Joe said nothing. Ed Crawford paused, and then continued, "Our firm has represented Mr. Laskowski for many years. He was one of our very first clients, dating back to when my father was just starting out. Mr. Laskowski said we reminded him of himself, lacking the unnecessary show of wealth you find in most firms." Joe had noticed the same. "He said he appreciated the fact that our offices were for practicing law, not impressing clients. He's been one ever since."

Joe listened and felt that he understood Mr. Laskowski a little better. He then asked a very obvious question: "But, why did he need a lawyer?"

"When he came to this country, it was very difficult for immigrants. He feared being taken advantage of, a legitimate fear, and retained us to protect his interests."

"Why am I here?" Joe asked.

"I'm going to share a secret with you, Joe. Mr. Laskowski wasn't who you thought he was. Yes, he was the maintenance man of a small apartment building on the west side of the city. But that's not all. He was also the owner."

"He what?" Joe gasped. "He owned it?"

"Yes," Ed said. "Your real landlord was Mr. Laskowski."

"All this time," Joe started, but finished with nothing but a shake of his head.

"Joe," Ed continued, "Mr. Laskowski married before he immigrated. His wife promised to follow him, but she never did. She passed away twenty-five years ago. They had no children."

Joe was unsure where Ed Crawford was taking him, but he followed along without interruption. "So you see, he had no heirs." Ed then produced a legal looking document and placed it on the table. "And according to his will," he said, pointing to the document, "the building now belongs to you."

Joe's mouth fell open. "What?" he managed to ask.

"He bought the building over fifty years ago with every cent he had. He knew that even while charging modest rents, he would be able to make the bank payments and still live a decent life, which is all he ever wanted. He screened his tenants carefully. He knew more about you by the time you moved in than most know about life-long friends." This explained a lot. "He wanted to provide a good home for good people. He cared about each of them, but especially you. One day, maybe a year ago, he came to me and said if you were still living in his building when he died, he wanted you to have it. The will was amended on the spot, and we never spoke of it again. There's of course some paperwork that needs to be taken care of, but we can attend to that later. He was a good man, Joe. My father used to say the best he ever knew. And he cared about people, they meant something to him. And you, you meant a great deal."

Joe was filled with as many emotions as questions, but could only verbalize one. "Who's the Manhattan Management Group?"

"You're looking at him, Joe. No one else knows Mr. Laskowski was the owner, just as they won't know you are now. I think he'd like it if you kept it that way."

Joe walked slowly home. He made his way through the park, past the very bench where he spent so many mornings. He looked at the trees. He again felt a wave of sorrow, but this time, it was only for them.

It was dark when he reached his building, and though the air was much colder, he did not enter. He stood outside, thinking of everything and nothing, and then he saw Mrs. Lunderberg. She exited the building and began to slowly descend the steps. As she neared, Joe could see she was crying. She walked to where Joe stood, unable to speak, and hugged him instead.

"Where've you been, Joe?" She finally asked, and then added, "Have you heard?"

"I have." Joe said. "I just found out." He then thought of the conversation he had with Mr. Laskowski after he had lost his job. He looked deeply into Mrs. Lunderberg's eyes, into her soul. "Are you okay?" He asked. "Do you want to talk about it?"

"Yes," she answered, "I do."

And Joe listened.

Giving

A Thoughtful Gift

It was just a small, white envelope stuck among the other gifts in our living room. No name, no identification, no inscription. It has been the highlight of our Christmas for the past ten years or so.

It all began because my husband Tim always dreaded Christmas—oh, not the true meaning of Christmas, but the commercial aspects of it: overspending, the frantic running around at the last minute to get a tie for Uncle Harry or perfume for Grandma, the gifts given in desperation because you couldn't think of anything else.

Knowing he felt this way, I decided one year to bypass the usual shirts, sweaters, ties, and so forth. I reached for something special, just for Tim. The inspiration came in an unusual way.

Our son, Jordan, who was twelve that year, was wrestling at the junior level at the school he attended and shortly before Christmas, there was a nonleague match against a team sponsored by an inner-city church. These youngsters, dressed in sneakers so ragged that shoestrings seemed to be the only thing holding them together, presented a sharp contrast to our boys in their spiffy blue and gold uniforms and sparkling new wrestling shoes. As the match began, I was alarmed to see that the other team was wrestling without headgear, a kind of light helmet designed to protect a wrestler's ears.

It was a luxury the ragtag team obviously could not afford. We ended up walloping them. We took every weight class. As each of their boys got up from the mat, he swaggered around in his tatters with false bravado, a kind of street pride that couldn't acknowledge defeat.

Tim, seated beside me, shook his head sadly, "I wish just one of them could have won," he said. "They have a lot of potential, but losing like this could take the heart right out of them."

Tim loved children—all children—and he knew them, having coached little league football, baseball, and lacrosse. That's when the idea for his present came.

That afternoon, I went to a local sporting goods store and bought an assortment of wrestling headgear and shoes and sent them anonymously to the inner-city church. On Christmas Eve, I placed the envelope among the other gifts with a note inside telling Tim what I had done and that this was his gift from me. His smile was the brightest thing about Christmas that year and in succeeding years. For each Christmas, I followed the tradition—one year sending a group of mentally handicapped youngsters to a hockey game, another year a check to a pair of elderly brothers whose home had burned to the ground the week before Christmas, and on and on.

The envelope became the highlight of our Christmas. It was always the last thing opened on Christmas morning and our children, ignoring their new toys, would stand with wide-eyed anticipation as their dad opened the envelope to reveal its contents.

As the children grew, the toys gave way to more practical presents, but the envelope never lost its allure. The story doesn't end there.

You see, we lost Tim a year ago due to cancer. When Christmas rolled around, I was still so wrapped in grief that I couldn't even seem to think about Christmas. Finally on Christmas Eve I filled out the card, sealed it in the usual white envelope and placed it carefully among the other gifts. The next morning, to my pleasant surprise, it was joined by three more white envelopes.

Each of our children, unbeknownst to the others, had placed an envelope for their dad. The tradition has grown and someday will expand even further with our grandchildren standing around with wide-eyed anticipation watching as their fathers open the envelope.

We learned that the spirit of giving to others in need always brings the greatest joy.

Brighten Your Corner

We cannot all be famous
Or be listed in "Who's Who",
But every person, great or small
Has important work to do.

For seldom do we realize
The importance of small deeds,
Or to what degree of greatness
Unnoticed kindness leads.

For it's not the big celebrity
In a world of fame and praise,
But it's doing unpretentiously
In an undistinguished way.

The work that God assigned to us,
Unimportant as it seems,
That makes our task outstanding
And brings reality to dreams.

So do not sit and idly wish
For wider, new dimensions,
Where you can put into practice
Your many good intentions.

But at the spot God placed you
Begin at once to do,
Little things to brighten up
The lives surrounding you.

If everybody brightened up
The spot where they are,
By being more considerate
And a little less demanding.

This dark old world would very soon
Eclipse the evening star,
If everybody brightened up
The corner where they are!

—Author Unknown

Give Freely

"Remember this—a farmer who plants only a few seeds will get a small crop. But, the one who plants generously will get a generous crop. You must each make up your mind as to how much you should give. Don't give reluctantly or in response to pressure, for God loves the person who gives cheerfully, and God will generously provide all you need. Then you will always have every thing you need and plenty left over to share with others."

The Real Test

Someone has said, "To determine how much a person loves God, look at his checkbook." It's possible to give without loving, but we cannot love without giving. True love for God will never say, "I can't afford to give." Love always finds a way. Love gives more than asked. The Bible speaks of tithes and offerings. How much do you love God? Enough to give Him tithes and offerings?

God's Word

Bible Through The Eyes Of Children

Story of Elijah

The Sunday school teacher was carefully explaining the story of Elijah the prophet and false prophets of Baal. She explained how Elijah built the altar, put wood upon it, cut the animal in pieces, and laid it on the altar. And then, Elijah commanded the people of God to fill four barrels of water and pour it over the altar. He had them do this four times. "Now", said the teacher, "can anyone in the class tell me why the Lord would have Elijah pour water over the animal on the altar?" A little girl in the back of the room started waving her hand. "I know! I know!" she said. "To make the gravy!"

Did Noah Fish?

A Sunday school teacher asked, "Johnny, do you think Noah did a lot of fishing when he was on the ark?"

"No," he replied, "How could he, with just two worms?"

The Lord is my Shepherd

A Sunday school teacher decided to have her youngest class memorize one of the most quoted passages in the Bible—Psalm 23. She gave the youngsters a month to learn the verses. Little Rick was excited about the task—but he just couldn't remember the Psalm. After much practice, he could barely get past the first line. On the day the children were scheduled to recite Psalm 23 in front of the congregation, Ricky was so nervous. When it was his turn, he stepped up to the microphone and said proudly "The Lord is my shepherd…and that's all that I need to know."

Christ Our Savior

Jesus is the greatest person that ever lived. The entire world remembers His birth, death, and resurrection.

1. Cradle. Born of a virgin (Isa. 7:14). This prophecy was given 700 years before He was born and is fulfilled in Matthew 1:20-23.
2. Character. The prophet describes some of His character in Isaiah 53. Peter said Jesus was without sin, fault and wrong (I Pet. 2:22).
3. Consecration. Though the Son of God, He humbled Himself, and became obedient to the Father and came into the world to live, teach, suffer, and die (Phil. 2:7, 8). He became human to understand our feelings (Heb. 4:15).
4. Control. He had control over sickness (Matt. 8:16). He had control over nature (Matt. 14:27). He had control over demons (Matt. 8:31-34). He had control over death (John 11:25, 26). He is above all (Phil. 2:9-11).
5. Coronation. On Palm Sunday, Jesus rode into Jerusalem as King (Matt. 21:1-13). Garments and palm branches were placed on the road to welcome Him. Though made their King, He would be crucified the following Friday.
6. Crucifixion. Isaiah predicts Christ's suffering (Isa. 53). The Psalmist tells of His sufferings (Psalm 22). These prophecies were fulfilled in Matt. 27. He suffered because of our sins (Rom. 3:23, Rom. 5:8).
7. Conqueror. Jesus said if they destroy His body, He would rise again in three days (John 2: 19). He fulfilled His words in Mark 16:1-14. Because He lives, we too shall live (John 14: 19).
8. Coming. He promised to return for His people (John 14:1-3). Later He ascended (Acts 1:9-11). Paul gave the details of His return (I Thes. 4:13-18). He could return at any time (Matt. 24:44).

This great Savior wants to be your personal Savior. He wants to live and dwell within your heart.

Coal Basket Bible

The story is told of an old man who lived on a farm in the mountains of eastern Kentucky with his young grandson. Each morning, Grandpa was up early sitting at the kitchen table reading from his old worn out Bible. His grandson who wanted to be just like him tried to imitate him in any way he could.

One day the grandson asked, "Papa, I try to read the Bible just like you but I don't understand it, and what I do understand I forget as soon as I close the book. What good does reading the Bible do?"

The Grandfather quietly turned from putting coal in the stove and said, "Take this coal basket down to the river and bring back a basket of water."

The boy did as he was told, even though all the water leaked out before he could get back to the house.

The grandfather laughed and said, "You will have to move a little faster next time," and sent him back to the river with the basket to try again.

This time the boy ran faster, but again the basket was empty before he returned home. Out of breath, he told his grandfather that it was impossible to carry water in a basket, and he went to get a bucket instead.

The old man said, "I don't want a bucket of water; I want a basket of water. You can do this. You're just not trying hard enough," and he went out the door to watch the boy try again.

At this point, the boy knew it was impossible, but he wanted to show his grandfather that even if he ran as fast as he could, the water would leak out before he got far at all. The boy scooped the water and ran hard, but when he reached his grandfather the basket was again empty. Out of breath, he said, "See Papa, it's useless!"

"So you think it is useless?" The old man said, "Look at the basket." The boy looked at the basket and for the first time he realized that the basket looked different. Instead of a dirty old coal basket, it was clean.

"Son, that's what happens when you read the Bible. You might not understand or remember everything, but when you read it, it will change you from the inside out.

That is the work of God in our lives. To change us from the inside out and to slowly transform us into the image of His son. Take time to read a portion of God's word each day.

Diary Of A Bible

January: A busy time for me. Most of the family decided to read me through this year. They kept me busy for the first two weeks, but they have forgotten me now.

February: Clean-up time. I was dusted yesterday and put in my place. My owner did use me for a few minutes last week. He had been in an argument and was looking up some references to prove he was right.

March: Had a busy day first of the month. My owner was elected president of the PTA & used me to prepare a speech.

April: Grandpa visited us this month. He kept me on his lap for an hour reading from 1 Peter 5:5-7. He seems to think more of me than do some people in my own household.

May: I have a few green stains on my pages. Some spring flowers were pressed between my pages.

June: I look like a scrapbook. They have stuffed me full of newspaper clippings—one of the girls got married.

July: They put me in a suitcase today. I guess we are off on vacation. I wish I could stay home; I know I'll be closed up in this thing for at least two weeks.

August: Still in the suitcase.

September: Back home at last and in my old familiar place. I have a lot of company. Two women's magazines and four comic books are stacked on top of me. I wish I could be read as much as they are..

October: They read me a little bit today. One of them is very sick. Right now I am sitting in the center of the coffee table. I think the pastor is coming by for a visit.

November: Back in my old place. Somebody asked today if I were a scrapbook.

December: The family is busy getting ready for the holidays. I guess I'll be covered up under wrapping paper and packages again just as I am every Christmas.

—Author Unknown

Emergency Phone Numbers

When in sorrow..call John 14
When people fail you..................................call Psalm 27
If you want to be fruitful...............................call John 15

If you have sinned..call Psalm 51
When you worry.............................call Matthew 6:19-34
When you are in danger................................call Psalm 91
When God seems far away.........................call Psalm 139
When your faith needs stirring................call Hebrews 11
When you are lonely and fearful...................call Psalm 23
When you grow bitter.......................call I Corinthians 13
Paul's secret of happiness.............call Colossians 3:12-17
What is Christianity?.............call 2 Corinthians 5:15-19
When feeling down and out...................call Romans 8:31
When you want peace and rest......call Matthew 11:25-30
When the world seems bigger than God......call Psalm 90
Wanting Christian assurance?...........call Romans 8:1-30
Leaving home for work or travel................call Psalm 121
When prayer becomes selfish........................call Psalm 67
For a great invention/opportunity................call Isaiah 55
When you want courage for a task...............call Joshua 1
How to get along with people...................call Romans 12
Thinking of investments returns?.................call Mark 10
If you are depressed.....................................call Psalm 27
If your pocketbook is empty..........................call Psalm 37
If losing confidence in people...........call 1 Corinthians 13
If people seem unkind....................................call John 15
If discouraged about your work..................call Psalm 126

Alternate Numbers
For dealing with fear.................................call Psalm 34:7
For security...call Psalm 121:3
For assurance...call Mark 8:35
For reassurance.....................................call Psalm 145:18

All numbers may be dialed direct. No operator assistance is necessary. All lines to Heaven are open 24 hours a day!

Facts About The Bible

- The word "Jehovah" or "Lord" occurs in the Old Testament 6,855 times, the word "reverend" but once. (Psalm 111:9)
- The word "and" occurs 46,277 times, the word "girl" but once in Joel 3:3.
- The words "everlasting fire" but twice, and "everlasting punishment" but once.
- The word "horseback" occurs 5 times.
- The word "bushel" is found in Matt. 5:15 and Luke 11:33.
- Ezra 7:21 contains all the letters of the alphabet except the letter 'j'.
- The 19th chapter of 2 Kings and the 37th chapter of Isaiah are alike.
- The shortest verse in the New Testament is John 11:35.
- The 8th, 15th, 21st and 31st verses of the 107th Psalm are alike.
- All the verses of the 136th Psalm end alike.
- The longest verse is Esther 8:9.
- One of the finest chapters to read is Acts 26.
- The most instructive and most beautiful, Matthew, the 5th, 6th, and 7th chapters.

Father's Love Letter

My Child...

- You may not know me, but I know everything about you (Psalm 139:1).
- I know when you sit down and when you rise up (Psalm 139:2).
- I am familiar with all your ways (Psalm 139:3).
- Even the very hairs on your head are numbered (Matthew 10:29-31).
- For you were made in my image (Genesis 1:27).
- In me you live and move and have your being (Acts 17:28).
- For you are my offspring (Acts 17:28).
- I knew you even before you were conceived (Jeremiah 1:4-5).
- I chose you when I planned creation (Ephesians 1:11-12).
- You were not a mistake, for all your days are written in my book (Psalm 139:15-16).
- I determined the exact time of your birth and where you would live (Acts 17:26).
- You are fearfully and wonderfully made (Psalm 139:14).
- I knit you together in your mother's womb (Psalm 139:13).
- And brought you forth on the day you were born... (Psalm 71:6).

- I have been misrepresented by those who don't know me (John 8:41-44).
- I am not distant and angry, but am the complete expression of love (1 John 4:16).
- And it is my desire to lavish my love on you (1 John 3:1).
- Simply because you are my child and I am your father (1 John 3:1).
- I offer you more than your earthly father ever could (Matthew 7:11).
- For I am the perfect father (Matthew 5:48).
- Every good gift that you receive comes from my hand (James 1:17).
- For I am your provider and I meet all your needs… Matthew (6:31-33).
- My plan for your future has always been filled with hope (Jeremiah 29:11).
- Because I love you with an everlasting love (Jeremiah 31:3).
- My thoughts toward you are countless as the sand on the seashore (Psalm 139:17-18).
- And I rejoice over you with singing (Zephaniah 3:17).
- I will never stop doing good to you (Jeremiah 32:40).
- For you are my treasured possession (Exodus 19:5).
- I desire to establish you with all my heart and all my soul (Jeremiah 32:41).
- And I want to show you great and marvelous things (Jeremiah 33:3).
- If you seek me with all your heart, you will find me… (Deuteronomy 4:29).
- Delight in me and I will give you the desires of your heart (Psalm 37:4).
- For it is I who gave you those desires
- (Philippians 2:13).
- I am able to do more for you than you could possibly imagine (Ephesians 3:20).
- For I am your greatest encourager
- (2 Thessalonians 2:16-17).
- I am also the Father who comforts you in all your troubles (2 Corinthians 1:3-4).
- When you are brokenhearted, I am close to you… (Psalm 34:18).
- As a shepherd carries a lamb, I have carried you close to my heart (Isaiah 40:11).
- One day I will wipe away every tear from your eyes (Revelation 21:3-4).
- And I'll take away all the pain you have suffered on this earth (Revelation 21:3-4).
- I am your Father, and I love you even as I love my son, Jesus (John 17:23).
- For in Jesus, my love for you is revealed (John 17:26).
- He is the exact representation of my being (Hebrews 1:3).
- He came to demonstrate that I am for you, not against you (Romans 8:31).
- And to tell you that I am not counting your sins (2 Corinthians 5:18-19).
- Jesus died so that you and I could be reconciled (2 Corinthians 5:18-19).
- His death was the ultimate expression of my love for you (1 John 4:10).
- I gave up everything I loved that I might gain your love (Romans 8:31-32).
- If you receive the gift of my son Jesus, you receive me 1 John 2:23
- And nothing will ever separate you from my love again (Romans 8:38-39).
- I have always been Father, and will always be Father (Ephesians 3:14-15).
- My question is… Will you be my child? (John 1:12-13).
- I am waiting for you (Luke 15:11-32).

Love,
Your Father,
Almighty God

God's Decrees

Laws. Rules. Absolutes. Morality. Ethics. These words are becoming less and less respected in our society. People proclaim that there are no absolutes; everything is relative. You can live however you desire, as long as you're happy and nobody else gets hurt. It's okay to take revenge if someone has offended you. There's nothing wrong with lying or cheating if you do so to protect yourself.

People often assume they will be happier with no restraints. Yet in reality, the opposite is true. God has given us a standard to live by, and that standard will lead us to a fruitful Christian life.

—Tia Cooper,
God's Word For Today

God's Minorities

- During the time Noah was building the ark, he was very much in the minority, but he won.
- When Joseph was sold into Egypt by his brothers, he was in a decided minority, but he won.
- When Gideon and his 300 followers, with their broken pitchers and lamps, put the Midianites to flight, they were in an insignificant minority, but they won.
- When Elijah prayed down fire from heaven and put the prophets of Baal to shame, he was in a notable minority, but he won.
- When David, ridiculed by his brothers, went out to meet Goliath, in size he was in a decided minority, but he won.
- When Martin Luther nailed his theses on the door of the cathedral, he was a lonesome minority, but he won.
- When Jesus Christ was crucified by the Roman soldiers, He was a conspicuous minority, but He won.
- One plus God is a majority.

Keeping Fit

There are three areas in which God wants us to keep fit, so we may be a better Christian

1. Fit Spiritually—Weekly in the Sunday School lesson, and in the Pastor's sermons, we are given helpful advice and counsel. The information is of little value unless we apply it to our lives. The more services we attend, the more help we receive. Daily we should read our Bible. Not only read it, but study it, memorize it, and meditate upon it. As we do this, His Word will speak to us. Besides God's word, we should take time daily to pray. The length of our prayer is not as important as being in an attitude of prayer. To remain fit spiritually, we must maintain God's touch upon our life.
2. Fit Physically—Our bodies are the temples of the Holy Ghost (I Cor. 6:19, 20). Visit your doctor twice a year. In some cases you may need more visits. Obey the instructions of the Doctors. Take your prescribed medication. Get proper sleep. Sometimes a 10-15 minute nap will do wonders. Learn to relax, even under pressure. Refrain from eating the foods that you are not permitted to eat. Be careful of overeating. Obesity can shorten your life in various ways. Develop some sort of exercise. Walking is free, and it does wonders. Note how we should glorify Christ in our bodies (I Cor. 6:20).
3. Fit Mentally—Solomon said we are what we think (Prov. 23:7). Thoughts quickly turn into action and behavior. To keep alert in mind, read daily. Of course, read your Bible. Read religious books and magazines. Read the newspaper daily. Visit the library. There are many books, magazines, and periodicals to read free of charge. Study the Sunday School lesson each week. Think of the many good things God has given you. Think positive. Keep in mind the words of Solomon, "You are what you think."

Learn to keep fit spiritually, physically, and mentally, and bring honor and glory to God.

Keeping In Touch

A young girl answered the phone and after speaking for about twenty minutes she hung up. Her father was pleasantly surprised by the brief conversation. Most times her phone conversations were an hour or longer. Given the shortness of the conversation he asked her which of her friends she was talking to. She replied, "It wasn't a friend. Someone dialed the wrong number."

While the story is rather humorous, it's also a reminder to me of the wasted time and frustrations the telephone, and now cell phones, bring to the society in which we live. Yes, there are benefits. We can get in touch with loved ones or important contacts virtually anywhere, anytime. Decisions can be made quickly. We can get answers to important questions. But therein lies the challenge. Is the question I have important enough to interrupt others at that moment? Do I make a call before trying to come to a decision on my own.

The frustrations the telephone brings begin with voice mail. Voice mail, I am convinced is a convenient way to say, "Don't bother me." I am also convinced it doesn't always tell the truth. "I am away from my desk or helping another customer at the moment," as many voice mail recordings go, may be genuinely the case, but it is also possible the person is sitting right there listening and deciding if he or she really wants to answer. A busy signal and automated answering machines that put you through a series of options instead of a live voice, also find their place in the frustration column.

The modern technology that brings us the Internet at faster and faster speeds, online services, text messaging, cell phones, instant access, and a whole host of programs is mind boggling. But even in an era of modern technical advances we still get put on hold or get dropped completely when someone transfers the call. "Your call will be answered by the next available customer service representative." I hold my breath every time. Given the popularity of cell phones, apparently, most of us have concluded that the frustration does not outweigh the convenience. It is something we just need to cope with.

In conjunction with that I got to thinking about all the "phone calls" that God fields every day. He never drops a connection. He never gives a busy signal. He never puts us on hold. He is never reluctant to answer. He does not have a "do not call list". No call is a nuisance. In Judges chapter 6, Gideon put in a call asking God to confirm his instructions. He put out a fleece and requested the dew to be on the fleece but the ground around it to be dry. God answered. Again, Gideon called. This time however he requested that the fleece be dry and the ground wet with the dew. Again, God answered. Gideon's request was important to God. Gideon was willing to put out a fleece and accept God's answer.

God wants us to bring our requests to him. He wants to engage in conversation with us. It is His delight. He wants us to realize our dependence on Him and He wants us to put out a fleece of submission. The greatest mistake we make is when we fail to call. God is our friend. Let's keep in touch.

—M. Gingrich

Marriage Communication Guidelines

1. Be a ready listener and do not answer until the other person has finished talking (*Proverbs 18:13; James 1:19*).
2. Be slow to speak. Think first. Don't be hasty in your words. Speak in such a way that the other person can understand and accept what you have to say (*Proverbs 15:23 & 28; 21:23; 29:20; James 1:19*).
3. Speak the truth always, but do it in love. Do not exaggerate (*Ephesians 4:15 & 25; Colossians 3:9*).
4. Do not use silence to frustrate the other person. Explain why you are hesitant to talk at this time.
5. Do not become involved in quarrels. It is possible to disagree without quarreling (*Proverbs 17:14; 20:3; Romans 13:13; Ephesians 4:31*).
6. Do not respond in anger. Use soft and kind responses (*Proverbs 14:29; 15:1; 25:15; 29:11; Ephesians 4:26 & 31*).
7. When you are in the wrong, admit it and ask for forgiveness. (*James 5:16*) When someone confesses to you, tell them you forgive them. Be sure it is forgotten and not brought up to the person (*Proverbs 17:9; Ephesians 4:32; Colossians 3:13; 1 Peter 4:8*).
8. Avoid nagging (*Proverbs 10:19; 17:9; 20:5*).
9. Do not blame or criticize the other person. Instead, restore…encourage…build up. If someone verbally attacks, criticizes, or blames you, do not respond in the same manner (*Romans 12:17 & 21; 1 Peter 2:23; 3:9*).
10. Try to understand the other person's opinion. Make allowances for differences. Be concerned about their interests (*Philippians 2:1-4*).

—Author Unknown

Mr. Common Sense

I received a 3x5 card with just a few lines of wisdom. It read, "There has been over the years, many times that Mr. Common Sense and Mr. Good Judgment were screaming in my ears, at the top of their lungs, telling me to think before I act; asking me if what I am about to do, is the correct thing or the correct time, or telling me not to delay that now is the time to act."

Webster defines common sense as ordinary good sense or sound practical judgement. In other words it is decision making that has a solid foundation, it is sound and in all probability has proven successful in the past. It has a good track record. Secondly, it is good and in the best interest of all the parties involved. Thirdly, it is practical or readily understood and easily administrated. It is a logical decision. Fourthly, it is common. It fits the occasion and the culture and meets the criteria necessary to resolve any issues. It just makes sense that it is the right decision. Why then is common sense seemingly in short supply?

Perhaps it comes back to the foundation. In order to have sound judgement or make sensible choices their needs to be a basis for them. Without a basis they cannot function. We must also consider, the word, "good". What is good? Good can be defined as morally uplifting, uncontaminated, honorable, respectable, healthy and producing favorable results. So much of what we see and hear through the media today runs counter to that. Much of the music is unfit for human consumption. Videos and video games in many cases are morally corrupted. It is further indication that the foundation has crumbled. If we expect to see common sense and good judgement prevail in our day, we must begin by rebuilding the foundation.

Most folks wouldn't consider for a moment the idea of constructing a house on the local landfill. They know it won't work. Why then do many of those same people allow their families to feed their minds on the contaminated, polluted, unhealthy garbage that is so prevalent? It is devastating to say the least! The lack of nutrition and the bacteria will eventually take its toll and the family structure will weaken until it breaks. And break it will, unless major changes take place in the daily diet!

When we build a house we dig down below frost line to find solid footing on ground that is stable and will not shift. There is no other source of stability and unchanging principles that have stood the test of time like the Bible. It has proven trustworthy time and again. It is reliable because it is God's Word to mankind. It is the source on which we must cast our anchor and thereby build the foundation necessary for common sense and good judgement to establish themselves.

The last lines on the 3x5 card reads like this, "Keep in close touch with Mr. Common Sense and Mr. Good Judgement and they will serve you well in many circumstances." Thank you, Richard, for your words of admonition. They are certainly good friends to have.

—M. Gingrich

Refining Silver

Malachi 3:3 says: "He will sit as a refiner and purifier of silver."

This verse puzzled some women in a Bible study and they wondered what this statement meant about the character and nature of God. One of them offered to find out the process of refining silver and get back to the group at their next Bible study.

That week, the woman called a silversmith and made an appointment to watch him at work. She didn't mention anything about the reason for her interest beyond her curiosity about the process of refining silver.

As she watched the silversmith, he held a piece of silver over the fire and let it heat up. He explained that in refining silver, one needed to hold the silver in the middle of the fire where the flames were hottest as to burn away all the impurities.

The woman thought about God holding us in such a hot spot; then she thought again about the verse that says: "He sits as a refiner and purifier of silver."

She asked the silversmith if it was true that he had to sit there in front of the fire the whole time the silver was being refined. The man answered that yes, he not only had to sit there holding the silver, but he had to keep his eyes on the silver the entire time it was in the fire. If the silver was left a moment too long in the flames, it would be destroyed.

The woman was silent for a moment. Then she asked the silversmith, "How do you know when the silver is fully refined?"

He smiled at her and answered, "Oh, that's easy—when I see my image in it."

If today you are feeling the heat of the fire, remember that God has his eye on you and will keep watching you until He sees His image in you.

Tax Free

A tax assessor came one day to a poor pastor to determine the amount of taxes the pastor would have to pay.

"What property do you possess?" asked the assessor.

"I am a very wealthy man," replied the minister.

"List your possessions, please," the assessor instructed. The pastor said:

- "First, I have everlasting life, (John 3:16).
- Second, I have a mansion in heaven, (John 14:2).
- Third, I have peace that passes all understanding, (Philippians 4:7).
- Fourth, I have joy unspeakable, (1 Peter 1:8.)
- Fifth, I have divine love which never fails, (I Corinthians 13:8.)
- Sixth, I have a faithful pious wife, (Proverbs 31:10).
- Seventh, I have healthy, happy, obedient children, (Exodus 20:12.).
- Eighth, I have true, loyal friends, (Proverbs 18:24).

- Ninth, I have songs in the night, (Psalms 42:8).
- Tenth, I have a crown of life, (James 1:1-2).

The tax assessor closed his book, and said, "Truly you are a very rich man, but your property is not subject to taxation."

—Author Unknown

The Bible

A small son said to his father, "I know what the Bibe means." The father asked the son, "Tell me what the Bible means." The son replied, "It's easy. It means, Best Instructions Before Leaving Earth."

The 7 Ups For Christians

1. Wake Up!
   Decide to have a good day. "This is the day that the Lord hath made: let us rejoice and be glad in it" (Psalms 118:24).
2. Dress Up!
   The best way to dress up is to put on a smile. A smile is an inexpensive way to improve your looks. "The Lord does not look at the things man looks at. Man looks at outward appearance, but the Lord looks at the heart" (1 Sam. 16:7).
3. Shut Up!
   Say nice things and learn to listen. God gave us two ears and one mouth, so He must have meant for us to do twice as much listening as talking. "He who guards his lips guards his soul" (Prov. 13:3).
4. Stand Up!
   Stand up for what you believe. Stand for something or you will fall for anything. "Let us not be weary in doing good; for at the proper time, we will reap a harvest if we do not give up. Therefore, as we have opportunity, let us do good" (Gal 6:910).
5. Look Up!
   Look up to the Lord. "I can do all things through Christ who strengthens me" (Phil. 4:13).
6. Reach Up!
   Reach for something higher. "Trust in the Lord with all your heart, and lean not unto your own understanding. In all your ways, acknowledge Him, and He will direct your path" (Prov. 3:5-6).
7. Lift Up!
   Lift up your prayers. "Do not worry about anything: instead pray about everything" (Phil. 4:6).

The Marriage Issue

There is a lot of controversy today regarding marriage. Why? What has brought this subject to the forefront? On one side there is a cry for equal rights and equal treatment while on the other is a cry for the sanctity and protection of marriage as we know it today, the union of one man and one woman. Perhaps a bit of history and a look at the origin of marriage will help us to see how this crisis has come about.

Marriage was instituted by God in Genesis 2:24. We also have recorded in Genesis the creation of the whole earth including the animal kingdom and man. To reject the fact of creation and theorize that man evolved is an undermining of all our foundational moorings. God gave specific instructions for how man is to live. He gave do's and don'ts for their well-being. He set man above the animal kingdom and gave him care-taking responsibility. He gave them instruction to replenish the earth. To do this he instructed man and woman to leave father and mother, become husband and wife and establish a new home.

History records some rather blatant rejections of God's instructions that have paved the way for the mentality we see in our American culture today.

First of all, is a rejection of creation which in reality erodes the authority of scripture. This is replaced with the theory of evolution, which, even though it has no scientific basis is taught in public schools as the way man came into being. Nothing could be further from the truth.

Secondly, is the broad based acceptance in society that divorce is a normal and acceptable way of resolving differences. God's instructions are one man and one woman as long as life shall last. Divorce in God's eyes is not acceptable and yet man continues to look the other way. It has reached epidemic proportions and become a plague on countless families. If only we could hear the cries of the children that come from broken homes.

Thirdly, is the removal of prayer and Bible reading in school. Children are starving for acceptance and accountability because their spiritual diet has been taken away. Their diet now consists of entertainment and sports to the extent many have become obese.

Fourthly, is the breakdown in the churches of America. Church leaders have given in to pressure, rejected the authority of scripture and allowed alternative lifestyles and divorce to permeate the pews. Jesus loved people but he denounced their sins. The church must do the same.

Fifthly, the media has bombarded the minds of people with filth and garbage and brainwashed them until they believe that they can do as they please. They believe there is no one to whom they need to answer. Anything goes.

Sixthly, is the "keep up with the Joneses" mentality. Lifestyles have gone high tech. Two incomes have become a must to meet financial obligations. Meals are microwaved rather than cooked because schedules are such that when one family member is there the rest aren't. Families are on the run to this game and that game with no time to sit and eat a meal together.

All of these things militate against the structure of the home. Instead of a place of refuge homes have far too often become a place of confusion.

In a society that has rejected many of God's teachings it seems rather ironic that some folks would insist on carrying out the command to marry. It is not surprising, however, that they also insist on doing it their way. Some folks go so far as to claim that a percentage of people are born with an alternative lifestyle nature. This is a rejection of God and his creation. God denounces such activity. Man is born with a sin nature ever since his disobedience in the garden of Eden. When that sin nature is not brought under the authority of God it will continue to digress.

When man throws out the authority of scripture and chooses to believe only what he wants, he has lost his sense of direction. Creation, The Ten Commandments, acknowledgment of sin and its consequences, repentance, the plan of salvation, and the authority of a supreme God are foundational principles that give substance to moral integrity. Without them, there are no morals. Marriage is the bonding of a man and a woman for the sake of establishing a home. True freedom and peace are found only as man accepts God's plan for their lives. Anything else will bring disappointment and heartache. There is hope, there is love, and there is happiness in marriage when we choose to abide by the principles God has outlined.

—M. Gingrich

The Presence of Angels

Angels are real. God created them (Col. 1:16). The Bible says it's impossible to count the angels (Heb. 12:22). There were 10,000 angels to confirm the presence of God on Sinai (Deut. 33:2). John says he heard the singing of 10,000 times 10,000 of angels (Rev. 5:11, LB). They are perfect heavenly beings.

Protection. "For he orders his angels to protect you wherever you go. They will steady you with their hands to keep you from stumbling against the rocks on the trail" (Psalm 91:11-12, LB).

Praise. "Then Ezra prayed, 'You alone are God. You have made the skies and the heavens, the earth and seas, and everything in them. You preserve it all; and all the angels of heaven worship you.'" (Nehemiah 9:6, LB).

Prophecy. An angel appears to Zacharias, telling him his wife Elisabeth would have a son, and his name would be John. This son would bring them much joy. This son would be John the Baptist, the great Evangelist. John would be a cousin to Jesus, and he would introduce Jesus as The Lamb of God (Luke 1:11-16).

Power. Daniel refused to stop praying and was thrown into the den of lions. God closed the mouths of the lions. Notice the words of Daniel to the king. "My, God has sent his angel," he said, "to shut the lion's mouths so they can't touch me. For I am innocent before God, nor sir, have I wronged you'" (Dan. 6:22, LB).

Provision. Peter and James are in prison because of preaching the gospel. An angel comes and frees Peter. Peter thinks it was a dream, but later he realized it wasn't a dream. See Acts 12:6-11.

The Ten Commandments

There was a very gracious lady who was mailing an old family Bible to her brother in another part of the country. "Is there anything breakable in here?" Asked the postal clerk. "Only the Ten Commandments," answered the lady.

Growth

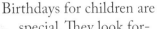

Birthday's Are Special!

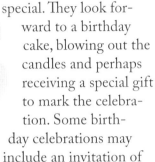

Birthdays for children are special. They look forward to a birthday cake, blowing out the candles and perhaps receiving a special gift to mark the celebration. Some birthday celebrations may include an invitation of several friends at a special party. Balloons, games, a piñata, and other festivities may be included. It is a time of recognition and celebration. Someone exclaims, "You're 2 years old!—or 3 or 4."

I remember a little girl saying when she was asked how old she is, "I'm 4, almost 5 and I'll soon be 6, and then I can go to school." Birthdays are often associated with privileges and they become milestones of achievements in our lives. A child reaches school age at 5 or 6 years old. Depending in which state you live you can get a drivers license at approximately 15 to 16 years of age. A child looks forward in anticipation to those events.

Birthdays for adults are special as well. If you don't think so, try forgetting your spouse's birthday and see if it isn't important. A bouquet of flowers, dinner for two, or just some time together are ways a person can sense the importance of their special day. It gives a sense of self-worth and belonging. While age has a tendency to diminish the excitement that a child associates with a birthday, it still holds a certain amount of regard. It provides a reference point in time to our existence. It is a mark of distinction. We have achieved a certain level of wisdom or a certain level of accomplishment by virtue of our age. God has allowed us the privilege to experience many things through the years. As we get older it seems like the years do run together and we are more inclined to prefer comments like "39 and holding" versus "almost 40", or "I'm 70 years young" instead of "70 years old". Almost before we know it we begin to qualify for retirement and senior citizens discounts. At times we may feel like time could slow up a bit, if at all possible.

One of the lessons I've learned when guessing a person's age is to make sure you guess low. It goes over a whole lot better, except for a young person. Young people like to be considered older than what they are. I suppose its the difference of wanting to be considered mature and actually reaching maturity.

Every birthday we have is a gift. It is a gift of life from God. It is another day in which we can thank Him and honor Him and that alone makes it special. Happy Birthday!

—M. Gingrich

Change Or Progress

An old timer once said, "I am in favor of progress just as long as nobody changes anything." In our society we are constantly bombarded with change. Some of the change that takes place is defined as progress. As the population increases the ripples of change have an ever widening impact. This has led to solicitation by "Special Interests." Folks are encouraged to jump on the band wagon and help promote their ideology. While these interests have some merit, there is always the danger of promoting a narrowly focused agenda and forgetting the bigger picture. What may be of utmost importance to me may be unimportant to someone else. There is no "one size fits all" answer to these situations. Probably all of us are somewhat like the old timer, in favor of progress as long as nothing affects me.

There are many things to be considered when a change is proposed. Things like, how much will it cost? How will it affect other people? What is the detriment to the environment? Are there other possible answers? What are the long and short term effects? Do the benefits outweigh the negatives? Unfortunately the outcome is more often determined, not by what may be the best, but by who has the bigger pockets.

We've all heard the stories of bog turtles and wetlands and how major projects have been sidetracked for months and even years. Is the alternative to recklessly abandon any type of preservation efforts and move our agenda forward. No! But neither is spending millions of taxpayer dollars because there might be a bog turtle or because it looks like their habitat. We must strike a balance that gives consideration to both sides and then render a decision.

While these "Special Interests" show up in the National and Political scene, they also infiltrate schools, businesses, churches, organizations, and any place decisions need to be made. Truth and common sense often play second fiddle to bribes and scandals. You've heard the phrase, "it isn't what you know, it's who you know". There are occasions where who you know may be okay but bribes and illegal actions are never right. Every person is entitled to an opinion but their opinions do not become legislature for everyone else. In a free society of millions and millions of people we have all kinds of opinions that cross and crisscross varied cultures and religions and present themselves in all kinds of different scenarios. There is a time and place to air our opinions and concerns, but there is also a time to relinquish our position and accept decisions, as long as they do not violate moral and scriptural principals.

This is illustrated by the story that is told of a congregation which had a maple tree growing next to the church building. A possible building project was on hold because the tree stood in the way. It was decided to take a vote to see whether the members were in favor of cutting it down. One old man cast the lone descending vote. On the day the church gathered to clear away the old tree, the old man was the first one there with his chain saw. He probably had many fond memories of that old tree. Perhaps he had even climbed in its branches as a little boy. It was hard to see it go. But laying aside his opinions and wishes he demonstrated to his fellow church members the way of peace. Perhaps we can all learn a lesson.

—*M. Gingrich*

Dad Through The Decades

This Article reflects the transition most of us have gone through in our assessment of father:

4 years: My daddy can do anything.
7 years: My dad knows a lot, a whole lot.
8 years: Dad doesn't know quite everything.
12 years: Dad just doesn't understand.
14 years: Dad? Hopelessly old fashioned.
21 years: My dad is truly out of date. But what would you expect?
25 years: He comes up with a good idea now and then.
30 years: I must find out what Dad thinks about it.
35 years: Wait, I want Dad's input first.
50 years: What would Dad have thought about that?
60 years: I wish I could talk it over with Dad once more.

Dangers In The Senior Years

The "senior years" can be the most happy and productive years of your life, but for some, they become miserable and nonproductive. Here are three dangers to consider.

Danger of Inactivity

Seniors should keep as active as possible. You now have plenty of time to do things you didn't have time to do in the past. Keep active physically and spiritually. Keep active in all the areas of life. Inactivity is like an unused car—it becomes rusty, hard to start, and soon is useless. The more active you are, the less time you will have to think you are a senior citizen.

Danger of Inferiority

Some senior citizens feel, "I'm no longer needed or wanted." They feel they are no longer valuable or important. You are not inferior to your family, your friends, the church, and God! You are valuable. You are wanted and needed. With your many years of experience, you can be mentors to family, friends, and God's people. In God's eyes you're not inferior—you're superior!

Danger of Indifference

Indifference robs many senior citizens from God's blessings. Don't take the attitude, "I've paid my dues—let others do it, and I'll take it easy." The Christian life requires dedication and faithfulness from the time you accept Christ until the grave. Your faithfulness to God is needed for both you and those who know you. In your senior years, keep active every day. Don't allow Satan to make you feel inferior in any way, and remain faithful to God.

Dangers Of Easy Living

A mother said, "I fear more the luxury and easy living given my children than the adversity and problems they face." She went on to say, "It is the adversity and hardness that develops character." Most all successful people faced problems and adversity. It appeared there was no hope, but they used opposition as stepping stones to succeed.

Don't Quit!

When things go wrong as they sometimes will,
When the road you're trudging seems all up hill,
When funds are low and debts are high,
And you want to smile, but have to sigh,

When care is pressing you down a bit—
Rest if you must, but don't quit.
Life is queer with its twists and turns,
And everyone of us sometimes learns;

And many a fellow turns about
When he might had won, had he stuck it out.
Don't give up though the pace seem slow
You may succeed with another blow.

Often the goal is nearer than it may seem
To a faint and faltering man;
Often the struggler has given up
When he might have captured the victor's cup.

And he learned too late when the night came down,
How close he was to winning the crown.
Success is failure turned inside out
The silver tint of the clouds of doubt,

You never can tell how close you are,
It may be near, when it seems afar;
So stick to the fight when you're hardest hit
It's when things seem worst that you mustn't quit.

—*Unknown*

Forgiveness

Corrie Ten Boom told of not being able to forget a wrong that had been done to her. She had forgiven the person, but she kept rehashing the incident and so couldn't sleep. Finally Corrie cried out to God for help in putting the problem to rest. "His help came in the form of a kindly Lutheran pastor," Corrie wrote, "to whom I confessed my failure after two sleepless weeks."

"Up in the church tower," he said, nodding out the window, "is a bell which is rung by pulling on a rope. But you know what? After the sexton lets go of the rope, the bell keeps on swinging. First ding, then dong. Slower and slower until there's a final dong and it stops. I believe the same thing is true of forgiveness. When we forgive, we take our hand off the rope. But if we've been tugging at our grievances for a long time, we mustn't be surprised if the old angry thoughts keep coming for a while. They're just the ding dongs of the old bell slowing down."

"And so it proved to be. There were a few more midnight reverberations, a couple of dings when the subject came up in my conversations, but the force—which was my willingness in the matter—had gone out of them. They came less and less often and at the last, stopped altogether: we can trust God not only above our emotions, but also above our thoughts."

Graduation

Graduation marks a culmination of study. It is a time of testing and verifying that individuals have successfully completed their studies. When the scores are in there is a sigh of relief, as the tension ebbs its way out of the body and is replaced with a feeling of accomplishment and satisfaction in knowing that the many hours of study were well worth the time and effort. The goal that looked so distant and future has been attained. It took time, effort, sacrifice, and commitment and a lot of energy was consumed. For some it is just a short break until they hit the books again. For others it is time to take that knowledge and begin utilizing it in the workplace environment. Therein lies the real test that will speak for itself whether the efforts were of value or not.

It is important as graduates navigate into the workplace that they do so with the understanding that they are still learning. A spirit of arrogance or a know-it-all attitude will quickly cause conflict with seasoned employees. An attitude that exuberates a willingness to learn and apply your skills will yield promotions and will nurture a pleasant work environment. We can learn from those who are experienced. If we walk around carrying a chip on our shoulders it won't take long to separate ourselves from our coworkers. Humility goes a long way in our work relationships. A supervisor's attitude will make a big difference in how those under his jurisdiction function. A humble spirit will kindle a desire for employees to put forth their best effort but a spirit of arrogance will quench and stymie the enthusiasm to do a good job.

Graduation is a culmination of past efforts but it is much more a time of new beginnings. Hopefully all the study and learning will pay off. A head full of knowledge is wasted if it is not put to good use, whereas, a head full of knowledge is a valuable asset and contribution to mankind if it is put to good use. We can then make the determination that education is important but it is not an end in itself. It is how an individual incorporates those education skills they have learned into every day life experiences that will produce results and determine some level of success.

My hat is off to everyone who graduates. May all your years of hard study be rewarded. We wish you success in the workplace but even more so we wish you success in your relationships with other people so that in years to come you can look back with fondness upon the acquaintances you have made and realize that while blessing others you have been blessed in return. Congratulations!

—M. Gingrich

Growing Up

My son Mark was only 5 feet 8 inches tall when he left for college in the fall. He worked through the Christmas holidays and didn't return home again until the February break.

When he got off the plane, I was stunned at how much taller he looked. Measuring him at home, I discovered he now stood at 5 feet 11 inches. My son was as surprised as I. "Couldn't you tell by your clothes that you'd grown?" I asked him.

"Since I've been doing my own laundry," he replied, "I just figured everything had shrunk."

Have You Looked In The Mirror?

One of the first tasks of each day is to stand in front of the mirror and observe how we look. Most of us are not the most presentable when we first get up after a night's sleep. We would not consider venturing out into public until we have washed our face and combed our hair. We look into the mirror to see how we appear to others. The mirror is the only way we can know what we look like. It is an accurate and true reflection of our image.

Mirrors are really quite useful. They allow dentists to see into the recesses of our mouth and observe things that are otherwise hidden from view. The mirrors on our vehicles give us a greater awareness of our surroundings. Mirrors are used in telescopes to magnify objects. They are used in copy machines to transfer images.. Sometimes nature itself will provide us with a mirror, for example, when a lake is very calm and still it will reflect the surrounding landscape. Camera's are a type of mirror that capture an express image at a given time.

A mirror does not create an image, it only reflects the object that it captures. If there are flaws in the object they will be reflected in the mirror. The mirror is unable to correct them. Even when the object itself is perfect it is possible for the mirror to reflect a flawed image. The reason lies in the condition of the mirror. I have had occasion to stand in front of mirrors that distorted my image. They were curved mirrors designed for that purpose. I have also stood in front of mirrors that were old and cracked or had damage to the reflective material. My image was incorrectly reflected because of flaws in the mirror.

In many ways people are like mirrors. Children reflect the actions and mannerisms of their parents. They carry certain genes and characteristics that identify them as part of a certain family lineage. They develop a distinct accent in speech that reflects their native culture. We re-elect our principles and values through our speech and conduct. A salesperson likewise reflects the integrity and ideology of their company. If the relationship between a salesperson and the company they are representing becomes strained it will soon become apparent to others. The same is true of a marriage or any type of relationship. We mirror on the outside what is taking place on the inside.

People mirror their religious beliefs and convictions as well. What they say they believe, must bear evidence in their deeds and actions. If these fail to correspond then the image being conveyed becomes distorted and difficult to envision.

In Jesus Christ we have an original, completely perfect and flawless character. Christian's must give due diligence to reflect that image in their lives. If our reflection of Christ is distorted, if our mirror is broken or flawed, then we do an injustice and bring insult to the God who created us(man) in His(God's) image and people who observe us will be misguided and deceived. If however our reflection of Christ is free of defects so that the image of Christ is truly visible without distortion, then others will be drawn to Him because of what they observe in us. When that happens, then we can know that we have mirrored Him.

—M. Gingrich

Horse Sense

Just up the road from my home is a field, with two horses in it. From a distance, each looks like every other horse. But if one stops the car, or is walking by, one will notice something quite amazing. Looking into the eyes of one horse will disclose that he is blind. His owner has chosen not to have him put down, but has made a good home for him. This alone is amazing. Listening, one will hear the sound of a bell. Looking around for the source of the sound, one will see that it comes from the smaller horse in the field. Attached to her bridle is a small bell.

It lets her blind friend know where she is, so he can follow her. As one stands and watches these two friends, one sees how she is always checking on him, and that he will listen for her bell and then slowly walk to where she is trusting that she will not lead him astray. Like the owners of these two horses, God does not throw us away just because we are not perfect or because we have problems or challenges. He watches over us and even brings others into our lives to help us when we are in need. Sometimes we are the blind horse being guided by God and those whom he places in our lives. Other times we are the guide horse, helping others see God.

—Author Unknown

If Teacups Could Talk

There was a couple who used to go to England to shop in a beautiful antique store. This trip was to celebrate their 25th wedding Anniversary. They both liked antiques and pottery, and especially teacups. Spotting an exceptional cup, they asked "May one see that? We've never seen a cup quite so beautiful."

As the lady handed it to them, suddenly the teacup spoke, "You don't understand." It said, "I have not always been a teacup. There was a time when I was just a lump of red clay. My master took me and rolled me, pounded and patted me over and over and I yelled out, Don't do that. I don't like it, it hurts! Let me alone.' But he only smiled, and gently said; 'Not yet.'"

"Then, WHAM!!! I was placed on a spinning wheel and suddenly I was spun around and around and around. 'Stop it! I'm getting so dizzy! I'm going to be sick!', I screamed. But the master only nodded and said, quietly; 'Not yet.' He spun me and poked and prodded and bent me out of shape to suit himself and then…then he put me in the oven. I never felt such heat. I yelled and knocked and pounded at the door. 'Help! Get me out of here!' I could see him through the opening and I could read his lips as he shook his head from side to side, 'Not yet.'

"When I thought I couldn't bear it another minute, the door opened. He carefully took me out and put me on the shelf, and I began to cool. Oh, that felt so good! 'Ah, this is much better,' I thought. But, after I cooled he picked me up and he brushed and painted me all over. The fumes were horrible. I thought I would gag. 'Oh, please; Stop it, Stop it!!' I cried. He only shook his head and said. 'Not yet!'

"Then suddenly he put me back in to the oven. Only it was not like the first one. This was twice as hot and I just knew I would suffocate. I begged. I pleaded. I screamed. I cried. I was convinced I would never make it. I was ready to give up. Just then the door opened and he took me out and again placed me on the shelf, where I cooled and waited…and waited…wondering what he was going to do to me next?

"An hour later he handed me a mirror and said 'Look at yourself.' And I did. I said, 'That's not me; that couldn't be me. It's beautiful. I'm beautiful!!'

"Quietly he spoke: 'I want you to remember, then,' he said, 'I know it hurt to be rolled and pounded and patted, but had I just left you alone, you'd have dried up. I know it made you dizzy to spin around on the wheel, but if I had stopped, you would have crumbled. I know it hurt and it was hot and disagreeable in the oven, but if I hadn't put you there, you would have cracked. I know the fumes were bad when I brushed and painted you all over, but if I hadn't done that, you never would have hardened. And you would not have had any color in your life. If I hadn't put you back in that second oven, you wouldn't have survived for long because the hardness would not have held. Now you are a finished product. Now you are what I had in mind when I first began with you.'"

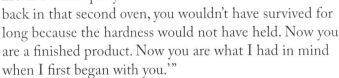

The moral of this story is this: God knows what He's doing for each of us. He is the potter, and we are His clay. He will mold us and make us, and expose us to just enough pressures of just the right kinds that we may be made into a flawless piece of work to fulfill His good, pleasing and perfect will. So when life seems hard, and you are being pounded and patted and pushed almost beyond endurance; when your world seems to be spinning out of control; when you feel like you are in a fiery furnace of trials; when life seems to "stink", try this…brew a cup of your favorite tea in your prettiest tea cup, sit down and think about this story and then have a little talk with the Potter.

If You Had But A Day

- Would you neglect your private and secret devotions?
- Would you leave your Bible unopened and unread?
- Would you find it prudent and highly desirable to cancel some engagement you have made?
- Would you hasten to correct some misunderstanding that had driven a friend from your side and filled your soul with bitterness?
- Would your mind be filled with anxious foreboding over vows solemnly made to God in your time of great need—and which you have carefully neglected to pay?
- Would you have occasion to pay some debts that have been outlawed, or make restitution of money wrongfully received, or recall some untruth declared?
- Would you be less gruff and grouchy in the home, manifesting a more tender and considerate, kindly spirit?
- Would your past, because uncovered by the blood, loom up before you like a hideous nightmare filling your last hours with languish and terror?
- Would the things for which you have been laboring and striving for years seem as much worthwhile when you were facing such a certainty as they do now?

In The Valleys

Sometimes life seems hard to bear,
Full of sorrow, trouble and woe;
It's then I have to remember
That it's in the valley's I grow.

If I always stayed on the mountain top
And never experienced pain,
I would never appreciate God's love
And would be living in vain.

I have so much to learn
And my growth is very slow;
Sometimes I need the mountain tops,
But it's in the valley's I grow.

I do not always understand
Why things happen as they do,
But I am very sure of one thing,
My Lord will see me through.

My little valley's are nothing
When I picture Christ on the cross
He went through the valley of death;
His victory was Satan's loss.

Forgive me Lord, for complaining
When I'm feeling so very low,
Just give me a gentle reminder
That it's in the valleys I grow.

Continue to strengthen me, Lord
And use my life each day,
To share your love with others
And help them find their way.

Thank you for the valley's Lord
For this one thing I know,
The mountain tops are glorious
But it's in the valley's I grow.

—Unknown

Just For Today

Just For Today, I will try to live through this day only, and not tackle all my life's problems at once. I can do something for 12 hours that would appall me if I felt I had to keep it up for a lifetime.

Just For Today, I will be happy. This assumes to be true what Abraham Lincoln said, that, "Most folks are as happy as they make up their minds to be."

Just For Today, I will try to strengthen my mind. I will study. I will learn something useful. I will not be a mental loafer. I will read something that requires effort, thought and concentration.

Just For Today, I will adjust myself to what is, and not try to adjust everything to my own desires. I will take my "luck" as it comes, and fit myself to it.

Just For Today, I will exercise my soul in three ways; I will do somebody a good turn, and not get found out. I will do at least two things I don't want to do—just for exercise; I will not show anyone that my feelings are hurt. They may be hurt, but today I will not show it.

Just For Today, I will be agreeable, I will look as well as I can, dress becomingly, talk kindly, act courteously, criticize not one bit, nor find fault with anybody and not try to improve or regulate anybody except myself.

Just For Today, I will have a program. I may not follow it exactly, but I will have it. I will save myself from two pests; Hurry and Indecision.

Just For Today, I will have a quiet half hour all by myself, and relax. During this half hour, sometime, I will try to get a better perspective of my life.

Just For Today, I will be unafraid. Especially I will not be afraid to enjoy what is beautiful, and to believe that as I give to the world, so the world will give to me.

Knowledge & Wisdom

Knowledge and wisdom may sometimes be referred to as the same thing, but too often we do not realize how different they really are. Webster's says that knowledge is having the ability to know facts and information. According to Webster's dictionary, wisdom is having the ability to understand what is right, true, or enduring. It is having good judgement and knowledge. Knowledge is the truth or facts of life that a person acquires either through experience or thought. Wisdom is the ability to judge correctly and to follow the best course of action, based on knowledge and understanding. Mental knowledge by itself is inadequate; it is capable of only producing pride. The classical view of wisdom was sought through philosophy and man's rational thought to determine the mysteries of existence and the universe. A man needs to humble himself before God to develop wisdom. Any man can gain knowledge whether he has God in his heart or not. Knowledge is gained by studying facts and information. Anyone with an education has a portion of knowledge. Wisdom is gained by humbleness, studying God's Word, and obeying Him. Knowledge is of the mind; wisdom is of the heart. A man of knowledge may know a lot about the things of this world, but will he know which path to take when it comes to choosing between right and wrong? A man of wisdom may have a high education too, but he will also have a heart that seeks after God. Knowledge is good if you learn to glorify God with it, but wisdom is always important.

—Melissa Shenk

Letting Go

I heard a story once about a group of scientists who were on a mission to capture a particular species of monkeys in the jungles of Africa. It was important that the monkeys be brought back alive and well. Knowing the ways of monkeys, the scientists devised a trap consisting of a small jar with a long neck. Into the jar was placed a handful of nuts. Several of these jars were staked out and anchored to the ground.

When the monkeys caught the scent of the nuts in the jars, they would reach in by way of the long neck and grab the handful of nuts. But when they tried to withdraw the prized nuts, they discovered that their clenched fist would not pass through the narrow neck of the bottle. So, there they were, trapped in the long-necked, anchored bottles, unable to escape with the nuts because of an unwillingness to let go.

I like that. It reminds me of us sometimes. How often are we trapped, or held back, or remain captive through an unwillingness to "let go" of the past and move forward confidently facing the magnificent future God has in store for us.

We all have problems. You do. I do. But sometimes I really do believe that so many of them stem from our own self-containment in long necked bottles, bound by our stubborn unwillingness to "let go."

The monkey had the power to open his fist and "let go" to be free. We, too, have the power to "let go" of fear, worry, resentment, regret, and whatever it is in the past which keeps us trapped and unable to live in the marvelous freedom God gives us each day.

Turn it loose! Live! Enjoy! "This is the day the Lord has made; rejoice and be glad in it!"

Not Quitting

A small boy bought ice skates and was learning to skate. He fell often, causing many bruises and cuts on his face and hands.

A person offered some advice, "Why don't you quit and give up?"

The small boy responded, "I didn't buy these skates to try and quit. I bought them to learn how to skate."

Reputation And Character

The circumstances amid which you live determine your reputation; the truth you believe determines your character.

- **Reputation** is what you are supposed to be; **Character** is what you are.
- **Reputation** is the photograph; **Character** is the face.
- **Reputation** comes over one from without, **Character** grows from within.
- **Reputation** is what you have when you come to a new community; **Character** is what you have when you go away.
- Your **reputation** is learned in an hour; **Character** may not come to light for a year.
- **Reputation** is made in a moment; **Character** is built over a lifetime.
- **Reputation** grows like a mushroom; **Character** grows like the oak.
- A single newspaper report gives you **reputation**; A life of toil gives you your **character**.
- **Reputation** makes you rich or makes you poor; **Character** makes you happy or makes you miserable.
- **Reputation** is what men say about you on your tombstone; **Character** is what the angels say about you before the throne of God.

—William Hersey Davis

Setting Goals For A New Year

The previous calendar year is now history. The activities and events of the past year are only a memory. They may be recorded in diaries, personal notebooks or as scribbled reminders on old calendar pages. Those of more importance may have made news headlines. For some, the years events may have included a much anticipated wedding day, an anniversary or a special vacation. Whatever events you looked forward to, are now small blips in history. They can never be repeated, redone or undone. They are finished except for reaping the results of decisions and actions and their historical record.

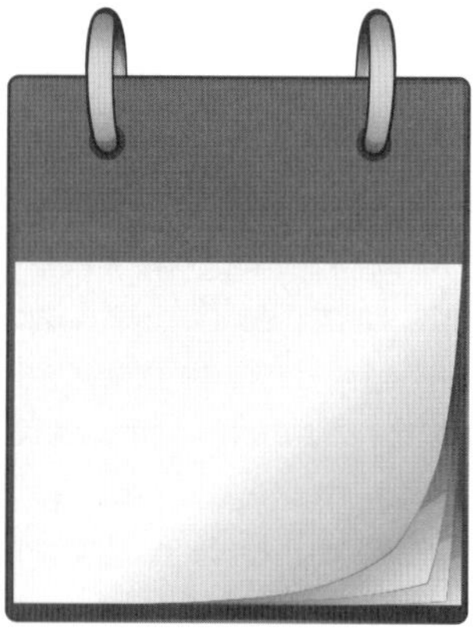

As you reflect back on the past year you may see some areas that could use improvement. You may feel good that some decisions you made were the right choice. You may have gone through difficult trials or you may have experienced great joy. You may have experienced financial failure, or the loss of a companion or friend. Some of these things are beyond our control. We have no say in them. Still others, however, are the result of decisions and choices we make.

Looking back on the past year and evaluating the events is a means of taking inventory. What could I change for the better? What was my response to things that were beyond my control? Could I have avoided some of the predicaments I found myself in by making wiser choices? Were some of the challenges I faced the result of greed or envy? Was I content or did I constantly wish for more? These are all questions we can ask as we look back and grade ourselves on the past year.

The greater challenge, however, lies in the coming year. Will I learn from my past mistakes? Am I willing to ask forgiveness of those I hurt? Will inventory next year find the same old habits and misgivings? Will I rise to greater heights of maturity and wisdom or will I succumb to the same pitfalls all over again?

The new year is a turning of the page. The clean page is waiting in anticipation to record the events as they unfold. It is without blemish, untainted and flawless. But it also lacks character and substance. With each passing day the pages will once again take on meaning. They will tell the story of all the activities one day at a time until, once more another year is complete.

Each year that empty page will record whether I succeed or fail in the goals I have set. Most people fail in reaching their goal because they set them too idealistic rather then within reach. It is important to set goals within range but also high enough to challenge. Don't give up because you failed one day. Failure comes when we no longer get up after a fall! Press on! Be courageous! Throw aside the notion that you are too old. Reject the idea that it never works anyway. Face each day with renewed vigor and determination!

It is also important to consider what our goals in life really are. Are the goals I set trivial and meaningless or are they goals that will bring lasting long term results? Are my goals designed to put me in the spotlight, or are they designed to challenge my character. Is my goal wealth or is it contentment? Will reaching my goals bring true joy and happiness? Do I pattern my goals in light of their eternal value or do I live for the present?

The apostle Paul wrote that he had learned in whatsoever state he was, therewith to be content. That included being thrown in prison for his boldness in preaching the gospel. Paul's goal and purpose in life were still intact even while in prison. He could still serve God! Was prison his choice? No! Was he bitter? No! Rather than despair Paul used the occasion to further the cause of the gospel. His goal in life was not personal exaltation or earthly prominence but a determination to challenge his fellow man to a closer walk with God. It was a goal with eternal value. A goal that is on record and is still challenging men centuries later.

As you turn the page of a new year consider your goals. Should they be reevaluated and altered? Are they within reach? Is their purpose fulfilling? Do they bring the kind of contentment that Paul talked about? Press on! Don't give up! Refuse to let history repeat its failures! Be courageous! Step out in faith! Ask God to be your strength! He will not let you down! Ask Him to help you set your goals. With His help your goals can become reality.

—M. Gingrich

Sowing & Reaping

A successful Christian business man was growing old and knew it was time to choose a successor to take over the business. Instead of choosing one of his directors or his children, he decided to do something different.

He called all the young executives in his company together. He said, "It is time for me to step down and choose the next CEO. I have decided to choose one of you."

The young executives were shocked, but the boss continued, "I am going to give each one of you a seed today—one very special seed. I want you to plant the seed, water it and come back here one year from today with what you have grown from the seed I have given you. I will then judge the plants that you bring, and the one I choose will be the next CEO."

One man, named Jim, was there that day and he, like the others, received a seed. He went home and, excitedly, told his wife the story. She helped him get a pot, soil, and compost and he planted the seed. Every day, he would water it and watch to see if it had grown. After about three weeks, some of the other executives began to talk about their seeds and the plants that were beginning to grow.

Jim kept checking his seed, but nothing ever grew. Three weeks, four weeks, five weeks went by, still nothing. By now, others were talking about their plants, but Jim didn't have a plant and he felt like a failure. Six months went by—still nothing in Jim's pot. He just knew he had killed his seed.

Everyone else had trees and tall plants, but he had nothing. Jim didn't say anything to his colleagues, however. He just kept watering and fertilizing the soil. He so wanted the seed to grow.

A year finally went by and all the young executives of the company brought their plants to the CEO for inspection. Jim told his wife that he wasn't going to take an empty pot. But she asked him to be honest about what happened. Jim felt sick at his stomach, it was going to be the most embarrassing moment of his life, but he knew his wife was right. He took his empty pot to the board room.

When Jim arrived, he was amazed at the variety of plants grown by the other executives. They were beautiful—in all shapes and sizes. Jim put his empty pot on the floor and many of his colleagues laughed. A few felt sorry for him!

When the CEO arrived, he surveyed the room and greeted his young executives. Jim just tried to hide in the back.

"My, what great plants, trees, and flowers you have grown," said the CEO. "Today one of you will be appointed the next CEO!"

All of a sudden, the CEO spotted Jim at the back of the room with his empty pot. He ordered the financial director to bring him to the front. Jim was terrified. He thought, "The CEO knows I'm a failure! Maybe he will have me fired!" When Jim got to the front, the CEO

asked him what had happened to his **seed**. Jim told him the story.

The **CEO** asked everyone to sit down except Jim. He looked at Jim, and then announced to the young executives, "Behold your next Chief Executive! His name is Jim!" Jim couldn't believe it. Jim couldn't even grow his seed.

How could he be the new **CEO**, the others said. Then the **CEO** said, "One year ago today, I gave everyone in this room a **seed**. I told you to take the **seed**, plant it, water it, and bring it back to me today. "But I gave you all boiled **seeds**; they were dead—it was not possible for them to grow. All of you, except Jim, have brought me trees and plants and flowers. "When you found that the **seed** would not grow, you substituted another seed for the one I gave you. Jim was the only one with the courage and honesty to bring me a pot with my **seed** in it. Therefore, he is the one who will be the new Chief Executive!"

- If you plant honesty, you will reap trust.
- If you plant goodness, you will reap friends.
- If you plant humility, you will reap greatness.
- If you plant perseverance, you will reap contentment.
- If you plant consideration, you will reap perspective.
- If you plant hard work, you will reap success.
- If you plant forgiveness, you will reap reconciliation.
- If you plant faith in Christ, you will reap a harvest.

So, be careful what you plant now; it will determine what you will reap later.

Two thousand years ago, Paul wrote to the church at Galatia the same story but with fewer words, "What you sow, so shall you reap." (Gal. 6:7) We are grass that will wither and die, but the incorruptible seed of God's Word will live forever. Sow it daily into the life of your family! (1 Peter 1:23-25)

Spring Fever

The skies are filled with the V-formations and honking of migrating geese. I've seen my first robins hopping around the yard with their unmistakable hop. The crocuses and daffodils are pushing their shoots. The sights and sounds of Spring are in the air once more.

Webster tells us that Spring is that season of the year in which plants begin to grow after lying dormant all winter. As I reflected on that definition I noticed that it contained the idea of life and action. Also, according to Webster, like so many other English words the word spring has a variety of meanings. It can mean to move suddenly and rapidly, for example, to spring to one's feet. It can mean to come into existence, like a town springing up or a plant springing up from a seed. Spring can refer to a coil device that is used to absorb shock and springs back to its original shape after being forced out of shape. It can also be a flow of water from out of the ground that is often the source of a stream or pond.

With all these different meanings it can get confusing. You see when I was a youngster, I envisioned having a pond in our backyard. I conveyed the idea to my father who informed me that you needed a spring in order to have a pond. My youthful mind could only envision a pond. Springs, that's not a problem, we have lots of them stacked out behind the shop. Oh, you mean truck springs won't work. You said we need springs. And so it was kindly explained that there is more than one kind of spring and no, a pond in our backyard probably wouldn't work out either. My balloon was deflated. I had already been dreaming of swimming and boating and catching frogs and all the other things a boy could do with a pond in his backyard. It was all for nothing because Spring had more than one meaning.

I must admit that even though I never got my pond that I envisioned, I am glad for another definition of the word spring. The one that refers to a season of the year. Although I enjoy the variety of seasons, Spring is one of my favorites. I enjoy seeing the grass turn green, smelling the fragrance of the flowers and listening to the singing of the birds. The longer days and the warmth of the sun are a welcome reprieve from the harshness of winter.

There is a parallel here to everyday life. Sometimes we go through difficulties and situations in life that are not of our choosing. There may be times of sickness, or times of being rebelled against by someone you love. There may be broken relationships. But hope springs eternal and even though the trials or circumstances you may face seem, oh so difficult, there is always a tomorrow. The difficulties of life are only temporary. They are for a

season. There are better days ahead because Spring is on the horizon.

May we be encouraged to face each day with new vigor, and new determination and zest for life. May we spring back from our Winter doldrums and grasp the future with vision. May our lives flow as a spring that brings life and refreshment to others along its path just as a spring gives birth to a stream and then a river, etc. I think I've got this spring thing straightened out, at least until someone comes up with yet another meaning for it, so for now there is a spring in my step because I do believe I've got Spring Fever.

—M. Gingrich

Stagnant!

The word stagnant conjures up images of green algae covering a pool of standing water. Stagnation takes place when there is little or no exchange of water. Water that is flowing, cleanses itself of harmful pollutants, but water that is stationary becomes contaminated and slimy. Stagnation can occur even in people. Board of Directors, committees, employees, etc., become stagnant when they have little or no incentive. They become lethargic and unmotivated if they have no involvement or responsibility in decision-making.

Stagnation in people is unfortunate. Stress, overload, micro-management, and undesirable work conditions are some factors that contribute to the cause. Assignments that are repetitious and monotonous are high risk for becoming stagnant. New board members or a change of responsibility can invigorate a stagnant committee, board member, or employee. It fosters new ideas and brings challenges that require thought process and decision making. Even small responsibilities such as ordering, inventory control, etc. help to give incentive. People want to be a part of the process. They want to feel needed. They want to be involved.

When they feel a part of the process, they respond with ideas. A piece of machinery we purchased has a feeding system integrated into the design that originated with a plant employee who has since been promoted. This employee had an idea he thought would help make a better system. His idea helped his company's product improve and provided job security as well.

We often hear the phrase "money talks". When it comes to keeping good employees, money has it's place but it is not the ultimate criteria. People who earn a lot of money can become stagnant, unproductive, and dissatisfied if their work is boring and unfulfilling. A person who finds fulfillment in his work will be a more productive and satisfied employee even if the pay is not exceptional.

The opposite of stagnation is fresh, active, and thriving. I would rather sit by a waterfall or a rushing stream then keep company with mosquitoes by a stagnant water hole. Likewise it is much more enjoyable to be around folks who have a positive attitude and contagious enthusiasm.

—M. Gingrich

Teenage Rules

Raising teenagers is a challenge, so my hubby and I came up with the following rules to help them understand what was expected of them during their pre-adult status.

Rules of this household

1. If you are not here for dinner, too bad. This is not a fast-food place where the cook is on duty at all times. The cook works full time and does not need a second job.
2. If you make a mess, clean it up. The dishwasher is open 24 hours a day to service you; as are the vacuum, broom, and sponge. Please help them to help you by using them. If you need assistance, ask the cook—she will be happy to give you training on any of the equipment.
3. The taxi service for this household is not on call 24 hours. You must make reservations at least 12 hours in advance. You have two good legs, skateboards, and bikes that are somewhat operational; one of you has a vehicle that works. Use them. By the way, skateboards are to be used on the outside of this house and are never to be used in the living room just because the landing is softer when you fall.
4. We are not a bank and you have no collateral to offer us. Face it: we own everything you have and I have receipts to prove it, so don't ask us for loans. Get jobs! We have them. Try it and you might like it (not so much the work as the money).
5. Curfew is negotiable, but try not to be late too often because it could go either way.
6. Tell us where you are going. I am way older than you, and I still tell my mother where I am going when I am at her house. Leave us a note or try to form words describing where you are going.

7. You know how to use a phone. Some of you even have cell phones. We like to hear your voice if you are going to be late. You can use a phone to find out what's for dinner, to let us know you made it to wherever all right, or just to let us hear your beautiful voice.
8. No food in your room, the living room, the bathroom, or anywhere in the house other than the kitchen or dining area ever! How many times do I have to say this?
9. You do not contribute financially in any way, shape, or form to this household, so try to pull your weight in other ways: clean something, put something away, surprise us by doing it before we ask. Otherwise, you may find yourself financially supporting yourself on the outside of this house.

The Blessing Of Thorns

Sandra felt as low as the heels of her shoes as she pushed against a November gust and the florist shop door. Her life had been easy, like a spring breeze. Then in the fourth month of her second pregnancy, a minor automobile accident stole her ease.

During this Thanksgiving week she would have delivered a son. She grieved over her loss. As if that weren't enough, her husband's company threatened a transfer. Then her sister, whose annual holiday visit she coveted, called saying she could not come. What's worse, Sandra's friend infuriated her by suggesting her grief was a God-given path to maturity that would allow her to empathize with others who suffer. "She has no idea what I'm feeling," thought Sandra with a shudder.

"Thanksgiving? Thankful for what?" she wondered aloud. For a careless driver whose truck was hardly scratched when he rear-ended her? For an airbag that saved her life but took that of her child?

"Good afternoon, can I help you?" The shop clerk's approach startled her.

" I…I need an arrangement," stammered Sandra.

"For Thanksgiving? Do you want beautiful-but-ordinary or would you like to challenge the day with a customer favorite I call the Thanksgiving Special?" asked the shop clerk. "I'm convinced that flowers tell stories," she continued. "Are you looking for something that conveys 'gratitude' this Thanksgiving?"

"Not exactly!" Sandra blurted out. "In the last five months, everything that could go wrong has gone wrong." Sandra regretted her outburst, and was surprised when the shop clerk said, "I have the perfect arrangement for you."

Then the door's small bell rang, and the shop clerk said, "Hi Barbara, let me get your order." She politely excused herself and walked toward a small workroom, then quickly reappeared, carrying an arrangement of greenery, bows, and long-stemmed thorny roses—except the ends of the rose stems were neatly snipped. There were no flowers.

"Want this in a box?" asked the clerk. Sandra watched for the customer's response. Was this a joke? Who would want rose stems with no roses!?! She waited for laughter, but neither woman laughed.

"Yes, please," Barbara replied with an appreciative smile. "You'd think after three years of getting the special, I wouldn't be so moved by its significance, but I can feel it right here, all over again," she said as she gently tapped her chest.

"Uhh," stammered Sandra, "that lady just left with, uhh.. she just left with no flowers!"

"Right—I cut off the roses. That's the Special—I call it the Thanksgiving Thorns Bouquet."

"Oh, come on, you can't tell me someone is willing to pay for that?!" exclaimed Sandra.

"Barbara came into the shop three years ago feeling very much like you feel today," explained the clerk. "She thought she had very little to be thankful for. She had lost her father to cancer, the family business was failing, her son was into drugs, and she was facing major surgery. That same year I had lost my husband, and for the first time in my life, I had to spend the holidays alone. I had no children, no husband, no family nearby, and too great a debt to allow any travel."

"So what did you do?" asked Sandra.

"I learned to be thankful for thorns," answered the clerk quietly. "I've always thanked God for good things in life and never thought to ask Him why those good things happened to me, but when the bad stuff hit, did I ever ask! It took time for me to learn that dark times are important. I always enjoyed the 'flowers' of life, but it took thorns to show me the beauty of God's comfort. You know, the Bible says that God comforts us when we're afflicted, and from His consolation we learn to comfort others."

Sandra sucked in her breath as she thought about the very thing her friend had tried to tell her. "I guess the truth is I don't want comfort. I've lost a baby and I'm angry with God."

Just then someone else walked into the shop. "Hey, Jim!" shouted the clerk to the balding, rotund man.

"My wife sent me in to get our usual Thanksgiving arrangement—twelve thorny, long stemmed stems!" laughed Jim as the clerk handed him a tissue wrapped arrangement from the refrigerator.

"Those are for your wife?" asked Sandra doubtingly. "Do you mind me asking why she wants something that looks like that?"

"No, I'm glad you asked," Jim replied. "Four years ago my wife and I nearly divorced. After forty years, we were in a real mess, but with the Lord's grace and guidance, we slogged through problem after problem. He rescued our marriage. Jenny here (the clerk) told me she kept a vase of rose stems to remind her of what she learned from 'thorny' times, and that was good enough for me. I took home some of those stems. My wife and I decided to label each one for a specific 'problem' and give thanks to Him for what that problem taught us."

As Jim paid the clerk, he said to Sandra, "I highly recommend the Special!"

"I don't know if I can be thankful for the thorns in my life." Sandra said to the clerk. "It's all too…fresh."

"Well," the clerk replied carefully, "my experience has shown me that thorns make roses more precious. We treasure God's providential care more during trouble than at any other time. Remember, it was a crown of thorns that Jesus wore so we might know His love. Don't resent the thorns."

Tears rolled down Sandra's cheeks. For the first time since the accident, she loosened her grip on resentment. "I'll take those twelve long-stemmed thorns, please," she managed to choke out.

"I hoped you would," said the clerk gently. "I'll have them ready in a minute."

"Thank you. What do I owe you?" asked Sandra.

"Nothing." said the clerk. "Nothing but a promise to allow God to heal your heart. The first year's arrangement is always on me." The clerk smiled and handed a card to Sandra. "I'll attach this card to your arrangement, but maybe you'd like to read it first."

It read: *"Dear God, I have never thanked you for my thorns. I have thanked you a thousand times for my roses, but never once for my thorns. Teach me the glory of the cross I bear; teach me the value of my thorns. Show me that I have climbed closer to you along the path of pain. Show me that, through my tears, the colors of your rainbow look much more brilliant."*

The Millionaire And The Scrub Lady

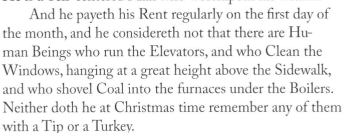

There is a certain Millionaire, who hath his offices on the Second Floor of the First National Bank Building. And when he goeth up to his offices he rideth in the Elevator, but when he goeth down, then he walketh.

And he is an Haughty Man, who once was poor, and hath risen in the World. He is a Self-centered Man who worshipeth his wealth.

And he payeth his Rent regularly on the first day of the month, and he considereth not that there are Human Beings who run the Elevators, and who Clean the Windows, hanging at a great height above the Sidewalk, and who shovel Coal into the furnaces under the Boilers. Neither doth he at Christmas time remember any of them with a Tip or a Turkey.

And there is in that Building a Poor Woman who Scrubbeth the Stairs and the Halls. And he hath walked past her often but hath never seen her until recently, for his head was high in the air, and he was thinking of More Millions.

Now it came to pass on a day that he left his Office, and started to walk down the Stairs. And the Scrub Lady was halfway down; for she had begun at the top and was giving the stairs their First Once over, And upon the topmost Stair, in a wet and soapy spot, there was a Large Cake of Soap, And the Millionaire steppeth on it.

Now the foot which he set upon the Soap flew eastward toward the sunrise, and the other foot started on an expedition of its own toward the going down of the Sun, And the Millionaire sat down on the Topmost Step, but he did not remain there. As it had been his intention to Descend, so he Descended, but not in the manner of his Original Design. And as he descended he struck each step with a sound as if it had been a Drum.

And the Scrub Lady stood aside courteously, and let him go. And at the bottom he arose, and considered whether he should rush into the Office of the Building and demand that the Scrub Lady should be fired, but he considered that if he should tell the reason there would be great Mirth among the occupants of the Building. And so he held his peace. But since that day he taketh notice of the Scrub Lady, and passeth her with Circumspection.

For there is no one so high or mighty that he can afford to ignore any of his fellow human beings. For a very Humble Scrub Lady and a very common bar of Yellow Soap can take the mind of a Great Man off his Business Troubles with surprising rapidity.

Wherefore, consider these things, and count not thyself too high above even the humblest of the children of God. Lest haply thou come down from thy place of pride and walk off with thy bruises aching a little more by reason of thy suspicion that the Scrubady is Smiling, and facing the day's work the more cheerfully by reason of the fun thou hast afforded her.

W. E. B.

Two Dead Sparrows

I was cruising along on the highway about 60 miles per hour when up ahead I saw two sparrows in a fierce battle at the side of the road. With feathers flying, they attacked each other with great fury.

As my car approached, they became locked in combat. Together they rose in the air and fluttered blindly into the path of the car. With a violent thud they smashed against the windshield, leaving a smear of blood and feathers. They were so preoccupied with their battle that they were blind to more serious dangers. Their quarrel cost them their lives.

How often we act like those two sparrows! We fail to realize that in a fight no one ever wins. Both are losers. We carry grudges, and our irritations get blown out of proportion. I don't know what those sparrows were fighting over, but it wasn't worth dying for. Neither are our quarrels.

Learn a lesson from the sparrows. Forget your grievances, be ready to forgive, and admit it when you're wrong. Ask God's Spirit to produce in you "love, joy, peace, long-suffering, kindness, goodness, faithfulness, gentleness, self-control" (Gal. 5:22-23).

When you feel like fighting, remember those two dead sparrows by the roadside.

Under Construction

When traveling the highways we often see the sign, "Under Construction." Work is being done on the highway. From the moment we accept Christ we could say, "We Are Under Construction." Or we might say, "Be patient—God Isn't Finished With Me Yet."

Regardless how long we serve God, we are in need of improvement. God wants to work on us to perfect us, making us what He wants us to be. God uses many things in perfecting us. He uses sickness, problems, troubles, setback, and loss. He doesn't send these, but allows these for our good and for His glory (Romans 8:28). There will be tears, testing, troubles, and trials. We will have many experiences in the valley. We will go through deep water, not to drown but to be cleansed. We'll go through the fire, not to be burned, but to be refined. These experiences don't hurt us, they help us!

Allow God to work in you, perfecting you. Remember, "No pain, no gain!" Construction will bring perfection, and then you won't be ashamed at His inspection.

Wang The Tiger

Wang was the son of a wealthy Chinese farmer. His father gave him interesting home and farm duties, provided him with all the food and clothing he needed, and taught him the sayings of Confucius; but Wang was selfish and wild. At night he would slip out of his house to join a group of hoodlums in town.

His father tried to keep him out of trouble. He bolted the gates, but Wang climbed over the walls. He tied him with ropes, but Wang broke the ropes and escaped. The father pleaded with him, but Wang just laughed in his face.

Wang finally ran away to stay, and the father heard of him only through rumor: "Wang is leader of the bandit tribe!" "Wang helped to sack a nearby village!" Everyone was afraid of him.

For a long time no news was heard of Wang. Then to the surprise of his home community, notice was given of his death and the time of his funeral. Great crowds assembled at the family burial ground. The funeral procession came with loud laments of hired mourners. The casket was placed ready for burial. Before the earth was lifted, Wang's father stepped forward and opened the casket. Wang himself stepped forth.

The awestruck villagers listened while Wang spoke: "You have heard of the life I was living among the bandits. The more homes I could destroy the smarter I thought I was. I was Wang the Tiger!

"One day I met a man who was not afraid of me. I threatened to destroy his home, but he said his God was able to deliver him. I was curious about this new God, and he told me that he was a Christian. As he spoke I had such a hunger in my soul for the peace that he had! When I despaired at the thought of ever controlling myself, he said that Christ, the Son of God, could change me.

"Oh, the wonder that came to my soul! What walls and chains had failed to do, Christ was able to do. Wang, the Tiger, is truly dead. This is a new man in Christ you see before you."

Wang went back to his father's home. He took his place on the farm. Through his leadership, many found Christ, and a church grew up in the village.

Weathered Old Barns

A stranger came by the other day with an offer that set me to thinking. He wanted to buy the old barn that sits out by the highway. I told him right off he was crazy. He was a city type, you could tell by his clothes, his car, his hands, and the way he talked. He said he was driving by and saw that beautiful barn sitting out in the tall grass and wanted to know if it was for sale. I told him he had a funny idea of beauty.

Sure, it was a handsome building in its day. But then, there's been a lot of winters pass with their snow and ice and howling wind. The summer sun beat down on that old barn till all the paint's gone, and the wood has turned silver gray. Now the old building leans a good deal, looking kind of tired. Yet, that fellow called it beautiful.

That set me to thinking. I walked out to the field and just stood there, gazing at that old barn. The stranger said he planned to use the lumber to line the walls of his den in a new country home he's building down the road. He said you couldn't get paint that beautiful. Only years of standing in the weather, bearing the storms and scorching sun, only that can produce beautiful barn wood.

It came to me then. We're a lot like that, you and I. Only it's on the inside that the beauty grows with us. Sure we turn silver, gray too, and lean a bit more than we did when we were young and full of sap. But the Good Lord knows what He's doing. And as the years pass He's busy using the hard wealth of our lives, the dry spells and the stormy seasons, to do a job of beautifying our souls that nothing else can produce. And to think how often folks fuss because they want life easy!

They took the old barn down today and hauled it away to beautify a rich man's house. And I reckon someday you and I'll be hauled off to Heaven to take on whatever chores the Good Lord has for us. And I suspect we'll be more beautiful then for the seasons we've been through here; and just maybe even add a bit of beauty to our Father's house.

Worry

Is there a magic cutoff period when offspring become accountable for their own actions? Is there a wonderful moment when parents can become detached spectators in the lives of their children and shrug, "It's their life," and feel nothing?

When I was in my 20s, I stood in a hospital corridor waiting for doctors to put a few stitches in my son's head. I asked, "When do you stop worrying?" The nurse said, "When they get out of the accident stage." My mother just smiled faintly and said nothing.

When I was in my 30s, I sat on a little chair in a classroom and heard how one of my children talked incessantly, disrupted the class, and was headed for a career making license plates. As if to read my mind, a teacher said, "Don't worry, they all go through this stage and then you can sit back, relax, and enjoy them." My mother just smiled faintly and said nothing.

When I was in my 40s, I spent a lifetime waiting for the phone to ring, the cars to come home, the front door to open. A friend said, "They're trying to find themselves. Don't worry, in a few years, you can stop worrying. They'll be adults." My mother just smiled faintly and said nothing.

By the time I was 50, I was tired of being vulnerable. I was still worrying over my children, but there was a new wrinkle. There was nothing I could do about it. My mother just smiled faintly and said nothing.

I continued to anguish over their failures, be tormented by their frustrations and absorbed in their disappointments. My friends said that when my children got married I could stop worrying and lead my own life. I wanted to believe that, but I was haunted by my mother's warm smile and her occasional, "You look pale. Are you all right? Call me the minute you get home. Are you depressed about something?"

Can it be that parents are sentenced to a lifetime of worry? Is concern for one another handed down like a torch to blaze the trail of human frailties and the fears of the unknown? Is concern a curse or is it a virtue that elevates us to the highest form of life?

One of my children became quite irritable recently, saying to me, "Where were you? I've been calling for three days, and no one answered! I was worried." I smiled a warm smile. The torch had been passed.

History

Advertising

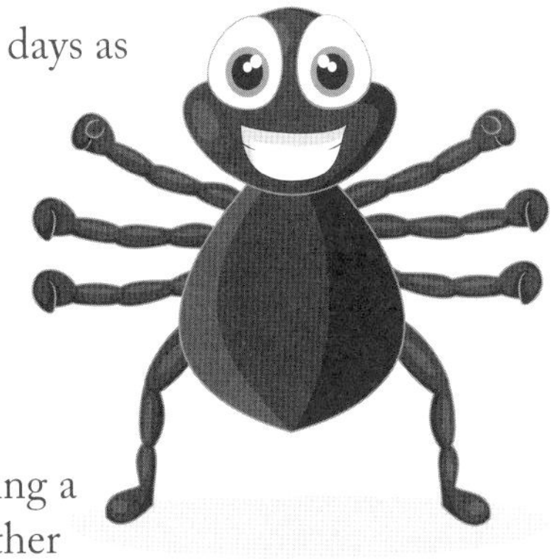

In Mark Twain's early days as the editor of a small Missouri newspaper he once received a letter from a reader who had found a spider in his paper. He wrote asking if this was an omen of good or bad luck.

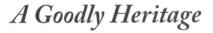

Replied Twain, "Finding a spider in your paper is neither good luck nor bad. The spider was merely looking over our paper to see which merchant was not advertising so that he could go to that store, spin his web across the door, and lead a life of undisturbed peace ever afterward."

A Goodly Heritage

It's hard to believe when Christmas arrives, but alas that is what the calendar says, so it must be so. Family get-togethers around the dinner table laden with all the fixings are a delightful experience. The conversation is often focused on the past year's events and highlights as everyone tries to update their family album of who is doing what and who is going where. Later in the day the conversation may turn to childhood memories such as the time we went to grandma and grandpa's house, the time all the cousins slept overnight at Uncle Roy's, the time Janie broke mom's favorite dish, the spilled peas, hide-and-seek, kick-the-tin can, jumping in the hay mow, swimming in the creek, and riding in grandpa's station wagon.

Oft times Uncle Bill will begin by saying, "When I was a boy", or Aunt Millie will say, "When I was a girl", and then proceed to explain how times were tough and how they made do with what they had. They may reminisce about growing up in an era when children were taught right from wrong and when the consequences for being disobedient meant a visit to the old woodshed. While that experience was not very pleasant, looking back, they value the lesson they learned. They may reflect on those "good old days" when everyone knew their neighbors and the evenings were spent visiting on the front porch. A time when the keys were always in the ignition, the house was never locked, and the stars in the sky were the only light at night. They walked to the one room school were they learned their "reading, 'riting and 'rithmetic". When a real snowstorm hit they were snowed in for several days and drove through the fields to get out.

As I thought about my own childhood it was a good reminder of the rich heritage I enjoy because of the lessons my parents and grandparents handed down to my generation. Time proven values of right and wrong. The importance of good morals and religious convictions. The principles of hard work, quality workmanship, and sticking to a job until it is finished. A time to work, a time to laugh, and a time to play. I thought about the decisions and choices that my forefathers made and how those choices affected where I am today. My ancestors moved from Pennsylvania to Canada and then Iowa and back to Pennsylvania, so I could have been a Canadian, or an Iowa native. Their choices had an effect on the people I learned to know, my place of employment, the person I married, the church I attend, how I view life, and a host of other things. I will always be indebted to my ancestors for the lasting impact they have made in my life. I have been blessed with a goodly heritage for which I am indeed grateful.

—M. Gingrich

Great Value In Disaster

Thomas Edison's laboratory was virtually destroyed by fire in December 1914. Although the damage exceeded $2 million, the buildings were only insured for $238,000 because they were made of concrete and thought to be fireproof. Much of Edison's life's work went up in spectacular flames that December night.

At the height of the fire, Edison's 24-year old son, Charles, frantically searched for his father among the smoke and debris. He finally found him, calmly watching the scene, his face glowing in the reflection, his white hair blowing in the wind.

"My heart ached for him," said Charles. "He was 67—no longer a young man—and everything was going up in flames. When he saw me, he shouted, "Charles, where's your mother?" When I told him I didn't know, he said, "Find her. Bring her here. She will never see anything like this as long as she lives."

The next morning, Edison looked at the ruins and said, "There is great value in disaster. All our mistakes are burned up. Thank God we can start anew."

Three weeks after the fire, Edison managed to deliver his first phonograph.

—The Sower's Seeds

It Could Have Been That Way All Along

Around 1890-1900 most homes were heated with a fireplace or wood stove. In a small town, there was a local citizen named Charles who cleaned chimneys (many chimneys). Charles was capable, dependable, and he cleaned most chimneys in the area. He was a member of the church and most church members were customers of his.

Charles was a black man, the only black man in this church. Each time he went up the ladder he asked the good Lord to take care of him. As Charles was getting older, he realized that some day he would pass away and he wanted to go to heaven. He also wanted to be buried in the cemetery. He told one of the church board that he wanted to buy a lot in the cemetery. The board talked about it. The result was that no black man can be buried in the church cemetery.

However, there was a hedge growing along the edge of the cemetery. They were willing to sell him a lot on the other side of the hedge. Charles had told the good Lord he wanted to be in this cemetery so he bought the lot on the other side of the hedge. When Charles passed away he was buried in the lot on the other side of the hedge.

The cemetery became larger and larger until it eventually went around Charles' lot. Today, Charles, the black man is in the center of the cemetery. It seems the good Lord wanted it to be this way from the start.

—as told to Ray Kraft

Mr. Lincoln—God's Man

Almost any American can tell you the birthday of Abraham Lincoln, but few can tell you very much about his church and religious life. Even the more than three thousand books which have been written about the sixteenth president give little information about his spiritual life. That "Honest Abe" was a praying man, many people know; but how much time he spent in praying or what prayer really meant in his life seems to be vague.

Mr. Lincoln was brought up on the Bible. Each night as the Lincoln children were put to bed, they would hear a Bible story read. "Grace" was always offered at the table by Abe's father. His parents feared the Lord, and taught their children to do the same.

In spite of this religious training, Abraham Lincoln did not make a personal acceptance of Christ until he was an adult. A pastor of one of the churches that Mr. Lincoln attended tells how he preached on the text, "Ye must be born again." Later that day Lincoln called the minister, telling him that he was impressed with the message and wanted to talk to him about it. "I talked and prayed with him for several hours," said the minister, and if ever a man was converted, Abraham Lincoln was converted that night.

In Washington, Lincoln attended the New York Avenue Presbyterian Church. In fact, the president had a paid pew there. Since people knew that Mr. Lincoln was a generous man, many of them would stand in the church lobby, waiting for the church pews to fill up; then when all the seats were taken, they were sure that Mr. Lincoln would allow them to share his pew. "Come right in here, brother," he would say, "there's plenty of room."

According to old records found in the church, Mr. Lincoln's pews rented for fifty dollars a year. Other records tell of his appearance in the church from Sunday to Sunday and at midweek services, too. While the president wanted to attend the weeknight services, he found it very difficult because his presence created a stir. So he asked the minister's permission to sit in the side room during the midweek prayer service, leaving the door open a little in order to hear. This was to have been a secret between the president and the preacher. But things didn't work out that way.

People soon realized that there was someone in the other room, because of the shadow in the glass door. On one prayer meeting night, the snow came down heavily. After the service, a couple of small and curious boys followed the big tracks from the side room of the church, directly to the president's house. When the preacher learned of this, he made the boys promise that they would not tell, or Mr. Lincoln would no longer be able to attend the week-night service.

When national affairs became more than he could bear, Mr. Lincoln knew where to turn. One night when he could not sleep, he got up from his bed, fell on his knees before God, and cried, "O God, I cannot guide the affairs of this nation without Thy help. I am poor and weak and sinful. O God, hear me and save this nation."

During the battle of Gettysburg, one of the great generals asked the president if he was worried about the way things were going, "No," said Mr. Lincoln. "I got down on my knees before almighty God and prayed for victory at Gettysburg. I told Him the war was His, and our cause was His cause."

With such a man leading the affairs of the nation, it is no wonder that he is remembered as one of the greatest leaders America has known.

—Ruth I. Johnson

Perseverance

At an early age, Milton dropped out of school and experienced one failure after another. While still a youth, he moved to Colorado where he answered an employment ad, only to find himself trapped in a labor camp. Although he escaped the camp, the experience affected him long into his adult life.

Returning home, he began making candy and selling it on the street. But opposition from competitors soon destroyed this endeavor. He then became an apprentice in a print shop but was fired after dropping the type on the floor and losing his hat in the press. Later, he opened candy stores in Chicago, New York and Philadelphia—all of which went out of business. It seemed everything Milton attempted ended in failure.

One day a businessman from England offered Milton an opportunity that changed his life forever. Through perseverance, Milton Hershey survived years of heartbreaking setbacks. His business became The Hershey Chocolate Company.

Persistence Overcomes Failure

Thomas A. Edison. He was told by his teachers, "You're stupid, and can't learn anything." Fired from 16 different jobs, because he was a dreamer, Edison has more patents in the U.S. Patents office than anyone.

Walt Disney. He was fired from his job working for a newspaper. The editor said, "He had no good ideas." Walt Disney is known worldwide for his creativity of the Disney characters, plus a number of Disney World Parks throughout the world.

F. W. Woolworth. He was fired while working in a store because he didn't have enough sense. He began the F. W. Woolworth Department Stores.

Michael Jordan. The all time great basketball player was unable to make the high school basketball team.

The Birth Of The Song "Precious Lord"

In 1932, I was 32 years old and a fairly new husband. My wife, Nettie and I were living in a little apartment on Chicago's south side. One hot August afternoon I had to go to St. Louis, where I was to be the featured soloist at a large revival meeting. I didn't want to go.

Nettie was in the last month of pregnancy with our first child. But a lot of people were expecting me in St. Louis. I kissed Nettie good-bye, clattered downstairs to our Model A, and, in a fresh Lake Michigan breeze, chugged out of Chicago on Route 66.

However, outside the city, I discovered that in my anxiety at leaving, I had forgotten my music case. I wheeled around and headed back. I found Nettie sleeping peacefully. I hesitated by her bed; something was strongly telling me to stay. But eager to get on my way, and not wanting to disturb Nettie, I shrugged off the feeling and quietly slipped out of the room with my music.

The next night, in the steaming St. Louis heat, the crowd called on me to sing again and again. When I finally sat down, a messenger boy ran up with a Western Union telegram. I ripped open the envelope. Pasted on the yellow sheet were the words: "Your wife just died."

People were happily singing and clapping around me, but I could hardly keep from crying out. I rushed to a phone and called home. All I could hear on the other end was "Nettie is dead. Nettie is dead."

When I got back, I learned that Nettie had given birth to a boy. I swung between grief and joy. Yet that same night, the baby died. I buried Nettie and our little boy together, in the same casket. Then I fell apart.

For days I closeted myself. I felt that God had done me an injustice. I didn't want to serve him anymore or write gospel songs. I just wanted to go back to that jazz world I once knew so well. But then, as I hunched alone in that dark apartment those first sad days, I thought back to the afternoon I went to St. Louis. Something kept telling me to stay with Nettie. Was that *something* God? Oh, if I had paid more attention to Him that day, I would have stayed and been with Nettie when she died.

From that moment on, I vowed to listen more closely to Him. But still I was lost in grief. Everyone was kind to me, especially a friend, Professor Fry, who seemed to know what I needed. On the following Saturday evening he took me up to Malone's Poro College, a neighborhood music school. It was quiet; the late evening sun crept through the curtained windows. I sat down at the piano, and my hands began to browse over the keys. Something happened to me then. I felt at peace. I felt as though I could reach out and touch God. I found myself playing a melody—once into my head, the notes just seemed to fall into place:

"Precious Lord, take my hand, lead me on, let me stand! I am tired, I am weak, I am worn. Through the storm, through the night lead me on to the light, take my hand, precious Lord, lead me home."

The Lord gave me the words and melody, and He also healed my spirit. I learned that when we are in our deepest grief, when we feel farthest from God, this is when He is closest, and when we are most open to His restoring power.

And so I go on living for God willingly and joyfully, until that day comes when He will take me and gently lead me home.

—Thomas A. Dorsey

The House That Never Was

In London, England, there is a strange house. It looks like any other house on the block but nobody ever comes out of 23 Leinster Gardens. There is neither a doorbell or a letter box. No one ever looks out the windows and no one ever sits on the balcony. Simply put, No. 23 Leinster Gardens, in the tree lined Bayswater section of London, is "The House That Never Was."

No. 23 is a sham. It's a dummy house whose door and windows are merely painted on a cement wall. Behind this facade there is nothing except a network of steel girders, some train tracks, and the entrance to a tunnel. Every so often a fresh coat of paint is applied to the facing wall to keep it looking exactly like the neighboring buildings.

"The house that never was" was put up by London's Metropolitan Railway (the so-called underground), whose officials decided it would be the best way to hide the entrance to the subway tunnel and fill the gap in the row of houses so as not to spoil the harmonious look of the street.

In another sham, a woman tried to pay her purchases with some bogus money—really bogus that is. It was a counterfeit one million dollar bill. I suppose she didn't realize the cashier might have trouble giving her the right amount of change for her less than $2000.00 purchase. Million dollar bills are not a part of the U. S. currency.

The U.S. began making a new twenty dollar bill designed with numerous safety features to make counterfeiting more difficult. But it didn't deter those who were bent on cheating in this way. Within hours of the new $20 bills release there were counterfeits as well.

Counterfeiting extends to more than just currency. Music CD's and video's are common targets, and more recently, identity theft. Identity theft is retrieving personal information, such as credit card numbers and social security numbers, and then using that information to make purchases and charging it to the stolen identity.

Counterfeiting costs the U.S. Government a lot of money. It costs you and I a lot of money. I think all of us would agree that counterfeiting is wrong. Really wrong. It's outright stealing. We would have no part of it. But what about cheating on our taxes? What about operating on a cash basis to conceal earnings? What about falsifying insur-

ance claims to get extra money? What about fraudulent lawsuits for personal gain? What about false claims on unemployment benefits or workmen's compensation? These are all forms of counterfeiting and yet I have heard the claims of individuals who say, "Hey, it's okay. Everybody does it."

Falsifying information or cheating on taxes may seem like a small thing and is often rationalized with comments like, "I can spend it more wisely than Uncle Sam," or "They get enough of my money." Small or not it is still wrong. It is cheating! It is dishonest!

Jesus told the Pharisees, "Render unto Caesar the things that are Caesar's and unto God the things that are God's." In other words, pay your dues.

Honesty and integrity have taken a hit in our present culture. Unfortunately, this is true even in many religious circles. Some folks try to hide behind a facade of Christianity but aren't willing to live it out in real life. Counterfeits are deceptive and tend to undermine the genuine. Claims of Christianity become counterfeit when we fail to practice Christ likeness in our lives. Genuine Christianity is a lifestyle. Christ's teachings must be observed in all areas of life otherwise those looking on become confused and uninterested. Honesty and integrity are a vital part of that makeup. Genuine or counterfeit, which are you?

—M. Gingrich

The Supreme Court

As you walk up the steps to the Capitol Building which houses the Supreme Court you can see near the top of the building a row of the world's law givers and each one is facing one in the middle who is facing forward with a full frontal view—it is Moses and the Ten Commandments!

As you enter the Supreme Court courtroom, the two huge oak doors have the Ten Commandments engraved on the lower portion of each door.

As you sit inside the courtroom, you can see on the wall right above where the Supreme Court judges sit, a display of the Ten Commandments!

There are Bible verses etched in stone all over the Federal Buildings and Monuments in Washington, D.C. James Madison, the fourth president, known as "The Father of Our Constitution" made the following statement, "We have staked the whole of all our political institutions upon the capacity of mankind for self-government, upon the capacity of each and all of us to govern ourselves, to control ourselves, to sustain ourselves according to the Ten Commandments of God."

Patrick Henry, that patriot and Founding Father of our country said, "It cannot be emphasized too strongly or too often that this great nation was founded not by religionists but by Christians, not on religions, but on the Gospel of Jesus Christ." Every session of Congress begins with a prayer by a paid preacher, whose salary has been paid by the taxpayers since 1777.

Fifty-two of the 55 founders of the Constitution were members of the established orthodox churches in the colonies. Thomas Jefferson worried that the Courts would overstep their authority and instead of interpreting the law would begin making law "an oligarchy"—the rule of a few over many.

The very first Supreme Court Justice, John Jay said, "Americans should select and prefer Christians as their rulers."

How then, has America gotten to the point that everything done for 200 years in this country is now suddenly wrong and unconstitutional?

The @ Symbol

A blue sky. The nature of love. A child's smile. The @ symbol. Some things are so common place that you scarcely notice them. But that doesn't make them any less fascinating. Take the humble @ symbol, for instance. It's something we use dozens—perhaps hundreds—of times a day. This little "a" with the curved tail is inextricably linked to the instantaneous communication that we, as a society, are dependent upon. But where did @ come from, exactly?

Let's go back to the 6th or 7th century. Latin scribes, rubbing their wrists with history's first twinges of carpal tunnel syndrome, tried to save a little effort by shortening the Latin word ad (at, to, or toward) by stretching the upstroke of "d" and curving it over the "a". Italian researchers unearthed 14th-century documents, where the @ sign represented a measure of quantity. The symbol also appeared in a 15th-century Latin Spanish dictionary, defined as a gauge of weight, and soon after, according to ancient letters, was referenced as an amphora, a standard-sized clay vessel used to carry wine and grain.

Over the next few hundred years our plucky @ sign was used in trade to mean "at the price of" before resting on the first Underwood typewriter keyboard in 1885, then later rubbing symbolic shoulders with QWERTY on modern keyboards in the 1940s.

Then, one day in late 1971, computer engineer Ray Tomlinson grappled with how to properly address what would be history's very first e-mail. After 30 seconds of intense thought, he decided to separate the name of his intended recipient and their location by using the @ symbol. He needed something that wouldn't appear in anyone's name, and settled on the ubiquitous symbol, with the added bonus of the character representing the word "at," as in, hey you @ wherever you happen to work.com."

In the English language, we know @ as the "at symbol"; it goes by many other unusual pseudonyms throughout the world.

- In South Africa, it means "monkey's tail."
- In Bosnia, Croatia, and Serbia it's the "Crazy I."
- In the Czech Republic, it's "pickled herring."
- The Danish refer to it as "alpha- sign", "elephant's trunk", or "pig's tail."
- The French often refer to it as "little snail."
- In Greece, it's "little duck."
- In Hungary, it's called "maggot."
- In Mandarin Chinese, it's the "mouse sign."
- The Poles say "little cat" or "pig's ear."
- Russians often refer to it as "little dog."
- There's no official word for it in Thailand, but "wiggling worm-like character."
- The Turks lovingly describe it as "ear."

But an @ by any other name is just as sweet. Online, it's at the heart of every user's identity. It represents the breathless urgency of our connected culture: clear, concise, typographical shorthand for lobbing our thoughts, needs, and ideas to nearly anyone else in the world, instantly.

Its ubiquity and urgency has transcended the Latin alphabet of its origins to worm its way into other language groups, including Arabic and Japanese.

And that, web wanderers, is where it's @.

The Year Is 1903

The year is 1903, over one hundred years ago...what a difference a century makes.

- The average life expectancy in the U.S. was 47.
- Only 14 percent of the homes in the U.S. had a bathtub.
- Only 8 percent of the homes had a telephone.
- A three-minute call from Denver to New York City cost $11.00.
- There were only 8,000 cars in the U.S. and only 144 miles of paved roads.
- The maximum speed limit in most cities was ten mph.
- Alabama, Mississippi, Iowa, and Tennessee were each more heavily populated than California. With a mere 1.4 million residents, California was only the 21st most populous state in the Union.
- The tallest structure in the world was the Eiffel Tower.
- The average wage in the U.S. was 22¢ an hour.
- The average U.S. worker made between $200 and $400 per year.
- A competent accountant could expect to earn $2,000 per year, a dentist $2,500 per year, a veterinarian between $1,500 and $4,000 per year, and a mechanical engineer about $5,000 per year.
- More than 95 percent of all births in the U.S. took place at home.
- Ninety percent of all U.S. physicians had no college education. Instead, they attended medical schools, many of which were condemned in the press and by the government as "substandard".

- Sugar cost 4¢ a pound. Eggs were 14¢ a dozen. Coffee cost 15¢ a pound.
- Most women only washed their hair once a month and used borax or egg yolks for shampoo.

- Canada passed a law prohibiting poor people from entering the country for any reason.
- The five leading causes of death in the US were:
  1. Pneumonia and influenza
  2. Tuberculosis
  3. Diarrhea
  4. Heart disease
  5. Stroke
- The American flag had 45 stars. Arizona, Oklahoma, New Mexico, Hawaii, and Alaska hadn't been admitted to the Union yet.
- The population of Las Vegas, Nevada, was 30.
- Crossword puzzles and iced tea hadn't been invented.
- There was no Mother's Day or Father's Day.
- One in ten U.S. adults couldn't read or write. Only six percent of all Americans had graduated from high school.
- Coca-Cola® contained cocaine. Marijuana, heroin, and morphine were all available over the counter at corner drugstores. According to one pharmacist, "Heroin clears the complexion, gives buoyancy to the mind, regulates the stomach and the bowels, and is, in fact, a perfect guardian of health."
- Eighteen percent of households in the U.S. had at least one full-time servant.
- There were only about 230 reported murders in the entire U.S.

Just think what things could be like in another 100 years.

Truth Unflattered

It may well be said that Abraham Lincoln is best remembered for his Gettysburg Address! It may be well for all to become acquainted with the last paragraph of his "second inaugural". "With malice toward none; with charity for all; with firmness in the right, as God gives us to see the right, let us strive on to finish the work we are in; to bind up the nation's wounds; to care for him who shall have borne the battle, and for his widow, and his orphan to do all which may achieve and cherish a just, and a lasting peace, among ourselves with all nations."

Lincoln evaluated the place his address would occupy in history.

Executive Mansion, Washington
March 15,1865
Thurlow Weed, Esq.

My Dear Sir:

Everyone likes a compliment. Thank you for yours on my little notification speech, and on the recent inaugural address. I expect the latter to wear as well as—perhaps better than—anything I have produced; but I believe it is not immediately popular. Men are not flattered by being shown that there has been a difference of purpose between the Almighty and them. To deny it, however, in this case, is to deny that there is a God governing the world. It is a truth which I thought needed to be told; and as whatever of humiliation there is in it, falls most directly on myself, I thought others might afford for me to tell it.

Yours truly,
A. Lincoln

Who Was Edward Kimball?

A Sunday School teacher named Edward Kimball thought he didn't have much impact as a Christian. In 1858, he at least was able to lead a shoe clerk to Christ. The clerk, Dwight L. Moody, became an evangelist, and in 1879 Moody awakened an evangelistic zeal in the heart of F.B. Meyer, the pastor of a small Church in New England. Meyer, preaching on a college campus won a student named J. Wilbur Chapman to Christ. While Chapman was engaged in YMCA work, he employed a former baseball player named Billy Sunday to help with evangelistic meetings. Sunday held a series of services in Charlotte, N.C. area, and a group of local men were so enthusiastic about the meetings that they planned another campaign. This time they brought preacher Mordecai F. Ham to town. During one of his meetings, a young man named Billy Graham yielded his life to Christ. Since then, millions have heard the gospel through Graham's meetings. Kimball had started quite a ripple effect! So can you. In fact, you're probably a touchtone already making a greater impact than you think.

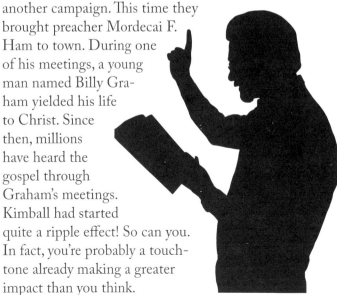

Humor

2nd Try

Arriving home from work at my usual hour of 5 P.M., I discovered that it had not been one of my wife's better days. Nothing I said or did seemed to be right.

By 7 P.M. things had not changed, so I suggested I go outside, pretend I had just got home, and start all over again. My wife agreed.

I went outside, came back in, and with a big smile, announced, "Honey, I'm home!"

"And just where have you been?" she replied sharply. "It's after seven o'clock!"

7 R's

Jimmy, an elementary school boy, had trouble pronouncing the letter "R" in class, so his teacher wrote a sentence on a piece of paper, handed the paper to him, and as an assignment, ordered him to practice the sentence, complete with 7 R's, at home: "Robert gave Richard a rap in the rib for roasting the rabbit so rare."

So, Jimmy went home to work on the troublesome R's and the annoying sentence, that had now become a pain, an anxiety, and a terror to him. Some days later, just as Jimmy had feared , the teacher asked him to say the sentence for her. Jimmy stored up his courage, took a deep breath, and recited the following, "Bob gave Dick a poke in the side for not cooking the bunny enough."

8 Ways to Weight Loss

1. Never weigh yourself with wet hair.
2. When weighing, remove everything, including glasses. In this case, blurred vision is an asset.
3. Use cheap scales only, never the medical kind, because they are always five pounds off…to your advantage, of course.
4. Stand with arms raised, making pressure on the scale lighter. (Waving them is optional but occasionally helps!)
5. Don't eat or drink in the morning until AFTER you've weighed in.
6. Weigh yourself after a hair-cut; this is good for at least half a pound of hair (hopefully).
7. Exhale with all your might BEFORE stepping onto the scale (air has to weigh something right?).
8. Start out with just one foot on the scale, then holding onto the towel rack in front of you, slowly edge your other foot on and slowly let off of the rack. Admittedly, this takes time, but it's worth it. You will weigh at least two pounds less than if you'd stepped on normally.

22 Mph

A state trooper spied a car puttering along at 22 mph, so he turned on his lights and pulled the driver over. Approaching the car, he noticed that five old ladies were inside, and they looked wide-eyed and terribly pale. The driver pleaded with him, "Officer, I don't understand, I was doing exactly the speed limit! What seems to be the problem?"

"Ma'am," the officer replies, "You weren't speeding, but driving slower than the speed limit can also be dangerous!"

"I beg to differ, sir. I was doing the speed limit exactly: twenty-two miles an hour!" the old woman said.

The state police officer, chuckling, explained to here that "22" was the route number, not the speed limit.

A bit embarrassed, the woman grinned and thanked the officer for pointing out her error.

"But before I let you go, ma'am, I have to ask…Is everyone in this car okay? These women seem awfully shaken," the officer asked.

"Oh, they'll be all right in a minute officer; we just got off Route 119."

50th Anniversary

At my grandparent's 50th wedding anniversary, I was looking through a photo album of their marriage ceremony. "Grandma, so many of these styles have come back over the years," I commented.

Grandma never hesitated. "That's why I've kept Grandpa all this time," she said. "I know he'll be back in style again one of these days."

A Birthday Wish

Laughing at herself when I got to her house, the 80-year-old matriarch of our family, my grandmother, touched my arm and said, "You're never going to believe what I just did."

Hard-of-hearing and tone-deaf, she unabashedly insists on carrying on her tradition of calling each of us on our birthday to sing "the birthday song." This time, it was my uncle's turn.

Unknowingly, she dialed the wrong number. Instead of my uncle, an innocent and confused man became the recipient of her embarrassing solo.

Amusing and a little uncomfortable it is to be on the receiving end of her out-of-tune melody—even for us. To interrupt her mid-song would be rude, I suppose—even for someone under no obligation to cringe and let her finish. I can't think of another reason this gentleman allowed her to sing until the final, "…and many more" before asking with the utmost sincerity, "Who is this?"

Still unaware of her blunder, but ever concerned for her 60-year-old son, Gram replied, "It's me, Ralph, mom. You sound like you have a cold."

Too hysterical to respond, the man gave the phone to his wife, who graciously informed my grandmother that she reached the wrong party.

A Cluttered Desk Is…

About a week ago, I came across an internet advice column that told me how to eliminate the paperwork clutter on my desk.

Great! So I printed out the five pages of how-to instructions, and placed them on top of the rest of the stuff on my desk. Now I can't find them.

Actual Classified Ads

These are actual classified ads taken out of newspapers.

- Auto Repair Service. Try us once, you'll never go anywhere again.
- Illiterate? Write today for help.
- Dog For Sale. Eats anything and is fond of children.
- Stock Up and Save! Limit one per customer.
- Cleaners. We do not tear your clothing with machinery. We do it carefully by hand.
- Vacation Special. Have your home exterminated. Get rid of aunts.
- Toaster. A gift that every member of the family appreciates. Automatically burns toast.
- For Rent. Six room hated apartment.
- We will oil your sewing machine, and adjust tension in your home for $1.00.
- Used Cars: Why go elsewhere and be cheated? Come here first.
- Found: Dirty white dog. Looks like a rat…been out a while. Better be reward.
- Nordic Track: $300—Hardly used, call Chubby.
- Hummers: Largest Selection Ever—If it's in stock, we have it!
- Georgia Peaches: California Grown—89¢/lb.
- Nice Parachute: Never Opened—Used Once
- Tired of Working for only $9.75 per hour? We offer Profit Sharing and Flexible Hours. Starting Pay: $7-$9 per hour.
- For Sale by Owner: Complete set of Encyclopedia Britannica. 45 volumes. Excellent condition. $1,000.00 or best offer. No longer needed. Got married last weekend. Wife knows everything.

Actual School Absence Excuse Notes

These are excuse notes from parents (including original spelling) collected by schools from all over the country.

1. Dear School: Please excuse John being absent on Jan. 28, 29, 30, 31, 32, and also 33.
2. Please excuse Roland from P.E. for a few days. Yesterday he fell out of a tree and misplaced his hip.
3. John has been absent because he had two teeth taken out of his face.
4. Chris will not be in school because he has an acre in his side.
5. I kept Billie cause she had to go Christmas shopping because I don't know what size she wears.
6. Please excuse Jennifer for missing school yesterday. We forgot to get the Sunday paper off the porch, and when we found it Monday, we thought it was Sunday.
7. Mary Ann was absent December 11-16, because she had a fever and sore throat. Her brother had a low grade fever and ached all over. I wasn't the best either, sore throat and fever. There must be something going around.

A Doctor And A Lawyer

A doctor and a lawyer met at a party. Their conversation was interrupted repeatedly by guests asking the doctor for medical advice. Finally, the exasperated doctor turned to the lawyer and said, "Tell me, what do you do to stop people from asking you for legal advice when you're out of the office?"

"When they ask, I give them advice," replied the lawyer, "And them I send them a bill in the morning."

The doctor decided to take the lawyer's advice and for the rest of the evening wrote down the names and addresses of everyone who approached him for advice. The next morning he took out the list, just as his secretary walked into his office and handed him a bill from the lawyer.

Advertising

I was at a yard sale one day and saw a box marked, "Electronic cat and dog caller— guaranteed to work."

I looked inside and was amused to see an electric can opener.

Affectionate Husband

We had made some changes in our lives.

My husband had lost fifty pounds, and after eight years of being a housewife, I had taken a job in a restaurant. When I returned home after my first day at work, I gave my husband a big hug. He seemed to cling to me longer than usual. "Did you really miss me that much today, dear?" I asked.

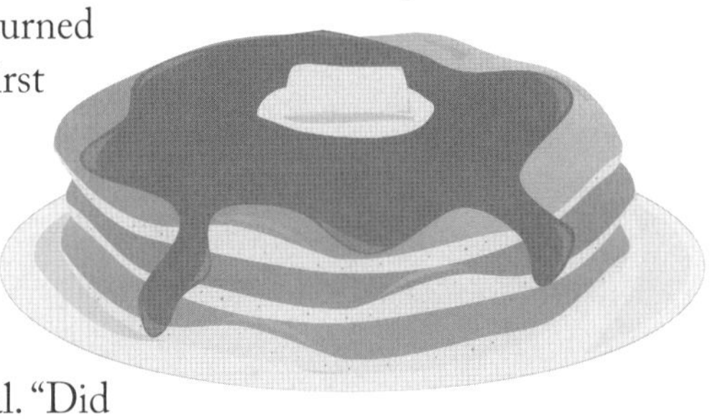

"No," came the reply. "But you smell so much like pancakes that I hate to let you go."

Air Conditioning

A customer was continually bothering the waiter in a restaurant; First, he'd asked that the air conditioning be turned up because he was too hot, then he asked it be turned down because he was too cold, and so on for about half an hour.

Surprisingly, the waiter was very patient, walking back and forth and never once getting angry. So finally, a second customer asked why didn't they just throw out the pest.

"Oh, I don't care," said the waiter with a smile. "We don't even have an air conditioner."

Airline Pricing

I couldn't decide whether to go to Salt Lake City or Denver for vacation, so I called the airlines to get prices.

"Airfare to Denver is $300," said a cheery salesperson.

"And what about Salt Lake City?"

"We have a really great rate Salt Lake—$99.00, but there is a stop-over."

"Where?" I asked.

"Denver," was the reply.

A Little Story

This is a story about four people named Everybody, Somebody, Anybody and Nobody. There was an important job to be done and Everybody was sure that Somebody would do it. Anybody could have done it, but Nobody did it. Somebody got angry about that because it was Everybody's job. Everybody thought Anybody could do it, but Nobody realized that Everybody would not do it. It turned out that Everybody blamed Somebody when Nobody did what Anybody could have done!

All I Need To Know About Life Learned By A Snowman

- It's okay if you're a little overweight.
- Hold your ground, even when the heat is on.
- Wearing white is always appropriate.
- Winter is the best of the four seasons.
- It takes a few extra rolls to make a good midsection.
- There's nothing better than a foul weather friend.
- The key to life is to be a jolly, happy soul.
- We're all made up of mostly water.
- You know you've made it when they write a song about you.
- Don't get too much sun.
- It's embarrassing when you can't look down and see your feet.
- It's fun to hang out in your front yard.
- Always put your best foot forward.
- There's no stopping you once you're on a roll

Always On Time

I had always prided myself in being an "on time" person. One morning I overslept and rushed around getting ready for Sunday School. As I ran out the door, my husband tried to say something,

"What?" I called back, "Don't slow me down, I'm late."

"No you're not," he responded, "it's Saturday."

Analogies And Metaphors

These are actual analogies and metaphors found in high school essays.

- Even in his last years, grandpappy had a mind like a steel trap, only one that had been left out so long, it had rusted shut.
- The plan was simple, like my brother-in-law, Phil. But unlike Phil, this plan just might work.
- The young fighter had a hungry look, the kind you get from not eating for a while.
- She walked into my office like a centipede with ninety-eight missing legs.

- Her voice had that tense grating quality, like a Generation thermal-paper fax machine that needed a band tightening.
- It hurt the way your tongue hurts after you accidentally staple it to the wall.

An Emergency Doctor Visit

A woman went to see her doctor, looking very much worried and all strung out.

She rattled off, "Doctor, take a look at me. When I woke up this morning, I looked at myself in the mirror and saw my hair all wiry and frazzled up, my skin was all wrinkled and pasty, my eyes were blood-shot and bugging out, and I had this corpse-like look on my face! What's wrong with me, Doctor?"

The doctor looked her over for a couple of minutes, then calmly said, "Well, I can tell you one thing…there ain't nothing wrong with your eyesight."

Another Word for Thesaurus?

Steven Wright is a comedian who delivers all his jokes as a series of absolutely dead pan, no expression statements. Imagine these statements being made in a quiet, almost monotone delivery…

- When I get real, real bored, I like to drive downtown and get a great parking spot, then sit in my car and count how many people ask me if I'm leaving.
- Do you think that when they asked George Washington for ID that he just whipped out a quarter?
- Don't you hate when your hand falls asleep and you know it will be up all night?
- Ever notice how irons have a setting for PERMANENT press? I don't get it.
- Everywhere is walking distance if you have the time.
- For my birthday I got a humidifier and a de-humidifier. I put them in the same room and let them fight it out.
- He was a multi-millionaire. Wanna know how he made all of his money? He designed the little diagrams that tell which way to put batteries in.
- I bought a house on a one-way, dead-end road: I don't know how I got there.
- I don't have to walk my dog anymore. I walked him all at once. He was fun when he was a puppy. I named him Stay. When I'd call him I'd say C'mere Stay C'mere Stay and he'd go like this…(FILL IN THE MOVEMENT YOURSELF). He's a lot smarter than that now. Now when I call him he just ignores me and keeps on typing.
- I got a new shadow. I had to get rid of the other one—it wasn't doing what I was doing.
- I got my driver's license photo taken out of focus on purpose. Now when I get pulled over, the cop looks at it [moving it nearer and farther, trying to see it clearly], and says, "Here, you can go."
- I had to stop driving my car for a while…the tires got dizzy…
- I have a hobby. I have the world's largest collection of sea shells. I keep it scattered on beaches all over the world. Maybe you've seen some of it.
- I have a map of the United States…It's original size…it says one mile equals one mile.
- I like to reminisce with people I don't know…
- I like to torture my plants by watering them with ice cubes.
- I lost a button hole today.
- I put contact lenses in my dog's eyes. They had little pictures of cats on them. Then I took one out and he ran around in circles.
- I recently moved into a new apartment, and there was this switch on the wall that didn't do anything…So anytime I had nothing to do, I'd just flick that switch up and down…up and down…up and down. Then one day I got a letter from a woman in Germany. It just said, "Cut it out."
- I saw a man with a wooden leg and a real foot.
- I spilled spot remover on my dog and now he's gone.
- I turned my air conditioner the other way around, and it got cold out. The weatherman said, "I don't understand it. It was supposed to be 80 degrees today," and I said, "Oops."
- I was pulled over for speeding today. The officer said, "Don't you know the speed limit is 55 miles an hour?" I replied, "Yes, but I wasn't going to be out that long."
- I was walking down the street and all of a sudden the prescription for my eyeglasses ran out.
- I went to a general store, but they wouldn't let me buy anything specific.
- I wrote a song, but I can't read music. Every time I hear a new song on the radio, I think, "Hey, maybe I wrote that."
- I'm moving to Mars next week, so if you have any boxes…
- I've got some powdered water, but I don't know what to add.
- I'm writing a book. I've got the page numbers done.
- If toast always lands butter-side down, and cats always land on their feet, what happens if you strap toast on the back of a cat and drop it?
- If you can't hear me, it's because I'm in parentheses.
- In my house, on the ceilings I have paintings of the rooms above…so I never have to go upstairs.
- Last night the power went out. Good thing my camera had a flash…I took 65 pictures of myself making a sandwich. My neighbors thought it was lightning in my house, so they called the police.
- My friend has a baby. I'm writing down all the noises he makes so later I can ask him what he meant.
- One time a cop pulled me over for running a stop sign. He said, "Didn't you see the stop sign?" I said, "Yeah, but I don't believe everything I read."
- There was a power outage at a department store yesterday. Twenty people were trapped on the escalators.

- There's a pizza place near where I live that sells only slices. In the back you can see a guy tossing a triangle in the air.
- Today I dialed a wrong number. The other side said, "Hello?" and I said, "Hello, could I speak to Joey?" They said, "Uh. I don't think so…he's only two months old." I said, "I'll wait…".

And finally, what is another word for thesaurus?

Answering Questions

A salesman was going door to door trying to sell his wares, As he walked up to the next house, he noticed a small boy sitting on the front steps.

"Is your mother home?" the salesman asked the small boy.

"Yeah, she's home," the boy said, scooting over to let him pass.

The salesman rang the doorbell, got no response, knocked once, then again. Still, no one came to the door. Turning to the boy, the fellow said, "I thought you said your mother was home!?"

The boy replied, "She is but this isn't where I live."

Appendix Worry

Old Jacob Johnson, raging hypochondriac, was convinced that the pain on his left side was appendicitis. Mrs. Johnson explained that the appendix is on the right.

"So, aha! THAT's why it hurts to much," said Jacob. "My appendix is on the wrong side!"

Art Value

An artist asked the gallery owner if there had been any interest in his paintings on display at that time.

"I have good news and bad news," the owner replied. "The good news is that a gentleman inquired about your work and wondered if it would appreciate in value after your death. When I told him it would, he bought all fifteen of your paintings."

"That's wonderful," the artist exclaimed. "What's the bad news?"

"The guy was your doctor."

A Teenager Is…

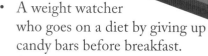

- Someone who can't remember to walk the dog each day but never forgets a phone number he heard once.
- A weight watcher who goes on a diet by giving up candy bars before breakfast.
- Someone who receives his allowance on Monday, spends it on Tuesday, and borrows from his best friend on Wednesday.
- Someone who can pick out the voice of a friend from three blocks away, but can't hear his mother calling from the next room.
- A computer whiz who can operate any new gadget within seconds but can't make the bed.
- A connoisseur of two types of fine music: loud and very loud.
- A person who can bike for miles but is usually too tired to help with the dishes.
- Painfully funny at times. At other times a teenager is just painful.
- Someone who will pitch in and help clean every room in the house, as long as it's the neighbor's house.

Attendance Credit

It used to be that it was required that in order for a college student to receive credit for a particular course, a card that listed his or her courses had to be signed by the instructor/lecturer. It was, at the time, policy that students attend their courses. But depending on the size of the class, it was often quite possible to receive credit, even after not attending the class regularly.

Not so, with this physics professor. If he didn't recognize you, you would have to repeat the course. On one occasion, a student handed his card to be signed. The professor looked at the name, then at the student, and said, "I've never seen you in my class," and handed back the card.

Now being a science student, he naturally thought quickly, and proceeded to the end of the line. When he was at the front again, he handed his card to the professor. The professor looked at the name, then at the student, and said, "You look familiar. Okay," and signed the card.

Auto Auction

The auto auction I attended was selling cars to benefit charity. Vehicles were classified as either "Running" or "No Start". On the block was a No Starter. It had a shattered windshield, two missing tires, a sagging front bumper, a cockeyed grille, a hood that was sprung up at an angle, and dings and dents all over the body.

Before he started the bidding, the auctioneer announced the car's year, make, and model, and then read the owner's comments: "Please note—the radio does not work."

Back To School

After raising four children, and having lost my husband, I decided to return to college and get the degree I had started working for, but never finished. On my first day back in college, eager with anticipation, and more than a little nervous, I took a front row seat in my first class in over forty years; a literature course.

The professor told us we would be responsible for reading five books over the course of the semester, and that he would provide us with a list of authors from which we could choose.

He ambled over to the lectern, took out his class book, and began "Baker, Black, Brooks, Carter, Cook…" I was working feverishly to get down all the names, when I felt a tap on my shoulder. The student behind me whispered, "Slow down! He's just taking Attendance!"

Banking Hiccup

While waiting in line at the bank, a coworker developed a very loud case of hiccups. By the time he reached the teller's window, the hiccups seemed to have worsened. The teller took my friend's check and proceeded to run a computer verification of his account.

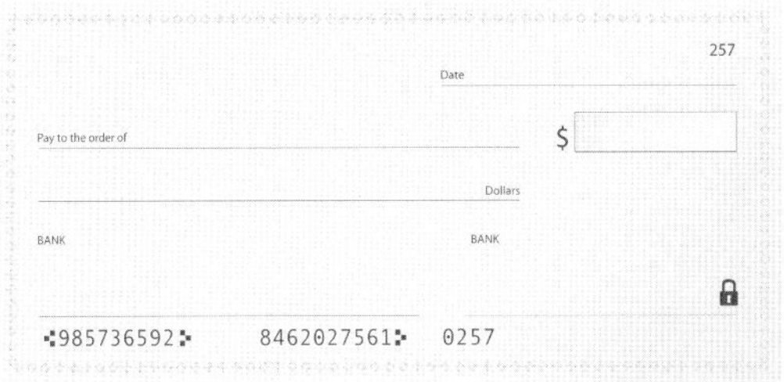

After a minute she looked up from her terminal with a frown and said that she would be unable to cash his check.

"Why not?" my friend asked incredulously.

"I'm sorry, sir," she replied, "but our computer indicates that you do not have sufficient funds to cover this amount. As a matter of fact," she continued, "our records show your account overdrawn in excess of $5000."

"It CAN'T be!" he cried. "You have GOT to be kidding!"

"Yes, I am," she answered with a big smile, counting out his cash. "But you will notice that your hiccups are gone."

Bank Line

With only two tellers working at the bank, the line I was standing in was moving very slowly. As I waited, I began to fill in my withdrawal slip. Not sure of the date, I turned and asked the woman behind me.

"It's the fifth," she replied.

A man from the back of the line advised, "Don't write it in yet!"

Bank Name

Mother decided that ten-year-old Cathy should get something 'practical' for her birthday.

"Suppose we open a savings account for you?" mother suggested. Cathy was delighted.

"It's your account, darling," mother said as they arrived at the bank, "so you fill out the application." Cathy was doing fine until she came to the space for 'Name of your former bank.' After a slight hesitation, she put down 'Piggy.'

Bank Trouble

The coed came running in tears to her father. "Dad, you gave me some terrible financial advice!" she cried.

"I did? What did I tell you?" asked the dad.

"You told me to put my money in that big bank, and now that big bank is in trouble."

"What are you talking about? That's one of the largest banks in the world," he said. "Surely there must be some mistake."

"I don't think so," she sniffed. "They just returned one of my checks with a note saying, 'Insufficient Funds.'"

Barbara Goes Horseback Riding

Barbara decided to try riding horseback, even though she had no lessons or prior experience. She mounted the horse unassisted and the horse immediately sprang into motion. It galloped along at a steady and rhythmic pace, but Barbara began to slip from the saddle. In terror, she grabbed for the horse's mane, but couldn't seem to get a firm grip. She tried to throw her arms around the horse's neck, but she slid down the side of the horse anyway. The horse galloped along, seemingly oblivious to its slipping rider. Finally, giving up her frail grip, she leapt away from the horse and tried to throw herself to safety. Unfortunately, her foot became entangled in the stirrup and she was now at the mercy of the horse's pounding hooves as she fell to the ground. Finally the Walmart® manager saw her, pulled the plug, and shut the ride off, leaving the others waiting in line for their turn, furious.

Baseball Doctor

As the manager of our hospital's softball team, I was responsible for returning equipment to the proper owners at the end of the season. When I walked into the surgery department carrying a bat that belonged to one of the surgeons, I passed several patients and their families in a waiting area. I heard one man say to his wife, "Look, honey, here comes your anesthesiologist."

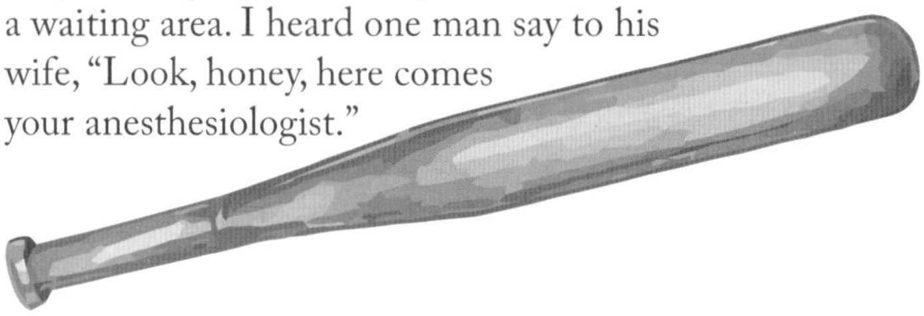

Bathroom Supply

In search of a new shower for our home, my wife and I went to a bathroom-supply store.

We discussed our needs with a young saleswoman. Since it was near closing time, we had to curtail our discussion and made plans to come back the next day to make our final decision.

Later that evening, my wife and I were at a restaurant, where the same young lady from the bathroom-supply store was now working a shift as a waitress.

As she passed our table, she suddenly recognized us and called to me in a loud voice, "Hey! You're the man who needs a shower!"

Being Polite

While I was working as a pediatric nurse, I had the difficult assignment of giving immunization shots to children. One day I entered the examining room to give four-year-old Lizzie her shot.

"No! No! No!" she screamed.

"Lizzie," her mother scolded. "That's not polite behavior." At that, the girl yelled even louder, "No, thank you! No, thank you! No, thank you!"

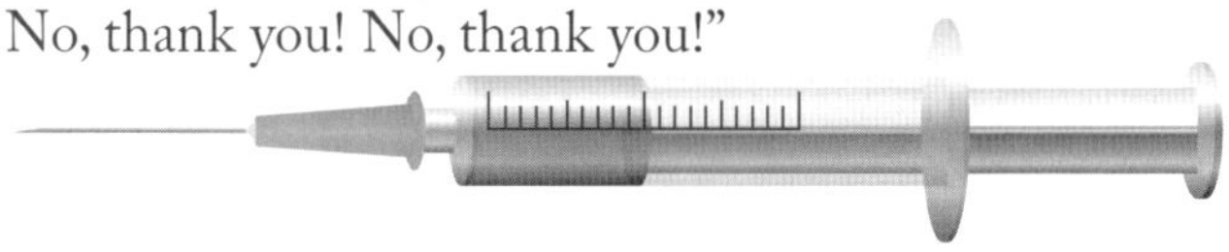

Best Newspaper Headlines of 2002

1. Something Went Wrong in Jet Crash, Expert Says
2. Teacher Strikes Idle Children
3. Miners Refuse to Work after Death
4. Juvenile Court to Try Shooting Defendant
5. War Dims Hope for Peace
6. If Strike Isn't Settled Quickly, It May Last Awhile
7. Cold Wave Linked to Temperatures
8. Red Tape Holds Up New Bridges
9. Typhoon Rips Through Cemetery; Hundreds Dead
10. Man Struck By Lightning Faces Battery Charge
11. New Study of Obesity Looks for Larger Test Group
12. Children Make Nutritious Snacks
13. Chef Throws His Heart into Helping Feed Needy
14. Local High School Dropouts Cut in Half
15. Hospitals are Sued by Seven Foot Doctors

Black Coffee in a Clean Cup

Bill and Doug went into a diner that looked as though it had seen better days. As they slid into a booth, Bill wiped some crumbs from the seat. Then he took a napkin and wiped some moisture from the table. The waitress came over and asked if they wanted some menus.

"No thanks," said Doug. "I'll just have a cup of black coffee."

"I'll have black coffee, too," Bill said. "And please make sure the cup is clean." The waitress shot him a nasty look. She turned and marched off into the kitchen.

Two minutes later, she was back.

"Two cups of black coffee," she announced, sternly. "Which one of you wanted the clean cup?"

Boat Compromise

My friend wanted a boat more than anything. His wife kept refusing, but he bought one anyway. "I'll tell you what," he told her, "In the spirit of compromise, why don't you name the boat?"

Being a good sport, she accepted. When her husband went to the dock for his maiden voyage, this is the name he saw painted on the side: "For Sale."

Boat Trouble

Last summer down on Lake Isabella, an hour east of Bakersfield, California, some folks, new to boating, were having a problem. No matter how hard they tried, they couldn't get their brand new twenty-two foot boat going. It was very sluggish in almost every maneuver, no matter how much power was applied. After about an hour of trying to make it go, they putted to a nearby marina, thinking someone there could tell them what was wrong.

A thorough topside check revealed everything in perfect working condition. The engine ran fine, the outdrive went up and down, the prop was the correct size and pitch. So, one of the marine guys jumped into the water to check underneath, he came up choking on water, he was laughing so hard. Under the boat, still strapped securely in place, was the trailer.

Boring Flight

Bored during a long flight, an eminent scholar leaned over and woke up the sleeping man next to him to ask if he would like to play a game.

"I'll ask you a question," the scholar explained, "and if you don't know the answer, you pay me \$5. Then you ask me a question, and if I don't know the answer, I'll pay you \$50."

When the man agreed to play, the scholar asked, "What's the distance from the earth to the moon?" Baffled, the man handed him \$5. "Ha!" said the scholar. "It's 238,857 miles. Now it's your turn."

The man was silent for a few moments. Then he asked, "What goes up a hill with three legs and comes down with four?"

Puzzled, the scholar racked his brain for an hour—but to no avail. Finally he took out his wallet and handed over \$50. "Okay, okay, what is the answer?" the scholar asked.

The man said, "I don't know," pulled out a \$5 bill, handed it to the scholar, and went back to sleep.

Bowling Tournament Bus Trip

Two bowling teams chartered a double-decker bus for a weekend tournament in Atlantic City.

The one team rode in the bottom deck of the bus and the other team rode on the top level. The team down below was whooping it up and having a great time when one of them realized she didn't hear anything from the team upstairs. She decided to go up and investigate.

When she reached the top, she found them frozen in fear, staring straight ahead at the road and clutching the seats in front of them. She asked, "What is going on up here? We're having a great time downstairs!"

One of them replied, "Yeah, but you've got a driver!"

Breakfast Special

We went to breakfast at a restaurant where the special was two eggs, bacon, hash browns, and toast for $1.99. "Sounds good," my wife said. "But I don't want the eggs."

"Then I'll have to charge you two dollars and forty-nine cents because you're ordering a la carte," the waitress warned her.

"You mean I'd have to pay for not taking the eggs?" my wife asked incredulously. "I'll take the special."

"How do you want your eggs?"

"Raw and in the shell," my wife replied. She took the two eggs home.

Brick Order

A man went into his local building supply store and ordered 10,000 bricks.

"May I ask what you're building?" asked the man behind the counter.

"It's going to be a barbecue."

"Wow, that's a lot of bricks for one barbecue."

"Not really; I live on the 12th floor."

Broken Lawnmower

When the power mower broke and wouldn't run, I kept hinting to my husband that he ought to get it fixed, but somehow the 'message' never sank in. Finally, I thought of a clever way to make my point. When my husband arrived home that day, he found me seated in the tall grass, busily snipping away with a tiny pair of sewing scissors. He watched silently for a short time and then went into the house. He was gone only a few moments when he came out again. He handed me a toothbrush. "When you finish cutting the grass," he said, "you might as well sweep the driveway." I guess from now on I'll let him mow the grass.

Bug Batteries

When our grandchildren were visiting late last summer, they went out to catch lightning bugs one night. As three-year-old Carl put one in a jar, he looked up at me and asked, "Grandma, what size batteries do these bugs take?"

Building Muscles

For those keyboard jockeys (those with jobs that require sitting at a computer all day) that don't want to spend the money for those fancy exercise machines, here is a little secret for building arm and shoulder muscles. Three days a week works well.

Begin by standing (in your cubicle) with a five pound potato sack in each hand extend your arms straight out to your sides and hold them there as long as you can. After a few weeks, move up to ten pound potato sacks and then fifty pound potato sacks, and finally get to where you can lift a one hundred pound potato sack in each hand and hold your arms straight for more than a full minute.

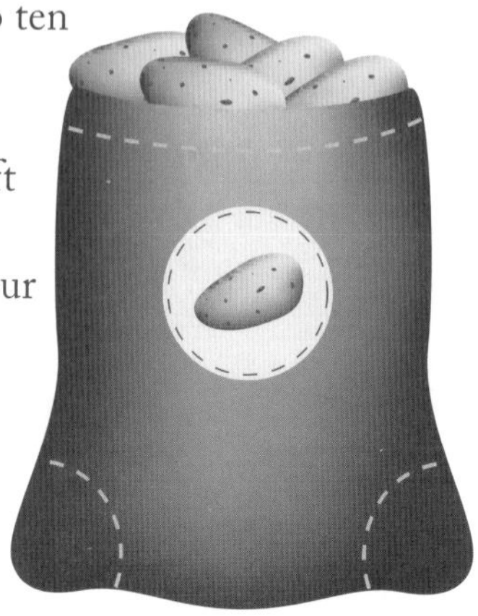

Next, start putting a few potatoes in the sacks, but be careful not to overdo it.

Build It And They Will Come

The telephone solicitor selling basement waterproofing must have thought she had a potential customer when she reached my very polite and patient son on the phone. At the end of her long sales pitch, she asked, "Do you mind if we send out someone to give you an estimate?"

"Not at all," my son said.

"When would be a good time?" she asked.

My son answered, "Just as soon as I dig a basement."

Bumpers

Most people hate to parallel park. The other day, I saw this woman trying to get out of a tight parking space. She bumped the car in front, then backed up and hit the car behind her. This went on for about two minutes.

I walked over to see if I could somehow help. My offer was declined. She said, "Why have bumpers if you're not going to use them once in a while?"

Burning Calories

Someone gave this advice on how to burn calories by doing these exercises. Here is the number of calories burned for each exercise.

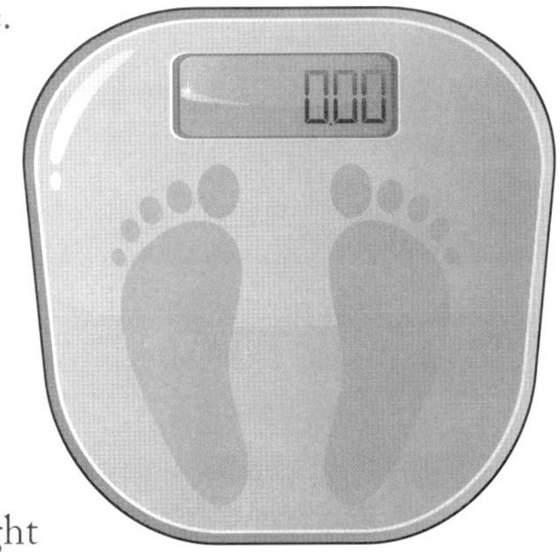

1. Beating around the bush: 75
2. Jumping to conclusions: 100
3. Climbing the walls: 250
4. Swallowing your pride: 150
5. Throwing your weight around (depending on your weight): 50-300
6. Dragging your heels: 75
7. Banging your head against the wall: 75
8. Pushing your luck: 235
9. Making mountains out of mole hills: 500
10. Hitting the nail on the head: 50
11. Running around in circles: 400
12. Bending over backwards: 125
13. Passing the buck: 35
14. Tooting your own horn: 25
15. Climbing the ladder of success: 1,000
16. Adding fuel to the fire: 120
17. Putting your foot in your own mouth: 300
18. Going over the edge: 50
19. Picking up the pieces: 600
20. Crossing the bridge before you get there: 200
21. Crying over spilled milk: 75
22. Running people down: 400
23. Going from home to home as a talebearer: 500
24. Tearing down what others built: 400
25. Changing your mind too often: 200
26. Climbing out of debt: 300
27. Carrying a grudge: 500
28. Using the remote control: 300

Though humorous, if these practices burned off calories, we would have very few overweight people.

Business Exhaustion

The businessman dragged himself home and barely made it to his chair before he dropped exhausted. His sympathetic wife was right there with a tall, cool drink and a comforting word. "My, you look tired," she said. "You must have had a hard day today. What happened to make you so exhausted?"

"It was terrible," her husband said. "The computer broke down and all of us had to do our own thinking."

Buying A Hat

My wife and I were visiting her 95-year-old grandfather when he asked us to take him to buy a new hat.

My wife took me aside. "I'm worried that he doesn't have enough money, and he'll be very embarrassed," she said. So I asked the salesperson to tell my wife's grandfather that whichever hat he chose cost $15. I would pay the difference. Grandpa picked out a hat and was charged $15. After he left, I paid the other $45 of the price.

Later grandpa said, "What a bargain! The last one I bought there cost me $60."

Cake Disaster

Many years ago my just married young cousin moved into an upstairs apartment and invited some of her women friends over for the evening. She put out snacks and then came out with a cake that looked like a disaster.

She apologized and said she didn't know what happened to the cake because, she explained, "I even used the high altitude directions because I live upstairs."

Calculate The Height Of A Flag Pole

A group of managers was trying to calculate the height of a flag pole. They tried to measure its height by lining up their thumbs and then turning the thumb 90 degrees and marking a spot on the ground. Then they tried to use its shadow and trig functions, but no luck.

An engineer came by and watched for a few minutes. He asked one of the managers what they were doing.

"We're trying to calculate the height of this flag pole."

The engineer watched a few minutes more and then, without saying a word, he walked over, pulled the pole out of the ground, laid it down, measured it, wrote the measurement on a piece of paper, gave it to one of the managers and walked away.

The manager looked at the paper, snickered and said to the other managers: "Isn't that just like an engineer?! We're trying to calculate the height and he gives us the length."

Call Center Conversations

Customer: "I've been ringing numbers for two days and can't get through to inquiries. Can you help?"
Operator: "Where did you get that number from, sir?"
Customer: "It was on the door to the Travel Centre."
Operator: "Sir, they are our office hours."

Caller: "I deleted a file from my PC last week and I have just realized that I need it. If I turn my system clock back two weeks, will I have my file back again?"

Samsung Electronics Caller: "Can you give me the telephone number for Jack?"
Operator: "I'm sorry, sir, I don't understand who you are talking about."
Caller: "On page 1, section 5, of the user guide, it clearly states that I need to unplug the fax machine from the AC wall socket and telephone jack before cleaning. Now, can you give me the number for Jack?"
Operator: "I think you mean the telephone socket on the wall."

RAC Motoring Services Caller: "Does your European Breakdown Policy cover me when I am traveling in Australia?"
Operator: "Doesn't the product give you a clue?"

Caller (enquiring about legal requirements while traveling in France): "If I register my car in France, do I have to change the steering wheel to the other side of the car?"

Then there was the caller who asked for a knitwear company in Woven.
Operator: "Woven? Are you sure?"
Caller: "Yes. That's what it says on the label: Woven in Scotland."

On another occasion, a man making heavy breathing sounds from a phone box told a worried operator: "I haven't got a pen, so I'm steaming up the window to write the number on."

Camels

A mother and baby camel were talking one day when the baby camel asked, "Mom, why have I got these huge three-toed feet?"

The mother replies, "Well, son, when we trek across the desert, your toes will help you to stay on top of the soft sand."

"Ok," said the son, but a few minutes later he asked, "Mom, why have I got these great long eyelashes?"

"They are there to keep the sand out of your eyes on the trips through the desert."

"Thanks, mom," replied the son. After a short while, the son inquired again, "Mom, why have I got these great big humps on my back?"

The mother, now a little impatient, replied, "They are there to help store fat for our long treks across the desert, and so we can go without water for long periods."

"That's great, mom. So we have huge feet to stop us from sinking, and long eyelashes to keep the sand from our eyes, and these humps to store water, but mom..."

"Yes, son?"

"Why are we in the San Diego Zoo?"

Car Ad, Meanings

If the ad claims...
It *really* means...

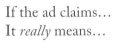

- "Parts Car"... beyond repair
- "Immaculate"...recently washed
- "Engine quiet"... if you use 90-weight oil
- "Needs minor overhaul"...needs engine
- "Needs major overhaul"...phone the junk yard
- "Burns no oil"...it all leaks out
- "Drive it away"...I live on a hill
- "Drive it anywhere"...within 10 miles
- "Desirable classic"...no one wants it.
- "Rare classic"...no one wanted it even when it was new.
- "Stored twenty years"...in a farmer's field
- "Ran when stored"...won't start

Car Names Explained

(My car is in here so don't be offended if yours is too!)

Audi
- Always Unsafe Designs Implemented

BMW
- Big Money Works
- Brutal Money Waster
- Break My Window

Buick
- Big Ugly Indestructible Car Killer

Chevrolet
- Can Hear Every Valve Rap On Long Extended Trips
- Cheap, Hardly Efficient, Virtually Runs On Luck Every Time
- Cheap Heap, Every Valve Rattles, Oil Leaks Every Time
- Condition Hopeless, Entire Vehicle Relies On Left Over Engine Technology

Dodge
- Drips Oil, Drops Grease Everywhere
- Dem Old Dudes Go Everywhere
- Dead Or Dying Gas Eater
- Dear Old Dad's Geriatric Express

Fiat
- Failed in Italian Automotive Technology
- Fix It All the Time
- Fix It Again, Tony!

Ford
- Fix Or Repair Daily
- Found On Road, Dead
- Fast Only Rolling Downhill
- Found On Russian Dump

GM
- General Maintenance
- Great Mistake

GMC
- Garage Man's Companion
- Got A Mechanic Coming?

Honda
- Had One Never Did Again

Hyundai
- Hope You Understand Nothing's Driveable And Inexpensive

Mazda
- Most Always Zipping Dangerously Along

Oldsmobile
- Old Ladies Driving Slowly Make Others Behind Infuriatingly Late Everywhere,
- Overpriced, Leisurely Driven Sedan Made Of Buick's Irregular Leftover Equipment

Pinto
- Put In New Transmission Often

Pontiac
- Poor Old Neanderthal Thinks It's A Cadillac

Saab
- Send Another Automobile Back
- Swedish Automobiles Always Breakdown

Toyota
- Too Often Yankees Overprice This Auto

Volvo
- Very Odd Looking Vehicular Object
- Vehicles Of Low Velocity Owners

VW
- Virtually Worthless

Car Privileges

David and Bernice had just given their teenage daughter family car privileges. One night she returned home very late from a party.

The next morning her father went out to the driveway to get the newspaper and came back into the house frowning. At 11:30 a.m. the girl sleepily walked into the kitchen, and her father asked her, "Sweetheart, what time did you get in last night?"

"Not too late, Dad." she replied nervously.

Dead-panned, her father said, "Then, my precious one, I'll have to talk with the paperboy about putting my paper under the front tire of the car."

Car Problems

Jill's car was unreliable and she called John for a ride every time it broke down. One day John got yet another one of those calls.

"What happened this time?" he asked

"My brakes went out," Jill said. "Can you come to get me?"

"Where are you?" John asked.

"I'm in the drugstore," Jill responded.

"And where's the car?" John asked.

"It's right here, with me."

Car Rental

On duty as a customer-service rep for a car-rental company, I took a call from a driver who needed a tow. He was stranded on a busy highway, but he didn't know the make of the car he was driving. I asked again for a more detailed description beyond "a blue four-door."

After a pause, the driver replied, "It's the one on fire."

Car Repair

Wayne, a friend of mine, owns an auto-repair business. One day a woman called to inquire when he could work on her car. "I'm not busy now," he replied. "Bring it right in."

A short time later, the woman pulled into the service bay, stopping her small car perfectly over the wide, deep grease pit.

"Wow!" Remarked Wayne. "That's great driving. Your wheels only have a couple of inches to spare on each side of the pit."

She looked blankly at him and asked, "What pit?"

Car Warning

A husband, the owner of a new car, was somewhat reluctant to allow his wife to drive his prize possession, even to the grocery store, which was a few blocks from the house.

After she insisted, he finally relented, cautioning her as she departed, "Remember, if you have an accident, the newspaper will print your age."

Cart Ads

My father is a skilled CPA who is not great at self-promotion. So when an advertising company offered to put my father's business placard in the shopping carts of a supermarket, my dad jumped at the chance. Fully a year went by before we got a call that could be traced to those placards.

"Richard Larson, CPA?" the caller asked.

"That's right," my father answered. "May I help you?"

"Yes," the voice said. "One of your shopping carts is in my yard, and I want you to come and get it."

Caution

A pharmacy major was taking a course in dispensing. One day they were discussing the various labels affixed to prescription containers, such as, "Take with food" and "Take with water".

At the end of class, the professor passed out a few sample labels.

Days later he noticed that one member of the class had stuck one of them onto his chemistry textbook. It read: "Caution: may cause extreme drowsiness."

Cave Soliciting

Dr. Schwartz decided to take a week off from the pressures of the office and went skiing. Alas, no sooner did he reach the slopes than he heard an ominous rumbling: moments later a sheet of snow came crashing toward him. Fortunately, Dr. Schwartz was able to jump into a cave just before the avalanche hit. Just as fortunately, he had matches with him and was able to light a fire. Hours later, when everyone but Dr. Schwartz had returned, a rescue team was sent to search for him. After several hours they saw smoke curling from the cave and went to investigate.

Poking his head into the entrance, one of the rescuers yelled "Dr. Schwartz, are you there? It's the Red Cross."

Bristling, the harried doctor called back, "I already gave at the office!"

Cell Phone

Cell service in our area was so rotten we told our service provider to cancel the contract.

About a week later, we received a letter saying they wanted to continue the relationship. The reason that they were writing? They had been unsuccessful in contacting us by phone. Hel-lo?

Check Signing

Mr. Greenberg was an illiterate immigrant, but he worked hard, saved his pennies, and started a small business. It did well, and soon he had enough money to send for the wife and children.

The work kept him very busy, so he never had time to learn to write, but the bank was happy to do business with him, even though his signature consisted of two "a"s.

He prospered, he opened more stores, the children were transferred to private schools, the family moved into a fancy house (with one staircase going nowhere just for show),...you get the idea.

One day his banker, Mr. Smith, asked him to drop by. "So vat's the problem?" Greenberg asked, a bit anxiously.

Smith waved a bunch of checks at him. "Perhaps nothing," he said, "but I wanted to be on the safe side. These recent checks of yours are all signed with three "a"s, but your signature of record has just two."

Greenberg looked embarrassed. "I'm sorry about making trouble," he said, "but my wife said that since I'm now such a high class rich guy, I should have a middle name!"

Chicken Farming

A life-long city man, tired of the rat race, decided he was going to give up the city life, move to the country, and become a chicken farmer. He found a nice, used chicken farm, which he bought. His next door neighbor was also a chicken farmer.

The neighbor came for a visit one day and said, "Chicken farming isn't easy. Tell you what. To help you get started, I'll give you 100 chickens."

The new chicken farmer was thrilled. Two weeks later the new neighbor stopped by to see how things were going. The new farmer said, "Not too good. All 100 chickens died."

The neighbor said, "Oh, I can't believe that. I've never had any trouble with my chickens. I'll give you 100 more."

Another two weeks went by, and the neighbor stopped in again. The new farmer said, "You're not going to believe this, but the second 100 chickens died too. "

Astounded, the neighbor asked, "what went wrong? What did you do to them?"

"Well," says the new farmer, "I'm not sure whether I'm planting them too deep or not far enough apart."

Children Are Quick

Teacher: Maria, go to the map and find North America.
Maria: Here it is.
Teacher: Correct. Now class, who discovered America?
Class: Maria.

~~~~~~~~~~~~~~~~~~~~~~~~~~

Teacher: Why are you late Frank?
Frank: Because of the sign.
Teacher: What sign?
Frank: The one that says, "School ahead. Go slow."

~~~~~~~~~~~~~~~~~~~~~~~~~~

Teacher: John, why are you doing your multiplication on the floor?
John: You told me to do it without using tables.

~~~~~~~~~~~~~~~~~~~~~~~~~~

Teacher: Greg, how would you spell "crocodile?"
Greg: K-R-O-K-O-D-I-A-L
Teacher: No Greg, that's incorrect.
Greg: Maybe it's incorrect, but you asked me how "I" spelled it.

~~~~~~~~~~~~~~~~~~~~~~~~~~

Teacher: Ryan, what is the chemical formula for water?
Ryan: H I J K L M N O
Teacher: Ryan, what are you talking about?
Ryan: Well, yesterday you said it was H to O.

~~~~~~~~~~~~~~~~~~~~~~~~~~

Teacher: Hunter, name one important thing that we have today that we didn't have 10 years ago.
Hunter: Me!

Teacher: Adam, why do you always get so dirty?
Adam: Well, I guess it's because I'm a lot closer to the ground than you are.

~~~~~~~~~~~~~~~~~~~~~~~~~~

Teacher: Beth, give me a sentence starting with "I".
Beth: I is…
Teacher: No Beth…Always say "I am"…not "I is".
Beth: All right…"I am the ninth letter of the alphabet."

~~~~~~~~~~~~~~~~~~~~~~~~~~

Teacher: Daniel, your composition on "My Dog" is exactly the same as your brother's composition. Did you copy off of him?
Daniel: No teacher, it's the same dog.

~~~~~~~~~~~~~~~~~~~~~~~~~~

Teacher: Parker, what do you call a person who keeps on talking to people who are no longer interested?
Parker: A teacher.

Children at Play

As newlyweds, my wife and I hosted a family get-together at our apartment, which had a large grassy field and superb children's playground next door. My wife organized games outdoors for our eight nieces and nephews, and the laughter and activity drew other children, until about thirty children were playing and clamoring for my wife's attention. After three hours, she called it quits.

The next morning while we were getting ready for work, two boys knocked on our patio door and asked if our children could come out and play. I told them we had no children; our nieces and nephews had just been visiting. Looking momentarily dejected, they brightened considerably as they asked, "Well, then, can your wife come out and play?"

Children's Exams

Enjoy these children's science exam answers.

Q: Name the four seasons.
A: Salt, pepper, mustard, and vinegar.

Q: What does the word 'benign' mean?'
A: Benign is what you will be after you be eight.

Q: How can you delay milk turning sour?
A: Keep it in the cow.

Q: What are steroids?
A: Things for keeping carpets still on the stairs.

Q: How are the main parts of the body categorized? (E.G., Abdomen)
A: The body is consisted into three parts—the brainium, the borax, and the abdominal cavity. The brainium contains the brain; the borax contains the heart and lungs; and the abdominal cavity contains the five bowels a, e, i, o, and u.

Q: How is dew formed?
A: The sun shines down on the leaves and makes them perspire.

Children's Kitchen Terms

Boil: The point a parent reaches upon hearing the automatic "Yuck" before a food is even tasted.
Casserole: Combination of favorite foods that go uneaten because they are mixed together.
Dessert: The reason for eating a meal.
Evaporate: Magic trick performed by children when it comes time to clear the table or wash dishes.
Fruit: A natural sweet not to be confused with dessert.
Refrigerator: A very expensive and inefficient room air conditioner when not being used as an art gallery.
Soda Pop: Shake 'N Spray.
Table Leg: Percussion instrument.

Chuckles

"Does your husband always live up to what he said when he was courting you?"

"Always. He used to say he wasn't good enough for me. He's been proving it ever since."

"What's for dinner?" asked the cannibal chief. Answered his wife: "Baked beings."

Did you hear about the fellow who fell into a lens-grinding machine and made a spectacle of himself?

"These sausages you sent me are meat at one end and breadcrumbs at the other," said Mrs. Andrews.

"Yes, madam," replied the butcher; "in these hard times it is difficult to make both ends meat."

Hotel Clerk: "I beg your pardon, but what is your name?"

Indignant guest, who had just signed the register: "Name? Don't you see my signature there on the register?"

Clerk: "I do, sir. That's what aroused my curiosity."

Clever

Cannibal: Someone who is fed up with people.
Chickens: The only animals you eat before they are born and after they are dead.
Committee: A body that keeps minutes and wastes hours.
Dust: Mud with the juice squeezed out.
Egotist: Someone who is usually me-deep in conversation.
Handkerchief: Cold Storage.
Inflation: Cutting money in half without damaging the paper.
Mosquito: An insect that makes you like flies better.
Secret: Something you tell to one person at a time.
Skeleton: A bunch of bones with the person scraped off.
Toothache: The pain that drives you to extraction.
Tomorrow: One of the greatest labor-saving devices of today.
Yawn: An honest opinion openly expressed.
Wrinkles: Something other people have.

Clunker Leak

As the owner of a clunker, I was used to dealing with a variety of car breakdowns. One day at the supermarket, just after I had filled my trunk with groceries, I noticed a stream of fluid pouring out of the bottom of the car. I knew I had to get home before the car was once again out of action.

When I arrived, I asked my husband to take a look at the problem. Expecting the worst, I braced myself for his diagnosis. When he came back in, he was smiling. "It's apple juice," he said.

Collecting Wood

It was autumn, and an Indian son at the remote reservation asked their new chief if the winter was going to be cold or mild. Since he was an Indian Chief in a modern society, he had never been taught the old secrets, and when he looked at the sky, he couldn't tell what the weather was going to be. Nevertheless, to be on the safe side, he replied to his tribe that the winter was indeed going to be cold and that the members of the village should collect wood to be prepared.

But, also being a practical leader, after several days he got an idea. He went to the phone booth, called the National Weather Service and asked, "Is the coming winter going to be cold?"

"It looks like this winter is going to be quite cold indeed," the meteorologist at the weather service responded. So he went back to his people and told them to collect even more wood in order to be prepared.

One week later he called the National Weather Service again. "Is it going to be a very cold winter?"

"Yes," the man at the National Weather Service again replied, "it's going to be a very cold winter." The chief again went back to his people and ordered them to collect every scrap of wood they could find.

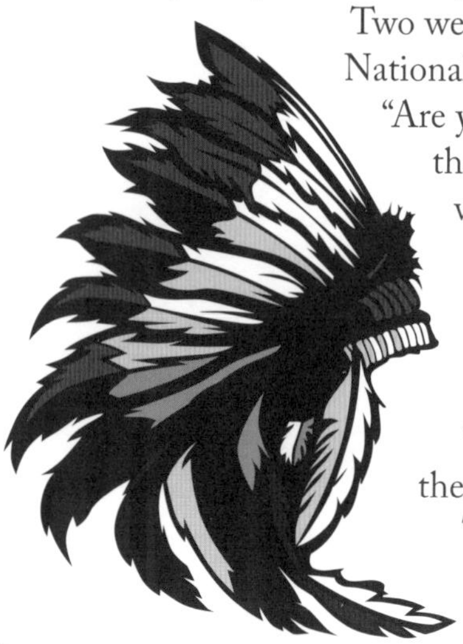

Two weeks later he called the National Weather Service again. "Are you absolutely sure that the winter is going to be very cold?"

"Absolutely," the man replied. "It's going to be one of the coldest winters ever."

"How can you be so sure?" the chief asked.

The weatherman replied, "The Indians are collecting wood like crazy."

Communication

A bricklayer at my husband's construction job routinely complained about the contents of his lunch box. "I'm sick and tired of getting the same old thing!" he declared one day. "Tonight I'll set my wife straight."

The next day the men could hardly wait until lunchtime to hear what happened. "You bet I told her," the bricklayer boasted. "I said, 'No more of the same old stuff. Be creative!' We had quite an argument, but I got my point across."

He had indeed. In front of an admiring audience, he opened his lunch box to find that his wife had packed a coconut—and a hammer.

Confusing Directions

We go up to Harrisburg, down to Allentown, out to Pittsburgh, in to Lebanon, front to Myerstown, back to Frystown, and over to Richland. What is it that determines whether we go up, down, out, in, front, back, or over? It gets even more complicated when some folks who live in a slightly different locality say they go up to Allentown or down to Harrisburg, or up to Richland. Are North and South identified with up and down? But then how do we identify East and West? It almost makes you want to jump up and down trying to figure it all out but that doesn't get you anywhere either. You keep ending up at the same place. Or is it down? When we let go of a balloon it goes up, literally. Now that is up. But we don't go that direction when we travel do we? Perhaps we ought to fly if we want to go up to Harrisburg. But that's confusing too, because if we go up we also need to come down.

Then there's the front and back issue to deal with. Who is facing front anyhow and how do we determine which way they are turned? Is it another North and South deal or what? Whichever direction I head, the town I travel to will be in front of me and when I leave it will be in back of me. So how do I decide if I'm going front or back? And over! What bizarre driving habits do we have? Over; is that sideways, or is it just a bumpy ride over the objects in your path? Hopefully we arrive with all four wheels on the ground!

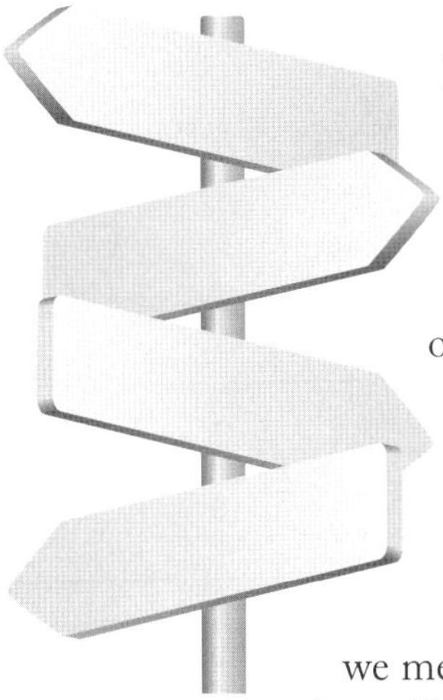

In and out. That must be East and West because we go out West and in East. Wow that works! Or does it? Isn't it back East? Don't we go in when we arrive at a place and out when we leave? If so, are we always leaving when we go West and arriving when we go East? If we go back East, why don't we go front West?

Hopefully we know what we mean when we say it. For the stranger trying to learn English don't ask me to explain it. Whether it's up, down, in, out, front, back, over, or whatever means you choose, I hope you arrive at your destination fully alert and unscathed and hopefully not too confused.

—M. Gingrich

Cookie Monster

Returning from a trip to visit my grandmother in Canada, I was stopped by a state trooper in New York for exceeding the speed limit. Grateful to have received a warning instead of a ticket, I gave him a small bag of my grandmother's delicious chocolate chip cookies and proceeded on my way.

Later, I was stopped by another trooper. "What have I done?" I asked.

"Nothing," the trooper said, smiling. "I heard you were passing out great chocolate chip cookies."

Cooking From Scratch

My mother never let me do much in the kitchen except things like making vegetable salad, or stirring the gravy so it wouldn't be lumpy. As a result, my cooking knowledge and ability was practically non-existent when I got married. But I did remember mother mentioning to her many friends that she'd made certain cakes, pies, and such from scratch. So, my first priority after the honeymoon was to locate some scratch.

With mother's delicious cakes in mind, my first trip to the supermarket was to buy some scratch. I found the aisle that read "baking items" and spent a good fifteen minutes looking at everything from Mazola oil to corn starch, sugar, flour, and chocolate, but no signs of scratch could I see. I was sure it couldn't be with pickles and mayonnaise or in the meat department.

I asked a clerk if they carried scratch. He looked at me rather oddly and finally said, "Oh, you'll have to go to the store at the corner of Colfax and Wadsworth."

When I got there, it turned out to be a feed store. I thought this rather odd (but I guess cakes are rather odd), but I guess cakes are food, so I went in and said, "I'd like to buy some scratch." When the clerk asked me how much I wanted, I suggested a pound or two. His reply was, "How many chickens do you have? It only comes in 20 pound bags." I really didn't understand why he mentioned chickens, but I had heard my mother say that she'd made some chicken casserole from scratch, so I bought 20 pounds and hurried on home, delighted with my purchase. My next problem was to find a recipe calling for scratch. I went through every single page of my lovely "Better Homes and Gardens Cookbook" given as a wedding present but didn't find even one recipe requiring scratch. Subsequently, I spent hours in the nearby library trying to end my search. No luck. There I was with 20 pounds of scratch and no recipe.

When I had opened the bag of scratch, I had some doubts that a beautiful, fluffy, moist cake could ever result from such hard looking ingredients, but then, I was sure that with the addition of liquids and the use of heat, the results would be successful. I had no need or desire to mention my problem to my husband as he had suggested very early in our marriage that he liked to cook, and would gladly take over that department. One day when I was raving about his chocolate pie, he proudly acknowledged that he had made it from scratch, so I was assured that it could be done.

Now, as many of you know, being a new bride is pretty scary, especially when three meals a day are on one's mind all the time. During the first week I learned that our muffins, waffles, pancakes, pies, cakes, and even lemon pudding he'd made from scratch. Well, if he'd made all those things from scratch, I was sure he'd bought a twenty pound bag of it, too. But I

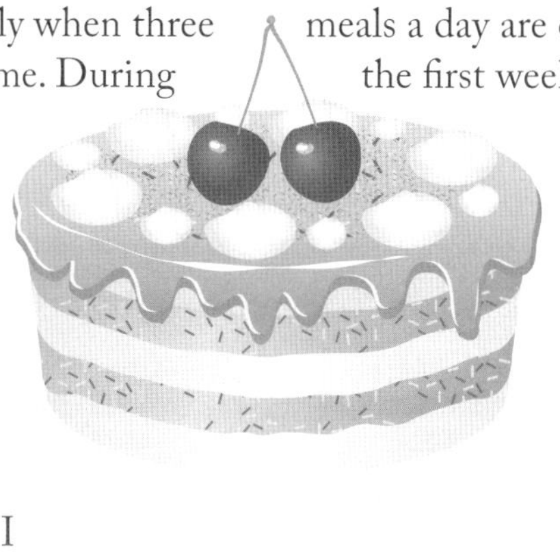

couldn't find where he stored it. I checked my own supply, which I kept hidden in the bedroom closet behind all my clothes, but it was still full. The mystery continued, but I was never one to give up or reveal my problem. The biggest jolt came one day when I heard a friend bragging to my husband that he'd built his house himself from scratch. In quick succession I heard via numerous acquaintances that they'd made dresses, costumes, and even jackets from scratch, in addition to their numerous desserts and pastries.

At this point, I was almost ready to give up because all the world seemed to know everything about scratch except me. But pride kept me silent. If paper can be made from wood, and glue from horses' hoofs, maybe wood or cloth could be made from scratch.

By now, the detective in me was getting weary, so I decided to try a different approach. One day when my husband was doing nothing in particular, I said, "Honey, I wish you'd teach me how to bake a cake." He got out the flour, sugar, eggs, milk, shortening, chocolate, and baking soda, but there was no sign of scratch. I watched him carefully blend it all together, pour it into a pan, then put it in the oven to bake. An hour later, when we were eating the cake, he couldn't understand my asking, "Honey, why don't we raise a few chickens?"

Country Tunes

My wife and I were browsing in a crafts store when I noticed a display of country-style musical instruments. After looking over the flutes, dulcimers, and recorders, I picked up a shiny, one stringed instrument I took to be a mouth harp. I put it to my lips and, much to the amusement of other shoppers, twanged a few notes on it.

After watching from a distance, my wife came up and whispered in my ear, "I hate to tell you this, honey, but you're trying to play a cheese slicer."

Crowded Bus

It was rush hour, and when the bus finally arrived, it was packed. I tried to force my way on, but no one would budge, although there was ample room in the back. Then the bus driver took over.

"Excuse me, Ladies and Gentlemen," he shouted. "Will all the beautiful, smart people please move to the back of the bus, and all the ugly stupid people stay up front?"

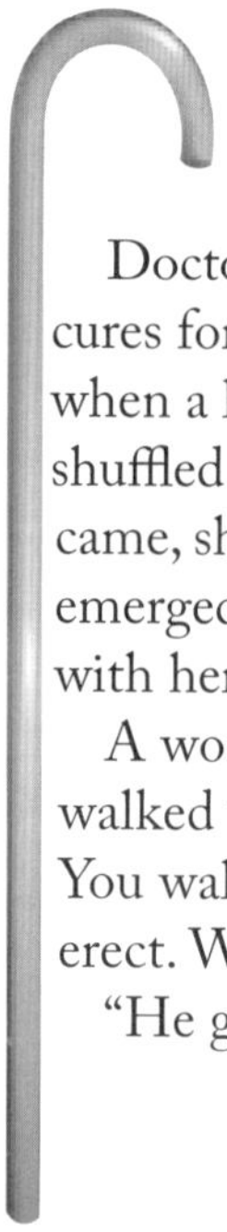

Cure For Arthritis

Doctor Bloomfield, who was known for miraculous cures for arthritis, had a waiting room full of people when a little old lady, completely bent over in half, shuffled in slowly, leaning on her cane. When her turn came, she went into the doctor's office, and, amazingly, emerged within five minutes walking completely erect with her head held high.

A woman in the waiting room who had seen all this walked up to the little old lady and said, "It's a miracle! You walked in bent in half and now you're walking erect. What did that doctor do?"

"He gave me a longer cane!" she replied.

Customer Service

After booking my 80-year-old grandmother on a flight from Florida to Nevada, I called the airline to go over her special needs. The representative listened patiently as I requested a wheelchair and an attendant for my grandmother because of her arthritis and impaired vision to the point of near blindness.

My apprehension lightened a bit when the woman assured me that everything would be taken care of. I thanked her.

"Oh, you're welcome," she replied. I was about to hang up when she cheerfully asked…"And will your grandmother need a rental car?"

Cute Baby

When we brought our newborn son to the pediatrician for his first check up, the doctor said, "You have a cute baby." Smiling, I said, "I'll bet you say that to all the new parents."

"No," he replied, "just to those whose babies are really cute."

"So what do you say to the others?" I asked.

"He looks just like you," he replied.

Dangerous Cargo

Our supply clerk at the factory where I work, discovered a box that was left on the loading dock with this warning printed on it: Danger! Do not touch!

Management was called and all employees were told to stay clear of the box until it could be analyzed.

When the foreman arrived, he donned gloves and safety glasses, and then, very carefully opened the box. Inside were 25 signs that read: Danger! Do not touch!

Dangling Participles

- The burglar was about 30 years old, white, 5' 10", with wavy hair weighing about 150 pounds.
- The family lawyer will read the will tomorrow at the residence of Mr. Hannon, who died June 19, to accommodate his relatives.
- Mrs. Shirley Baxter, who went deer hunting with her husband, is very proud that she was able to shoot a fine buck as well as her husband.
- Organ donations from the living reached a record high last year, outnumbering donors who are dead for the first time.
- The dog was hungry and made the mistake of nipping a 2-year-old that was trying to force feed it in his ear.
- We spent most of our time sitting on the back porch watching the cows playing Scrabble and reading.
- Hunting can also be dangerous, as in the case of pygmies hunting elephants armed only with spears.

Dead Donkey

Morris, a city boy, moved to the country and bought a donkey from an old farmer for $100. The farmer agreed to deliver the mule the next day. The next day, the farmer drove up and said, "Sorry, but I have some bad news. The donkey died."

"Well, then, just give me my money back."

"Can't do that. I went and spent it already."

"Okay, then. Just unload the donkey."

"What ya gonna do with him?"

"I'm going to raffle him off."

"You can't raffle off a dead donkey!"

"Sure I can. I just won't tell anybody he's dead."

A month later the farmer met up with the city boy and asked, "Whatever happened with that dead donkey?" "I raffled him off. I sold five hundred tickets at $2 a piece and made a profit of $998."

"Didn't anyone complain?"

"Just the guy who won, so I gave him his $2 back."

Dean's List

College student: "Hey dad! I've got some great news for you!"

Father: "What, son?"

College student: "Remember that $500 you promised me if I made the dean's list?"

Father: "I certainly do."

College student: "Well, you get to keep it."

Decision

A group of junior-level executives were participating in a management training program. The seminar leader pounded home his point about the need to make decisions and then take action on them.

"For instance," he said, "If you had five frogs on a log and three of them decided to jump, how many frogs would you have left on the log?"

The answers from the group were unanimous: "Two."

"Wrong," replied the speaker, "There would still be five because there is a difference between deciding to jump and jumping."

Deputy Sheriff Interview

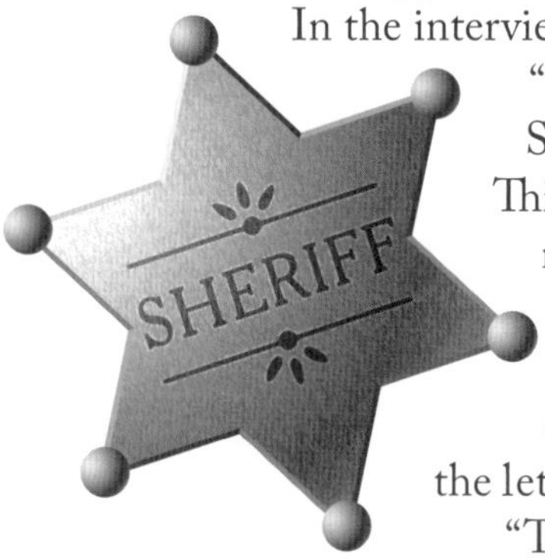

Simon applied for a deputy sheriffs job. In the interview, the sheriff asked him, "What's one and one?"

Simon answered, "Eleven." This wasn't what the sheriff meant, but he had to admit the boy was right. Next question: "What two days of the week start with the letter T?"

"Today and tomorrow."

The sheriff was impressed by the way Simon thought outside the box, so he challenged him. "Who killed Abraham Lincoln?"

Simon looked surprised and admitted, "I don't know."

"Well, go home and work on that for a while," replied the sheriff, satisfied that he'd stumped him.

Simon went home and told his mother, "The interview went great! First day on the job and I'm already working on a murder case!"

Details

A man walked into a very expensive bakery shop where they specialized in making cakes to order.

"I'd like you to bake me a cake in the shape of the letter 'S'," he said. "Can you do that?"

"Why certainly!" said the baker. "We can make a cake in any shape. When would you like it to be ready?"

"Have it ready by tomorrow at three o'clock. I'll call for it," said the man.

The next day at three o'clock, the man came in for his cake. The baker proudly displayed the cake he had made. It was shaped like the letter and decorated beautifully.

"Oh!" cried the man. "That's all wrong! That's not what I want. You made it in the shape of a regular printed 'S'. I wanted a graceful script 'S'. That won't do at all!"

"I'm terribly sorry you're so disappointed," said the baker. "We aim to please. I'll make you another cake at no extra charge. Don't worry."

"All right, then," said the man. "I'll be back at six o'clock for the cake. And this time I hope it's right."

At six o'clock the man came in. The baker brought in the new cake. He was all smiles. "Isn't this a beauty!" he exclaimed.

The man looked at the cake. His face lit up.

"That's perfect!" he said. "Just what I wanted."

"I'm delighted," said the baker. "Now tell me, sir, what kind of a box shall I put it in?"

"Oh, don't bother wrapping it up," said the man, "I'll eat it here."

Diagnosis

One afternoon, a man went to his doctor and told him that he hadn't been feeling well lately. The doctor examined the man, left the room, and came back with three different bottles of pills.

The doctor said, "Take the green pill with a big glass of water when you wake up. Take the blue pill with a big glass of water after you eat lunch. Then just before going to bed, take the red pill with another big glass of water."

Startled to be put on so much medicine, the man stammered, "Wow Doc, exactly what is my problem?"

The doctor replied, "You're not drinking enough water."

Did I Read That Sign Right?

- In a London department store:
  Bargain Basement Upstairs

- Notice in health food shop window:
  Closed Due To Illness

- Spotted in a safari park:
  Elephants Please Stay In Your Car

- Notice in a farmer's field:
  The Farmer Allows Walkers To Cross The Field For Free, But The Bull Charges.

- On a repair shop door:
  We Can Repair Anything. (Please Knock Hard On The Door—The Bell Doesn't Work)

Dishwasher Repair

Wanda's dishwasher quit working so she called a repairman. Since she had to go to work the next day, she told the repairman, "I'll leave the key under the mat. Fix the dishwasher, leave the bill on the counter, and I'll mail you a check.

"Oh, by the way don't worry about my bulldog Spike. He won't bother you. But, whatever you do, do NOT, under ANY circumstances, talk to my parrot! I REPEAT, DO NOT TALK TO MY PARROT!!!

"When the repairman arrived at Wanda's apartment the following day, he discovered the biggest, meanest looking bulldog he had ever seen. But, just as she had said, the dog just lay there on the carpet watching the repairman go about his work.

The parrot, however, drove him nuts the whole time with his incessant fussing. Finally the repairman couldn't contain himself any longer and yelled, "Shut up, you stupid bird!"

To which the parrot replied, "Get him, Spike!"

Doctor Mistake

During the course of being interviewed by the press, the noted doctor was asked by a reporter: "Doctor, did you ever make a serious mistake?"

"Yes," was the reply, "I once cured a millionaire in three visits!"

Doctor's Orders

A man was showing his friend a new set of matching golf clubs he had just bought.

"Doctor's orders," the man told his friend. "My wife and I have been gaining too much weight, and we went to see the doctor about it. He said we needed more exercise, so I joined the country club and bought myself this set of golf clubs."

"What did you buy your wife?" the friend asked.

The man said, "A new matching bicycle and lawn mower."

Does He Have a License?

During a county-wide drive to round up all unlicensed dogs, a patrolman signaled a car to pull over to the curb. When the driver asked why he had been stopped, the officer pointed to the big dog sitting on the seat beside him. "Does your dog have a license?" He asked. "Oh, no," the man said, "He doesn't need one. I always do the driving."

Dog Food

After our friend Tom had been a temporary bachelor for several weeks, we stopped by his home to visit him. My wife asked if he was eating properly. "Well, I do eat a lot of dog food," Tom told her.

"Dog food!" My wife exclaimed, horrified. "I can't believe you would be eating anything like that!"

"Come to the kitchen and I'll show you," Tom replied.

Opening the refrigerator door, he waved his hand at a row of doggie bags from half of the restaurants in town.

Dog Growth

A distraught dog owner called his vet pleading for an immediate appointment. He explained that his dog had a large growth or swelling near the corner of its mouth. The vet told him to bring the animal right over.

When the man came in, the vet examined the dog as the man stood by, anxiously waiting. At last the vet turned to him and asked, "Do you have any children?"

"Oh, is it contagious?" The man gasped.

"No," the doctor answered. "It's bubblegum."

Dog Nap

A dog came into the garden. I could tell from his collar and well-fed belly that he had a home.

He followed me into the house, down the hall, and fell asleep in a corner. An hour later, he went to the door and I let him out.

The next day he was back, resumed his position in the hall, and slept for an hour. This continued for several weeks.

Curious, I pinned a note to his collar: "Every afternoon your dog comes to my house for a nap."

The next day he arrived with a different note pinned to his collar: "He lives in a home with ten children. He's trying to catch up on his sleep. May I come with him tomorrow?"

Dog Wash

A young boy, about eight years old, was at the corner Mom & Pop grocery picking out a pretty good size box of laundry detergent. The grocer walked over, and trying to be friendly, asked the boy if he had a lot of laundry to do.

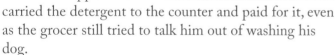

"Oh, no laundry," the boy said, "I'm going to wash my dog."

"But you shouldn't use this to wash your dog. It's very powerful and if you wash your dog in this, he'll get sick. In fact, it might even kill him."

But the boy was not to be stopped and carried the detergent to the counter and paid for it, even as the grocer still tried to talk him out of washing his dog.

About a week later the boy was back in the store to buy some candy. The grocer asked the boy how his dog was doing.

"Oh, he died," the boy said.

The grocer, trying not to be an I-told-you-so, said he was sorry the dog died but added, "I tried to tell you not to use that detergent on your dog."

"Well," the boy replied, "I don't think it was the detergent that killed him."

"Oh? What was it then?"

"I think it was the spin cycle!"

Doilies

As a new bride, Aunt Edna moved into the small home on her husband's ranch near Snowflake. She put a shoe box on a shelf in her closet and asked her husband never to touch it.

For 50 years Uncle Jack left the box alone, until Aunt Edna was old and dying.

One day when he was putting their affairs in order, he found the box again and thought it might hold something important.

Opening it, he found two doilies and $82,500 in cash. He took the box to her and asked about the contents.

"My mother gave me that box the day we married," she explained. "She told me to make a doily to help ease my frustrations every time I got upset at you." Uncle Jack was very touched that in 50 years she'd only been upset at him twice.

"What's the $82,500 for?" he asked. "Oh, well that's the money I've made selling the doilies."

Dollar Measure

Our mom needed a new mattress for her antique bed, so my brother, Josh, and I decided to buy her one as a gift. The problem was we weren't sure what to get, because it was an odd size. Fortunately, my brother happened to be visiting my mother one day when I called home. "Measure the bed frame before you leave," I told him.

"I don't have a tape measure."

"You can use a dollar bill," I suggested, "each one is six inches long."

"Can't," he replied after digging through his wallet, "I only have a ten."

Donkey Purchase

A man bought a donkey from a preacher. The preacher told the man that this donkey had been trained in a very unique way (being the donkey of a preacher). The only way to make the donkey go, is to say, "Hallelujah!" The only way to make the donkey stop, is to say, "Amen!"

The man was pleased with his purchase and immediately got on the animal to try out the preacher's instructions.

"Hallelujah!" shouted the man. The donkey began to trot. "Amen!" shouted the man. The donkey stopped immediately. "This is great!" said the man. With a "Hallelujah," off he rode very proud of his new purchase. The man traveled for a long time through some mountains. Soon he was heading towards a cliff. He could not remember the word to make the donkey stop. "Stop," said the man. "Halt!" he cried. The donkey just kept going. "Oh, no... Bible...Church!...Please Stop!!" shouted the man. The donkey just began to trot faster. He was getting closer and closer to the edge of the cliff.

Finally, in desperation, the man said a prayer... "Please, dear Lord. Please make this donkey stop before I go off the end of this mountain, In Jesus name, Amen."

The donkey came to an abrupt stop just one step from the edge of the cliff.

"Hallelujah!" shouted the man.

Don't Jump

While ferrying workers back and forth from our offshore oil rig, the helicopter I was in lost power and went down. Fortunately, it landed safely in the lake. Struggling to get out, one man tore off his seat belt, inflated his life vest, and jerked open the exit door.

"Don't jump!" the pilot yelled. "This thing is supposed to float!" As the man leapt from the helicopter into the lake, he yelled back, "Yeah, and it's supposed to fly too!"

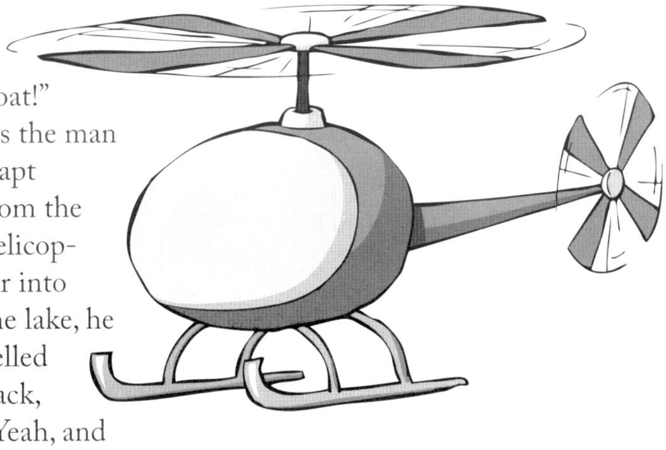

Double Checking The Locks

My dad was on a trip in New York City, and was very careful about double checking the locks on his pickup truck because his laptop computer was inside.

Business completed, he came back, unlocked, and drove off. Being a warm day, he reached over to crank down the window, only to discover he had never closed it!

The laptop was fine, but his self-confidence was a little hurt.

Drawing Of God

A kindergarten teacher was observing her classroom of children while they drew. She would occasionally walk around to see each child's artwork. As she got to one little girl who was working diligently, she asked what the drawing was.

The girl replied, "I'm drawing God."

The teacher paused and said, "But no one knows what God looks like."

Without missing a beat, or looking up from her drawing the girl replied, "They will in a minute."

Driving Around

I tell you, men drivers are a hazard to traffic. Driving to work this morning on Highway 11 from Albert Street, I looked over to my left and there's this man in a Mustang doing 95 miles per hour with his face up next to his rear view mirror...shaving...

I looked away for a couple seconds and when I looked back, he's halfway over in my lane. Scared me so bad I almost dropped my donut in my coffee.

Early Bird Rant

Okay, what is the deal with "The early bird gets the worm"? He gets up early, and all he gets is a worm? It says "the worm," which means one single worm. That doesn't seem very fair, for a bird that goes through the trouble of getting up early.

Myself, I would rather sleep late and get the "worm and grub" brunch special at the local diner. I can't imagine that an early 5:00 a.m. worm is going to taste that much better than a plate of later 11:00 a.m. worms! And, speaking of which, what's the deal with the early worm? He gets up early to get a start on the day, because he has loads of work to do, and he gets eaten by a bird! Where is the moral of the story, when the lazy worms don't get eaten? Isn't that hypocritical? Seems to me that all the smart worms either work nights, or sleep late and get up after lunch. Isn't that sending the wrong message? Who made up these rules?

Elk Hunting

Two hunters got a pilot to fly them into the far north for elk hunting. They were quite successful in their venture and bagged six big bucks. The pilot came back, as arranged, to pick them up.

They started loading their gear into the plane, including the six elk. The pilot objected and said, "The plane can only take four of your elk; you will have to leave two behind."

They argued with him; the year before they had shot six and the pilot had allowed them to put all aboard. The plane was the same model and capacity. Reluctantly, the pilot finally permitted them to put all six aboard. When they attempted to take off and leave the valley, the little plane could not make it and they crashed into the wilderness.

Climbing out of the wreckage, one hunter said to the other, "Do you know where we are?"

"I think so," replied the other hunter. "I think this is about the same place where we crashed last year."

English Essay

Jimmy's English teacher was a perfectionist and demanded the very best of his pupils. So it was only to be expected that he would get furious when little Jimmy handed in a poor paper.

"This is the worst essay that has ever been my misfortune to read," ranted the teacher. "It has too many mistakes. I can't understand how one person would have made all these mistakes."

"One person didn't," replied little Jimmy defensively. "My father helped me."

ESP Banking

Tired of having to balance his wife's checkbook, Mike made a deal with her (Cindy); he would only look at it after she had spent a few hours trying to wrestle it into shape. Only then would he lend his expertise.

The following night, after spending hours poring over stubs and figures, Cindy said proudly, "There! I've done it! I made it balance!"

Impressed, Mike came over to take a look.

"Let's see…mortgage 550.00, electricity 70.50, phone 35.00." His brow wrinkled as he read the last entry. "It says here ESP, 615.00. What is that?"

"Oh," she said, "That means, Error Some Place!!!"

Executive Approval

For many years I worked as a receptionist and switchboard operator at a busy company. After a good annual review, my supervisor told me I was up for a raise, pending approval of the vice president.

A month later, my supervisor called me into his office and told me the VP had refused to approve the raise. His reason? I clearly wasn't doing my job. Every time he saw me, I was either chatting with someone in the lobby or on the phone.

Expen$ive $chool

Dear Dad,

I gue$$ you $ee why I'm $ending you thi$ me$$age. Plea$e $end me $ome as $oon a$ po$$ible. $chool $ure i$ expen$ive.

$o long. It'$ che$$ time.

Your $on,
$am

Dear $on,

Thanks for your note. Nothing much noteworthy is happening here now.

No one notified us of your need. It was noble of you to send another note.

We will not be able to come in November. That's all for now.

Dad

Face Warning

Finding one of her students making faces at others on the playground, Ms. Smith stopped to gently reprove the child.

Smiling sweetly, she said, "You know, Bobby, when I was a little girl, I was told that if I made ugly faces, my face would freeze and always stay like that."

Bobby looked up into her face and replied, "Well, Ms. Smith, you can't say you weren't warned."

Factory Supplies

At the end of my factory shift, I was asked to purchase some supplies. The machine's conveyor belts needed talcum powder to prevent them from sticking, and we had run out of aspirin for workers with noise-induced tension headaches.

I drove to the nearest store and loaded a shopping cart with four cases of baby powder and several boxes of aspirin.

As the man behind me in the checkout line peered at my purchases, he laughed and exclaimed, "Must be quite the family!"

Outsmarted

A woman walked into a bank in New York City and asked for the loan officer. She said she's going to Europe on business for two weeks and needs to borrow $5,000. The bank officer explained that the bank will need some kind of security for the loan, so the woman handed over the keys to a new Rolls Royce (the car was parked on the street in front of the bank, she had the title and everything checked out. The bank agreed to accept the car as collateral for the loan.

The bank's president and its officers all enjoyed a good laugh at the woman for using a $250,000 Rolls as collateral against a $5,000 loan. An employee of the bank then proceeded to drive the Rolls into the banks' underground garage and parked it there.

Two weeks later, the woman returned, repaid the $5,000 and the interest which came to $15.41. The loan officer said, "Miss, we are very happy to have had your business, and this transaction has worked out very nicely, but we are a little puzzled. While you were away, we checked you out and found that you are a multimillionaire. What puzzles us is, why would you bother to borrow $5,000?"

The woman replied, "Where else in New York City can I park my car for two weeks for only $15.41 and expect it to be there when I return?"

Failing Eyesight

An older lady was expecting a gentleman friend to call on her later in the day. She was nervous because her eyesight was failing and was afraid her friend might reject her because she was less than perfect. So, she came up with a plan to prove to him that she could see perfectly.

She put a straight pin in a tree that was about 200 feet from her front porch.

When her beau arrived, they sat in the porch swing and were talking when she suddenly stopped the conversation and asked, "Is that a pin sticking in that tree?"

Her friend squinted his eyes and said, "I don't see a thing."

"Well, I'm going to go see," she said as she jumped up, ran toward the tree, and stumbled over the dog.

Faithfulness

The front door was accidentally left open and our dog was gone. After unsuccessfully whistling and calling, my husband got in the car and went looking for him. He drove around the neighborhood for some time with no luck. Finally he stopped beside a couple out for a walk and asked if they had seen our dog.

"You mean the one following your car?" They asked.

Father Takes His Turn

My sister works as a secretary for a number of medical doctors. One doctor was the father of ten children. One night it was his turn to stay home and take care of the house and the children while his wife got out to relax.

The doctor settled down in the living room to read his newspaper and magazines. There were children running all around, up and down stairs and just having a grand time. Finally about 8:00 p.m. the doctor called out with a loud voice," Okay, everybody upstairs and start getting ready for bed!"

There was a stampede of children heading up the stairs as they were ordered. The doctor settled down in his chair with a bit more of peace and quiet. Only a few minutes passed when he heard the distinct footsteps fall of someone coming down the stairs. He hollered out, "I told you to get upstairs and get ready for bed." The next thing he heard was the sound of feet running upstairs.

Once again, the doctor settled into his reading. Not two minutes passed until he heard the steps of someone coming down the stairs. He got up out of his chair and stood at the bottom of the stairs. With hands on his hips he looked up at the child and said, "Didn't I tell you to get upstairs and get ready for bed?"

Sheepishly the child looked at the doctor and said, "But Mister, I don't even live here!"

Fat Man Directions

You go to the Burger King® and turn right. Go two blocks to Wendy's® and turn left. Go three blocks and make a left turn at Taco Bell®. Follow for several hundred yards and turn right at Kentucky Fried Chicken®.

Final Exam

At Duke University, there were four sophomores taking chemistry and each of them had an "A" so far.

These four friends were so confident, that the weekend before finals, they decided to visit some friends and have a big party. They had a great time, but after all the partying, they slept all day Sunday and didn't make it back to Duke until early Monday morning.

Rather than taking the final at that time, they decided that after the final was over they would explain to their professor why they missed it.

They said that they visited friends but on the way back they had a flat tire. As a result, they missed the final.

The professor agreed they could make up the final the next day.

The guys were excited and relieved. They studied that night for the exam.

After taking their cell phones, the Professor placed each of them in separate rooms and gave each their test booklet. They had only one hour to complete the test.

They quickly answered the first essay problem worth 5 points. Cool, they thought, thinking this was going to be easy…they turned the page.

On the second page was written, "For 95 points: Which tire? _____".

Finances

My mother, who is 93, lives simply, but comfortably in an assisted-living home. Even though she has ample savings, she is always worried about the state of her finances.

My brother-in-law tried to ease her mind by telling her, "I've calculated that, given your expenses, you have enough money for at least the next 16 years."

"That's fine," Mom replied, "but how will I manage after that?"

First Driving Lesson

My teenaged niece, Elizabeth, was nervous as she took the wheel for her first driving lesson. As she was pulling out of the parking lot, the instructor said, "Turn left here, and don't forget to let the people behind you know what you're doing."

Elizabeth turned to the students sitting in the back seat and announced, "I'm going left."

Fish Heads

A customer at Green's Gourmet Grocery marveled at the proprietor's quick wit and intelligence.

"Tell me, Green, what makes you so smart?"

"I wouldn't share my secret with just anyone," Green replied, lowering his voice so the other shoppers wouldn't hear. "But since you're a good and faithful customer, I'll let you in on it. Fish heads. You eat enough of them, you'll be positively brilliant."

"You sell them here?" the customer asked.

"Only $4 apiece," said Green. The customer bought three. A week later, he was back in the store complaining that the fish heads were disgusting and he isn't any smarter.

"You didn't eat enough," said Green. The customer went home with twenty more fish heads. Two weeks later, he was back and this time he was really angry.

"Hey, Green," he said, "You're selling me fish heads for $4 a piece when I can buy the whole fish for $2. You're ripping me off!"

"You see?" said Green. "You're smarter already."

Fishing Advice

Two buddies were fishing, but they hadn't caught anything all day. Then another fisherman walked by with a huge load of fish. They asked him, "Excuse me, but where did you get all those fish?"

The other fisherman replied, "If you just go down the stream until the water isn't salty, you will find a ton of hungry fish."

They thanked him and went on their way. Fifteen minutes later, one fisherman said to the other, "Fill the bucket up with water and see if the water is salty."

He dipped the bucket in the stream and drank some. "Nope. Still salty." Thirty minutes later, he asked him to check again.

"Nope, still salty." One hour later they checked again. "Nope. Still salty."

"This isn't good," one fisherman finally said. "We have been walking for almost two hours and the water is still salty!"

"I know," replied the other. "And the bucket is almost empty!"

Floral Arrangement

The customer ordering a floral arrangement from my shop was giving me very specific guidelines. "Nothing fragrant," she instructed. "Nothing too tall or too wild. And no bright colors please. My house is decorated in beige and cream. Here is a wallpaper sample." She handed me a plain square of tan-colored paper.

"Your name?" I asked.

"Mrs. Bland," the woman replied.

Fishing Mirror

A fisherman from the city was out fishing on a lake in a small boat. He noticed another man in a small boat open his tackle box and take out a mirror. Being curious the man rowed over and asked, "What is the mirror for?"

"That's my secret way to catch fish," said the other man. "Shine the mirror on the top of the water. The fish notice the spot of sun on the water above and they swim to the surface. Then I just reach down and net them and pull them into the boat."

"Wow! Does that really work?"

"You bet it does."

"Would you be interested in selling that mirror? I'll give you $30 for it."

"Well, okay."

After the money was transferred, the city fisherman asked, "By the way, how many fish have you caught this week?"

"You're the sixth," he said.

Flat Tire Etiquette

The other day while driving in southwest Oklahoma I ran across this ol' boy who had a flat tire. He had pulled off on the side of the road and proceeded to put a bouquet of flowers in front of the car and one behind it. Then he got back in the car to wait. When I drove by, I studied the scene and noticed the Mississippi tag, but was so curious I turned around and went back.

I asked the ol' boy what the problem was. He replied, I have a flat tar."

Then I asked him, "But what's with the flowers?"

He told me, "When ya break down they tell ya to put flares in the front and flares in the back; I never understood it neither."

For Sale

A real-estate agent was driving around with a new trainee when she spotted a charming little farmhouse with a hand-lettered "For Sale" sign out front.

After briskly introducing herself and her associate to the startled occupant, the agent cruised from room to room, opening closets and cupboards, testing faucets, and pointing out where a new light fixture here and a little paint there would help. Pleased with her assertiveness, the woman was hopeful that the owner would offer her the listing.

"Ma'am," the man said, "I appreciate the home-improvement tips and all, but I think you read my sign wrong. It says, 'HORSE for sale.'"

Four Little Words

Heather and Marcy hadn't seen each other in awhile, so they decided to meet for lunch. The talk naturally got around to their respective love lives. Marcy confided that there really wasn't anyone special in her life.

Heather, on the other hand, was beaming about the new man she had found. "He's perfect. He's handsome, he's sweet, and last night when we went out to dinner, he said the four little words I've been waiting to hear a man say to me!"

"He said, 'Will you marry me'?" Marcy asked.

Heather replied, "No, he said, 'Put your money away'."

Free Almanac

One day I noticed an elderly man approach the counter, hat in hand, and asked the druggist for one of the store's free almanacs. Receiving the almanac, he thanked the druggist and added, "I sure do appreciate this. Last year I didn't get a copy and had to take the weather just as it came."

French Dream

A boy was having a lot of difficulty in French class. To encourage him, his teacher said, "You'll know you're really beginning to get it when you start dreaming in French."

The boy ran into class all excited one day, saying, "Teacher, teacher! I had a dream last night and everyone was talking in French!"

"Great!" Said the teacher; "what were they saying?"

"I don't know," the boy replied. "I couldn't understand them."

Fresh Fruit

A picky customer went into a small food shop and saw a new delivery of fresh fruit. "Give me two kilograms of oranges and wrap every orange up in a separate piece

Gated Community

Security and peace of mind were part of the reason we moved to a gated community. Both flew out the window the night I called a local pizza shop for a delivery.

"I'd like to order a large pepperoni pizza, please," I said, then gave him the address of our condominium. "We'll be there in about half an hour," the guy at the other end replied. "Your gate code is still 1238, right?"

Geography Jokes

Teacher: It's clear that you haven't studied your geography. What's your excuse?
Pupil: Well, my dad says the world is changing every day. So I decided to wait until it settles down!

Teacher: What are the small rivers that run into the Nile?
Pupil: The juve-niles!

Teacher: Why is the Mississippi such an unusual river?
Pupil: Because it has four eyes and can't see!

Teacher: What are the Great Plains?
Pupil: 747, Concorde, and F-16!

Pupil: My teacher was upset with me because I didn't know where the Rockies were.
Mother: Well, next time remember where you put things!

Teacher: Why does the Statue of Liberty stand in New York Harbor?
Pupil: Because it can't sit down!

Getting in Shape

Somewhat skeptical of his son's newfound determination to get into shape, the father nevertheless followed the teenager over to the sporting goods department to admire a set of weights.

"Please, dad," pleaded the boy, "I promise I'll use 'em every day."

"I don't know, Michael. It's really a commitment on your part," the father pointed out.

"Please, dad?" the boy continued.

"They're not cheap either," the father came back.

"I'll use 'em dad, I promise. You'll see."

Finally won over, the father paid for the equipment and headed for the door.

From the corner of the store he heard his son yelp, "What! You mean I have to carry them to the car?"

Getting Rid Of Pests

My husband works as a service technician for a large exterminating company. One of the rules of the company is that he has to confirm each appointment by phone the night before his service call to that household.

One evening he made such a call, and when a man answered the phone, he said, "Hi, this is Gary from A-Z Pest Control Company. Your wife phoned us."

There was a long silence, and then my husband heard the man on the other end say, "Honey, it's for you. Someone wants to talk to you about your relatives."

Gift Disappointment

The rich aunt was hurt and said to her nephew, "I'm sorry you don't like your gift. I asked you if you preferred a large check or a small check."

"I know, auntie," the nephew said contritely, "But I didn't know you were talking about neckties."

Gifts For Men

Buying gifts for men is not nearly as complicated as it is for women. Follow these rules and you should have no problems.

Rule **#1:** When in doubt—buy him a cordless drill. It does not matter if he already has one. I have a friend who owns seventeen, and he has yet to complain. As a man, you can never have too many cordless drills. No one knows why.

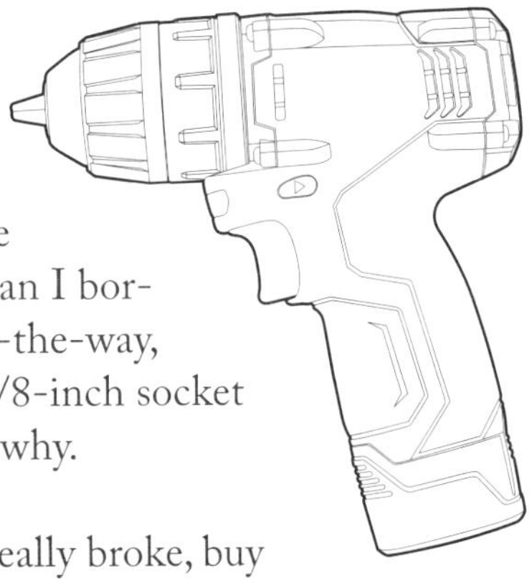

Rule #2: If you cannot afford a cordless drill, buy him anything with the word ratchet or socket in it. Men love saying those two words. "Hey George, can I borrow your ratchet?" "Ok. By-the-way, are you through with my 3/8-inch socket yet?" Again, no one knows why.

Rule #3: If you are really, really broke, buy him anything for his car. A 99¢ ice scraper, a small bottle of de-icer, or something to hang from his rear view mirror. Men love gifts for their cars. No one knows why.

Rule #4: Do not buy men socks. Do not buy men ties. And never buy men bathrobes.

Rule #5: Do not buy any man industrial-sized canisters of after shave or deodorant. I'm told they do not stink—they are earthy.

Rule #6: Buy men label makers. Almost as good as cordless drills. Within a couple of weeks there will be labels absolutely everywhere. "Socks. Shirts. Cups. Saucers. Door. Lock. Sink." You get the idea. No one knows why.

Rule #7: Never buy a man anything that says "Some assembly required" on the box. It will ruin his day and he will always have parts left over.

Rule #8: Good places to shop for men include NorthWest Iron Works, Parr Lumber, Home Depot, John Deere, Valley RV Center, and Les Schwab Tire. Napa Auto Parts and Sear's Clearance Centers are also excellent men's stores. It doesn't matter if he doesn't know what it is. "From Napa Auto, eh? Must be something I need. Hey! Isn't this a starter for a '68 Ford Fairlane? Wow! Thanks."

Rule #9: Men enjoy danger. That's why they never cook—but they will barbecue. Get him a monster grill

Rule #10: Men love chainsaws. Never, ever, buy a man you love a chainsaw. If you don't know why—please refer to rule #6 and what happens when he gets a label maker.

Rule #11: It's hard to beat a really good wheelbarrow or an aluminum extension ladder. Never buy a real man a step ladder. It must be an extension ladder. No one knows why.

Rule #12: Rope. Men love rope. It takes them back to their cowboy origins, or at least the boy scouts. Nothing says love like a hundred feet of 3/8" manilla rope.

Gift to Dad

A lumberjack had raised his only son and had managed to finance the young man's college education by the only way he knew how—cutting down trees, by hand.

The young man had helped his father cut down some of those trees. He knew how hard his father had to work to put him through college.

When the son started college, he promised himself that the first thing he would do was to buy his father a present that would make the old man's life easier. The son saved and scrimped and finally had enough money to purchase the finest chainsaw in the world.

On a school vacation, the son asked his dad how many trees he could cut down in one day. The father, a large husky man, thought and said on a good day he was able to bring down 20 trees. The son gave his father the brand-new chainsaw and said from now on he would be able to triple the amount and work only half as hard.

The old man was very pleased and said he had the best son in the world. The young man left for school the next morning and wasn't able to return until the next school break, three months later.

When he arrived, he immediately noticed that his dad appeared tired. He asked if his father was feeling all right. The old man replied that cutting trees was getting harder and harder and now with the new chainsaw he was working longer hours but not cutting as many trees as before.

The son knew there was something wrong and thought perhaps the saw he purchased wasn't as good as advertised. He asked to check it out. Upon examining it, he checked the oiler and it was full. He checked the gas and it too was full. He yanked on the cord and immediately it roared to life.

His father grabbed him by the shirt and hollered, "What's that noise!?!?"

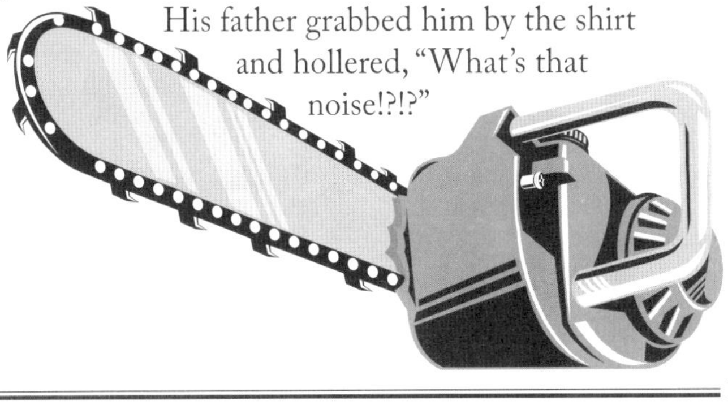

Girl With A Bag On The Beach

A couple lived near the ocean and used to walk the beach a lot. One summer they noticed a girl who was at the beach almost every day. She wasn't unusual, nor was the travel bag she carried, except for one thing; she would approach people who were sitting on the beach, glance around furtively and then speak to them.

Generally, the people would respond negatively and she would wander off, but occasionally someone would nod and there would be a quick exchange of money for something she carried in her bag. The couple assumed she was selling drugs and debated calling the cops, but since they didn't know for sure they just continued to watch her.

After a couple of weeks the wife asked, "Honey, have you ever noticed that she only goes up to people with boom boxes and other electronic devices?" He said he hadn't. Then she said, "Tomorrow I want you to get a towel and our big radio and go lie out on the beach. Then we can find out what she's really doing."

Well, the plan went off without a hitch, and the wife was almost hopping up and down with anticipation when she saw the girl talk to her husband and then leave. The man walked up the beach and met his wife. "Well, is she selling drugs?" she asked excitedly.

"No, she's not," he said, enjoying this probably more than he should have. "Well, what is it, then?" his wife fairly shrieked.

The man grinned and said. "She's a battery salesperson."

"Batteries?" cried the wife.

"Yes," he replied. "She sells C cells by the seashore."

Glad I'm Not A Tech

Tech support: What kind of computer do you have?
Customer: A white one...

Customer: Hi, this is Celine. I can't get my diskette out.
Tech support: Have you tried pushing the button?
Customer: Yes, sure, it's really stuck.
Tech support: That doesn't sound good; I'll make a note.
Customer: No wait a minute...I hadn't inserted it yet... it's still on my desk...sorry...

Tech support: Click on the 'my computer' icon on the left of the screen.
Customer: Your left or my left?

Tech support: Good day. How may I help you?
Customer: Hello...I can't print.
Tech support: Would you click on "start" for me and...
Customer: Listen pal, don't start getting technical on me! I'm not Bill Gates!

Customer: Hi, good afternoon, this is Martha, I can't print. Every time I try, it says 'Can't find printer'. I've even lifted the printer and placed it in front of the monitor, but the computer still says he can't find it...

Customer: I have problems printing in red...
Tech support: Do you have a color printer?
Customer: Aaaah...thank you.

Tech support: What's on your monitor now, ma'am?
Customer: A teddy bear my boyfriend bought for me at the 7-11.

Customer: My keyboard is not working anymore.
Tech support: Are you sure it's plugged into the computer?
Customer: No. I can't get behind the computer.
Tech support: Pick up your keyboard and walk 10 paces back.
Customer: OK
Tech support: Did the keyboard come with you?
Customer: Yes
Tech support: That means the keyboard is not plugged in. Is there another keyboard?
Customer: Yes, there's another one here. Ah...that one does work...

Tech support: Your password is the small letter 'a' as in apple, a capital letter 'V' as in Victor, the number '7.'
Customer: Is that '7' in capital letters?

Customer: I can't get on the Internet.
Tech support: Are you sure you used the right password?
Customer: Yes, I'm sure. I saw my colleague do it.
Tech support: Can you tell me what the password was?
Customer: Five stars.

Tech support: What anti-virus program do you use?
Customer: Netscape.
Tech support: That's not an anti-virus program.
Customer: Oh, sorry...Internet Explorer.

Customer: I have a huge problem. A friend has placed a screen saver on my computer, but every time I move the mouse, it disappears.

Tech support: How may I help you?
Customer: I'm writing my first e-mail.
Tech support: OK, and what seems to be the problem?
Customer: Well, I have the letter 'a' in the address, but how do I get the circle around it?

A woman customer called the Canon help desk with a problem with her printer.
Tech support: Are you running it under windows?
Customer: No, my desk is next to the door, but that is a good point. The man sitting in the cubicle next to me is under a window, and his printer is working fine.

Goat Down The Hole

Two guys were walking through the woods and came across this big deep hole.

"Wow…that looks deep," said one.

"Sure does," replied the other. "Toss a few pebbles in there and see how deep it is."

They picked up a few pebbles and threw them in and waited. No noise!

"That is REALLY deep. Here, throw one of these great big rocks down there. That should make a noise," said the first guy.

They picked up a couple football sized rocks and tossed them into the hole and waited…and waited. Nothing.

They looked at each other in amazement. One got a determined look on his face and said, "Hey", over here in the weeds, there's a railroad tie. Help me carry it over here. When we toss THAT thing in, it's GOTTA make some noise!"

They drug the heavy tie over to the hole and heaved it in. Not a sound came from the hole.

Suddenly, out of the nearby woods, a goat appeared, running like the wind. It rushed toward the two men, then right past them, running as fast as its legs would carry it. Suddenly it leaped in the air and down into the hole.

The two men were astonished with what they'd just seen. Then, out of the woods came a farmer who spotted the men and ambled over.

"Hey, have you two guys seen my goat out here?" he asked.

"You bet we did! The craziest thing I've ever seen! It came running like crazy and just jumped into this hole!"

"Naw", said the farmer, "That couldn't have been my goat. My goat was chained to a railroad tie."

Gold, Common Sense, And Fur

My husband and I had been happily married for five years but hadn't been blessed with a baby. I decided to do some serious praying and promised God that if he would give us a child, I would be a perfect mother, love it with all my heart and raise it with His Word as my guide.

God answered my prayers and blessed us with a son. The next year God blessed us with another son. The following year, he blessed us with yet another son. The year after that we were blessed with a daughter. My husband thought we'd been blessed right into poverty. We now had four children, and the oldest was only four years old. I learned never to ask God for anything unless I meant it. As a minister once told me, "If you pray for rain, make sure you carry an umbrella."

I began reading a few verses of the Bible to the children each day as they lay in their cribs. I was off to a good start. God had entrusted me with four children and I didn't want to disappoint Him.

I tried to be patient the day the children smashed two dozen eggs on the kitchen floor searching for baby chicks. I tried to be understanding when they started a hotel for homeless frogs in the spare bedroom, although it took me nearly two hours to catch all twenty-three frogs.

When my daughter poured ketchup all over herself and rolled up in a blanket to see how it felt to be a hot dog, I tried to see the humor rather than the mess.
In spite of changing thousands of diapers, never eating a hot meal and never sleeping for more than thirty minutes at a time, I still thanked God daily for my children.

While I couldn't keep my promise to be a perfect mother (I didn't even come close) I did keep my promise to raise them in the Word of God.

I knew I was missing the mark just a little though when I told my daughter we were going to church to worship God, and she wanted to bring a bar of soap along to "wash up" Jesus, too.

My proudest moment came during the children's Christmas pageant. My daughter was playing Mary, two of my sons were shepherds and my youngest son was a wise man. This was their moment to shine. My five-year-old shepherd had practiced his line, "We found the babe wrapped in swaddling clothes." But he was nervous and said, "The baby was wrapped in wrinkled clothes."

My four-year-old "Mary" said, "That's not 'wrinkled clothes,' silly. That's dirty, rotten clothes." A wrestling match broke out between Mary and the shepherd that was eventually stopped by an angel.

I slouched a little lower in my seat when Mary dropped the doll representing Baby Jesus, and it bounced down the aisle crying, "Mama-mama." Mary grabbed the doll, wrapped it back up and held it tightly as the wise men arrived.

My other son stepped forward wearing a bathrobe and a paper crown, knelt at the manger and announced, "We are the three wise men, and we are bringing gifts of gold, common sense, and fur."

The audience dissolved into laughter, and the pageant got a standing ovation.

"I've never enjoyed a Christmas program as much as this one," Father laughed, wiping tears from his eyes. "For the rest of my life, I'll never hear the Christmas story without thinking of gold, common sense, and fur."

"My children are my greatest blessing," I said as I dug through my purse for another aspirin.

Golfer's Tall Tale

A group of golfers were telling tall stories. At last came a veteran's turn. "Well," he said, "I once drove a ball, accidentally off course, through a cottage window. The ball knocked over an oil lamp and set the place on fire!"

"What did you do?" asked his friends.

"Oh," said the veteran, "I immediately teed another ball, took careful aim, and hit the fire alarm on Main Street. That brought out the fire engine before any major damage was done."

Government Farm Visit

A cocky Department of Agriculture representative stopped at a farm and talked with the old farmer; "I need to inspect your farm."

The old farmer said, "You better not go in that field."

The Agriculture representative said in a "wise" tone, "I have the authority of the U. S. Government with me. See this card, I am allowed to go wherever I wish on agricultural land."

So the old farmer went about his farm chores.

Later, the farmer heard loud screams and saw the Department of Agriculture man running for the fence; close behind was the farmer's prize bull. The bull was madder than a nest full of hornets, and the bull was gaining at every step.

"Help," the rep shouted to the farmer, "what should I do?" he screamed helplessly.

The old farmer, hooking his thumbs in his overalls, called out, "Show him your card!"

Grandpa Lost

I remember the day when a police car pulled up to Grandma's house and Grandpa got out.

The officer explained that this elderly gentlemen said he was lost in the park.

"Why, Bill," said Grandma, "You've been going there for over 30 years! How could you get lost?"

Leaning close to Grandma so the police officer couldn't hear, he whispered, "I wasn't exactly lost. I was just too tired to walk home."

Great Ad

When F. W. Woolworth opened his store, a merchant down the street ran an ad in the local paper. It read: Do your local shopping here. We have been in business for fifty years!

Woolworth countered with an ad of his own. It read: We've been in business only one week—all of our merchandise is brand new!

Grouchiness

While on a road trip, an elderly couple stopped at a roadside restaurant for lunch. After finishing their meal, they left the restaurant and resumed their trip. When leaving, the elderly woman unknowingly left her glasses on the table and she didn't miss them until they had been driving about twenty minutes.

By then, to add to the aggravation, they had to travel quite a distance before they could find a place to turn around, in order to return to the restaurant to retrieve her glasses.

All the way back, the elderly husband became the classic grouchy old man. He fussed and complained and scolded his wife relentlessly during the entire return drive. The more he chided her, the more agitated he became. He just wouldn't let up one minute.

To her relief, they finally arrived at the restaurant. As the woman got out of the car and hurried inside to retrieve her glasses, her husband yelled to her, "While you're in there, you might as well get my hat and our credit card."

Hand Signals

A Florida officer pulled over an eighty-year-old teacher because her hand signals were confusing.

"First you put your hand up, like you're turning right, then you waved your hand up and down, then you turned left," said the officer.

"I decided not to turn right," she explained.

"Then why the up and down?" asked the officer.

"Officer," she sniffed, "I was erasing!"

Happy Birthday

A couple phoned a neighbor to extend birthday greetings. They dialed the number and then sang "Happy Birthday" to him. But when they finished their off-key rendition, they discovered that they had dialed the wrong number.

"Don't let it bother you," said a strange but amused voice. "You folks need all the practice you can get."

Hard-Nosed Mr. Swiller

Mr. Swiller was known far and wide as a hard-nosed boss who watched his employees like a hawk. He was making one of his regular tours of the factory when he spotted a young man leaning against a pile of boxes just outside the foreman's office. Since George, the foreman, wasn't around, Swiller stood off to the side and watched to see just how long the young man would stand around doing nothing.

The young man yawned, scratched his head, looked at his watch, and sat on the floor. He took out a nail file and began cleaning his nails. Then he stretched, yawned again, and leaned back on the pile of boxes. Swiller stepped from his hiding place and walked up to the young man. "You!" he boomed. "How much do you make a week?"

The young man looked up indifferently. "Two hundred and fifty dollars," he said. Swiller swooped into the cashier's office, took $250 from the cash box, and returned. "Take it," he said, "and get out! Don't let me see you around here again!"

The young man took the cash, put it in his pocket, and left.

Swiller snorted at his lack of remorse, embarrassment, or any other feeling. Then he went looking for George.

When he found him, Swiller was red with anger. "That idler in front of your office," Swiller said. "I just gave him a week's pay and fired him. What's the matter with you, letting him stand around as though he had nothing to do?"

"You mean the guy in the red shirt?" George asked.

"Yes! The guy in the red shirt!"

"He was waiting for the twenty dollars we owe him for lunch," George said. "He works for the coffee shop around the corner."

Head Check

One weekend my friend, a nurse, was looking after her six-year-old nephew when he fell off a playground slide and hit his head.

Worried that he might have a concussion, she checked him all night. Every hour, she'd gently shake him and ask, "What's your name?" Soon, he began moaning in protest each time she entered the room.

When Sally went in at 5:00 a.m., she found something white on his forehead. Leaning close, she saw a crayon-scrawled message taped to his forehead.

It read: "My name is Daniel."

He Ain't My Dog!

A salesman was traveling through Berks County and got a little lost. Seeing a store he decided to stop and ask for directions. As he approached the store he saw a farmer sitting on a bench with a dog at his feet. He asked if his dog bites, to which the farmer replied, "Nope!"

With that the salesman reached down to pet the dog. He was promptly bit on the hand.

The salesman asked, "I thought you said your dog didn't bite?"

The farmer responded, "He ain't my dog!"

Healthy News Reporter

A young news reporter once visited an elderly man on his ninety-ninth birthday to interview him about his longevity. The interview over, the reporter said to the elderly man, as he was about to leave: "I hope to see you again, sir, on your hundredth birthday." The old gentleman carefully looked the young reporter over and then said: "I can't see any reason why you shouldn't, young man, you look healthy enough to me."

Heavy Housework

Smith went to see his supervisor. "Boss," he said, "we're doing some heavy house-cleaning at home tomorrow, and my wife needs me to help with the attic and the garage, moving and hauling stuff."

"We're short-handed, Smith," the boss said, " I can't give you the day off."

"Thanks, boss," Smith said, "I knew I could count on you!"

He Is Watching

In the cafeteria of a school, the children were lined up for lunch. At the head of the line was a large pile of apples. Someone had made a note and placed it in front of the apples. The note read: "Take only one, God is watching."

Further down the cafeteria line was a large pile of chocolate chip cookies…

One of the boys had written a note of his own. The note he placed in front of the cookies read: "Take all you want, God is watching the apples."

Helping Hand

A man writing at the post office desk was approached by an older fellow with a post card in his hand. The old man said, "Sir, I'm sorry to bother you but could you address this post card for me? My arthritis is acting up today, and I can't even hold a pen."

"Certainly sir," said the younger man. "Glad to."

He wrote out the address and also agreed to write a short message and sign the card for the man. Finally, the younger man asked, "Now, is there anything else I can do for you?"

The older fellow thought about it for a moment and said, "Yes, at the end could you just add, 'P.S.: Please excuse the sloppy handwriting.'?"

Holiday Eating Tips

1. Avoid carrot sticks. Anyone who puts carrots on a buffet table knows nothing of the holiday spirit. In fact, if you see carrots, leave immediately. Go next door, where they're serving real snack food.
2. If something comes with gravy, use it. That's the whole point of gravy. Gravy does not stand alone. Pour it on. Make a volcano out of your mashed potatoes. Fill it with gravy. Eat the volcano. Repeat.
3. As for mashed potatoes, always ask if they're made with skim milk or whole milk. If it's skim, pass. Why bother? It's like buying a sports car with an automatic transmission.
4. Do not have a snack before going to a party in an effort to control your eating. The whole point of going to a party is to eat other people's food for free. Lots of it. Hello?

5. Under no circumstances should you exercise between now and New Year's. You can do that in January when you have nothing else to do. This is the time for long naps, which you'll need after circling the buffet table while carrying a ten-pound plate of food.
6. If you come across something really good at a buffet table, like frosted Christmas cookies in a variety of shapes and sizes, position yourself near them and don't budge. Have as many as you can before becoming the center of attention. They're like a beautiful pair of shoes. If you leave them behind, you're never going to see them again.
7. Same for pies. Apple. Pumpkin. Mincemeat. Have a slice of each. Or, if you don't like mincemeat, have two apples and one pumpkin. Always have three. When else do you get to have more than one dessert? Labor Day?
8. Did someone mention fruitcake? Granted, it's loaded with the mandatory celebratory calories, but avoid it at all cost. I mean, have some standards.
9. One final tip: if you don't feel terrible when you leave the party or get up from the table, you haven't been paying attention. Reread tips; start over, but hurry, January is just around the corner.

Home-Cooked Meal

When the power failed at the elementary school, the cook couldn't serve a hot meal in the cafeteria, so at the last minute she whipped up great stacks of peanut-butter-and-jelly sandwiches.

As one little boy filled his plate, he said, "It's about time. At last—a home-cooked meal!"

Home Freezer

Jane would carefully note in large clear letters, "Meatloaf" or "Pot Roast" or "Steak and Vegetables" or "Chicken and Dumplings" or "Beef Pot Pie".

Every day when she asked her husband what he wanted for dinner, he never asked for any of those meals. She decided to stock the freezer with his various requests. In Jane's freezer now you'll see a whole new set of labels. You'll find dinners with neat little tags that say: "Whatever", "Anything", "I Don't Know", "I Don't Care", "Something Good", or "Food".

No more frustration for Jane because no matter what her husband replies when she asks him what he wants for dinner, it's there waiting.

Honk The Horn

As I drove into a parking lot, I noticed that a pickup truck with a dog sitting behind the wheel was rolling toward a female pedestrian. She seemed oblivious, so I hit my horn to get her attention, She looked up just in time to jump out of the way of the truck's path, and the vehicle bumped harmlessly into the curb and stopped.

I rushed to the woman's side to see if she was all right. "I'm fine," she assured me, "but I hate to think what could have happened to me if that dog hadn't honked."

Hospital Charts By Doctors:

1. Patient has chest pain if she lies on her left side for over a year.
2. On the second day the knee was better, and on the third day it disappeared.
3. The patient is tearful and crying constantly. She also appears to be depressed.
4. The patient has been depressed since she began seeing me in 1993.
5. Discharge status: Alive but without my permission.
6. Healthy appearing decrepit 69 year old male, mentally alert but forgetful.
7. The patient refused autopsy.
8. The patient has no previous history of suicides.
9. Patient has left white blood cells at another hospital.
10. Patient's medical history has been remarkably insignificant with only a 40 pound weight gain in the past three days.
11. Patient had waffles for breakfast and anorexia for lunch.
12. She is numb from her toes down.
13. The skin was moist and dry.
14. Occasional, constant infrequent headaches.
15. Patient was alert and unresponsive.
16. I saw your patient today, who is still under our care for physical therapy.

17. Skin: somewhat pale but present.
18. Patient has two teenage children, but no other abnormalities.

Hospital Regulations

Hospital regulations require a wheelchair for patients being discharged. However, while working as a student nurse, I found one elderly gentleman already dressed and sitting on the bed with a suitcase at his feet, who insisted he didn't need my help to leave the hospital. After a chat about rules being rules, he reluctantly let me wheel him to the elevator. On the way down I asked him if his wife was meeting him.

"I don't know," he said. "She's still upstairs in the bathroom changing out of her hospital gown."

Hospital Visit

A lady came to the hospital to visit a friend. She had not been in a hospital for several years and felt very ignorant about all the new technology. A technician followed her onto the elevator, wheeling a large, intimidating looking machine with tubes and wires and dials.

"Boy, would I hate to be hooked up to that thing," she said.

"So would I," replied the technician. "It's a floor-cleaning machine."

Hotel Humor

During my stay at an expensive hotel in New York City, I woke up in the middle of the night with an upset stomach. I called room service and ordered some soda crackers. When I looked at the charge slip, I was furious. I called room service and raged, "I know I'm in a luxury hotel, but $11.50 for six crackers is ridiculous!"

"The crackers are complimentary," the voice at the other end coolly explained. "I believe you are complaining about your room number."

Hotel Security

At a hotel in Washington, the bride asked, "What if the place is bugged?"

The groom said, "I'll look for a bug." He looked behind the drapes, behind the pictures, and under the rug. Finally, he said, "Aha!"

Under the rug was a disc with four screws. He got his Swiss army knife, unscrewed the screws, and threw them and the disc out the window.

The next morning, the hotel manager asked the newlyweds, "How was your room? How was the service? How was your stay?"

The groom said, "Why are you asking me all of these questions?"

The hotel manager said, "Well, the room under you complained of the chandelier falling on them."

How Can A Student Pass?

It's not the fault of the student if he fails, because the year only has 365 days. Typical academic year for a student:

1. Sundays: 52 Sundays in a year—you know Sundays are for rest—313 days left.
2. Summer holidays: 50 where weather is very hot and difficult to study—263 days left.
3. 8 hours daily sleep: 130 days gone—141 days left.
4. 1 hour for daily playing: (good for health) means 15 days—126 days left.
5. 2 hours daily for food & other delicacies (chewing properly & swallowing) means 30 days—96 days left.
6. 1 hour for talking (man is a social being) means 15 days—81 days left.
7. Exam days per year—at least 35 days—46 days left.
8. Quarterly, Half yearly and festival (holidays)—40 days. Balance—6 days.
9. For sickness at least 3 days. Remaining days = 3.
10. Various Activities—at least 2 days. 1 day left.
11. That 1 day is your birthday. How can you study on that day? Days left = 0.

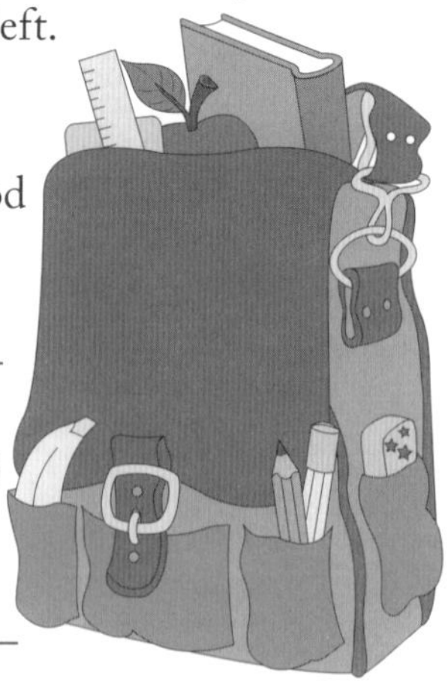

How can any student pass?

How High Is It?

An engineering student, a physics student, and a mathematics student were each given $150 dollars and were told to use that money to find out exactly how tall a particular hotel was.

All three ran off, extremely keen on how to do this. The physics student went out, purchased some stop-watches, a number of ball bearings, a calculator, and some friends. He had them all time the drop of ball bearings from the roof, and he then figured out the height from the time it took for the bearings to accelerate from the rest until they impacted with the sidewalk.

The math student waited until the sun was going down, then she took out her protractor, plumb line, measuring tape, and scratch pad, measured the length of the shadow, found the angle the buildings roof made from the ground, and used trigonometry to figure out the height of the building.

Of course, with all that was involved in getting this experiment done, they were up plenty late studying for other courses' exams. These two students bumped into the engineering student the next day, who looked quite refreshed. When asked what he did to find the height of the building he replied: "Well, I walked up to the bell hop, gave him ten bucks, asked him how tall the hotel was, and went inside for supper!"

How Many Bricks?

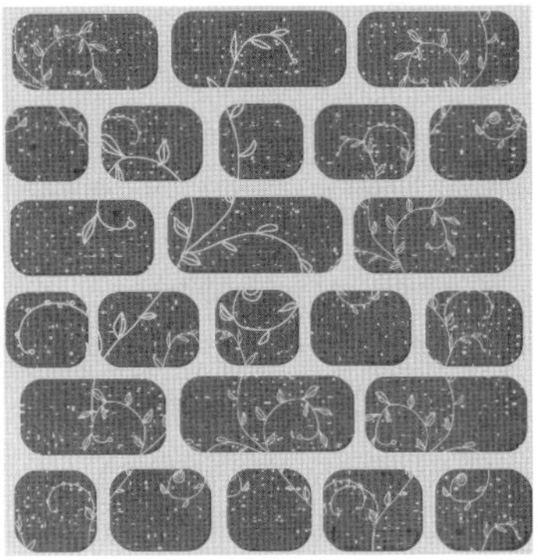

While a friend and I were visiting Annapolis, we noticed several students on their hands and knees assessing the courtyard with pencils and clipboards in hand. "What are they doing?" I asked our tour guide. "Each year," he replied with a grin, "The upperclassmen ask the freshmen how many bricks it took to finish paving this courtyard."

"So what's the answer?" my friend asked him when we were out of earshot of the freshmen. The guide replied, "One."

How Quickly Things Change

While traveling through the jungle, a missionary met a lion. Seeing that his plight was hopeless, he fell to his knees in anxious prayer.

A few moments later he was greatly comforted to see the lion on its knees beside him.

"Dear Brother," said the relieved missionary, "how delightful it is to join you in prayer when a moment ago I feared for my life."

"Don't interrupt," said the lion, "I'm saying grace."

How Long

The company I work for offers tours through the historic district of Annapolis, Maryland, led by guides dressed in Colonial clothing. While leading a group, Felix, one of our guides, tripped and fell, breaking his wrist.

He went to the hospital, and as he sat waiting in the emergency room, a policeman walked by. Doing a double take at Felix in his 18th-century garb, he asked, "Just how long have you been waiting?"

How Smart Is Your Right Foot

This is so funny that it will boggle your mind, and you will keep trying it several times to see if you can outsmart your foot—but you can't!

1. While sitting down, lift your right foot off the floor and make clockwise circles with it.
2. Now, while doing this, draw the number "6" in the air with your right hand. Your foot will change direction!
3. Told you so—and there's nothing you can do about it!

How To Brighten Your Day By Annoying Others

1. Leave the copy machine set at 99 copies; reduce 200%; extra dark; 17" paper.
2. Specify that your drive through order is: "to go."
3. If you have a glass eye, tap on it occasionally with your pen while talking to others.
4. Insist on keeping your windshield wipers running in all weather conditions to "Keep them tuned up."
5. Reply to everything someone says with, "That's what *you* think."
6. Practice making fax and modem noises.
7. Highlight irrelevant information in scientific papers and copy.
8. Make beeping noises when you back up.
9. Finish all your sentences with the words: "in accordance with the prophecy."
10. Signal that a conversation is over by clamping your hands over your ears.
11. Disassemble your pen or whiteout and "accidentally" flip the ink cartridge across the room.
12. Holler random numbers while someone is counting.
13. When watching a video adjust the tint so that all the people are green and insist to others "I like it that way."
14. Staple papers in the middle of the page.
15. Scotch tape down the "hang-up button" on your coworkers phone.
16. Publicly investigate just how slowly you can make a croaking noise.
17. Honk and wave to strangers.
18. TYPE ONLY IN UPPERCASE.
19. type only in lowercase.
20. Dontuseanypunctuationorspaceseither
21. Repeat the following conversation a dozen times: "Do you hear that?"…"What?"…"Never mind, it's gone now."
22. Try tapping out a song on the bottom of your chin. When nearly done, announce, "No, wait. I messed it up" and repeat.
23. While making presentations, occasionally bob your head like a parakeet.
24. Sit in your front yard pointing a hair drier at passing cars.
25. Sing along at the opera.
26. Go to a poetry recital and ask why each poem doesn't rhyme.
27. Ask your coworkers mysterious questions and then scribble their answers in a notebook and mutter something about "psychological profiles."
28. Tell your friends five days prior that you can't attend their party because you are not in the mood.
29. Type all "X's" to fill a page, in 9 point size; then on the same piece of paper repeat with 12 point; increase the point size to 16 point; change to uppercase "W's". When you have a complete page of garble, make 2 additional copies and fax them to someone that just got a new fax machine. Wait 3 minutes and fax 3 blank pages.
30. AND THE FINAL WAY TO ANNOY PEOPLE…Send this to everyone you know, even if they sent it to you.

How to Speak English Properly

1. Verbs has to agree with their subjects.
2. Prepositions are not words to end sentences with.
3. And don't start a sentence with a conjunction.
4. It is wrong to ever split an infinitive.
5. Avoid cliches like the plague (they're old hat).
6. Also, always avoid annoying alliteration.
7. Be more or less specific.
8. Parenthetical remarks (however relevant) are (usually) unnecessary.
9. Also too, never, ever use repetitive redundancies.
10. No sentence fragments.
11. Contractions aren't necessary and shouldn't be used.
12. Foreign words and phrases are not apropos.
13. Do not be redundant; do not use more words than necessary; it's highly superfluous.
14. One should never generalize.
15. Comparisons are as bad as cliches.
16. Eschew ampersands & abbreviations, etc.
17. One-word sentences? Eliminate.
18. Analogies in writing are like feathers on a snake.
19. The passive voice is to be ignored.
20. Eliminate commas, that are, not necessary. Parenthetical words however should be enclosed in commas.
21. Never use a big word when a diminutive one would suffice.
22. Use words correctly, irregardless of how others use them.
23. Understatement is always the absolute best way to put forth earth-shaking ideas.
24. Eliminate quotations. As Ralph Waldo Emerson said, "I hate quotations. Tell me what you know."
25. If you've heard it once, you've heard it a thousand times: Resist hyperbole; not one writer in a million can use it correctly.

26. Puns are for children, not groan readers.
27. Go around the barn at high noon to avoid colloquialisms.
28. Even if a mixed metaphor sings, it should be derailed.
29. Who needs rhetorical questions?
30. Exaggeration is a billion times worse than understatement.
31. Proofread carefully to see if you any words out.

How To Train A Cat

Our young daughter had adopted a stray cat. To my distress, he began to use the back of our new sofa as a scratching post. "Don't worry," my husband reassured me. "I'll have him trained in no time."

I watched for several days as my husband patiently "trained" our new pet. Whenever the cat scratched, my husband deposited him outdoors to teach him a lesson.

The cat learned quickly. For the next 16 years, whenever he wanted to go outside, he scratched the back of the sofa.

Humility

A colleague was invited to hold a speech in Japan. Aware of his reputation as a very good speaker, he was surprised that his audience did not react at all to any of his perfectly timed jokes and witticisms. In fact, the audience did not react to anything he said. Somewhat put down, he went back to his seat and a Japanese gentleman appeared on the stage. This man had a terrific success! People laughed and applauded, and although the original speaker could not understand one bit of what was said, still he started to applaud, as the man evidently deserved praise for this perfect speech.

He was interrupted by the chairman of the conference, "No no, sir. You must not applaud."

Dumbfounded, he protested: "But why? This man is obviously a very good speaker."

"No sir, you must not applaud. He is translating your speech."

Hunting License

The Game Warden stopped a deer hunter and asked to see his hunting license. "This is last year's license," the warden informed him.

"I know," said the hunter, "but I shouldn't need a new license, I am only shooting at the deer I missed last year."

Husbands & Shopping

This is why women should not take men shopping against their will.

After Mr. and Mrs. Fenton retired, Mrs. Fenton insisted her husband accompany her on her trips to the local store. Unfortunately, Mr. Fenton was like most men—he found shopping boring and preferred to get in and get out. Equally unfortunately, Mrs. Fenton was like most women—she loved to browse.

One day Mrs. Fenton received the following letter from her local store:

Dear Mrs. Fenton,

Over the past six months, your husband has been causing quite a commotion in our store. We cannot tolerate this behavior and may be forced to ban both of you from the store. Our complaints against Mr. Fenton are listed below and are documented by our video surveillance cameras.

1. June 15: Took 24 boxes of Polident and randomly put them in people's carts when they weren't looking.
2. July 2: Set all the alarm clocks in Housewares to go off at 5-minute intervals.
3. July 19: Walked up to an employee and told her in an official voice, "Code 3 in Housewares. Get on it right away."
4. August 4: Went to the Service Desk and tried to put a bag of M&M's® on layaway.
5. September 14: Moved a "CAUTION—WET FLOOR" sign to a carpeted area.
6. September 15: Set up a tent in the camping depart ment and told other shoppers he'd invite them in if they would bring pillows and blankets from the bedding department.
7. September 23: When a clerk asked if she could help him, he began crying and screamed, "Why can't you people just leave me alone?"

8. October 4: Looked right into the security camera and used it as a mirror while he picked his nose.
9. December 18: Hid in a clothing rack and when people browsed through, yelled "PICK ME! PICK ME!"

Regards,
The Management

I Always Wondered About That

During a summer break from my studies at an engineering university, I worked in a scrap yard repairing construction equipment. One afternoon, I was taking apart a piling hammer that had some very large bolts holding it together. One of the nuts had corroded onto the bolt, so I started heating the nut with an oxyacetylene torch. As I was doing this, one of the dimmest apprentices I have ever known came along and asked me what I was doing. I patiently explained that if I heated the nut, it would grow larger and release its grip on the bolt so I could then remove it.

"So things get larger when they get hot, do they?" he asked.

Suddenly, an idea flashed into my mind. "Yes," I said, "that's why days are longer in summer and shorter in winter."

There was a long pause, then his face cleared. "You know, I always wondered about that," he said.

Iams Hot Line

"How many calories in a mouse?" and "What should I feed a borderline collie?" are just a few of the wacky questions that the Iams Pet Professionals have fielded from pet owners. Here are some of the team's favorite calls in recent years to 800-863-IAMS (4267):

- "My two-year-old daughter loves the taste of Iams—is it okay for her to eat it?"—mother, Staten Island, NY.
- "What's the best way to get super glue off my dog's paws?"—dog owner, Arlington, TX.
- "Can a dog get claustrophobia?"—dog owner, Cambridge, MA.
- "My dog growls in his sleep. Do you think he could have a vitamin B deficiency?"—dog owner, Puyallup, WA.
- "How can I get the secret recipe for your Iams Chunks dog food?"—dog owner, Anchorage, AK.
- "I think if my dog received mail, it would build his character. Can I register him on your mailing list?"—dog owner, Richmond, VA.
- "Where can I get a six-toed cat?"—cat owner, El Paso, TX.
- "How do I potty train my pot belly pig?"—pot belly pig owner, Vero Beach, FL.
- "What's up with my cat? She looks at me strangely when I sing and dance for her."—cat owner, New York, NY.
- "Is it normal for a dog to shed?"—dog owner, Miami, FL.
- "I have two new kittens and I don't want to leave them home alone. Can I carry them around in my gym bag?"—new kitten owner, Brooklyn, NY.
- "How do I stop my cat from giving food to the dog?"—pet owner, Ephrata, WA.
- "My son just sold me a subscription to the Iams Your Cat magazine. But you tell me it's free?"—concerned mom, Englewood, OH.
- "Will chewing pop cans remove enamel from my puppy's teeth?"—puppy owner, Chico, CA.
- "I raise worms—the world's most perfect protein source. How about using them in your food?"—worm farmer, Long Barn, OH.
- "How can I keep my cat from stealing my husband's toothbrush?"—cat owner, Los Angeles, CA.

"When these type of calls come in, it's hard to keep a straight face," says Sally Northcutt, manager of Customer Service, The Iams Company. "But we know that most of the time, we have a customer on the phone who is genuinely concerned for his or her pet. Our sole purpose is to help pet owners with their questions, so however strange those questions may seem, we try our best to answer them."

I Didn't Do My Homework Because…

- I didn't do my history homework because I don't believe in dwelling on the past.
- I didn't want the other students in the class to look bad.

- A sudden gust of wind blew my homework out of my hand and I never saw it again.
- Another pupil fell in a lake and I jumped in to rescue him. Unfortunately, my homework drowned.
- Our furnace broke and we had to burn my homework to keep ourselves from freezing.
- I'm not at liberty to say why.
- I have a solar-powered calculator, and it was cloudy.
- My mom used it as a dryer sheet.
- I felt it wasn't challenging enough.
- My parents were sick and unable to do my homework last night. Don't worry, they have been suitably punished.
- We had homework?!
- I didn't want to add to your already heavy workload.
- I spent the night at a rally supporting higher pay for our hard-working teachers.

If You'll Be Quiet

It was a hectic day of running errands with my wife and son. As if the stress weren't enough, four-year-old Christopher insisted on asking questions about everything, told me how to drive better, and sang every song he knew.

Finally, growing impatient with the incessant chatter, I made him an offer: "Christopher, if you'll be quiet for just a few minutes, I'll give you a quarter." It worked.

But when we stopped for lunch, I unknowingly began to harp on him. "Christopher, sit up straight…Don't spill your drink…Don't talk with your mouth full."

Finally he said seriously, "Dad, if you'll be quiet for just a few minutes, I'll give you a quarter."

Illegal Turn

A man in a hurry taking his eight-year-old son to school, made a turn at a red light where it was prohibited.

"Uh-oh, I just made an illegal turn!" the man said.

"Aw, Dad, it's okay" the son said. "The police car right behind us did the same thing."

Imported Cheese

The customer in the Italian restaurant was so pleased that he asked to speak to the chef. The owner proudly led him into the kitchen and introduced him to the chef.

"Your veal parmigiana was superb," the customer said. "I just spent a month in Italy, and yours is better than any I ever had over there."

"Naturally," the chef said. "Over there, they use domestic cheese. Ours is imported from Italy."

Innocent

A young girl of four was told she needed an x-ray after an accident. Her mother tried to calm her down, but she was still nervous when the time came for the x-ray.

When she came out of the x-ray room, however, she seemed relaxed and just fine. "They took a picture of my bones," she told her mother.

"Yes, dear," replied the mother. "Did everything go all right?"

"Yeah," said the girl. "It was great! I didn't even have to take my skin off, or anything!"

Interpreting Hotel Brochures

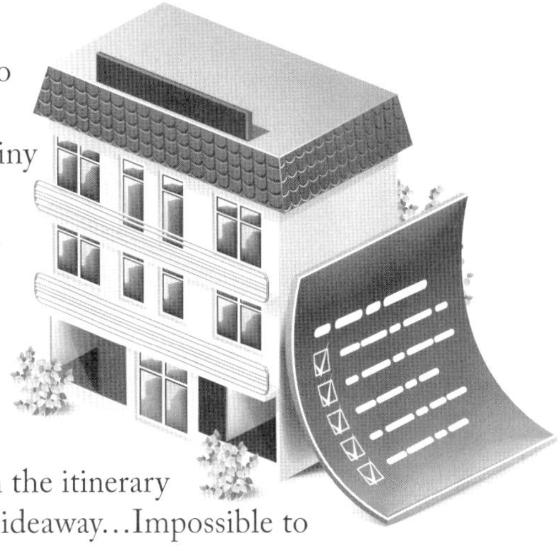

- Old world charm…No bath
- Tropical rainy majestic setting…A long way from town
- Options galore… Nothing is included in the itinerary
- Secluded hideaway…Impossible to find or get to
- Pre-registered rooms…Already occupied
- Explore on your own…Pay for it yourself
- Knowledgeable trip hosts…They've flown in an airplane before

- No extra fees…No extras
- Nominal fee…Outrageous charge
- Standard…Substandard
- Deluxe…Standard
- Superior…One free shower cap
- Cozy…Small
- All the amenities…Two free shower caps
- Plush…Top and bottom sheets
- Gentle breezes…Occasional Gale-force winds
- Light and airy…No air conditioning
- Picturesque…Theme park nearby
- Concierge…Stand with tourist brochures
- Continental breakfast…Free muffin

In The News

Burglars broke in to an unoccupied house that was being renovated for sale. Among the items they stole were roofing shingles, a lawn mower, weed whackers, and lumber.

They broke into a storage area under the deck and also a shed in the back. Before leaving, though, they mowed the lawn of the residence.

Neighbors reported seeing strange men walking around the home, but they never called the police because they figured the men were hired to do the lawn.

The owners are quoted as saying they will leave a pressure washer and painting equipment for the thieves next week as they did a better job than the lawn care company they had hired, and they were cheaper also.

IRS Questions

This is a list of IRS-directed questions from an often-confused public.

Caller: I got a letter from you guys and I want to know what you want.
IRS: What does it say?
Caller: Just a minute, I'll open it.

Caller: I'm a bookkeeper and I need to know if ten $100 bills make a thousand dollars or only ten hundred dollars.
IRS: Both. It's the same amount.
Caller: So why do I get a different answer every time I move the decimal point?

Caller: What does the law say about people who are renting to relatives and taking a loss on the property?
IRS: You are required to charge them fair market value.
Caller: It's very fair. If we rented to someone else we could get a lot more.

Caller: Could you please send me some of those WD-40's?

IRS Theme Song

Tax his cow, tax his goat;
Tax his pants, tax his coat.

Tax his crop, tax his work;
Tax his ties, tax his shirt.

Tax his tractor, tax his mule;
Tell him, "Taxing is the rule."

Tax his oil, tax his gas;
Tax his notes, tax his cash.

Tax him good and let him know
That after taxes, he has no dough.

If he hollers, tax him more;
Tax him 'til he's good and sore.

Tax his coffin, tax his grave,
Tax the sod 'neath which he's laid.

Put these words upon his tomb:
"Taxes drove him to his doom."

After he's gone, we won't relax;
We'll still collect inheritance tax.

It Comes With The Dinner

Have you ever considered the awesome power of the spoken word? For instance:

Waiter: What'll you have for dessert?
First diner: Nothing for me.
Second diner: I'm stuffed.
Third diner: Couldn't eat another bite.
Waiter: It comes with the dinner.
First Diner: Ice Cream.
Second Diner: Pecan Pie.
Third Diner: Chocolate Layer Cake.

Jar Number 47

A new miracle doctor had just arrived in town, He could cure anything and anybody, and everyone was amazed with what he could do—everyone except for Mr. Thompson, the town skeptic.

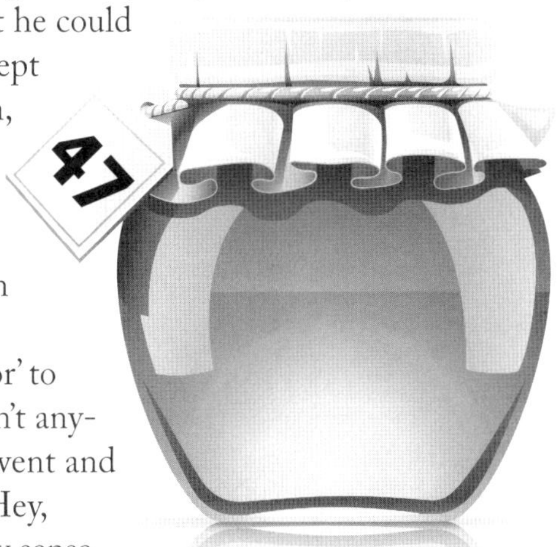

Grumpy old Mr. Thompson went to this 'miracle doctor' to prove that he wasn't anybody special. He went and told the doctor, "Hey, doc, I have lost my sense of taste. I can't taste nothin', so what are ya goin' to do?"

The doctor scratched his head and mumbled to himself a little, then told Mr, Thompson, "What you need is jar number 47."

So the doctor brought the jar and told Mr. Thompson to taste it. He tasted it and immediately spit it out, "This is gross!" he yelled. "I just restored your sense of taste Mr. Thompson," said the doctor.

So Mr. Thompson went home very mad.

One month later, Mr. Thompson went back to the doctor along with a new problem, "Doc," he started, "I can't remember anything!"

Thinking he had the doctor stumped now, he waited as the doctor scratched his head, mumbled to himself a little, and told Mr. Thompson, "What you need is jar number 47."

Immediately Mr. Thompson was cured and fled the room!

Job Description—Parent

Position:

Mom, Mommy, Mama, Ma
Dad, Daddy, Dada, Pa, Pop

Job Description:

Long-term team players needed for challenging permanent work in an often chaotic environment.

Candidates must possess excellent communication and organizational skills and be willing to work variable hours, which will include evenings and weekends and frequent 24-hour shifts on call.

Some overnight travel required, including trips to primitive camping sites on rainy weekends and endless excursions around the countryside doing fundraisers.

Travel expenses not reimbursed.

Extensive courier duties also required.

Responsibilities:

The rest of your life.

Must be willing to be considered as hopeless, at least temporarily, until someone needs $5.

Must be willing to bite tongue repeatedly.

Also, must possess the physical stamina of a pack mule and be able to go from zero to sixty mph in three seconds flat in case, this time, the screams from the backyard are not someone just crying wolf.

Must be willing to face stimulating technical challenges, such as small gadget repair, mysteriously sluggish toilets, and stuck zippers.

Must screen phone calls, maintain calendars, and coordinate production of multiple homework projects.

Must have ability to plan and organize social gatherings for clients of all ages and mental outlooks.

Must be willing to be indispensable one minute and an embarrassment the next.

Must be ready to host overnight guests without prior notice.

Must handle assembly and product safety testing of a half million cheap plastic toys and battery-operated devices.

Must always hope for the best but be prepared for the worst.

Must assume final, complete accountability for the quality of the end product.

Responsibilities also include floor maintenance and janitorial work throughout the facility.

Possibility For Advancement And Promotion:

If you are fortunate, you may be promoted to the position of Grandparent. Of course, you must still retain and fulfill all the responsibilities of Parent while assuming the new title and job responsibilities of Grandparent.

Previous Experience:

None required. On-the-job training is offered on a continually exhausting basis.

Wages And Compensation:

Get this! You pay them!

Offering frequent raises and bonuses.

A balloon payment is due when they turn 18 because of the assumption that college will help them become financially independent.

When you die, you give them whatever is left.

The oddest thing about this reverse-salary is that you actually enjoy it and wish you could only do more.

Benefits:

While no health or dental insurance, no pension, no tuition reimbursement, no paid holidays, and no stock options are offered, this job supplies limitless opportunities for personal growth and free hugs and kisses for life if you render the love only a parent can give.

Job Impressions

I had always talked about my job a lot at home, and my young daughter had always expressed great interest. So I thought it would be a treat for her to spend the day with me at the office. Since I wanted it to be a surprise, I didn't tell her where we were going, just that it would be fun. Although usually a bit shy, she seemed excited to meet each colleague I introduced. On the way home, however, she seemed somewhat down.

"Didn't you have a nice time?" I asked.

"Well, it was okay." she responded. "But I thought it would be more like a circus."

Confused, I asked, "Whatever do you mean?"

She said, "Well, you said you work with a bunch of clowns, and I never got to see them!"

Job Interview

Jennifer had applied for a job and when she returned home, her mother asked how the interview went.

"Pretty good, I think," replied Jennifer, "but if I go to work there I won't get a vacation until I'm married."

Her mother, of course, had never heard of such a thing. "Is that what they told you?"

"No," replied Jennifer, "but right on the application it said 'vacation time may not be taken until you've had your First tersary.'"

Joggers

A man had been driving all night and by morning was still far from his destination. He decided to stop at the next city he came to and park somewhere quiet so he could get an hour or two of sleep. As chance would have it, the quiet place he chose happened to be on one of the city's major jogging routes.

No sooner had he settled back to snooze when there came a knocking on his window.

He looked out and saw a jogger running in place.

"Yes?"

"Excuse me, sir," the jogger said, "do you have the time?"

The man looked at the car clock and answered, "8:15."

The jogger said thanks and left. The man settled back again and was just dozing off when there was another knock on the window and another jogger.

"Excuse me, sir, do you have the time?"

"8:25!"

The jogger said thanks and left. Now the man could see other joggers passing by and he knew it was only a matter of time before another one disturbed him.

To avoid the problem, he got out a pen and paper and put a sign in his window saying, "I do not know the time!"

Once again he settled back to sleep. He was just dozing off when there was another knock on the window.

"Sir? It's 8:45."

Jogging Shoes

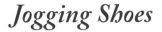

Deciding to take up jogging, the middle-aged man was astounded by the wide selection of jogging shoes available at the local sports shoe store.

While trying on a basic pair of jogging shoes, he noticed a minor feature and asked the clerk about it. "What's this little pocket thing here on the side for?"

"Oh, that's to carry spare change so you can call your wife to come pick you up when you've jogged too far."

Johnny And The School Teacher

Teacher: Well Johnny, here it is, three o'clock and you have to stay after school. You know I am only punishing you because I like you.

Johnny: I wish I could say the same for you.

Teacher: This makes the fifth time I've punished you this week. What have you got to say about that?

Johnny: I'm sure glad it's Friday, ma'am.

Teacher: Well Johnny, why don't you work hard and get ahead?

Johnny: But I've already got a head.

Teacher: Johnny, all you need is a little push and you will succeed in everything you do. Just push, push, push!

Johnny: SURE! Who should I push?

Teacher: Really, Johnny, aren't you ashamed of yourself? You've been going to school for three years now, and you can only count to ten. What will you ever be able to do in life, if you keep on at this rate?

Johnny: I could be a referee at a boxing match.

Teacher: Sure, a fine thing. Why can't you be more like Gerald? He's an all around boy. He even won the swimming match last week. Of course, he's been swimming now for three years.

Johnny: Really!? He sure must be tired.

Teacher: You know, I don't really think you're that stupid. Now, tell me, Where is Mexico?

Johnny: Oh, that's easy. On page 20 of the geography book.

Teacher: Very smart, see if you can answer this question. Who discovered America?

Johnny: Simple -Ohio!

Teacher: Ohio? Are you crazy? Don't you know it was Columbus!

Johnny: Yeah! But I didn't think it was proper to use his first name.

Teacher: Okay, let's see if you know this one. What happened in 1776.

Johnny: 1776! Why, I can't even remember what happened last week!

Teacher: It's no wonder you failed the history test!

Johnny: Well, I would have passed if it weren't for one thing.

Teacher: What was that?

Johnny: The boy who sits next to me was at home, sick.

Teacher: You're impossible! Let's see how good you are in grammar. Correct this sentence! "It was me that spilled the ink."

Johnny: "It was not me that spilled the ink. I don't even know what ink you're talking about!"

Teacher: Let's go on. Is it correct to say, "I et my supper."

Johnny: No, it is not correct.

Teacher: Why not?

Johnny: 'Cause I ain't et yet.

Teacher: Okay, that's enough grammar for now. What's drama?

Johnny: Oh, that's easy. My drama lives on a farm, and I go to see her every Christmas.

Teacher: Oh Johnny, you're terrible! How old are you?

Johnny: Nine.

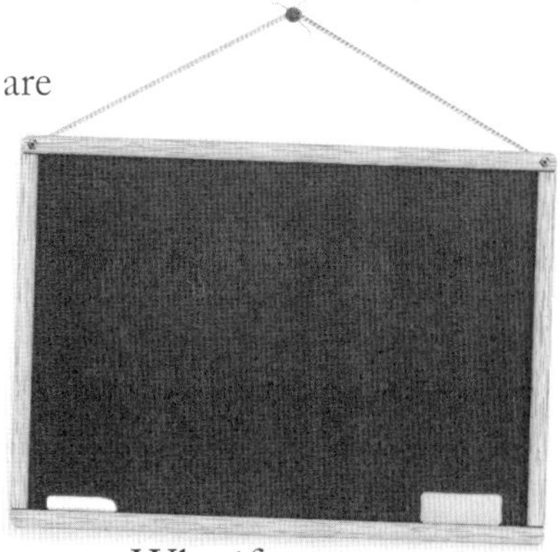

Teacher: At this rate you are never going to make anything of yourself. What are you going to be in 20 years?

Johnny: Twenty-nine

Teacher: I still say you're not as bad as you seem. Why, if you really tried you could be my right hand man.

Johnny: Just my luck—I'm left-handed.

Teacher: Oh, you are so very clever. Why don't you get wise to yourself? You're not fooling anybody. Why, this composition you handed in about your dog is word for word, just like your brothers.

Johnny: Why shouldn't it be? It's about the exact same dog.

Teacher: For certain, you are ignorant! But you must know something! Tell me, do you know what an operetta is?

Johnny: An operetta is the girl who answers the phone when you dial "0".

Teacher: I see you know nothing about music, history, geography, or grammar. Let's try this—take 13 from 21. "What's the difference?"
Johnny: That's what I say—What's the difference?
Teacher: You're impossible! What would your father have to pay if he owed $34.00 to the grocer, and $5.00 to the milkman?
Johnny: He'd pay nothing. He'd move!
Teacher: Well Johnny, you surely must know some arithmetic. What is 3x3?
Johnny: Nine.
Teacher: Well, that's pretty good.
Johnny: Pretty good nothing—that's perfect!
Teacher: Johnny, I wanted to tell you that your hand writing is absolutely impossible. You simply must learn to write better.
Johnny: Well, if I did you'd only get me for my spelling.
Teacher: Tell me, Johnny, what is a synonym?
Johnny: I'm not sure, but I think its the word you use when you can't spell the other one.
Teacher: Let's go back to geography. Can you tell me what shape the world is?
Johnny: Well, they say it's in pretty bad shape right now.
Teacher: Okay, okay, that's enough.

Just Couldn't Help Myself

For a computer programming class, I sat directly across from someone, and our computers were facing away from each other. A few minutes into the class, she got up to leave the room. I reached between our computers and switched the inputs for the keyboards.

She came back and started typing, and immediately got a distressed look on her face. She called the teacher over and explained that no matter what she typed, nothing would happen. The teacher tried everything.

By this time I was hiding behind my monitor and quaking, red-faced. I started to type, "Leave me alone!"

They both jumped back, silenced. "What…" the teacher said.

I typed, "I said leave me alone!"

The girl got real upset. "I didn't do anything to it!" she exclaimed.

It was all I could do to keep from laughing out loud. The conversation between them and her went on for an amazing five minutes.

Me: "Don't touch me!"

Her: "I'm sorry, I didn't mean to hit your keys that hard."

Me: "Who do you think you are anyway?!"

Finally, I couldn't contain myself any longer and fell out of my chair laughing. After they realized what I had done, they both turned beet red.

Funny, I never got more than a C- in that class.

Keep Walking

A boy was walking down the road one day when his dad pulled up next to him.

"If you get in the car," his dad said, "I'll give you $10 and a piece of candy."

The boy said, "I'd rather walk."

A few moments later, not to take no for an answer, his dad pulled over again. "How about $20 and two pieces of candy?"

The boy said, "I'd rather walk."

Still further down the road his dad pulled over to the side road. "Okay," he said, "I'll give you $50 and all the candy you can eat."

The little boy stopped, walked over to the car and leaned in.

"Look Dad," he said. "You bought the Ford. You'll have to live with it!"

Kentucky Mom To Her Son

Dear Son,

I am writing this slow cause I know you can't read fast. We don't live where we did when you left, your Dad read in the paper where most accidents happened within twenty miles of home, so we moved. I won't be able to send you the address 'cause the last Kentuckian family that lived here took the numbers with them for their next house so they wouldn't have to change their address.

This place has a washing machine. The first day I put four shirts in it, pulled the chain and haven't seen them since.

It's only rained twice this week, three days the first time and four days the second time.

The coat you wanted me to send you, your Aunt Sue said it would be a little too heavy to send in the mail with big heavy buttons, so we cut them off and put them in the pockets.

We got a bill from the funeral home, said if we didn't make the last payment on Grandma's funeral bill, up she comes.

About your father, he has a lovely new job, he has over five hundred people under him. He is cutting the grass at the cemetery. And your sister, she had a baby this morning. I haven't found out whether it's a boy or a girl, so I don't know whether you are an aunt or uncle.

Three of your friends went off the bridge in a pick-up truck. One was driving, the other two were in the back. The driver got out, he rolled down the window and swam to safety. The other two drowned, they couldn't get the tailgate down.

Not much news this time, nothing much has happened.

Love, Mom

P.S. I was going to send you some money, but the was already sealed.

Kitchen Help

My brother-in-law came home to an empty house one day and decided he would start dinner. First, he would make the salad. He searched high and low for the big bowl for making the salad and finally found it in the refrigerator, half full of Kool-Aid®.

"Who put Kool-Aid® in a bowl?" He looked around and found some empty pop bottles, rinsed them out and using a funnel, transferred the Kool-Aid® to the pop bottles and returned them to the fridge. He then made the salad and started the rest of the dinner.

Later, my sister came home. She had been to the store and was putting some things in the fridge, when suddenly she asked her husband, "Who put my Jell-O® in pop bottles?"

Kitchen Signs

- Kitchen closed—I've had it!
- Martha Stewart doesn't live here!!
- I'm creative; you can't expect me to be neat, too!
- Ring Bell for Maid Service. If no answer, do it yourself!
- You may touch the dust in this house, but please don't write in it!
- If you write in the dust, please don't date it!
- I would cook dinner, but I can't find the can opener!
- I came, I saw, I decided to order take out.
- If you don't like my standards of cooking, lower your standards.
- A messy kitchen is a happy kitchen, and this kitchen is delirious.
- Help keep the kitchen clean—eat out.
- Countless numbers of people have eaten in this kitchen and gone on to lead normal lives.
- My house was clean last week; too bad you missed it!

Label Warning

My in-laws gave us a beautiful knife set—top quality. The accompanying cutting board, however, was a different story. On the wrapping around it was printed this warning: "Opening with sharp object may damage this product."

Late Preacher

A young preacher was asked by the local funeral director to hold a grave-side burial service at a small local cemetery for someone with no family or friends. The preacher started early but quickly got himself lost, making several wrong turns. Eventually, a half-hour late, he saw a backhoe and its crew, but the hearse was nowhere in sight,and the workmen were eating lunch.

The diligent young pastor went to the open grave and found the vault lid already in place.

Taking out his book and feeling guilty because of his tardiness, he preached an impassioned and lengthy service.

As he was returning to his car, he overheard one of the workmen say: "I've been putting in septic tanks for twenty years and I ain't never seen anything like that."

Laws:

- Law of Mechanical Repair
  After your hands become coated with grease, your nose will begin to itch or you'll suddenly need to use the restroom.
- Law of the Workshop
  Any tool, when dropped, will roll to the least accessible corner.
- Law of Probability
  The probability of being watched is directly proportional to the stupidity of your act.
- Law of the Telephone
  If you dial a wrong number, you never get a busy signal.
- Law of the Alibi
  If you tell the boss you were late for work because you had a flat tire, the very next morning you will have a flat tire.
- Variation Law
  If you change lanes, the one you were in will start to move faster than the one you are in now (works every time).
- Law of the Bath
  When the body is fully immersed in water, the telephone rings.
- Law of Close Encounters
  The probability of meeting someone you know increases dramatically when you are with someone you don't want to be seen with.
- Law of the Result
  When you try to prove to someone that a machine won't work, it will.
- Law of Bio-mechanics
  The severity of the itch is inversely proportional to the reach.
- Law of the Theatre
  At any event, the people whose seats are furthest from the aisle arrive last.
- Law of Coffee
  As soon as you sit down to a cup of hot coffee, your boss will ask you to do something which will last until the coffee is cold.
- Murphy's Law of Lockers
  If there are only two people in a locker room, they will have adjacent lockers.
- Law of Rugs/Carpets
  The chances of an open-faced jelly sandwich landing face down on a floor covering are directly correlated to the newness and cost of the carpet/rug.
- Law of Location
  No matter where you go, there you are.
- Law of Logical Argument
  Anything is possible if you don't know what you are talking about.
- Brown's Law
  If the shoe fits, it's ugly.
- Oliver's Law
  A closed mouth gathers no feet.
- Wilson's Law
  As soon as you find a product that you really like, they will stop making it
- Doctors' Law
  If you don't feel well, make an appointment to go to the doctor, by the time you get there you'll feel better. Don't make an appointment and you'll stay sick.

Laws of the Toddler

1. If I like it, it's mine.
2. If it's in my hand, it's mine.
3. If I can take it from you, it's mine.
4. If I had it a little while ago, it's mine.
5. If it's mine, it must never appear to be yours in any way.
6. If I'm doing or building something, all the pieces are mine.
7. If it looks just like mine, it's mine.
8. If I think it's mine, it's mine.

Lawyers

A very successful lawyer parked his brand new Lexus in front of the office, ready to show it off to his colleagues. As he got out, a truck came along, too close to the curb, and completely tore off the driver's door.

The lawyer immediately grabbed his cell phone, dialed 911, and it wasn't more than five minutes before a policeman pulled up. Before the cop had a chance to ask any questions, the lawyer started screaming hysterically.

His Lexus, which he had just picked up the day before, was now completely ruined and would never be the same, no matter how the body shop tried to make it new again.

After the lawyer finally wound down from his rant, the cop shook his head in disgust and disbelief. "I can't believe how materialistic you lawyers are," he said. "You are so focused on your possessions that you neglect the most important things in life."

"How can you say such a thing?" asked the lawyer.

The cop replied, "Man, don't you even realize that your left arm is missing? It got ripped off when the truck hit you!!"

"Oh my!" screamed the lawyer, looking down at his missing arm. "Where's my Rolex?"

Leaning Slightly

I have a friend who always seemed to lean slightly to the left all the time.

It used to bother me, so I suggested he see a doctor and have his legs checked out. For years, he refused and told me I was crazy.

But last week, he finally went, and sure enough, the doctor discovered his left leg was 1/4 inch shorter than his right.

A quick bit of orthopedic surgery later, he was cured. Both legs are exactly the same length now, and he no longer leans.

"So," I said, "you didn't believe me when I told you a doctor could fix your leg."

He just looked at me and said, "I stand corrected."

Leaky Pipe

A lady answered her front door to find a plumber standing there. "I'm here to fix the leaky pipe," he announced.

"I didn't call a plumber," said the lady.

"What?" huffed the plumber. "Aren't you Mrs. Frobisher?"

"The Frobishers moved out of this house over a year ago," explained the lady.

"How do you like that," grunted the plumber. "They call you up and tell you it's an emergency and then they move away!"

Learning How to Ride a Bicycle

Never having learned to ride a bicycle as a child, I finally decided to do it in my late twenties. My boyfriend, William, offered to teach me, and we headed to the park for my first lesson. He held on to the seat as I wobbled down a path. My self consciousness was just beginning to disappear when I saw a father, teaching his little daughter to ride a bike, approaching. As we passed, I was mortified when William said to the dad, "They grow up so fast, don't they?"

Leaky Roof

Mr. Gable had a leak in the roof over his dining room, so he called a repairman to take a look at it.

"When did you first notice the leak?" the repairman inquired.

Mr. Gable scowled. "Last night, when it took me two hours to finish my soup!"

Lessons From A Tree

1. It's important to have roots.
2. In today's complex world, it pays to branch out.
3. Don't pine away over old flames.
4. If you really believe in something, don't be afraid to go out on a limb.
5. Be flexible so you don't break when a harsh wind blows.
6. Sometimes you have to shed your old bark in order to grow.
7. If you want to keep accurate records, keep a log.
8. To be politically correct, don't wear firs.
9. Grow where you are planted.
10. It's perfectly okay to be a late bloomer.
11. Avoid people who would like to cut you down.

12. If the party is boring, just leaf.
13. You can't hide your true colors as you approach the autumn of your life.
14. It's more important to be honest than poplar.

—Submitted by Gary Fike

Lessons I Learned From A Cow

1. Wake up in a happy mooo-d.
2. Don't cry over spilled milk.
3. When chewing your cud, remember: There's no fat, no calories, no cholesterol, and no taste!
4. The grass is greener on the other side of the fence.
5. Turn the udder cheek and mooo-ve on.
6. Seize every opportunity and milk it for all its worth!
7. It's better to be seen and not herd.
8. Honor thy fodder and thy mother and all your udder relatives.
9. Always let them know who's the bossy.
10. Black and white is always an appropriate fashion statement.
11. Don't forget to cow-nt your blessings every day.

Letters to God from Children

Dear God,

Thank you for the baby brother but what I asked for was a puppy. I never asked for anything before. You can look it up.

—Joyce

Dear Mr. God,

I wish you would not make it so easy for people to come apart. I had to have three stitches and a shot.

—Janet

Dear God,

How did you know you were God?

—Charlene

Dear God,

My Grandpa says you were around when he was a little boy. How far back do you go?

—Love, Dennis

Dear God,

I bet it's very hard for you to love everybody in the whole world. There are only four people in our family and I can never do it.

—Nan

Dear God,

Who draws the lines around the countries?

—Nan

Dear God,

Did you mean for a giraffe to look like that or was it an accident?

—Norma

Dear God,

What does it mean you are a jealous God? I thought you had everything.

—Jane

Dear God,

In Sunday School they told us what you do. Who does it when you are on vacation?

—Jane

Life In Los Angeles

A man was sitting in an airplane when another guy took the seat beside him. The new guy was a wreck—pale, hands shaking, biting his nails and moaning in fear.

"Hey, pal, what's the matter?" said the first guy.

"I've been transferred to Los Angeles, California," he answered nervously. "They've got race riots, drugs, the highest crime rate in the country…"

"Hold on," said the first. "I've been in Los Angeles all my life, and it's not as bad as the media says. Find a nice home, go to work, mind your own business, enroll your children in a good school, and it's as safe as anywhere in the world."

The second guy stopped shaking for a moment and said, "Oh, good. I was really worried! But if you live there and say it's ok, I'll take your word for it. By the way, what do you do for a living?"

"Me?" said the first, "I'm a security guard on a bread truck."

Limp Duck

A woman brought a very limp duck into a veterinary surgeon. As she lay her pet on the table, the vet pulled out his stethoscope and listened to the bird's chest. After a moment or two, the vet shook his head sadly and said, "I'm so sorry, your pet has passed away."

The distressed owner wailed, "Are you sure?"

"Yes, I'm sure. The duck is dead," he replied.

"How can you be so sure," she protested. "I mean, you haven't done any testing on him or anything. He might just be in a coma or something."

The vet rolled his eyes, turned around and left the room. He returned a few moments later with a black Labrador Retriever. As the duck's owner looked on in amazement, the dog stood on his hind legs, put his front paws on the examination table and sniffed the duck from top to bottom. He then looked at the vet with sad eyes and shook his head. The vet patted the dog and took it out and returned a few moments later with a beautiful cat. The cat jumped up on the table and also sniffed the bird from its beak to its tail and back again. The cat sat back on its haunches, shook its head, meowed softly, jumped down and strolled out of the room.

The vet looked at the woman and said, "I'm sorry, but as I said, this is most definitely, 100% certifiably, a dead duck." Then the vet turned to his computer terminal, hit a few keys, and produced a bill, which he handed to the woman.

The duck's owner, still in shock, took the bill. "$150!" she cried. "$150 just to tell me my duck is dead?!!"

The vet shrugged. "I'm sorry. If you'd taken my word for it, the bill would have been $20. But with the Lab Report and the Cat Scan, it all adds up."

Little Tim

Little Tim was in the garden filling in a hole when his neighbor peered over the fence. Interested in what the rosy-cheeked youngster was up to, he politely asked, "What are you up to there, Tim?"

"My goldfish died," replied Tim tearfully, without looking up, "and I've just buried him."

The neighbor was concerned, "That's an awfully big hole for a goldfish, isn't it?"

Tim patted down the last heap of earth then replied, "That's because he's inside your cat!"

Lobster Tails

A guy was down on Fisherman's Wharf in San Francisco when he saw a seafood restaurant and a sign on the Specials Board which read, "Big Lobster Tales, $5 each."

Amazed at the great value, he said to the waitress, "$5 each for lobster tails…is that correct?"

"Yes", she said, "It's our special just for today."

"Well", he said, "they must be little lobster tails."

"No," she replied, "they're really big!"

"Are you sure they aren't green lobster tails—and a little bit tough?"

"No", she said, "they're really big, red lobster tails"

"Big red lobster tails, $5 each?" he said, amazed. "They must be old lobster tails!"

"No, they're definitely today's."

"Today's big red lobster tails—$5 each?" he repeated, astounded.

"Yes", she insisted.

"Well, here's my five dollars," he said, "I'll take one."

She took the money and led him to a table where she invited him to sit down. She then sat down next to him, put her hand on his shoulder, leaned over close to him and said,

"Once upon a time there was a really big red lobster…"

Logic

Explaining luggage regulations to passengers can be aggravating for flight attendants. One day a woman tried to board with an enormous bag. The lead flight attendant told her why it would not fit, but the woman argued that her bag was a carry-on because it had wheels and a handle.

Without blinking the attendant said, "My Ford has wheels and a handle, but that doesn't make it a carry-on."

Lost In Bookstore

A friend and her young son, Reid, were browsing in a large bookstore. Engrossed in making a selection, my friend had lost sight of her child.

"Reid!" she called out, racing through the aisles. "Reid!"

Just as she spotted the boy, she bumped into another customer. "Pardon me, ma'am," he said, "but most folks come here because they already like to read. No sense in wasting your time trying to convince them."

Lost In The Library

Arriving back at the dorm late one evening, my roommate explained that she had gotten lost in the school library. No one was surprised, since the library is large and has a confusing layout.

When asked how long it took her to find an exit, she admitted she hadn't actually found the exit herself. She had used an emergency phone to call for help. Puzzled, I asked, "How did your rescuers find you if you didn't know where you were?"

"Easy," she said. "I started reading titles of books around me, and they located my position from the card catalogue."

Love Campaign

The young suitor was determined to win the heart of the girl he wanted to marry, in spite of her rejection of his proposals a number of times.

He began what can only be called "campaigning" and sent her a small token of his affection every day for a month to her house.

Soon, the young lady fell in love with the UPS man.

Luggage Pick-Up At The Airport

Robert was a traveling salesman and frequent flyer, so he was always very, VERY careful to mark his luggage so that no one would mistakenly take his bags. He always did this carefully, with bright ribbons and tape, so he was quite surprised to see his bags grabbed by a well dressed man.

Robert pointed out the colored ribbons tied to the handle, and the fluorescent tape on the sides. "Were your bags marked like this?" he asked. "Actually," the man replied, "I was wondering who did this to my luggage."

Lumberjack Wanted

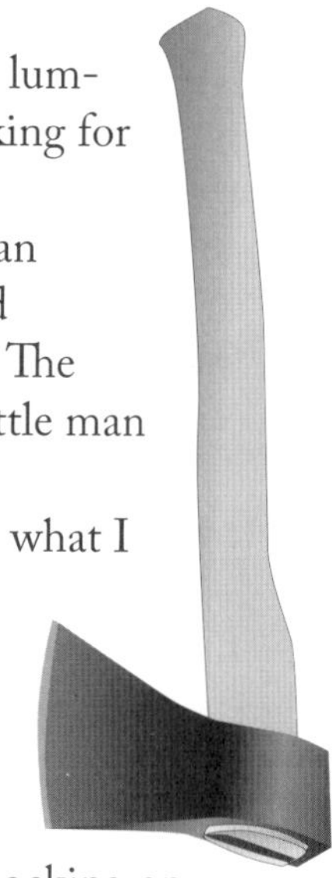

A large, well-established Canadian lumber camp advertised that they were looking for a good lumberjack.

The very next day, a skinny little man showed up at the camp with his axe and knocked on the head lumberjack's door. The head lumberjack took one look at the little man and told him to leave.

"Just give me a chance to show you what I can do," said the skinny man.

"Okay, see that giant redwood over there?" said the lumberjack.
"Take your axe and go cut it down."

The skinny man headed for the tree, and in five minutes he was back knocking on the lumberjack's door. "I cut the tree down," said the man.

The lumberjack couldn't believe his eyes and said, "Where did you get the skill to chop down trees like that?"

"In the Sahara Forest," replied the puny man.

"You mean the Sahara Desert," said the lumberjack.

The little man laughed and answered back, "Oh sure, that's what they call it now!"

Lumber Needed

Some men in a pickup truck drove into a lumberyard. One of the men walked in the office and said, "We need some four-by-twos."

The clerk asked, "You mean two-by-fours, don't you?"

The man said, "I'll go check," and went back to the truck. He returned and said, "Yeah, I meant two-by-fours."

"All right. How long do you need them?"

The customer paused for a minute and said, "I'd better go check."

After a while, the customer returned to the office and said, "A long time. We're gonna build a house."

Mail Worker

A young man named Clarence got a part time job at the post office. The first assignment his supervisor gave him was the job of sorting the mail. Clarence separated the letters so fast that his motions were literally a blur. Extremely pleased by this, the supervisor approached Clarence at the end of his first day.

"I just want you to know," the supervisor said, "that I'm very pleased with the job you did today. You're one of the fastest workers we've ever had."

"Thank you, sir," said Clarence, beaming, "and tomorrow I'll try to do an even better job."

"Better?" the supervisor asked with astonishment. "How can you possibly do any better than you did today?"

Clarence replied, "Tomorrow I'm going to read the addresses."

Maine Veterinarian

Dr. Cutter is the local veterinarian, known for his wry humor. He surpassed himself one summer day when a city dog was brought to him after an encounter with a porcupine. After almost an hour of prying, pulling, cutting, and stitching, he returned the dog to its owner, who asked what she owed.

"Fifteen dollars, Ma'am," he answered.

"Why that's simply outrageous!" she stormed. "That's what's wrong with you Maine people, you're always trying to over charge summer visitors. Whatever do you do in the winter, when we're not being gypped here?"

"Raise porcupines, Ma'am," he replied.

Major Oops!

Tired of the inconvenience of driving from the airport to his country cottage, a man equipped his small plane with pontoons so he could land on the lake directly in front of his cottage. On his next trip however, he made his approach down the airport runway as usual.

Alarmed, his wife cried out, "Are you crazy? You can't land this plane here without wheels!" The startled husband yanked the nose up, narrowly averting certain disaster.

Continuing home, he landed the plane on the lake without mishap. As he sat there, visibly shaken, he said to his wife, "I don't know what on earth got into me. That's the stupidest thing I've ever done in my life!"

And with that, he opened the door and stepped out…right into the water.

Man's Greatest Invention

In my opinion the dishwasher is one of man's greatest inventions. It is a little too presumptuous to say it is the best, because many other inventions had to be invented to even make such a machine possible.

Although many machines save us time, the dishwasher must rank near the top. It can save us an hour and a half of work each day and possibly more. When the air is hot and sticky outside, a dishwasher can save you the task of putting your already hot arms into a pan of boiling water. The dishwasher can be extremely handy when you have guests to entertain, or you feel tired and sick. To be able to place your dishes in a machine, press some buttons, and then walk away leaving it to do the job is an immense treat.

By all of this I am not suggesting that we totally eradicate the old method of washing dishes by hand, but I am pointing out the usefulness of this machine if we allow it to occupy a small part of our kitchen. Since washing dishes is something that needs to be learned and can even be therapeutic at times, the dishwasher should be used sparingly while fully appreciating the treats we are given by it.

So every time you load that wonder machine and simply press the magic button, be thankful that you have it and take some time to pity those that don't. You see, I don't have one!

Marital Argument

A young couple drove several miles down a country road, not saying a word. An earlier discussion had led to an argument, and neither wanted to concede their position.

As they passed a barnyard of mules and pigs, the husband sarcastically asked, "Are they relatives of yours?"

"Yes," his wife replied. "I married into the family."

Math Symbols

While reviewing math symbols with my second-grade pupils, I drew a greater-than (>) and a less-than sign (<) on the chalkboard and asked, "Does anyone remember what these mean?"

A few moments passed, and then a boy confidently raised his hand. "One means fast-forward," he exclaimed, "And the other means rewind!"

"Mature"

Today at the drugstore, the clerk was a gent.
From my purchase, this chap took off ten percent.
I asked for the cause of a lesser amount;
and he answered, "Because of the Seniors Discount".
I went to McDonald's® for a burger and fries;
And there, once again, got quite a surprise.
The clerk poured some coffee which he handed to me,
He said, "For you Seniors the coffee is free."

But some things are changing, temporarily, I'm sure.
Understand, I'm not old, I'm merely mature;
The newspaper print gets smaller each day,
And people speak softer—can't hear what they say.
My teeth are my own (I have the receipt)
and my glasses identify people I meet.
Oh, I've slowed down a bit…not a lot, I'm sure.
You see, I'm not old, I'm only mature.

The gold in my hair has been bleached by the sun.
You should see all the damage that chlorine has done.
Washing my hair has turned it all white,
But don't call it gray, saying 'blonde' is just right.
My car is all paid for, not a nickel is owed.
Yet a child yells, "Old duffer…get off of the road!"
My car has no scratches, not even a dent,
Still I get all that mean stuff that's not worth a cent.
My friends all get older, much faster than me.
They seem much more wrinkled, from what I can see.
I've got 'character lines', not wrinkles, for sure,
But don't call me old, just call me mature.

The steps in the houses they're building today
Are so high that they take your breath all away;
And the streets are much steeper than ten years ago,
That should explain why my walking is slow.
But I'm keeping up on what's in and what's new,
And I think I can still dance a jig or two.
I'm still in the running in this I'm secure,
I'm not really old, I'm only mature.

Measuring

A man saw four men measuring a pole. Three of them were holding the pole straight up and another fellow was climbing it with a tape measure measuring it. "What are you doing?" he asked. They answered, "We are measuring this pole. The onlooker said, "Why not lay it down on the ground?" They replied, "We are not trying to find out how long it is, we want to know how high it is."

Message Puzzle

April was puzzled recently by the odd messages she kept getting on her voice mail. Day after day, all she'd hear, from friends, family, and customers alike, would be their message and then they'd all say, "BEEP."

We were talking about something else and I had her check her voice mail message to find something out. She discovered the solution to the BEEP riddle.

Her message said, "I'm not available right now, so, please leave a beep after the message."

Missed Bus

The new family in the neighborhood overslept, and their six-year-old daughter missed her school bus.

The father, though late for work, had to drive her. Not knowing where the school was, he asked if she'd direct him.

They rode several blocks before she told him to turn the

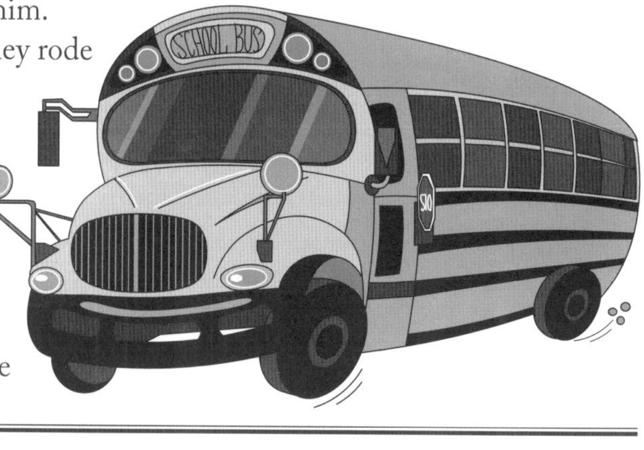

first time, several more before she indicated another turn. This went on for twenty minutes—but when they finally reached the school, it proved to be only a short distance from their home.

The father, much annoyed, asked his daughter why she'd led him around in such a circle.

The child explained, "That's the way the school bus goes, Daddy. It's the only way I know."

Missed Ferry

This guy loved living in Staten Island, but he wasn't crazy about the ferry. If he missed a ferry late at night, he would have to spend the next hour or so wandering the deserted streets of lower Manhattan.

When he spotted a ferry no more than fifteen feet from the dock, he decided he wouldn't subject himself to an hour's wait. He made a running leap and landed on his hands and knees, a little bruised maybe, but safe on deck.

He got up, brushed himself off, and announced proudly to a bystander, "Well, I made that one, didn't I?"

"Sure did," the bystander said. "But you should have waited a minute or two. The ferry is just about to dock."

Missing Bags

I couldn't find my luggage at the airport baggage area so I went to the lost luggage office and told the woman there that my bags never showed up. She smiled and told me not to worry because they were trained professionals and I was in good hands.

"Now," she asked me, "has your plane arrived yet?"

Money Worries

Fresh out of business school, the young man answered a want ad for an accountant. He was being interviewed by a very nervous man who ran a three-man business.

"I need someone with an accounting degree," the man said. "But mainly, I'm looking for someone to do my worrying for me."

"Excuse me?" the young accountant said.

"I worry about a lot of things," the man said. "But I don't want to have to worry about money. Your job will be to take all the money worries off my back."

"I see," the young accountant said. "And how much does the job pay?"

"I will start you at eighty-five thousand dollars."

"Eighty-five thousand dollars!" the young man exclaimed. "How can such a small business afford a sum like that?"

"That," the owner said, "is your first worry."

More Computer Literate

Don't feel stupid about using your computer—read on...(This is an excerpt from a Wall Street Journal article):

1. Compaq is considering changing the command "Press Any Key" to "Press Return Key" because of the flood of calls asking where the "Any Key" is.
2. AST technical support had a caller complaining that her mouse was hard to control with the dust cover on. The cover turned out to be the plastic bag the mouse was packaged in.
3. Another AST customer was asked to send a copy of her defective diskettes. A few days later a letter arrived from the customer along with photocopies of the floppies.
4. Dell customer called to say he couldn't get his computer to fax anything. After 40 minutes of troubleshooting, the technician discovered the man was trying to fax a piece of paper by holding it in front of the monitor screen and hitting the "send" key.
5. A Dell technician received a call from a customer who was enraged because his computer had told him he was "bad and an invalid." The tech explained that the computer's "bad command" and "invalid" responses shouldn't be taken personally.
6. A confused caller to IBM was having trouble printing documents. He told the technician that the computer said it "couldn't find printer." The user had also tried turning the computer screen to face the printer but that his computer still couldn't "see" the printer.
7. An exasperated caller to Dell Computer Tech Support couldn't get her new Dell Computer to turn

on. After ensuring the computer was plugged in, the technician asked her what happened when she pushed the power button. Her response, "I pushed and pushed on this foot pedal and nothing happens." The "foot pedal" turned out to be the mouse.

8. Another customer called Compaq tech support to say her brand-new computer wouldn't work. She said she unpacked the unit, plugged it in and sat there for 20 minutes waiting for something to happen. When asked what happened when she pressed the power switch, she asked "What power switch?"
9. IBM customer had trouble installing software and called in for support. "I put in the first disk, and that was okay. It said to put in the second disk, and that's when I began encountering problems with the disk. When it said to put in the third disk, I couldn't even fit it in…" The user hadn't realized that "Insert Disk 2" meant to remove Disk 1 first.
10. In a similar incident, a customer had followed the instructions for installing software. The instructions said to remove the disk from its cover and insert into the drive. The user had physically removed the casing of the disk and wondered why there were problems.
11. True story from a Novell NetWare Sysop:
    Caller: "Hello, is this Tech Support? The cup holder on my PC is broken and I am within my warranty period. How do I go about getting that fixed?"
    Tech: "I'm sorry, but did you say a cup holder?"
    Caller: "Yes, it's attached to the front of my computer."
    Tech: "Please excuse me. If I seem a bit stumped, it's because I am. Did you receive this as part of a promotional at a trade show? How did you get this cup holder? Does it have any trademark on it?"
    Caller: "It came with my computer. I don't know anything about a promotion. It just has '4X' on it."
    At this point, the Tech Rep had to mute the caller because he was laughing too hard. The caller had been using the load drawer of the CD ROM drive as a cup holder and snapped it off.

Now don't you feel better about your skill level??

Most Difficult Case

Two psychiatrists were at a convention. As they conversed over dinner, one asked, "What was your most difficult case?"

The other replied, "I had a patient who lived in a pure fantasy world. He believed that an uncle in South America was going to die and leave him a fortune. All day long he waited for a letter to arrive from an attorney. He never went out, he never did anything, he merely sat around and waited for this fantasy letter from this fantasy uncle. I worked with this man eight years."

"What was the result?"

"It was an eight-year struggle, every day for eight years, but I finally cured him. And then that stupid letter arrived!"

Motivating Others

John, a neighbor of mine, was annoyed because he had to search for his newspaper each morning after the paperboy tossed it. Often he would find it covered with dirt under the car in the gravel driveway. Then one day the paperboy's mother mentioned that her son's ambition was to play professional basketball. John had an idea.

When he got home, he attached a basketball hoop to a post on the front porch. Sure enough, the next morning there was a resounding "Plunk" as the newspaper sailed through the hoop and landed by the door.

John never had to search for his paper again.

Mouse Mom

A mother mouse and a baby mouse were walking along, when all of a sudden, a cat attacked them. The mother mouse yelled, "Bark!" And the cat ran away.

"See?" Said the mother mouse to her baby. "Now do you understand why it's important to learn a foreign language?"

Moving Labels

Having moved fifteen times during our 37-year marriage, my husband and I appreciate movers who take the time to label carefully boxes they pack for us.

The accuracy of labels can make a huge difference when we try to find something right away.

My favorite was done by one guy who attached this sticker to a box—obviously not knowing how to spell the best one word description: "Animals you hit with a stick at a Mexican party."

Musical Note

The first graders were attending their first music lesson. The teacher was trying to start at the beginning. She drew a musical staff on the blackboard and asked a little girl to come up and write a note on it.

The little girl went to the blackboard, looked thoughtful for a minute and wrote, "Dear Aunt Emma, just a short note to tell you I'm fine."

Nail Biting

Two elderly women were fussing about their husbands over tea one day.

"I do wish my Leroy would stop biting his nails. That makes me terribly nervous!" The first one said.

"Oh, my Elmer used to do the same thing," the other woman commented. "But I broke him of that habit real quick."

"What did you do?"

"I hid his teeth!"

Name Puns

Baby Name Ideas, Based On Your Occupation…

Profession: Name

- Lawyer's daughter: Sue
- Thief's son: Rob
- Lawyer's son: Will
- Doctor's son: Bill
- Meteorologist's daughter: Haley
- Steam shovel operator's son: Doug
- Hair stylist's son: Bob
- Homeopathic doctor's son: Herb
- Justice of the Peace's daughter: Mary
- Sound stage technician's son: Mike
- Iron worker's son: Rusty
- Barber's son: Harry
- Housewife's son: Dusty
- Manicurist's son: Hans
- Athlete's son: Victor
- Plumber's son: John
- Accountant's son: Ira
- Musician's daughter: Melody
- Museum curator's son: Art
- Book printer's daughter: Paige
- Trout fisher's daughter: Brook
- Woodworker's daughter: Peg
- Clothing manufacturer's daughter: Polly Esther
- Teacher's son: Mark
- Singer's twin daughters: Harmony & Melody
- Patrolman's son: Chase
- Hot-dog vendor's son: Frank

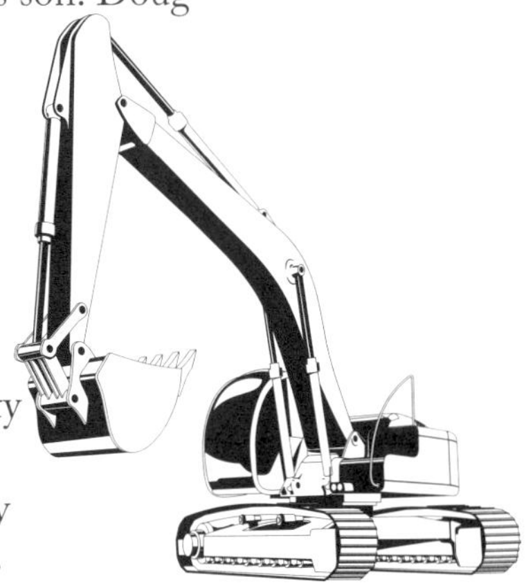

Neither Borrower Nor A Lender

My next-door neighbor and I frequently borrow things from each other. Not long ago, when I requested his ladder, he told me he had lent it to his son. Recalling a saying my grandmother used to repeat, I recited, "You should never lend anything to your children, because you will never get it back."

With that, he responded, "Well, it's not even my ladder. It's my dad's."

Newborn Price Tag

A mother came home from the hospital with her newborn son still wearing his hospital identification tag. The mother's three-year-old son asked the mother, "Mamma, when you gonna take off his price tag?"

New Diet

Needing to shed a few pounds, my wife and I went on a diet that had specific recipes for each meal of the day. We followed the instructions closely, dividing the finished recipe in half for our individual plates. We felt terrific and thought the diet was wonderful. We never even felt hungry!

But soon we realized we were gaining weight, not losing it. Checking the recipes again, we found it. There, in fine print, was: "Serves 6."

New Patio

My husband, Ray, was attempting to build a patio for the first time. He bought one hundred cement blocks. Laying them out in a pattern, he discovered the chosen area was too small.

He stacked the blocks against the house and cleared more space. The next day Ray put the cement blocks back down, only to find that the ground was too hard to keep the patio level.

He ordered a truckload of sand to be delivered the following morning. Again he stacked the 100 blocks against the house.

Observing all this, our next door neighbor asked, "Ray, are you going to put your patio away every night?"

Newlywed Repairs

A man came home from the office and found his new bride sobbing convulsively. "I feel terrible," she told him. "I was pressing your suit and I burned a big hole in the seat of your trousers."

"Oh, just forget it," consoled her husband. "Remember that I've got an extra pair of pants for that suit."

"Yes, I know. And it's lucky you have!" Said the woman, drying her eyes. "I was able to use a piece from them to patch the hole!"

New Wing

Recently, when a Panel of Doctors at our local hospital was asked to vote on adding a new wing, this is what happened…

- The allergists voted to scratch it.
- The dermatologists preferred no rash moves.
- The gastroenterologists had a gut feeling about it.
- The neurologists thought the administration had a lot of nerve.
- The ophthalmologists considered the idea shortsighted.
- The pathologists yelled, "Over my dead body!"
- The pediatricians said, "Grow up."
- The psychiatrists thought it was madness.
- The surgeons decided to wash their hands of the whole thing.
- The radiologists could see right through it.
- The internists thought it was a hard pill to swallow.
- The plastic surgeons said, "This puts a whole new face on the matter."
- The podiatrists thought it was a big step forward.
- The urologists felt the scheme wouldn't hold water.
- The anesthesiologists thought the whole idea was a gas.
- And the cardiologists didn't have the heart to say no.
- The HMOs killed it anyway.

No Novocaine

A woman and her husband interrupted their vacation to go to the dentist. "I want a tooth pulled, and I don't want novocaine because I'm in a big hurry," the woman said. "Just extract the tooth as quickly as possible, and we'll be on our way."

The dentist was quite impressed. "You're certainly a courageous woman," he said. "Which tooth is it?"

The woman turned to her husband and said, "Show him your tooth, dear."

No Pun In Ten Did

1. Two vultures board an airplane; each is carrying two dead raccoons. The stewardess looks at them and says, "I'm sorry, gentlemen, only one carrion allowed per passenger."
2. Two Eskimos sitting in a kayak were chilly, but when they lit a fire in the craft it sank, proving once again that you can't have your kayak and heat it, too.
3. A group of chess enthusiasts checked into a hotel and were standing in the lobby discussing their recent tournament victories. After about an hour, the manager came out of the office and asked them to disperse. "But why?" they asked, as they moved off. "Because," he said, "I can't stand chess nuts boasting in an open foyer."

4. And finally, there was the person who sent ten different puns to friends, with the hope that at least one of the puns would make them laugh. Unfortunately, no pun in ten did.

Note from the Judge

During court one busy day, the judge quietly passed the clerk a note reading: "Blind on right side, may be falling. Please call someone."

Understandably alarmed, the clerk called for help before whispering to the judge that paramedics were on their way.

Puzzled, the judge pointed to a sagging venetian blind on the right side of the room and explained, "I was thinking maybe someone from maintenance!"

Not for Lunch

My husband retired, and for the first time in over 40 years I had to think about preparing midday meals. Tired of it after several months, I said, "I married you for better or worse, but not for lunch."

"Fair enough. From now on I'll make my own," he replied.

A few weeks later he had to go downtown on business and invited me to join him afterwards. "We could have lunch at that Chinese place we both like," he suggested.

I happily agreed. At the restaurant the next day we were seated, and the waiter came to take our order. My husband looked up, a twinkle in his eyes and said, "Separate checks, please…"

Not So Wild Please

These are actual comments left on U. S. Forest Service registration sheets and comment cards by backpackers upon completion of their wilderness camping trips:

- A small deer came into my camp and stole my bag of pickles. Is there a way I can get reimbursed? Please call.
- Escalators would help on steep uphill sections.
- Instead of a permit system or regulations, the Forest Service needs to reduce world-wide population growth to limit the number of visitors to wilderness.
- Trails need to be wider so people can walk while holding hands.
- The coyotes made too much noise last night and kept me awake. Please eradicate these annoying animals.
- All the mile markers are missing this year.
- A McDonald's® would be nice at the trailhead.
- Trails need to be reconstructed. Please avoid building trails that go uphill.
- Too many bugs and leeches and spiders and spider webs. Please spray the wilderness to rid the area of these pests.
- Please pave the trails so they can be plowed of snow in the winter.
- Chair lifts need to be in some places so that we can get to wonderful views without having to hike to them.
- Reflectors need to be placed on trees every fifty feet so people can hike at night with flashlights.
- Need more signs to keep area pristine.
- Too many rocks in the mountains.
- Ban walking sticks in the wilderness. Hikers that use walking sticks are more likely to chase animals.
- The places where trails do not exist are not well marked.

Now, Now, Ellen

A man observed a woman in the grocery store with a three-year-old girl in her basket. As they passed the cookie section, the child asked for cookies, and her mother told her "No." The little girl immediately began to whine and fuss, and the mother said quietly, "Now, Ellen, we just have half of the aisles left to go through; don't be upset. It won't be long."

He passed the mother again in the candy aisle. Of course, the little girl began to shout for candy. When she was told she couldn't have any, she began to cry. The mother said, "There, there, Ellen, don't cry. Only two more aisles to go, and then we'll be checking out."

The man happened to be behind the pair in the checkout line, where the little girl began to clamor for gum and burst into a terrible tantrum upon discovering her mother would not buy any gum. "Ellen, we'll be through this checkout stand in five minutes, and then you can go home and have a nice nap," the mom said.

The man followed them out to the parking lot and stopped the woman to compliment her. "I couldn't help noticing how patient you were with little Ellen," he said.

The mother replied, "My little girl's name is Tammy. I'm Ellen."

Nutritious Eating

According to a recent article I just read on nutrition, they said eating right doesn't have to be complicated. Nutritionists say there is a simple way to tell if you're eating right. Colors. Fill your plates with bright colors. Greens, reds, yellows.

In fact, I did that this morning. I had an entire bowl of M&M's®. It was delicious! I never knew eating right could be so easy.

I now have a whole new outlook on life.

Old-Timer Woes

At a nursing home in Florida, a group of senior citizens were sitting around talking about their aches and pains. "My arms are so weak I can hardly lift this cup of coffee," said one. "I know what you mean. My cataracts are so bad I can't even see my coffee," replied another. "I can't turn my head because of the arthritis in my neck," said a third, to which several nodded weakly in agreement. "My blood pressure pills make me dizzy," another contributed. "I guess that's the price we pay for getting old," winced an old man as he slowly shook his head. Then there was a short moment of silence. "Well, it's not that bad," said one woman cheerfully. "At least we can all still drive."

Ol' Spot

A group of country neighbors wanted to get together on a regular basis and socialize. As a result, about ten couples formed a dinner club and agreed to meet for dinner at a different neighbors' house each month. When it came time for Jimmy and Susie Brown to have the dinner at their house, Susie wanted to outdo all the others and prepare a meal that was the best that any of them had ever had. A few days before the big event, Susie got out her cookbook and decided to have mushroom smothered steak.

When she went to the store to buy some mushrooms, she found the price for a small can was more than she wanted to pay. She then told her husband, "We aren't going to have mushrooms, because they are too expensive."

He said, "Why don't you go down in the pasture and pick some of those mushrooms? There are plenty of them right in the creek bed."

She said, "No, I don't want to do that, because I have heard that wild mushrooms are poisonous."

He then said, "I don't think so. I see the varmints eating them all the time and it never has affected them."

After thinking about this, Susie decided to give this a try and got in the pickup and went down in the pasture and picked some. She brought the wild mushrooms back home and washed them, sliced and diced them to get them ready to go over her smothered steak. Then she went out on the

back porch and got Ol' Spot's (the yard dog) bowl and gave him a double handful. She even put some bacon grease on them to make them tasty. Ol' Spot didn't slow down until he had eaten every bite. All morning long, Susie watched him and the wild mushrooms didn't seem to affect him, so she decided to use them. The meal was a great success, and Susie even hired a lady from town to come out and help her serve. It was first class. After everyone had finished, they all began to kick back and relax and socialize. The men were visiting and the women started to gossip a bit.

About this time, the lady from town came in from the kitchen and whispered in Susie's ear. She said, "Mrs. Brown, Spot just died." With this news, Susie went into hysterics. After she finally calmed down, she called the doctor and told him what had happened. The doctor said, "It's bad, but I think we can take care of it. I will call for an ambulance and I will be there as quick as I can get there. We will pump out everyone's stomach and everything will be fine. Just keep them all there and keep them calm." It wasn't long until they could hear the wail of the siren as the ambulance was coming down the road. When they got there, the EMTs got out with their suitcases and a stomach pump and the doctor arrived shortly thereafter. One by one, they took each person into the master bedroom and pumped out their stomach. After the last one was finished, the doctor came out and said, "I think everything will be fine now, and he left."

They were all looking pretty peaked sitting around the living room, and about this time, the town lady came in and said, "You know, that fellow that ran over Ol' Spot never even stopped."

One Hard Question

There was a student who wanted to be admitted to the university.

He was smart enough to get through the written test, a GED, and was to appear for the personal interview. Later, as the interview progressed, the interviewer found this boy to be bright since he could answer all the questions correctly. The interviewer got impatient and decided to corner the boy.

"Tell me your choice," he said to the boy, "what's your choice: I shall either ask you ten easy questions or one real difficult. Think well before you make up your mind."

The boy thought for a while and said, "My choice is one real difficult question."

"Well, good luck to you, you have made your own choice!" Said the man on the opposite side, "Tell me: what comes first, day or night?"

The boy was jolted at first but he waited for a while and said: "It's the day, sir."

"How???????" The interviewer shot back, smiling. ("At last, I got you!" he said to himself.)

"Sorry sir, you promised me that you will not ask me a second difficult question!"

The student was admitted to the university.

Opening

A man went to apply for a job.

After filling out all of the application, he waited anxiously for the outcome.

The employer read his application and said, "We have an opening for people like you."

"Oh, great," he said, "what is it?"

"It's called the door!" replied the employer.

Organization

My sister was bemoaning the fact that she had procrastinated cleaning and organizing her house for a long time. Since she was planning to entertain, she felt a lot of pressure to get moving. That afternoon she phoned, sounding glum.

"I went to the bookstore," she explained, "And I bought a book on how to get organized. I was all fired up, and I decided to clean out all the shelves in the living room. While I was cleaning, I found the same stupid book. I had bought it a couple of years ago!"

Outhouse Confession

A little boy lived in the country.

For facilities, they had to use an outhouse, and the little boy hated it because it was hot in the summer, cold in the winter and stank all the time. The outhouse was sitting on the bank of a creek and the boy determined that one day he would push that outhouse into the water.

One day after a spring rain, the creek was swollen so the little boy decided today was the day to push the outhouse into the creek. So he got a large stick and pushed, Finally, the outhouse toppled into the creek and floated away. That night his dad told him they were going to the woodshed after supper. Knowing that meant a spanking, the little boy asked, "Why?"

The dad replied, "Someone pushed the outhouse into the creek today. It was you, wasn't it, son?"

The boy answered, "Yes." Then he thought a moment and said, "Dad, I read in school today that George Washington chopped down a cherry tree and didn't get into trouble because he told the truth."

The dad replied, "Well, son, George Washington's father wasn't in that cherry tree!!"

Out Of The Mouths Of Babes

Little Sarah was sitting on her grandfather's lap as he read her a bedtime story. From time to time, she would take her eyes off the book and reach up to touch his wrinkled cheek. She was alternately stroking her own cheek, then his again.

Finally she spoke up, "Grandpa, did God make you?"

"Yes, sweetheart," he answered, "God made me a long time ago."

"Oh," she paused, "Grandpa, did God make me too?"

"Yes, indeed, honey," he said, "God made you just a little while ago."

Feeling their respective faces again, she observed, "God's getting better at it, isn't he?"

Out Of Office Replies

1. I am currently out at a job interview and will reply to you if I fail to get the position. Be prepared for my mood.
2. You are receiving this automatic notification because I am out of the office. If I was in, chances are you wouldn't have received anything at all.
3. I will be unable to delete all the unread, worthless emails you send me until I return from vacation on September 30th. Please be patient and your mail will be deleted in the order it was received.
4. Thank you for your email. Your credit card has been charged $10.99 for the first ten words and $5.99 for each additional word in your message.
5. The e-mail server is unable to verify your server connection and is unable to deliver this message. Please restart your computer and try sending again.
6. Thank you for your message, which has been added to a queuing system. You are currently in 352nd place, and can expect to receive a reply in approximately 19 weeks.

Packed Lunch

One day Jake, a nine-year-old, asked to pack his own lunch for school. His mom agreed. But they couldn't agree on what he should pack, so they both made lists.

This was the mom's list:
- One sandwich
- One apple
- Pretzels
- A carton of milk

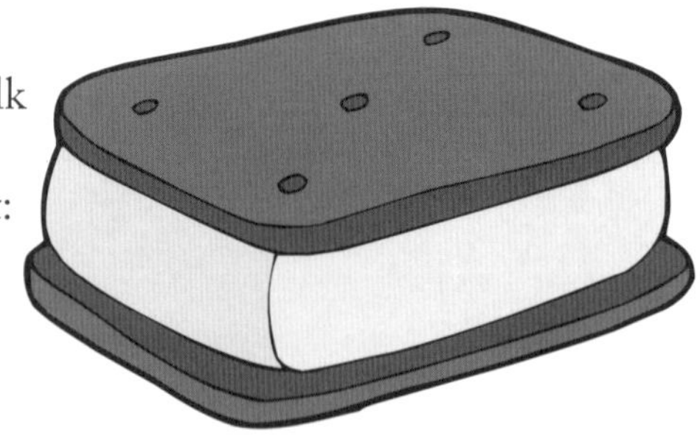

This was Jake's list:
- Candy
- Candy
- Candy

Jake agreed to compromise. Sure enough, the next morning, Jake was ready for school and he packed his lunch. His mom came to check his lunch, and this is what he had:

- An ice cream sandwich
- A caramel apple
- White chocolate-covered pretzels with sprinkles on top
- A carton of Nesquik® chocolate milk
- And a bag of candy, of course, for dessert.

Paper Walls

As a young married couple, a husband and a wife lived in a cheap housing complex near the military base where he was working.

Their chief complaint was that the walls were paper-thin and that they had no privacy. This was painfully obvious when one morning the husband was upstairs and the wife was downstairs on the telephone. She was interrupted by the doorbell and went to greet her neighbor.

"Give this to your husband," he said thrusting a roll of toilet paper into her hands. "He's been yelling for it for fifteen minutes!"

Parental Rules

A teacher at a parochial school was trying to elicit from the youngsters rules that their parents might give before taking them to a nice restaurant.

"Don't play with your food," one second grader cited.

"Don't be loud," said another, and so on.

"And what rule do your parents give you before you go out to eat?" the teacher inquired of one little boy.

Without batting an eye, the child replied, "Order something cheap!"

Parking Lot Speed Limit

Safety is a major concern at the manufacturing company where I work. So I'm constantly preaching caution to the workers I supervise. "Does anyone know," I asked a few guys, "what the speed limit is in our parking lot?"

The long silence that followed was interrupted when one of them piped up. "That depends. Do you mean coming into work or leaving?"

Parking Lot Stay

I pulled into the crowded parking lot at a Super Walmart® Shopping Center and rolled down the car windows to make sure my Labrador Retriever Pup had fresh air.

She was stretched, full-out, on the back seat and I wanted to impress upon her that she must remain there. I walked to the curb backward, pointing my finger at the car and saying emphatically, "Now you stay. Do you hear me? Stay! Stay!"

The driver of a nearby car, a young lady, gave me a strange look and said, "Why don't you just put it in park?"

Parts Search

I was living in the mountains above Denver when my college buddy, Gary, arrived in his ancient Maserati sports car. He had just driven it from Ohio, and as he pulled into my driveway, the car broke down.

Calls to auto-supply houses and garages in search of replacement parts proved futile. The 1962 model was simply too rare. Responses ranged from "Mas-a-what?" to "You've got to be kidding."

One guy just laughed.

I was at the end of the listings in the Yellow Pages when I dialed Victor's Garage. "Vic," I said, "you're my last hope. Do you carry any parts for a 1962 Maserati?"

There was a long pause. Finally, Victor cleared his throat. "Yes," he replied. "Oil."

Penguin Breakdown

A truck driver had to deliver five hundred penguins to the state zoo. As he was driving his truck through the desert, the truck broke down.

After waiting by the side of the road for about three hours, he waved another truck down and offered the driver $500 to take the penguins to the state zoo for him.

The next day, the first truck driver arrived in town and saw the second truck driver crossing the road with 500 penguins walking in single file behind him.

The first truck driver jumped out of his truck and said, "What's going on? I gave you $500 to take these penguins to the zoo!"

The second truck driver replied, "I did take them to the zoo. And I had money left over, so now we're going to get some ice cream."

People And Mistakes

- People who do lots of work…
  Make lots of mistakes
- People who do less work…
  Make less mistakes
- People who do no work…
  Make no mistakes
- People who make no mistakes…
  Get promoted

I need a promotion.

Perfectly Made

When we put our house up for sale, I stressed emphatically that my sons make their beds each morning. I left for work before they left for school, and I wanted to be sure that the house looked presentable when the agent showed it to prospective buyers.

I was surprised and impressed that my 15-year-old son's bed was perfectly made each day. One night when I went into his room, I discovered his secret.

He was fast asleep on the floor in his sleeping bag.

Pie Manners

In a country home that seldom had guests, the young son was eager to help his mother after his father appeared with two dinner guests from the office.

When the dinner was nearly over, the boy went to the kitchen and proudly carried in the first piece of apple pie, giving it to his father, who passed it to a guest. The boy came in with a second piece of pie and again watched his father give it to a guest.

This was too much for the boy, who said, "It's no use, Dad. The pieces are all the same size."

Pilot Pride

As one of relatively few female airline pilots, I've often been mistaken for a flight attendant, ticket agent, or even a snack bar employee. Occasionally people will see me in uniform and ask if I'm a "real" pilot. Still others congratulate me for making it in a male-dominated field. One day, I was in the restroom before a flight. I was at the sink, brushing my teeth, when a woman walked through the door and looked over at me. "My sister would be so proud of you!" she remarked. I figured her sister must also be in the airline business, so I smiled and asked why. Replied the woman, "She's a dentist."

Pizza

Operator: "Thank you for calling Pizza Hut. May I have your…"
Customer: "Hi, I'd like to order."
Operator: "May I have your NIDN first, sir?"
Customer: "My National ID Number, yeah, hold on, eh, it's 6102049998-45-54610."
Operator: "Thank you, Mr. Sheehan. I see you live at 1742 Meadowland Drive, and the phone number's 494-2366. Your office number over at Lincoln Insurance is 745-2302 and your cell number's 266-2566. Which number are you calling from, sir?"
Customer: "Huh? I'm at home. Where d'ya get all this information?"
Operator: "We're wired into the system, sir."
Customer: (Sighs) "Oh, well, I'd like to order a couple of your All-Meat Special Pizzas…"
Operator: "I don't think that's a good idea, sir."
Customer: "Whaddya mean?"
Operator: "Sir, your medical records indicate that you've got very high blood pressure and extremely high cholesterol. Your National Health Care provider won't allow such an unhealthy choice."
Customer: "What do you recommend, then?"
Operator: "You might try our low-fat Soybean Yogurt Pizza. I'm sure you'll like it."
Customer: "What makes you think I'd like something like that?"
Operator: "Well, you checked out 'Gourmet Soybean Recipes from your local library last week, sir. That's why I made the suggestion."

Customer: "All right, all right. Give me two family-sized ones, then. What's the damage?"
Operator: "That should be plenty for you, your wife, and your four children, sir. The 'damage,' as you put it, heh, heh, comes to $49.99."
Customer: "Lemme give you my credit card number."
Operator: "I'm sorry sir, but I'm afraid you'll have to pay in cash. Your credit card balance is over its limit."
Customer: "I'll run over to the ATM and get some cash before your driver gets here."
Operator: "That won't work either, sir. Your checking account's overdrawn."
Customer: "Never mind. Just send the pizzas. I'll have the cash ready. How long will it take?"
Operator: "We're running a little behind, sir. It'll be about 45 minutes, sir. If you're in a hurry you might want to pick 'em up while you're out getting the cash, but carrying pizzas on a motorcycle can be a little awkward."
Customer: "How do you know I'm riding a bike?"
Operator: "It says here you were behind on your car payments, so your car got repo'ed. But your Harley's paid up, so I just assumed that you'd be using it."
Customer: "This is ridiculous."
Operator: "I'd advise taking it easy with your driving, sir. You've already got one ticket for speeding."
Customer: (Speechless)
Operator: "Will there be anything else, sir?"
Customer: "No, nothing. Oh, yeah, don't forget the two free liters of Coke your ad says I get with the pizzas."
Operator: "I'm sorry sir, but our ad's exclusionary clause prevents us from offering free soda to diabetics."

Plane Crash

A plane containing a pilot and his only passenger was circling high above a small playing field. Suddenly the pilot cut his motor and began gliding. "Do you know what?" chuckled the pilot as he looked down. "I'll bet all the people down there right now think we're going to crash." The passenger gulped nervously. "Half of us up here do, too," he said weakly.

Planning Their Wedding

George, age 92, and Edith, age 89, had been seeing each other for two years when they decided that life was too short and they might as well be together for the rest of their lives. Excited about their decision to become newlyweds they went for a stroll to discuss the wedding and what plans needed to be made.

Along the way they found themselves in front of the drugstore. George said to his bride to be "Let's go in. I have an idea." They walked to the rear of the store and addressed the man behind the counter.

George: "Are you the owner?"
Pharmacist: "Yes sir, I am. How can I help you?"
George: "Do you sell heart medications?"
Pharmacist: "Of course we do."
George: "How about support hose for circulation?"
Pharmacist: "Definitely."
George: "What about meds for rheumatism, osteoporosis, and arthritis?"
Pharmacist: "All kinds."
George: "How about hearing aids, denture supplies, and reading glasses?"

Pharmacist: "Yes sir."
George: "What about eye drops, sleeping pills, Geritol, Preparation-H, and Ex-lax?"
Pharmacist: "Absolutely."
George: "You sell wheelchairs, walkers, and canes?"
Pharmacist: "All kinds and sizes."

The pharmacist asked, "Why are you asking me all these questions?"

George smiled, glanced at Edith and replied to the pharmacist. "We've decided to get married and we'd like to use your store as our BRIDAL REGISTRY!

Poison Control Center

Becky prepared a pasta dish for a dinner party she was giving. In her haste, however, she forgot to refrigerate the spaghetti sauce, and it sat on the counter all day. She was worried about spoilage, but it was too late to cook up another batch.

She called the local Poison Control Center and voiced her concern. They advised Becky to boil the sauce again.

That night, the phone rang during dinner, and one of the guests volunteered to answer it. Becky's face dropped as the guest called out, "It's the Poison Control Center. They want to know how the spaghetti sauce turned out."

Pole Power

I was getting ready for work when I looked out the window and saw the utility company starting to erect a pole in front of my house. They were going to position it directly in front of my picture window. No way, absolutely no way, was I going to permit this. I gulped down my coffee and went directly to the crew supervisor and told him, in no uncertain terms, that I was not going to stand for his crew putting that stupid electrical pole directly in front of my picture window.

He took out a plot map, a map for pole locations, and a right of way document. He went on to explain that the chosen location was the best spot for the pole. I told him it was not the best location for me and that when I came home from work that day I certainly did not expect to see that pole in front of my window.

He asked where I did want them to put it and I told him I didn't give a hoot, as long as it was not in front of my window. I felt pretty smug as I drove off to work because I felt I got my point across. I knew he was afraid to put it there now.

Ah, the feeling of power; at least until I got home and found the pole in the middle of my driveway.

Political Wrangling

Charlie, a politician, decided to take a sightseeing vacation to Europe. While visiting Europe, he is privileged to have tea with the Queen. He asks her what her leadership philosophy is. She says that it is to surround herself with intelligent people. He asks how she knows if they're intelligent. "I do so by asking them the right questions," says the Queen. "Allow me to demonstrate."

She phones Tony Blair and says, "Mr. Prime Minister, please answer this question: Your mother has a child, and your father has a child, and this child is not your brother or sister. Who is it?"

Tony Blair responds, "It's me, ma'am."

"Correct. Thank you and goodbye, sir," says the Queen. She hangs up and says, "Did you get that, sir?"

"Yes ma'am. Thanks a lot. I'll definitely be using that!"

Upon returning home, he decides he'd better put some of his old friends to the test. He calls his close friend, Ed, and says, "Hi, Ed, I wonder if you can answer a question for me."

"Why, of course, Charlie. What's on your mind?"

"Uhh, your mother has a child, and your father has a child, and this child is not your brother or sister. Who is it?"

Ed hems and haws and finally asks, "Can I think about it and get back to you?" Charlie agrees and Ed hangs up.

Ed immediately calls members of his staff, and they puzzle over the question for several hours, but nobody can come up with an answer.

Finally, in desperation, Ed calls Colin Powell at the State Department and explains his problem. "Now look here, your mother has a child, and your father has a child, and this child is not your brother or sister. Who is it?"

Powell answers immediately, "It's me, of course."

Much relieved, Ed rushes back to call Charlie and exclaims. "I know the answer Charlie! I know who it is! It's Colin Powell!!"

And Charlie replies in disgust, "Wrong, it's Tony Blair."

Ponder This

A bus station is where
A bus stops.

A train station is where
A train stops.

On my desk I have
A work
station…

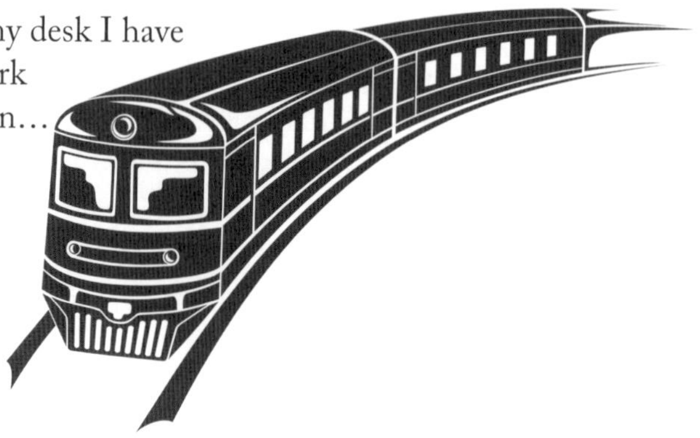

Popping Ears

Aboard a plane from Los Angeles to New York, Grandma Esther was taking her very first flight. They had only been aloft a few minutes when the elderly lady complained to the flight attendant that her ears were popping. The young woman smiled and gave the older woman some chewing gum, assuring her that many people experienced the same discomfort. When they landed in New York, Grandma thanked the flight attendant. "The chewing gum worked fine," she said, "but tell me, how do I get it out of my ears?"

Positive Feedback

After trying a new shampoo for the first time, Morris mailed off an enthusiastic letter of approval to the manufacturer.

Several weeks later he came home from work to a large carton in the middle of the floor. Inside were free samples of the many products the same company produced: soaps, detergents, tooth paste, and paper items…with a "thank you" note from the manufacturer.

"Well, what do you think?" asked his smiling wife, Ruth.

"I think that next time," Morris replied, "I'm writing to General Motors."

Potato Problem

Upon going away to college, my brother-in-law received a hand mixer from his mother because of his fondness for mashed potatoes. Later that semester, she asked him how the mixer was working for him.

"Not very good," Terry said, "The potatoes keep flying all over the kitchen."

After a perplexed pause, his mother asked, "Terry, did you cook the potatoes first?"

To which a surprised Terry responded, "You have to cook the potatoes first?"

Pray For Me

One Sunday a young child was "acting up" during the morning worship hour. The parents did their best to maintain some sense of order in the pew but were losing the battle. Finally, the father picked the little fellow up and walked sternly up the aisle on his way out. Just before reaching the safety of the foyer, the little one called loudly to the congregation, "Pray for me! Pray for me!"

Printer Repair

When the office printer's type began to grow faint (this was one of the old dot-matrix printers), the office manager called a local repair shop where a friendly man informed him that the printer probably needed only to be cleaned. Because the store charged $50 for such cleanings, he said, the manager might try reading the printer's manual and doing the job himself.

Pleasantly surprised by his candor, the office manager asked, "Does your boss know that you discourage business?"

"Actually it's my boss's idea," the employee replied. "We usually make more money on repairs if we let people try to fix things themselves first."

Procrastinators Creed

You may wish to delay reading this until you have more free time.

1. I believe that if anything is worth doing, it would have been done already.
2. I shall never move quickly, except to avoid more work or find excuses.
3. I will never rush into a job without a lifetime of consideration.
4. I shall meet all of my deadlines directly in proportion to the amount of bodily injury I could expect to receive from missing them.
5. I firmly believe that tomorrow holds the possibility for new technologies, astounding discoveries, and a reprieve from my obligations.

6. I truly believe that all deadlines are unreasonable regardless of the amount of time given.
7. If at first I don't succeed, there is always next year.
8. I shall always decide not to decide, unless of course I decide to change my mind.
9. I shall always begin, start, initiate, take the first step, and/or write the first word, when I get around to it.
10. I will never put off tomorrow, what I can forget about forever.

Produce Profit

Two guys wanted to invest $100 they had won. They went to a watermelon farmer they knew and bought 100 watermelons at $1.00 Each. After finding a good place to park and sell the watermelons from their truck bed, they started selling them at $1.00 Each. When they sold that load they went back to the farmer for more.

After selling several truck loads they counted their money and realized they still had only $100. After counting it several more times to be sure, Charlie said to Bobby, "This is getting us nowhere! We're just not making any more money here. We sold all our watermelons but we still only have $100. Something's wrong but I surely can't figure it out."

Finally Bobby said to Charlie, "I was gonna let you figure it out, but you're just too dumb since you didn't even finish the third grade. It's as plain as the nose on your face that the only way we can make money is to get a bigger truck!"

Proper Job Placement

Methods from human resources...

1. Put 400 bricks in a closed room.
2. Put your new hires in the room and close the door.
3. Leave them alone and come back after six hours.
4. Then analyze the situation.

A. If they are counting the bricks, put them in the accounting department.
B. If they are recounting them, put them in auditing.
C. If they have messed up the whole place with the bricks, put them in engineering.
D. If they are arranging the bricks in some strange order, put them in planning.
E. If they are throwing the bricks at each other, put them in operations.
F. If they are sleeping, put them in security.
G. If they have broken the bricks into pieces, put them in information technology.
H. If they are sitting idle, put them in human resources.
I. If they say they have tried different combinations and they are looking for more, yet not a brick has been moved, put them in sales.
J. If they have already left for the day, put them in management.
K. If they are staring out of the window, put them in strategic planning.
L. If they are talking to each other, and not a single brick has been moved, congratulate them and put them in top management.
M. Finally, if they have surrounded themselves with bricks in such a way that they can neither be seen nor heard from, put them in congress.

Quarter Horse

One evening while I was preparing dinner, my daughter came into the kitchen asking for homework help on her vocabulary words. "Mom," she asked, "what's a quarter horse?"

As I thought of a simple explanation, my five-year-old son piped up, "It's the one they have in front of the grocery store."

Quarter Rush

On a busy Friday night at the restaurant where I'd recently started waiting tables, the owner suddenly emerged from the kitchen and handed me money.

"We're in trouble!" He said. "We're out of quarters, and customers are waiting. Go next door and get me $40 worth."

I ran to the supermarket next door, but a cashier said she wasn't allowed to give out that many quarters. Determined, I sprinted to a convenience store two blocks away, but it was closed. At a gas station farther down the road, the clerk took pity and gave me the four rolls of quarters. Twenty minutes after I'd left, I handed the coin rolls to my boss.

"Where are the quarters?" he asked.

"Right here," I said breathlessly.

His face sank. "I meant chicken quarters."

Questions Asked By Banff Park Tourists

1. How do the elk know they're supposed to cross at the "Elk Crossing" signs?
2. At what elevation does an elk become a moose?
3. Tourist: "How do you pronounce 'E-l-k'?"
   Park Information Staff: "Elk."
   Tourist: "Oh."
4. Are the bears with collars tame?
5. Is there anywhere I can see the bears pose?
6. Is it okay to keep an open bag of bacon on the picnic table, or should I store it in my tent?
7. Where can I find Alpine Flamingos?
8. I saw an animal on the way to Banff today—could you tell me what it was?
9. Are there birds in Canada?
10. Did I miss the turnoff for Canada?
11. Where does Alberta end and Canada begin?
12. Do you have a map of the State of Jasper?
13. Is this the part of Canada that speaks French, or is that Saskatchewan?
14. If I go to B.C., do I have to go through Ontario?
15. Which is the way to the Columbia rice fields?
16. How far is Banff from Canada?
17. What's the best way to see Canada in a day?
18. Do they search you at the B.C. border?

Quick Thinking

During a hectic night of mail processing at the post office, a number of letters fell off an elevated conveyor belt and scattered onto the floor. Before the area supervisor came, James had a chance to pick them up, but the facility manager, who had a reputation for being stern, came upon the scene.

"James, why is this mail on the floor?" he demanded angrily.

Without hesitation, James replied, "Gravity, sir."

Reading Glasses

I took my five-year-old grandson to the optometrist to pick up his new glasses. The glasses were prescribed, "To help him read and be able to see the computer better."

When we got back home, he got on the computer to play a game. In a few minutes he called me and said there was something wrong with his glasses.

I asked him what was the problem and he said, "I still can't read."

Real 911 Calls, Believe It Or Not!

Note: only call 911 in case of emergency

Dispatcher: 9-1-1 what is your emergency?
Caller: Someone broke into my house and took a bite out of my ham and cheese sandwich.
Dispatcher: Excuse me?
Caller: I made a ham and cheese sandwich and left it on the kitchen table and when I came back from the bathroom, someone had taken a bite out of it.
Dispatcher: Was anything else taken?
Caller: No, but this has happened to me before and I'm sick and tired of it.

Dispatcher: 9-1-1 What is your emergency?
Caller: Hi, is this the police?
Dispatcher: This is 9-1-1. Do you need police assistance?
Caller: Well, I don't know who to call. Can you tell me how to cook a turkey? I've never cooked one before.

Dispatcher: 9-1-1 fire or emergency?
Caller: Fire, I guess.
Dispatcher: How can I help you sir?
Caller: I was wondering…Does the fire department put snow chains on their trucks?
Dispatcher: Yes sir, do you have an emergency?
Caller: Well, I've spent the last four hours trying to put these chains on my tires and…well…Do you think the fire department could come over and help me?
Dispatcher: Help you what?
Caller: Help me get these chains on my car!

Dispatcher: 9-1-1, what is the nature of your emergency?
Caller: I'm trying to reach nine eleven but my phone doesn't have an eleven on it.

Dispatcher: This is nine eleven.
Caller: I thought you just said it was nine-one-one
Dispatcher: Yes, ma'am nine-one-one and nine-eleven are the same thing.
Caller: Honey, I may be old, but I'm not stupid.

And the winner is…

Dispatcher: 9-1-1.
Caller: Yeah, I'm having trouble breathing. I'm all out of breath. I think I'm going to pass out.
Dispatcher: Sir, where are you calling from?
Caller: I'm at a pay phone. North and Foster.
Dispatcher: Sir, an ambulance is on the way. Are you an asthmatic?
Caller: No
Dispatcher: What were you doing before you started having trouble breathing?
Caller: Running from the police.

Really, Really Bad Traffic

- Freeway congestion is getting so bad, you can change a tire without losing your place in line.
- All across the country rush hour traffic is bumper to bumper. The next thing they'll be selling is antiperspirant to put under your car's fenders.
- Traffic is always heavy in both directions. There are just as many people trying to get to whatever you're trying to get away from.

- It's useless to print roadmaps anymore. You just get on the highway and go wherever the other cars take you.
- The only way to get home from work on time is to take the day off…even then, you're cutting it close.
- Traffic is so bad nowadays, a pedestrian is someone in a hurry.
- You can sit on the highways forever. In fact, some places have little exit ramps where you can pull over and make a car payment.
- During rush hour the only way you can change lanes is to buy the car driving next to you.

Redecorating Help

A young woman decided to redecorate her bedroom. She wasn't sure how many rolls of wallpaper she would need, but she knew that her friend next door had recently done the same job and the two rooms were identical in size.

"Buffy," she said, "how many rolls of wallpaper did you buy for your bedroom?"

"Ten," said Buffy.

So the girl bought the ten rolls of paper and did the job, but she had two rolls leftover.

"Buffy," she said. "I bought ten rolls of wallpaper for the bedroom, but I've got two leftover!"

"Yeah!" said Buffy. "So did I."

Refrigerator Goals

When I returned home from college for a break, I noticed a paper posted on the refrigerator. It listed some goals my dad had set for himself: Help wife more; lose weight; be more productive at work.

I promptly added: "Send Michelle money every month."

A few days later my brother wrote: "Make payments on car for Jason."

Then my boyfriend joined in with: "Buy Tom a Jeep."

Finally my father added a new goal to his amended list: "Wean children."

Relativism

An older woman recently returned from her hometown in North Carolina and told a friend they'd spruced up the churchyard cemetery since her last visit several years past. "Lots of new greenery," she said. "And families are together now."

"All together?" her friend asked, puzzled.

"Well," the first replied, "years ago they never much worried where they buried someone because everyone was a neighbor anyhow. They'd just dig a grave wherever it seemed to balance things. But they've redone it so people are with their children and grandchildren, instead of scattered."

The friend was still puzzled. "You mean they exhumed all those people and reburied them?"

"Oh my, no," was the reply. "We just shifted the headstones. Everyone agrees it looks ever so much nicer."

Restaurant Signs

- A man in a restaurant said, "I could eat a horse."
  The waitress responded, "You came to the right place."

- Sign: Our pies are homemade.
  The customer asked, "In whose home were they made?"

- A restaurant sign said, "Our tongue sandwiches speak for themselves."

- A man called a restaurant asking, "Do you serve crabs?"
  The waitress responded, "Yes, we serve all kinds of people."

- A man questioned the waitress, "What's that foreign object doing in my soup?
  The waitress replied, "It's not foreign, we grow them in the kitchen."

- A waitress asked, "How did you find your steak?"
  The man responded, "Easy, I moved two peas and found it."

- Sign outside a restaurant: "Don't eat your wife's burnt food—eat ours."

Return Policy

The store's policy on returns was prominently posted at every register as well as throughout the store. Every receipt also had the same information. A store credit would be given on all returns, but there were no cash refunds.

After explaining this policy to the grouchy customer, the woman blew up at the clerk, finally demanding the name of the president and his address. The clerk replied George Bush, 1600 Pennsylvania Avenue, Washington, D.C.

The woman promptly wrote this information down and stuffed it into her purse. "He will hear from me!" She announced as she stormed out of the store.

Roof Chicken

One day a state trooper was pulling off an expressway near Chicago. When he turned onto the street at the end of the ramp, he noticed someone at a chicken place getting into his car. The driver placed the bucket of chicken on top of his car, got in and drove off with the bucket still on top of his car.

So the trooper decided to pull him over and perform a community service by giving the driver his chicken. So he pulled him over, walked up to the car, pulled the bucket off the roof and offered it to the driver. The driver looked at the trooper and said, "No thanks, I just bought some."

Rules For Bank Robbers

According to the FBI, most modern-day bank robberies are "unsophisticated and unprofessional crimes," committed by young male repeat offenders who apparently don't know the first thing about their business. For instance it is reported that in spite of the widespread use of surveillance cameras, 76 percent of bank robbers use no disguise, 86 percent never study the bank before robbing it, and 95 percent make no long-range plans for concealing the loot. Thus, this tongue-in-cheek advice is offered to would-be bank robbers, along with examples of what can happen if the rules aren't followed:

1. Pick the right bank. Clark advises that you don't follow the lead of the fellow in Anaheim, CA, who tried to hold up a bank that was no longer in business and had no money. On the other hand, you don't want to be too familiar with the bank. A California robber ran into his mother while making his getaway. She turned him in.
2. Approach the right teller. Granted, this is harder to plan. One teller in Springfield, MA, followed the holdup man out of the bank and down the street until she saw him go into a restaurant. She hailed a passing police car, and the police picked him up. Another teller was given a holdup note by a robber, and her father, who was next in line, wrestled the man to the ground and sat on him until authorities arrived.
3. Don't sign your demand note. Demand notes have been written on the back of a subpoena issued in the name of a bank robber in Pittsburgh, PA, on an envelope bearing the name and address of another in Detroit, MI, and on the back of a withdrawal slip giving the robber's signature and account number in East Hartford, CT.
4. Beware of dangerous vegetables. A man in White Plains, NY, tried to hold up a bank with a zucchini. The police captured him at his house, where he showed them his "weapon".
5. Avoid being fussy. A robber in Panorama City, CA, gave a teller a note saying, "I have a gun. Give me all your twenties in this envelope." The teller said, "All I've got is two twenties." The robber took them and left.
6. Don't advertise. A holdup man thought that if he smeared mercury ointment on his face, it would make him invisible to the cameras. Actually, it accentuated his features, giving authorities a much clearer picture. Bank robbers in Minnesota and California tried to create a diversion by throwing stolen money out of the windows of their cars. They succeeded only in drawing attention to themselves.
7. Take right turns only. Avoid the sad fate of the thieves in Florida who took a wrong turn and ended up on the Homestead Air Force Base. They drove up to a military police guardhouse and, thinking it was a tollbooth, offered the security men money.
8. Provide your own transportation. It is not clever to borrow the teller's car, which she carefully described to police. This resulted in the most quickly-solved bank robbery in the history of Pittsfield, Mass.
9. Don't be too sensitive. In these days of exploding dye packs, stuffing the cash into your pants can lead to embarrassing stains, not to mention severe burns—as bandits in San Diego and Boston painfully discovered.

10. Consider another line of work. One nervous criminal in Swansea, Mass., fainted when the teller told him she had no money. He was still unconscious when the police arrived.

Editor's Note: We do not advise options 1-9. Always select option 10.

Rules of Chocolate

1. If you've got melted chocolate all over your hands, you're eating it too slowly.
2. Chocolate covered raisins, cherries, oranges, and strawberries all count as fruit, so eat as many as you want, they're good for you.
3. When you have a problem getting two pounds of chocolate home from the store in your hot car, just eat it in the parking lot instead.
4. For dieters—eat a chocolate bar before each meal. It'll spoil your appetite.
5. A box of chocolates can provide your total daily intake of calories in one place. Isn't that handy?
6. If you can't eat all your chocolate, there's something wrong with you.

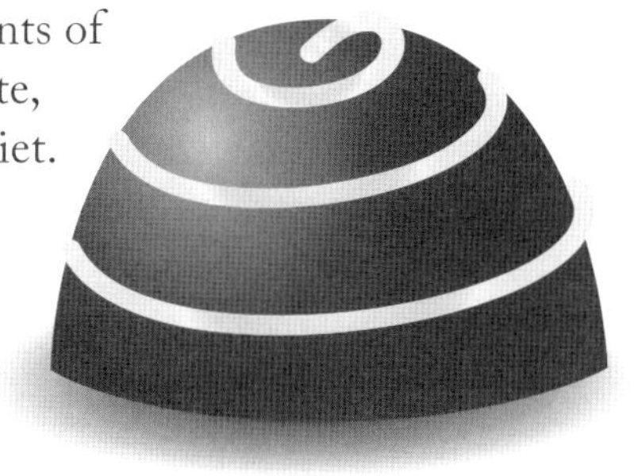

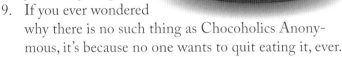

7. If you eat equal amounts of white & dark chocolate, you have a balanced diet.
8. Chocolate contains many preservatives. Preservatives make you look young.
9. If you ever wondered why there is no such thing as Chocoholics Anonymous, it's because no one wants to quit eating it, ever.
10. If you put "Eat Chocolate" on your daily list of things to do you'll always accomplish one thing you set out to do, every day.

—Compliments of Reppert's Candy

Rules of the Air

1. Every takeoff is optional. Every landing is mandatory.
2. Flying isn't dangerous. Crashing is what's dangerous.
3. The only time you have too much fuel is when you're on fire.
4. It's always better to be down here wishing you were up there than up there wishing you were down here.
5. If you push the stick forward, the houses get bigger. If you pull the stick back, they get smaller. That is, unless you keep pulling the stick all the way back, then they get bigger again.
6. The propeller is just a big fan in front of the plane used to keep the pilot cool. When it stops, you can actually watch the pilot start sweating.
7. A 'good' landing is one from which you can walk away. A 'great' landing is one after which they can use the plane again.
8. Learn from the mistakes of others. You won't live long enough to make all of them yourself.
9. You know you've landed with the wheels up if it takes full power to taxi to the ramp.
10. The probability of survival is inversely proportional to the angle of arrival. Large angle of arrival, small probability of survival and vice versa.
11. Stay out of clouds. The silver lining everyone keeps talking about might be another airplane going in the opposite direction. Reliable sources also report that mountains have been known to hide out in clouds.
12. Always try to keep the number of landings you make equal to the number of take offs you've made.
13. There are three simple rules for making a smooth landing. Unfortunately no one knows what they are.
14. If all you can see out of the window is ground that's going round and round and all you can hear is commotion coming from the passenger compartment, things are not at all as they should be.
15. In the ongoing battle between objects made of aluminum going hundreds of miles per hour and the ground going zero miles per hour, the ground has yet to lose.
16. Good judgment comes from experience. Unfortunately, the experience usually comes from bad judgment.
17. It's always a good idea to keep the pointy end going forward as much as possible.
18. Keep looking around. There's always something you've missed.
19. Remember, gravity is not just a good idea. It's the law. And it's not subject to repeal.
20. The three most useless things to a pilot are the altitude above you, runway behind you, and a tenth of a second ago.

Salesmanship

My buddy applied for a job as an insurance salesman. Where the form requested "Prior experience," he wrote "Lifeguard." That was it. Nothing else.

"We're looking for someone who can not only sell insurance, but who can sell himself as well," said the hiring manager. "How does working as a lifeguard pertain to salesmanship?"

My friend replied, "I couldn't swim."

He got the job.

Same Condition

One day a customer walked into a pet shop and told the clerk,"I need two small mice, and about five dozen roaches." Puzzled, the clerk asked the reason for the strange request.

"Well," replied the man, "I'm moving out of my apartment, and my lease stipulates that I must leave the premises in exactly the same condition as when I moved in."

Same Landlord

A young woman, pursuing a graduate degree in art history, was going to Italy to study the country's greatest works of art. Since there was no one to look after her grandmother while she was away, she took the old lady with her. At the Sistine Chapel in the Vatican, she pointed to the painting on the ceiling.

"Grandma, it took Michelangelo a full four years to get that ceiling painted."

"Oh my," the grandmother says. "He and I must have the same landlord."

Sand Traps

An octogenarian who was an avid golfer moved to a new town. He went to the golf course for the first time to play but was told there wasn't anybody he could play with because they were already out on the course.

He repeated several times that he really wanted to play. Finally, the Assistant Pro said he would play with him and would give him a 12 stroke handicap. The 80- year-old said, "I really don't need a handicap as I have been playing quite well. The only real problem I have is getting out of sand traps."

And he did play well in one of the sand traps around the hole. Shooting from the sand trap he hit a very high ball which landed on the green and rolled into the hole!

The Pro walked over to the sand trap where his opponent was still standing. He said "Nice shot, but I thought you said you have a problem getting out of sand traps?"

Replied the octogenarian, "I do! Please give me a hand."

Scale Conversion

At the scale manufacturers' convention, people often wanted to weigh themselves on different scales to see if they agreed. However, some visitors abstained, not wishing to advertise their weight.

A smooth-talking representative coaxed a woman onto his scale by promising her that he would not look and that she could even cover the digital display so only she could see her weight.

She finally stood on the scale, whereupon a loud, mechanical voice from within the machine announced: "One hundred and sixty-three pounds."

School Zone

An off-duty police officer, familiar with radar speed checking equipment, drove through a school zone within the legal speed limit when suddenly the flash of a camera went off, taking a picture of his car and license plate.

The officer, thinking the radar was in error, drove by again; even more slowly. Another flash. He did it again for a third time, at an even slower speed. Same result. So, he made a note to himself to contact the traffic department and tell them that their machine wasn't working properly.

A few weeks later, the off-duty police officer received an envelope from the police department containing three traffic citations, each of them were for NOT wearing a seat belt.

Science Lesson

Miss Jones had been giving her second-grade students a lesson on science. She had explained about magnets and showed how they could pick up nails and other bits of iron. Now it was question time, and she asked, "My name begins with the letter 'M' and I pick up things. What am I?" A little boy on the front row stood up proudly and said, "You're a mother!"

Seattle Rain

A newcomer to Seattle arrived on a rainy day. She got up the next day and it rained, and the day after that. She went out to lunch and saw a young boy and, out of despair, asked, "Hey, you, does it ever stop raining around here?"

The boy replied, "How should I know? I'm only six."

Senior Exercises

The Doc told me to start an exercise program. Not wanting to harm this old body, I've devised the following:

Monday
- Beat around the bush
- Jump to conclusions
- Climb the walls
- Wade through the morning paper

Tuesday
- Drag my heels
- Push my luck
- Make mountains out of mole hills
- Hit the nail on the head

Wednesday
- Bend over backwards
- Jump on the Band Wagon
- Run around in circles

Thursday
- Advise the President on how to run the country
- Toot my own horn
- Pull out all the stops
- Add fuel to the fire

Friday
- Open a can of worms
- Put my foot in my mouth
- Start the ball rolling
- Go over the edge

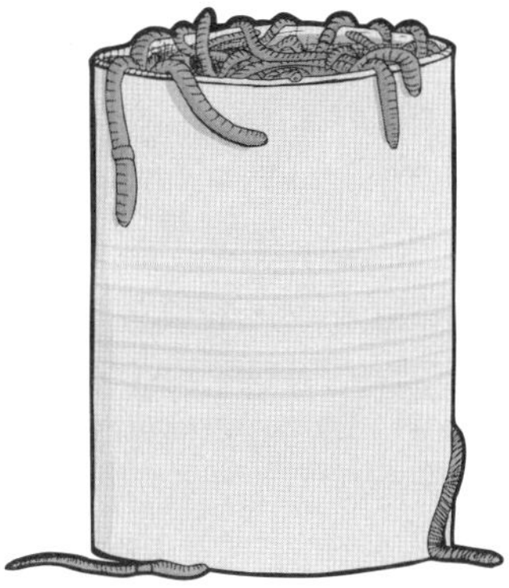

Saturday
- Pick up the pieces.

Sunday
- Kneel in prayer
- Bow my head in thanksgiving
- Uplift my hands in praise
- Hug someone and encourage them

What a Workout!

Senior Moments

As a senior citizen was driving down the freeway, his car phone rang. Answering, he heard his wife's voice urgently warning him, "Herman, I just heard on the news that there's a car going the wrong way on I-95. Please be careful!"

"It's not just one car," said Herman. "It's hundreds of them!"

Sermon Sub

A minister was called away unexpectedly by the illness of a close family member. He entrusted his new assistant with filling the pulpit. The Pastor's wife stayed home. When he returned, the minister asked his wife what she thought of the young man's sermon.

"The poorest I've ever heard," she said. "There was nothing in it, nothing at all. It didn't even make sense. It was very unorganized. I was disappointed."

Later that day, the concerned minister met his assistant and asked him, "How'd the Sunday service and sermon go? Did all go well? How did you manage?"

"All went very well, sir, absolutely wonderful," he said. "I didn't have time to prepare a new sermon of my own on such short notice, so I got on your computer and pulled up one of your old sermons from last year."

Setting Himself Right

George Washington Thomas, an able-bodied man of Sleepy Hollow, appeared before Magistrate Nussbaum charged with stealing chickens. The man was accompanied by his lawyer, Col. Simmons, a rising young attorney.

The old judge sauntered into the dingy court room, where he had reigned for more than twenty years, and, after calling for order, looked around on the little company there assembled. Seeing George Washington Thomas, he

pointed to him and said: "Be you the defendant in this case?"

Quick as a flash George was on his feet, and, not understanding legal terms, he exclaimed politely: "No, sir; no, sir; I am not the defendant; there's the defendant over there." And he pointed to his lawyer. There was a general laugh about the room, in which the queer old judge joined heartily.

The man felt abashed. He was visibly embarrassed, and, thinking to correct the mistake, if mistake it were, said again, pointing at his lawyer: "Yes, sir; he's the defendant," and pointing to himself, he said, "I'm the gentleman who stole the chickens."

Setting the Table

Little Susan was mother's helper.

She helped set the table when company was due for dinner. Presently everything was on, the guest came in, and everyone sat down. Then mother noticed something was missing.

"Susan," she said, "You didn't put a knife and fork at Mr. Smith's place."

"I thought he wouldn't need them," explained Susan. "Daddy says he always eats like a horse!"

Shipwrecked Sailor

The shipwrecked sailor had spent several years on a deserted island. Then one morning he was thrilled to see a ship offshore and a smaller vessel pulling out toward him.

When the boat grounded on the beach, the officer in charge handed the marooned sailor a bundle of newspapers and told him, "With the captain's compliments. He said to read through these and let us know if you still want to be rescued."

Shoe Repair

Arnold and his wife were cleaning out the attic one day when he came across a ticket from the local shoe repair shop. The date stamped on the ticket showed it was over eleven years old. They both laughed and tried to remember which of them might have forgotten to pick up a pair of shoes over a decade ago.

"Do you think the shoes will still be in the shop?" Arnold asked.

"Not very likely," his wife said.

"It's worth a try," Arnold said, pocketing the ticket.

Short One

Q. What do you get when you cross an elephant with a crow?

A. Downed power lines.

Sign Language For Your Dentist

You know how hard it is to talk to your dentist when your teeth are being cleaned or you are getting a filling? Well, I decided I would make up a sort of sign language that you could use to express yourself without having to mumble.

Below are 10 common things you might wish to say, numbered 1-10. These would be printed on a poster and mounted on the ceiling above the dentist chair.

It would give you something to read since procedures can be boring. When a phrase seems appropriate, you would just hold up the corresponding number of fingers to express yourself. The dentist would not need to stop to ask you to repeat yourself and could fix the problem right away.

1. Everything is fine, but my nose itches.
2. When you get a chance, there seems to be saliva running down my neck.
3. So, I guess you had garlic again for lunch today?
4. You realize that wasn't my tooth that you just poked with that incredibly sharp tool of yours.
5. I would really prefer you didn't do that again.
6. Could you please suction the chunk of debris that you missed before I gag?
7. Remember how I said I was numb? I think I may have been mistaken.
8. Wait a minute—maybe I am allergic to latex.

9. Just so you know, if I don't get to take a break soon, I may bite you.
10. Please stop asking me stupid questions about myself. I can't answer anyway.

Signs Of The Time

- On a plumber's truck: "We repair what your husband fixed."
- At a towing company: "We don't charge an arm and a leg. We want tows."
- In a non-smoking area: "If we see smoke, we will assume you are on fire and take appropriate action.
- At an optometrist's office: "If you don't see what you're looking for, you've come to the right place."
- On a taxidermist's window: "We really know our stuff."
- In a podiatrist's office: "Time wounds all heels."
- On a fence: "Salesmen welcome! Dog food is expensive."
- At a car dealership: "The easiest way to get back on your feet—miss a car payment."
- Outside a muffler shop: "No appointment necessary. We hear you coming."
- In a veterinarian's waiting room: "Be back in 5 minutes. Sit! Stay!"
- At the electric company: "We would be de-lighted if you send in your payment. However, if you don't, you will be."
- In a restaurant window: "Don't stand there and be hungry. Come on in and get fed up."

Signs Your SUV Is Too Big

- The last time you took your children to a Monster Truck Pull the parking attendants directed you right onto the stadium racetrack.
- When you replaced your tires, Goodyear stock went up five dollars a share for the quarter.
- Your garage is larger than your house.
- One of those "Oversize Load" escort trucks has to precede you down the interstate.
- Your children refer to riding the bus to school as "downsizing."
- Before you go out, you have to file for a parade permit.
- There is a successful Starbucks franchise located in the back.
- It doubles as a carport for your Taurus.
- Your buddy riding shotgun is in a different time zone.
- Mortgage payment = $2200, Texaco card payment = $2201.
- The fuel gauge doubles as a fan.

Silent Descent

Teddy came thundering down the stairs, much to his father's annoyance. "Teddy," he called, "how many more times do I need to tell you to come downstairs quietly? Now, go back upstairs and come down like a civilized human being."

There was a silence, and Teddy reappeared in the front room. "That's better," said his father, "now in the future will you always come downstairs like that."

"Really," said Teddy. "I slid down the railing."

Singing Fish

Jimmy: "Hey, Mike! How's your new pet fish doing? You told me he was really something special."

Mike: "To tell the truth, I'm really disappointed in him. The guy who sold him to me said I could teach him to sing like a bird."

Jimmy: "What? Let me get this straight…You bought a fish because you thought you could teach him to sing like a bird?"

Mike: "Well, yeah. After all, you know, he's a parrotfish."

Jimmy: "Now listen, Mike, while you might be able to teach a parrot to sing, you're never going to get any where with a parrotfish.'"

Mike: "That's what you think! It just so happens this fish CAN sing. The thing is, he's terribly off key and it's driving me crazy. Do you know how hard it is to tuna fish?"

Skim Milk

To help a friend lose weight, I told her that she should switch to lower-fat foods, including skim milk. When she said her family would drink only whole milk, I suggested that she keep their regular container and refill it with skim milk. This worked for quite a while, until her daughter asked one morning whether the milk was okay.

"Sure, it's fine," my friend answered, fearing she had been found out. "Why do you ask?"

The daughter explained, "Well, according to the expiration date, this milk expired two years ago!"

Sleep Pun

A wife and husband both talked in their sleep. She loved auctions; his hobby was golf.

The other night, the man yelled, "Fore!"

His wife yelled back, "Four Fifty!"

Slow Train

A passenger train was creeping along, until slowly and finally it creaked to a halt. A passenger saw a conductor walking by outside.

"What's going on?" she yelled out the window.

"Cow on the track!" replied the conductor.

Ten minutes later, the train resumes its slow pace. Within five minutes, however, it stopped again. The woman saw the same conductor walk by again.

She leaned out the window and yelled, "What happened? Did we catch up with the cow again?"

Smarter Than You Think

There was a little boy named Johnny who used to hang out at the local corner market. The owner didn't know what Johnny's problem was, but the boys would constantly tease him.

They would always comment that he was two bricks shy of a load or two pickles short of a barrel. To prove it, sometimes they would offer Johnny his choice between a nickel (five cents) and a dime (ten cents) and Johnny would always take the nickel (they said) because it was bigger.

One day after Johnny grabbed the nickel, the store owner took him aside and said "Johnny, those boys are making fun of you. They think you don't know the dime is worth more than the nickel. Are you grabbing the nickel because it's bigger, or what?"

With a big grin on his face, Johnny slowly turned toward the store owner. "Well," he answered, "if I took the dime, they'd stop doing it, and so far I've saved $20!"

Snoring Husband

"The day he came a-wooing,"
Says his most devoted wife,
"I used to think 'twould easy be
With him to spend my life.

"His speech was oh, so gentle,
And so tall and straight was he.
I never dreamed how terrible
He'd some day prove to be.

"I never dreamed I'd wake at night
To give his ribs a whack
With 'Darlin, please turn over—
You are sleeping on your back!'"

"When life was all before us
And our single path up-hill
I never dreamed the time would come
I'd wish his voice were still.

"And when, 'for better or for worse,'"
To cling to him I vowed.
I never dreamed so nice a man
Could make a noise so loud.

"Now night long through I elbow him
Until he's blue and black.
And say: 'Turn over darling, please!
You're sleeping on your back.'"

"At times it's like a whistle's shriek;
At times a grunt and groan,
And then buzz saw at a knot,
And then a fearful moan!

"There comes a second's silence
When I think he must be dead,
To find he's merely paused for breath
To start full-steam ahead.

"And this must last my lifetime
Through for how can I forsake,
This ghastly creature fast asleep
Who is so nice awake."

—Edgar A. Guest

Sock Concern

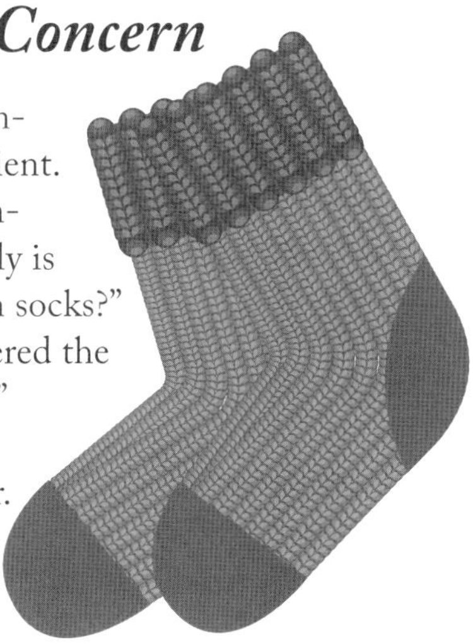

The psychiatrist was interviewing a first-time patient. "You say you're here," he inquired, "because your family is worried about your taste in socks?"

"That's correct," muttered the patient. "I like wool socks."

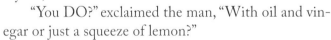

"But that's perfectly normal," replied the doctor. "Many people prefer wool socks to those made from cotton or acrylic. In fact, I myself, like wool socks."

"You DO?" exclaimed the man, "With oil and vinegar or just a squeeze of lemon?"

Software Engineering

At a recent computer software engineering course, the participants were given an awkward question to answer:

"If you had just boarded an airliner and discovered that your team of programmers had been responsible for the flight control software, how many of you would disembark immediately?"

Among the ensuing forest of raised hands only one man sat motionless. When asked what he would do, he replied that he would be quite content to stay aboard. With his team's software, he said, the plane was unlikely to even taxi as far as the runway, let alone take off.

Someone Knocking At My Door

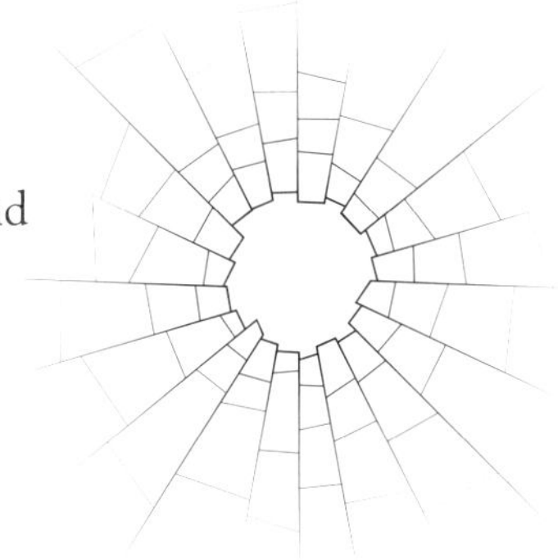

There was a knock at the door. It was a small boy, about six years old. Something of his had found its way into my garage, he said, and he wanted it back. Upon opening the garage door, I noticed two additions: a baseball and a broken window sporting a baseball-sized hole. "How do you suppose this ball got in here?" I asked the boy.

Taking one look at the ball, one look at the window, and one look at me, the boy exclaimed, "Wow! I must have thrown it right through that hole!"

Some People

Some people should have to wear signs that just say, "I'm not very smart"; that way you wouldn't rely on them, would you? You wouldn't ask them anything. It would be like, "Excuse me…oops, never mind. I didn't see your sign."

It's like before my wife and I moved. Our house was full of boxes and there was a U-Haul truck in our driveway. My neighbor comes over and says "Hey, you moving?" "Nope. We just pack our stuff up once or twice a week to see how many boxes it takes. Here's your sign."

A couple of months ago I went fishing with a buddy of mine, we pulled his boat into the dock, I lifted up this big 'ol stringer of bass and this guy on the dock goes, "Hey, y'all catch them fish?" "Nope. Talked 'em into giving up. Here's your sign."

Last time I had a flat tire, I pulled my truck into one of those side-of-the-road gas stations. The attendant walks out, looks at my truck, looks at me, and says, "Tire go flat?" I couldn't resist. I said, "Nope. I was driving around and those other three just swelled right up on me. Here's your sign."

We were trying to sell our car about a year ago. A guy came over to the house and drove the car around for about 45 minutes. We get back to the house, he gets out of the car, reaches down and grabs the exhaust pipe, then says, "Ouch that's hot!" See? If he'd been wearing his sign, I could have stopped him.

I learned to drive an 18-wheeler in my days of adventure. Wouldn't you know I misjudged the height of a bridge. The truck got stuck and I couldn't get it out no matter how I tried. I radioed in for help and eventually a local police showed up to take the report. He went through his basic questioning.. ok.. no problem. I thought for sure he was clear of needing a sign…until he asked, "So.. is your truck stuck?" I couldn't help myself! I looked at him, looked back at the rig and then back to him and said, "No I'm delivering a bridge…Here's your sign."

I stayed late at work one night and a coworker looked at me and said "Are you still here?" I replied, "No. I left about ten minutes ago. Here's your sign."

Sounds

A teacher arranged her young students into a circle. She then went around the circle and asked each one a question.

"Davey, what sound does a cow make?"

Davey replied, "It goes 'moo.'"

"Alice, what sound does a cat make?"

Alice said, "It goes 'meow.'"

"Jamie, what sound does a lamb make?"

Jamie said, "It goes 'baaa.'"

"Jennifer, what sound does a mouse make?"

Jennifer paused, and said, "Uhh…it goes…'click!'"

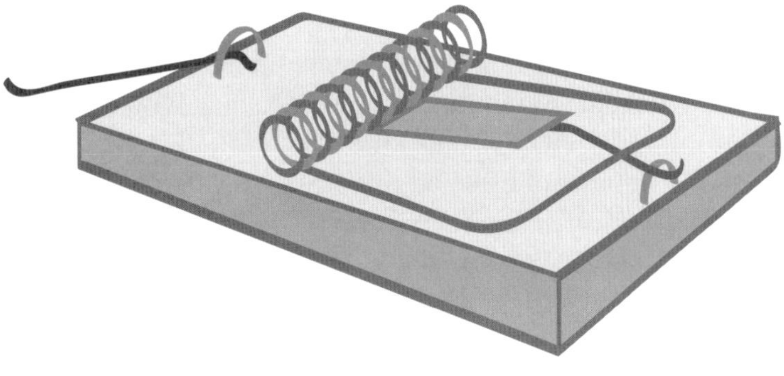

Soup Objects

The truck driver looked suspiciously at the soup he had just been served in an eatery. It contained dark flecks of seasoning, but two of the spots were suspicious.

"Hey," he called out to the waitress, "these particles in my soup, aren't they foreign objects?"

She scrutinized his bowl.

"No, sir!" she reassured him. "Those things live around here."

Station Help

An elderly man was standing in front of the ticket office in Grand Central Station. A picture of utter helplessness, it was clear something was horribly wrong with him. He stood with his elbows pressed closely at his side. His forearms were rigidly extended before him and his palms were turned towards each other about ten inches apart. Apparently, the man was paralyzed.

A young woman approached him. "Can I do anything to help you?" she asked.

"Oh, thank you. Please put your hand in my coat pocket and take out money to buy me a ticket to Philadelphia."

The woman complied. She bought the ticket and accompanied the crippled man on the train, to make sure he was settled before leaving him.

"I hope you have a complete recovery. Are you visiting an out of town specialist?"

"A specialist," replied the cripple. "Why should I go to a specialist?"

"To treat you for the trouble with your hands."

"But, I have no trouble with my hands."

"Of course you have trouble with your hands. Why, you couldn't even reach into your pocket to get the money to buy your ticket."

"Oh, you're wondering why my hands are like this. My wife asked me when I go to Philadelphia, to buy her a pair of shoes. This is her size."

Staying Awake

Tech support people like me spend our days on the phone with customers. Many like to chat while waiting for their computers to reboot. One man told me he'd been a long-haul truck driver.

"I'd love to drive a big rig," I said, "but I'd worry about falling asleep at the wheel."

"Here's a tip to stay awake," he offered. "Put a $100 bill in your left hand and hold it out the window."

Stranded On A Desert Island

A ragged individual stranded for several months on a small desert island in the middle of the Pacific Ocean noticed a bottle lying in the sand with a piece of paper in it. Rushing to the bottle, he pulled out the cork and with shaking hands withdrew the message.

"Due to lack of maintenance," he read, "we regretfully have found it necessary to cancel your e-mail account."

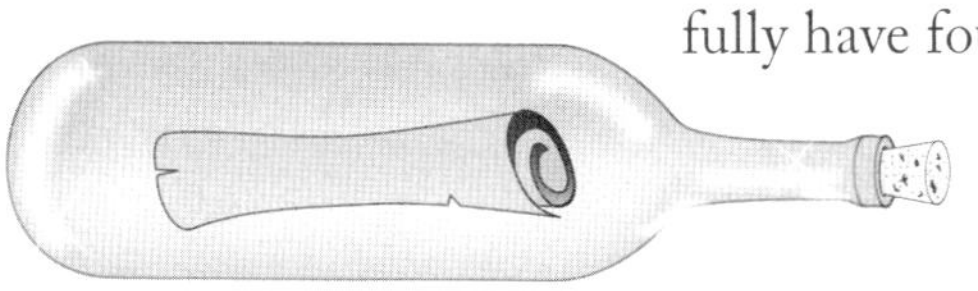

Strange 911 Calls

- A man called 911 and said: "Please connect me to Switzerland."
- Another person called to report he had the hiccups.
- A man called and requested police call gas stations on all exits of I-95 to find out which ones were open.
- A woman called to report she had seen a wild mouse in her house.
- Someone called 911 to report the parrot got out of his cage and is in a tree outside.
- A man called to report he had a roach stuck in his ear.

Strong Coffee

A former roommate baked a coffee cake and asked me to sample it.

It was very tasty but I asked her what the small crunchy things were in the cake. She said the recipe called for 2 cups of strong coffee.

You guessed it. She put two cups of pure coffee in—not perked coffee!!! Quite a buzzzzzzzz from that cake.

Stuck Between Floors

Soon after our high-tech company moved into a new building, we had trouble with the elevators. A manager got stuck between floors and, after some door banging, finally attracted attention. His name was taken and rescue promised.

It took two hours before the elevator mechanic arrived and got the manager out. When he returned to his desk, he found this note from his efficient secretary: "The elevator people called and will be here in two hours."

Supervision

My grandson, Chris, has worn glasses since the age of three. When he was in the first grade he came home one day very distressed. Wanting to find out what was the matter his mother asked, "Chris, what happened today to upset you so?"

He answered, "It's not fair that I'm not allowed to go to the library."

His mother became very concerned and asked, "Why aren't you allowed to go to the library?"

With a tearful reply he said, "Because, in order to go to the library you must have supervision, and I wear glasses!"

Supporting a Family

The prospective father-in-law asked, "Young man, can you support a family?"

The surprised groom-to-be replied, "Well, no. I was just planning to support your daughter. The rest of you will have to fend for yourselves!"

Surgeon Feedback

Surgeons invited to dinner parties are often asked to carve the meat or worse yet, to watch the host carve while commenting on the surgeon's occupation. At one party, a surgeon friend was watching the carving while Harry, his host, kept up a running commentary: "How am I doing, doc? How do you like that technique? I'd make a pretty good surgeon, don't you think?"

When the host finished and the slices of meat lay neatly on the serving platter, the surgeon spoke up: "Anybody can take them apart, Harry. Now let's see you put them back together again."

Surgical Tools

To address an emergency call a doctor came to see a rich patient at his home, who was screaming with extreme stomach pain and was surrounded by many anxious relatives. The doctor kicked all the relatives out of the room, closed the door with the patient and him inside.

After a while he came out and asked, "Please give me a pair of scissors." Someone gave him a stainless steel scissors. He again went inside, closed the door and soon came back. He said, "Please give me a hammer." He got one. A number of times he repeated the routine of going inside, closing the door and then coming back again for a new tool.

Finally he came outside one more time and asked, "Please give me a screw driver." The oldest son could not stand it any more and lost his patience. In a crying voice he pleaded, "Doctor please tell us what has happened to our dear Dad. Will he live? Could we open his will?"

The doctor said, "No, I don't know that yet. I am still trying to open my medical bag—I lost the key."

Sweetheart

An elderly gent was invited to his old friends' home for dinner one evening. He was impressed by the way his buddy preceded every request to his wife with endearing terms: Honey, My Love, Darling, Sweetheart, Pumpkin, etc. The couple had been married almost 70 years and, clearly they were still very much in love.

While the wife was in the kitchen, the man leaned over and said to his host, "I think it's wonderful that, after all these years, you can still call your wife those loving pet names."

The old man hung his head. "I have to tell you the truth," he said. "I forgot her real name ten years ago."

Talking Turkey

What does a turkey say?

"Gobble, gobble, gobble." Right? Not always!

What does a turkey in the shoe repair shop say? "Cobble, cobble, cobble."

What does a turkey with a sore leg say? "Hobble, hobble, hobble."

What does a football turkey say? "Huddle, huddle, huddle."

A dieting turkey: "Nibble, nibble nibble."

A turkey who argues a lot: "Squabble, squabble, squabble."

What does Dr. Seuss' turkey say? "Tweedle, beetle, paddle, battle, puddle, wobble, hobble, gobble."

Then there was the dizzy Turkey who just went: "Wobble, wobble, wobble!"

Talk Of The South

The following is a pre-approved posting whose purpose is to offer insight and advice to Northerners moving South.

1. Save all manner of bacon grease. You will be instructed on how to use it shortly.

2. Just because you can drive on snow and ice does not mean Southerners can. Stay home the two days of the year it snows.
3. If you do run your car into a ditch, don't panic. Four men in the cab of a four-wheel drive pick-up and a tow chain will be along shortly. Don't try to help them. Just stay out of their way. This is what they live for.
4. You can ask Southerners for directions, but unless you already know the positions of key hills, trees, and rocks, you're better off trying to find it yourself.
5. Remember: "Y'all" is singular. "All y'all" is plural. "All y'all's" is plural possessive.
6. Get used to hearing, "You ain't from around here, are you?"
7. Don't be worried that you don't understand anyone. They don't understand you, either.
8. The first Southern expression to creep into a transplanted Northerner's vocabulary is the adjective "big ole", as in "big ole truck", or "big ole boy". "Fixin'", as in "I'm fixin' to go to the store", is second. And "Y'all" is third.
9. When following a person driving 15 mph in a 55 mph zone directly in the middle of the road, remember: ALL Southern folks learned to drive on a John Deere, and this is the proper speed and lane position for that vehicle.
10. If you hear a Southerner exclaim, "Hey, y'all, watch this!" stay out of his way. These are likely the last words he will ever say, or worse still, that you will ever hear.
11. Most Southerners do not use turn signals; they ignore those who do. In fact, if you see a signal blinking on a car with a Southern license plate, you may rest assured that it was already turned on when the car was purchased.
12. If it can't be fried in bacon grease, it ain't worth cooking, let alone eating.
13. The wardrobe you always brought out in September can wait until December.

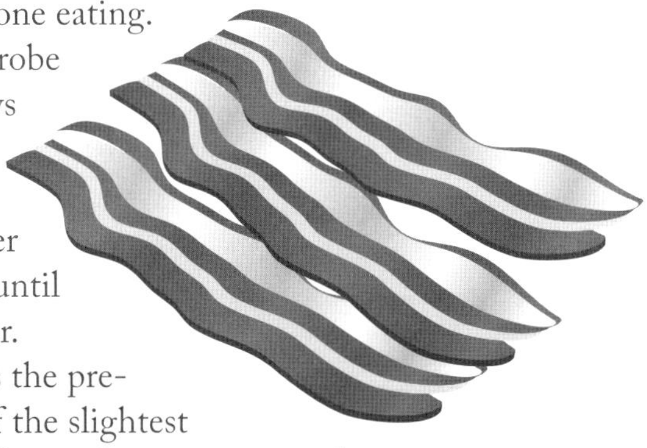

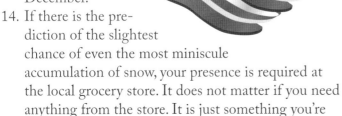

14. If there is the prediction of the slightest chance of even the most miniscule accumulation of snow, your presence is required at the local grocery store. It does not matter if you need anything from the store. It is just something you're supposed to do. Okay? Show of hands…who's tired of snow?
15. Satellite dishes are very popular in the South. When you purchase one, it is positioned directly in front of the house. This is logical, bearing in mind that the dish cost considerably more than the house and should, therefore, be prominently displayed.

Tall Animal

A woman clerk discovered a youngster wandering forlornly in the lobby of the Department of Agriculture Building in Washington D.C., and in a spirit of kindness, said to him, "Perhaps you'd like to see the 40-foot mural on the floor above. It's quite interesting."

With an expression of awed-anticipation, the small boy hot-footed his way upstairs. A few minutes later there came a despairing call from the Bureau of Animal Husbandry upstairs. "What is the big idea?" A voice demanded. "Just who sent a little fellow up here looking for a 40-foot mule?"

Teaching Your Children How To Change A Light Bulb

First, mom checks three books on electricity out of the library, then the children make models of light bulbs, read a biography of Thomas Edison, and do a skit based on his life. Next, everyone studies the history of lighting methods, wrapping up with dipping their own candles. Next, everyone takes a trip to the store where they compare types of light bulbs as well as prices and figure out how much change they'll get if they buy two bulbs for $1.99 and pay with a five dollar bill. On the way home, a discussion develops over the history of money and also Abraham Lincoln, as his picture is on the five dollar bill. Finally, after building a homemade ladder out of branches dragged from the woods, the light bulb is installed. And there is light.

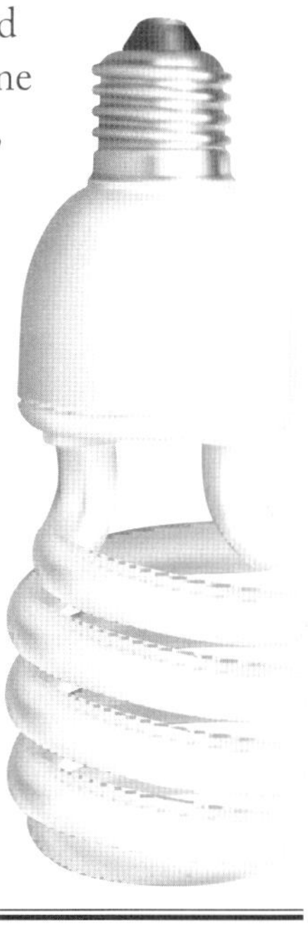

Tea Party

There was this day that I had a tea party
When I was three.
'Twas very small, three guests in all.
Just "I", "Myself", and "Me".

"Myself" ate all the sandwiches
While "I" drank all the tea.
'Twas also "I" who ate the pie,
And passed the cake to "Me".

Tea Service

One day my mother was out and my dad was in charge of me and my brother who is four years older than I am. I was maybe 1 and a half years old and had just recovered from an accident in which my arm had been broken. Someone had given me a little 'tea set' as a get-well gift and it was one of my favorite toys. Daddy was in the living room engrossed in the evening news and my brother was playing nearby in the living room when I brought daddy a little cup of 'tea', which was just water.

After several cups of tea and lots of praise for such yummy tea, my mom came home. My dad made her wait in the living room to watch me bring him a cup of tea, because it was "Just the cutest thing!!"

My mom waited, and sure enough, here I come down the hall with a cup of tea for daddy and she watches him drink it up, then says, "Did it ever occur to you that the only place that she can reach to get water is the toilet??"

Technology

When a customer left his cell phone in my store, I scrolled through his saved numbers, stopped at "Mom" and pushed send. His mother answered, and I told her what happened.

"Don't worry," she said, "I'll take care of it."

A few minutes later, the cell phone rang. It was "Mom."

"Martin," she said, "you left your cell phone at the convenience store."

Teenagers Are Always Hungry

The parents in our cycling group were discussing the subject of teenagers and their appetites. Most agreed that teenagers would eat anything, anywhere, and at anytime. Some were concerned that such appetites always made it hard to judge when you should feed them because they were always eating.

A veteran parent of six children told us of his method for judging the true hunger of teenagers. "I would hold up a piece of cold, cooked broccoli, and if they were jumping and snapping at it, I figured they were hungry enough to be fed."

Teenagers Celebrating

Dining out one evening, I noticed six teenagers boisterously celebrating some event at a nearby table. Toward the end of their meal, one of them got up and produced a camera.

"Hey, wait a minute," one of her companions said. "You have to be in the picture too." When I approached and asked if I could help, the girl who owned the camera was delighted. I snapped a picture of the group and then, being unfamiliar with the camera, I asked her, "Do you want me to take another in case that one doesn't come out?"

"Oh, no, that's okay," she chirped innocently. "I always get double prints."

Ten Minute Wait

I called to make airline reservations and was put on hold. After several minutes of taped music, a recorded voice came on:

"If you have been waiting longer than ten minutes, you may press eight. This will not speed up your call, but it will give you something to do while you wait."

Tennis Ball Lesson

A college professor had the mysterious habit of walking into the lecture hall each morning, removing a tennis ball from his jacket pocket, and setting it on the corner of the podium. After giving the lecture for the day, he would once again pick up the tennis ball, place it into his jacket pocket, and leave the room. No one ever understood why he did this, until one day…

A student fell asleep during the lecture. The professor never missed a word of his lecture while he walked over to the podium, picked up the tennis ball and threw it, hitting the sleeping student squarely on the top of the head.

The next day, the professor walked into the room, reached into his jacket, removed a baseball… No one ever fell asleep in his class the rest of the semester!

Tense

An English teacher at Michigan State University spent a lot of time marking grammatical errors on her students' written work. She wasn't sure how much impact she was having until one overly busy day when she sat at her desk rubbing her temples.

A student asked, "What's the matter, Mrs. Sheridan?"

"Tense," she replied, describing her emotional state.

After a slight pause the student tried again. "What was the matter? What has been the matter? What might have been the matter?…???"

Texan Talk

A boy and his mom were walking on the sidewalk in Dallas. The boy, being 100% Texan, upon seeing some cowboys, said, "Hey Maw, look at them thar men with them thar bowed laigs."

She said that if he didn't start speaking correct English, she was going to send him to a Shakespearean English school.

A little further along, they saw some more cowboys. "Hey maw! Look at them thar men with them thar bowed legs!" he said.

So, true to her word, she sent him off to a Shakespearean English school to learn correct English.

He came home several months later on vacation. As they walked together down the sidewalk, they saw some cowboys. "Hark!" he said, "What manner of men are these who wear their legs in parentheses?"

Thanksgiving Forecast

Turkeys will thaw in the morning, then warm in the oven to an afternoon high near 190°F. The kitchen will turn hot and humid, and if you bother the cook, be ready for a severe squall or cold shoulder.

During the late afternoon and evening, the cold front of a knife will slice through the turkey, causing an accumulation of one to two inches on plates. Mashed potatoes will drift across one side while cranberry sauce creates slippery spots on the other. Please pass the gravy. A weight watch and indigestion warning have been issued for the entire area, with increased stuffiness around the beltway. During the evening, the turkey will diminish and taper off to left-overs, dropping to a low of 34°F in the refrigerator. Looking ahead to Friday and Saturday, high pressure to eat sandwiches will be established. Flurries of leftovers can be expected both days with a fifty percent chance of scattered soup late in the day. We expect a warming trend where soup develops. By early next week, eating pressure will be low as the only wish left will be the bone.

Thanksgiving Recipes By Children

Mrs. Geraghty's kindergarten class Thanksgiving cookbook: *Note, Mrs. Geraghty will not be responsible for medical bills resulting from use of her cookbook.*

- Ivette—Banana Pie
  You buy some bananas and crust. Then you mash them up and put them in the pie. Then you eat it.

- Russell—Turkey
  You cut the turkey up and put it in the oven for ten minutes and 300°. You put gravy on it and eat it.

- Geremy—Turkey
  You buy the turkey and take the paper off. Then you put it in the refrigerator and take it back out and cut it with a knife and make sure all the wires are out and take out the neck and heart. Then you put it in a big pan and cook it for half an hour at 80°. Then you invite people over and eat.

- Andrew—Pizza
  Buy some dough, some cheese and pepperoni. Then you cook it for 10 hours at 5°. Then you eat it.

- Shelby—Applesauce
  Go to the store and buy some apples, and then you squish them up. Then you put them in a jar that says, "Applesauce". Then you eat it.

- Megan—Chicken
  You put it in the oven for 25 minutes and 25° and put gravy on it and eat it.

- Christa—Cookies
  Buy some dough and smash it and cut them out. Then put them in the oven for 2 hours at 100°. Then take them out and dry them off. Then it's time to eat them.

- Grace—Turkey
  First you add some salt. Then you put it in a bowl. Then you put brown sugar on it. Then you mix it all together with a spoon and then you add some milk and mix it again. And then you put it in a pan. Then you put it in the oven for 15 minutes and 16°. Then you take it out of the oven and then you eat it.

- Alan—Turkey
  First you shoot it and then you cut it. And then you put it in the oven and cook it for 10 minutes and 20°. You put it on plates and then you eat it.

- Jordan—Chocolate Pudding
  Buy some chocolate pudding mix. Then you add the milk. Then you add the pudding mix. Then you stir it. Then you put it in the refrigerator and wait for it to get hard. Then you eat it.

- Christopher—Pumpkin Pie
  First you buy a pumpkin and smash it. Then it is all done. And you cook it in the oven for 12 minutes and 4°. Then you eat it.

- Jarryd—Deer Jerky
  Put it in the oven overnight at 20°. Then you go hunting and bring it with you. Then you eat it.

- Joplyn—Apple Pie
  Take some apples, mash them up. Take some bread and make a pie with it. Get some dough and squish it. Shape the dough into a pie shape. Put the apples in it. Then bake it at 9° for 15 minutes.

- Isabelle—Spaghetti
  Put those red things in it. Then put the spaghetti in it. Then cook it in the oven for 2 minutes at 8°.

- Nicholas—White and Brown Pudding
  First you read the wrapper. Get a piece of water. Stir. Then you eat it.

- Lauren—Turkey
  First you find a turkey and kill it. Cut it open. Put it in a pan. Pour milk in the pan. Put a little chicken with it. Put salsa on it. Take out of pan. Put it on the board. Cut into little pieces. Put on a rack. Put in the oven for 7 minutes at 10°. Take out of the oven and put eensy weensy bit of sugar on it. Put a little more salsa on it. Then you eat it.

Thanksgiving Riddles

Q. What is the best thing to put into stuffing?
A. Your teeth!

Q. What is the key to a good Thanksgiving dinner?
A. The turkey!

Q. Did the little Pilgrims eat the turkey with their fingers?
A. No, they never ate their fingers!

Q. Why didn't the Pilgrim want to make the bread?
A. It's a crummy job!

Q. Why didn't the turkey want any lunch?
A. He was already stuffed!

Q. What part of the turkey can play in a band?
A. The drum-stick!

Q. What can you never eat for Thanksgiving dinner?
A. Breakfast or lunch!

The Cowboy's New Car

Three cowboys were hanging out in the bunkhouse.

"I know that smart alec, Tex," said the first. "He's going to start bragging about that new foreign car he bought as soon as he gets back."

"Not Tex," said the second. "He'll always be just a good ol' boy. When he walks in, I'm sure all he'll say is hello."

"I know Tex better than any of you," said the third. "He's so smart, he'll figure out a way to do both. Here he comes now."

Tex swung open the bunkhouse door and shouted "Audi, partners!"

The Diet

A lady is terribly overweight, so her doctor put her on a diet. "I want you to eat regularly for 2 days, then skip a day, and repeat this procedure for 2 weeks. The next time I see you, you'll have lost at least 5 pounds."

When the lady returned, she shocked the doctor by losing nearly 20 pounds.

"Why, that's amazing!" the doctor said, "Did you follow my instructions?"

The lady nodded, "I'll tell you though, I thought I was going to drop dead that third day."

"From hunger, you mean?" asked the doctor.

"No, from skipping."

The Duel

Aaron came home from school one day all banged up, bloodied, and bruised. His father asked him what had happened.

"Well, dad, it's like this," Aaron began. "I challenged Larry to a duel and you know how that goes…I gave him his choice of weapons."

"Uh huh," said the father. "That seems fair."

"I know, but I never thought he'd choose his sister!"

The English Language, Homographs

If you ever feel stupid, then just read on. If you've learned to speak fluent English, you must be a genius! This little treatise on the lovely language we share is only for the brave. Peruse at your leisure, English lovers.

1. The bandage was wound around the wound.
2. The farm was used to produce produce.
3. The dump was so full that it had to refuse more refuse.
4. We must polish the Polish furniture.
5. He could lead if he would get the lead out.
6. The solider decided to desert his dessert in the desert.
7. Since there is no time like the present, he thought it was time to present the present.
8. A bass was painted on the head of the bass drum.
9. When shot at, the dove dove into the bushes.
10. I did not object to the object.
11. The insurance was invalid for the invalid.
12. There was a row among the oarsmen about how to row.

13. They were too close to the door to close it.
14. The buck does funny things when the does are present.
15. A seamstress and a sewer fell down into a sewer line.
16. To help with the planting, the farmer taught his sow to sow.
17. The wind was too strong to wind the sail.
18. After a number of injections my jaw got number.
19. Upon seeing the tear in the painting I shed a tear.
20. I had to subject the subject to a series of tests.
21. How can I intimate this to my most intimate friend?

P.S. Why doesn't Buick rhyme with quick?

Take your time and see if you can read each line aloud without a mistake. The average person can't.

This is this cat
This is is cat
This is how cat
This is to cat
This is keep cat
This is the cat
This is staff cat
This is busy cat
This is for cat
This is forty cat
This is seconds cat

Now, go back and read the third word in each line from the top down :)

The English Language Twisters

Most of us speak English, or at least the American version of the language we inherited from our so-called mother country, Great Britain. Let's check some similarities, differences, and absurdities in the way we speak and write, and see what we come up with (ending a sentence with a preposition is a good start).

- Where is the ham in hamburger? Or the egg in eggplant? Or the apple in pineapple? Or the pine, either?
- English muffins weren't invented in England, and if you asked for French fries in Paris they wouldn't know what you were talking about.
- Cold Duck is a drink, and hot peppers are cold.
- Your alarm clock goes off by going on.
- We belong to the human race which isn't a race at all.
- Does a barn burn up or down?
- We fill in a form by filling it out.
- Why say "R" in colonel?
- We drive on a parkway and park on a driveway.
- How can overlook and oversee be opposites?
- We ship by truck and send cargo by ship.
- We recite at a play and play at a recital.
- Quicksand works very slowly, and a boxing ring is square.
- A slim chance and a fat chance mean the same thing.
- When the stars come out they are plain to be seen, but when the lights are out they are invisible.
- We speak of brother and also of brethren, and though we say mother, we never say methren.
- The masculine pronouns are he, his and him.
- Imagine the feminine—she, shis, and shim.
- End of page coming up. You take it from here. I'm coming to a red light. Do I slow up or slow down?

The Experts Speak

- Electric Light—"Good enough for our transatlantic friends, but unworthy of the attention of practical or scientific men" (British Parliament report on Edison's work, 1878).
- The Telephone—"That's an amazing invention, but who would ever want to use one of them?" (Pres. Rutherford Hayes, 1876).
- Computers—"There is no reason for any individual to have a computer in their home" (Ken Olson, Pres. of Digital Equipment Corp., 1977).
- Aviation—"The popular mind often pictures gigantic flying machines speeding across the Atlantic and carrying innumerable passengers…it seems safe to say that such ideas are wholly visionary" (Harvard astronomer Wm. Henry Pickering, 1908).

- Nuclear Energy—"Nuclear powered vacuum cleaner will probably be a reality within 10 years" (Vacuum cleaner manufacturer, Alex Lewyt, 1955).
- Medicine—"The abdomen, the chest, and the brain will be forever shut from the intrusion of the wise and humane surgeon" (British surgeon Erichsen, 1837).

The Farmers

A farmer from Texas went to Australia on vacation. There he met an Australian farmer and got talking. The Australian was showing off his big wheat field when the Texan said, "Oh! We have wheat fields that are at least twice that size!"

The Australian was annoyed at the Texan but didn't say anything. They walked around the farm a little, and the Australian farmer pointed out his herd of cattle. The Texan immediately replied, "We have longhorns that are at least twice as large as your cows." The conversation died down when the Texan saw some kangaroos hopping through the field. He asked the Aussie, "What are those?"

The Australian replied with an incredulous look, "Don't you have any grasshoppers in Texas?"

The Greatest

A little boy was overheard talking to himself as he strutted through the backyard, wearing his baseball cap and toting a ball and bat. "I'm the greatest hitter in the world," he announced. Then, he tossed the ball into the air, swung at it, and missed. "Strike One !" he yelled. Undaunted, he picked up the ball and said again, "I'm the greatest hitter in the world!"

He tossed the ball into the air. When it came down he again missed. "Strike Two!" he cried. The boy then paused a moment to examine his bat and ball carefully. He spit on his hands and rubbed them together. He straightened his cap and said once more, "I'm the greatest hitter in the world!"

Again he tossed the ball up in the air and swung at it. He missed. "Strike Three! Wow!" he exclaimed. "I'm also the greatest pitcher in the world!"

The Happy Trucker

My brother, a trucker, is often caught in commuter rush hour traffic. One morning when everything came to a standstill, he sat high up in his eighteen-wheeler singing and whistling. A passenger in a nearby car, frustrated by the delay, yelled up at my brother, "What are you so happy about?"

"I'm already at work!" he cheerfully replied.

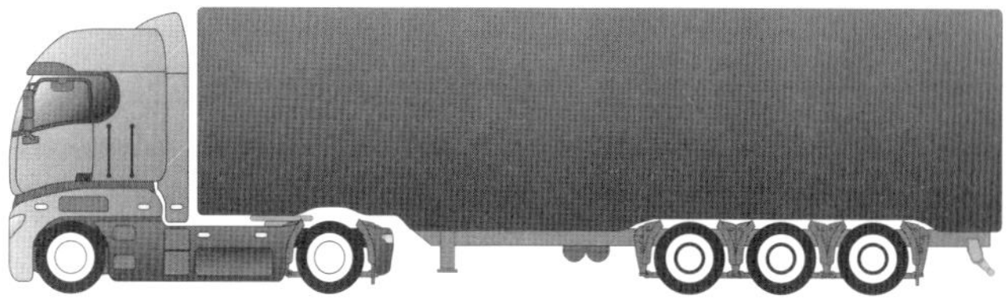

The Household Handyman's Guide

1. If you can't find a screwdriver, use a knife. If you break off the tip, it's an improved screwdriver.
2. Try to work alone. An audience is rarely any help.
3. Above all, if what you've done is foolish, but it works, then it isn't foolish.
4. Work in the kitchen whenever you can…many fine tools are there, its warm and dry, and you are close to the refrigerator.
5. If it's electronic, get a new one…or consult a twelve-year-old.
6. Stay simple minded: Get a new battery; replace the bulb or fuse; see if the tank is empty; try turning the switch "on" ; or just paint over it.
7. Always take credit for miracles. If you dropped the alarm clock while taking it apart and it suddenly starts working, you have healed it.
8. Regardless of what people say, kicking, pounding, and throwing sometimes DOES help.
9. If something looks level, it is level.
10. If at first you don't succeed, redefine success.
11. Time is the most valuable thing a man spends.

The Kind Lawyer?

One afternoon, a wealthy lawyer was riding in the back of his limousine when he saw two men eating grass by the side of the road side. He ordered his driver to stop and he got out to investigate.

"Why are you eating grass?" he asked one man.

"We don't have any money for food," the poor man replied.

"Oh, come along with me then."

"But sir, I have a wife with two children!"

"Bring them along! And you, come with us too!" he said to the other man.

"But sir, I have a wife with six children!" the second man answered.

"Bring them as well!"

They all climbed into the car, which was no easy task, even for a car as large as the limo. Once underway, one of the poor fellows said, "Sir, you are too kind. Thank you for taking all of us with you."

The lawyer replied, "No problem; the grass at my home is about two feet tall!"

The Modern Little Red Hen

Once upon a time, there was a little red hen who scratched about the barnyard until she uncovered some grains of wheat, She called her neighbors and said, "If I plant this wheat, we shall have bread to eat. Who will help me plant it?"

"Not I," said the cow.

"Not I," said the duck

"Not I," said the pig.

"Not I," said the goose.

"Then I will," said the little red hen. And she did. The wheat grew tall and ripened into golden grain. "Who will help me reap my wheat?" asked the little red hen.

"Not I," said the duck.

"Out of my classification," said the pig.

"I'd lose my seniority," said the cow.

"I'd lose my unemployment compensation," said the goose.

"Then I will," said the little red hen, and she did.

At last it came time to bake the bread.

"Who will help me bake the bread?" asked the little red hen.

"That would be overtime for me," said the cow.

"I'd lose my welfare benefits," said the duck.

"I'm a dropout and never learned how," said the pig.

"If I'm the only helper, that's discrimination," said the goose.

"Then I will," said the little red hen. She baked five loaves and held them up for her neighbors to see.

They all wanted some and, in fact, demanded a share. But the little red hen said, "No, I can eat the five loaves myself."

"Excess profits!" cried the cow.

"Capitalist leech!" screamed the duck.

"I demand equal rights!" yelled the goose.

And the pig just grunted.

When the government agent came, he said to the little red hen, "You must not be greedy."

"But I earned the bread," said the little red hen.

"Exactly," said the agent. "That is the wonderful free enterprise system. Anyone in the barnyard can earn as much as he wants. But under our modern government regulations, the productive workers must divide their product with the idle."

And they lived happily ever after, including the little red hen, who smiled and clucked, "I am grateful. I am grateful."

But her neighbors wondered why she never again baked any more bread.

The Nativity Scene

A seven-year-old child was drawing a picture of the Nativity. The picture was very good, including Mary, Joseph, and, of course, baby Jesus.

However, there was a fat man standing in the corner of the stable, that just did not seem to fit in. When the child was asked about it, she replied, "Oh, that's Round John Virgin."

The Optimist & The Pessimist

There is a story of identical twins. One was a hope-filled optimist. "Everything is coming up roses!" he would say. The other twin was a sad and hopeless pessimist. He thought that Murphy, as in Murphy's Law, was an optimist. The worried parents of the boys brought them to the local psychologist.

He suggested to the parents a plan to balance the twins' personalities. "On their next birthday, put them in separate rooms to open their gifts. Give the pessimist the best toys you can afford, and give the optimist a box of manure." The parents followed these instructions and carefully observed the results.

When they peeked in on the pessimist, they heard him audibly complaining, "I don't like the color of this computer…I'll bet this calculator will break…I don't like the game…I know someone who's got a bigger toy car than this"

Tiptoeing across the corridor, the parents peeked in and saw their little optimist gleefully throwing the manure up in the air. He was giggling. "You can't fool me! Where there's this much manure, there's gotta be a pony!"

The Perfect Prize

A lady went into a restaurant and noticed a "peel and win" sticker on her coffee cup. So, she's peeled it off and started screaming, "I've won a motor home! I've won a motor home!"

The waitress said, "That's impossible. The biggest prize is a free lunch."

But the lady kept screaming, "I've won a motor home! I've won a motor home!"

Finally the manager came over and said, "Ma'am, I'm sorry, but you're mistaken. You couldn't possibly have won a motor home because we didn't have that as a prize!"

The lady said, "No, it's not a mistake. I've won a motor home!"

She handed the ticket to the manager and he read, "W I N A B A G E L"

The Poor Tailor And The French Restaurant

Old Abraham was a poor tailor whose shop was next door to a very upscale French restaurant. Every day at lunch time, Abraham would go out the back of his shop and eat his black bread and herring while smelling the wonderful odors coming from the restaurant's kitchen.

One day, Abraham was surprised to receive an invoice from the restaurant for "enjoyment of food". So, he went to the restaurant to point out that he had not bought anything from them. The manager said, "You're enjoying our food, so you should pay us for it."

Abraham refused to pay and the restaurant sued him. At the hearing, the judge asked the restaurant manager to present his side of the case. The manager said, "Every day, this man comes and sits outside our kitchen and smells our food while eating his. It is clear that we are providing added value to his poor food and we deserve to be compensated for it."

The judge turned to Abraham and said, "What do you have to say to that?" Abraham didn't say anything but stuck his hand in his pocket and rattled the few coins he had inside. The judge asked him, "What is the meaning of that?" Abraham replied, "I'm paying for the smell of this food with the sound of my money."

The Portrait

One semester when my brother, Peter, attended the University of Minnesota in Minneapolis, an art-student friend of his asked if he could paint Peter's portrait for a class assignment. Peter agreed, and the art student painted and submitted the portrait, only to receive a C-.

The art student approached the professor to ask why the grade was so poor.

The teacher told him that the proportions in the painting were incorrect.

"The head is too big," the professor explained. "The shoulders are too wide, and the feet are enormous."

The next day, the art student brought Peter to see the professor. He took one look at my brother. "Okay, A-," he said.

The Right To Write

When you write copy, you have the right to copyright the copy you write, if the copy is right. If however, your copy falls over, you must right your copy. If you write religious services you write rite, and have the right to copyright the rite you write. Very conservative people write right copy, and have the right to copyright the right copy they write. A right wing cleric would write right rite, and has the right to copyright the right rite he has the right to write. His editor has the job of making the right rite copy right before the copyright can be right. Should Thom Wright decide to write right rite, then Wright would write right rite, which Wright has the right to copyright. Duplicating that rite would copy Wright's right rite, and violate copyright, which Wright would have the right to right. Right?

The Six Men And The Elephant

"It's very like a wall," said the first man as he touched the side of the elephant.

"It's very like a spear," said the second man as he stroked the elephant's tusk.

And the third man, taking the elephant's squirming trunk in hand, said, "It's very like a snake!"

"Nonsense!" the fourth man shouted. Stretching his arms about one of the legs, he concluded, "This wondrous beast is very like a tree!"

The fifth man, touching the elephant's ear, cried, "Even the blindest can tell this animal is very like a fan."

And the sixth, grabbing the tail, assured his friends that, "The elephant is really very like a rope!"

This Is Not My Dog

A woman had checked her baggage thru, except for the cage carrying her dog, for which she wanted special handling and checking, which she received. The flight was uneventful. After landing, the baggage appeared after a normal wait. However, the dog cage was not there. The baggage handlers had checked the cage earlier and noticed that the dog was not moving. They thought that the dog must have died in the cold baggage compartment. It looked like an ordinary cocker spaniel, so they decided to find another cocker spaniel to put in the cage. In the meantime, the woman kept asking about the rest of her luggage. She was told that it was delayed because of the special handling required and to be patient. Time dragged on for her while the baggage handlers found a replacement dog in a pet shop, which they put into the cage. They finally brought the cage with the dog to her and she looked into the cage. She jumped back with a horrified look and screamed out, "This is not my dog!! My dog was dead and I was bringing her here for a proper burial!!!"

Three Tickets

Three lawyers and three engineers are traveling by train to a conference. At the station, the three lawyers each buy tickets and watch as the three engineers buy only a single ticket.

"How are three people going to travel on only one ticket?" asked one of the three lawyers. "Watch and you'll see," answers one of the engineers.

They all board the train. The lawyers take their respective seats but all three engineers cram into a restroom and close the door behind them.

Shortly after the train has departed, the conductor came around collecting tickets. He knocks on the restroom door and says, 'Ticket, please." The door opens just a crack and a single arm emerges with a ticket in hand. The conductor takes it and moves on. The lawyers saw this and agreed it was quite a clever idea.

So after the conference, the lawyers decide to copy the engineers on the return trip and save some money.

When they get to the station, they buy a single ticket for the return trip. To their astonishment, the engineers don't buy a ticket at all. "How are you going to travel without a ticket," asks one perplexed lawyer. "Watch and you'll see," says one of the engineers.

When they board the train the three lawyers cram into a restroom and the three engineers cram into another one nearby. The train departs. Shortly afterward, one of the engineers leaves his restroom and walks over to the restroom where the lawyers are hiding. He knocks on the door and says, "Ticket, please."

Editor's Note: Cheating catches up eventually. Pay your dues and then there is nothing to worry about.

Ticket Collection

"What am I supposed to do with this?" grumbled a motorist as the policeman handed him a speeding ticket.

"Keep it," the cop said, "when you collect four of them you get a bicycle.

Time Travel

Unaware that Indianapolis is on Eastern Standard Time and Chicago on Central Standard Time, Bob inquired at the Indianapolis airport about a plane to Chicago.

"The next flight leaves at 1:00 p.m.," a ticket agent said, "and arrives in Chicago at 1:01 p.m."

"Would you repeat that, please?" Bob asked.

The agent did so and then inquired, "Do you want a reservation?"

"No," said Bob, "But I think I'll hang around and watch that thing take off!"

Tired Of Waiting

The two ladies were sitting in the living room waiting for their hostess, who was slightly delayed. The daughter of the family was with them, on the theory that she would keep the visitors occupied during the wait.

The child was about six years old, snub nosed, freckled, buck toothed, and bespectacled. She maintained a deep silence and the two ladies peered doubtfully at her. Finally, one of them muttered to the other, "Not very p-r-e-t-t-y, I fear," carefully spelling the key word. Whereupon the child piped up, "But awful s-m-a-r-t."

Tired Son

A man, walking down a country lane, saw a young farmer struggling to load hay back onto a cart after it had fallen off.

"You look tired, my son," said the man. "Why don't you rest a moment, and I'll give you a hand."

"No thanks," said the young man. "My father wouldn't approve."

"Don't be silly," the man said. "Everyone is entitled to a break. Come and have a drink of water."

Again the young man protested that his father would be upset.

Losing his patience just a little, the man said, "Your father must be a real slave driver. Tell me where I can find him and I'll give him a piece of my mind!"

"Well," replied the young farmer, "you can tell him whatever you like just as soon as I get this hay off of him."

Toast

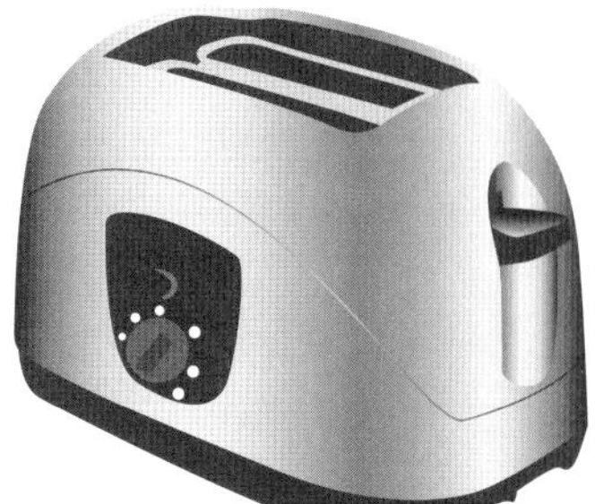

One of my daughter's wedding presents was a toaster. Soon after the honeymoon, she and her husband tried it out. Almost immediately, smoke billowed out of the toaster. "Get the owner's manual!" her husband shouted. "I can't find it anywhere!" she cried, searching through the box. "Oops!" came a voice from the kitchen. "Well, the toast is fine, but the owner's manual is burnt to a crisp."

To Boil Water

First find a pot or pan. Colanders are impractical for this purpose. With the pot held firmly in left hand, address sink, insert pot under faucet, and turn water on with right hand. Fill to desired depth or until it becomes too heavy to hold, transport utensil containing liquid to stove, place on nearest burner. Turn lever of the stove in whichever direction it will turn. If stove has pilot light, one of the burners will ignite. If utensil happens to be over that burner leave it there. Otherwise move it to the one with a flame. If stove has no pilot light, strike a match and hold it as close as you dare to a burner, but be prepared to leap for your life. Striking a match will be of little effect if your stove is electric. Do nothing more. In time the liquid will become agitated and you will have boiling water!

Variations: Use for instant coffee, birthing babies, or freeze for ice.

Toilet Repair

Because I couldn't unclog the toilet with a plunger, I had to dismantle the entire fixture; no small feat for a non-plumber. Jammed inside the drain was a purple rubber dinosaur, which belonged to my five-year-old son. I painstakingly got all the toilet parts together again, the tank filled, and I flushed it. However, it didn't work much better than before! As I pondered what to do next, my son walked into the bathroom. I pointed to the purple dinosaur I had just dislodged and told him that the toilet still wasn't working.

"Did you get the green one, too?" he asked.

Tomatoes

A small boy was looking at the red ripe tomatoes growing in the farmer's garden. "I'll give you my two pennies for that tomato," said the boy pointing to a beautiful, large, ripe fruit hanging on the vine.

"No," said the farmer, "I get a dime for a tomato like that one."

The small boy pointed to a smaller green one, "will you take two pennies for that one?"

"Yes," replied the farmer, "I'll give you that one for two cents."

"Ok," said the lad, sealing the deal by putting the coins in the farmer's hand, "I'll pick it up in about a week."

Too Fast For Germs

An elderly lady at 78 kept very busy cooking, cleaning, and caring for her home and mowing her yard. When asked the reason for her good health and strength, she replied, "I move so fast the germs can't catch me."

Top Stories of the Year

1. The president of a large company was fired after nine months, because he lacked intellectual leadership. He received a $26 million severance package.
2. Police in California spent two hours attempting to subdue a gunman who had barricaded himself inside his home. After firing ten tear gas canisters, officers discovered that the man was standing beside them in the police line, shouting "Please, come out and give yourself up."
3. Police in Los Angeles had good luck with a robbery suspect who just couldn't control himself during a lineup. When detectives asked each man in the lineup to repeat the words, "Give me all your money," the man shouted, "That's not what I said!"

Top Ten Silliest Questions Asked On A Cruise Ship

10. Do these steps go up or down?
9. What do you do with the beautiful ice carvings after they melt?
8. Which elevator do I take to get to the front of the ship?
7. Does the crew sleep on the ship?
6. Is this island completely surrounded by water?
5. Does the ship make its own electricity?
4. Is it salt water in the toilets?
3. What elevation are we at?
2. There's a photographer on board who takes photos and displays them the next day...the question asked: If the pictures aren't marked, how will I know which ones are mine?
1. What time is the Midnight Buffet being served?

—Paul Grayson,
Cruise Director for the Royal Caribbean Cruise Line

Totally Twisted Proverb

A 4th grade teacher collected well known proverbs. She gave each child in the class the first half of the proverb, and asked them to come up with the rest. Here is what they came up with.

- Better to be safe than...punch a 5th grader.
- Strike while the...bug is close.
- It's always darkest before...daylight savings time.
- Never underestimate...the power of termites.
- You can lead a horse to water but...how?
- Don't bite the hand that...looks dirty.
- A miss is as good as a...Mr.
- You can't teach an old dog...math.

- If you lie down with dogs…you will stink in the morning.
- The pen is mightier than… the pigs.
- An idle mind is…the best way to relax.
- Where there is smoke, there's…pollution.
- Happy is the bride who…gets all the presents.
- A penny saved is…not much.
- Children should be seen and not…spanked or grounded.
- If at first you don't succeed…get new batteries.
- You get out of something what's…pictured on the box.
- When the blind lead the blind…get out of the way.
- Laugh and the whole world laughs with you…cry and you have to blow your nose.

Tough Boys

Three little boys were bragging about how tough they were.

"I'm so tough," said the first boy, "That I can wear out a pair of shoes in a week."

"Well," said the second little boy, "I'm so tough, I can wear out a pair of jeans in a day."

"That's nothing," said the third boy. "When my parents take me to see my grandma and grandpa, I can wear them out in just one hour."

Traits Passed From Parents To Children

Father, Mother, and their three sons, John (oldest), Mike (middle), and Steve (youngest) are conversing around the table after dinner. The subject of traits of parents being passed on to children comes up.

The Father says, "John has my eyes, Mike has my creativity, and Steve has my intelligence."

Steve responds, "Daddy, what's intelligence?"

Travel Quip

Story from Travel Agent

I had someone ask for an aisle seat on the plane so that her hair wouldn't get messed up by being near the window.

Treasure

Someone in our neighborhood put a huge sofa out by the curb for trash collection. Since it was in good shape, many motorists slowed down for a look. But when they saw how enormous it was, they'd leave.

Eventually a compact car pulled up, and two men got out.

"This I've got to see," I thought.

They removed the cushions, turned the sofa upside down, and shook it hard. Then they picked up all the coins that tumbled out and drove off.

Tree Trouble

Unexpected cold snaps had destroyed the buds on my father's young peach tree for two years in a row. This spring, Dad was ready. He replanted the sapling in a large box, mounted it on wheels, and put the tree in the garage whenever the temperature dropped.

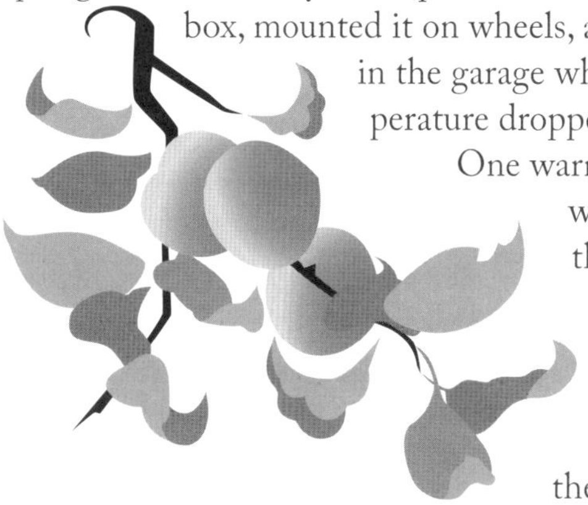

One warm April day, Dad was wheeling the tree out into the yard, and he stopped to give our dog a drink from the garden hose. A neighbor watched the scene with amusement. "Frank," he finally commented, "you're the only man I know who walks his tree and waters his dog!"

Trouble At The Zoo

Three mischievous boys went to the zoo one day for an outing, since they had been at school all week. They decided to visit the elephant cage, but soon enough, they were picked up by a cop for causing a commotion. The officer hauled them off to security for questioning. The supervisor in charge asked them to give their names and tell what they were doing at the elephant cage.

The first boy innocently said, "My name is Gary and I was just throwing peanuts into the elephant cage."

The second added, "My name is Larry, and all I was doing was throwing peanuts into the elephant cage."

The third boy was a little shaken up and said, "Well, my name is Peter, but my friends call me Peanuts."

Truth In Taxes

When Pastor Ovall picked up the phone, Special Agent Struzik from the IRS was on the line.

"Hello, Pastor Ovall?"

"Yes, this is."

"I'm calling to inquire about a member of your congregation, a Dr. Shipe. Do you recognize the name?"

"Yes, he is a member of our congregation. How can I be of service?"

"Well, on last year's tax return, the doctor claimed that he made a sizable tax-deductible contribution to your church? Is it true?"

"Well, I'll have to have my bookkeeper verify this information for you. How much did Dr. Shipe say he contributed?"

"Twenty five thousand dollars," answered Agent Struzik. "Can you tell me if that's true?"

There was a long pause. "I'll tell you what," replied Pastor Ovall, "Call back tomorrow. I'm sure it will be."

True Tales Of InDUHviduals

- I went to the registry of motor vehicles to renew my license. When I handed the clerk a check to pay for the license she asked for some identification. I pointed to the renewed picture license that she was holding in her hand.
- While talking to a colleague IN PERSON I mentioned that I colored my hair. He asked me what color.
- Last week my co-worker was traveling on business to a very small town. They found a restaurant in the phone book and asked the woman working at the hotel desk how to get there. The desk clerk told them all about it and gave them directions. After driving around for half an hour they could not find it. When they returned to the hotel, the woman at the hotel desk told them, "Oh, I forgot; they never did build that restaurant."
- I went into a major retail establishment and asked an employee in the garden section whether they sold hyacinth vases. Seeing her blank look, I described a hyacinth vase, explaining that it has a narrow neck, with space for a flower bulb on top and water on the bottom. Said the employee, "Have you looked in Electronics?"

Turnip

I put some turnip, his least-favorite vegetable, on my eleven-year-old son's dinner plate and instructed him to eat everything. He cleaned his plate, except for the turnip.

I pointed out to him that if he'd eaten it earlier, he wouldn't have been left with its taste in his mouth at the end of the meal.

Thoughtfully, he replied, "I guess I was just trying to delay the inedible."

Twisting His Arm

While I was visiting my sister one evening, I took out a candy dispenser that was shaped like a miniature person.

"How does that thing work?" she asked.

As I turned the figurine's arm to pop candy out, my sister laughed.

"I see…it's a lot like my husband," she said. "You have to twist his arm to get anything out of him, too!"

Two Brothers

Two brothers inherit the family ranch. Unfortunately, after just a few years, they are in financial trouble. To keep the bank from repossessing the ranch, they need to purchase a bull from the stockyard in a far town so they can breed their own stock.

They have only $600 left. Upon leaving, the one brother said to the other brother, "When I get there, if I decide to buy the bull, I'll contact you to drive out after me and haul it home."

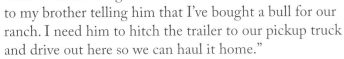

He arrived at the stockyard, inspected the bull, and decided he wanted to buy it. The man said he would sell it for $599, no less. After paying him, he drove to the nearest town to send his brother a telegram to tell him the news. He walked into the telegraph office and said, "I want to send a telegram to my brother telling him that I've bought a bull for our ranch. I need him to hitch the trailer to our pickup truck and drive out here so we can haul it home."

The telegraph operator explains that he'll be glad to help, then adds, "It's just 99¢ a word." Well, after paying for the bull, he had only $1 left. He realized that he'd be able to send just one word.

After a few minutes of thinking, he said, "I want you to send the word 'comfortable.'"

The operator shakes his head. "How is he ever going to know that you want him to hitch the trailer to your pickup truck and drive out here to haul that bull back to your ranch if you send just the word 'comfortable'?"

He explained, "My brother reads slow and the word's big, so he'll read it very slowly: 'com-for-da-bull'!"

Unique Sayings

1. A bicycle can't stand on its own because it is two-tired.
2. What's the definition of a will? (It's a dead giveaway).
3. Time flies like an arrow. Fruit flies like a banana.
4. A back-wards poet writes inverse.
5. In democracy it's your vote that counts. In feudalism it's your count that votes.
6. A chicken crossing the road is poultry in motion.
7. With her marriage she got a new name and a dress.
8. When a clock is hungry, it goes back four seconds.
9. The man who fell into an upholstery machine is fully recovered.
10. You feel stuck with your debt if you can't budge it.
11. Local Area Network in Australia: the LAN down under.
12. He often broke into song because he couldn't find the key.
13. Every calendar's days are numbered.
14. A lot of money is tainted. It taint yours and it taint mine.
15. A boiled egg in the morning is hard to beat.
16. He had a photographic memory that was never developed.
17. A plateau is a high form of flattery.
18. Once you've seen one shopping center you've seen a mall.
19. Those who jump off a Paris bridge are in Seine.
20. Bakers trade bread recipes on a knead to know basis.
21. Acupuncture is a jab well done.
22. Marathon runners with bad footwear suffer the agony of defeat.

Unusual Haircut

A man went into his regular barbershop, sat down on the chair and the barber asked him how he would like his hair cut this time.

The customer replied, "Well, lets see. Leave the left side long, take quite a bit off the right side to make it really short. I want the very back and top to be crew cut."

The barber was astonished and said he could not cut hair that way.

"Why not," the customer replied, "you cut it that way last time!"

Unusual Labels

- Fan belt: Don't change fan belt while motor is running.
- Hair Dryer: Don't use while sleeping.
- Sleeping Tablets: Warning—may cause drowsiness.

- Owner's Manual of Car: Do not shift into reverse while driving forward.
- Airline Package of Nuts: Open packet, eat the nuts.
- Bread Pudding Packet: Product will be hot after eating.

Used Books For Sale

Cards offering used textbooks for sale are posted on the college notice board at the beginning of each semester. One read: "Introduction to Psychology, $8, never used." The card was signed, "Must sell."

The next day a note had been added: "Good price. Are you sure it's never been used?" Signed, "Prospective buyer."

Below in a different hand was: "Positive!" signed, "Professor who graded his exam."

Use Of Car

A young boy had just gotten his driver's permit and inquired of his father, an evangelist, if they could discuss his use of the car.

His father took him into his study and said to the boy, "I'll make a deal with you, son. You bring your grades up from a C to a B average, study your Bible a little, get your hair cut, and we'll talk about the car." Well, the boy thought about that for a moment, and decided that he'd settle for the offer, and they agreed on it. After about six weeks, the boy came back and again asked his father about using the car.

Again, they went to the study, where his father said, "Son, I've been real proud of you. You've brought your grades up, and I've observed that you have been studying your Bible, and participating a lot more in the Bible study class on Sunday morning. But, I'm real disappointed, since you haven't gotten your hair cut."

The young man paused a moment, and then said, "You know, Dad, I've been thinking about that, and I've noticed in my studies of the Bible that Samson had long hair. It is possible that John the Baptist had long hair. Moses had long hair and some would even argue that Jesus had long hair."

His father replied, "You're right, son. Did you also notice that they all walked everywhere they went?"

Vacation Reflection

A neighbor of mine took off with his family to see the country. When he returned, I asked how he enjoyed the vacation.

He replied, "Have you ever spent three weeks in a minivan with those you thought you loved?"

Vacuum Salesman

An enthusiastic door-to-door vacuum cleaner salesman goes to the first house in his new territory. He knocks, and a lady opens the door. Before she has a chance to say anything, he runs inside and dumps garden soil all over the carpet.

He says, "Lady, if this vacuum cleaner don't do wonders cleaning this up, I'll eat every bit of it."

She turns to him with a smirk and says, "You want ketchup on that?"

The salesman says, "Why do you ask?"

She says, "We just moved in and we haven't got the electricity turned on yet."

Van Problem

The fist knocking on the door belonged to a cop. Bracing for the worst, the yard foreman opened the door. "Is that yours?" asked the officer, pointing to a company van that was jutting out into the narrow street.

"Uhh, yes it is," said the foreman. "That is, it's our company's."

"Would you mind moving it?" asked the officer. "We've set up a speed trap, and the van's causing everyone to slow down."

Visa® Pun

A business man called a travel agent and had a question about the documents he needed in order to fly to China. After a lengthy discussion about passports, the travel agent reminded him he needed a Visa®.

"Oh, no, I don't. I've been to China many times and never had to have one of those."

The travel agent double checked, and sure enough, his stay required a Visa®. When the travel agent told him this he said, "Look, I've been to China four times and every time they have accepted my American Express® or Master Card®."

Waiter Feedback

The diner was furious when his steak arrived too rare. "Waiter," he barked, "Didn't you hear me say 'well done'?"

"I can't thank you enough, sir," replied the waiter. "I hardly ever get a compliment."

Volunteers

On the way back to New York as I was sitting in the Phoenix airport, they announced that a flight to Las Vegas was full. The airline was looking for volunteers to give up their seats. In exchange, they'd give you a $100 voucher for your next flight and a first class seat in the plane leaving an hour later. About eight people ran up to the counter to take advantage of the offer. About fifteen seconds later all eight of those people sat down grumpily as the lady behind the ticket counter said, "If there is anyone else OTHER than the flight crew who'd like to volunteer, please step forward."

Walk On Water

Joey had heard a family rumor that his father, his grandfather, and even his great-grandfather, all "walked on water" on their 21st birthday. Well, today was his 21st birthday and if they could do it, so could he.

So, off he went in a boat with his friend Eric. When he reached the middle of the lake, he got up and stepped out of the boat…and nearly drowned.

The next day, Joey asked his grandmother why he wasn't given the same gift as the others in his family. The grandmother told him that his father, grandfather, and great-grandfather had all been born in February…not in August as was he.

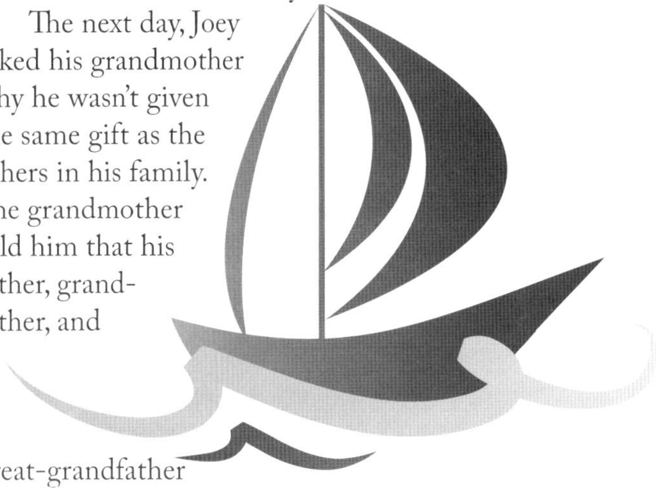

Wages

A man owned a small farm in North Carolina. The Wage and Hour Department of North Carolina claimed he was not paying proper wages to his help and sent an agent to interview him.

"I need a list of your employees and how much you pay them," demanded the agent.

"Well, there's my hired hand who's been with me for three years. I pay him $600 a week plus free room and board. The cook has been here for eighteen months, and I pay her $500 a month plus free room and board. Then there's the half-wit that works about eighteen hours a day. He makes $10 a week," replied the farmer.

"That's the guy I want to talk to, the half-wit," says the agent.

The farmer said, "That would be me."

Warning

As he was driving home from work, a man in a rural community was stopped by a local police officer. The motorist, informed that he had failed to come to a full stop at a stop sign, was handed a ticket.

"Don't I get a warning?" He protested.

The officer replied, "Sure. Here's your warning: If you don't come to a complete stop next time, I'll give you another ticket."

Warning Sign

Vacationing in Alaska, I couldn't help but notice all the warnings about bears posted in campgrounds, visitors' centers, and rest areas advising people not to feed the bears, how to avoid bears, what to do if a bear sees you, what to do if a bear attacks, and so on.

My favorite, however, was a hand-lettered sign on the door of a small gas station in a remote area. It said: "Warning! If you are being chased by a bear, don't come in here!"

Water In The Carburetor

When the husband came home, the wife said, "There's water in the carburetor."

The husband said, "You don't know the difference between a carburetor, generator, or muffler."

Then he asked, "Where is the car?"

The wife replied, "At the bottom of the lake."

We Always Go The Extra Mile

Driving down the highway one day, I saw this slogan on the back of a well known trucking company's vehicle: "We Always Go the Extra Mile".

Then I noticed another phrase scrawled in the dirt just below it: "That's Because We Missed the Last Exit."

Wedding

Selma and Irving received an invitation in the mail. Since it was many years since they were invited anywhere, they read it with glee, very excited that they were asked to attend a wedding.

All was fine until they reached the last line. Confused, Irving asked Selma, "Selma, vat does this "RSVP" mean?"

Selma was at a loss, as for the life of her, she simply couldn't remember.

Finally, she cried out: "Vait! I remember! I remember! RSVP!! It means "Remember, Send Vedding Present!"

Wedding Gift

She had a wedding to go to, and needed a wedding gift. "Aha," she thought, "I have that monogrammed silver tray from my wedding that I never use. I'll just take it to a silversmith and have him remove my monogram and put hers on it. Viola, one cheap wedding present."

She took it to the silversmith and asked him to remove her monogram and put the new one on. The silversmith examined the tray carefully, shook his head and said, "Lady, this can only be done so many times!"

Welcome To The Neighborhood

After living in our house for four years, we were moving out of state. My husband had backed the truck up to our garage door so that we could start loading all of the boxes. Just then one of our neighbors came walking across the lawn carrying a plate full of muffins.

"Isn't that thoughtful," my husband said to me. "They must have realized that we packed our kitchen stuff."

The neighbor stuck out his hand and boomed, "Welcome to the neighborhood!"

What a Hoot

Each evening a bird lover, Tom, stood in his backyard, hooting like an owl. One night an owl called back to him.

For a year, Tom and his feathered friend hooted back and forth. He even kept a log of the "conversation".

Just as he thought he was on the verge of a break-through in inter-species communication, his wife had a chat with her neighbor.

"My husband spends his nights calling out to owls," she said. "That's odd," the neighbor replied, "so does mine."

Dad told Doug, "While we are gone, I want you boys to clean away the dirty dishes, clean your room, and mow the grass."

When they returned, nothing had been done. Dad was very upset. He asked Doug, "What have you been doing while we were gone?"

Doug replied, in a low voice, "Nothing."

Dad then turned to Jason, and asked, "What have you been doing?"

Jason replied, "Helping Doug."

What Do They Do?

Two youngsters were closely examining bathroom scales on display at the department store.

"What's it for?" one asked.

"I don't know," the other replied. "I think you stand on it and it makes you mad. At least it does that for mom and dad."

What Do You Want To Be?

The teacher asked her class what each wanted to become when they grew up. A chorus of responses came from all over the room. "A football player," "A doctor," "An astronaut," "The president," "A fireman," "A teacher," "A race car driver." Everyone that is, except Tommy. The teacher noticed he was sitting there quiet and still. So she said to him, "Tommy, what do you want to be when you grow up?"

"Possible," Tommy replied.

"Possible?" asked the teacher.

"Yes," Tommy said. "My mom is always telling me I'm impossible. So when I get to be big, I want to be possible."

What Have You Been Doing?

Doug and Jason were brothers. One day, mom and dad had to go to town.

What Makes Men And Women So Different?

Nicknames

- If Laura, Suzanne, Debra, and Rose go out for lunch, they will call each other Laura, Suzanne, Debra, and Rose.
- If Mike, Charlie, Bob, and John go out, they will affectionately refer to each other as Fat Boy, Knuckle-head, Peanut, and Scrappy.

Eating out

- When the bill arrives, Mike, Charlie, Bob, and John will each throw in \$20, even though it's only \$32.50. None of them will have anything smaller, and none will actually admit they want change back.
- When the women get their bill, out come the pocket calculators.

Money

- A man will pay \$2 for a \$1 item he wants.
- A woman will pay \$1 for a \$2 item that she doesn't want.

Bathrooms

- A man has six items in his bathroom: a toothbrush, comb, shaving cream, razor, a bar of soap, and a towel.
- The average number of items in the typical woman's bathroom is 337. A man would not be able to identify most of these items.

Arguments

- A woman has the last word in any argument. Anything a man says after that is the beginning of a new argument.

Cats
- Women love cats.
- Men say they love cats, but when women aren't looking, men kick cats.

Future
- A woman worries about the future until she gets a husband.
- A man never worries about the future until he gets a wife.

Success
- A successful man is one who makes more money than his wife can spend.
- A successful woman is one who can find such a man.

Marriage
- A woman marries a man expecting he will change, but he doesn't.
- A man marries a woman expecting that she won't change, and she does.

Dressing up
- A woman will dress up to go shopping, water the plants, empty the garbage, answer the phone, read a book, and get the mail.
- A man will dress up for weddings and funerals.

Offspring
- Ah, children. A woman knows all about her children. She knows about dentist appointments, best friends, favorite foods, secret fears, and hopes and dreams.
- A man is vaguely aware of some short people living in the house.

What Not To Say To A Police Officer!

1. I can't reach my license unless you hold my soda.
2. Sorry, officer, I didn't realize my radar detector wasn't plugged in.
3. Hey, you must've been doin' about 125 mph to keep up with me. Good job!
4. I thought you had to be in relatively good physical condition to be a police officer.
5. You're not gonna check the trunk, are you?
6. I pay your salary!
7. Hey, Officer! That's terrific. The last officer only gave me a warning, too!
8. Do you know why you pulled me over? Okay, just so one of us does.
9. I was trying to keep up with traffic. Yes, I know there are no other cars around. That's how far ahead of me they are.

What Puzzles Me?

My Grandmother says I've Daddy's nose,
Before I came he had two, I suppose,
She always adds, "And what is more,
You've Mother's eyes." Did she have four?

Folks say I've got my mouth and chin
From Grandma's husband, Benjamin.
He died before I came, you see
And must have willed them both to me.

I understand about my hair,
'Cause Daddy's head is kinda bare;
But I'd really like to know
It puzzles me and tries me so.

Am I just some odds and ends?
Parts of relatives and friends?
Or do you think that it can be,
There's something left that's really me?

What Size?

A woman came into my pharmacy with a shopping list. As she asked for items such as hair spray and toothpaste, I inquired what size of each she wanted. Everything was going well until she requested a bottle of Pepto-Bismol®.

I was surprised when, in response to my usual question, "What size?" she said, "What size would you suggest? I'm only having four for dinner."

What's The Medical Term?

A man told his doctor that he wasn't able to do all the things around the house that he used to do.

When the doctor was done examining him, the patient said, "Now, doc, I can take it. Tell me in plain English what is wrong with me."

"Well, in plain English," the doctor replied, "you're just lazy."

"Okay," said the man. "Now give me the medical term, so I can tell my wife."

What Tax Problem?

The owner of a small New York sandwich deli was being questioned by an IRS agent about his tax return. He had reported a net profit of $80,000 for the year.

"Why don't you people leave me alone?" the deli owner said. "I work like a dog, everyone in my family helps out, the place is only closed three days a year, and you want to know how I made $80,000?"

"It's not your income that bothers us," the agent said. "It's these travel deductions. You listed six trips to Florida for you and your wife."

"Oh, that," the owner said smiling. "It is a legitimate business expense because we also deliver."

When I'm An Old Lady

When I'm an old lady, I'll live with each child,
And bring so much happiness,
just as they did.
I want to pay back all the
joy they've provided.
Returning each deed! Oh,
they'll be so excited!
(When I'm an old lady and live
with my children).

I'll write on the wall with reds, whites, and blues,
And I'll bounce on the furniture wearing my shoes.
I'll drink from the carton and then leave it out.
I'll stuff all the toilets, and oh, how they'll shout!
(When I'm an old lady and live with my children).

When they're on the phone and just out of reach,
I'll get into things like sugar and bleach.
Oh, they'll snap their fingers and then shake their head,
And when that is done, I'll hide under the bed!
(When I'm an old lady and live with my children).

When they cook dinner and call me to eat,
I'll not eat my green beans or salad or meat,
I'll gag on my okra, spill milk on the table,
And when they get angry, I'll run, if I'm able!
(When I'm an old lady and live with my children).

I'll sit under the tables and I'll lick on lollipops,
I'll cross both eyes just to see if they stick.
I'll take off my socks and throw one away,
And play in the mud till the end of the day!
(When I'm an old lady and live with my children).

And later in bed, I'll lay back and sigh,
I'll thank God in prayer and then close my eyes.
My children will look down with a smile slowly creeping,
And say with a groan, "She's so sweet when she's sleeping!"

When Visiting The Midwest

Because of misunderstandings that frequently develop when Easterners and Californians cross states such as Arkansas, Nebraska, Kansas, Iowa, Missouri, Illinois, etc., those states' tourism councils have adopted a set of information guidelines. In an effort to help outsiders understand the Midwest, the following list is available to all visitors:

1. That farm boy standing next to the feed bin did more before breakfast than you do all week at the gym.
2. It's called a gravel road. No matter how slow you drive you're going to get dust on your Navigator. Drive it or get it out of the way.
3. We all started hunting and fishing when we were seven years old.
4. Go ahead and bring your $600 Orvis fly rod. Just don't cry to us if a flathead catfish breaks it off at the handle. We have a name for those little trout you fish for—bait.
5. If that cell phone rings while a bunch of mallards are making their final approach, we will shoot it.

6. No, there's no "Vegetarian Special" on the menu. Order steak. Or you can order the chef's salad and pick off two pounds of ham and turkey.
7. So you have a $60,000 car you drive on weekends. We're real impressed. We have a quarter of a million dollar combine that we use two weeks a year.
8. Let's get this straight. We have one stoplight in town. We stop when it's red. We may even stop when it's yellow.
9. They are pigs. That's what they smell like. Get over it. Don't like it? Interstates 80 and 90 go two ways; interstates 29 and 35 go the other two. Pick one and use it.
10. So every person in every pickup waves. It's called being friendly. Understand the concept?
11. That highway patrol officer that just pulled you over for driving like an idiot—his name is Sir—no matter how old he is.

Where Ya From?

A policeman saw a man dressed in full cowboy garb—hat, chaps, duster, six-shooters, boots and spurs—standing on a street corner in a busy city. He approached the cowboy and asked him his name.

"Call me Tex!" was the cowboy's reply.

"Well, Tex, where are you from, Texas?" the policeman asked.

"Nah, I'm from Louisiana, but I didn't want you to call me Louise!"

Why Men Are Just Happier People

- Your last name stays the same.
- The garage is all yours.
- Wedding plans take care of themselves.
- Chocolate is just another snack.
- You can be president.
- Car mechanics tell you the truth.
- You don't have to stop and think of which way to turn a nut on a bolt.
- Same work, more pay.
- Wrinkles add character.
- New shoes don't cut, blister, or mangle your feet.
- One mood—all the time.
- Phone conversations are over in thirty seconds flat.
- A five-day vacation requires only one suitcase.
- You can open all your own jars.
- You get extra credit for the slightest act of thoughtfulness.
- If someone forgets to invite you, he or she can still be your friend.
- Three pairs of shoes are more than enough.
- You are unable to see wrinkles in your clothes.
- Everything on your face stays its original color.
- The same hairstyle lasts for years, maybe decades.
- You can play with toys all your life.
- One wallet and one pair of shoes—one color for all seasons.
- You can do Christmas shopping for twenty-five relatives on December 24 in twenty-five minutes.
- No wonder men are happier!

Why, Oh Why?

- When they invented the Internet why did they decide to use "w-w-w" when every other letter of the alphabet is just one syllable and much easier to say?
- Why do our parents get so much smarter as we get older?
- What is it about car keys and remote controls that make them so hard to find?
- Why is it so important to a Mac user to convince me that his computer is better than mine?
- Why do we have answers to our friend's problems and not our own?
- Since all the excitement of a basketball game happens in the last minute, why don't they just start the game with a minute left?
- Why do Sundays fly by and Mondays last forever?
- Why do banks charge a fee on "insufficient funds" when they know there is not enough money?
- Why does someone believe you when you say there are four billion stars, but check when you say the paint is wet?
- Whose idea was it to put an "s" in the word "lisp"?
- Why is it that no matter what color bubble bath you use the bubbles are always white?
- Is there ever a day that mattresses are not on sale?
- Why do people constantly return to the refrigerator with hopes that something new to eat will have materialized?

- Why do people keep running over a string a dozen times with their vacuum cleaner, then reach down, pick it up, examine it, then put it down to give the vacuum one more chance?
- Why is it that no plastic bag will open from the end on your first try?
- How do those dead bugs get into those enclosed light fixtures?
- When we are in the supermarket and someone rams our ankle with a shopping cart then apologizes for doing so, why do we say, "It's all right", when, it isn't all right?
- Why is it that whenever you attempt to catch something that's falling off the table you always manage to knock something else over?
- In winter, why do we try to keep the house as warm as it was in summer when we complained about the heat?

Will It Be Long?

When my husband and I showed up at a very popular restaurant, it was crowded. I went up to the hostess and asked, "Will it be long?" The hostess, ignoring me, kept writing in her book. I asked again, "How much of a wait?" The woman looked up from her book and said, "About ten minutes."

A short time later, I heard an announcement over the loudspeaker: "Willette B. Long, your table is ready."

Window Washer

There was a gentleman in the hospital bed next to me. He was covered with bandages from head to toe. I said to him, "What do you do for a living?" He said, "Well, I used to be a window washer." I asked, "When did you give it up?" He replied, "Halfway down."

Wise Pupil

A teacher was giving a lesson on the circulation of the blood. Trying to make the matter clearer, she said, "Now, class if I stood on my head, the blood, as you know, would run into it, and I would turn red in the face."

"Yes," the class said.

"Then why is it while I am standing in the upright position the blood doesn't run into my feet?"

A little fellow shouted, "Cause your feet ain't empty."

Withheld Pay

After being laid off from five different jobs in four months, my Uncle Joe was hired by a warehouse. One day he lost control of a forklift and drove it off the loading dock. Surveying the damage, the owner shook his head and said he'd have to withhold ten percent of Uncle Joe's wages to pay for the repairs.

"How much will it cost?" asked my uncle.

"About $4,500," said the owner. "What a relief!" exclaimed Uncle Joe, "I've finally got job security!"

Woman Drivers

A state trooper was driving along in the country when he noticed a small black coupe swerving all over the lonely back road. He put on his flashers and pulled the car over. Hopping out of his cruiser, he then approached the driver. "Ma'am, is there a reason that you're weaving all over the road?" The woman replied, "Oh, officer, thank goodness you're here!! I almost had an accident! I looked up and there was a tree right in front of me. I swerved to the left and there was another tree in front of me. I swerved to the right and there was another tree in front of me!" Reaching through the side window to the rear view mirror, the officer replied, "Ma'am…That's your air freshener."

Women's Stress Diet

This is a specially formulated diet designed to help women cope with stress.

Breakfast
- 1 Grapefruit
- 1 Slice whole wheat toast
- 1 Cup skim milk

Lunch
- 1 Small portion lean, steamed chicken
- 1 Cup spinach
- 1 Cup herbal tea
- 1 Hershey Kiss

Afternoon Tea
- The rest of the Hershey Kisses in the bag
- 1 Tub of Hagen-daaz ice cream with chocolate chip topping

Dinner
- 4 Glasses of iced tea
- 2 Loaves garlic bread
- 1 Family size supreme pizza
- 3 Snickers bars

Late Night Snack
- 1 Whole Sarah Lee cheesecake (Eaten directly from the Freezer)

Words That Really Should Exist:

- Abracadabbler: an amateur magician.
- Badaptation: a bad movie version of a good book.
- Carbage: the trash found in your automobile.
- Dadicated: being the best father you can be.
- Ecrastinate: checking your e-mail just one more time.
- Faddict: someone who has to try every new trend that comes along.
- Gabberflasted: the state of being speechless due to someone else talking too much.
- Hackchoo: when you sneeze and cough at the same time.
- Iceburg: an uppity, snobbish neighborhood.
- Jobsolete: a position within a company that no longer exists.
- Knewlyweds: a marriage between long time acquaintances.
- Lamplify: turning on (or up) the lights within a room.
- Mandals: sandals for men.
- Nagivator: someone who constantly assists with driving directions in an overly critical manner.
- Obliment: an obligatory compliment.
- Pestariffic: adjective describing a particularly pesty person.
- Qcumbersome: a salad that contains too many cucumbers.
- Ramdumbtious: a rowdy, energetic person who's not too bright.
- Sanktuary: a graveyard for ships.
- Testimoney: fees paid to expert witnesses.

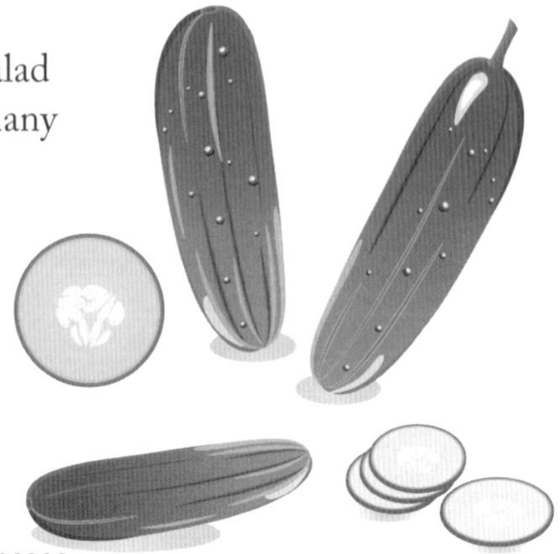

- Unbrella: an umbrella that the wind has turned inside-out.
- Vehiculized: you own a vehicle.
- Wackajacky: very messed up.
- Xerocks: two identical pieces of stone.
- Yawnese: the language of someone trying to speak while yawning.
- Zingle: a single person with a lot of pep in his or her step.

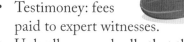

Word Study

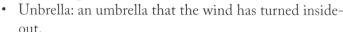

A husband, proving to his wife that women talk more than men, showed her a study which indicated that men use about 15,000 words a day, whereas women use 30,000 words a day. She thought about this, then told her husband that women use twice as many words as men because they have to repeat everything they say. Looking stunned, he said, "What?"

Worried Housewife

The worried housewife sprang to the telephone when it rang and listened with relief to the kindly voice in her ear. "How are you, darling?" she said. "What kind of a day are you having?"

"Oh, mother," said the housewife, breaking into bitter tears "I've had such a bad day. The baby won't eat and the washing machine broke down. I haven't had a chance to go shopping, and besides, I've just sprained my ankle and I have to hobble around. On top of that, the house is a mess and I'm supposed to have two couples to dinner tonight."

The mother was shocked and was at once all sympathy. "Oh, darling," she said, "sit down, relax, and close your eyes. I'll be over in half an hour. I'll do your shopping, clean up the house, and cook your dinner for you. I'll feed the baby and I'll call a repairman I know who'll be at your house to fix the washing machine promptly. Now stop crying. I'll do everything. In fact, I'll even call George at the office and tell him he ought to come home and help out for once."

"George?" said the housewife. " Who's George?"

"Why, George! Your husband!…is this 223-1374?"

"No, this is 223-1375."

"Oh. I'm sorry. I guess I have the wrong number."

There was a short pause and the housewife said, "Does this mean you're not coming over?"

Wrong Again

On Coast Guard cutters, low-ranking crewmembers take turns in the galley helping the cooks. One young seaman aboard was always dropping dishes and spilling food.

One day, alone in the galley, he noticed an unfrosted yellow sheet-cake cooling on a counter. Determined to rectify past errors, the seaman made chocolate icing and carefully decorated the cake with it. The seaman stood proudly by the dessert as the head cook returned to the galley.

Frantically, the cook began to look around. "Where did my cornbread go?" he shouted.

X-Rays Of A Trauma Patient

While working as a radiology technician in a hospital emergency room, I took x-rays of a trauma patient. I brought the films to our radiologist, who studied the multiple fractures of both femurs and pelvis. "What happened to this patient?" he asked in astonishment.

"He fell out of a tree," I reported.

The radiologist wanted to know what the patient was doing up a tree. "I'm not sure, but his paperwork states he works for Acme Tree Experts."

Gazing intently at the x-rays, the radiologist blinked and said, "Cross out experts."

Yes, That's Me Officer!

When I went to get my driver's license renewed, our local motor vehicle bureau was packed. The line inched along for almost an hour until the man ahead of me finally got his license. He inspected his photo for a moment and commented to the clerk, "I was standing in line so long, I ended up looking pretty grouchy in this picture."

The clerk looked at his picture closely, and reassured him, "It's okay. That's how you're going to look when the cops pull you over anyway."

Yosemite Vacation

A couple was vacationing in Yosemite. The wife expressed her concern about camping because of bears and said she would feel more comfortable in a motel. The husband said that he'd like to camp and to calm her concerns, they'd talk to the park ranger to see what the likelihood of a bear encounter would be.

The ranger told them, "Well, we haven't seen any grizzlies in this area so far this year, or black bears for that matter."

The wife shrieked, "There's two types of bears out here? How can you tell the difference? Which one is more dangerous?"

The ranger replied, "Well, that's easy. See, if the bear chases you up the tree and it comes up after you, it's a black bear. If it shakes the tree until you fall out, it's a grizzly."

The motel room was quite nice.

You Are A Lousy Cook If...

- Your family automatically heads for the table every time they hear a fire alarm.
- Anyone has ever broken a tooth eating your homemade yogurt.
- Your family know what "peas porridge in a pot nine days old" tastes like.
- Your son goes outside to make mud pies, and the rest of the family grabs forks and follows him.
- Your children get even with the neighborhood bully by inviting him over for dinner.
- Your husband refers to the smoke detector as the oven timer.
- No matter what you do to it, the gravy still turns bright purple.

You Can Tell It's Going To Be A Bad Day When:

- You see a "60 Minutes" news team waiting in your office.
- Your birthday cake collapses from the weight of the candles.
- You turn on the news and they're giving emergency routes out of the city.
- Your twin sister forgot your birthday.
- Your car horn goes off accidentally and remains stuck as you follow a group of motorcycles on the freeway.
- Your boss tells you not to bother to take off your hat.
- The bird singing outside your window is a buzzard.
- You wake up and your braces are locked together.
- You call your answering service and they tell you it's none of your business.
- Your income tax refund check bounces.
- You put both contact lenses in the same eye.
- Your pet rock snaps at you.
- Your wife says, "Good morning, Bill," and your name is Henry.

You Gotta Read These

I am a medical student currently doing a rotation in toxicology at the poison control center. Today, this woman called in very upset because she caught her little daughter eating ants. I quickly reassured her that the ants are not harmful and there would be no need to bring her daughter into the hospital. She calmed down and at the end of the conversation happened to mention that she gave her daughter some ant poison to eat in order to kill the ants. I told her that she better bring her daughter into the emergency room right away.

Early this year, some Boeing employees on the airfield decided to steal a life raft from one of the 747s. They were successful in getting it out of the plane and home. Shortly after they took it for a float on the river, they noticed a Coast Guard helicopter coming towards them. It turned out that the chopper was homing in on the emergency locator beacon that activated when the raft was inflated. They are no longer employed at Boeing.

A true story out of San Francisco: A man, wanting to rob a downtown Bank of America, walked into the branch and wrote: "This iz a stikkup. Put all your muny in this bag," while standing in line, waiting to give his note to the teller. He began to worry that someone had seen him write the note and might call the police before he reached the teller's window. So, he left the Bank of America and crossed the street to Wells Fargo. After waiting a few minutes in line, he handed his note to the Wells Fargo teller. She read it, and, surmising from his spelling errors that he wasn't the brightest light in the harbor, told him that she could not accept his stickup note because it was written on a Bank of America deposit slip and that he would either have to fill out a Wells Fargo deposit slip or go back to Bank of America. Looking somewhat defeated, the man said, "OK" and left. He was arrested a few minutes later, as he was waiting in line back at Bank of America.

A motorist was unknowingly caught in an automated speed trap that measured his speed using radar and photographed his car. He later received in the mail a ticket for $40 and a photo of his car. Instead of payment, he sent the police department a photograph of $40. Several days later, he received a letter from the police that contained another picture, this time of handcuffs. He immediately mailed in his $40.

The Ann Arbor News crime column reported that a man walked into a Burger King® in Ypsilanti, Michigan, at 12:50 and flashed a gun and demanded cash. The clerk turned him down because he said he couldn't open the cash register without a food order. When the man ordered onion rings, the clerk said they weren't available for breakfast. The man, frustrated, walked away.

You Know You Live…

You live in Alaska when…

- You only have four spices: salt, pepper, ketchup, and Tabasco.
- You have more than one recipe for moose.
- The four seasons are: winter, still winter, almost winter, and construction.

You live in California when…

- You make over $250,000 and you still can't afford to buy a house.
- The high school quarterback calls a time-out to answer his cell phone.
- The fastest part of your commute is going down your driveway.
- You know how to eat an artichoke.
- You drive to your neighborhood block party.
- Someone asks you how far away something is, you tell them how long it will take to get there rather than how many miles away it is.

You live in Colorado when…

- You carry your $3,000 mountain bike atop your $500 car.
- You tell your husband to pick up Granola on his way home, and he stops at the Day Care Center.

You live in the Deep South when…

- You get a coffee and bait in the same store.
- "Ya'll" is singular and "all ya'll" is plural.
- After fifteen years you still hear, "You ain't from 'round here, are ya?"
- Everyone has two first names.

You live in Florida when…

- You eat dinner at 3:15 in the afternoon.
- All purchases include a coupon of some kind, even houses and cars.
- Everyone can recommend an excellent dermatologist.
- Road construction never ends anywhere in the state.
- "Down south" means "Key West."
- You think no one over 70 should be allowed to drive.
- Flip-flops are everyday wear.
- Sweet tea can be served at any meal.
- An alligator once walked through your neighborhood.
- You smirk when a game show's "Grand Prize" is a trip or cruise to Florida.
- You measure distance in minutes.
- You get annoyed at the tourists who feed seagulls.
- A mountain is any hill 100 feet above sea level.

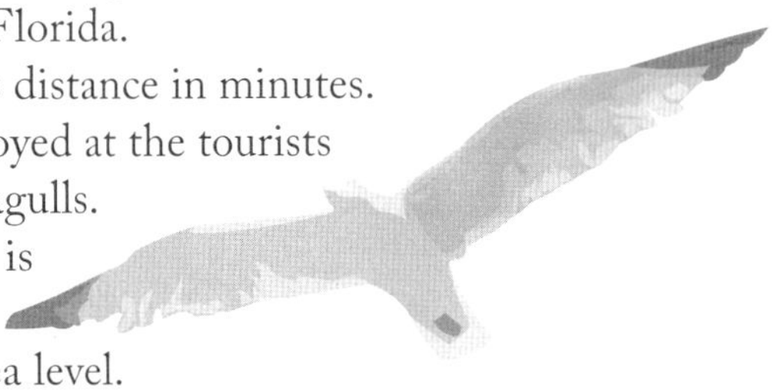

- You think everyone from a bigger city has a northern accent.
- You've hosted a hurricane party.
- You pass on the right and honk at the elderly.
- You understand the futility of exterminating cockroaches.
- You can pronounce Okeechobee, Kissimmee, and Withlacoochee.
- You understand why it's better to have a friend with a boat than have a boat yourself.
- You were eight years old before you realized they made houses without pools.
- You were 12 when you first met someone who couldn't swim.
- You get angry when people say, "Florida isn't really part of the South."

You live in the Midwest when…

- You've never met any celebrities, but the mayor knows your name.
- Your idea of a traffic jam is ten cars waiting to pass a tractor.
- You have had to switch from "heat" to "AC" on the same day.
- You end sentences with a preposition: "Where's my coat at?"
- When asked how your trip was to any exotic place, you say, "It was different!"

You live in New England when…

- If your local Dairy Queen is closed from September through May.
- If someone in a Home Depot store offers you assistance and they don't work there.

- If you've had a lengthy telephone conversation with someone who dialed a wrong number.
- If "Vacation" means going anywhere south of New York City for the weekend.
- If you measure distance in hours.
- If you know several people who have hit a deer more than once.
- If you have switched from "Heat" to "A/C" in the same day and back again.
- If you can drive 75 mph through 2 feet of snow during a raging blizzard without flinching.
- If you install security lights on your house and garage, but leave both unlocked.
- If you carry jumper cables in your car and your wife knows how to use them.
- If the speed limit on the highway is 55 mph, you're going 80, and everybody is passing you.
- If driving is better in the winter because the potholes are filled with snow.
- If you know all four seasons: almost winter, winter, still winter, and road construction.
- If your snowblower has more miles on it than your car.
- If you find 10° "A little chilly."

You live in New York when…

- You say "the city" and expect everyone to know you mean Manhattan.
- You have never been to the Statue of Liberty.
- You can get into a four-hour argument about how to get from Columbus Circle to Battery Park, but can't find Wisconsin on a map.
- You think Central Park is "nature."
- You've worn out a car horn.
- You think eye contact is an act of aggression.

You know you live in a small town when…

- The "road hog" in front of you on Main Street is a farmer's combine.
- The local phone book has only one yellow page.
- Third Street is on the edge of town.
- You leave your jacket on the back of the chair in the cafe, and when you go back the next day, it's still there, on the same chair.
- You don't signal turns because everyone knows where you're going anyway.
- No social events can be scheduled when the school gym floor is being varnished.
- You call a wrong number and are supplied with the correct one.
- Everyone knows all the news before it's published; residents read the hometown paper just to see whether the publisher got it right.

You know you're from Tennessee when…

- "Vacation" means going to the family reunion.
- You know all four seasons: almost summer, summer, still summer, and Christmas.
- You laugh when people from anywhere north of Tennessee try to say or spell "Y'all."
- It's "Mar-vull", not "Mary-ville".
- It's "Knox-vull", not "Knox-ville".
- A toboggan is a hat, not a sled.
- You butter your hot biscuit by cutting it open, putting a slab of butter inside, and closing it back up again.
- Gatlinburg does have an "L" in it, and it should be pronounced.
- Sales tax is 9.75%.
- You think it's worth it driving to Alabama just to save 1.25% on the sales tax.
- You eat "Dinner" at noon and "Supper" in the evening.
- You barely get snow days because there's hardly ever any snow. Better yet, you get snow days if your local weather stations predict even the slightest bit of snow!
- Everything is coke, and if you don't like it, tough. Ex: "You want a coke?" "Sure." "Which kind?" "Dr. Pepper."
- Everyone you know owns a truck, and at least one of those trucks is just painted with primer or more colors than the rainbow.
- You measure distance in minutes, not miles.
- Sweet tea is the drink…No questions, no exceptions. Most people from Tennessee begin drinking sweet tea even before they can drink out of sippy cups. Iced tea is appropriate for all meals, and you start drinking it when you're two. We do like a little tea with our sugar!
- You use "fix" as a verb. Example: "I'm fixing to go to the store."
- You install security lights on your house and garage and leave both unlocked.
- You know what a "Dawg" is.
- You carry jumper cables in your car—for your own car.
- You own only four spices: salt, pepper, tabasco, and ketchup.
- You think that the first day of deer season is a national holiday.
- Fried catfish is "the other white meat."
- You're convinced you don't need driver's ed—your father's and uncles' pickup trucks were training enough.
- Possums sleep in the middle of the road with their feet in the air.

- There are 5,000 types of snakes, and 4,998 live in Tennessee.
- There are 10,000 types of spiders. All 10,000 live in Tennessee plus a couple no one's seen before.
- If it grows, it sticks; if it crawls, it bites.
- Onced and twiced are words.
- It is not a shopping cart; it is a buggy.
- People actually grow and eat okra.
- "Fixinto" is one word.
- Backwards and forwards means, "I know everything about you."
- "Jeet?" is actually a phrase meaning, "Did you eat?"
- You don't have to wear a watch because it doesn't matter what time it is. You work until you're done, or it's too dark to see.

You live in Texas when…

- The birds have to use potholders to pull worms out of the ground.
- The best parking place is determined by shade and not by distance.
- Hot water now comes out of both taps.
- You can make sun tea instantly.
- You learn that a seat belt buckle makes a pretty good branding iron.
- The temperature drops below 95, and you feel a little chilly.
- You discover that in July it only takes 2 fingers to steer your car.
- You discover that you can get sunburned through your car window.
- You actually burn your hand opening the car door.
- You break into a sweat the instant you step outside at 7:30 a.m.
- Your biggest bicycle wreck fear is, "What if I get knocked out and end up lying on the pavement and cook to death?"
- You realize that asphalt has a liquid state.
- The potatoes cook underground, so all you have to do is pull one out and add butter, salt, and pepper.
- Farmers are feeding their chickens crushed ice to keep them from laying hard-boiled eggs.
- The cows are giving evaporated milk.

You Qualify As A Certified Eccentric If…

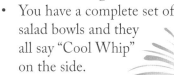

- You can entertain yourself for more than 15 minutes with a flyswatter.
- You burn your yard rather than mow it.
- The Salvation Army declines your mattress.
- You offer to give someone the shirt off your back and they don't want it.
- You have the local taxidermist on speed dial.
- You come back from the dump with more than you took.
- You keep a can of Raid on the kitchen table.
- You keep flea and tick soap in the shower.
- You know how many bales of hay your car will hold.
- You have a rag for a gas cap.
- Your house doesn't have curtains, but your truck does.
- You consider your license plate personalized because your father made it.
- Your lifetime goal is to own a fireworks stand.
- You have a complete set of salad bowls and they all say "Cool Whip" on the side.
- The biggest city you've ever been to is Walmart®.
- You've used your ironing board as a buffet table.
- A tornado hits your neighborhood and does a $100,000 worth of improvements
- You've used a toilet brush to scratch your back.
- You think fast food is hitting a deer at 65 mph.
- Somebody tells you that you've got something in your teeth, so you take them out to see what it is!

Young Patients

A pediatrician in town always plays a game with some of his young patients to put them at ease and test their knowledge of body parts.

One day, while pointing to a little boy's ear, the doctor asked him. "Is this your nose?"

Immediately the little boy turned to his mother and said, "Mom, I think we'd better find a new doctor!"

Your Lucky Day

I pulled up to a parking meter recently, only to realize I didn't have any coins. As I got out of my car I saw a meter maid heading my way.

"I'm just going to get change," I called out to her. "If there's no quarter in the meter by the time I get there, I'll have to give you a ticket," she yelled back to me.

Quickly running into a nearby coffee shop, I ordered a coffee. The waitress seeing the $20 bill in my hand, asked if I had anything smaller.

"I'm sorry, I don't."

"It's your lucky day, then," she said, handing me the coffee. "We don't have any change, so your coffee is on the house!"

Zoo Thank-You

As a volunteer who conducts educational tours of the zoo, Sally occasionally receives thank-you notes from members of school groups.

One of her favorites said: "Dear Sally, I am a third grader. I loved all the animals in the zoo. You were the best of all."

Influence

21st Century Teacher Applicant

Let me see if I've got this right? You want me to go into that room with all those students and fill their every waking moment with a love for learning. Not only that, I'm supposed to instill a sense of pride in their ethnicity, behaviorally modify disruptive behavior, observe them for signs of abuse and T-shirt messages.

I am to fight the war on drugs and sexually transmitted diseases, check their backpacks for illegal items, and raise their self-esteem. I'm to teach them good citizenship, sportsmanship, and fair play, how to balance a checkbook, and how to apply for a job.

I am to check their heads occasionally for lice, maintain a safe environment, recognize signs of potential antisocial behavior, offer advice, write letters of recommendation for student employment and scholarships, encourage respect for the cultural diversity of others, and, oh yeah, always make sure that I give the girls in my class 50 percent of my attention.

I'm required by my contract to be working toward an advance certificate and a master's degree on my own time during the summer and evenings and at my own expense. After school, I am to attend committee and faculty meetings and participate in staff development training to maintain my employment status.

I am to be a paragon of virtue larger than life, such that my very presence will awe my students into being obedient and respectful of authority. I am to pledge allegiance to supporting family values, a return to the basics, and to my current administration. I am to incorporate technology into the learning and monitor all web sites while providing a personal relationship with each student. I am to decide who might be potentially dangerous and/or liable to commit crimes in school or who is possibly being abused, and I can be sent to jail for not mentioning these suspicions.

I am to make sure all students pass the state and federally mandated testing and all classes, whether or not they attend school on a regular basis or complete any of the work assigned. Plus, I am expected to make sure that all of the students with handicaps are guaranteed a free and equal education, regardless of their mental or physical handicap. I am to communicate frequently with each student's parent by letter, phone, newsletter, and grade card.

I'm to do all of this with just a piece of chalk, a computer, a few books, a bulletin board, a 45 minute more-or-less plan time, and a big smile, all on a starting salary that qualifies my family for food stamps in many states.

Is that all? You want me to do all of this and expect me NOT TO PRAY?

A Cow's Leg

President Lincoln never lacked the ingenuity to catch his opponents unawares. Once when a stubborn disputer seemed unconvinced, Lincoln said, "Well, let's see, how many legs has a cow?"

"Four, of course," came the reply disgustedly.

"That's right," agreed Lincoln. "Now suppose you call the cow's tail a leg. How many legs would the cow have?"

"Why, five of course," was the confident reply.

"Now that's where you're wrong," said Lincoln. Calling a cow's tail a leg doesn't make it a leg."

A Little New Wood

When Henry Longfellow was well along in years, his head as white as snow but his cheeks as red as a rose, an ardent admirer asked him how it was that he was able to keep so vigorous and write so beautifully.

Pointing to a blooming apple tree nearby, he replied, "That apple tree is very old, but I never saw prettier blossoms on it than those it now bears. The tree grows a little new wood every year, and I suppose it is out of that new wood that those blossoms come. Like the apple tree, I try to grow a little new wood every year."

A little new wood every year—yes, that's the key! Never give up, mind you, but just keep at it little by little, bit by bit. As we age, the body grows weaker and we need to let some chores for younger more able hands, but we should never cave in to the idea that we are no longer useful. Retirement isn't a time to just fold your hands and count the minutes, but it is a time that can be very rewarding and very productive.

A little new wood every year is certainly in order for people of all ages. Just as Spring brings on new growth in the trees and plants so the various seasons of life bring new growth and maturity both physically and spiritually. The old wood gives the stability of past experiences while the new wood gives us vision and hope for the future.

The new wood allows us to blossom that others may enjoy the beauty. It gives us purpose, fulfillment, and joy. Each facet of our lives is woven with intricate detail, the memories, the joys, the sorrows, friends, family and neighbors, work and pleasure, providing a beautiful and delicate tapestry.

As the blossom eventually fades and falls to the ground we find in its place fruit beginning to form. New wood provided the nutrients so the tree could blossom. Without the blossom there would be no fruit. So it is with each of our lives. We must continue to grow new wood and blossom. Then we, as well as others, will be able to enjoy the fruit of our labors.

—M. Gingrich

A Look at the Critic

A critic is usually right in what she/he criticizes, but a critic does not have many friends. The dictionary defines a critic as one who tends too readily to find fault or to make judgment—a faultfinder.

A critic is usually an intelligent and observant person, a keen observer of human nature and habit, and knowledgeable in many areas of life; one who has been around. But a critic does not get compliments for being intelligent or wise. In fact, people cringe even at the sight of a carping critic.

A critic has an inner desire to change persons and situations and feels she/he is really helping by pointing out failures and mistakes and what would help, giving unasked for advice and suggestions.

A common phrase of a critic is "I don't mean to be critical, but..." The "but" is followed by some critique of a person, about what was said, or what one should do or should not do.

It's good for each of us to remember that people are looking for friends, not critics—for persons who affirm, not fault finders—for persons who encourage, and not for persons who think they help by dwelling on failures.

One solution in seeking to overcome a critical spirit is to begin to make at least ten positive statements for every negative one. An old phrase says, "Accentuate the positive, and eliminate the negative."

We need always remember there are two things one never forgets; a compliment and a criticism. Choose how you want to be remembered.

—John M. Drescher

An Open Letter To A Candidate For A Missionary Appointment

Jerusalem
Province of Judea
January 1, 66 A.D.

Rev. Saul (the apostle Paul)
Independent Missionary
Corinth, Greece

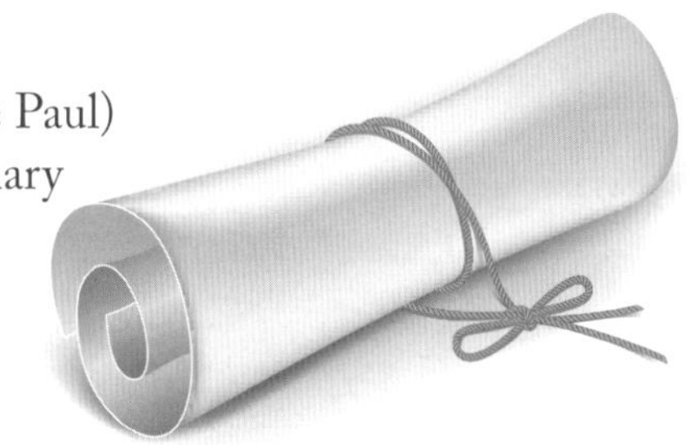

Dear Rev. Paul:

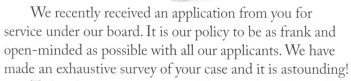

We recently received an application from you for service under our board. It is our policy to be as frank and open-minded as possible with all our applicants. We have made an exhaustive survey of your case and it is astounding!

To be clear, we are surprised that you have been able to "pass" as a bona fide missionary. We are told that you are afflicted with severe eye trouble. This is certain to be a definite handicap to an effective ministry. We require 20-20 vision.

Do you think it proper for a missionary to do part-time secular work? We hear that you are making tents on the side. In a letter to the church at Philippi, you admitted that they were the only church supporting you. We wonder why.

Is it true that you have a jail record? Certain brethren report that you did two years' time at Caesarea and were imprisoned at Rome. How much time have you spent in jail? Really now!

You made so much trouble for the businessmen at Ephesus that they refer to you as "the man who turned the world upside down." Sensationalism has no place in missions! We also deplore the lurid "over-the-wall-in-a-basket" escapade at Damascus.

We are appalled at your obvious lack of conciliatory behavior. Diplomatic men are not stoned and dragged out of the city gate or assaulted by furious mobs. Have you ever considered that gentler words might gain you more friends? I enclose a copy of Dallus Carnagus' book, *How to Win Barbarians and Influence Greeks*.

In one of your letters you refer to yourself as "Paul the aged." Our mission policies do not anticipate a surplus of elderly recipients, we feel the hope is in youth.

We understand too, that you are given to fantasies and dreams. You said at Troas you saw "a man of Macedonia," and, at another time, "were caught up into the third heaven," and even claimed "the Lord stood by you." We reckon that more realistic and practical minds are needed in the task of world evangelization. We consider our work to be more serious.

You have caused much trouble everywhere you have gone. You opposed the honorable women at Berea and the leaders of your own nationality in Jerusalem. If a man cannot get along with his own people, how can he serve foreigners?

You admit that while you were serving time at Rome, "all forsook you." Good men are not left friendless. Three fine brothers by the names of Diotrephes, Demas, and Alexander the coppersmith have notarized affidavits to the effect that it is impossible for them to cooperate with either you or your program.

We have heard as well that you had a bitter quarrel with a fellow missionary named Barnabas. Harsh words do not further God's work. Wouldn't it be wise if you tried getting along better with people?

You have written many letters to churches where you formerly pastored. In one of these letters you accused a church member of living with his father's wife. As a result you caused the whole church to feel badly and the poor fellow was expelled from membership.

You spend far too much time talking about, "the second coming of Christ." Your letters to the people of Thessalonica were almost entirely devoted to this theme. From now on, you should put first things first. Our strategy calls for thorough organization and long range planning. We can't be distracted by other issues.

Your ministry has been far too flighty to be successful: first, Asia Minor; then, Macedonia, Greece, Italy, and now you are talking about a wild goose chase into Spain. Concentration is more important than dissipation of one's powers. There is wisdom in settling down to do some work of a permanent nature.

In a recent sermon you stated, "God forbid that I should glory, save in the cross of our Lord Jesus Christ." It seems to us that you ought to glory in our heritage, our denominational program, the unified budget, and the world federation of churches.

Your sermons are much too long for our modern culture. At one place, you rambled until after midnight and a young man was so sleepy that he fell out of the window and broke his neck. You know that nobody is saved after the first twenty minutes. "Stand up, speak up, and then shut up," is our advice.

Dr. Luke reports that you are a thin little man, bald, frequently sick, and always so agitated over your churches that you sleep very poorly. He reports that you pad around the house praying half the night. A healthy mind in a robust body is our ideal for all applicants. A good night's sleep will give you zest and zip so that you wake up full of zing.

You wrote recently to Timothy that "you had fought a good fight." Fighting is hardly a recommendation for a missionary! No fight is a good fight. Jesus came not to bring a sword but peace. You boast that, "I fought with wild beasts at Ephesus." What do you mean?

It hurts me, brother Paul, but in all my 25 years of experience I have never met a man so opposite to the requirements of our mission board. If we accept you, we would break every rule of modern missionary practice. We are sending a copy of this letter to other mission boards in case you try them. We will be sending this letter to local churches throughout the area so that all may be aware of your "fly by night" unorthodox methods.

Most sincerely yours,
J. Flavius Fluffyhead

Better Trainer

A fellow computer programmer for a consulting group had designed some software for one of our largest accounts. He asked my help in putting it into operation. At first, he handled most of the work. Eventually, though, he asked me to help with the last phase of the training. When I sat down with one woman and told her I would be showing her how to make changes to the files, she sighed with relief. "I'm so glad you're teaching me instead of him."

Surprised, I said that my colleague was far more experienced than I was. "Yes," she said, "but I feel much more comfortable with you. I get nervous around really smart people."

Children Learn What They Live

- If a child lives with criticism, he learns to condemn.
- If a child lives with hostility, he learns to fight.
- If a child lives with fear, he learns to be apprehensive.
- If a child lives with pity, he learns to feel sorry for himself.
- If a child lives with ridicule, he learns to be shy.
- If a child lives with jealousy, he learns to be envious.
- If a child lives with shame, he learns to feel guilty.
- If a child lives with encouragement, he learns to be confident.
- If a child lives with tolerance, he learns to be patient.
- If a child lives with praise, he learns to be appreciative
- If a child lives with approval, he learns to like himself.
- If a child lives with recognition, he learns that it is good to have a goal.
- If a child lives with sharing, he learns about generosity.
- If a child lives with honesty and fairness, he learns what truth and justice are.
- If a child lives with security, he learns to have faith in himself and those about him.
- If a child lives with friendliness, he learns that the world is a nice place in which to live.
- If you live with serenity, your child will live with peace of mind.

Cloud Nine Doesn't Last

It's hard to stay excited about a constant. Inherit a million dollars and you are ecstatic for a few weeks. Eventually, you come down to earth. No one who has been a millionaire for years goes around in a state of euphoria. The most beautiful girl in town agrees to marry you, and you're on cloud nine. But a year or ten years into the marriage, you're back to normal. Let a young businessman get promoted to the second-highest place in the business and he is overwhelmed with excitement. A year later, he is overwhelmed and overwrought with the expectations placed on him. Life has returned to normal. No one can live on a mountain of excitement.

Fortunately, the Lord has not asked euphoria or even excitement from us, just faithfulness and steadfastness. Those who measure a worship service by its emotional highs are missing the mark. As the old preacher used to say, "It's not how high you jump that impresses God but how straight you walk after you hit the ground."

Contemplation

If you find yourself stuck in traffic, don't despair. There are people in this world for whom driving is an unheard of privilege.

Should your car break down, leaving you miles away from assistance. Think of the paraplegic who would love the opportunity to take that walk.

Should you notice a new gray hair in the mirror; think of the cancer patient in chemo who wishes she had hair to examine.

Should you find yourself at a loss and pondering what life is about, asking what is my purpose? Be thankful. There are those who didn't live long enough to get the opportunity.

—*The Energizer*

Core Issues

As we evaluate many of the troubles in life we often focus our efforts and attention on the symptoms rather than the core issues. Perhaps this is because the surface issues are more evident and appear easier to deal with. Perhaps it is a fear of the resulting consequences when dealing with core issues. Or, perhaps it is simply an unwillingness to admit our mistakes and make the changes necessary to correct the problem. Whatever the situation, when the core issue is not addressed it will result in a return to more problems. We can clear away the mold and mildew but it will return if there is nothing done to provide better air circulation and get rid of the dampness.

When you pick up an apple with a worm hole in it, you are inclined to think that a worm crawled onto the surface, liked it, and bore a hole from the outside. However, this is generally not the case. Rather, the worm lays an egg in an apple blossom and the egg is hatched in the core of the apple. The hole you see indicates that the worm has bored its way out from within.

In a very similar way we see many issues of society being addressed with the premise that the transgressor is boring its way in from the outside when in reality the real culprit is hatching from within. We swat away at flies as they buzz about because they are annoying and bothersome. As we rid ourselves of a few pesky ones it seems there are others waiting to replace them. It is only when we destroy their breeding grounds that we can really get control of the situation. Swatting them one by one is a losing battle that will, in the very least, provide a temporary reprieve.

May I suggest then some core issues that I believe are plaguing our society today and will continue to do so unless we address them.

#1. Lack of respect for God—someone once said, "God said it, I believe it, and that settles it," but the reality is this; God said it, that settles it, and I believe it. When God says something, it is settled regardless of whether or not it fits our way of thinking. God is sovereign. You can choose to disregard Him, you can choose to dishonor Him, but ultimately you will bow at His feet. He is your Creator, the potter who gives you life and breath. You are simply clay, a miracle of life in His hands. Lack of respect then, for God and His authority on our life permeates the blood stream in every element of society. It affects our attitude toward the laws of the country, the role of the church, the responsibility of the home, the lessons that are taught in our schools, etc. Lack of respect for the school teacher, the parents, the police officer, the government official, etc., is a direct correlation of a lack of respect for God.

#2. Dishonesty—the idea that I can get away with it by fooling society has caused many to forge the path of dishonesty. It is a quest for promotion of self through a reckless abandonment of Godly principles. You can fool people, but you can't fool God. He is the author of truth and requires it of all people. As disgusting and obnoxious as they are, cheating, stealing, lying, etc., have all weaseled their way into the highest dictates of authority, including the church and government. That doesn't mean they will go unrewarded. The criminal may go to his grave thinking he has outsmarted the magistrates but his guilty conscience will incriminate him when he stands before God in judgement. In all his recklessness he forgot that God must be reckoned with and he would ultimately pay an awful price for his foolishness.

#3. Misplaced values—bigger incomes, along with more time on our hands than ever before, has contributed to a society that eats and drinks pleasure. Children are transported to all kinds of events and sports activities starting at a young age. There is precious little time to spend alone as family. Mealtime around the dinner table is unknown. In order to pay off debts from over spending, both parents need to work. Grandparents and day care centers are raising the next generation. In a pursuit of pleasure and keeping up with society, children become a pawn. God places the responsibility of raising children squarely on the shoulders of parents. Discipline, respect, and obedience must first be taught in the home and then reinforced by the church, the school, and society. When the family unit is in disarray, society will quickly follow.

#4. Selfishness—"What's in it for me?" One of the first questions a prospective candidate for a job is likely to ask, is how much does the job pay. While that is a legitimate question, it begs farther consideration of how hard you are going to work. The scale has tilted too far to one side because we have become a greedy people. There is a lack of appreciation for the many blessings that are ours to enjoy. The mentality that "the world owes it to me" is far too prevalent and is illustrated by the excess of frivolous law suits. It shows up in people's attitudes. Provide a plan, be it medical care, financial assistance, etc., and you will find those who abuse it for selfish gain. It's all about me! God's way is far different. His is a spirit of love that says, "What can I do to help you?"

#5. Sanctity of life—the value of human life has been largely undermined by many. When God breathed into man's nostrils the breath of life, man became a living soul. For that reason, man is far superior to the animal kingdom. Man has a precious eternal soul. Abortion, murder, and suicide are evil atrocities. Jesus said, "I am come to give life and to give it more abundantly!" When He hung upon the cross He gave his life so others might live. He had the resources of ten thousand angels at His command, but He chose to die that man might have life through Him. His blood alone is the atonement for our sins. Without His blood mankind is hopelessly doomed. But God so loved the world that he gave His only son that we might have life. Through his word and by His example He taught us to daily give our lives a living sacrifice for the sake of others. All of human life is sacred!

#6. Immorality—we have become victims of gradualism. If the immorality that is seen today had been displayed fifty years ago it would have met with punishment and censorship. Why is it now so readily accepted? Have we become immune? I trust not. We are reaping the seed that was sown. There are valid reasons why children are abused and victimized. Divorce affects one out of every two marriages, and many children are born out of wedlock. Follow the trail of most murder and abuse cases and it will lead back to jealousy and rage in a marriage separation or a live in partnership. Children become the innocent victims. God outlined a plan for marriage that provides a solid foundation and a secure place for children to grow up. A place where love and forgiveness are emphasized and embraced by mom and dad. Immorality feeds the carnal desires while it poisons our spiritual sensitivity. Rat bait is made up of only 3% poison. The rest is delicious corn meal. The end result is still deadly. Can we expect to feast at the table of immorality and come away unscathed? The answer is no.

#7. Fantasy—most children are exposed to a world of fantasy at a very young age. Television shows with characters ranging from the cute and cuddly to the gruesome and ghostly are a daily part of their lives. Products such as stationery, toys, and trinkets promote their favorite character. While you may argue the fact that it is part of their childhood and that they will separate fact from fiction you cannot argue that it doesn't have an impact on their lives. I see it in their actions at the grocery store. I see it in the clothes they wear and how they wear them. I see it in their respect for authority. The violence of video games to which many children are exposed destroys their sense of right and wrong. They attempt to duplicate the action of their favorite character and wonder why they get in trouble. They turn to drugs and fantasy as a way of trying to escape reality, but the reality is, they can't escape.

This may appear as a harsh commentary and I must confess that there are some things I would like to delete. I would much prefer to write an article that is upbeat and positive but at times we've got to look in a mirror and be honest. If the apples are treated, we can expect a good harvest, but if the blossoms go untreated the apples will be full of worms. I prefer apples without the worms.

Likewise, if we fail to treat the underlying worms that are destroying much of society we will reap the consequences. Scratching away at the surface will not restore the fruit. It will be permanently scarred. Any apple farmer will assure you that treating the core issue is much less costly and far more effective. We must begin the treatment process by giving God his due respect. We have waited far too long.

—M. Gingrich

Credit Cards

Hardly a day goes by that I don't receive a credit card application in the mail. Some days I receive several. Visa®, Master Card®, and American Express®, to name a few. Most of the time they are discarded into the waste can. Recently, however, I was considering getting another card and so I began researching the different offers. Some of the offers were 0% APR for five months, 5% Cash Back, No Annual Fee, Free Awards Program, Points for Free Air Line Tickets, 5% off the purchase of a New GM vehicle and they even lauded the fact that I am "pre-approved".

I began to sort the different offers according to their appeal. 0% APR meant nothing because I wasn't planning on transferring any money and the interest rate although exorbitant in most cases, was irrelevant since I planned to pay any purchases before interest was charged. No Annual Fee sounded okay, but most cards offered that. 5% toward the purchase of a new vehicle wasn't a consideration either since I had no intention of buying a new vehicle. 5% Cash Back made sense, so I began reading. 5% on all purchases at supermarkets, gas stations, and drug stores. Wonderful! I found one that meant something. 5% off my grocery bill, 5% savings when I fill-up my vehicle or purchase a prescription. Great! But wait! What does it say in the fine print? Qualifying purchases at retail establishments that classify their merchant locations as gas stations or grocery stores. Convenience stores and warehouse or discount stores are not eligible. How do they figure? So, I guess the first thing I need to do to get the best results from my credit card is walk into the store and ask them, are you a gas station or a convenience store? I wonder if my card qualifies if I pay at the pump? Why must they make it all so difficult. Why not just pay cash? But it is so convenient to just carry a card and so much safer they argue. Oh yes, did I mention that once I've spent $6000.00 I will have saved a whopping $300.00. I will also have maxed out my savings for the calendar year and I will need to call in a request or I won't get my rebate at all. Reading further I discovered that my being pre-approved was based on criteria contained on

my personal credit report and that after I apply and upon further review I may be refused. What! I thought I was pre-approved!

Credit cards are convenient, however, they carry with them some dangers as well. Over extend your credit limit and you may get a $35.00 fee. Late payment will also incur a $35.00 fee and an interest rate of 10% or higher. There is also the temptation to buy on impulse and spend far more than you had planned. The savings are soon lost in the interest paid out. The figures I hear regarding credit card debt are almost beyond belief. Like any other good thing, its misuse must be controlled and guarded against.

Wouldn't it be a lot easier to go back to paying cash or check? In a lot of ways it would. However, the increasing fees for processing checks versus No Annual Fee credit cards has swung the pendulum in favor of credit cards. Probably the biggest reason for credit card acceptance is the idea that it is a safer method of conducting transactions. This is especially true when traveling in areas where tourists can be a target. A stolen credit card can be cancelled where as stolen cash is gone for good. Another benefit is its acceptance worldwide. Try renting a car without a credit card. You can't. They won't accept cash.

Perhaps the greatest danger of all is the subtle step we have taken as a society to really accept any new form of payment that touts its ease of use and excellent security features. Our forefathers shook hands and traded a cow or chicken for a plot of land or food for the family. The next generation used cash and a checkbook. Today's generation relies on credit cards, debit cards, and ATM machines. As fraudulent use of credit cards continues to rise, what will be the next step?

Will we readily accept any new method that has merit.

Has our acceptance of credit card use taken us to the brink of becoming a cashless society? Is it really for the better? The jury is still out.

—M. Gingrich

Delinquency

Once there was a little boy.

- When he was three weeks old his parents turned him over to a babysitter.
- When he was two, they dressed him up like a cowboy and gave him a gun.
- When he was three everybody said, "How cute," as he went about lisping a commercial jingle.
- When he was six, his father occasionally dropped him off at Sunday School on his way to the golf course.
- When he was eight they bought him a BB gun and taught him to shoot sparrows. He learned to shoot windshields by himself.
- When he was ten he spent his after school time squatting at a drugstore newsstand reading comic books.
- His mother wasn't home, and his father was busy.
- When he was thirteen, he told his parents other boys stayed out as late as they wanted to so they said he could too. It was easier that way.
- When he was fourteen they gave him a deadly two-ton machine, wrangled a license for him to drive it, and told him to be careful.
- When he was fifteen, the police called his home one night and said, "We have your boy. He's in trouble." "In trouble?" screamed the father. "It can't be my boy!" But it was!

MORAL: As the twig is bent, it is apt to snap back in your face!

Did God Create Evil?

The university professor challenged his students with this question: "Did God create everything that exists?"

A student bravely replied, "Yes, He did!"

"God created everything?" the professor asked.

"Yes, sir," the student replied.

The professor answered, "If God created everything, then God created evil since evil exists, and according to the principle that our works define who we are, then God is evil."

The student became quiet before such an answer. The professor was quite pleased with himself and boasted to the students that he had proven once more that the Christian faith was a myth.

Another student raised his hand and said, "May I ask you a question, professor?"

"Of course," replied the professor. The student stood up and asked, "Professor, does cold exist?"

"What kind of question is this? Of course it exists. Have you never been cold?"

The students snickered at the young man's question.

The young man replied, "In fact, sir, cold does not exist. According to the laws of physics, what we consider cold is in reality the absence of heat. Everybody and every object is susceptible to study when it has or transmits energy, and heat is what makes a body or matter have or transmit energy. Absolute zero (-460 degrees F) is the total absence of heat; all matter becomes inert and incapable of reaction at that temperature. Cold does not exist. We have created this word to describe how we feel if we have too little heat.

The student continued, "Professor, does darkness exist?"

The professor responded, "Of course it does."

The student replied, "Once again you are wrong, sir, darkness does not exist either. Darkness is in reality the absence of light. Light we can study, but not darkness. In fact, we can use Newton's prism to break white light into many colors and study the various wavelengths of each color. You cannot measure darkness. A simple ray of light can break into a world of darkness and illuminate it. How can you know how dark a certain space is? You measure the amount of light present. Isn't this correct? Darkness is a term used by man to describe what happens when there is no light present."

Finally the young man asked the professor, "Sir, does evil exist?"

Now uncertain, the professor responded, "Of course, as I have already said. We see it every day. It is in the daily example of man's inhumanity to man. It is in the multitude of crime and violence everywhere in the world. These manifestations are nothing else but evil."

To this the student replied, "Evil does not exist, sir, or at least it does not exist unto itself. Evil is simply the absence of God. It is just like darkness and cold, a word that man has created to describe the absence of God. God did not create evil. Evil is not like faith, or love, that exists just as does light and heat. Evil is the result of what happens when man does not have God's love present in his heart. It's like the cold that comes when there is no heat or the darkness that comes when there is no light."

The professor sat down.

The young man's name was Albert Einstein.

Drop A Pebble In The Water

Drop a pebble in the water:
Just a splash and it is gone;
But there's half-a hundred ripples
Circling on and on and on,

Spreading, spreading from the center,
Flowing on and out to sea.
And there is no way of telling
Where the end is going to be.

Drop a pebble in the water:
In a minute you forget,
But there's little waves a-flowing,
And there's ripples circling yet,

And those little waves a-flowing,
To a great big wave have grown;
You've disturbed a mighty river
Just by dropping in a stone.

Drop an unkind word, or careless:
In a minute it is gone;
But there's half-a-hundred ripples
Circling on and on and on.

They keep spreading, spreading, spreading
From the center as they go,
And there is no way to stop them,
Once you've started them to flow.

Drop an unkind word, or careless:
In a minute you forget;
But there's little waves a-flowing,
And there's ripples circling yet,

And perhaps in some sad heart
A mighty wave of tears you've stirred,
And disturbed a life was happy
Ere you dropped that unkind word.

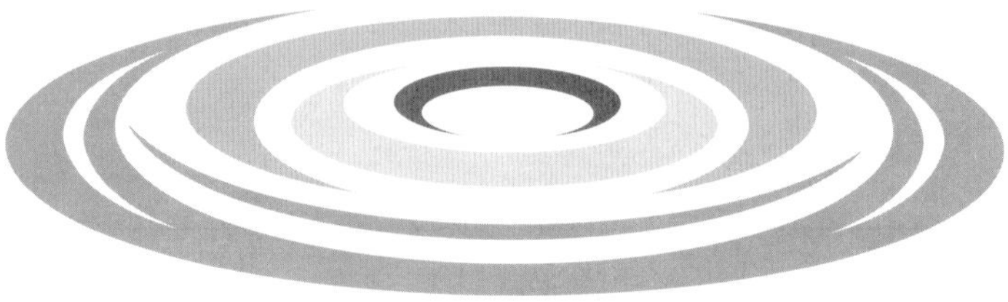

Drop a word of cheer and kindness:
Just a flash and it is gone;
But there's half-a-hundred ripples
Circling on and on and on,

Bearing hope and joy and comfort
On each splashing, dashing wave,
Till you wouldn't believe the volume
Of the one kind word you gave.

Drop a word of cheer and kindness:
In a minute you forget;
But there's gladness still a-swelling
And there's joy a-circling yet;

And you've rolled a wave of comfort
Whose sweet music can be heard,
Over miles and miles of water
Just by dropping one kind word.

—James W. Foley

Fishing With Dad

It was a beautiful day as we headed for a part of the Brodhead Creek that I had never been to before. My father had fished the Brodhead many times and knew most of the stream, but my memory is not clear whether he had ever fished this section. He was fully "equipped" with vest, rod, reel, net, polarized glasses, silicon spray, leader, tippet, clippers, knife, bag, rain gear, extendable walking stick, and boxes containing what must have been 10,000 flies and nymphs to match every size, color, and species to come out of any body of water in the United States. Needless to say, he was loaded down—not to mention we both had large rubber chest waders on. My father always kept an extra rod and vest on hand for days when I could join him, and we always looked forward to the times we could spend together on the stream, even if we didn't catch any fish.

As customary, we fished our way downstream. My father always felt you would disturb the waters less by walking with the current. It was a beautiful section of winding stream with large boulders and lots of trout in the beautiful Pocono mountains of Northeastern Pennsylvania. The water was still cool and the flies weren't quite hatching out, and as luck would have it, the fish weren't biting real well, either.

As the day progressed we happened upon an area that was a little more rural, with a few houses and large green fields. The stream rounded a large bend and opened up into a clear shallow pool about thirty to forty yards wide. A large rock that was almost the full width of the stream slowed the current with the exception of the far shore where the water flowed off the end into a huge dark hole that was probably at least twenty feet deep. From years of water gently washing over the rock surface it had become perfectly smooth and out at the end, you could see a school of fish sitting along the bottom feeding on

whatever the current washed their direction. Being the object of our desire, we waded out as far as the waders would allow and began long slow casts allowing our flies to float down over them. We weren't sure whether they were the trout we were hoping for or if it was just a few suckers feeding on the bottom, but we were willing to give them a try either way.

After a time of casting I happened to look down at the smooth stone surface and noticed a peculiar pattern. It appeared like tire tracks had been somehow cut into the rock right where we were standing. I pointed it out to my father and together we realized that the rock we were on was covered with a very thin film of algae and the marks were being left by our boots as the current was slowly pushing us downstream. The rock had been so smooth we hadn't even realized we were moving and now we began to realize the dangerous situation we were in. If the chest waders were to fill with water in the deep hole toward which we were moving, we would not have been able to swim and the task of trying to pull them off over our feet was difficult enough when we were sitting on dry ground.

We turned toward the shore and quickly found that we were too buoyant to compete with the ever increasing current. We continued moving slowly and being slightly less deep in the water, I was able to slowly work my way out. I began to look for a stick or anything long enough to be able to reach my father who was now moving even faster. I quickly realized I didn't have time. There was nothing I could find nearby so I dropped my rod and went back into the water. My dad reached for me with his rod. I pulled gently on the end only to have it separate in the middle. We were now held together only by the thin fishing line. We pulled on the line gently so as not to tear it and slowly came closer together, but were not at a point where we could get footing enough to move toward the shallow water. As we held onto each other we inevitably moved toward the dark hole where the water increased its current.

I was positioned just downstream of my dad when I felt my boot slide over a crack in the rock. I shifted my weight upstream to catch my other foot on the crack. My dad at arms length, was still sliding. I tried to explain where the crack was and that it was vital that he too, would get hold of this crack. We supported each other so as not to fall as he slid onto the crack and caught it with the edge of his boot. We had stopped but we were balanced precariously between the current and leaning too far upstream. Cautiously we took turns trying to move one foot at a time. When I picked up my foot I immediately felt the current try to take me but my father's hold was strong and in turn we slowly worked our way up the crack in the rock to dry land where we put the rod back together and decided to head back to the vehicle. It had been enough fishing for one day. We both knew we had stared death in the face and we were quite shaken. About halfway back to the car we met a couple of men headed for the same area with fly rods in hand "Watch out for that hole! It looks tempting but the rock is slippery and if you wade out too far you'll soon find out you can't get back in," we warned. It was then that we found out two children had lost their lives there to the same fate only a couple weeks earlier.

We didn't talk about the day much after that, realizing that no one would be able to understand it without actually having been there. Over time I thought of the event less and less until one day on my way home from work. My father had been battling cancer from years of working in an asbestos plant and had passed away. It was two days before his memorial service and the pastor wanted to get together with us to rehash some of the events of his life. Suddenly this day came rushing back to me and it occurred to me how much our life is like that walk in the stream.

We often get caught up in the day and while striving for our goals we tend to forget the importance of simply living and observing the beauty of our surroundings and the importance of the company of the ones we love. That day as we struggled for achievement we found we had wandered out too far. Our material things failed to save us and only through holding on to one another and keeping our balance and focus were we able to get out alive. The crack in the rock is like faith. It may be very thin at times, but it's there when you need it most, in the deeper water.

—Rob Yost

Gossip—Remember Me

My name is gossip.

- I have no respect for justice.
- I maim without killing. I break hearts and ruin lives.
- I am cunning and malicious and gather strength with age.
- The more I am quoted, the more I am believed.
- I flourish at every level of society.
- My victims are helpless. They cannot protect themselves against me because I have no name and no face.
- To track me down is impossible. The harder you try, the more elusive I become.
- I am nobody's friend.
- Once I tarnish a reputation, it is never the same.
- I topple governments and wreck marriages.
- I make innocent people cry on their pillows.

My name is gossip.

Grandpa's Hands

Grandpa, some ninety plus years, sat feebly on the patio bench. He didn't move, just sat with his head down staring at his hands. When I sat down beside him, he didn't acknowledge my presence, and the longer I sat, I wondered if he was okay. Finally, not really wanting to disturb him, but wanting to check on him at the same time, I asked him if he was okay.

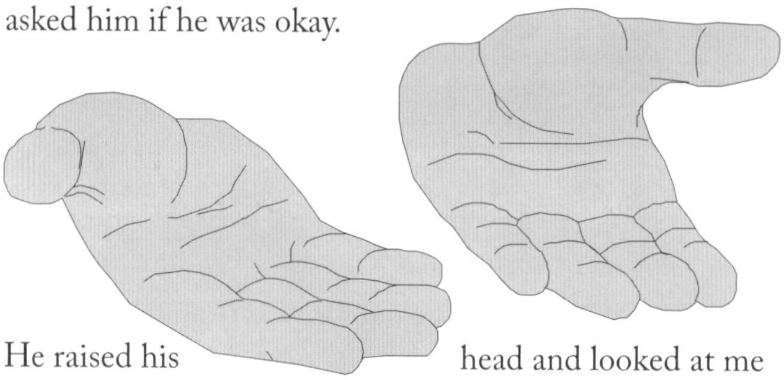

He raised his head and looked at me and smiled. "Yes, I'm fine, thank you for asking," he said in a clear strong voice.

"I didn't mean to disturb you, Grandpa, but you were just sitting here staring at your hands and I wanted to make sure you were okay."

He explained to me, "Have you ever looked at your hands?" he asked. "I mean really looked at your hands?" I slowly opened my hands and stared down at them, I turned them over, palms up and then palms down. No, I guess I had never really looked at my hands as I tried to figure out the point he was making. Grandpa smiled and related this story:

"Stop and think for a moment about the hands you have, how they have served you well throughout your years. These hands, though wrinkled, shriveled, and weak have been the tools I have used all my life to reach out and grab and embrace life. They braced and caught my fall when as a toddler I crashed upon the floor. They put food in my mouth and clothes on my back. As a child, mother taught me to fold them in prayer. They tied my shoes and pulled on my boots. They wiped my tears when I cried with grief.

They have been dirty, scraped and raw, swollen, and bent. They were uneasy and clumsy when I tried to hold my newborn son. They wrote letters home when I was away and trembled and shook when I buried my parents and spouse and walked my daughter down the aisle. Yet, they were strong and sure when I dug my buddy out of a foxhole and lifted a plow off of my best friend's foot. They have held children, consoled neighbors, and shook in fists of anger when I didn't understand. They have covered my face, combed my hair, and washed and cleansed the rest of my body. They have been sticky and wet, bent and broken, dried and raw.

And to this day when not much of anything else of me works real well, these hands hold me up, lay me down, and again continue to fold in prayer. These hands are the mark of where I've been and the ruggedness of my life. But more importantly it will be these hands that God will reach out and take when He leads me home. And with my hands He will lift me to His side and there I will use these hands to touch the face of Christ."

I will never look at my hands the same again. But I remember God reached out and took my grandpa's hands and led him home. When my hands are hurt or sore or when I stroke the face of my children and wife I think of grandpa. I know he has been stroked and caressed and held by the hands of God. I, too, want to touch the face of God and feel His hands upon my face.

Gullible Anyone?

In Belo Horizonte, Brazil, a farmer was duped into investing his life savings in a "money making machine" which he was assured would turn out 100 cruzeiro (about $20) notes. Four slick salesmen demonstrated the machine loaded with real notes, and convinced the farmer to hand over $45,000 for it. After failing to print himself a fortune, the farmer took it to the police and pleaded with them to "make it work"!

Louis Stone, a reporter discovered that a lot of people believe everything they read so he began to invent and sell stories about such things as a tree that produced baked apples, a squirrel that brushed its master's shoes with its tail every morning, and so on.

The Sante Prison in France is so well built and constructed that since its completion in 1867, only six prisoners have escaped. Leon Oaudet, however, walked out through the front gates in 1927 with hardly any effort. A friend telephoned the warden that Oaudet had been pardoned. The credulous official, without checking, immediately released him.

These accounts sound far fetched and utterly ridiculous. But many folks, although they wouldn't admit it, are really quite gullible. They have a tendency to believe what they hear without taking time to reason it out in their minds.

A lot of sales gimmicks are designed to take advantage of our gullibility. They are constructed in such a way that makes them sound appealing. Promotions are painted as super deals and are effective because they play on the emotions and interests of the consumer. Limited time offer! Sale! Free—these have an almost magical effect with many people. People forget that there is a cost hidden somewhere.

Another place where folks get caught up is in games of chance. Games of chance are successful because they are based on many folks participating, but only a few winning. Folks tend to downplay in their mind the fact that their chance of winning anything significant is remote while their chance of losing is almost a guarantee. There is always that carrot hanging at the end of the stick to entice them on. Maybe this time!

Our level of trust in people can make us more gullible as well. The more straightforward and honest a person is the more of a tendency there is to believe that other people are that way too. We tend to believe that no-one would feed us a line, that is at least, until we get hooked. A high level of trust and honesty is commendable but it must be fused with caution.

One technique that has helped me to avert buying into a salesperson's line is to postpone a decision, and to call back. If they insist on an immediate response, you probably don't want their product.

The old adage, "You can fool some of the people some of the time, some of the people all of the time, but you can't fool all the people all the time" still holds true.

Remember, "If it sounds too good to be true, it probably isn't."

—M. Gingrich

Haircut

A man and a little boy entered a barbershop together.

After the man received the full treatment—shave, shampoo, manicure, haircut, etc.—he placed the boy in the chair. "I'm going to buy a green tie to wear for the parade," he said. "I'll be back in a few minutes."

When the boy's haircut was completed and the man still hadn't returned, the barber said, "Looks like your daddy's forgotten all about you."

"That wasn't my daddy," said the boy. "He just walked up, took me by the hand and said, 'Come on, son, we're gonna get a free haircut!'"

Holding On To God's Hand

I just returned from New Jersey. While en route there, I was stuck in traffic on Interstate 81, just below the Virginia state line (Bristol, Tennessee), due to a traffic accident with a fatality involved. This accident involved a tanker truck hauling a hazardous material load that developed a leak, which meant that we weren't going anywhere for several hours. After being told by the Tennessee State Troopers that we would be sitting still until the cleanup was completed, I set my brakes on the truck and got out to stretch my legs. Other truck drivers did the same, and at one point there were five of us standing there by my truck, complaining.

Sitting right beside me in the left lane, were two elderly people in a Silverado pickup truck, which was loaded quite well. The man, Joe, lowered his window and asked what was going on regarding the traffic situation.

Soon we were all talking with this couple. I mentioned that if I had known about this, I would have brought some water to drink, for I was becoming thirsty. The lady, Anna, said that they had plenty of water, and sodas in the cooler in the bed of the truck, and offered everyone present something. While she was back there, she said that she had plenty of tuna salad made up, and asked if we would be interested in a sandwich.

After some urging from Joe, we agreed to a sandwich. While Anna was making the sandwiches on the tailgate of the truck, she was singing like a songbird. To be close to seventy, (I guess), she had a remarkable voice.

When she finished making the sandwiches, and putting everything up, Joe raised the tailgate of the truck to close it. I noticed a Mississippi license plate on it. I inquired as to what part of Mississippi they were from. Joe said Biloxi. Knowing that Biloxi had been ravaged also by hurricane Katrina, I asked if they sustained any damage. Joe said that they lost everything but what they had on and what was in the pickup. All of us drivers tried unsuccessfully to pay them for their drinks and the sandwiches. They would have nothing to do with it.

Joe said that their son was living around Harrisonburg, Virginia, and that they were going there. He was in the real estate business and that there was a home that became open, and that they were going to start all over there. Starting over at their age would not be easy.

I will soon be forty-eight years old, and I have to say that I have never eaten a tuna sandwich with side orders of reality and humility. These people lost everything except the pictures, important documents, and some clothes. Joe had managed to get their antique heirloom grandfathers clock into the bed of the truck, and Anna got her china and silverware, but that was all. These wonderful people lost practically everything they owned and still would not accept any money for their food and drinks. Joe told us, "It is better to give than to receive."

They had sought refuge behind a block wall that he had built years ago, and they watched their belongings and their home disappear in the winds of Hurricane Katrina. Joe said that during all this he had one hand holding onto Anna and the other holding on to God. Their truck and themselves came out of Katrina unscathed.

As I stated before, Anna was singing a song while making the sandwiches.

The song is titled "I Know Who Holds Tomorrow," an old gospel song. She knew every word, and was quite a gifted singer of it. Have you ever heard it?

The chorus of this song is, "Many things, about tomorrow, I don't seem to understand. But I know who holds tomorrow, and I know who holds my hand."

There is no doubt in my mind who was holding both their hands. I know there have been many, many stories that have circulated over the years about things that will touch your heart, but this one I personally was involved in.

Forget all of the politics that the news is thriving on, and think about people just like Joe and Anna. If you can, help out with the victims relief funds. If you cannot, at least offer a prayer for everyone.

I know these two elderly people got this old boy. I will always remember them. Joe and Anna, if by some strange way, you or someone you know gets this and shows it to you, God bless you!

—Mike Dowdy, Hartselle, Alabama

Hospital Waiting

A nurse took the tired, anxious serviceman to the bedside. "Your son is here," she said to the old man.

She had to repeat the words several times before the patient's eyes opened. Heavily sedated because of the pain of his heart attack, he dimly saw the young uniformed Marine standing outside the oxygen tent. He reached out his hand. The Marine wrapped his toughened fingers around the old man's limp ones, squeezing a message of love and encouragement. The nurse brought a chair so that the Marine could sit beside the bed. All through the night, the young Marine sat there in the poorly lighted ward, holding the old man's hand and offering him words of love and strength.

Occasionally, the nurse suggested that the Marine move away and rest awhile. He refused. Whenever the nurse came into the ward, the Marine was oblivious of her and of the night noises of the hospital—the clanking of the oxygen tank, the laughter of the night staff members exchanging greetings, the cries and moans of the other patients. Now and then, she heard him say a few gentle words. The dying man said nothing, only held tightly to his son all through the night.

Along towards dawn, the old man died. The Marine released the now lifeless hand he had been holding and went to tell the nurse. While she did what she had to do, he waited. Finally, she returned. She started to offer words of sympathy, but the Marine interrupted her.

"Who was that man?" he asked.

The nurse was startled, "He was your father," she answered.

"No, he wasn't," the Marine replied. "I never saw him before in my life."

"Then why didn't you say something when I took you to him?"

"I knew right away there had been a mistake, but I also knew he needed his son, and his son just wasn't here. When I realized that he was too sick to tell whether or not I was his son, knowing how much he needed me, I stayed."

If You Can't Sing, Whittle

I Corinthians 12:4—"To each is given the manifestation of the Spirit for the common good."

He was a lad in the town of Cremona, Italy, in the middle of the 17th century. Cremona was a musical town and great acclaim was given to those who could sing or play. Wanting to be accepted and given some recognition for his musical talents, he tried singing. His friends called him "squeaky voice," and he soon realized that his singing would never be anything special.

The young lad then tried to learn to play, but his success wasn't much better than his singing. So he was a dejected lad as he walked through the streets of Cremona with his friends and listened to their beautiful voices. About the only thing the lad could do was to whittle on a block of wood with his knife.

One day he was sitting on the edge of the street whittling as three of his friends played and sang beautiful songs for the people passing by. Appreciating the musical ability of his friends, many people dropped some coins into their hands to reward their efforts. One gentlemen stopped longer than many of the others and even asked the friends to sing a song again. After they finished he dropped a coin into the hand of the singer. Then he moved on down the street.

Upon looking, the boys discovered that it was a gold coin! It was quite a piece of money to give a street singer. But the man who gave it could afford to do so. "Who was he?" asked the lad who whittled. "It was Amati," his friend with the beautiful voice replied. "Amati who?" asked the lad. "Nicolo Amati," the friend replied. "He is the greatest violin maker in all of Italy!"

That evening at home the lad thought about the man named Nicolo Amati. He was a man who succeeded in the musical field. But he neither sang nor played! The more he thought about the violin maker, the more he became convinced that he wanted to become a violin maker. He wanted to become the best violin maker in Italy!

Early the next morning the lad hurried off to the home of Nicolo Amati. Inquiring about the way, he sat on the doorsteps after arriving and waited for the great violin maker to come out. When Amati came out, the lad told him that he wanted to become a violin maker and asked Amati if he would teach him to make violins. He explained to Amati that he couldn't sing or play, but that he could whittle. And, more than anything else, he wanted to make violins.

Amati accepted the young lad as a pupil. Day after day, week after week, month after month, year after year the young man studied from the master. In due time his work became known in Cremona, then Italy, and finally throughout the whole world.

We may not have the talent to do some things as well as other people. But God has given us all a very special talent which, if we develop, can help us help others. Antonio Stradivari found this to be true. Even to this very day men still make music with his violins. And they pay upwards of $100,000 to do so!

Just because you can't sing or play doesn't mean you can't make music.

In A Perfect World:

- Everyone would smile and say, "Have a great day!" and mean it.
- No One would tailgate, pull out in front of you or yell at you when you pass them on the road.
- Everyone would really care when they ask you, "How are you doin?"
- No One would make fun of you or criticize you for thinking differently than they do.
- Everyone would be on time for every appointment, etc., and doctors would see you according to schedule.
- No One would oversleep, get lost or not care about being on time.
- All Unborn Babies would be treated with love and respect and given an opportunity to be born.
- No Unborn Baby, at any age, would be aborted.
- Every Family would live in harmony and treat each other with love and care.
- No Families would be broken by violence, selfishness, drug or alcohol abuse, separation, or divorce.
- All Sports activities would be for fun, with no score being kept (like "t-ball").
- No Sports activities would be held on Sundays, have long seasons, or conflict with family time.
- All Schools would allow students to bring Bibles and read them during "free times".
- No Schools would allow "bullies" to pick on students.
- Every Knee "will bow…and every tongue confess that Jesus Christ is Lord, to the glory of God the Father" (Philippians 2:10-11).

—Pastor Jim Bauer

Instruments In God's Hand

Suppose we lay one of our gloves on the table and then tell the glove to pick up a pen and write out a letter for us. It cannot do that. But when we put our hand inside the glove and through the glove use the pen, then the glove has become a useful instrument in our hand.

We are just like that glove. We are instruments in the hand of the living God.

Lessons on Life

There was an Indian Chief who had four sons. He wanted his sons to learn not to judge things too quickly. So he sent them each on a quest, in turn, to go and look at a pear tree that was a great distance away. The first son went in the winter, the second in the spring, the third in summer, and the youngest son in the fall.

When they had all gone and come back, he called them together to describe what they had seen. The first son said that the tree was ugly, bent, and twisted. The second son said no, it was covered with green buds and full of promise. The third son disagreed; he said it was laden with blossoms that smelled so sweet and looked so beautiful, it was the most graceful thing he had ever seen. The last son disagreed with all of them; he said it was ripe and drooping with fruit, full of life and fulfillment.

The man then explained to his sons that they were all right, because they had each seen but only one season in the tree's life. He told them that you cannot judge a tree, or a person, by only one season, and that the essence of who they are and the pleasure, joy, and love that come from that life can only be measured at the end, when all the seasons are up.

If you give up when it's winter, you will miss the promise of your spring, the beauty of your summer, fulfillment of your fall.

Moral: Don't let the pain of one season destroy the joy of all the rest. Don't judge life by one difficult season. Persevere through the difficult patches and better times are sure to come…

Listen To The Whisper

A young and successful executive was traveling down a neighborhood street going a bit too fast in his new Jaguar. He was watching for children darting out from between parked cars and slowed down when he thought he saw something. As his car passed, no children appeared. Instead, a brick smashed into the Jag's side door! He slammed on the brakes and spun the Jag back to the spot where the brick had been thrown. He jumped out of the car, grabbed some child and pushed him up against a parked car shouting, "What was that all about and why did you do it?"

"Please mister, please. I'm sorry, I didn't know what else to do," pleaded the youngster. "I threw the brick because no one else would stop. "Tears were dripping down the boy's chin as he pointed around the parked car. "It's my brother," he said. "He rolled off the curb and fell out of his wheelchair and I can't lift him up." Sobbing the boy asked the executive, "Would you please help me get him back into his wheelchair? He's hurt and he's too heavy for me."

Moved beyond words, the driver tried to swallow the rapidly swelling lump in his throat. He lifted the young man back into the wheelchair and took out his handkerchief and wiped the scrapes and cuts, checking to see that everything was going to be okay.

"Thank you and may God bless you," the grateful child said to him.

The man watched the little boy push his brother down the sidewalk toward his home. He never did repair the side door. He kept the dent to remind him not to go through life so fast that someone has to throw a brick at you to get your attention.

God whispers in your soul and speaks to your heart. Sometimes when you don't have time to listen, He has to throw a brick at you. It is your choice: Listen to the whisper—or wait for the brick.

Make Music With What You Have Left

On Nov. 18, 1995, Itzhak Perlman, the violinist, came on stage to give a concert at Avery Fisher Hall at Lincoln Center in New York City. If you have ever been to a Perlman concert, you know that getting on stage is no small achievement for him. He was stricken with polio as a child, and so he has braces on both legs and walks with the aid of two crutches—to see him walk across the stage one step at a time, painfully and slowly, is an unforgettable sight. He walks painfully, yet majestically, until he reaches his chair. Then he sits down, slowly puts his crutches on the floor, undoes the clasps on his legs, tucks one foot back and extends the other foot forward. Then he bends down and picks up the violin, puts it under his chin, nods to the conductor and proceeds to play. By now, the audience is used to this ritual. They sit quietly while he makes his way across the stage to his chair. They remain reverently silent while he undoes the clasps on his legs. They wait until he is ready to play. But this time, something went wrong. Just as he finished the first few bars, one of the strings on his violin broke.

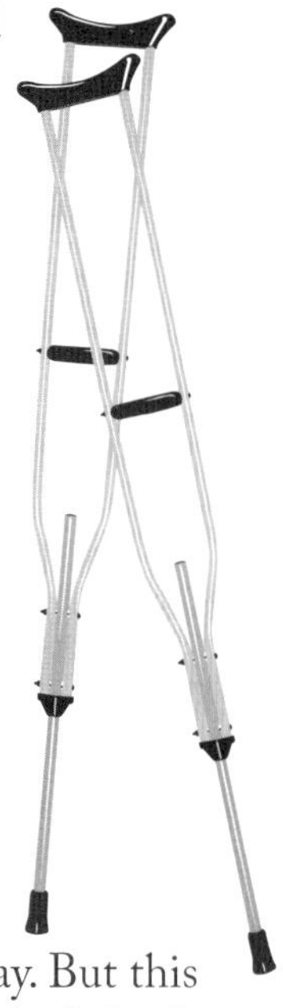

You could hear it snap—it went off like gunfire across the room. There was no mistaking what that sound meant. There was no mistaking what he had to do.

People who were there that night thought to themselves: We figured that he would have to get up, put on the clasps again, pick up the crutches and limp his way off stage—to either find another violin or else find another string for this one.

But he didn't. Instead, he waited a moment, closed his eyes and then signaled the conductor to begin again. The orchestra began, and he played from where he had left off. And he played with such passion and such power and such purity as they had never heard before. Of course, anyone knows that it is impossible to play a symphonic work with just three strings. I know that, and you know that, but that night Itzhak Perlman refused to know that. You could see him modulating, changing, recomposing the piece in his head. At one point, it sounded like he was detuning the strings to get new sounds from them that they had never made before.

When he finished, there was an awesome silence in the room. And then people rose and cheered. There was an extraordinary outburst of applause from every corner of the auditorium. We were all on our feet, screaming and cheering, doing everything we could to show how much we appreciated what he had done. He smiled, wiped the sweat from his brow, raised his bow to quiet us, and then he said, not boastfully, but in a quiet, pensive, reverent tone, "You know, sometimes it is the artist's task to find out how much music you can still make with what you have left." What a powerful line that is. It has stayed in my mind ever since I heard it. And who knows? Perhaps that is the way of life—not just for artists but for all of us. So, perhaps our task in this shaky, fast-changing, bewildering world in which we live is to make music, at first with all that we have, and then, when that is no longer possible to make music with what we have left.

—Jack Riemer, Houston Chronicle (April, 2001)

"Minor" Traveling Unattended

Right before the jet way door closed, I scrambled aboard the plane going from LA to Chicago, lugging my laptop and overstuffed briefcase. It was the first leg of an important business trip a few weeks before Christmas, and I was running late. I had a ton of work to catch up on. Half wishing, half praying, I muttered, "Please God, do me a favor; let there be an empty seat next to mine. I don't need any distractions."

I was at the aisle in a two seat row. Across sat a businesswoman with her nose buried in a newspaper. No problem. But in the seat beside mine, next to the window, was a young boy wearing a big red tag around his neck: Minor Traveling Unattended.

The boy sat perfectly still, hands in his lap, eyes straight ahead. He'd probably been told never to talk to strangers. Good, I thought. Then the flight attendant came by. "Michael, I have to sit down because we're about to take off," she said to the little boy. "This nice man will answer any of your questions, okay?"

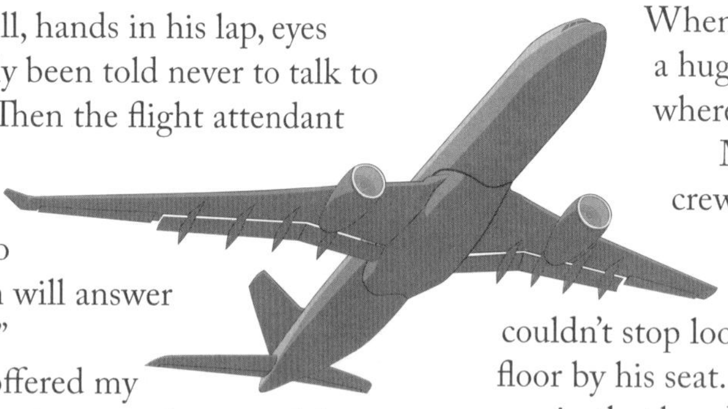

Did I have a choice? I offered my hand, and Michael shook it twice, straight up and down.

"Hi, I'm Jerry," I said. "You must be about seven years old."

"I'll bet you don't have any children," he responded.

"Why do you think that? Sure I do." I took out my wallet to show him pictures.

"Because I'm six."

"I was way off, huh?"

The captains' voice came over the speakers, "Flight attendants, prepare for takeoff." Michael pulled his seat belt tighter and gripped the armrests as the jet engines roared. I leaned over, "Right about now, I usually say a prayer. I asked God to keep the plane safe and to send angels to protect us."

"Amen," he said, then added, "but I'm not afraid of dying. I'm not afraid because my mama's already in Heaven."

"I'm sorry." I said.

"Why are you sorry?" he asked, peering out the window as the plane lifted off.

"I'm sorry you don't have your mama here." My briefcase jostled at my feet, reminding me of all the work I needed to do.

"Look at those boats down there!" Michael said as the plane banked over the Pacific. "Where are they going?"

"Just going sailing, having a good time. And there's probably a fishing boat full of guys like you and me."

"Doing what?" he asked.

"Just fishing, maybe for bass or tuna. Does your dad ever take you fishing?"

"I don't have a dad," Michael sadly responded.

Only six years old and he didn't have a dad, and his Mom had died, and here he was flying halfway across the country all by himself. The least I could do was make sure he had a good flight. With my foot I pushed my briefcase under my seat.

"Do they have a bathroom here?" he asked, squirming a little.

"Sure," I said, "let me take you there." I showed him how to work the "Occupied" sign, and what buttons to push on the sink, then he closed the door.

When he emerged, he wore a wet shirt and a huge smile. "That sink shoots water everywhere!" The attendants smiled.

Michael got the VIP treatment from the crew during snack time. I took out my laptop and tried to work on a talk I had to give, but my mind kept going to Michael. I couldn't stop looking at the crumpled grocery bag on the floor by his seat. He'd told me that everything he owned was in that bag. Poor boy.

While Michael was getting a tour of the cockpit the flight attendant told me his grandmother would pick him up in Chicago. In the seat pocket a large manila envelope held all the paperwork regarding his custody. He came back explaining, "I got wings! I got cards! I got more peanuts. I saw the pilot and he said I could come back anytime!" For a while he stared at the manila envelope.

"What are you thinking?" I asked Michael. He didn't answer.

He buried his face in his hands and started sobbing. It had been years since I'd heard a little one cry like that. My children were grown—still I don't think they'd ever cried so hard. I rubbed his back and wondered where the flight attendant was. "What's the matter, buddy?" I asked.

All I got were muffled words "I don't know my grandma. Mama didn't want her to come visit and see her sick. What if Grandma doesn't want me? Where will I go?"

"Michael, do you remember the Christmas story? Mary and Joseph and the baby Jesus? Remember how they came to Bethlehem just before Jesus was born? It was late and cold, and they didn't have anywhere to stay, no family, no hotels, not even hospitals where babies could be born. Well, God was watching out for them. He found them a place to stay; a stable with animals."

"Wait, wait," Michael tugged on my sleeve. "I know Jesus. I remember now." Then he closed his eyes, lifted his head and began to sing. His voice rang out with a strength that rocked his tiny frame. "Jeeesus looooves me thiiiiiis I knowwwwwww. For the Biiiiiible tells meeeee sooooo...

Passengers turned or stood up to see the little boy who made the large sound. Michael didn't notice his audience. With his eyes shut tight and voice lifted high, he was in a good place.

"You've got a great voice," I told him when he was done. "I've never heard anyone sing like that."

"Mama said God gave me good pipes just like my grandma's," he said. "My grandma loves to sing in her church choir."

"Well, I'll bet you can sing there, too. The two of you will be running that choir."

The seat belt sign came on as we approached O'Hare. The flight attendant came by and said we just have a few minutes now, but she told Michael it's important that he put on his seat belt. People started stirring in their seats, like children before the final school bell. By the time the seat belt sign went off, passengers were rushing down the aisle. Michael and I stayed seated. "Are you gonna go with me?" he asked.

"I wouldn't miss it for the world, buddy!" I assured him.

Clutching his bag and the manila envelope in one hand, he grabbed my hand with the other. The two of us followed the flight attendant down the jet way. All the noises of the airport seemed to fill the corridor. Michael stopped, flipping his hand from mine, he dropped to his knees. His mouth quivered. His eyes brimmed with tears.

"What's wrong Michael? I'll carry you if you want."

He opened his mouth and moved his lips, but it was as if his words were stuck in his throat. When I knelt next to him, he grabbed my neck. I felt his warm, wet face as he whispered in my ear, "I want my mama!"

I tried to stand, but Michael squeezed my neck even harder. Then I heard a rattle of footsteps on the corridor's metal floor. "Is that you, baby?" I couldn't see the woman behind me, but I heard the warmth in her voice.

"Oh baby," she cried. "Come here. Grandma loves you so much. I need a hug, baby. Let go of that nice man."

She knelt beside Michael and me. Michael's grandma stroked his arm. I smelled a hint of orange blossoms. "You've got folks waiting for you out there, Michael. Do you know that you've got aunts and uncles and cousins?"

She patted his skinny shoulders and started humming. Then she lifted her head and sang. I wondered if the flight attendant told her what to sing, or maybe she just knew what was right. Her strong, clear voice filled the passageway, "Jesus loves me, this I know..."

Michael's gasps quieted. Still holding him, I rose, nodded hello to his grandma and watched her pick up the grocery bag. Just before we got to the doorway to the terminal, Michael loosened his grip around my neck and reached for his grandma.

As soon as she walked across the threshold with him, cheers erupted. From the size of the crowd, I figured family, friends, pastors, elders, deacons, choir members, and most of the neighbors had come to meet Michael. A tall man tugged on Michael's ear and pulled off the red sign around his neck. It no longer applied.

As I made my way to the gate for my connecting flight, I barely noticed the weight of my overstuffed briefcase and laptop. I started to wonder who would be in the seat next to mine this time...and I smiled.

—Jerry Seiden

Money Is A Tool

There is nothing wrong with money. The love and desire for more and more of it however has caused many to become despondent and enemies of their own selves.

We shake our heads at times as we observe folks spending it faster than they get it. We see people charging up credit cards to exorbitant amounts. There are countless seminars and classes on how to get rich. Too many times we lose our focus that money is simply a tool.

The tragic story is given of a seventy-one year old Bertha Adams who died in 1976, according to the coroner's report, of malnutrition. Her body had wasted away. When investigators went to her home they found a pigpen. The biggest mess you can imagine. The pitiful woman had begged food from neighbors and gotten what clothes she had from the Salvation Army. Amid the clutter there were found two keys for safe deposit boxes at two different banks. Investigators found a net worth of well over a million dollars. What was the focus of her life?

While that story is tragic and perhaps extreme, it is a scene that is repeated to a lesser degree over and over and over. People spend their money for things they don't need and then don't have money to pay for things they do need. I see people spending precious grocery money for gambling in hopes of hitting the Jackpot. I see people who take advantage of others by not paying their bills while buying personal luxuries. I see still others who charge things to their credit cards with no hope of ever being able to pay. And then, there are those who like the preceding story are misers who hoard up when they could be paying for some better health care and better living conditions or even reaching out to those in need.

All of these are tragic. Each scenario demonstrates a focus that has been skewed to think that happiness is found in money and things. It doesn't take us long to change mechanics if he never uses his tools or if he doesn't use them properly. In fact, if all he ever does is polish them they will do him absolutely no good. So it is with money. Properly used it is a tool to exchange goods and to provide for our basic needs in life. It is a necessary part of our lives that we must keep under control so that it doesn't control us. I like the terms outlined on a sign posted in a store window, "Use our new easy credit plan—100% down, nothing to pay each month." Perhaps that would help to answer some of our financial woes and help keep our spending in check. Is your money a tool or a taskmaster?

—M. Gingrich

My Home—A Place I Love

I look outside and all I see,
Is my own special home.
A peaceful place, a place to be,
That no one else calls their own.

My home is filled with laughter,
Each and every day,
And one day I asked my father,
"What makes my home this way?"

He looked at me and smiled and said,
"Our joy it comes from God,
When we praise and honor and worship him,
He fills our home with his love."

I smiled knowingly,
Because many people say,
"Your home is so peaceful here,
Like heaven on earth in a way."

Then I whisper a silent prayer to God,
And he always hears me say,
"Thank you God, praise to your name,
For making my home this way."

—Suzanne Harnish
Age 15

One Dropped Out

Dr. Pierce Harris, pastor of the First Methodist Church, Atlanta, Georgia, was invited to preach in a prison camp. The men in their prison garb were seated on the ground or standing in the shade of the trees, when one of them mounted the back of a truck to introduce the preacher.

He said, "Several years ago two boys lived in the same community in North Georgia, attended the same school, played with the same bunch of fellows, and went to the same Sunday school. One of them dropped out of s because he felt he had outgrown it, and that it was 'sissy stuff.' The other boy kept on going because he felt that it really meant something in his life.

"The boy who dropped out is the one who is making this introduction today. The boy who kept going to Sunday school is the famous preacher who will preach to us this morning."

Parent's Dictionary of Meanings

DUMB WAITER: one who asks if the children would care to order dessert.

FEEDBACK: the inevitable result when the baby doesn't appreciate the strained carrots.

FULL NAME: what you call your child when you want his attention.

GRANDPARENTS: the people who think your children are wonderful even though they're sure you're not raising them right.

INDEPENDENT: how we want our children to be as long as they do everything we say.

OW: the first word spoken by children with older siblings

PUDDLE: a small body of water that draws other small bodies wearing dry shoes into it.

SHOW OFF: a child who is more talented than yours.

STERILIZE: what you do to your first baby's pacifier by boiling it, and to your last baby's pacifier by blowing on it and wiping it with saliva.

VERBAL: able to whine in words

WHO DUNIT: none of the children that live in your house.

Sand & Stone

Two friends were walking through the desert. During some point of the journey they had an argument, and one friend slapped the other one in the face.

The one who got slapped was hurt, but without saying anything, wrote in the sand: TODAY MY BEST FRIEND SLAPPED ME IN THE FACE.

They kept on walking until they found an oasis, where they decided to take a bath. The one who had been slapped got stuck in the mire and started drowning, but the friend saved him.

After he recovered from the near drowning, he wrote on a stone: TODAY MY BEST FRIEND SAVED MY LIFE.

The friend who had slapped his best friend asked him, "After I hurt you, you wrote in the sand and now, you write on a stone, why?"

The other friend replied, "When someone hurts us we should write it down in the sand where winds of forgiveness can erase it away. But, when someone does something good for us, we should engrave it in stone where no wind can ever erase it."

Learn to write your hurts in the sand and to carve your benefits in stone.

They say it takes a minute to find a special person, an hour to appreciate them, a day to love them, but then an entire life to forget them.

Saturdays

The older I get, the more I enjoy Saturday mornings. Perhaps it's the quiet solitude that comes with being the first to rise, or maybe it's the unbounded joy of not having to be at work. Either way, the first few hours of a Saturday morning are most enjoyable.

A few weeks ago, I was shuffling toward the garage with a steaming cup of coffee in one hand and the morning paper in the other. What began as a typical Saturday morning turned into one of those lessons that life seems to hand you from time to time.

Let me tell you about it: I turned the dial up into the phone portion of the band on my ham radio in order to listen to a Saturday morning swap net. Along the way, I came across an older sounding chap, with a tremendous signal and a golden voice. You know the kind; he sounded like he should be in the broadcasting business. He was telling whomever he was talking with something about "A thousand marbles." I was intrigued and stopped to listen to what he had to say…

"Well, Tom, it sure sounds like you're busy with your job. I'm sure they pay you well but it's a shame you have to be away from home and your family so much. Hard to believe a young fellow should have to work sixty or seventy hours a week to make ends meet. It's too bad you missed your daughter's music recital," he continued. "Let me tell you something that has helped me keep my own priorities."

And that's when he began to explain his theory of a thousand marbles. "You see, I sat down one day and did a little arithmetic. The average person lives about seventy-five years. I know, some live more and some live less, but on average, folks live about seventy-five years. Now then, I multiplied 75 times 52 and I came up with 3900, which is the number of Saturdays that the average person has in their entire lifetime.

"Now, stick with me, Tom, I'm getting to the important part. It took me until I was fifty-five years old to think about all this in any detail," he went on, "and by that time I had lived through over twenty-eight hundred

Saturdays. I got to thinking that if I lived to be seventy-five, I only had about a thousand of them left to enjoy.

"So I went to a toy store and bought every single marble they had. I ended up having to visit three toy stores to round up 1000 marbles. I took them home and put them inside a large, clear plastic container right here in the shack next to my gear.

"Every Saturday since then, I have taken one marble out and thrown it away. I found that by watching the marbles diminish, I focused more on the really important things in life. There is nothing like watching your time here on this earth run out to help get your priorities straight.

"Now let me tell you one last thing before I sign-off with you and take my lovely wife out for breakfast. I took the very last marble out of the container. I figure that if I make it until next Saturday then I have been given a little extra time. And the one thing we can all use is a little more time. It was nice to meet you, Tom, I hope you spend more time with your family, and I hope to meet you again here on the band. This is a 75-year-old man, K9NZQ, clear and going QRT, good morning!"

You could have heard a pin drop on the band when this fellow signed off. I guess he gave us all a lot to think about. I had planned to work on the antenna that morning, and then I was going to meet up with a few hams to work on the next club newsletter.

Instead, I went upstairs and woke my wife up with a kiss. "C'mon honey, I'm taking you and the children to breakfast"

"What brought this on?" She asked with a smile.

"Oh, nothing special, it's just been a long time since we spent a Saturday together with the children. And hey, can we stop at a toy store while we're out? I need to buy some marbles."

Seven Wonders

A group of students were asked to list what they thought were the seven wonders of the world. The following list received the most votes.

1. Egypt's Great Pyramids
2. Taj Mahal
3. Grand Canyon
4. Panama Canal
5. Empire State Building
6. St. Peter's Basilica
7. China's Great Wall

While gathering the votes the teacher noted one girl hadn't turned in her paper yet so she asked the girl if she was having trouble with her list. The girl replied, "Yes, because there are so many."

"Well, tell us what you have and maybe we can help."

The girl hesitated, then read,

"I think the seven wonders of the world are:

1. To see
2. To hear
3. To touch
4. To taste
5. To feel
6. To laugh
7. And to love."

The room was so quiet you could have heard a pin drop.

Show Appreciation!

If you want results, show appreciation! Every person likes to feel wanted and needed. They like to hear that expressed to them verbally. It offers them a sense of self worth, a sense of satisfaction, and provides needed encouragement to try even harder. People naturally like to feel important. Recognizing their achievements gives a person emotional and social stability. Pause for a moment and evaluate yourself personally. Reflect on specific instances in your own life. Were there times when you thought you had accomplished something important or substantial but no one seemed to notice? Were there times you gave somebody a gift or lent them a hand but there was no expression of appreciation. Perhaps you even felt snubbed or cheated through it all. Small expressions of sincere appreciation go a long way in building and solidifying relationships. Unfortunately, we often have the consideration but then fail to make the application. We think about sending a thank you note but never get it done.

Why is that? One reason is because we become to self focused. We tend to zero in on things that benefit us. Common repetitive practices tend to be taken for granted. Because these things are readily at our disposal they tend to lose their importance and value. The more value something has the more likely we will treat it with respect. In that aspect then it is important to kept our value system up to date.

To whom then should we show appreciation? Let me suggest that if we started off showing more appreciation to our spouse there would likely be a decline in the divorce rate. Do our children feel affection or are they made to feel unwanted. Do we show respect for civil authority? Do we appreciate all they do on our behalf? Have you thanked your employer for giving you a place of employment? Have you thanked mom and dad for all they taught you? Have you thanked your local grocer, the banker, the fuel delivery man, the school teacher, the pharmacist, the cashier, the mechanic, etc. Any person who renders a service to you or others is worthy of appreciation. That service may be tangible, like opening a door, or intangible, like being a positive influence. Both are worthy of appreciation.

When is the right time? There is never a wrong time except never. It is always the right time. I have on occasion rebuked myself for not expressing appreciation. Time and location made it no longer possible, but as I reflected on the missed opportunity I was disappointed in myself for being so inconsiderate. I can't recall ever having felt that displeasure with myself for having shown excess appreciation. Our tendency is to err on the side of missing opportunities rather than being too lavish with our praise.

Where is the right place? Consideration must be given as to how we appropriate our praise in relation to the place we are at the given moment. While a slap on the back may be okay in some situations it could be totally inappropriate in others. Consideration should be taken not to embarrass the individual and should be a determining factor in choosing our method of appreciation as well. Should it be done publicly or privately? Ultimately there is no place where some appropriate recognition is out of place as long as it is carried out discreetly.

What are some ways we can express our appreciation. The greater the sacrifice the more sincere your appreciation will appear to the recipient. Actions speak louder than words. Words can be cheap. They are easily rendered. But to pick up the phone and call the florist, order a bouquet, and give them your credit card shows genuine appreciation. You made a conscious effort to recognize that individual. Obviously, the expression of appreciation should be relative to the situation. You don't send a $100.00 gift certificate just because someone took your cart back at the grocery store. But a hearty "Thank You" is most certainly in order.

The question may come, won't too much praise make us proud and boastful. To answer that I would pose another question? What is the result of too little appreciation? As with many things in life there needs to be a healthy balance. There is a ditch on both sides of the road. It is in the best interest of all parties to stay out of the ditch. Our appreciation must come from the heart as an expression of our gratitude. Appreciation from the heart is not likely to become fodder for bragging rights but will rather be received in a spirit of humility.

Sincere praise from the heart will not go unrewarded. It will bless others, improve your health, and bring joy to your life.

—M. Gingrich

Something To Think About

- What if, God decided to stop leading us tomorrow because we didn't follow Him today?
- What if, God couldn't take the time to bless us today because we couldn't take the time to thank Him yesterday?
- What if, we never saw another flower bloom because we grumbled when God sent the rain?
- What if, God didn't walk with us today because we failed to recognize it as His day?
- What if, God took away the Bible tomorrow because we would not read it today?
- What if, God took away His message because we failed to listen to the messenger?
- What if, the door of the church was closed because we did not open the door of our heart?
- What if, God stopped loving and caring for us because we failed to love and care for others?
- What if, God would not hear us today because we would not listen to Him?
- What if, God answered our prayers the way we answer His call to service?
- What if, God met our needs the way we give Him our lives???

The Art Of Self-Defense

"Do you think it wrong for me to learn the art of self-defense?" asked a young man of his pastor.

"Certainly not," answered the minister. "I learned it in youth myself, and I have found it of great value during my life."

"Indeed, sir! Did you learn the Old English system or Sullivan's system?"

"Neither. I learned Solomon's system."

"Solomon's system?"

"Yes. You will find it laid down in the first verse of the 15th chapter of Proverbs, 'A soft answer turneth away wrath.' It is the best system of self-defense I know."

The Carpenter And The Little End Table

Once there was a young carpenter. His father was a master craftsman and had taught him how to make the finest furniture in the country.

The young carpenter decided to create a small end table for his room. He worked for several days making every little detail just perfect. It was absolutely the most beautiful table he had ever seen and he loved it with all his heart.

And then one day while the young carpenter was away, a wealthy banker came to visit. When he saw the table he just had to have it.

"It is the most beautiful table I've ever seen," said the banker. "What do you want for it? I'll pay anything!"

The salesman at first was reluctant, but when he saw the banker counting out money, he quickly forgot how much the young carpenter loved the table.

"It is worth at least $500, probably more," said the salesman. "I'll give you twice that," said the banker. "Never in my life have I seen such perfection." The banker carefully carried the table out to his carriage and drove off into the dark night.

The next day the young carpenter returned to the workshop. "Father, where is my table?" asked the young carpenter. The two searched everywhere, but the table was gone. Soon, the salesman arrived. "Do you know what happened to my son's table?" asked the father. A big smile came over the salesman's face, "I sold it for $1,000!" He saw the disappointment in his face, "Did I not do well?"

"You did," said the father. "Do you know who purchased the table? I wish to purchase it back." The salesman thought for a moment. I don't know his name. He said he was a banker, but I have never seen him around here."

"Very good," said the father. "Go on and watch the store. I'll take care of everything." The father walked to the back where his son was waiting. He put his arm around his son. "Don't worry. We will find your table," said the father. "Get focused on your work."

Many years passed and the father never found the table. After his father's death, the young carpenter took over the family business and it became a major enterprise, employing hundreds of craftsmen. He became very wealthy and known throughout the world for his fine work and generosity.

But no matter what success he had, he could never forget his little end table.

After a long and happy life, the now old carpenter was enjoying his final years. His son now ran the business. The old carpenter enjoyed the simple things in life like spending time with his grandson.

One day the two were visiting a flea market checking out the merchandise. Off in the corner of a booth, covered in dust, the old carpenter saw something familiar.

"It just can't be," said the old carpenter as he carefully wiped the cobwebs and dust away.

Although missing a leg and neglected for years, the old carpenter instantly recognized his little end table.

"What is it, Grandpa?" asked his grandson.

"This is the best piece I ever made," said the old carpenter.

"That old thing?" asked his grandson.

The old carpenter turned to his grandson with a smile on his face and tears in his eyes. "I love this table dearly and have looked for it for many years. It is perfect in my eyes."

The grandson was confused. All he saw was a broken piece of junk. "Come back to my workshop and let me show you what love can do," said the old carpenter.

For several days the old carpenter carefully worked on his end table. He removed all the scars and blemishes and fixed all the broken parts. With his grandson at his side, the two perfectly restored the end table.

"It's beautiful grandpa!"

The old carpenter put his arm around his grandson and the two admired their work.

"Let's take it inside," said the old carpenter.

Several days later, the old carpenter had a big banquet at his house. All the guests gathered around the little end table and admired its beauty. The old carpenter's grandson explained how they had taken a broken piece of junk and made this perfect little table.

"It's so beautiful. I must have it!" said one of the guests.

"I'll pay whatever price you require," said another.

Soon the guests were bidding against each other over the little end table.

The old carpenter raised his hand and a hush fell on the room.

"Friends, thank you for your kind offers and admiration. But this table is not for sale. It was lost and neglected for many years and I never stopped searching for it. Now that it is back where it belongs, I will never lose it again. I love this little end table and it will stay with me forever."

And so the little end table stayed with the old carpenter. Each time someone inquired about it, the old carpenter would happily recount the story of the table that was lost, but later found. It was broken, but now it was again and forever perfect.

The Empty Egg

Jeremy was born with a twisted body and a slow mind. At the age of 12 he was still in second grade, seemingly unable to learn. His teacher, Doris Miller, often became exasperated with him. He would squirm in his seat, drool, and make grunting noises. At other times, he spoke clearly and distinctly, as if a spot of light had penetrated the darkness of his brain. Most of the time, however, Jeremy just irritated his teacher.

One day she called his parents and asked them to come in for a consultation. As the Forrester's entered the empty classroom, Doris said to them, "Jeremy really belongs in a special school. It isn't fair to him to be with younger children who don't have learning problems. Why, there is a five year gap between his age and that of the other students."

Mrs. Forrester cried softly into a tissue, while her husband spoke.

"Miss Miller," he said, "there is no school of that kind nearby. It would be a terrible shock for Jeremy if we had to take him out of this school. We know he really likes it here."

Doris sat for a long time after they had left, staring at the snow outside the window. Its coldness seemed to seep into her soul. She wanted to sympathize with the Forresters. After all, their only child had a terminal illness. But it wasn't fair to keep him in her class. She had eighteen other youngsters to teach, and Jeremy was a distraction. Furthermore, he would never learn to read and write. Why waste any more time trying?

As she pondered the situation, guilt washed over her. Here I am complaining when my problems are nothing compared to that poor family, she thought. Lord, please help me to be more patient with Jeremy. From that day on, she tried hard to ignore Jeremy's noises and his blank stares.

Then one day, he limped to her desk, dragging his bad leg behind him. "I love you, Miss Miller," he exclaimed, loud enough for the whole class to hear. The other students snickered, and Doris' face turned red. She stammered, "Wh-why that's very nice, Jeremy. N-now please take your seat."

Spring came, and the children talked excitedly about the coming of Easter. Doris told them the story of Jesus, and then to emphasize the idea of new life springing forth, she gave each of the children a large plastic egg. "Now," she said to them, "I want you to take this home and bring it back tomorrow with something inside that shows new life. Do you understand?"

"Yes, Miss Miller," the children responded enthusiastically—all except for Jeremy. He listened intently; his eyes never left her face. He did not even make his usual noises. Had he understood what she had said about Jesus' death and resurrection? Did he understand the assignment? Perhaps she should call his parents and explain the project to them.

That evening, Doris' kitchen sink stopped up. She called the landlord and waited an hour for him to come by and unclog it. After that, she still had to shop for groceries, iron a blouse, and prepare a vocabulary test for the next day. She completely forgot about phoning Jeremy's parents.

The next morning, nineteen children came to school, laughing and talking as they placed their eggs in the large wicker basket on Miss Miller's desk. After they completed their math lesson, it was time to open the eggs. In the first egg, Doris found a flower. "Oh yes, a flower is certainly a sign of new life," she said. "When plants peek through the ground, we know that spring is here." A small girl in the first row waved her arm. "That's my egg, Miss Miller," she called out. The next egg contained a plastic butterfly, which looked very real. Doris held it up. "We all know that a caterpillar changes and grows into a beautiful butterfly. Yes, that's new life, too." Little Judy smiled proudly and said, "Miss Miller, that one is mine." Next, Doris found a rock with moss on it. She explained that moss, too, showed life. Billy spoke up from the back of the classroom, "My daddy helped me," he beamed. Then Doris opened the fourth egg. She gasped. The egg was empty. Surely it must be Jeremy's she thought, and of course, he did not understand her instructions. If only she had not forgotten to phone his parents.

Because she did not want to embarrass him, she quietly set the egg aside and reached for another. Suddenly, Jeremy spoke up, "Miss Miller, aren't you going to talk about my egg?" Flustered, Doris replied, "But Jeremy, your egg is empty." He looked into her eyes and said softly, "Yes, but Jesus' tomb was empty, too." Time stopped.

When she could speak again, Doris asked him, "Do you know why the tomb was empty?"

"Oh, yes," Jeremy said, "Jesus was killed and put in there. Then His Father raised Him up." The recess bell rang. While the children excitedly ran out to the school yard, Doris cried. The cold inside her melted completely away.

Three months later Jeremy died. Those who paid their respects at the mortuary were surprised to see nineteen eggs on top of his casket, all of them empty.

The Gift Of Encouragment

One of the most powerful things one person can share with another is encouragement. Encouragement can stop a suicide, a divorce, and countless other tragedies. A word of encouragement can heal someone who is broken and wounded. It can give someone the courage to keep trying.

Our world is full of negative, bitter, uncaring people who can't say anything good about anyone or anything. The people of God should be a radiant contrast to the people of the world. We should bubble over with the joy of the Holy Spirit. We should find it easy to be positive and uplifting. Are you an encouragement to those around you? Don't let someone die from neglect and lack of encouragement. Share your Christian joy by encouraging those around you on a regular basis!

The Most Creative Job In The World

It involves...
Taste,
Fashion,
Decorating,
Recreation,
Education,
Transportation,
Psychology,
Romance,
Cuisine,
Designing,
Literature,
Medicine,
Handicraft,
Art,
Horticulture,
Economics,
Government,
Community relations,
Pediatric,
Geriatrics,
Entertainment,
Maintenance,
Purchasing,
Direct mail,
Law,
Accounting,
Religion,
Energy,
And Management.

Anyone who can handle all these things has to be somebody special. Who is that person? She's a homemaker.

The Old Man And The Dog

"Watch out! You nearly broadsided that car!" My father yelled at me. "Can't you do anything right?" Those words hurt worse than blows. I turned my head toward the elderly man in the seat beside me, daring me to challenge him. A lump rose in my throat as I averted his eyes. I wasn't prepared for another battle.

"I saw the car, dad. Please don't yell at me when I'm driving." My voice was measured and steady, sounding far calmer than I really felt.

Dad glared at me, then turned away and settled back. At home I left dad in the family room and went outside to collect my thoughts. Dark, heavy clouds hung in the air with a promise of rain. The rumble of distant thunder seemed to echo my inner turmoil.

What could I do about him?

Dad had been a lumberjack in Washington and Oregon. He had enjoyed being outdoors and had reveled in pitting his strength against the forces of nature. He had entered grueling lumberjlack competitions, and had placed often. The shelves in his house were filled with trophies that attested to his prowess.

The years marched on relentlessly. The first time he couldn't lift a heavy log, he joked about it; but later that same day I saw him outside alone, straining to lift it. He became irritable whenever anyone teased him about his advancing age, or when he couldn't do something he had done as a younger man.

Four days after his sixty-seventh birthday, he had a heart attack. An ambulance sped him to the hospital while a paramedic administered CPR to keep blood and oxygen flowing. At the hospital, dad was rushed into an operating room. He was fortunate; he survived.

But something inside dad died. His zest for life was gone. He obstinately refused to follow doctor's orders. Suggestions and offers of help were turned aside with sarcasm and insults. The number of visitors thinned, then finally stopped altogether. Dad was left alone.

My husband, Dick, and I asked dad to come live with us on our small farm. We hoped the fresh air and rustic atmosphere would help him adjust. Within a week after he moved in, I regretted the invitation. It seemed nothing was satisfactory. He criticized everything I did. I became frustrated and moody.

Soon I was taking my pent-up anger out on Dick. We began to bicker and argue. Alarmed, Dick sought out our pastor and explained the situation. The clergyman set up weekly counseling appointments for us. At the close of each session he prayed, asking God to soothe dad's troubled mind. But the months wore on and God was silent. Something had to be done and it was up to me to do it.

The next day I sat down with the phone book and methodically called each of the mental health clinics listed in the yellow pages. I explained my problem to each of the sympathetic voices that answered. In vain. Just when I was giving up hope, one of the voices suddenly exclaimed, "I just read something that might help you! Let me go get the article." I listened as she read. The article described a remarkable study done at a nursing home. All of the patients were under treatment for chronic depression. Yet their attitudes had improved dramatically when they were given responsibility for a dog.

I drove to the animal shelter that afternoon. After I filled out a questionnaire, an officer led me to the kennels. The odor of disinfectant stung my nostrils as I moved down the row of pens. Each contained five to seven dogs. Long-haired dogs, curly-haired dogs, black dogs, spotted dogs all jumped up, trying to reach me. I studied each one but rejected one after the other for various reasons; too big, too small, too much hair. As I neared the last pen a dog in the shadows of the far corner struggled to his feet, walked to the front of the run and sat down. It was a pointer, one of the dog world's aristocrats. But this was a caricature of the breed. Years had etched his face and muzzle with shades of gray. His hipbones jutted out in lopsided triangles. But it was his eyes that caught and held my attention. Calm and clear, they beheld me unwaveringly.

I pointed to the dog. "Can you tell me about him?" The officer looked, then shook his head in puzzlement.

"He's a funny one. Appeared out of nowhere and sat in front of the gate. We brought him in, figuring someone would be right down to claim him. That was two weeks ago and we've heard nothing. His time is up tomorrow." He gestured helplessly.

As the words sank in I turned to the man in horror. "You mean you're going to kill him?"

"Ma'am," he said gently, "That's our policy. We don't have room for every unclaimed dog."

I looked at the pointer again. The calm brown eyes awaited my decision. "I'll take him," I said.

I drove home with the dog on the front seat beside me. When I reached the house I honked the horn twice. I was helping my prize out of the car when dad shuffled onto the front porch.

"Ta-da! Look what I got for you, dad!" I said excitedly.

Dad looked, then wrinkled his face in disgust. "If I had wanted a dog I would have gotten one. And I would have picked out a better specimen than that bag of bones. Keep it! I don't want it!" Dad waved his arm scornfully and turned back toward the house.

Anger rose inside me. It squeezed together my throat muscles and pounded into my temples.

"You'd better get used to him, Dad. He's staying!" Dad ignored me. "Did you hear me, Dad?" I screamed. At those words dad whirled angrily, his hands clenched at his sides, his eyes narrowed and blazing.

We stood glaring at each other like duelists, when suddenly the pointer pulled free from my grasp. He wobbled toward my dad and sat down in front of him. Then slowly, carefully, he raised his paw.

Dad's lower jaw trembled as he stared at the uplifted paw. Confusion replaced the anger in his eyes. The pointer waited patiently. Then dad was on his knees hugging the animal.

It was the beginning of a warm and intimate friendship. Dad named the pointer Cheyenne. Together he and Cheyenne explored the community. They spent long hours walking down dusty lanes. They spent reflective moments on the banks of streams, angling for tasty trout. They even started to attend Sunday services together, dad sitting in a pew and Cheyenne lying quietly at his feet.

Dad and Cheyenne were inseparable throughout the next three years. Dad's bitterness faded, and he and Cheyenne made many friends. Then late one night I was startled to feel Cheyenne's cold nose burrowing through our bed covers. He had never before come into our bedroom at night.

I woke Dick, put on my robe and ran into my father's room. Dad lay in his bed, his face serene. But his spirit had left quietly sometime during the night.

Two days later my shock and grief deepened when I discovered Cheyenne lying dead beside dad's bed. I wrapped his still form in the rag rug he had slept on. As Dick and I buried him near a favorite fishing hole, I silently thanked the dog for the help he had given me in restoring dad's peace of mind.

The morning of dad's funeral dawned overcast and dreary. This day looks like the way I feel, I thought, as I walked down the aisle to the pews reserved for family. I was surprised to see the many friends dad and Cheyenne had made filling the church. The pastor began his eulogy. It was a tribute to both dad and the dog who had changed his life. And then the pastor turned to Hebrews 13:2. "Be not forgetful to entertain strangers."

"I've often thanked God for sending that angel," he said.

For me, the past dropped into place, completing a puzzle that I had not seen before: the sympathetic voice that had just read the right article…

Cheyenne's unexpected appearance at the animal shelter…His calm acceptance and complete devotion to my father.. And the proximity of their deaths. And suddenly I understood. I knew that God had answered my prayers after all.

The Poem

I knelt to pray but not for long,
I had too much to do.
I had to hurry and get to work
For bills would soon be due.

So I knelt and said a hurried prayer,
And jumped up off my knees.
My Christian duty was now done
My soul could rest at ease.

All day long I had no time
To spread a word of cheer
No time to speak of Christ to friends,
They'd laugh at me I'd fear.

No time, no time, too much to do,
That was my constant cry,
No time to give to souls in need
But at last the time, the time to die.

I went before the Lord, I came,
I stood with downcast eyes.
For in his hands God held a book;
It was the Book of Life.

God looked into his book and said
"Your name I cannot find;
I once was going to write it down…
But never found the time."

The Quiet Sermon

A member of a certain church, who previously had been attending services regularly, stopped going. After a few weeks, the pastor decided to visit him.

It was a chilly evening. The pastor found the man at home alone, sitting before a blazing fire. Guessing the reason for his pastor's visit, the man welcomed him, led him to a comfortable chair near the fireplace, and waited.

The pastor made himself at home but said nothing. In the grave silence, he contemplated the dance of the flames around the burning logs. After some minutes, the pastor took the fire tongs, carefully picked up a brightly burning ember and placed it to one side of the hearth all alone. Then he sat back in his chair, still silent. The host watched all this in quiet contemplation. As the one lone ember's flame flickered and diminished, there was a momentary glow and then its fire was no more. Soon it was cold and dead.

Not a word had been spoken since the initial greeting. The pastor glanced at his watch and realized it was time to leave. He slowly stood up, picked up the cold, dead ember, and placed it back in the middle of the fire. Immediately, it began to glow, once more with the light and warmth of the burning coals around it.

As the pastor reached the door to leave, his host said with a tear running down his cheek, "Thank you so much for your visit and especially for the fiery sermon. I shall be back in church next Sunday."

We live in a world today, which tries to say too much with too little. Consequently, few listen. Sometimes the best sermons are the ones left unspoken.

If you don't stand for something, you'll fall for anything!

The Room

Seventeen-year-old Darren Clark had only a short time to write something. It was his turn to lead the discussion so he sat down and wrote the "The Room." He showed the essay, titled "The Room" to his mother, Kathy, before he headed out the door.

"I wowed 'em." he later told his father, Brian. It's the best thing I ever wrote." It also was the last he ever wrote. Darren's parents had forgotten about the essay when a cousin found it while cleaning out the teenager's locker.

Darren had been dead only hours, but his parents desperately wanted every piece of his life near them—the crepe paper that had adorned his locker during his senior football season, notes from classmates and teachers, his homework.

Only two months before, he had handwritten the essay about encountering Jesus in a file room full of cards detailing every moment of the teen's life.

But it was only after Darren's death that Kathy and Brain Clark realized that their son had described his view of heaven. "It makes such an impact that people want to share it. You feel like you are there," Mr. Clark said.

Darren died the day before his 18th birthday. He was driving home from a friend's house when his car went off the road and struck a utility pole. He emerged from the wreck unharmed but stepped on a downed power line and was electrocuted.

"Darren seemed to excel at everything he did. He was an honor student. He told his parents he loved them a hundred times a day," Mrs. Clark said.

He was a star wide receiver on the football team and had earned a scholarship because of his athletic and academic abilities.

He took it upon himself to learn how to help a fellow student who used a wheelchair at school.

During one homecoming ceremony, Darren walked on his tiptoes so that the girl he was escorting wouldn't be embarrassed about being taller than him. He adored his younger brother, Tim. He often escorted his grandmother, Grace Kearn, to church.

"I always called him the 'deep thinker,'" Grace said of her eldest grandson.

The Clark's framed a copy of Darren's essay and hung it among the family portraits in the living room. "I think God used him to make a point. I think we were meant to find it and make something out of it," Mrs. Clark said, of the essay.

She and her husband want to share their son's vision of life after death. "I'm happy for Darren. I know he's in heaven. I know I'll see him again someday." Mrs. Clark said. "It just hurts so bad right now."

Essay—The Room

In that place between wakefulness and dreams, I found myself in the room. There were no distinguishing features except for the one wall covered with small index card files. They were like the ones in libraries that list titles by author or subject in alphabetical order. But these files, which stretched from floor to ceiling and seemingly endless in either direction, had very different headings.

As I drew near the wall of files, the first to catch my attention was one that read "Girls I have liked." I opened it and began flipping through the cards. I quickly shut it, shocked to realize that I recognized the names written on each one. And then without being told, I knew exactly where I was. This lifeless room with its small files was a crude catalog system for my life. Here were written the actions of my every moment, big and small, in a detail my memory couldn't match.

A sense of wonder and curiosity, coupled with horror, stirred within me as I began randomly opening files and exploring their content. Some brought joy and sweet memories; others a sense of shame and regret so intense that I would look over my shoulder to see if anyone was watching.

A file named "Friends" was next to one marked "Friends I have betrayed". The titles ranged from the mundane to the outright weird. "Books I have read," "Lies I have told," "Comfort I have given," "Jokes I have laughed at."

Some were almost hilarious in their exactness: "Things I've yelled at my brothers." Others I couldn't laugh at: "Things I have done in anger," "Things I have muttered under my breath at my parents." I never ceased to be surprised by the contents.

Often there were many more cards than I expected. Sometimes fewer than I hoped. I was overwhelmed by the sheer volume of the life I had lived.

Could it be possible that I had the time in my years to write each of these thousands or even millions of cards? But each card confirmed this truth. Each was written in my own handwriting. Each signed with my signature.

When I pulled out the file marked "Songs I have listened to," I realized the files grew to contain their contents. The cards were packed tightly, and yet after two or three drawers, I hadn't found the end of the file. I shut it, shamed, by the quality of music and vast time I knew that file represented.

When I came to a file marked "Lustful thoughts," I felt a chill run through my body. I pulled the file out only an inch, not willing to test its size, and drew out a card. I shuddered at its detailed content. I felt sick to think that such a moment had been recorded.

An almost animal rage broke on me. One thought dominated my mind: "No one must ever see these cards! No one must ever see this room! I have to destroy them!"

In insane frenzy I yanked the file out. Its size didn't matter now. I had to empty it and burn the cards! But as I took it at one end and began pounding it on the floor, I could not dislodge a single card. I became desperate and pulled out a card, only to find it as strong as steel when I tried to tear it. Defeated and utterly helpless, I returned the file to its slot. Leaning my forehead against the wall, I let out a long, self-pitying sigh.

And then I saw it. The title bore "People I have shared the gospel with". The handle was brighter than those around it, newer, almost unused. I pulled on its handle and a small box of not more than three inches long fell into my hands. I could count the cards it contained on one hand. And then the tears came. I began to weep. Sobs so deep that they hurt. They started in my stomach and shook through me. I fell on my knees and cried. I cried out of shame, from the overwhelming shame of it all. The rows of file shelves swirled in my tear-filled eyes. No one must ever, ever know of this room. I must lock it up and hide the key.

But then as I pushed away the tears, I saw Him. No, please, not Him. Not here. Oh, anyone but Jesus. I watched helplessly as He began to open the files and read the cards. I couldn't bear to watch His response. And in the moments I could bring myself to look at His face, I saw a sorrow deeper than my own. He seemed to intuitively go to the worst boxes.

Why did He have to read every one? Finally He turned and looked at me from across the room. He looked at me with pity in His eyes. But this was a pity that didn't anger me.

I dropped my head, covered my face with my hands, and began to cry again. He walked over and put His arm around me. He could have said so many things. But He didn't say a word. He just cried with me.

Then He got up and walked back to the wall of files. Starting at one end of the room, He took out a file and, one by one, began to sign His name over mine on each card. "No!" I shouted rushing to Him. All I could find to say was "No, no," as I pulled the card from Him. His name shouldn't be on these cards. But there it was, written in red so rich, so dark, so alive. The name of Jesus covered mine. It was written with His blood. He gently took the card back. He smiled a sad smile and began to sign the cards.

I don't think I'll ever understand how He did it so quickly, but the next instant it seemed I heard Him close the last file and walk back to my side. He placed His hand on my shoulder and said, "It is finished."

I stood up and He led me out of the room. There was no lock on its door. There were still cards to be written.

—Darren Clark

The Smile

It costs nothing, but creates much. It enriches those who receive without making those who give poor. It happens in a flash and the memory sometimes lasts forever. None are so rich they can get along without it and none so poor but are much richer for a smile. It creates happiness and is the counter sign of friendship. Yet it cannot be bought, begged, borrowed, or stolen; for it is something that is no earthly good to anybody till it is given away. And if it ever happens that someone should be too tired to give you a smile, why not give them yours? For nobody needs a smile so much as those who have none left to give.

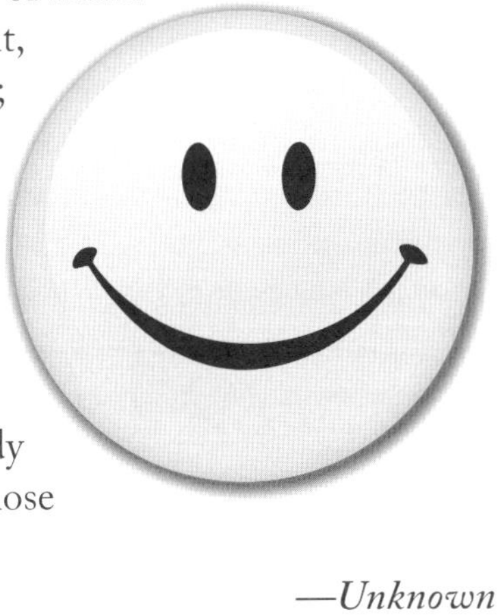

—*Unknown*

The Sneeze

They walked in tandem, each of the ninety-three students filing into the already crowded auditorium. With rich maroon gowns flowing and the traditional caps, they looked almost as grown up as they felt. Dads swallowed hard behind broad smiles, and moms freely brushed away tears. This class would not pray during the commencement…not by choice but because of a recent court ruling prohibiting it. The principal and several students were careful to stay within the guidelines allowed by the ruling. They gave inspirational and challenging speeches, but no one mentioned divine guidance and no one asked for blessings on the graduates or their families. The speeches were nice, but they were routine, until the final speech received a standing ovation. A solitary student walked proudly to the microphone. He stood still and silent for just a moment, and then he delivered his speech…an astounding SNEEZE! The rest of the students rose immediately to their feet, and in unison they said, "GOD BLESS YOU."

The audience exploded into applause. The graduating class found a unique way to invoke God's blessing on their future, with or without the court's approval.

The Wet Noodle Of Politics

In 1803, the American Congress granted to General Lafayette 11,520 acres of land in what was then called the Territory of New Orleans; but by some inadvertency, a portion of the same land was afterwards granted to the Corporation of New Orleans. Lafayette was advised to bring forward his claim and eminent lawyers assured him it was perfectly legal. Lafayette replied, "I cannot consent even to inquire into the validity of my title. It was gratuitously bestowed by congress, and it is for them to say what was given. I cannot for a moment think of entering into litigation." On this tract that Lafayette so gallantly relinquished was built the city of New Orleans.

It is with a bit of reluctance that I even mention the word politics as it may sound like I have a political agenda. My agenda is not politics but rather a call to restore character and integrity. Politics conjures up images of name calling, character bashing, and party wrangling. As always, we need to be careful not to put all politicians in the same basket just because of one or two bad apples. Politicians have their rightful place as government leaders. It is their responsibility to make the laws of the land. As a leader, it is their responsibility to set a good example for the people.

I have a high regard and a deep appreciation for our government. It is our responsibility to be law abiding citizens. It is our responsibility to "render unto Caesar the things that are Caesar's." It is important to honor those in leadership. The office they hold commands our respect. Each President's Day is set aside to honor the presidents of the United States. As one looks back on history the opinions would vary on who was a good president and who wasn't. Regardless of our opinion, the office they held demands our admiration. They have helped to set the course of history. May we ever be grateful for their contribution.

Over the years, politics has gained a reputation of being corrupt and arrogant. Political leaders are in a precarious position. They are elected into office by their constituents and so they are reluctant to make choices that would turn away votes. Therefore issues have a tendency to be affected by special interest groups who carry a lot of clout. These groups further reinforce their cause by offering special perks and "under the table" money if politicians will support their interests.

Someone described government like a gigantic bowl of wet noodles. Trying to get something done is like pushing on one end of the noodle. Nobody knows where the noodle is connected—where it goes in the mass—and what, if anything, will move. Many politicians resemble wet noodles. They go with the flow. They bend when pushed. They succumb to the pressure of their parties ttt. They vote along party lines rather than follow their conscience. In the mass of party wrangling they often lose sight of the issues and their constituents are left dangling.

One example of a political wet noodle is the legislature's inability to appoint new judges. The well being and the governing of the people has been set aside and derailed by right wing and left wing politics while the real needs of the people are left in limbo.

Is the integrity that was demonstrated by General Lafayette some 200 years ago a part of the political landscape today? Integrity is a virtue that needs to be earned. Certainly General Lafayette earned that respect. The choices that need to be made are not always easy nor are they always popular. Integrity is the result of making choices you know in your heart are right regardless of popular opinion. Integrity involves honesty, character, dignity, and honor. Perhaps we could all learn a lesson from Lafayette's example by standing firm on principle and not be swayed by special interests, greed, and popularity.

—M. Gingrich

Thinking Outside The Box

When it comes to being creative and innovative we are sometimes our own worst enemies. There are many things we do each and every day simply because that is how we have always done them. We form habits because of the repetitive nature of some tasks. When we get used to doing a task a certain way it then becomes more difficult to suddenly change course and do it differently. There is nothing wrong with being habitual in certain tasks, in fact it has some good qualities. Being habitual means it is more likely to get done and it will probably we done to satisfaction. Having a method for how we do it also speeds up the process so we accomplish more in less time. Being habitual also has its drawbacks. It can cause us to become so focused we lose our vision and perspective. We become blinded to opportunities. We fail to see beyond the task at hand. We can't see the forest for the trees. We can't see the bigger picture because the menial tasks of the moment have our undivided attention. When those are finished we can move on to something else. We have a tendency to box ourselves in and limit our own potential because we are task driven rather than visionary driven. Perhaps it's time to think outside the box.

Before we venture too far into this subject may I insert a bit of caution. There are certain tasks that merit our undivided attention. Driving is one of them. Cell phones are convenient tools but they are proven to be a distraction to drivers and have been the direct cause of many accidents. We must not become careless when thinking outside the box lest we lose all the ground we gain. Thinking outside the box is simply asking oneself the question, "Could this task be accomplished better, faster, and with less energy than what it is currently? Is there a better way?"

In many ways we are the recipients of modern conveniences because people thought outside the box. They asked that question, "Is there something better?" They developed refrigerators, the internal combustion engine, tubeless tires, computers, submersible pumps, etc. Our ancestors drew water from a well. Then they developed a hand pump. Then a motor was invented and they learned how to draw the water up with it. Later they learned that putting the pump down in the well and pumping it up was even better. Most of us would be reluctant to regress to carrying our water in buckets from the well down the street. Water readily available from the tap is a result of thinking outside the box.

Every time I do some remodeling work and subject myself to lugging around some oversized drywall sheets I think there must be a better way, a better product. I suppose the relatively low cost of drywall is what makes it a viable choice along with the fact that no one has come up with something better. It certainly is a tremendous improvement over its predecessor, horsehair plaster. If you've never tore any of that out of an old house you ought to, just for the experience. I tend to think that someday something will replace drywall just like drywall replaced horsehair plaster. Someone will find or develop a more durable, more soundproof, lightweight product; perhaps out of recycled plastic. Can you picture that? A lot less

dirt and a lot less mess. Easy to glue in place. No screws. Even larger sheet size for less finishing. Ridiculous? I don't think so! There has got to be a better way. Most inventions are a direct result of dissatisfaction with what is currently available. The guy that figures it out will be set financially for a long time. The rest of us will wonder why we didn't think of it.

Thinking outside the box doesn't mean we need to be inventors. It simply means that we ought to take a look at the how and why of what we do. Look at the little tasks as well as the big ones. Consider your attitudes about them. Ask yourself if the task is even relevant or necessary anymore. Time and change have a way of eliminating old necessities and creating new ones. Have you adapted your methods accordingly?

Many folks hesitate to think outside the box for fear of change. They feel comfortable where they are and with what they are doing. They become complacent. They become lethargic and lose their motivation. A willingness to look outside the box brings zeal and energy back into life. It makes more efficient use of time. It eliminates non-essential tasks and streamlines the necessary ones. It is productive.

Thinking outside the box is not a process of trying to reinvent the wheel, but rather finding ways to make the wheel roll more smoothly.

—M. Gingrich

Through The Eyes Of A Child

An eye witness account from New York City, on a cold day in December:

A little boy about ten years old was standing before a shoe store on the roadway, barefooted, peering through the window, and shivering with cold.

A lady approached the boy and said, "My little fellow, why are you looking so earnestly in that window?"

"I was asking God to give me a pair of shoes," was the boy's reply.

The lady took him by the hand and went into the store and asked the clerk to get half a dozen pairs of socks for the boy. She then asked if he could give her a basin of water and a towel.

He quickly brought them to her. She took the little fellow to the back part of the store and, removing her gloves, knelt down, washed his little feet, and dried them with a towel.

By this time the clerk had returned with the socks. Placing a pair upon the boy's feet, she then purchased him a pair of shoes.

She tied up the remaining pairs of socks and gave them to him. She patted him on the head and said, "No doubt, my little fellow, you feel more comfortable now?"

As she turned to go, the astonished lad caught her by the hand, and looking up in her face, with tears in his eyes, answered, "I thought God was a man."

Tiny Tim

It was a relatively calm day in my hospital's Neonatal Intensive Care Unit. Two other nurses and I were trying to have a conversation amid the customary sounds of ventilators and heart monitors. I was in mid-sentence when the shrill ring of the red emergency phone halted all conversation. "Come fast," the voice said urgently. "We need a neonatal nurse!"

Fear gripped my heart as I ran into the delivery room. Instantly, I knew the situation was critical. "What's happening here?" I asked.

"It's an 'oops abortion,' and now it's your problem!" responded one of the nurses.

For us, an "oops abortion" meant the mother's due date was miscalculated, and the fetus survived the abortion procedure. A pediatrician was called to the scene. He ran by me with the fetus (now called a baby) in his hand and yelled in my direction, indicating he wanted me to follow him into the resuscitation room adjoining the delivery room. I looked into the bed of the warmer as I grabbed equipment. Before my eyes was a baby boy. A very, very tiny baby boy.

The doctor and I immediately made an attempt at intubation (inserting a tube down the trachea from the mouth or nose of the infant to the tip of the lungs to ventilate, expand, and oxygenate them). The doctor's effort at intubation failed, which further traumatized the baby. I glanced at the doctor and hesitantly asked, "Will you attempt intubation again?"

"You've got to be kidding," he replied. "It would be inhumane to attempt to intubate this poor little thing again. This infant will never survive."

"No, doctor, I'm not kidding," I said, "and it's my job to ask." The doctor softened for a moment. "I'm sorry, Sharon. I'm just angry. The mother doesn't want the inconvenience of a baby, so she comes to the hospital so she can pay somebody to get rid of it—all neat and tidy. Then the whole thing gets messed up when the fetus has the audacity to survive. Then everybody takes it seriously, and they call the pediatrician, who's supposed to fix it or get rid of it."

With anger in his voice, he went on, "Some lawyers will fight for the right to do whatever we want to our bodies, but watch out for what they will do when these abortions aren't so neat and tidy! A failed homicide—and oops! Then all of a sudden everybody cares, and it's turned from a 'right' into a 'liability' that someone is blamed for!"

We looked at our pathetic little patient. He was lying in the fetal position in the wrong environment, trying to get air into underdeveloped lungs that couldn't do the job. In a calmer voice, the doctor said, "Okay, nurse, I'm going back to the office. Keep him comfortable and let me know when it's over. I'm sorry about this. Call me if you need me. I know this is a hard one. If it helps, please know it's tough for me, too." Holding the baby's hand, I watched the doctor retreat and then glanced back at the infant before me. He was gasping for air. "Lord, help!" I prayed. Almost instinctively, I took the baby's vitals. His temperature was dangerously low. I pushed the warmer settings as high as they could go. His heart rate was about 180-200 beats per minute. I could count the beats by watching his little chest pulsate. I settled down a bit and began to focus on this tiny little person. He had no name, so I gave him one. Suddenly, I found myself speaking to the baby. "Tiny Tim, who are you? I am so sorry you weren't wanted. It's not your fault."

I placed my little finger in his hand, and he grasped it. As I watched him closely, I marveled that all the minute parts of a beautiful baby were present and functioning in spite of the onslaught. I touched his toes and discovered he was ticklish!

He had a long torso and long legs. I wondered if he would have become a baseball player. Perhaps he would have been a teacher or doctor. Emotions swept over me as I thought of my friends who had been waiting and praying for years for a baby to adopt. I spoke aloud once again to the miniature baby. "They would have given you a loving and a happy home. Why would people destroy you before ever considering adoption? Ignorance is not bliss, is it, Tiny Tim?"

Hanging on meanwhile, Tim put his thumb into his mouth and sucked. I hoped that gave him comfort. I continued to talk to him. "I'm sorry, Tim. There are people who would risk their lives for a whale or an owl before they'd even blink about what just happened to you." Tiny Tim gasped, and his little chest heaved as if a truck were sitting on it. I took my stethoscope and listened to his tiny, pounding heart. At the moment it seemed easier to focus on physiology rather than on this baby's humanity.

He wet, and with that my mind took off again. Here was Tiny Tim with a whole set of kidneys, a bladder, and connecting tubes that functioned with a very complex system of chemistry. His plumbing was all working! I turned the overhead light up and Tim turned from it, in spite of eyelids that were fused together to protect his two precious little eyes. I thought about them. They would never see a sunset, a mother's smile, or the wagging tail of a dog. I took his temperature again. It was dropping. He was gasping for air and continued to fight for life. I stroked him gently and began to sing : "Jesus loves the little children, all the children of the world; red and yellow, black and white, they are precious in His sight. Jesus loves the little children of the world."

A nurse walked in. "How's the mother?" I asked. "Oh, she's fine. She's back in her room resting. The family said they don't want to see or hear about anything. They said, "Just take care of it." The nurse retreated with one last glance at the tiny patient. "For such a little person, he's sure putting up a big fight."

I looked at Tiny Tim and wondered if he knew that what he was fighting for so hard was life—and I knew he was losing it. He was dying and his family was resting. Their words tormented me. 'Just take care of it! 'No mess and no fuss. Then Tiny Tim moved and caught hold of my little finger. I let him hang on. I didn't want him to die without being touched and cared for. As I saw him struggle to breathe, I said, "It's okay, Tim. You can let go now. You can go back to God."

His gasping started slowing down, but he still clung to my finger. I stroked the baby ever so slowly and watched him take his last breath. "Good-bye, Tiny Tim," I whispered. "You did matter to someone."

Epilogue

A few years later, Sharon became the manager of a psychiatric unit. One day, Kathy, a young, severely depressed woman, came to see Sharon following an unsuccessful suicide attempt. As Sharon interviewed her, Kathy said she had gone through an abortion three years before and she was having recurring nightmares. A baby was crying for help and kept calling her name. In her dreams, Kathy searched for the baby, but she could never find him or her. As Kathy gave the name of the hospital and the names of the doctors, a disturbing realization dawned on Sharon. Kathy was Tiny Tim's mother. Because of hospital regulations, she couldn't tell her what she knew. Time passed. Sharon was no longer a nurse or a therapist. Kathy was no longer a psychiatric patient. They ran into each other at a restaurant, where Sharon gently unfolded the story that had been hidden for so long. Tears flowed as she gave Kathy the gift of answers. Her baby was touched and loved by a mother. He was given a name. He didn't die alone. He was sent back to a loving God. As the visit neared an end, they held each other and wept. Sharon looked into Kathy's eyes and saw new strength and calm. There were scars, but she was beginning to heal. The nightmares were being put to rest. Sharon still lives with the haunting impact of this experience. A choice that was intended to be "no big deal" turned out to be a very big deal indeed for everybody.

Traveling Afar

Henry D. Thoreau wrote: "I have traveled much in Concord." Now Concord is so small a town you can travel from one end to the other in a few minutes. Yet, Thoreau, who saw little of the world beyond Concord, Massachusetts, saw much more of the world and nature in Concord than many see traveling the world. If we have an alert mind, seeing eyes, and hearing ears, we can "travel much" anywhere we live.

A woman, who became the authority on wild flowers in the state of Arkansas, was an invalid, unable to walk. But she had eyes to see and to reach out and observe. She learned from others until she knew more about wild flowers in Arkansas than any other.

She "traveled much" in her own home and yard.

If we have eyes to see and ears to hear we can learn much right where we are of Jesus, of others, and of the world around us. We also can "travel much" right where we live.

—John M. Drescher

To Each His Own

I cannot change the way I am,
I never really try,
God made me different and unique,
I never ask him why.

If I appear peculiar,
There's nothing I can do,
You must accept me as I am,
As I've accepted you.

God made a casting of each life,
Then threw the mold away,
Each child is different from the rest,
Unlike as night from day.

So often we will criticize,
The things that others do,
But, do you know, they do not think,
The same as me and you.

So God in all his wisdom,
Who knows us all by name,
He didn't want us to be bored,
That's why we're not the same

—Author Unknown

Trust

As a new school principal, Mr. Mitchell was checking over his school on his first day. Passing the stock room, he was startled to see the door wide open and teachers bustling in and out, carrying off books and supplies in preparation for the arrival of students the next day.

The school where he had been a principal the previous year had used a check-out system only slightly less elaborate than that at Fort Knox.

Cautiously, he asked the school's long time custodian, "Do you think it's wise to keep the stock room unlocked and to let the teachers take things without requisitions?"

The custodian looked at him gravely. "We trust them with the children, don't we?"

Trying To Please Everyone

An old man, a boy, and a donkey were going to town. The boy rode on the donkey and the old man walked. As they went along they passed some people who remarked it was a shame the old man was walking and the boy was riding. The man and boy thought maybe the critics were right, so they changed positions.

Later, they passed some people that remarked, "What a shame, he makes that little boy walk." They then decided they both would walk!

Soon they passed some more people who thought they were stupid to walk when they had a decent donkey to ride. So, they both rode the donkey. Now they passed some people that shamed them by saying how awful to put such a load on a poor donkey. The boy and man said they were probably right, so they decided to carry the donkey. As they crossed the bridge, they lost their grip on the animal and he fell into the river and drowned.

The moral of the story? If you try to please everyone, you'll never win.

Walk A Little Plainer, Daddy

Walk a little plainer, daddy
Said a little boy so frail,
I'm following in your footsteps
And I don't want to fail.

Sometimes your steps are very plain
Sometimes they're hard to see,
So walk a little plainer, daddy
For you are leading me.

I know that once you walked this way
Many years ago,
And what you did along the way
I'd really like to know.

For sometimes when I'm tempted
I don't know what to do,
So walk a little plainer, daddy
For I must follow you.

Someday when I'm grown up
You are like I want to be,
Then I will have a little boy
Who will want to follow me.

And I would want to lead him right
And help him to be true,
So walk a little plainer, daddy
For we must follow you.

Walk In The Garden

Did you ever walk in a garden
In the early morning hours
When the birds were sweetly singing
And the dew was on the flowers?

Did you look inside the petals
Of a brightly colored bloom
To see the heart of the flower,
And to smell its rare perfume?

When you'd looked at all the beauty
That was growing from the sod,
Did you stop to think for a moment
That you had walked with God?

Warning Sign

I recently attended a small business marketing seminar at which the speaker used actual examples to reinforce her teaching points. She told a delightful story about a coffee shop that distinguished itself from the competition by prominently displaying a warning sign that read: "Unattended children will be given a double espresso and a free puppy!"

What Am I Good For?

"What am I good for? Nothing," sighed the rose. "My thorns prick people, and they used thorns to make a crown for my Creator's head."

The butterfly decided that "I'm good for absolutely nothing! All I can do is flutter around and show off my beautiful colors."

"Look at me," buzzed the bee, "I have nothing to be thankful for. I have a stinger for protection, and people are scared of me every time I come around!"

Wake up, wake up, why are we all comparing ourselves with one another? When we are all created uniquely with a special purpose. Though it may not look like it at times!

Roses speak volumes and give off a wonderful scent for others to savor!

And you, Mr. Butterfly, your bright colors are used to bring cheer to so many hearts, wherever you flutter, whether you're going from flower to flower, or you may be in a picture!

And never fear, dear bee, you are important too. The honey you give the world lasts longer and is sweeter than your sting!

—Rosene Hoover

This was written by a 36-year-old cerebral palsy girl on a computer since she can't write by hand and her eye sight is limited.

What Are We Teaching?

A quick glance at the calendar reminded me that another school year was just around the corner. The halls and classrooms would once more echo the sounds of children as they enter to learn.

The dictionary tells us that school is a place for teaching, training, and learning. Learning is a never ending process. Children entering the classroom have many opportunities to learn. They learn to read in only a short time. They learn to write. They learn to associate with others. Those early years of a child's life are years of molding and shaping and training that will go with them into adulthood.

The age old saying, "There is more caught then taught," still stands true in the classroom and in the home. We ignore many of our problems in society when we refuse to recognize the dilemma in many homes. When children don't know who to call dad and who to call mom, or if parents are constantly fighting, they lose their sense of security and feeling of acceptance they need in those formative years.

If school, then, is a place of teaching and learning and training, we must conclude that the home, the school, and all of life is actually a school. That in turn brings us to the most important question: "What are we teaching?" Children need to be taught that there are consequences to be reckoned with as a result of their actions. The entertainment and music industry is a mega bucks conglomerate that is interested solely in your pocketbook. Parents must guard their children from its evil tentacles. Bombarding children with violence and seduction under the guise that they know it's not for real or the presumption that it won't hurt them is insane.

It is dangerous, too, because of its addictive nature. A child left alone with videos and computer games will become wrapped up in it to the point where literally hours are wasted. How many real life situations does it take where someone says they were doing just like they saw on TV until we get the picture.

Parents must realize that having children is a privilege and a blessing from God. With it comes the responsibility to teach and train that child so that he will be an asset to others. Expecting others to fill a mother's and father's role is to invite disaster. Parents must take an active interest in their children and teach them in the very young years. Practice discipline and they will learn to be submissive to authority. Practice encouragement and they will build self esteem. Practice good etiquette and they will catch it. Practice love and forgiveness and they will learn to love and forgive. Practice honesty at all costs and they will sense the peace that it brings. Practice patience and they will be patient with others. Practice hard work and they will become a good employee.

Teaching and training children is a noble work. We will make mistakes but we can't let that discourage us. It is a 24/7 task where parents, teachers, pastors, neighbors, and friends must serve as role models. Children are a reflection of parents. Can we look in the mirror without regret?

—M. Gingrich

What is a Grandma?

The following was written by a 3rd grader for a school assignment:

A grandma is a lady who has no children of her own so she likes other people's little girls. A grandfather is a man grandmother. He goes for walks with boys and they talk about fishing and things like that. Grandmas don't have anything to do except be there. They are so old they should not play hard. It is enough that they drive us to the supermarkets where the pretend horse is and have lots of dimes ready, or if they take us for walks, they should slow down past pretty things like leaves and caterpillars. They should never say "hurry up." Usually they are fat, but not too fat. They can take their teeth and gums off. They don't have to be smart, only answer questions like why dogs hate cats and how come God isn't married. They don't talk baby-talk like visitors do because it is hard to understand. When they read to us they don't skip words or mind if it is the same story again. Every body should try to have a grandma, because grandmas are grown-ups who have got time.

What Might Have Been

"What might have been" had I made a different choice? Could I have averted unwelcome and harsh consequences. "What might have been" if I had refrained from uttering those unkind words? Did that argument alter my relationship with that individual for life? "What might have been" if I had been just a few minutes earlier? Would the accident have happened? Might I have avoided serious injury? What if I had been the first to quote that job? Might I have had a better opportunity of getting the order? "What might have been" if I had saved that bonus check rather than spend it? Might I now be debt free? "What might have been" if I had decided to stop and help rather than zoom on by? Was guilt now stealing what could have been a blessing?

"What might have been" is a question we can ponder many times over. Most of the time there will be no definitive answer. We can only suppose how different things might have been if we had taken that job offer, or gotten out of bed a few minutes earlier, or spent our hard earned money with a bit more discretion. We can ponder "what might have been" in regards to our own decisions and choices but we are also affected by the choices made by our parents and peers. We might have grown up in another culture with different friends, with different manners, with different interests, and the list goes on.

Many of the "what might have been's" may be somewhat insignificant, but sometimes even little things can make a huge difference. Consider the account of one of America's presidents, William McKinley, when he was planning to appoint an ambassador to a foreign country. There were two candidates under consideration whose qualifications were almost equal. President McKinley searched his mind for some sort of measurement whereby he might be able to decide the true greatness of the men in question. He later confided that the self-centeredness of the one and the kindness of the other were the deciding factors in his decision. Many years before when he was still a representative in congress, Mr. McKinley had boarded a street car at rush hour and managed to get the last vacant seat. Shortly thereafter an elderly woman carrying a large basket boarded the train. She walked the length of the car and stood in the aisle clutching her basket, hardly able to stand as the car swayed from side to side as it sped down the tracks. No one offered her a seat. One of the men whom the president was now considering was sitting opposite where she was standing. Mr. McKinley noticed that he shifted his newspaper in order to avoid eye contact with the lady. Seeing the lady's predicament, McKinley rose to his feet, walked down the aisle, took her basket, and offered his seat in the back of the car. The candidate never knew that this small act of selfishness had deprived him of perhaps the crowning honor of his lifetime. As the president considered his options, he recalled this incident and decided to appoint the other man as his ambassador.

"What might have been," wasn't, because of a failure to show kindness when the opportunity afforded itself. Every minute of everyday opportunities are before us. If we choose wisely how to handle them there is no need to fret and wonder "what might have been," but we can move ahead with confidence that "what is" is good, and "what might have been" will need to be left to the imagination.

—M. Gingrich

Where Is Everybody Going?

As I stood in line for check-in at Orlando International Airport, that was the question. Then I stop to ponder the fact that this is just one airport in one city in one state and that there are literally hundreds of airports with even more people scurrying about, scattered across the globe. That doesn't take into account all the train stations, bus stations, and car and pedestrian traffic. People are going places, but where? To get groceries, to do banking, to shop, to visit friends, to their work, to the doctor, to eat out, or just for something to do. The reasons are many and varied.

I couldn't help but ponder the thought that comes to mind so many times when I'm driving down the highway. What would happen if everybody would switch occupations around or move close to work so that we wouldn't scoot past each other in opposite directions everyday? Or, what would happen if we just stayed home after work rather than needing to go to the shopping malls, the sporting events, the entertainment venues, etc? Would it give less congestion? Couldn't I switch jobs with the guy I pass each day on my way to work who is doing the same thing I do? Could we switch houses?

On my trip to Orlando I was attending an expo at the convention center. Others on our plane were going to visit relatives and friends. One group was enroute to a college football game. Some were just on vacation and heading for a warmer climate.

Obviously, we are a people on the go. Whether it be to the grocery store, the bank, the doctor, school, or to work, most of us use some type of transportation to get there. In a recent U.S. News and World Report there was an article on how to fix the transportation mess in New York City. Having been there numerous times I would heartily agree it needs fixing. It seems you need to learn quickly to drive like they do and make sure your horn is in proper working order if you want to get anywhere. But then I ask myself the question, "Am I adding to the problem?" I was there to pick up a piece of equipment so I had a purpose, but I suppose everyone else had a purpose, as well. In essence, I was part of New York City's transportation problems that day. While contributing to its economy I was also contributing to it's transportation woes. I was one person with an agenda. In order to complete my plans for the day, I needed to respect other folks' plans, too. With much patience I completed my task. What else can you do but wait, when you are boxed in on all sides?

Some cities are using computerization to control traffic signals. They can observe traffic flow that is captured on camera and adjust the signals to keep traffic moving. Technology such as this will most likely continue to play a larger role in combating traffic congestion on the highways. Getting stuck in traffic is no one's idea of fun, especially when our flight is soon scheduled to take off or the venue we are attending has already started.

So where is everybody going? They are going uptown, downtown, across town. Everyone has plans and so they take the route and mode that best fits their agenda. They want to arrive as quickly as possible, with the fewest interruptions, and the least inconvenience while keeping the cost of doing so within budget. Such was the case with my excursion to Orlando. I drove to Baltimore instead of Harrisburg because of better rates and a larger selection of flight times.

Is all this going necessary? Is it good? Yes, we must "Go" to meet our basic needs, and to do our jobs. We must eat to survive. We need to visit the doctor, the dentist, etc., to maintain our health. It's simply a part of life. Could we cut out some excess "Go"? Absolutely! Could we be more frugal and make our "Go's" more efficient? Sure! But will we? Perhaps the cost of fuel will force the issue. Otherwise we like our independence to come and go as we please.

—M. Gingrich

Who?

Someone started the whole day wrong
Was it you?
Someone robbed the day of its song—
Was it you?

Early this morning someone frowned,
Someone sulked until others scowled,
And soon harsh words were passed around—
Was it you?

Someone started the day aright—
Was it you?
Someone made it happy and bright—
Was it you?

Early this morning we were told
Someone smiled, and all day through
This smile encouraged young and old—
Was it you?

So always remember, whether you are short or tall
Doesn't determine your size at all.
You are measured by the width of your grin,
And the depth and breadth of what is within.

Who Is Your Daddy?

A seminary professor was vacationing with his wife in Gatlinburg, TN. One morning, they were eating breakfast at a little restaurant, hoping to enjoy a quiet, family meal. While they were waiting for their food, they noticed a distinguished looking, white-haired man moving from table to table, visiting with the guests. The professor leaned over and whispered to his wife, "I hope he doesn't come over here." But sure enough, the man did come over to their table.

"Where are you folks from?" he asked in a friendly voice.

"Oklahoma," they answered.

"Great to have you here in Tennessee," the stranger said. "What do you do for a living?"

"I teach at a seminary," he replied.

"Oh, so you teach preachers how to preach, do you? Well, I've got a really great story for you." And with that, the gentleman pulled up a chair and sat down at the table with the couple.

The professor groaned and thought to himself, "Great…just what I need…another preacher story!"

The man started, "See that mountain over there?" (Pointing out the restaurant window) "Not far from the base of that mountain, there was a boy born to an unwed mother. He had a hard time growing up, because every place he went, he was always asked the same question, 'Hey, boy, who's your daddy?' Whether he was at school, in the grocery store or drug store, people would ask the same question, 'Who's your daddy?'

"He would hide at recess and lunchtime from other students. He would avoid going into stores because that question hurt him so bad. When he was about 12 years old, a new preacher came to his church. He would always go in late and slip out early to avoid hearing the question, 'Who's your daddy?'

"But one day, the new preacher said the benediction so fast that he got caught and had to walk out with the crowd.

"Just about the time he got to the back door, the new preacher, not knowing anything about him, put his hand on his shoulder and asked him, 'Son, who's your daddy?'

"The whole church got deathly quiet. He could feel every eye in the church looking at him. Now everyone would finally know the answer to the question, 'Who's your daddy?'

"This new preacher, though, sensed the situation around him and using discernment that only the Holy Spirit could give, said the following to that scared little boy, 'Wait a minute! I know who you are! I see the family resemblance now. You are a child of God.'

"With that he patted the boy on his shoulder and said, 'Boy, you've got a great inheritance. Go and claim it.'

"The boy smiled for the first time in a long time and walked out the door a changed person. He was never the same again. Whenever anybody asked him, 'Who's your daddy?' he'd just tell them, 'I'm a child of God.'"

The distinguished gentleman got up from the table and said, "Isn't that a great story?"

The professor responded that it really was a great story!

As the man turned to leave, he said, "You know, if that new preacher hadn't told me that I was one of God's children, I probably never would have amounted to anything!" and he walked away.

The seminary professor and his wife were stunned. He called the waitress over and asked her, "Do you know who that man was—the one who just left that was sitting at our table?"

The waitress grinned and said, "Of course. Everybody here knows him. That's Ben Hooper. He's Governor of Tennessee!"

Someone in your life today needs a reminder that they're one of God's children!

Words!

The three hardest words to say…,"I am wrong."
The two most appreciated words…, "Thank you."
The four most encouraging words…, "Let me help you."
The five most inspirational words…,"I'm praying for you."
The four most negative words…,"You can't do it."
The four most positive words…,"You can do it."
The three most needed words to hear…,"I love you."

Integrity

Decision Making

While desperately in need of money in 1890, a Stockholm man sold the ownership of his body after death to the Royal Swedish Institute for dissecting purposes. Twenty years later he inherited a fortune, and being unable to buy back his contract, he sued the organization for it. The institute not only successfully defended its position but requested, and was awarded, damages for two of the man's teeth which had been extracted without its permission.

Esau, in Bible times, sold his birthright for a bowl of porridge. In a moment of famished hunger his only thought was for some food to eat and he foolishly traded his birthright. Afterwards he realized his grave mistake, and though he sought desperately to buy it back, he could not.

These two accounts are a solemn reminder that radical decision making on the spur of the moment is not wise and often carries with it undesirable consequences. There are times when decisions must be made quickly; however, when possible I have made it a personal policy to sleep over it before making a final decision. More than once this has saved me from making an unwise choice.

A general practice of door-to-door salespeople is to try and get you to buy immediately. If you mention talking it over with your husband or wife or thinking it over until the next day they will often try to pressure you. They may use tactics such as, "I'm only in the area today" or "This deal is only good for so long", etc. They know their chances of securing a sale are greatly diminished if you have time to think it over and compare it with other products or perhaps decide that it is totally unnecessary.

Dealing with a door-to-door salesperson is just a small thing. Life is full of decisions that need to be made that carry with them far-reaching consequences. Decisions regarding moral purity, choosing a life companion, an occupation, friends, etc., are all of vital importance. The results can be seen in future generations. As these two stories prove, poor decisions can be costly and devastating. Taking the time that is needed, seeking counsel, and considering carefully the end result can help us make wise decisions that we can feel good about and that will be beneficial in the end.

—M. Gingrich

How Reads Your Book?

Most of us would not consider ourselves to be an author. We look at people who write books as having a special gift just as an artist has a gift for drawing. While we may not be talented in writing out our thoughts and putting them on paper, we are in essence writing an autobiography by the daily occurrences in our lives. Many of these occurrences may be repetitious and seem rather insignificant, but along the way there are highlights such as a birthday, a special surprise, becoming a parent, a vacation, etc. These are recorded on our pages of memory and we can look back on them at will. Each one of us is writing a story complete with real life characters, relationships, opportunities, failures, joys, and disappointments. Every moment of everyday is a comma, a period, a question mark, a sentence, or a paragraph that collectively makes a complete historical account of our life. It is all about you, your character, and your personality. You are the main character.

So how does your book read? What do your friends and acquaintances read when they get a glimpse inside the cover of your autobiography? Is it filled with adventure? Are they intrigued and motivated to read more? Are they captivated by your personality? Are they challenged by your generosity and dedication? Do they see in your book a person of character? Is your book boring and uninviting? Does it turn them off because it is self-centered, opinionated, or even a bit sarcastic? Does it contain episodes of anger, resentment, or bitterness? Are there things perhaps you would really like to edit out but can't because history keeps a complete list of the good and bad? How does your book read?

This book you are writing is one of a kind. It will not be mass produced or even duplicated. It can only be written once as you go through life. There are no remakes or do overs so take care to make your book the best it can be.

—M. Gingrich

Leadership Principles

Leadership is an important aspect of any business or organization. Without leadership things quickly fall apart. Without leadership there is indecisiveness, there is uncertainty, there is loss of communication and a lack of a sense of responsibility. Successful businesses or organizations have a leader who says yes or no, who makes decisions whether right or wrong and stands by them, is willing to accept responsibility for personal mistakes, and frequently praises his or her subordinates for their personal accomplishments. Leadership requires a visionary approach, a willingness to try new ideas, and the courage to test uncharted waters. A leader is one who is not afraid to attempt something for fear of failure because he knows that it is far worse to fail because you never tried. Good leaders surround themselves with others who have a similar vision and motivation. Many failures have come as a result of divided loyalty and vision within the organization. Good leaders will recognize the value of diversity and prod it in the right direction. At the same time they are alert to dangerous undercurrents and have the courage to subdue them before they have an adverse effect. In short, a good leader will align his or her team so that they are united in their vision, united in their efforts, and are equally devoted to the cause. Leadership is not doing everything yourself but it is using the resources around you; disciplining, educating, and motivating those resources to accomplish far more than you could individually. A good leader will never become complacent but will continue to seek and find ways to improve.

Here is a list of things a good leader should do so that he or she becomes an even better leader.

1. Seek self-improvement—Continually strengthen your attributes through study, classes, and interacting with others.
2. Be proficient—Have a good knowledge of and be familiar with the operation and functions of the organization.
3. Seek responsibility and take responsibility for your actions—Search for ways to guide your organization to new heights. When things go wrong—they always do sooner or later—do not blame others. Analyze the situation, take corrective action, and move on to the next challenge.
4. Make sound and timely decisions—Use good problem solving, decision making, and planning tools.
5. Set the example—Be a good role model for your employees. Don't just tell them what to do but be willing to lend a hand and show them you know how to get your hands dirty, too.
6. Know your people and look out for their well-being—Know human nature and the importance of sincerely caring for your workers.
7. Keep your workers informed—Communication is always important. Keep others abreast of the details rather than making them second guess as to what is going on.
8. Develop a sense of responsibility in your workers—Help to develop good character traits that will help them carry out their professional responsibilities.
9. Ensure that tasks are understood, supervised, and accomplished—Communication again. Assign tasks, lend support, and do follow up. Assumptions will get you in trouble.
10. Train as a team—Good leaders see the need for ongoing training and refresher courses throughout the organization. Every team member is an important and integral part of the finished product.
11. Use the full capabilities of your organization—By developing a team spirit, you will be able to employ your organization to its fullest.

Leadership principles will thread their way down through the channels of any organization. They reflect the integrity and values that are at the very heart of the organization. Croft Pentz in his book, *The Complete Book of Zingers*, has this quote, "A good leader inspires others with confidence in him—a great leader inspires them with confidence in themselves."

—M. Gingrich

Look Up

A father and small son crawled into a watermelon field to steal some watermelons. The father told the son to watch for him as he put several watermelons in a burlap bag. The father told the son to look north, south, east, and west. The son replied, "Dad, don't you think we should also look up?"

Now What?

A lady went to the butcher shop looking for a chicken for dinner. She asked the butcher to see his selection. He only had one chicken left but did not disclose this to the lady. He kept the chickens in the bin below the showcase and so he reached down and pulled out his last chicken. He put it on the scale, the lady eyed the weight and asked if he had one a little larger.

"Yes," he replied. He took the chicken and lowered it down to the empty bin, shook it against the side and brought it back out. This time when he placed it on the scale his trained thumb hung just a little bit on the edge of the scale.

The lady eyed the weight and said, "That is fine, I'll take both of them."

Note: Be sure your sin will find you out.

Personal Responsibility

He made me do it! It was his fault! Pointing a finger or passing the buck are references to people trying to blame their actions or lack of action on someone else. Little children get into a squabble and soon are heard the cries of, "He took my toy," "He hit me," etc. Older children make all kinds of excuses regarding incomplete home work assignments and unfinished chores. "I lost my paper!" "I forgot!" Adults make all kinds of excuses as well. They blame others for pulling in front of them. They cite negligence as a factor in causing them to trip and fall. They fault authorities. They fault municipalities. They fault manufacturers. They fault townships and schools. They fault doctors and teachers. Out of this blaming and fault finding epidemic we now have no-fault insurance on vehicles and malpractice insurance for doctors.

Whatever happened to personal accountability and personal responsibility? While certainly there are cases of negligence and there are cases where an individual is at fault, there are also many cases where people are simply unwilling to admit their own mistake. Recently, a professional ballplayer blamed the umpire for his season ending injury. The injury happened when his manager tried to intervene and keep him from going after the umpire. While the umpire may have spoken inappropriately it was the inability of the ballplayer to control his temper that was to blame. Had he turned and walked away without a word the injury would not have happened. The temper tantrum, rather than the umpire, was the cause of the injury. However, the ballplayer refused to acknowledge his problem with anger, choosing rather to blame circumstances around him. This is a scenario repeated over and over in life. People who haven't learned to take personal responsibility will cast their woes on anyone who happens to get in their way. They blame society, parents, authorities, circumstances, and a host of other things but refuse to admit their own mistake. While other things may factor into and influence decisions and actions there is still a choice that is made. That choice is the pivotal point of personal responsibility. I am responsible for that choice whether it is good or bad. I am responsible regardless of the external influences and inner pressures I am confronted with. I can blame other things and other people but ultimately I bring hurt to myself and others by refusing to admit I made a mistake.

This does not refute the fact that we are sometimes the victim of other peoples mistakes. We are mistake and accident prone and so a wrong turn, excessive speed, or a failure to brake can result in injury or death to ourselves and others. Most accidents are the result of either mechanical failure or operator error. Every day there are people injured and killed through no fault of their own. They are simply victims of circumstances. That is a part of life and always will be. In these situations our mentality is too often such that we want to hold others accountable for their mistakes but expect mercy for our own.

As parents we should try to teach our children at an early age lessons of sharing and appropriate conduct. Teach them that wrong choices bring hurt and pain while good choices bring joy and happiness. Teach them that they have a choice to make regardless of the situation they find themselves in. They can choose anger and hatred and animosity or they can choose peace and love and kindness.

Immature millionaires with uncontrolled tempers blaming others for their inappropriate conduct don't get much playing time in my league. Maybe they know how to play ball but they sure don't know how to live life.

—M. Gingrich

Promises, Promises, Promises!

Every day we make promises. We promise to meet someone at a specified time. We promise to return a phone call. We promise to write a letter. We promise to deliver some goods. We promise to follow the guidelines. We promise to tell the truth. We promise to keep a secret. We promise to help a neighbor. We promise to clean out the garage. We promise to try and do better. We promise our employer, our friend, our spouse, our children, our business associates, our banker, our pastor, etc.

Why do we make all these promises. It is because we want people to be able to depend on us. We want them to trust us. It is all a part of bringing structure to our lives. It is returning the commitment that others have given to us. It is all about relationships with those of our acquaintances. We make promises to alert others of our intentions. We make promises in response to a request from someone. We make promises for the sake of convenience (appointments). The reasons we make promises are many and varied but they all carry with them a degree of expectation.

Broken promises wreak havoc. Imagine a large group of people waiting to hear a well-known speaker that promised to come and then doesn't show up. Imagine how long the bank will lend you credit if you don't pay your bills. Imagine how your spouse feels when you fail to come through on something you committed to. Imagine the disappointment in your children when you fail to play ball with them like you promised. Imagine the dismay when your best friend discovers that the secret they entrusted to you is no longer a secret. Broken promises wreak havoc.

Are promises important? Absolutely! Does failure to keep them lessen our integrity? Yes indeed! History would tell us that a handshake was good enough to seal many agreements in the past. Once a promise was made you could expect that it would be carried out. It should still be sufficient. However, history also records many cases were men have failed to fulfill their commitments. One result of that is page after page of legal documents for even simple agreements. In a recent survey it was noted that a large percentage of the population believes it is okay to lie a little bit in certain situations. They did note, however, that if you get caught it may jeopardize your integrity. Interesting! That mentality severely weakens the fabric of society and its ability to function effectively.

Yes, promises are important, but even more important is the keeping of them. Promises were meant to be kept, not broken. If we have no intention of keeping our promise then we do everyone, including ourselves, a favor by not making the promise in the first place.

—*M. Gingrich*

Pros & Cons Of Secrets

I would suppose that many of us can remember that time when we dared to share a secret with someone only to discover that they couldn't keep a secret. Suddenly, our secret was no longer a secret because everyone else knew it too. It was an instant education that if you wanted to keep a secret the only sure way is to keep it to yourself. As we go through the experiences of life we learn to trust others to varying degrees. That level of trust between two people or a group of people then determines when and if we will share a secret with them.

Secrets are commonplace. In business, employees are given confidential information that is not to be shared with the general public or competition. It is information that helps the employee perform his duties but gives the competition an advantage if they find out. Secrets are used in family life for birthday parties, anniversaries, etc., where it is public knowledge to many individuals but it is kept secret from one person so as to surprise them. It is always a disappointment when the secret slips out and they become aware of the impending surprise. There are secret recipes, secret formulas, secret inventions, ideas, conversations, strategies, decisions, etc. We could devote ourselves 24/7 to discover all the secrets around us and we would still come up way short. There are simply some things that we will never know and it becomes futile to attempt to discover them. It is far more important to respond properly to things that are revealed to us.

Secrets have a proper and rightful place in life. They are used in practical ways to teach and to train. They are used as a form of discipline in law enforcement. Watch the brake lights come on when drivers discover that a policeman is conducting radar. His secret presence causes a proper change in their actions. The secrecy or uncertainty of where a police officer is keeps speed limits in check. It produces positive results. Surprising someone with a party when they least expect it conveys a message of love and caring. Secrets add drama to life. They keep things interesting and challenging.

While secrets have a good and rightful place they can also be very detrimental. A secret can be very burdensome when someone commits a wrong action and no one else knows about it. Often a thief or criminal will eventually share his secret with someone else simply because keeping it a secret becomes too heavy. Sharing his secret helps to shift some of the weight to another persons shoulders. Keeping things secret from a spouse can hinder a relationship. A willingness to share with our spouse runs parallel with our level of trust in each other. When a spouse senses that information is being withheld or there is an unwillingness to share details immediately it raises a flag of disloyalty. Secrecy can become a double edged sword.

In building relationships it is therefore necessary that we consider secrets. We must contemplate when, where, how, and why we would keep a secret or if we should reveal it. We also do well to remember that with God there are no secrets. While man is subject to secrets and limited knowledge, God is not. He is all knowing. There is not one thing hidden from His watchful eye. He sees each sparrow that falls to the ground. When we think for a moment that what we did is hidden and no one else knows, remember that no secret is hidden from God.

—M. Gingrich

Sowing & Reaping

It is the time of year when we see the sights of freshly tilled ground being readied for spring planting. Necessary fertilizer and nutrients are added and tilled in. The ground is a rich dark brown color and is ready for planting. The farmer or gardener then chooses what kind of seed he or she will plant. That choice is based on the desired harvest that is anticipated. We never plant without expecting a harvest. It would be a foolish waste of time. After the type of seed is selected, we begin the planting process. From experience we know something of the nature of what we are planting and so we space the seed accordingly. We know that peas are planted closer together than corn, and corn is closer together than potatoes and certainly we wouldn't want to plant cucumbers as close as any of those. There is a method to our planting. We plan our layout according to the space we have and the particular crops we want. We also plant certain things at certain times to take advantage of the proper growing conditions. Some plants will freeze out if they are planted too early or won't mature if planted too late. Preparing the soil and planting is a lot of hard work. It takes a lot of sweat and toil. After the plants are up the weeds must be kept in check. There is an ongoing battle against insects and disease. Only as we begin to harvest the fruit do we begin to realize the worth of our efforts. Nothing can beat garden fresh vegetables and fruit. A fresh garden salad, juicy strawberries, or the first potatoes are very nutritious and simply delicious.

Without some effort to prepare the soil and plant there would be no harvest. There are times when growing conditions are not always favorable and we experience disappointment when it comes time to harvest. We cannot control the weather, but we can do our part in preparation and cultivating.

I couldn't help but notice some of the parallels between planting our gardens and raising our families. In order for our children to become what we desire we need to nurture them and provide the proper soil and nutrients they need to grow. We must begin with a home where love is practiced. We must give them nutrients of loving discipline and proper morals. Left to choose their own way will result in stunted growth. We must surround them with gentleness, kindness, and happiness. We must water them with truth and honesty. We must cultivate their friendships so they are not overrun with the weeds of peer pressure and influence of unwanted character traits. If we are careless in how we plant and neglect our duty to cultivate we can expect nothing short of a disastrous harvest. As parents we need to do all we can to create the proper growing conditions, for in just a short time our children will become mature plants ready to bear fruit. The fruit they produce will bear the traits of our efforts. Will it be desirable? Will it resemble that seed we planted? Yes, it takes effort! It takes hard work! It takes sweat! When you as a parent take a stand and you hear that familiar phrase; "No one else does it," don't give up. Remember, the rewards only come when it's time to harvest.

—M. Gingrich

Sticking

There was a little postage stamp
No bigger than your thumb,
But still it stuck right on the job
Until its work was done.

They licked it and they pounded it
'Til it would make you sick,
But the more it took a licken'
Why, the tighter it would stick.

So friend, let's be like the postage stamp
In playing life's rough game,
And just keep on a sticking
Though we hide our heads in shame.

For the stamp stuck to the letter
'Til it saw it safely through,
There's no one could do better,
Let's keep sticking and be true.

Life

Before You Go, Stop, Look, And Listen

The age old advice of "Stop, look and listen," before crossing the street is a good principle we do well to apply to our personal lives. As we embark on the journey of a new year, there are a thousand different roads that we could take. Some will lead us away from our destination. Some will have curves and hills that we didn't anticipate. There is always the possibility of making a wrong turn or missing a road and then needing to turn around and retrace our steps. We will need to check our road map on a daily basis and choose the route that we want to go. Our final destination must always be the focal point. The route that we choose is always determined by where we wish to end up.

In our society there are many folks speeding down the highway of life with no real sense of direction. They don't know where they are going. They don't know what they will do when they get there. They simply follow the crowd. If it feels good, if it is easy, if it satisfies my desires, they reason, it must be the way to go. Unfortunately, many of them find themselves going the wrong way on a one way street, caught in traffic jams, or at the end of a dead end street. They are confused, disoriented, and exhausted because their journey took a disastrous detour. Why? They failed to stop. Life came at them so fast. There were so many things to do. There were so many places to go. There was peer pressure to succeed and be accepted. So with little thought of who's feelings they run over, they step on the throttle full speed ahead. It is a "Me first" mentality. I am the one that is important. I've got to get there.

Stop! Life has many uncertainties. Slow down so you are prepared to face them! Take time to evaluate your goals and to plan your route. Keep your destination in view as you go. Constantly check the map and make sure you are still on course. Stop sign violations are certain to cause an accident.

Look! Always look both ways. Defensive driving is every bit as important as offensive driving. Be alert to what is happening around you. Failure to brake when the traffic in front of you stops will have serious consequences. Look out for obstacles that will flatten your tire and cause unnecessary delays. They can often be avoided if we keep our eyes on the road. Look out for others. They are on a journey too and neglect or rashness on our part could cause them harm. Always look before you pull out onto the street or you may be impacted in ways you hadn't anticipated.

Listen! The warning whistle of the train should not go unheeded. We are no match for tons of steel traveling at that speed. It is in our best interest to wait until it passes. That's why they blow the whistle.

Stop! Where are you spiritually? What is your destination?

Look! Evaluate yourself! Look in the mirror! Who are you? Are you trying to be a different person on the outside than what you are inside? Spiritual neglect is like trying to cross the street without ever stopping, looking, and listening. Both will prove to be fatal.

Listen! This is your conscience speaking. Jesus wants to be your guide. He will lead you to eternal life if you follow his instructions. He will take away your heartaches, calm your fears, and give you peace and happiness. Give your life to him. Stop, look, listen! If you take that route you won't be disappointed.

—M. Gingrich

Delayed

Delays are those moments when our progress is slowed. We are on the way to work and traffic comes to a standstill. We hurry to the airport to catch a flight only to find that our flight is delayed. We layout plans to build a building but the construction of it is delayed because the paperwork is not complete. Sometimes a client may delay their payment. A shipment of goods may be delayed in transit. A machine breaks down. The car lets us sit. A health issue stops us in our tracks. Delays are those moments when our plans are put on hold.

Delays are not very welcome in a demanding, "I want it now society!" We grow accustomed to overnight shipment, instant credit, fast food, microwaves, cell phones, and GPS devices. Computers and internet services that process and transfer data at incredible speeds are soon considered to be dinosaurs. Technology seeks faster and faster ways of getting things done. As we experience the mega speeds, we begin to wonder how we ever did it the old way.

One time a group of us were returning home from Chicago. When we got through security we discovered that our flight into Philadelphia was delayed by three hours due to strong winds and heavy rain in the Philadelphia area. We arrived at the airport in good time even though we were held up in typical rush hour traffic. After passing through the security checkpoint we suddenly found ourselves with plenty of time on our hands.

Our delayed return to Philadelphia affected the eight of us in our group. Others on the flight were delayed as well, but our focus and our concern was directed to our group. At the time of our delay, baseball's World Series was also delayed. Fans were sent home. The visiting team had to find a motel some 25 miles away. They had planned on returning home but their plans were changed. Delays can affect a lot of people, but we tend only to look at how it affects us. Delays are usually caused by things or circumstances beyond our control. The weather, traffic congestion, regulatory paperwork, and mechanical failure are just a few of the culprits that cause delay on a daily basis.

How do we respond to delays? In rush hour traffic some resort to blowing the horn. Others weave in and out of their lane of traffic to try and get a few car lengths ahead. Some grow restless and impatient. Some become irritable and vent their anger on innocent bystanders. Some resort to shouting or arguing. Others take delays in stride. They expect them. They plan for them. They show patience. They relax and submit themselves to the circumstances they know they have no power to change. They find ways to make their time useful. They talk. They read. They make phone calls. They schedule appointments. They make a positive out of the negative.

Someone once said, "The reason people are late is because they plan to be on time. If they planned to be early, they would still be on time in the event there is a short delay." I can attest that it is much more relaxing sitting in the airport an hour ahead of time then to be tied up in traffic on the expressway with a flight scheduled to take off in 15 minutes. Delays tend to be a lot more stressful when we are running against the clock.

Delays are a fact of life. We do well to allow for them in our schedule. Expect them, and be prepared to make good use of them. Remember that as inconvenient as the delay is it could be far worse. Most times we still arrive at our destination albeit a bit later than we had planned.

—M. Gingrich

I Have Learned

- That no matter how much I care, some people just don't care back.
- That it takes years to build up trust, but only seconds to destroy it.
- That you can get by with charm for about fifteen minutes. After that, you better know something.
- That you can do something in an instant that will give you heartache for life.
- That it's taking me a long time to become the person I want to be.
- That you should leave loved ones with loving words. It may be the last time you see them.
- That you can keep going long after you can't.
- That we are responsible for what we do, no matter how we feel.
- That either I control my attitude or it will control me.
- That sometimes when I'm angry I have the right to be angry, but that doesn't give me the right to be cruel.
- That it isn't always enough to be forgiven by others. Sometimes you must learn to forgive yourself.
- That the people you care about most in life are taken from you too soon.
- That we don't have to change friends if we understand that friends change.
- That credentials on the wall do not make you a decent human.
- That money is a terrible way of keeping score.

Life Is Too Short

Often we allow ourselves to be upset by small things we should despise and forget. Perhaps some man we helped has proven ungrateful, some woman we believed to be a friend has spoken ill of us, some regard we thought we deserved has been denied us. We feel such disappointments so strongly that we can no longer work or sleep. But isn't that absurd? Here we are on this earth, with only a few more decades to live, and we lose many irreplaceable hours brooding over grievances that in a year's time will be forgotten by us and by everybody else. No, let us devote life to worthwhile actions and feelings, to great thoughts, real affections, and enduring understandings. For life is too short to belittle.

Life's Little Nuisances

- The person behind you in the supermarket who keeps running their cart into the back of your ankle.
- The way everyone drives slower when you're in a hurry.

- Trying on sunglasses with the tag still attached to the bridge.
- The way everyone drives right on your bumper when you slow down to look for an address.
- You open a can of soup—or anything, really—and the lid falls in.
- Slicing your tongue while licking an envelope.
- The tire gauge that lets out half the air in your tire while you're trying to get a reading.
- Realizing you never washed that bright red shirt by itself before…after everything else in the load comes out pink.
- Setting your alarm clock for P.M. instead of A.M.
- Having to say to five different salespeople, "No thanks, I'm just looking."
- You reach under a table to pick something up and whack your head coming back up.
- The candy bar or bag of chips that gets stuck on the rotating clip in a vending machine.

One of Those Days

Ever have one of these days?

Did you hear about the teacher who was helping one of her kindergarten students put his boots on? He asked for help and she could see why. With her pulling and him pushing, the boots still didn't want to go on.
When the second boot was finally on, she had worked up a sweat. She almost whimpered when the little boy said, "Teacher, they're on the wrong feet."

She looked and sure enough, they were. It wasn't any easier pulling the boots off than it was putting them on. She managed to keep her cool as together they worked to get the boots back on—this time on the right feet. He then announced, "These aren't my boots."

She bit her tongue rather than scream, "Why didn't you say so?" like she wanted to. Once again she struggled to help him pull the ill-fitting boots off. He then said, "They're my brother's boots. My mom made me wear them." She didn't know if she should laugh or cry.

She mastered up the grace to wrestle the boots on his feet again. She said, "Now, where are your mittens?" He said, "I stuffed them in the toes of my boots."

Preventive Maintenance

The benefits and the importance of preventive maintenance programs impact every area of life. The idea behind preventive maintenance is to preserve our investment. In some ways it is like an insurance policy in that it protects against or lessens the possibility of a major breakdown. We make a purchase and we want it to last so we service it in a way that will give us longevity. We know that a car with regular oil changes or a piece of machinery that is greased periodically is most likely to run smoother and longer than one that is neglected. Keeping tires inflated properly will translate into longer tire life. A coat of wax protects a floor against the constant exposure of harsh elements and shuffling feet. Even washing our clothes, brushing our teeth, etc., is an investment in personal hygiene that guards against disease and sickness.

Friendships, marriages, and all interpersonal relationships are dependent upon regular maintenance, as well. If a friendship is neglected it will dissolve. If a marriage is not oiled and greased properly it will generate plenty of friction and eventually fall apart. Interpersonal relationships will become strained when there is a lack of communication and appreciation.

It doesn't take long to recognize that having a good maintenance plan in place will reap huge benefits. The cost from major breakdowns and work loss can be devastating. And yet most of us have areas where preventive maintenance has been neglected. Why? Is it a time factor? Is it failure to give it priority? Is it carelessness? Whatever the reason for its neglect, we do know that failure to do routine maintenance will have its consequences.

How does this subject relate to society? Do we perhaps find ourselves picking up the pieces rather than practicing prevention? How different would society be if more marriages were intact and children had a real mom and dad? Would prisons be less crowded if proper discipline was administered in a child's formative years? Can honesty and integrity be expected of children when it's not evident in adults? The laws of nature teach us that we will reap what we sow. Society has promoted promiscuity, violence, infidelity, theft and greed, in increasing brazenness across the television screen until it is viewed by many as an acceptable norm. In the aftermath, we find children and youth struggling physically, mentally, and emotionally. The costs are astronomical in dollars and cents, but even more sobering are the statistics for those who are caught in the crossfire.

Is it too much to ask for a return to the things that have worked in the past? Marital faithfulness, so children have their real parents to teach and train them. Discipline by spanking, so the will is broken when the heart of a child is tender so that they can be taught. Financial responsibility, where children learn that if they want something they must work for it. Personal responsibility, that doesn't try to shift blame on someone else but accepts the consequences of mistakes and learns from it. Can society continue to snub the principles God set forth in His Word and not reap the consequences? The answer is no!

Will society change its course? Only as individual families begin the journey back to God and adhere to his preventive maintenance plan is it possible that the fabric of society will begin to change. Until then society will most likely continue its frustrating and lackluster attempts at reform, and resort instead to picking up the pieces. A new tire on a broken wheel will be short lived if the spokes of the wheel are twisted and broken. The wheel needs to be fixed and maintained if there is any hope of getting the wagon out of the ditch and back on the road. The spokes give the wheel its strength much the same as principles and values give a society its strength. The hope of the next generation is at stake. I pray that history will record families and people who saw the necessity of fixing the wheel and turned their hearts to God. Therein lies hope of reaching our intended destination!

—M. Gingrich

Seasons Of The Heart

The heart has many seasons
Just as this good old earth,
And they all combine together to
Comprise what we are worth.

There is a childhood innocence
In which we dream and play,
There is a time for growing up
And making our own way.

There is a time for keeping
And a time for letting go.
A time for moving swiftly
And a time for walking slow.

There is a time for learning
And a time for teaching, too,
And there is a time for resting
When all the chores are through.

We all know joy and sorrow,
'Tis written in the plan,
But heaven waits beyond life's gates
For every earnest man.

Each life has many pictures
And all a work of art,
But what a silver symphony
The seasons of the heart.

—Grace E. Easley

Sixteen Facts I Learned In My Life

1. Available credit is not available cash. Just because I can borrow it is not proof I can repay.
2. Credit is not income. Sooner or later I have to give it back.
3. A maxed out credit card is not "Full," it is "Empty." It is like taking water out of a bucket that I must put back into the bucket.
4. When I rob Peter to pay Paul, they both might go broke. It's like trying to keep a leaking bucket filled with the water from the good one.
5. If I sell something that I financed, I need to pay something that is financial. If I use it for expansion or vacation I run into problems.
6. Lost income is a big part of the actual cost of taking a vacation. And it is well hidden behind the pressure to visit kin and going places of interest.
7. I have to work for a living. Mankind had it pretty good in the Garden of Eden. Their fall and expulsion from the garden brought a big change. Now they had to work to make a living, and it hasn't changed much since.
8. I can save too much. It doesn't really matter how much "Off" the price is. If I buy a $10 item for 1/2 price, $5 leaves my possession. Question #1 is: Do I need it? Question #2 is: Do I have $5 for this?

9. Anybody with money can spend it. It takes no "smarts" at all. Very small children, the fool, the blind, the lunatics, and the illiterate, all can do it. Knowing when and on what to spend it is a lot harder.

10. 90 Days same cash is no special deal. If I don't have the money to pay for it now, I probably won't then either. I will buy now and pay later…and later…and later…and later…and later…and later…and later…
11. Getting from point A to point B costs money, no matter how I go. If I am going on foot, by bike, by horse, by car, plane, truck, or train. Plan to pay.
12. To get two birds with one stone, the birds have to be in the same tree. One can easily end up getting no birds with three stones. I can always blame somebody else. Even the worst criminal justifies his actions before he does the crime.
13. If I resist, it only makes it worse. Whether it is too hot, too cold, too long, too short, too painful, too little, or too much—fighting back makes it worse.
14. People remember 50% of what they hear and 90% of what they see. If I say something foolish, they may retell it, if I write it, they may fax it all over the place.
15. If I do something unorthodox to get attention, that is all I usually get. Respect is harder to come by.
16. Being "taught a lesson" is not the same as "learning a lesson." It is possible to have ten year's experience or have only one year's experience ten times.

The Holes In Life

- I've learned…That the best classroom in the world is at the feet of an elderly person.
- I've learned…That when you're in love, it shows.
- I've learned…that just one person saying to me, "You've made my day!," makes my day.
- I've learned…That having a child fall asleep in your arms is one of the most peaceful feelings in the world.
- I've learned…That being kind is more important than being right.
- I've learned…That you should never say no to a gift from a child.
- I've learned…That I can always pray for someone when I don't have the strength to help him in some other way.
- I've learned…That no matter how serious your life requires you to be, everyone needs a friend to act goofy with.
- I've learned…That sometimes all a person needs is a hand to hold and a heart to understand.
- I've learned…That simple walks with my father around the block on summer nights when I was a child did wonders for me as an adult.
- I've learned…That we should be glad God doesn't give us everything we ask for.
- I've learned…That money doesn't buy class.
- I've learned…That it's those small daily happenings that make life so spectacular.
- I've learned…That under everyone's hard shell is someone who wants to be appreciated and loved.
- I've learned…That the Lord didn't do it all in one day. What makes me think I can?
- I've learned…That to ignore the facts does not change the facts.
- I've learned…That when you plan to get even with someone, you are only letting that person continue to hurt you.
- I've learned…That love, not time, heals all wounds.
- I've learned…That the easiest way for me to grow as a person is to surround myself with people smarter than I am.
- I've learned…That everyone you meet deserves to be greeted with a smile.
- I've learned…That no one is perfect until you fall in love with them.
- I've learned…That life is tough, but I'm tougher.
- I've learned…That opportunities are never lost; someone will take the ones you miss.
- I've learned…That when you harbor bitterness, happiness will dock elsewhere.
- I've learned…That one should keep his words both soft and tender, because tomorrow he may have to eat them.
- I've learned…That a smile is an inexpensive way to improve your looks.
- I've learned…That I can't choose how I feel, but I can choose what I do about it.
- I've learned…That everyone wants to live on top of the mountain, but all the happiness and growth occurs while you're climbing it.
- I've learned…That it is best to give advice in only two circumstances; when it is requested and when it is a life threatening situation.
- I've learned…That the less time I have to work with, the more things I get done.

There once was a little boy who had a bad temper. His father gave him a bag of nails and told him that every time he lost his temper, he must hammer a nail into the back of the fence. The first day the boy had driven thirty-seven nails into the fence.

Over the next few weeks, as he learned to control his anger, the number of nails hammered daily gradually dwindled down.

He discovered it was easier to hold his temper than to drive those nails into the fence.

Finally the day came when the boy didn't lose his temper at all.

He told his father about it and the father suggested that the boy now pull out one nail for each day that he was able to hold his temper.

The days passed and the young boy was finally able to tell his father that all the nails were gone.

The father took his son by the hand and led him to the fence.

He said, "You have done well, my son, but look at the holes in the fence. The fence will never be the same. When you say things in anger, they leave a scar just like this one.

"You can put a knife in a man and draw it out. It won't matter how many times you say I'm sorry, the wound is still there.

"A verbal wound is as bad as a physical one."

—Andy Rooney

The Rock

The imagination and clarity of thought in youth can come back to us years later to help us see with child-like openness the greatness of our God.

In my youth, when I had liberty to roam and ramble through the countryside, I once happened upon an immense boulder perched, seemingly, in a precarious position on a hill. At once fascinated, I clambered up to the crest to examine it. Almost instantly the thought seized me that it would be a magnificent sight to see that huge rock go thundering down the slope, clearing a lane through the underbrush. Even though I pushed and strained to move that rock, which looked as if it should easily be made to move, I did not succeed. Sinking wearily to the ground, I gave myself over to daydreams. At first they consisted of new plans to replace my frustrated attempt, but eventually the thought struck me that the rock could aptly represent great strength and stability, I no longer wanted to move that rock. It became to me a symbol of the peace and contentment of my life. As time passed I made trips to the hill to make sure my rock was still there, but as I grew older they became less frequent. My life became filled with the changes that come in early adulthood, until I completely forgot it.

Years passed, the majority of which were filled with worry, depression, and a growing despair. When both my parents died, I was left with the family's country estate, which I planned to sell to a land-developer despite the county's opposition. I had pushed God out of my life and had no interest in seeking him. I did not know why I was doing it (I now realize it was God's hand), but I traveled back to the homestead, which I considered to hold nothing but bittersweet memories. Deep in despair, I started out on a purposeless hike. Without my help or encouragement, my feet moved down the trail then left it to seek a slope in the woods. All the while questions raced through my mind: Why was there no stability in my life? Why was my life so meaningless? Then I stopped, transfixed, for there in front of me was the answer. It was my childhood symbol of strength and stability: the rock! At that moment a thought crossed my mind that I tried desperately to push away, but could not: "God is the rock." I made a lunge at the rock, trying to dislodge it. I knew that if it would give, it could not represent the attributes of stability and strength. It would not give, and as in long days before, I sank to the ground, this time on my knees, realizing that I needed the rock to give me the true stability in life and the strength to hold fast.

Many times in years after, Satan came and pushed me. Many times I started to roll down the hill, but God always caught me before I reached the bottom, and brought me back to the top.

—Carmen Martin

Three Things

Three things in life that, once gone, never come back:
- Time
- Words
- Opportunity

Three things in life that must never be lost:
- Peace
- Hope
- Honesty

Three things in life that are most valuable:
- Love
- Self-confidence
- Friends

Three things in life that are never certain:
- Dreams
- Success
- Fortune

Three things that make a man/woman:
- Hard work
- Sincerity
- Commitment

Three things in life that can destroy a man/woman:
- Alcohol
- Pride
- Anger

Three things that are truly constant:
- Father
- Son
- Holy Ghost

I ask the Lord to bless you, as I pray for you today; to guide you and protect you as you go along your way. His love is always with you, His promises are true. And when you give Him all your cares, you know He'll see you through.

And as we seek for fun and ease
Our bodies to renew,
Let's draw yet closer to the Lord
Who died for me and you.

—*W.G. Ester*

What Cancer Cannot Do

Cancer is so limited…
- It cannot shatter love,
- It cannot corrode faith,
- It cannot destroy peace,
- It cannot kill friendship,
- It cannot suppress memories,
- It cannot silence courage,
- It cannot invade the soul,
- It cannot steal eternal life,
- It cannot conquer the spirit.

Vacation Time

Vacation time is here once more,
With all its joys and thrills;
The time to scale the mountains heights
And roam the lovely hills.

The time to go down to the beach
And learn to fish and swim;
But let's not forget the Lord of all
And what we owe to Him.
Vacation time is the time to rest
To relax and be at ease,
To forget our worries and our cares
And do just what we please.

'Tis true our bodies need some rest,
From worry, work, and care.
But let's remember God each day
And go to Him in prayer.

Our bodies need our constant care
To keep them fit and trim;
But God alone can help the soul
So let us trust in Him.

What If?

What if I'm involved in an accident? What if my house is destroyed by a tornado? What if I lose my health? What if my best friend turns their back? What if I get hurt and can't work? What if I lose my job? What if I can't pay my bills? What if I lose a major business client? What if economic losses cause severe financial strain? What if?

You will notice that every sentence in the previous paragraph had one common denominator, "what if," or the unknown. It is the foundational basis for every insurance company. Their business is built on the "what if." If people knew their house would never catch fire or they would never be involved in an accident you can certainly bet they wouldn't buy insurance to cover the loss. Why is fire insurance more expensive in the forests of the midwest? Why is hurricane insurance more feasible along the gulf coast? The answer is obvious. There is more risk of loss. Why is flood insurance more costly when you live next to a river? Why are vehicle insurance rates higher in metropolitan areas? Again, the answer is obvious. There is a direct correlation between insurance coverage and the "what if" risk factor.

The "what if" question is endless. What if my family had moved to another state? Would I have met my wife?

Would growing up in a different culture have affected my values and choices? What if I had gone to a different school or church? What if I had grown up on a farm, or in the city? What if?

What if our vehicles were the same as 50 years ago? What if the roads weren't paved? What if there was no law and order? What if there was no electric? What if there was no mail service? What if there were no trees or flowers? What if the sun refused to come up in the morning? What if?

The "what if" question reaches into the spiritual realm as well. What if my parents hadn't taken me to church? What if I had never heard the gospel message? What if Christ had not come to this earth for the salvation of mankind? What if He hadn't given His life on Calvary's cross? What if He hadn't triumphed over death on that Easter morning? What if?

But He did! He is risen indeed! But "what if" I refuse to accept his gift of salvation? Why go through life asking the question, "what if?", and insuring oneself "just in case", and then refusing the Savior in the face of certain calamity that is certain! The gift of God is eternal life. It is an insurance policy that outperforms all others. It lays claim to eternal benefits. It's not a question of "what if," but a question of "will you" refuse or accept. It resonates with eternal implications.

"Because He lives I can face tomorrow! Because He lives all fear is gone! Because I know He holds the future, life is worth the living just because He lives!" *(Gloria Gaither)*

—M. Gingrich

What's Now?

Before you rush away from this moment, take a look around and see its beauty. Instead of worrying about what's next, see the immense value that's already yours in what's now.

Savor the time you're in and the place where you are. Appreciate all that you have instead of being obsessed with how to get more.

You are already wealthy beyond all measure. Open your eyes to now, open your heart to purpose, and experience in rich detail the miracle that is your life.

There's nothing to be gained by racing furiously away from this moment in search of more. Instead, put your energy into accepting all that is and you'll find it is more than enough.

Put your focus, care, love, attention, interest, curiosity, purpose, and passion into where you are right now. This is your time and place to live, to achieve, to feel, to learn, and to experience.

Everything you are, you are right now. Be here and live the richness.

—Ralph Marston

You're Getting Older If...

- Everything hurts and what doesn't hurt, doesn't work.
- The gleam in your eyes is from the sun hitting your bifocals.
- You get winded playing chess.
- Your children begin to look middle-aged.
- You finally reach the top of the ladder, and find it leaning against the wrong wall.
- You join a health club and don't go.
- You begin to outlive enthusiasm.
- You decide to procrastinate but then never get around to it.
- You need glasses...to find your teeth.
- You know all the answers, but nobody asks you the questions.
- You look forward to a dull evening.
- You walk with your head held high trying to get used to your bifocals.
- Your favorite part of the newspaper is "25 Years Ago Today."
- You sit in a rocking chair and can't make it go.
- Your knees buckle and your belt won't.
- You stop looking forward to your next birthday.
- Dialing long distance wears you out.
- You're startled the first time you are addressed as "Old Timer."—
- You remember today that yesterday was your wedding anniversary.
- You burn the midnight oil after 9:00 P.M.
- Your back goes out more than you do.
- The little gray haired lady you helped across the street is your wife.
- You have too much room in the house and not enough in the medicine cabinet.
- You sink your teeth into a steak and they stay there.

Love

A Christmas Gift-A Baby's Love

We were the only family with children in the restaurant. I sat Erik in a high chair and noticed everyone was quietly eating and talking. Suddenly, Erik squealed with glee and said, "Hi there." He pounded his fat baby hands on the high chair tray. His eyes were wide with excitement, and his mouth bared a toothless grin, and he wriggled and giggled with merriment. I looked around and saw the source of his merriment. It was a man whose pants were baggy, and his toes poked out of would-be shoes. His shirt was dirty, and his hair was uncombed and unwashed. His whiskers were too short to be called a beard, and his nose was so varicose it looked like a road map. We were too far from him to smell, but I was sure he smelled. His hands waved and flapped on loose wrists. "Hi there, baby; hi there, big boy. I see ya, buster," the man said to Erik. My husband and I exchanged looks, "What shall we do?" Erik continued to laugh and answered "Hi, hi there." Everyone in the restaurant noticed and looked at us and then at the man. The old geezer was creating a nuisance with my beautiful baby.

Our meal came, and the man began shouting from across the room, "Do ya know pattycake? Do you know peek-a-boo? Hey, look, he knows peek-a-boo." Nobody thought the old man was cute. He was obviously drunk. My husband and I were embarrassed. We ate in silence; all except for Erik, who was running though his repertoire for the admiring skid-row bum, who in turn, reciprocated with his cute comments.

We finally got through the meal and headed for the door. My husband went to pay the check and told me to meet him in the parking lot. The old man sat poised between me and the door. "Lord, just let me out of here before he speaks to Erik or me," I prayed. As I drew closer to the man, I turned my back trying to sidestep him and avoid any air he might be breathing. As I did, Erik leaned over my arm, reaching with both arms in a baby's "pick-me-up" position. Before I could stop him, Erik had propelled himself from my arms to the man's.

Suddenly, a very old smelly man and a very young baby consummated their love relationship. Erik, in an act of total trust, love, and submission laid his tiny head upon the man's ragged shoulder. The man's eyes closed, and I saw tears hover beneath his lashes. His aged hands full of grime, pain, and hard labor, gently, so gently, cradled my baby and stroked his back.

No two beings have ever loved so deeply for so short a time. I stood awestruck. The old man rocked and cradled Erik in his arms for a moment, and then his eyes opened and set squarely on mine. He said in a firm commanding voice, "You take care of this baby." Somehow I managed, "I will," from a throat that contained a stone.

He pried Erik from his chest unwillingly, longingly, as though he were in pain. I received my baby, and the man said, "God bless you ma'am, you've given me my Christmas gift."

I said nothing more than a muttered thanks. With Erik in my arms, I ran for the car. My husband was wondering why I was crying and holding Erik so tightly, and why I was saying, "God, forgive me." I had just witnessed Christ's love shown though the innocence of a tiny child who saw no sin, who made no judgement; a child who saw a soul, and a mother who saw a suit of clothes.

I realized that I was a Christian who was blind, holding a child who was not. I felt it was God asking, "Are you willing to share your son for a moment?" when he shared his for all eternity. The ragged old man, unwittingly, had reminded me, "To enter the kingdom of God, we must become as little children."

A Lesson From A Retired Pastor

Many years ago, a church in Atlanta was honoring one of its senior pastors who had been retired many years.

He was 92 at that time, and I wondered why the church even bothered to ask the old gentleman to preach at that age. After a warm welcome, the speaker was introduced. As the applause quieted down he rose from his high back chair and walked slowly, with great effort and a sliding gait to the podium. Without a note or written paper of any kind, he placed both hands on the pulpit to steady himself and then quietly and slowly he began to speak.

"When I was asked to come here today and talk to you, your pastor asked me to tell you what was the greatest lesson ever learned in my fifty odd years of preaching. I thought about it for a few days and boiled it down to just one thing that made the most difference in my life and sustained me through all my trials. The one thing that I could always rely on when tears and heartbreak and pain and fear and sorrow paralyzed me…the only thing that would comfort was this verse."

"Jesus loves me this I know, For the Bible tells me so.
Little ones to him belong, We are weak but he is strong.
Yes, Jesus loves me, The Bible tells me so."

When he finished, the church was quiet.

You actually could hear his foot steps as he shuffled back to his chair. I don't believe I will ever forget it.

A pastor once stated, "I always noticed that it was the adults who chose the children's hymn 'Jesus Loves Me' (for the children, of course) during a hymn sing.

Here is a version of "Jesus Loves Me" just for seniors, middle age, and everyone else who has white hair, or no hair at all and for those over.

JESUS LOVES ME
Jesus loves me, this I know,
Though my hair is white as snow.
Though my sight is growing dim,
Still He bids me trust in Him.

(*Chorus*)
Yes, Jesus loves me, yes, Jesus loves me;
Yes, Jesus loves me, the Bible tells me so.

Though my steps are oh, so slow,
With my hand in His I'll go;
On through life, let come what may,
He'll be there to lead the way. (*Chorus*)

Though I am no longer young,
I have much which He's begun.
Let me serve Christ with a smile,
Go with others the extra mile. (*Chorus*)

When the nights are dark and long,
In my heart He puts a song;
Telling me in words so clear,
"Have no fear, for I am near." (*Chorus*)

When my work on earth is done,
And life's victories have been won.
He will take me home above,
Then I'll understand His love. (*Chorus*)

I love Jesus, does He know?
Have I ever told Him so?
Jesus loves to hear me say,
That I love Him every day. (*Chorus*)

A Long Walk

In a remote village in Central America, the word got out among the peoples of the region that one of the American missionaries that had served this country for many years was about to return to the U.S. to live out the remaining years of her life.

The nationals desired to honor her for her years of service with a public time of appreciation. News of the event went to all parts of the country in which the missionary was known to the people. One very old and very poor man walked to the ceremony over mountainous terrain for four days to bring his gift to the missionary.

The gift consisted of two coconuts, but it was all the man had. The missionary recognized the man as coming from the remote village in the mountains.

"Brother, I cannot believe that you would walk so far to present me with this gift," said the missionary to the man.

His response? "Long walk part of gift."

—Author Unknown

Bury The Hatchet!

Have you ever heard the expression, "I'll never forgive him"? I have, and I cringe when I hear it. Feelings of ill will, resentment, spite, animosity, or hatred are all symptoms of an unforgiving spirit. People who carry these feelings with them suffer loss of sleep and deprive themselves of peace and happiness. Unfortunately there are countless folks who suffer serious health problems simply because they hold other people at arms length. They don't want to go to the same party. They cross to the other side of the street to avoid meeting them on the sidewalk. They refuse to associate with them. They refuse to wave, say hi, or engage in any kind of conversation. They allow their feelings to fester and spread. The irony of it all is the fact that the person carrying the grudge is the one who suffers the most. While their feelings of animosity are meant to hurt the other individual, they themselves receive the greater hurt. The stress, the inconvenience, and the discontentment can often be traced back to trivial happenings. Little things such as misunderstandings, something taken out of context, a few harsh words, or even differences of opinion that are not corrected can lead to major conflicts. Years of happiness and contentment are lost.

When we learn to "bury the hatchet," or in other words we learn to forgive and forget, we bury with it the stress and mental anguish associated with it. Then as we walk down the street we don't need to worry about who we might meet. We can enjoy the blessings of life because we are at peace and in turn our health will improve. The time to bury the hatchet is now! Not tomorrow! Not next week, but now! Improve your health and quality of life by determining today that you will unload those burdensome characters of ill will, resentment, and hatred. Go back to those folks that you have not forgiven and seek their forgiveness. If they refuse to accept, that goes with them. Forgive them anyway. That is a choice you can make. It is a choice that will greatly enhance your quality of life.

—M. Gingrich

Can I Borrow $25?

Arthur Clemens arrived home from work late, tired and irritated, to find his five-year old son, Greg, waiting for him at the door.

"Daddy, may I ask you a question?" Greg asked.

"Yeah sure, what it is?" replied Arthur.

"Daddy, how much do you make an hour?"

"That's none of your business. Why do you ask such a thing?"

"I just want to know. Please tell me, how much do you make an hour?" replied Greg.

"If you must know, I make $50 an hour."

"Oh," Greg replied, with his head down.

"Daddy, may I please borrow $25?"

Arthur was furious!

"If the only reason you asked that is so you can borrow some money to buy a silly toy or some other nonsense, then you march yourself straight to your room and go to bed. Think about why you are being so selfish. I don't work hard everyday for such childish frivolities."

Greg quietly went to his room and shut the door.

Arthur sat down and started to get even angrier about his little boy's questions. How dare he ask such questions only to get some money? After about an hour or so, he began to calm down, and started to think: maybe there was something his son really needed to buy with that $25, and he really didn't ask for money very often.

Slowly he tiptoed to his little son's room and opened the door. "Are you asleep, son?" he asked.

"No daddy, I'm awake," replied Greg.

"I've been thinking, maybe I was too hard on you earlier. It's been a long day and I took out my aggravation on you. Here's the $25 you asked for."

Greg sat straight up, smiling. "Oh, thank you, daddy!" He shouted. Then, reaching under his pillow he pulled out some crumpled up bills.

Arthur seeing that his son already had money, started to get angry again. Greg slowly counted out his money, and then looked up at his father.

"Why do you want more money if you already have some?" Arthur grumbled.

"Because I didn't have enough, but now I do," Greg replied. "Daddy, I have $50 now. Can I buy an hour of your time? Please come home early tomorrow. I would like to have dinner with you."

Arthur was crushed. He put his arms around his little son, and begged for his forgiveness.

Remember to share that $50 worth of your time with someone you love.

If you die tomorrow, the company that you are working for could easily replace you. The family and friends you leave behind will feel the loss for the rest of their lives. Time is precious!

I Wish You Enough

I overheard a father and daughter in their last moments together. They had announced her departure and standing near the security gate, they hugged and he said, "I love you. I wish you enough."

She in turn said, "Daddy, our life together has been more than enough. Your love is all I ever needed. I wish you enough, too, Daddy."

They kissed and she left. He walked over toward the window where I was seated. Standing there I could see he wanted and needed to cry. I tried not to intrude on his privacy, but he welcomed me in by asking, "Did you ever say goodbye to someone, knowing it would be forever?" "Yes, I have," I replied. Saying that brought back memories I had of expressing my love and appreciation for all my Dad had done for me. Recognizing that his days were limited, I took the time to tell him face to face how much he meant to me. So I knew what this man was experiencing.

"Forgive me for asking, but why is this a forever good-bye?" I asked.

"I am old, and she lives much too far away. I have challenges ahead and the reality is, the next trip back would be for my funeral," he said.

"When you were saying goodbye I heard you say, 'I wish you enough.' May I ask what that means?"

He began to smile. "That's a wish that has been handed down from other generations. My parents used to say it to everyone." He paused for a moment and looking as if trying to remember it in detail, he smiled even more.

"When we said 'I wish you enough,' we were wanting the other person to have a life filled with just enough good things to sustain them," he continued and then turning toward me he shared the following as if he were reciting it from memory:

"I wish you enough sun to keep your attitude bright.
I wish you enough rain to appreciate the sun more.
I wish you enough happiness to keep your spirit alive.
I wish you enough pain so that the smallest
joys in life appear much bigger.
I wish you enough gain to satisfy your wanting.
I wish you enough loss to appreciate all that you possess.
I wish enough "hello's" to get you
through the final "goodbye."

He then began to sob and walked away.
My friend, I wish you enough!

Just An Old Man?

When I met him he was past sixty and a bit unsteady on his feet. He was the only grandfather I ever knew. I was only four, and had been sent off to kindergarten. I was an only child, never away from my mother, and scared. Everything was new and strange to me. I did not know more than one or two of my fellow students. That first day, when we went into the cafeteria for our milk, I got my first glimpse of Grandad. He was leaning on his broom, singing softly to himself. The song he sang was something like, "leaning on the everlasting arms." I never knew my real grandfathers. They had both passed away years ago. This man loved little children. He spoke to each of us. Many were too shy and tried to getaway, but his words were seasoned with love. I missed my mother and wanted to go home. When he spoke it was of the love of God, how He sent His son Jesus to go about doing good and to die for our sins on the cross. He told us that God watches over us and takes care of us. This is what I needed to hear. I wasn't scared anymore. Most mornings he was there when we went to the cafeteria. He would sing to us and quote from the Bible. Someone told me he was a preacher. I looked forward to seeing him and talking to him, even in first and second grade. He retired a few years later, and when I asked an older student what happened to him, he said, "What do you care? He was just a old man!"

Years went by and I forgot about Granddad. In my late teens, working at a hospital, I met a nursing student, and we became friends. One day she called and said she was dropping by with her Grandfather and wanted me to meet him. He sure looked familiar and suddenly I remembered he was the old gentleman who cleaned our school and, in fact, he hadn't changed much since he worked at the school. His hands shook a lot more, and what little hair he had was white, as was his beard. He did not remember me. I was a lot bigger. Now I sure remembered him. What impressed me about him was the fact that his subject matter had not changed. He still talked about Jesus, and His love for sinners. He asked me if I was a child of God. I wasn't at the time, but God had his hand on me. Not too many years later, his granddaughter and I were married, and soon after, when the brethren came to visit, I was ready to give my heart to the Lord. I had learned that when people reach out in genuine love to you, that love comes from God. "For God so loved the world, that He gave His only begotten Son, that whosoever believeth in Him should not perish, but have everlasting life" (John 3:16).

Years later, when Granddad was in the old folk's home and we went to see him, he would tell me that someday I would be a preacher like he was. He sang hymns and would share the gospel with everyone that visited him and everyone that took care of him. You could hear him singing before you got to the front door. Some people said that Granddad was senile. It was true that he often could not remember your name, or maybe he thought you were someone else. But the love he showed me, as well as everything else, was real, because it came from above.

Just an old man? If that is true, the world needs more old men like him. He has been gone over twenty years, yet a day does not go by that I do not think of him, because one day he took away a little boy's fear and replaced it with love.

"There is no fear in love, but perfect love casteth out fear" (I John 4:18).

Love Is…

Slow to suspect—quick to trust;
Slow to condemn—quick to justify;
Slow to offend—quick to defend;
Slow to expose—quick to shield;
Slow to reprimand—quick to forbear;
Slow to demand—quick to give;
Slow to provoke—quick to conciliate;
Slow to hinder—quick to help;
Slow to resent—quick to forgive.

Love Letters

To "walk in love" means that we continually do the little acts of kindness that can make life bearable and better for another person.

One practical way to express our love costs only the price of a postage stamp—plus paper, ink, and a little thought.

All of us have felt the nudge to write a letter—an unexpected note that could brighten another person's day. Perhaps, it is a note of appreciation, an expression of concern, or a compliment for a task well done. Too often the letter goes unwritten and the impulse is unexpressed. We convince ourselves that we don't have time or that our letter won't matter.

A young minister cherished a note he received from a busy architect in his congregation. The letter said simply, "Your sermon met me where I was on Sunday—at the crossroads of confusion and hurt. Thanks for preaching it." Those words met the pastor where he lived—at the intersection of discouragement and pain—and encouraged him to keep on in the ministry. The note took less than five minutes to write.

Can you think of someone who needs encouragement? "Walk in love" to the mailbox today.

Love Through The Eyes Of Children

A group of professional people posed this question to a group of 4 to 8 year-olds, "What does love mean?" The answers they got were broader and deeper than anyone could have imagined. See what you think:

- Rebecca, age 8—"When someone loves you, the way they say your name is different. You know that your name is safe in their mouth."
- Chrissy, age 6—"Love is what makes you smile when you're tired."
- Bobby, age 7—(wow!) "If you want to learn to love better, you should start with a friend who you hate."
- Nikka, age 6—"There are two kinds of love. Our love. God's love. But God makes both kinds of them."
- Noelle, age 7—"Love is like a little old woman and a little old man who are still pals even after they know each other so well."
- Clare, age 6—"Love is when mommy gives daddy the biggest piece of chicken."
- Elaine, age 5—"Love is when mommy sees daddy smelly and sweaty and still says he is handsome."
- Mark, age 6—"You really shouldn't say 'I love you' unless you mean it. If you mean it, you should say it a lot. People forget."

An author and lecturer once talked about a contest he was asked to judge. The purpose of the contest was to find the most loving child. The winner was a four-year-old child whose next door neighbor was an elderly gentleman who had recently lost his wife. Upon seeing the man cry, the little boy went into the old gentleman's yard, climbed up onto his lap, and just sat there. When his mother asked him what it was that he had said to the neighbor, the little boy said, "Nothing, I just helped him cry."

Pancakes

Brandon wanted to make his parents pancakes. He found a big bowl and spoon, pulled a chair to the counter, opened the cupboard, and pulled out the heavy flour canister, spilling it on the floor. He scooped some of the flour into the bowl with his hands, mixed in most of a cup of milk, and added some sugar, leaving a floury trail on the floor which by now had a few tracks left by his kitten.

Brandon was covered with flour and getting frustrated. He wanted this to be something very good for Mom and Dad, but it was getting very bad.

He didn't know what to do next, whether to put it all into the oven or on the stove (and he didn't know how the stove worked!). Suddenly he saw his kitten licking from the bowl of mix and reached to push her away, knocking the egg carton to the floor.

Frantically he tried to clean up this monumental mess but slipped on the eggs, getting his pajamas white and sticky. And just then he saw Dad standing at the door.

Big crocodile tears welled up in Brandon's eyes. All he'd wanted to do was something good, but he'd made a terrible mess. He was sure a scolding was coming, maybe even a spanking. But his father just watched him. Then, walking through the mess, he picked up his crying son, hugged him and loved him, getting his own pajamas white and sticky in the process.

That's how God deals with us. We try to do something good in life, but it turns into a mess. Our marriage gets all sticky or we insult a friend or we can't stand our job or our health goes sour.

Sometimes we just stand there in tears because we can't think of anything else to do. That's when God picks us up and loves us and forgives us. even though some of our mess gets all over Him. But, just because we might mess up, we can't stop trying to "make pancakes" for God or for others.

Puppy Size

"Danielle keeps saying it over and over again. We've been back to this animal shelter at least five times," mother told the volunteer.

"What is it she keeps asking for?" the volunteer asked.

"Puppy size!" replied mother.

"Well, we have plenty of puppies, if that's what she's looking for."

"I know, we have seen most of them," mother said in frustration.

Just then Danielle came walking into the office.

"Well, did you find one?" asked mom. "No, not this time," Danielle said with sadness in her voice. "Can we come back on the weekend?"

The two women looked at each other and shook their heads.

"You never know when we will get more dogs. There's always a good supply," said the volunteer.

Danielle took her mother by the hand and headed to the door. "Don't worry, I'll find one this weekend," she said.

Over the next few days both mom and dad had long conversations with Danielle. They both felt she was being too particular. "It's this weekend, or we're not looking any more," Dad finally said in frustration.

"We don't want to hear anything more about puppy size either," Mom said. Sure enough, they were the first ones in the shelter on Saturday morning. By now Danielle knew her way around, so she ran right for the section that housed the smaller dogs.

Tired of the routine, mom sat in the small waiting room at the end of the first row of cages. There was an observation window so you could see animals during times when visitors weren't permitted.

Danielle walked slowly from cage to cage, kneeling periodically to take a closer look. One by one the dogs were brought out, and she held each one.

One by one she said, "Sorry, you're not the one."

It was the last cage on this last day in search of the perfect pup. The volunteer opened the cage door, and Danielle carefully picked up the dog and held it closely. This time she took a little longer.

"Mom, this is it! I found the right puppy! He's the one! I know it!" she screamed with joy. "It's the puppy size!"

"But it's the same size as all the other puppies you held over the last few weeks," Mom said.

"No, not size—the sighs. When I held him in my arms, he sighed," she said.

"Don't you remember? When I asked you one day what love is, you told me love depends on the sighs of your heart. The more you love, the bigger the sigh!"

The two women looked at each other for a moment. Mom didn't know whether to laugh or cry. As she stooped down to hug her daughter, she did a little of both.

"Mom, every time you hold me, I sigh. When you and Daddy come home from work and hug each other, you both sigh. I knew I would find the right puppy if it sighed when I held it in my arms," she said.

Then holding the puppy up close to her face she said, "Mom, he loves me. I heard the sighs of his heart!"

Raindrops From Heaven

It was one of the hottest days of the dry season. We hadn't seen rain in almost a month. The crops were dying. The cows had stopped giving milk. The creeks and streams were long gone back into the earth. It was a dry season that would bankrupt several farmers before it was through. Every day, my husband and his brothers would go about the arduous process of trying to get water to the fields. Lately this process had involved taking a truck to the local water plant and filling it up with water. But severe rationing had cut everyone off. If we didn't see some rain soon, we would lose everything. It was on this day that I learned the true lesson of sharing and witnessed a miracle with my own eyes. I was in the kitchen making lunch for my husband and his brothers when I saw my six-year-old son, Billy, walking toward the woods. He wasn't walking with the usual carefree abandon of a youth but with a serious purpose. I could only see his back. He was obviously walking with a great effort, trying to be as still as possible. Minutes after he disappeared into the woods, he came running out again, toward the house. I went back to making sandwiches thinking that whatever task he had been doing was completed. A short time later, however, he was once again walking in that slow purposeful stride toward the woods. This activity went on for an hour—walking carefully to the woods, running back to the house.

Finally, I couldn't take it any longer and I crept out of the house and followed him on his journey (being very careful not to be seen, as he was obviously doing important work and didn't need his Mommy checking up on him). He was cupping both hands in front of him as he walked, being very careful not to spill the water he held in them, maybe two or three tablespoons in his tiny hands. I crept close as he went into the woods. Branches and thorns slapped his little face, but he just ignored them. As I leaned in to spy on him, I saw the most amazing site.

Several large deer stood in front of him. Billy walked right up to them. I almost screamed for him to get away. A huge buck with enormous antlers was dangerously close. But the buck did not threaten him, he didn't even move as Billy knelt down. Then I saw a tiny fawn lying on the ground; obviously suffering from dehydration and heat exhaustion. It lifted its head with great effort to lap up the water cupped in my little boy's hand. When the water was gone, Billy jumped up to run back to the house and I hid behind a tree. I followed him back to the side of the house where there was a spigot. We had shut off the water because of the drought. Billy opened it all the way up and a small trickle began to creep out. He knelt there, letting the drip, drip slowly fill up his makeshift "cup," as the sun beat down on his little back. Billy had gotten into trouble for playing with the hose the week before. He had received a lecture about the importance of not wasting water. It took several minutes for the drops to fill his hands. When he stood up and began the trek back, I was there in front of him.

His little eyes just filled with tears. "I'm not wasting," was all he said. As he began his walk, I joined him with a small pot of water from the kitchen. I let him tend to the fawn. I stayed away. It was his job. I stood on the edge of the woods watching as he worked so hard to save the fawn's life. As the tears that rolled down my face began to hit the ground, other drops…and more drops…and more suddenly joined them. I looked up at the sky. It was as if God, himself, was weeping. Some will probably say that this was all just a huge coincidence. Those miracles don't really exist; that it was bound to rain sometime. And I can't argue with that. I'm not going to try. All I can say is that the rain that came that day saved our farm, just like the actions of one little boy saved that fawn's life.

Rescued Goose

Where we live, on the eastern shore of Maryland, the gentle waters run in and out like fingers slimming at the tips. They curl into the smaller creeks and coves like tender palms. The Canadian geese know this place, as do the white swans and the ducks who ride an inch above the waves of Chesapeake Bay as they skim their way into harbor. In the autumn, by the thousands, they come home for the winter. The swans move toward the shores in a stately glide, their tall heads proud and unafraid. They lower their long necks deep into the water, where their strong beaks dig through the river bottoms for food. And there is, between the arrogant swans and the prolific geese, an indifference, almost a disdain. Once or twice each year, snow and sleet move into the area. When this happens, if the river is at its narrowest, or the creek shallow, there is a freeze which hardens the water to ice. It was on such a morning, near Osford, Maryland, that a friend of mine set the breakfast table beside the huge window, which overlooked the Tred Avon River. Across the river, beyond the dock, the snow laced the rim of the shore in white. For a moment she stood quietly, looking at what the night's storm had painted. Suddenly she leaned forward and peered close to the frosted window. "It really is," she cried out loud, "There is a goose out there." She reached to the bookcase and pulled out a pair of binoculars. Into their sights came the figure of a large Canadian goose, very still, its wings folded tight to its sides, its feet frozen to the ice. Then from the dark skies, she saw a line of swans. They moved in their own singular formation, graceful, intrepid, and free. They crossed from the west of the broad creek high above the house, moving steadily to the east.

As my friend watched, the leader swung to the right, then the white string of birds became a white circle. It floated from the top of the sky downward. At last, as easy as feathers coming to earth, the circle landed on the ice. My friend was on her feet now, with one unbelieving hand against her mouth. As the swans surrounded the frozen goose, she feared what life he still had might be pecked out by those great swan bills. Instead, amazingly instead, those bills began to work on the ice. The long necks were lifted and curved down, again and again, it went on for a long time. At last, the goose was rimmed by a narrow margin of ice instead of the entire creek. The swans rose again, following the leader, and hovered in that circle, awaiting the results of their labors.

The goose's head lifted. Its body pulled. Then the goose was free and standing on the ice. He was moving his big webbed feet slowly. And the swans stood in the air watching. Then, as if he had cried, "I cannot fly," four of the swans came down around him. Their powerful beaks scraped the goose's wings from top to bottom, scuttled under its wings and rode up its body, chipping off and melting the ice held in the feathers. Slowly, as if testing, the goose spread its wings as far as they would go, brought them together, accordion-like, and spread again.

When at last the wings reached their fullest, the four swans took off and joined the hovering group. They resumed their eastward journey, in perfect formation, to their secret destination.

Behind them, rising with incredible speed and joy, the goose moved into the sky. He followed them, flapping double time, until he caught up, until he joined the last end of the line, like a small child at the end of a crack-the-whip of older boys. My friend watched them until they disappeared over the tips of the farthest trees. Only then, in the dusk, which was suddenly deep, did she realize that tears were running down her cheeks and had been for how long she didn't know. This is a true story. It happened. I do not try to interpret it. I just think of it in the bad moments, and from it comes only one hopeful question: "If so for birds, why not for man?"

The Dime

Bobby was getting cold sitting out in his backyard in the snow. He didn't wear boots; he didn't like them, and anyway he didn't own any. The thin sneakers he wore had a few holes in them and they did a poor job of keeping out the cold.

Bobby had been in his backyard for an hour already, and try as he might, he could not come up with an idea for his mother's Christmas gift. He shook his head as he thought. "This is useless, because even if I do come up with an idea, I don't have any money to spend." Ever since his father had died three years before, the family of five had struggled. Bobby's mother worked nights at the hospital, but the small wage could only be stretched so far. What the family lacked in money and material things, they more than made up for in love and family unity. Bobby had two older sisters and one younger sister who ran the household in their mother's absence. All three sisters had already made beautiful gifts for their mother, now here it was Christmas Eve and he had nothing.

Wiping a tear from his eye, Bobby kicked the snow and started to walk down the street where the shops and stores were. It wasn't easy being six without a father, especially when he needed a man to talk to. He walked from shop to shop, looking into each decorated window. Everything seemed so beautiful and so out of reach. It was starting to get dark and Bobby reluctantly turned to walk home when suddenly his eye caught the glimmer of the setting sun's rays reflecting off something along the curb. He reached down and discovered a shiny dime. Never before had anyone felt as wealthy as Bobby did at that moment. As he held his new found treasure, a warmth spread throughout his entire body and he went into the first store he saw. His excitement quickly turned cold when the salesperson told him he couldn't buy anything with only a dime. He saw a flower shop and went inside to wait in line. When the shop owner asked if he could help him, Bobby presented the dime and asked if he could buy one flower for his mother's Christmas gift. The shop owner looked at Bobby and his ten cent offering. He then put his hand on Bobby's shoulder and said to him, "You just wait here and I'll see what I can do for you."

As Bobby waited he looked at the beautiful flowers and even though he was a boy, he could see why mothers and girls liked flowers. The sound of the door closing as the last customer left jolted Bobby back to reality. All alone in the shop, he began to feel alone and afraid. Suddenly the shop owner returned and came to the counter. There before Bobby's eyes lay twelve long-stem red roses with leaves of green and tiny white flowers all tied together with a big silver bow. Bobby's heart sank as the owner picked them up and placed them gently into a long white box. "That will be ten cents young man," the shop owner said reaching out his hand.

Slowly Bobby moved his hand to give the man his dime. Could this really be true? No one else would sell him a thing for his dime! Sensing the boy's reluctance, the man added, "I just happened to have some roses on sale for ten cents a dozen. Would you like them?" This time Bobby did not hesitate, and when the man placed the long box in his hands, he knew it was true. Walking quickly toward the door that the owner held for him, he heard him say, "Merry Christmas, son."

As he returned inside, the shop owner's wife walked out. "Who were you talking to back there and where are the roses you were fixing?" Staring out the window, and blinking back tears from his eyes, he replied, "A strange thing happened to me this morning. While I was setting up things to open the shop, I thought I heard a voice telling me to set aside a dozen of my best roses for a special gift. I wasn't sure at the time whether I had lost my mind or what, but I set them aside anyway. Then just a few minutes ago, a little boy came into the shop and wanted to buy a flower for his mother with one small dime."

"When I looked at him, I saw myself many years ago. I too was poor with nothing to buy my mother a Christmas gift. A bearded man, who I didn't know, stopped me on the street and told me that he wanted to give me ten dollars. When I saw that little boy tonight, I knew who's voice that was, and I put together a dozen of my best roses." The shop owner and his wife hugged each other tightly, and as they stepped out into the bitter night air, they somehow didn't feel the cold at all.

The Wooden Bowl

A frail old man went to live with his son, daughter-in-law, and four-year-old grandson. The old man's hands trembled, his eyesight was blurred, and his step faltered. The family ate together at the table.

But the elderly grandfather's shaky hands and failing sight made eating difficult. Peas rolled off his spoon and onto the floor. When he grasped the glass, milk spilled on the tablecloth. The son and daughter-in-law became irritated with the mess.

"We must do something about Grandfather," said the son. "I've had enough of his spilled milk, noisy eating, and food on the floor." So the husband and wife set a small table in the corner. There, Grandfather ate alone while the rest of the family enjoyed dinner. Since Grandfather had broken a dish or two, his food was served in a wooden bowl. When the family glanced in Grandfather's direction, sometimes he had a tear in his eye as he sat alone.

Still, the only words the couple had for him were sharp admonitions when he had dropped a fork or spilled food. The four-year-old watched it all in silence.

One evening before supper, the father noticed his son playing with wood scraps on the floor. He asked the child curiously, "What are you making?" Sweetly, the boy responded, "Oh, I am making a little bowl for you and Mama to eat your food in when I grow up." The four-year-old smiled and went back to work.

The words so struck the parents that they were speechless. Then tears started to stream down their cheeks. Though no word was spoken, both knew what must be done. That evening, the husband took Grandfather's hand and gently led him back to the family table. For the remainder of his days he ate every meal with the family. And for some reason, neither husband nor wife seemed to care any longer when a fork was dropped, when milk was spilled, or when the tablecloth was soiled.

This Is What Love Is All About

It was a busy morning, approximately 8:30 a.m., when an elderly gentleman in his 80's arrived to have stitches removed from his thumb. He stated that he was in a hurry as he had an appointment at 9:00 a.m.

I took his vital signs and had him take a seat, knowing it would be over an hour before someone would be able to see him. I saw him looking at his watch and decided, since I was not busy with another patient, I would evaluate his wound. On exam it was well healed, so I talked to one of the doctors, got the needed supplies to remove his sutures and redress his wound.

While taking care of his wound, we began to engage in conversation. I asked him if he had a doctor's appointment this morning, as he was in such a hurry.

The gentleman told me no, that he needed to go to the nursing home to eat breakfast with his wife.

I then inquired as to her health. He told me that she had been there for a while and that she was a victim of Alzheimer's disease. As we talked, and I finished dressing his wound, I asked if she would be worried if he was a bit late. He replied that she no longer knew who he was, that she had not recognized him in five years now.

I was surprised and asked him, "And you still go every morning, even though she doesn't know who you are?"

He smiled as he patted my hand and said, "She doesn't know me, but I still know who she is."

I had to hold back tears as he left. I had goose bumps on my arm, and thought, "That is the kind of love I want in my life."

True love is neither physical, nor romantic. True love is an acceptance of all that is, has been, will be, and will not be.

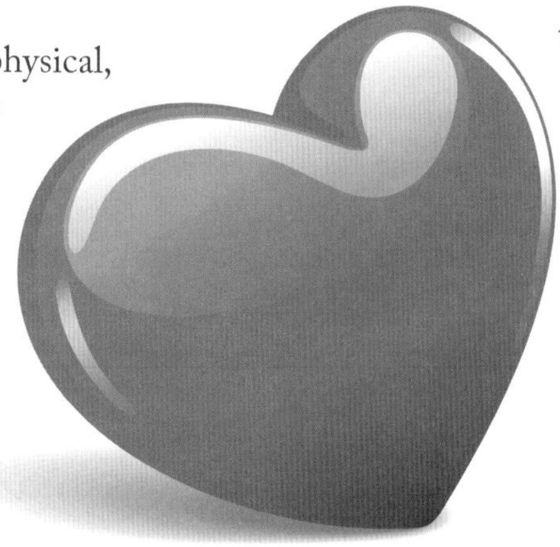

True Love

Two artists were once told to each draw a picture that would portray the word "Love".

The first artist drew a golden sunset, still waters, and cool mountains in the background.

The second artist drew his with a grey thunderstorm and winds whipping a pine tree till it slightly bent over. At the very top of the pine tree was a bird's nest with four little birds and a mother bird keeping them under her wings to protect them from the storm.

Which portrays a picture of true love?

What Really Matters

Date: Wednesday, December 27, 2000, 1:37 p.m. and they call some of these people "retarded." A few years ago, at the Seattle Special Olympics, nine contestants, all physically or mentally disabled, assembled at the starting line for the 100-yard dash. At the gun, they all started out, not exactly in a dash, but with a relish to run the race to the finish and win. All, that is, except one little boy who stumbled on the asphalt, tumbled over a couple of times, and began to cry. The other eight heard the boy cry. They slowed down and looked back. Then they all turned around and went back. Every one of them. One girl with Down's Syndrome bent down and kissed him and said: "This will make it better." Then all nine linked arms and walked together to the finish line. Everyone in the stadium stood, and the cheering went on for several minutes. People who were there are still telling the story. Why? Because deep down we know this one thing: What matters in this life is more than winning for ourselves. What matters is helping others win, even if it means slowing down and changing our course.

Miracles

Caller ID

Isn't it amazing how God works in our lives! On a Saturday night, this pastor was working late, and decided to call his wife before he left for home. It was about 10:00 PM, but his wife didn't answer the phone. The pastor let it ring many times.

He thought it was odd that she didn't answer, but decided to wrap up a few things and try again in a few minutes. When he tried again she answered right away. He asked her why she hadn't answered before, and she said that it hadn't rung at their house. They brushed it off as a fluke and went on their merry ways.

The following Monday, the pastor received a call at the church office, which was the phone that he'd used that Saturday night. The man that he spoke with wanted to know why he'd called on Saturday night. The pastor couldn't figure out what the man was talking about. Then the man said, "It rang and rang, but I didn't answer." The pastor remembered the mishap and apologized for disturbing him, explaining that he'd intended to call his wife.

The man said, "That's okay. Let me tell you my story. You see, I was planning to commit suicide on Saturday

night, but before I did, I prayed, 'God if you're there, and you don't want me to do this, give me a sign now.' At that point my phone started to ring, I looked at the caller ID, and it said, Almighty God. I was afraid to answer!"

The reason why it showed on the man's caller ID that the call came from 'Almighty God' is because the name of the church is Almighty God Tabernacle!!

God Still Heals

We moved to Kentucky in 1968, to work at Flat Creek Mission. When we arrived there with a big load of furniture, etc., a nineteen-year-old neighbor boy, Richard Hubbard, showed up and helped to unload the truck. When he was twelve years old he was riding a friend's bicycle. He stopped, stepped down with one foot, and went onto the ground with a broken leg. He was taken to Lexington Children's Hospital. When they operated they found that something was eating holes in the bone. They operated and scraped the bone and put his leg in a cast for six months. He came home, and had trouble and went back for a check up. The same thing was happening again. Each time they grafted bone in; another six months in the hospital, and then another six months at home. This was repeated for six years.

After we lived there a few months he came and asked if I would take him to Lexington for a check up. The hospital was a hundred miles away (one way), and he had no way to get there. I said I'd take him. There they x-rayed him before they would admit him. They found another hole, but didn't have bone to fix it. They said, "Go home, and we'll call you when we have bone." They called about a week and a half later. We took him back, and they x-rayed him again. They said, "The hole has grown so much that we don't have enough bone to fix it. You go home and we'll put in a rush order and we'll call you when we have it." We waited about a week till they called and said they have more bone and that we should bring him in tomorrow morning by eight o'clock. We told him to sleep at our place, and that we would try to leave by four o'clock. The next morning when we sat down at the table, I asked him if he believed that God could heal that leg. He said he believed God could. We prayed that God would guide the doctors as they would do a good job, and that it would heal solid, so this would be the last time he would have to go back. We took him to Lexington, and they x-rayed him again several times. The doctors said, "We don't know what happened, but we can't find the hole. We know that it was there, because we have the other x-rays. Go home, and if you have any more trouble, get back up here quick."

Richard was nineteen-years-old, and now he is fifty-two and has never had any more trouble. God did more than we asked him to.

Highway 109

A drunk man in an Oldsmobile
They said had run the light,
That caused the six-car pileup
On 109 that night.

A mother, trapped inside her car,
Was heard above the noise;
Her plaintive plea near split the air;
"Oh, God, please spare my boys!"

She fought to loose her pinioned hands
She struggled to get free;
But mangled metal held her fast
In grim captivity.

Her frightened eyes then focused on
Where the back seat once had been;
But all she saw was broken glass and
Two children's seats crushed in.

Her twins were nowhere to be seen
She did not hear them cry,
And then she prayed they'd been thrown free;
"Oh, God, don't let them die!"

Then firemen came and cut her loose,
But when they searched the back,
They found therein no little boys,
But the seat belts were intact.

They thought the woman had gone mad
And was traveling alone,
But when they turned to question her,
They discovered she was gone.

Policemen saw her running wild
And screaming above the noise,
In beseeching supplication;
"Please, help me find my boys!

They're four-years-old and wear blue shirts
Their jeans are blue to match."
One cop spoke up, "They're in my car,
And they don't have a scratch.

They said their daddy put them there
And gave them each a cone;
Then told them both to wait for Mom
To come and take them home.

I've searched the area high and low,
But I can't find their dad.
He must have fled the scene, I guess,
And that is very bad."

The mother hugged the twins,
And said, while wiping at a tear,
"He could not flee the scene, you see,
For he's been dead a year."

The cop just looked confused and asked,
"Now, how can that be true?"
The boys said, "Mommy, Daddy
Came and left a kiss for you.

He told us not to worry
And that you would be all right,
And then he put us in this car
With the pretty, flashing light.

We wanted him to stay with us,
Because we miss him so,
But Mommy, he just hugged us tight
And said he had to go.

He said someday we'd understand
And told us not to fuss,
And he said to tell you, Mommy,
He's watching over us."

The mother knew without a doubt
That what they spoke was true,
For she recalled their dad's last words;
"I will watch over you."

The firemen's notes could not explain
The twisted, mangled car,
And how the three of them escaped
Without a single scar.

But on the cop's report was scribed,
In print so very fine,
An angel walked the beat tonight
On Highway 109.

Jesus And The Mud Puddle

Howard County Sheriff Jerry Marr got a disturbing call one Saturday afternoon a few months ago. His six-year-old grandson Mikey had been hit by a car while fishing in Greentown with his dad. The father and son were near a bridge by the Kokomo Reservoir when a woman lost control of her car, slid off the bridge, and hit Mikey at a rate of about fifty mph. Sheriff Marr had seen the results of

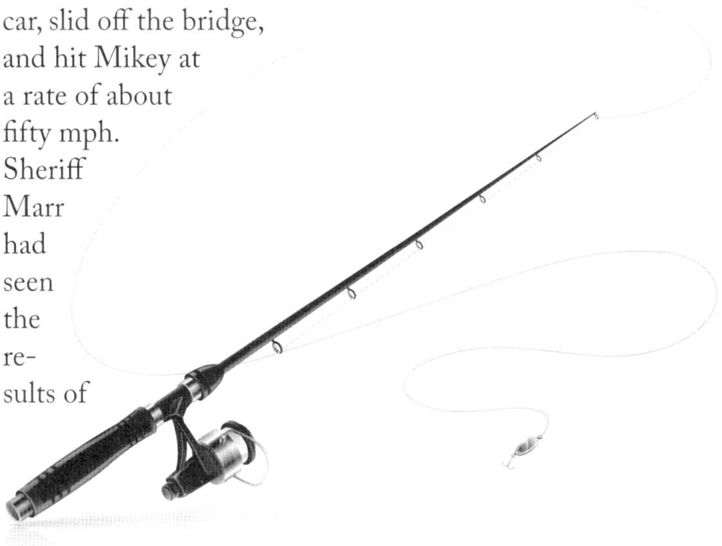

accidents like this and feared the worst. When he got to Saint Joseph Hospital, he rushed through the emergency room to find Mikey conscious and in fairly good spirits. "Mikey, what happened?" Sheriff Marr asked.

"Well, Papaw, I was fishin' with Dad, and some lady runned me over, and I flew into a mud puddle, and broke my fishin' pole, and I didn't get to catch no fish!" As it turned out, the impact propelled Mikey about 500 feet, over a few trees and an embankment and into the middle of a mud puddle. His only injuries were to his right femur bone which had broken in two places. Mikey had surgery to place pins in his leg. Otherwise, the boy was fine. Since the entire time, the only thing the boy could talk about was that his fishing pole was broken, the Sheriff went out to a store and bought him a new one while he was in surgery, so he could have it when he came out.

The next day the Sheriff sat with Mikey to keep him company in the hospital. Mikey was enjoying his new fishing pole and talked about when he could go fishing again, as he cast into the trash can. When they were alone, Mikey, just as a matter-of-fact, said, "Papaw, did you know Jesus is real?"

"Well," the Sheriff replied, a little startled. "Yes, Jesus is real to all who believe in Him and love Him in their hearts."

"No," said Mikey. "I mean Jesus is REALLY real."

"What do you mean?" asked the Sheriff.

"I know He's real, 'cause I saw Him," said Mikey, still casting into the trash can.

"You did?" asked the Sheriff.

"Yep," said Mikey. "When that lady runned me over and broke my fishing pole, Jesus caught me in His arms and laid me down in the mud puddle."

Journey

Diane, a young university student, was home for the summer. She had gone to visit some friends one evening and time passed quickly as each shared their various experiences of the past year. She ended up staying longer than planned, and had to walk home alone. She wasn't afraid because it was a small town and she lived only a few blocks away. As she walked along under the tall elm trees, Diane asked God to keep her safe from harm and danger. When she reached the alley, which was a shortcut to her house, she decided to take it. However, halfway down the alley she noticed a man standing at the end as though he were waiting for her. She became uneasy and began to pray, asking for God's protection. Instantly a comforting feeling of quietness and security wrapped around her; she felt as though someone was walking with her. When she reached the end of the alley, she walked right past the man and arrived home safely. The following day, she read in the newspaper that a young girl had been raped in the same alley, just twenty minutes after she had been there. Feeling overwhelmed by this tragedy and the fact that it could have been her, she began to weep.

Thanking the Lord for her safety and to help this young woman, she decided to go to the police station. She felt she could recognize the man, so she told them her story. The police asked her if she would be willing to look at a lineup to see if she could identify him. She agreed and immediately pointed out the man she had seen in the alley the night before. When the man was told he had been identified, he immediately broke down and confessed. The officer thanked Diane for her bravery and asked if there was anything they could do for her. She asked if they would ask the man one question. Diane was curious as to why he had not attacked her. When the policeman asked him, he answered, "Because she wasn't alone. She had two tall men walking on either side of her."

Never underestimate the power of prayer or angels.

Mommy's Little Angel Girl

There came a frantic knock
At the doctor's office door,
A knock, more urgent than
He had ever heard before.

"Come in, Come in,"
The impatient doctor said,
"Come in, Come in,
Before you wake the dead."

In walked a frightened little girl,
A child no more than nine,
It was plain for all to see,
She had troubles on her mind.

"Oh doctor, I beg you,
Please come with me,
My mother is surely dying,
She's as sick as she can be."

"I don't make house calls,
Bring your mother here,"
"But she's too sick, so you must come
Or she will die I fear."

The doctor, touched by her devotion,
Decided he would go;
She said he would be blessed,
More than he could know.

She led him to her house
Where her mother lay in bed,
Her mother was so very sick
She couldn't raise her head.

But her eyes cried out for mercy
As if pleading for a cure,
She would have died that very night
Of that they were quite sure.

The doctor got her fever down
And she lived through the night,
And morning brought the doctor signs,
That she would be all right.

The doctor said he had to leave
But would return again by two,
And later he came back to check,
Just like he said he'd do.

The mother praised the doctor
For all the things he'd done;
He told her she would have died,
Were it not for her little one.

"How proud you must be
Of your wonderful little girl,
It was her pleading that made me come,
She is really quite a pearl!"

"But doctor, my daughter died
Over three years ago,
Is the picture on the wall
Of the little girl you know?"

The doctors legs went limp
For the picture on the wall,
Was the same little girl
For whom he'd made this call.

The doctor stood motionless,
For quite a little while,
And then his solemn face,
Was broken by his smile.

He was thinking of that frantic
Knock heard at his office door,
And of the beautiful little angel
That had walked across his floor.

Out Of the Ordinary

He was no ordinary man. From the day of His birth to the day of His death, His life caused a stir among the people. Over 2000 years have passed and His life continues to be the central focus of civilization. The crowds of accusers continue to chant, "Away with Him, Away with Him," but try as they might they cannot silence Him. His life began in an out of the ordinary way. He was born of a virgin in a lowly stable room because there was no room in the inn. His birth was announced by angels on high. Shepherds and wisemen came to see Him. Miraculous indeed!

He began His out of the ordinary ministry at the age of thirty. What was different about his ministry? He taught as one having authority. The religious leaders could not refute Him. He exposed their hypocrisy. He cried out against their form of religion that was void of life. He healed the sick, made the lame to walk, and caused the blind to see. He fed the hungry multitude, He calmed the raging sea. He brought hope to the helpless, comfort to the hurting, and rest to the weary. Love was lived out in the ordinary circumstances of everyday life. He lived the life of a servant. He ministered to the needs of the common people.

His popularity caused jealousy among the religious leaders. They tried to snare Him with trick questions. They garnered the support of the local authorities. They bribed, they mocked, they scorned, they ridiculed. Their attempts to trap Him and corner Him were futile. They became the victims of their own traps.

Finally, He was sentenced to die on a cruel cross. Guiltless was He, innocent of any crime, condemned without a cause. Nailed to a cross between two thieves, He gave His life in death that men might live. The skies became dark although it was day. As His last breath was drawn, the earth shook, rocks broke in pieces, and the veil of the temple was rent from top to bottom. One of those looking on, said, "Truly this was the Son of God." Out of the ordinary! Miraculous indeed! Finally the religious authority of that day thought they had done away with this impostor who turned their tables of greed upside down and brought pangs of guilt to their self-righteous hearts. Now they could once more go about their business as usual.

His body was taken down from the cross and laid in an empty tomb. The tomb was sealed with a large stone and armed guards stood watch. Even a sealed tomb, armed guards, and death itself were no match for His out of the ordinary power. Triumphant, He rose victorious over death and the grave. The guards became as dead men. Angels sang the news. "He is not here! He is risen indeed!" Out of the ordinary! Previously unheard of! The tomb was empty, empty, empty!

The religious authority was defeated again. Even the bars of death could not hold Him. He was (is) alive! Forty days later he ascended to Heaven as His disciples watched Him go. He left with a promise of "I will never leave thee nor forsake thee. I go to prepare a place for you. I will come again and receive you unto myself that where I am there ye may be also." Occupy till I come! Indeed this was an out of the ordinary man who came to meet the needs of ordinary people so that they could live out-of-the-ordinary lives. In giving His life He gave an out of the ordinary gift. A gift that extended to every creed, every race, every culture, the rich, the poor, the young, and the old. It was given that all men, everywhere, could have life after death. Miraculous! Out of the ordinary love for ordinary people. Indeed!

—M. Gingrich

Special Delivery

Sally jumped up as soon as she saw the surgeon come out of the operating room. She said: "How is my little boy? Is he going to be okay? When can I see him?" The surgeon said, "I'm sorry, we did all we could."

Sally said, "Why do little children get cancer? Doesn't God care any more? God, where were you when my son needed you?"

The surgeon said, "One of the nurses will be out in a few minutes to let you spend time with your son's remains before it's transported to the university."

Sally asked that the nurse stay with her while she said good-bye to her son. Sally ran her fingers through his thick red curly hair. The nurse said, "Would you like a lock of his hair?" Sally nodded yes. The nurse cut a lock of his hair and put it in a plastic bag and handed it to Sally. Sally said, "It was Jimmy's idea to give his body to the university for study. He said it might help somebody else, and that is what he wanted. I said, 'No,' at first, but Jimmy said, 'Mom I won't be using it after I die, maybe it will help some other little boy to be able to spend one more day with his mother.'"

Sally said, "My Jimmy had a heart of gold, always thinking of someone else and always wanting to help others if he could."

Sally walked out of the Children's Hospital for the last time now after spending most of the last six months there.

She sat the bag with Jimmy's things in it on the seat beside of her in the car. The drive home was hard and it was even harder to go into an empty house. She took the bag to Jimmy's room and started placing the model cars and things back in his room exactly where he always kept them. She laid down across his bed and cried herself to sleep holding his pillow.

Sally woke up about midnight and laying beside of her on the bed, was a letter folded up. She opened the letter; it said:

"Dear Mom, I know you're going to miss me, but don't think that I will ever forget you or stop loving you because I'm not around to say I LOVE YOU. I'll think of you every day mom, and I'll love you even more each day. Some day we will see each other again. If you want to adopt a little boy so you won't be so lonely, he can have my room and my old stuff to play with. If you decide to get a girl instead, she probably wouldn't like the same things as us boys do, so you will have to buy her dolls and stuff girls like. Don't be sad when you think about me, this is really a great place.

"Grandma and Grandpa met me as soon as I got here and showed me around some, but it will take a long time to see everything here. The angels are so friendly, and I love to watch them fly. Jesus doesn't look like any of the pictures I saw of Him, but I knew it was Him as soon as I saw Him. Jesus took me to see God! And guess what mom? I got to sit on God's knee and talk to Him like I was somebody important. I told God that I wanted to write you a letter and tell you good-bye and everything, but I knew I couldn't do that. God handed me some paper and His own personal pen to write you this letter with. I think Gabriel is the name of the angel that is going to drop this letter off to you. God said for me to give you the answer to one of the questions you asked Him about…'Where was He when I needed him?'

"God said, 'The same place He was when Jesus was on the cross. He was right there, as He always is with all His children.'

"Oh, by the way Mom, nobody else can see what is written on this paper but you. To everyone else, it looks like a blank piece of paper. I have to give God His pen back now, He has some more names to write in the Book Of Life.

"Tonight I get to sit at the table with Jesus for supper. I'm sure the food will be great.

"I almost forgot to let you know—Now I don't hurt anymore, the cancer is all gone. I'm glad because I couldn't stand that pain anymore and God couldn't stand to see me suffer the pain either, so He sent The Angel of Mercy to get me. The Angel said I was Special Delivery!"

The All Seeing Eye Of God

It happened at a very busy place called "Bonded Warehouse" in Basel, Switzerland—my native country where there are lots of cars, trucks, trailers, and railways always moving around.

I wanted to back up with my van, but a "voice", not audible but very clear and kind of authoritative, said, "Stop, get out, and check behind the van!"

I saw no reason why I should do so and wanted to proceed, but again that voice told me, "Stop, get out, and check behind the van!"

I still wouldn't heed that "command" but that same voice ordered me the third time, "Stop, get out, and check behind the van!"

So, at last I followed that voice, got out, and checked behind the van, and lo and behold, a little boy, about six or seven years old was sitting on the ground right behind the van, playing! I could have killed him or crippled him! It was indeed an outstanding experience proving the existence of a never-to-be-forgotten superior being, God.

The Big Wheel

In September 1960, I woke up one morning with six hungry babies and just 75 cents in my pocket. Their father was gone. The boys ranged from three months to seven years; their sister was two. Their dad had never been much more than a presence they feared. Whenever they heard his tires crunch on the gravel driveway they would scramble to hide under their beds. He did manage to leave $15 a week to buy groceries. Now that he had decided to leave, there would be no more beatings, but no food either.

If there was a welfare system in effect in southern Indiana at that time, I certainly knew nothing about it. I scrubbed the children until they looked brand new and then put on my best homemade dress. I loaded them into the rusty old '51 Chevy and drove off to find a job. The seven of us went to every factory, store, and restaurant in our small town. No luck.

The children stayed in the car and tried to be quiet while I tried to convince whomever would listen that I was willing to learn or do anything. I had to have a job. Still no luck. The last place we went to, just a few miles out of town, was an old Root Beer Barrel Drive-in that had been converted to a truck stop. It was called the Big Wheel. An old lady named Granny owned the place and she peeked out of the window from time to time at all those children. She needed someone on the graveyard shift, eleven at night until seven in the morning. She paid sixty-five cents an hour, and I could start that night. I raced home and called the teenager down the street that baby-sat for people. I bargained with her to come and sleep on my sofa for a dollar a night. She could arrive with her pajamas on, and the children would already be asleep. This seemed like a good arrangement to her, so we made a deal.

That night when the little ones and I knelt to say our prayers, we all thanked God for finding Mommy a job. And so I started at the Big Wheel. When I got home in the mornings I woke the baby-sitter up and sent her home with one dollar of my tip money—fully half of what I averaged every night. As the weeks went by, heating bills added a strain to my meager wage. The tires on the old Chevy had the consistency of penny balloons and began to leak. I had to fill them with air on the way to work and again every morning before I could go home. One bleak fall morning, I dragged myself to the car to go home and found four tires in the back seat. New tires! There was no note, no nothing; just those beautiful brand new tires. Had angels taken up residence in Indiana? I wondered. I made a deal with the local service station. In exchange for his mounting the new tires, I would clean up his office. I remember it took me a lot longer to scrub his floor than it did for him to do the tires. I was now working six nights instead of five and it still wasn't enough. Christmas was coming and I knew there would be no money for toys for the children. I found a can of red paint and started repairing and painting some old toys. Then I hid them in the basement. Clothes were a worry too. I was sewing patches on top of patches on the boys pants and soon they would be too far gone to repair. On Christmas Eve the usual customers were drinking coffee in the Big Wheel. These were the truckers, Les, Frank, and Jim and a state trooper named Joe. The regulars all just sat around and talked through the wee hours of the morning and then left to get home before the sun came up. When it was time for me to go home at seven o'clock on Christmas morning I hurried to the car.

I was hoping the children wouldn't wake up before I managed to get home and get the presents up from the basement. It was still dark and I couldn't see much, but there appeared to be some dark shadows in the car—or was that just a trick of the night? Something certainly looked different, but it was hard to tell what. When I reached the car I peered warily into one of the side windows. Then my jaw dropped in amazement. My old battered Chevy was filled full to the top with boxes of all shapes and sizes. I quickly opened the driver's side door, crawled inside and knelt in the front facing the back seat. Reaching back, I pulled off the lid of the top box. Inside was a whole case of little blue jeans, sizes 2-10! I looked inside another box: It was full of shirts to go with the jeans. Then I peeked inside some of the other boxes. There was candy and nuts and bananas and bags of groceries. There was an enormous ham for baking, and canned vegetables and potatoes. There was pudding and Jell-O® and cookies, pie filling, and flour. There was a whole bag of laundry supplies and cleaning items. And there were five toy trucks and one beautiful little doll.

As I drove back through empty streets as the sun slowly rose, I was sobbing with gratitude. And I will never forget the joy on the faces of my little ones that precious morning. Yes, there were angels in Indiana that long-ago December, and they made a visit to the Big Wheel truck stop.

The Grocery List

Louise Bender, a poorly dressed lady with a look of defeat on her face, walked into a grocery store. She approached the owner of the store in a most humble manner and asked if he would let her charge a few groceries.

She softly explained that her husband was very ill and unable to work, they had seven children and they needed food.

John Zartman, the grocer, scoffed at her and requested that she leave his store at once.

Visualizing the family needs, she said: "Please, sir! I will bring you the money just as soon as I can."

John told her he could not give her credit, since she did not have a charge account at his store.

Standing beside the counter was a customer who overheard the conversation between the two. The customer walked forward and told the grocer that he would stand good for whatever she needed for her family.

The grocer said in a very reluctant voice, "Do you have a grocery list?"

Louise replied, "Yes sir."

"Okay," he said, "put your grocery list on the scales and whatever your grocery list weighs, I will give you that amount in groceries."

Louise hesitated a moment with a bowed head, then she reached into her purse and took out a piece of paper and scribbled something on it. She then laid the piece of paper on the scale carefully with her head still bowed.

The eyes of the grocer and the customer showed amazement when the scales went down and stayed down.

The grocer, staring at the scales, turned slowly to the customer and said begrudgingly, "I can't believe it."

The customer smiled and the grocer started putting the groceries on the other side of the scales. The scale did not balance so he continued to put more and more groceries on them until the scales would hold no more.

The grocer stood there in utter disgust. Finally, he grabbed the piece of paper from the scales and looked at it with greater amazement.

It was not a grocery list, it was a prayer, which said: "Dear Lord, you know my needs and I am leaving this in your hands."

The grocer gave her the groceries that he had gathered and stood in stunned silence. Louise thanked him and left the store. The other customer handed a fifty-dollar bill to the grocer and said; "It was worth every penny of it. Only God knows how much a prayer weighs."

Walking Recovery

An old fellow came into the hospital truly at death's door due to an infected gallbladder. The surgeon who removed the gallbladder was adamant that his patients be up and walking in the hall the day after surgery, to help prevent blood clots forming in the leg veins. The nurses walked the patient in the hall as ordered, and after the third day the nurse told how he complained bitterly each time they did. The surgeon told them to keep walking him.

After a week, the patient was ready to go. His family came to pick him up and thanked the surgeon profusely for what he had done for their father. The surgeon was pleased and appreciated the thanks, but told them that it was really a simple operation and we had been fortunate to get him in time.

"But doctor, you don't understand," they said. "Dad hasn't walked in over a year!"

Where God Wants Me To Be

After September 11, I happened to call a man on business that I didn't know and have not, nor will ever, talk to again. But this day, he felt like talking. He was Head of Security for a company that had invited the remaining members of a company who had been decimated by the attack on the Twin Towers to share their office space. With his voice full of awe he told me stories of why these people were alive and their counterparts were dead...and all the stories were just "little things."

As you might know, the head of the company got in late that day because his son started kindergarten.

Another fellow was alive because it was his turn to bring donuts.

There were other stories that I hope and pray will someday be gathered and put in a book.

The one that struck me was the man who put on a new pair of shoes that morning, took the various means to get to work but before he got there, he developed a blister on his foot. He stopped at a drugstore to buy a Band-Aid®. That is why he is alive today.

Now when I am stuck in traffic, miss an elevator, turn back to answer a ringing telephone—all the "little things" that annoy me—I think to myself, this is exactly where God wants me to be at this very moment.

—Author Unknown

Miscellaneous

Nature reveals poetic scenes,
Man cannot duplicate,
And when it's time, to leave the scene,
Our heart would rather wait.

For in this joy, we feel as though,
Our heart has skipped a beat,
For we have seen God's hand at work,
Making our day complete.

—Robert K. Phillips

Apology Letter

Lisa, my coworker at the travel agency, needed to send a letter of apology to a customer whose trip was a complete fiasco from start to finish. I reminded her of a similar situation a year earlier and dug out the letter I'd written then.

"All you have to do," I told her, "is to change the details, the date, and the name."

She looked it over and smiled wryly. "We won't even need to change the name."

Autumn Beauty

Nature reveals its color scheme,
When autumn rolls around,
Tree leaves display their beauty,
They trickle to the ground.

Our eyes gaze in
awesome wonder,
Unwilling to
retreat,
In these moments,
nature's beauty,
Has locked
Our eyes
and feet.

Our eyes dwell
upon this beauty,
That man cannot create,
Beauty from a higher power,
It's not an act of fate.

This beauty that nature displays,
Is beauty at its best,
It leaves us lasting impressions,
That place our soul at rest.

Eluding God

In 1981, a Minnesota radio station reported a story about a stolen car in California. Police were staging an intense search for the vehicle and the driver, even to the point of placing announcements on local radio stations to contact the thief. On the front seat of the stolen car sat a box of crackers that, unknown to the thief, were laced with poison. The car owner had intended to use the crackers as rat bait.

The police and the owner of the VW Bug were more interested in apprehending the thief to save his life than to recover the car. So often when we run from God, we feel it is to escape His punishment. But what we are actually doing is eluding His rescue.

Express Checkout

It was a Saturday afternoon, and Ray had rushed down to the local supermarket to hurriedly pick up some hamburger rolls, chips and a few condiments. He was having a few friends over to play games for the evening.

The store was loaded with shoppers and as he headed for the six item express lane, the only one that didn't have a long line, a woman completely ignoring the overhead sign slipped into the check-out line just in front of him pushing a cart piled high with groceries.

Ray was quietly fuming at the anticipated delay. But the elderly cashier beckoned the woman to come forward, looked into the cart and asked ever so sweetly, "So Dearie, which six items would you like to buy?"

Family Relationships

I ran short of money while visiting my brother and borrowed $50 from him.

After my return home, I wrote him a short letter every few weeks, enclosing a $5 check in each one. He called me up and told me how much he enjoyed the letters, regardless of the money; I had never written regularly before. Eventually, I sent off a letter and the last five-dollar check.

In my mail box the next week I found an envelope from my brother. Inside was another $50.

Five Little Chickens

Said the first little chicken,
With a queer little squirm,
"Oh, I wish I could find
A fat little worm!"

Said the next little chicken,
With an odd little shrug,
"Oh, I wish I could find
A fat little bug!"

Said the third little chicken
With a sharp little squeal,
"Oh, I wish I could find
Some nice yellow meal!"

Said the fourth little chicken,
With a small sigh of grief,
"Oh, I wish I could find
A green little leaf!"

Said the fifth little chicken,
With a faint little moan,
"Oh, I wish I could find
A wee gravel-stone!"

"Now, see here," said the mother
From the green garden-patch,
"If you want any breakfast,
You must come and scratch."

Foot Pill

A man limped into a hospital to have his foot X-rayed, and was asked to wait for the results. Some time later an orderly appeared and handed the man a large pill.

Just then a mother with a small child in need of immediate attention entered. After the orderly disappeared with the new patient, the man hobbled over to get a glass of water, swallowed the pill, and sat down to wait. Some time later the orderly reappeared carrying a bucket of water.

"Okay," he said, "Let's drop the pill in this bucket and soak your foot for a while."

Get the Facts!

Supposition is a word that Webster describes as, merely thought to be such; imagined or supposed. Recently I was reminded again of how far our imagination can take us, and I wondered if many of you have had a similar experience. While traveling with several other folks, someone made a comment about something they saw. Immediately someone else made a suggestion of what they assumed may have happened while another inserted something else and the story was off and running. Supposition on top of supposition was given with each one building their case until a final probability was concluded never to be proven and a far cry from what had actually transpired.

Let me explain what I'm talking about. You're driving along when a farmer pulls out on the road with his pickup loaded down with lumber. You follow him for several miles until he finally turns off into a farm lane. As you go around him you notice that farther in the farm lane there are a lot of cars and people are there working. It appears as though they may be building a barn. A little farther distant is a column of smoke rising from some charred embers. Immediately you assume there was a barn fire and neighbors have come together to help.

What is wrong with this picture? Well, nothing really as long as it remains as an unsolved supposition. You can imagine all you want as long as you don't begin to make statements that are not factual. The problem with this whole thing is that you have just received a few snapshots that caused you to put together a story that seemed probable. The snapshots, however, may not even have been related. The farmer may not have been a farmer at all but simply looked like one with his bib overalls and straw hat because that is what farmers wear. Secondly, the smoke rising in the distance may have actually been from a neighboring property not the property where you saw people working. The farm lane may have continued on past the place you saw to several other properties as well. The load of lumber may not even have been going to the destination you thought. Our minds take the snapshots and put together a story that seems a likely scenario. Unfortunately, the missing snapshots can distort the story and completely alter it.

That is just one example. We can put a lot of stories together this way and we can cause a lot of trouble as well when we begin to share them with others as though they were factual. We see two people together somewhere and we question the purpose of it. Without much thought we make a few guesses and arrive at a conclusion. Kept to itself it may be harmless, but somehow our tendency is to spill the beans, and the tale begins, and people's feelings get hurt.

A supposition or an imagination is probably best kept to oneself unless it is shared as a humorous reflection of yourself and how far off base you really were. The lesson to be learned is "Get the facts!" It takes all the snapshots to complete a story. Having just a few of them can be very misleading.

—M. Gingrich

Going To The Art Gallery

Ann went to her first show at an art gallery and was looking at the paintings. One was a huge canvas that was black with yellow blobs of paint splattered all over it. The next painting was a murky gray color that had drips of purple paint streaked across it. Ann walked over to the artist and said, "I don't understand your paintings."

"I paint what I feel inside me," explained the artist.

Ann asked, "Have you ever tried Alka-Seltzer?"

Gullible People

Many years ago, a man was going from door to door collecting money for the widow of the unknown soldier. People were so gullible they gave over $15,000.00 before he was stopped.

ICE Idea

A recent article from the Toronto Star, "The ICE Idea," is catching on and it is a very simple, yet important method of contact for you or a loved one in case of an emergency. As cell phones are carried by the majority of the population, all you need to do is program the number of a contact person or persons and store the name as "ICE."

The idea was thought up by a paramedic who found that when they went to the scenes of accidents, there were always mobile phones with patients, but they didn't know which numbers to call. He therefore thought that it would be a good idea if there was a nationally recognized name to file "next of kin" under.

Following a disaster in London, The East Anglican Ambulance Service has launched a national "In case of Emergency (ICE)" campaign. The idea is that you store the word "ICE" in your mobile phone address book, and with it enter the number of the person you would want to be contacted "In Case of Emergency". In an emergency situation, Emergency Services personnel and hospital staff would then be able to quickly contact your next of kin, by simply dialing the number programmed under "ICE."

It really could save your life or put a loved one's mind at rest. For more than one contact name simply enter ICE1, ICE2, ICE3, etc.

Just A Ditch Digger

I had occasion to move a substantial amount of ground from a crawl space underneath our house. The only way to get it done feasibly was with a jack hammer and a shovel. After a day or two of sweating and digging and not being able to stand up straight, I jokingly inquired as to how much ground you need to move before you can put "excavator" behind your name. I thought perhaps I had moved enough dirt to claim that title. My enthusiasm and "pride" were short lived however as one man remarked, as long as you do it by hand you're just a ditch digger. I guess my promotion is still on hold.

This little incident made me think about the importance and meaning of a title. A title says something about the person. It indicates what services he may provide whether it be doctor, lawyer, excavator, technician, or any other occupation. The title indicates that the individual has a certain amount of experience or schooling that qualifies them for the job. Having that title means they have met certain requirements, and they have the ability to do the work. I was short on experience and knowledge, therefore, I didn't qualify to be given the title of an excavator.

One certainly would not call an excavator for a toothache or likewise a doctor to do some carpentry work. The title one carries indicates the type of work they do. One drawback to a title, however, is that it only requires a minimum amount of experience or knowledge to earn it. Behind that title are many and varied levels of experience, knowledge, and expertise. Simply turning to the yellow pages does not guarantee that the contact you make will satisfy your wishes. There are other things to consider such as quality of workmanship, equipment, and price. Far too often people get hung up on price. They fail to consider that a higher rate per hour may be less in the end if it takes less time. There is also the issue of workmanship. What may at first seem to be more expensive may actually be less because it saves time later in the project. There is also the factor of durability and longevity. How long will it hold up before it needs repairs?

A title points us in the right direction and gives credit where credit is due, but proper research and reference regarding the one who will do your work is still necessary. That is why a second opinion is often requested, especially in the medical field. Failure to check out the workmanship may result in you just getting a ditch digger with an excavator title. That could be a disaster, especially when it comes to your health. Check out the quality of work and level of customer satisfaction. If your ego gets too big, someone is sure to put you back in your proper place!

—M. Gingrich, Just a ditch digger

Kindness

In the days when an ice cream sundae cost much less, a 10-year-old boy entered a hotel coffee shop and sat at a table. A waitress put a glass of water in front of him.

"How much is an ice cream sundae?"

"Fifty cents," replied the waitress.

The little boy pulled his hand out of his pocket and studied a number of coins in it. "How much is a dish of plain ice cream?" he inquired.

Some people were now waiting for a table and the waitress was a bit impatient. "Thirty-five cents," she said brusquely.

The little boy again counted the coins. "I'll have the plain ice cream," he said.

The waitress brought the ice cream, put the bill on the table and walked away. The boy finished the ice cream, paid the cashier and departed.

When the waitress came back, she began wiping down the table and then swallowed hard at what she saw. There, placed neatly beside the empty dish, were two nickels and five pennies—her tip.

Labor Rates

Usual Rate	$40 per hour
If you wait	$50 per hour
If you watch	$60 per hour
If you help	$70 per hour
If you laugh	$80 per hour
If you worked on it first	$150 per hour

Laziness

The young woman sat in her stalled car, waiting for help. Finally two men walked up to her. "I'm out of gas," she purred. "Could you push me to the gas station?"

The men readily put their muscles to the car and rolled it several blocks. After a while, one looked up, exhausted, to see that they had just passed a filling station.

"How come you didn't turn in?" he yelled.

"I never go there," the girl shouted back. "They don't have full service."

Making A Cake With Johnny

- Light oven.
- Get out utensils and ingredients.
- Remove blocks and toys from washtable.
- Grease pan and crack nuts.
- Measure two cups of flour.
- Remove Johnny's hand from flour; wash flour off him.
- Remeasure flour.
- Put flour, baking powder, and salt into sifter.
- Get pieces of bowl Johnny knocked on floor.
- Get another bowl.
- Answer doorbell.
- Return to kitchen. Remove Johnny's hands from bowl.
- Wash Johnny.
- Answer phone.
- Return and remove ¼" salt from greased pan.
- Look for Johnny.
- Grease another pan.
- Answer phone.
- Return to kitchen and find Johnny; remove his hands from the bowl.
- Find a layer of nutshells in greased pan.
- Head for Johnny who flees, knocking bowl off table.
- Wash kitchen floor, table, walls, and dishes.
- Call baker and lie down.

"Mint"

I "Mint" to call and thank you
But my time is in demand;
I "Mint" to say "I love you",
But I knew you'd understand.

I "Mint" to send you flowers,
But they cost so much you know.
I "Mint" to pray for you this morning
But had some place to go.

I "Mint" to say "Forgive me"
But that's so hard to do.
I heard my Lord say,
"Bless you child".
I hope He "Mint" me, too!

Mosquitoes

- Use Bounce Fabric Softener Sheets—just wipe on and go. Best thing ever used in Louisiana and great for babies.
- Bob, a fisherman, takes one vitamin B-1 tablet a day April through October. He said it works. He was right. He hasn't had a mosquito bite in 33 years. Try it. Every one he has talked into trying it, says it works for them. Vitamin B-1(Thiamine Hydrochloride 100 mg).
- If you eat bananas, the mosquitoes like you—something about the banana oil as your body processes it. Stop eating bananas for the summer and the mosquitoes will be much less interested.
- This is going to floor you, but one of the best insect repellents someone found (who is in the woods every day) is Vick's Vaporub.
- Plant marigolds around the yard. The flowers give off a smell that bugs do not like. Plant some in that garden also to help ward off bugs without using insecticides.
- "Tough guy" marines who spend a great deal of time "camping out" say that the very best mosquito repellent you can use is Avon Skin-So-Soft bath oil mixed about half and half with alcohol.
- One of the best natural insect repellents that I've discovered is made from the clear real vanilla. This is the pure Vanilla that is sold in Mexico. It works great for mosquitoes and ticks. Don't know about other insects.
- When all else fails—get a frog!

Moving The Car For The Snowplow

Norman and his wife live in Prince George. One winter morning while listening to the radio, they heard the announcer say, "We are going to have 3 to 4 inches of snow today. You must park your car on the even-numbered side of the street so the snowplow can get through."

Norman's wife went out and moved her car. A week later while they were eating breakfast, the radio announcer said, "We are expecting 4 to 5 inches of snow today. You must park your car on the odd numbered side of the street so the snowplow can get through." Norman's wife

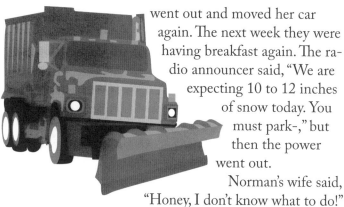

went out and moved her car again. The next week they were having breakfast again. The radio announcer said, "We are expecting 10 to 12 inches of snow today. You must park-," but then the power went out.

Norman's wife said, "Honey, I don't know what to do!"

Norman said, "Why don't you just leave it in the garage this time?"

Mule Solution

A Missouri farmer passed away and left 17 mules to his three sons. The instructions left in the will said that the oldest boy was to get one-half, the second oldest one-third, and the third oldest one-ninth. The three sons, recognizing the difficulty of dividing 17 mules into these fractions, began to argue.

Their uncle heard about the argument, hitched up his mule and drove out to settle the matter. He added his mule to the 17, making 18. The oldest therefore got one-half; or nine, the second oldest got one-third, or six; and the youngest son got one-ninth, or two. Adding up 9, 6 and 2 equals 17. The uncle, having settled the argument, hitched up his mule and drove home.

Not In My Contract

Two brawny men came to my house to install some new floor covering in the kitchen. Once they had moved the stove and refrigerator out of the way, it was not long before the job was done.

As they were getting ready to leave, I asked them to put the heavy appliances back in place.

The two men demanded $45 for this service, stating it was not in their contract.

I really had no choice but to pay them. As soon as they left, however, the doorbell rang. It was the two men. They asked me to move my car, which was blocking their van.

I told them my fee: $45.

Now She Wasn't Quite That Hungry

Our favorite restaurant offers all-you-can-eat for one price. They have a rule, however, that you cannot take any food home with you.

I didn't know this rule when I stepped in the door on my first visit. Imagine my surprise when I read the cheerful sign that says: "Please eat everything on the premises!"

Only A Woman Can

As the bus pulled away, I realized I had left my purse under the seat. Later, I called the company and was relieved that the driver had found my bag. When I went to pick it up, several off-duty bus drivers surrounded me. One man handed me my pocketbook, two typewritten pages, and a box containing the contents of my purse.

"We're required to inventory lost wallets and purses," he explained. "I think you'll find everything there." As I started to put my belongings back into the pocketbook, the man continued, "I hope you don't mind if we watch? Even though we all tried, none of us could fit everything into your purse and we'd like to see just how you do it."

Opportunities

When someone makes a lot of money in a business deal we often say that he was in the right place at the right time. When someone changes occupations and gets into a company at ground level just before it blossoms, we say they got in at just the right time.

Every day people are faced with opportunities. These may came in various forms, such as, a job promotion, an employment change, a property purchase, a sales promotion, etc. These are opportunities to do good, to show appreciation, and to better oneself in life. Sometimes we are alerted to opportunities by a more urgent note. The wail of an approaching siren, the blowing of a horn, the screeching sound of brakes, a shout of warning, the thunder of distant storm clouds, or even the ringing of a telephone. These are opportunities to respond, to get out of the way, to spur us to action, and to avoid danger.

Opportunities do not come with a label attached saying, "this is an opportunity," but rather they come as events and circumstances of everyday life. Our response to them can make a difference in our life and the lives of those around us. Some opportunities come because of our response to other opportunities. For example, a person who does well at their work is more likely to have the opportunity to move up in the organization than one who is careless. While some opportunities just happen others will not unless we work at making them happen. Some opportunities present themselves for a considerable amount of time while others are only available for a fleeting moment. For example, a property may be for sale for a number of months while the opportunity to give a smile as someone passes is an opportunity that lasts for just a moment. A quick glance at my own experiences tells me that I have missed many opportunities. However, to sit and pout and wonder about what if, will only result in more missed opportunities. We cannot undo the past but all the future lies before us. We have the opportunity to do good, to make a difference in others, to reach out, to lend, to warn, to calm, to respect, to honor, and to build. We will also have the opportunity to tear down, to ignore, to mock, to deceive, to steal, to harm, and to destroy. These opportunities will present themselves again and again in varied and candid ways. What you make of those opportunities and how you respond to them will speak volumes about your character and what kind of a person you are. Let us look for opportunities to encourage, for ways to honor, for a chance to lift a discouraged heart, and for the privilege to help carry someone's load. If we all put forth our best effort in every opportunity, life will be more pleasant and enjoyable for ourselves and others.

—*M. Gingrich*

Parts Is Parts

A parts manager for a small electronics shop had occasion to order part No. 669 from the factory. But when he received it he noticed that someone had sent part No. 699 instead.

Furious at the factory's incompetence, he promptly sent the part back along with a letter giving them a piece of his mind.

Almost a week later, he received the same part back with a letter containing just four words: "Turn the part over."

Patches

Lisa Alger of Roy, WA, had to take her claim all the way to state judge Paul Treyz in June, but she finally got a dismissal of one of the municipal citations against her for housing an unlicensed cat named "Patches."

Reason: "Patches" is a stuffed animal. The local Humane Society monitors for violations of licensing law by knocking on doors and asking children the names of their pets, so it can check license lists. When Alger's 7-year-old son mentioned the highly regarded "Patches," and the Humane Society found no license for it, it wrote Alger up without investigating.

Plan Retirement

From a retiree—with the average cost for a Nursing Home reaching $188.00 per day, there is a better way to spend our savings when we get old and feeble. I have already checked on reservations at the Holiday Inn for a combined long-term-stay discount and a senior discount. It comes to only $49.23 per night. That leaves $138.77 a day for:

1. Breakfast, lunch, and dinner in any restaurant I want or room service.
2. They offer free toothpaste and razors, shampoo and soap. Also, most have a pool, a workout room, a lounge, washer, dryer, etc.
3. They treat you like a customer, not a patient. $5 worth of tips a day will have the entire staff scrambling to help you.
4. There is city bus stop out front, and seniors ride free. The handicap bus will also pick you up (if you fake a decent limp).
5. To meet other nice people, call a church bus on Sundays. For a change of scenery, take the airport shuttle bus and eat at one of the nice restaurants there. While you're at the airport, fly somewhere. Otherwise the cash keeps building up.
6. It takes months to get into decent nursing homes. Holiday Inn will take your reservation today. And you are not stuck in one place forever. You can move from Inn to Inn, or even from city to city. Want to see Hawaii? They have a Holiday Inn there, too.

7. Something broken? Light bulbs need changing? Need a mattress replaced? No problem. They fix everything and apologize for the inconvenience.
8. The Inn has a night security person and daily room service. The maid checks to see if you are okay. If not, they will call an ambulance. If you fall and break a hip, Medicare will pay for the hip, and Holiday Inn will upgrade you to a suite for the rest of your life.
9. Don't worry about visits from family. They will always be glad to find you and will probably check in for a few days mini-vacation. The grandchildren can use the pool. What more can you ask for?
10. So, when I reach the golden age, I'll face it with a grin. Just forward all my e-mail to: me@Holiday Inn.

Politically Correct Statements

- Your bedroom isn't cluttered. It's just "passage restrictive."
- Children don't get grounded anymore. They merely hit "social speed bumps."
- You're not late. You just have a "rescheduled arrival time."
- You're not having a bad hair day. You're suffering from "rebellious follicle syndrome."
- No one's tall anymore. He's "vertically enhanced."
- You're not shy. You're "conversationally selective."
- You're not long-winded. You're just "abundantly verbal."
- It's not called gossip anymore. It's "the speedy transmission of near-factual information."
- The food at the school cafeteria isn't awful. It's "digestively challenged."
- No one fails a class anymore. He's merely "passing impaired."
- You don't have detention. You're just one of the "exit delayed."
- These days, a student isn't lazy. He's "energetically declined."
- Your locker isn't overflowing with junk. It's just "closure prohibitive."
- Your homework isn't missing. It's just having an "out-of-notebook experience."
- You're not sleeping in class. You're "rationing consciousness."
- You weren't passing notes in class. You were "participating in the discreet exchange of penned meditations."
- You're not being sent to the principal's office. You're "going on a mandatory field trip to the administrative building."

Power Failure

Every month I get a bill that I have a tendency to complain about. Six hours without electric on a warm sticky night quickly changes my criticism. Six hours is not a long time but it is long enough to realize how dependent on electricity we as Americans have become. We can't get any water. We can't flush the commodes. We can't take a shower. We can't run the air conditioners. We can't use the stove or the oven. We can't use any appliances. The sweeper doesn't work. Fans don't work. The furnace doesn't work. The lights don't work. The computer shuts down. Cordless phones don't function. Clocks go on the blink. The automatic garage door opener doesn't work. The things in the freezer begin to thaw. Our ability to accomplish anything is greatly diminished. We have become so accustomed to plugging in the cord and things work. When that power is interrupted so are we.

So, while the electric is off we grab flashlights and light a candle or a lantern to give us some light. We sit around in the dark and talk. We wonder how many others are out of electric, too. We wonder how long it will be until it comes back on. We talk about the storm that brought the interruption in power and watch the lightning continue to flash as it moves farther away. As darkness settles in there isn't a whole lot left to do except go to bed and try to catch a few winks.

Once more we have been reminded of how much easier life is when we have electricity. Suddenly the bill that comes every month doesn't seem quite as harsh. We have a clearer picture of what all that bill really represents. The inconvenience it brought is a testament to the fact that we don't fully appreciate the conveniences we have. When their source of power is removed many of our conveniences are rendered useless.

About 2:00 A.M. things return to normal. Power is restored. The lights come on with a simple flick of the switch. The air conditioner runs. The things in the freezer will be okay. Our water supply is functioning. About the only thing that has changed is my attitude. I have learned once again to appreciate the power of electricity and the convenience it brings to my life. Paying my next bill won't seem so bad after all because I have been reminded how inconvenient things are when we don't have electric. Sometimes it takes doing without something to better appreciate it when it returns. Electricity is one of those things.

—M. Gingrich

Power Nap

I am amazed at how quickly the human body can overcome fatigue. A short nap, a night's rest, or a short period of relaxation can transform a person from exhausted to vibrant. When Salvador Dali needed a short nap he would place a tin plate on the floor, then sit on a chair next to it, hold a spoon over the plate and relax into a doze. At the precise moment of the onset of sleep the spoon would slip from his fingers, clatter onto the plate and he would awaken. He claimed to be completely refreshed by the sleep he got from the time the spoon slipped from his fingers until it hit the plate. I guess you could call that a super power nap.

Lack of sleep has been the cause of many ailments and sicknesses. It has caused many accidents in the workplace and on the highway. Decision making and the ability to think are hindered by a lack of proper rest. When we become drowsy our response time is slowed. We are not as alert to what is going on around us. Attention to detail and productivity lessen. It is a proven fact that our ability to function proficiently is hindered when we are sleep deprived.

Someone has noted that there is a parallel we can draw from the rests in a score of music and life itself. In music the rests are silent, but they are of utmost importance. Consider a song that had no rests. The human voice couldn't sing it, simply because there is no opportunity to draw your next breath. Not only do the rests give opportunity to get your breath, they also provide clarity and resonance to the notes around it. A song without rests would become a jumble of monotonous and bland notes. The rests are unsung heroes. They vary in length of duration and are placed at strategic intervals throughout the music. While the notes seemingly get all the attention, the rests help set the tone and give the song its rhythm.

God created the human body with a need for rest. When we come to the end of a hard day our energy is spent. Rest rejuvenates us till morning and then once again we produce a few more notes. To go on and on without rest would quickly take its toll. We simply couldn't function. A good nights sleep is sufficient reward for a hard days work, and it gives the needed motivation to tackle the next days tasks. Life without proper rests, becomes a steady drum beat of the same old tunes. We quickly become discouraged and disgruntled. When we honor them, life becomes a beautiful song. We are more cheerful, more forgiving, more attentive, and more courteous. Proper rests add clarity and tone to our character. It helps us to hit the notes and stay on tune.

—M. Gingrich

Rationale

Jones was driving past the state mental hospital when his left rear tire suffered a flat. While Jones was changing the tire, another car went by, running over the hub cap in which Jones was keeping the lug nuts. The nuts were all knocked into a nearby storm drain.

Jones was at a loss for what to do and was about to go call a cab when he heard a shout from behind the hospital fence, where one of the patients had been watching the whole thing.

"Hey, pal! Why don't you just take one lug nut off each of the other three wheels? That'll hold your tires on until you can get to a garage or something."

Jones was startled by the patient's seeming rationality, but realized the plan would work, and installed the spare tire without incident.

Before he left, he called back to the patient. "You know, that was pretty sharp thinking. Why do they have you in there?"

The patient smiled and said, "I'm in here because I'm crazy, not because I'm stupid."

Read A Good Book

Wilbur Smith once said, "Through the years I have often been asked, at conferences and gatherings, "How do you get so much reading done? May I say here, again, that there is only one way to get any reading done, and that is to read. Whatever reading I may do, I do not deprive myself of needed sleep, and am always in bed for at least eight hours every night; I do not withdraw myself from society; and I am not a man free from obligations, that is, I have been a minister or professor all my adult life, and thus many hours of the day are not my own. There is only one way to get any reading done and that is to read. If one does not wish to read, he will not read—and if he does not, his ministry will be impoverished indeed."

The last phrase of that quote stands out. Many of the things we say are not original thoughts of our own, but were inspired or impressed upon our minds by others. Reading is a valuable resource for gaining knowledge, however, knowledge alone does not build a house. It must be accompanied with wisdom and skill. Knowledge can be self-destructing if it is not used for its specified purpose. For example, dynamite can be productive in excavating large rocks, but is very destructive if it is not handled properly or if it is used as a weapon. It is of utmost importance that we are careful and discerning of what we read. A constant diet of the local police log or political bickering can lead to depression and discouragement. Reading ought to inspire us and cause us to think. It should lead us to a higher level of fulfillment. It ought to teach us. Life is too short to learn everything there is to learn but that is no excuse not to learn all we can. Learn to read, and read to learn. The doors of opportunity and the gates of learning will open if you will but delve into a good book. As Wilbur Smith said, "The only way it will happen is to read." We need to make it a priority. We need to insist upon it. It is only as we sense its value that we will give reading a good book its rightful place.

—M. Gingrich

Running From God

Running from God
Will cost you more than you want to pay.

Running from God
Will hurt you more than you can say.

Running from God
Will keep you longer than you want to stay.

Sales Technique

A minister concluded that his church was getting into serious financial troubles. Coincidentally, by chance, while checking the church storeroom, he discovered several cartons of new Bibles that had never been opened and distributed. So, at his Sunday sermon, he asked for three volunteers from the congregation who would be willing to sell the Bibles door-to-door for $10 each to raise the desperately needed money for the church.

Peter, Paul, and Louie all raised their hands to volunteer for the task. The reverend knew that Peter and Paul earned their living as salesmen and were likely capable of selling some Bibles but he had serious doubts about Louie. Louie was just a local farmer, who had always kept to himself because he was embarrassed by his speech impediment. Poor Louis stuttered very badly. But, not wanting to discourage poor Louis, the minister decided to let him try anyway.

He sent the three of them away with the back seat of their cars stacked with Bibles and asked them to meet with him and report the results of their door-to-door selling efforts the following Sunday.

Anxious to find out how successful they were, the minister immediately asked Peter, "Well, Peter, how did you make out selling our Bibles last week?"

Proudly handing the minister an envelope, Peter replied, "Sir, using my sales prowess, I was able to sell 20 Bibles, and here's the $200 I collected on behalf of the church."

"Fine job, Peter!" the minister said, vigorously shaking his hand. "You are indeed a fine salesman and the church is indebted to you."

Turning to Paul, he asked "And Paul, how many Bibles did you manage to sell for the church last week?"

Paul, smiling and sticking out his chest, confidently replied, "Sir, I am a professional salesman and was happy to give the church the benefit of my sales expertise. Last week I sold 28 Bibles on behalf of the church, and here's the $280 I collected."

The minister responded, "That's absolutely splendid, Paul. You are truly a professional salesman and the church is also indebted to you."

Apprehensively, the reverend turned to little Louie and said, "And Louie, did you manage to sell any Bibles last week?"

Louie silently offered the minister a large envelope. He opened it and counted the contents. "What is this?" he exclaimed. "Louie, there's $3200 in here! Are you suggesting that you sold 320 Bibles for the church, door to door, in just one week?

Louie just nodded.

"That's impossible!" both Peter and Paul said in unison. "We are professional salesmen, yet you claim to have sold ten times as many Bibles as we could."

"Yes, this does seem unlikely," the minister agreed. "I think you'd better explain how you managed to accomplish this, Louie."

Louie shrugged. "I-I-I-re-rereally do-do-don't kn-kn-know f-f-f-for sh-sh-sh-sure," he stammered. Impatiently, Peter interrupted.

"For crying out loud, Louie, just tell us what you said to them when they answered the door!"

"A-a-a-alll I-I s-s-said wa-wa-was," Louis replied, "W-w-w-wwould y-y-y-you I-I-I-I-I-like t-t-to b-b-b-buy th-th-th-this B-B-B-B-Bible f-f-for t-t-ten b-b-b-bucks or wo-wo-would yo-you j-j-j-just like me t—to st-st-stand h-h-here and r-r-r-r-r-read it t-to y-y-you?"

So God Made A Farmer

God looked down on His planned paradise and said, "I need a caretaker." So He made a farmer.

God said, "I need somebody willing to get up before dawn, milk cows, work all day in the field, milk cows again, eat supper, then go to town and stay past midnight at a meeting of the school board." So God made a farmer.

"I need somebody with arms strong enough to wrestle a calf and yet gentle enough to play with his grandchild," God continued. "Somebody to call hogs, tame cantankerous machinery, and sit up all night with a newborn colt. When the colt dies, I need somebody who will dry his eyes and try again next year.

"I need somebody who can shape an ax handle from a persimmon sprout and shoe a horse with a hunk of car tire…somebody who can make harness out of baling wire and scraps of feed sacks…somebody who, during planting and harvest, will finish his 40-hour week by Tuesday noon, then put in another 72 hours, even with a painful case of tractor back." So God made a farmer.

God wanted somebody who'd race across bumpy ruts to get a load of hay in before the rain started, yet leave the load standing in mid-field if he saw his neighbor needed help. So God made a farmer. God said, "I need somebody who'll plow deep and straight and not cut corners…somebody who'll seed, weed, feed, and breed…somebody to disk and plant and tie the fleece and strain the milk and replenish the self-feeder.

"I need somebody who, after a hard week's work, will drive twenty miles to church…somebody who will bale a family together with the soft, strong bonds of sharing…somebody who will laugh, sigh, and then reply with smiling eyes when his son says he wants to spend his life doing what his Dad does."

So God made a farmer!

Stuff

Every Fall I start stirring in my stuff. There is closet stuff, drawer stuff, attic stuff, and basement stuff. I separate the good stuff from the bad stuff, then I stuff the bad stuff anywhere the stuff is not too crowded until I decide if I will need the bad stuff.

When the Lord calls me home, my children will want the good stuff, but the bad stuff, stuffed wherever there is room among all the other stuff, will be stuffed in bags and taken to the dump to join all the other people's stuff.

Whenever we have company they always bring bags and bags of stuff. When I visit my son, he always moves his stuff so I will have room for my stuff. My daughter-in-law always clears a drawer of her stuff so I will have room for my stuff. Their stuff and my stuff. It would be so much easier to use their stuff and leave my stuff at home, with the rest of my stuff.

This Fall I had an extra closet built so I would have a place for all the stuff too good to throw away and too bad to keep with my good stuff. You may not have this problem, but I seem to spend a lot of time with stuff…food stuff, cleaning stuff, medicine stuff, clothes stuff, and outside stuff. Whatever would life be like if we didn't have all this stuff?

Now there is all that stuff we use to make us smell better than we do. There is stuff to make our hair look good. Stuff to make us look younger. Stuff to make us look healthier. Stuff to hold us in, and stuff to fill us out. There is stuff to read, stuff to play with, stuff to entertain us, and stuff to eat. We stuff ourselves with the food stuff.

Well, our lives are filled with stuff…good stuff, bad stuff, little stuff, big stuff, useful stuff, junky stuff, and everyone's stuff. Now when we leave all our stuff and go to heaven, whatever happen to our stuff won't matter. We will still have the good stuff God has prepared for us in heaven.

Tallness

I was in the kitchen one day, trying to reach the baking powder on the top shelf of a cabinet. Being only five feet tall, I had to stretch, but still couldn't grab the box.

Fortunately, I have two six-foot-tall sons whom I often call to come to my rescue.

"Hey, Brian!" I yelled to my second son, who was in the living room. "Will you get your tallness in here and get this for me?"

"Sure, Mom," he remarked as he bounded into the kitchen. "But next time, I'd prefer the title 'Your Highness.'"

Taxes

Accounts Receivable Tax
Building Permit Tax
Capital Gains Tax
CDL License Tax
Cigarette Tax
Corporate Income Tax
Court Fines (indirect taxes)
Dog License Tax
Federal Income Tax
Federal Unemployment Tax (FUTA)
Fishing License Tax
Food License Tax
Fuel Permit Tax
Gasoline Tax (42 cents per gallon)
Hunting License Tax
Inheritance Tax
Interest Expense (tax on the money)
Inventory Tax
IRS Interest Charges (tax on top of tax)
IRS Penalties (tax on top of tax)
Liquor Tax
Local Income Tax
Luxury Taxes
Marriage License Tax
Medicare Tax
Property Tax
Real Estate Tax
Recreational Vehicle Tax
Road Toll Booth Taxes
Road Usage Taxes (truckers)
Sales Taxes
School Tax
Septic Permit Tax
Service Charge Taxes
Social Security Tax
State Income Tax
State Unemployment Tax (SUTA)
Telephone Federal Excise Tax
Telephone Federal Universal Service Fee Tax
Telephone Federal State And Local Surcharge Taxes
Telephone Recurring And Nonrecurring Charges Tax
Telephone State And Local Tax
Telephone Usage Charge Tax
Toll Bridge Taxes
Traffic Fines (indirect taxation)
Trailer Registration Tax
Utility Taxes
Vehicle License Registration Tax
Vehicle Sales Tax
Watercraft Registration Tax
Well Permit Tax
Workers Compensation Tax

Comments

Not one of these taxes existed one hundred years ago and the U.S. was the most prosperous in the world, had absolutely no national debt, had the largest middle class in the world, and mom stayed home to raise the children. What do you think changed?

Thank You Cards

My first stop on my vacation was my sister's house in Montana. She's extremely organized. Before she leaves on a trip, she always types up address labels for her postcards.

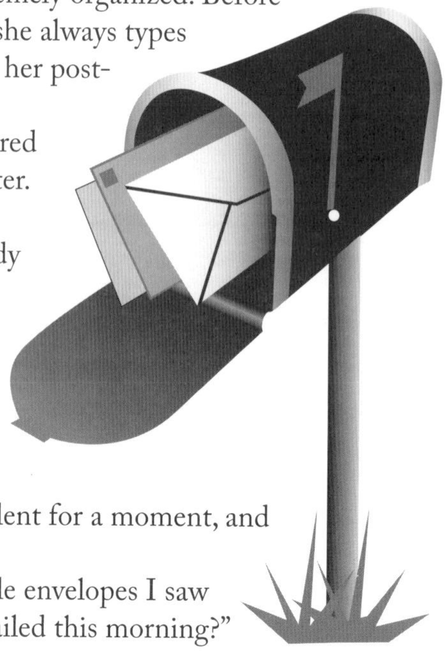

This time, I figured I'd done her one better. I boasted, "You'll be impressed. I've already written thank-you notes to everyone with whom I'll be staying. They're all stamped and ready to go."

My sister was silent for a moment, and then she said, "You mean those little envelopes I saw in your room and mailed this morning?"

The King & Court Jester

The familiar story of an ancient king and his court jester shows the folly of drifting and not deciding. The jester captivated the fancy of his monarch in such a way that he was presented by him with an elegant baton. The king said, "You keep this rod until you find a man more foolish than yourself." Time passed and the king fell sick. The jester was called in. He found his monarch in great agony.

"What is the trouble," the jester asked.

"Oh," said the king, "I feel very ill and fear I am about to go on a long journey."

"When will you return," asked the jester.

"Never," said the king.

"What do you know about the country to which you are going?"

"Nothing."

"What preparation have you made for the journey?"

"None."

There was a pause. Solemnly the jester extended the elegant baton. "Your Excellency," he began, "you told me to keep this rod until I found a man more foolish than myself. Now you tell me you are about to take a trip from which you will never return, to a country about which you know nothing, and for which you have made no preparation. Here, take the rod."

The Lure Of The Hunt

Every fall hunters take to the woods and fields of Pennsylvania with the hope of bagging some of its abundant supply of wild game. Their quest for game varies from trophy whitetail deer, black bear, cottontail rabbit, turkey, ducks, and geese, to squirrels or even the elusive fox. They hike for miles over rocks and fallen trees. They meander through the valleys, across the streams and climb their way to the top of the highest peaks until they are completely out of breath. They crawl on hands and knees through thick brush and tangled undergrowth. They get up hours before sunrise and spend the entire day afield. They brave the biting wind, the blowing snow, and driving rain as the weather at times turns downright miserable. When the temperatures drop well below freezing, they begin to wonder if their fingers and toes are still attached as all feeling disappears. Their legs get stiff from hours of sitting motionless on a rock or attached to the side of a tree some 30 feet up in the air. They lug along a truckload of gear that usually includes tree stand, rifle or bow, knife, rope, compass, deer call, lure, license, gloves, and a conglomerate of other things, just in case.

It is a yearly ritual of camo and orange clad contingents taking for the back country and less civilized terrain. In an almost uncanny way it seems the game know too what is taking place. Animals that were a regular show suddenly vanish. It is as though they have an emergency phone chain set up to let each other know that here come those funny looking creatures that invade our living room for a couple of days each year. So, into hiding they go and soon those out of shape funny looking creatures lose interest and everything goes back to normal.

Needless to say there are always those lame excuses of why the big one got away. The gun wouldn't go off. A twig caused the arrow to ricochet. The scope was fogged up or I had some bad ammo. Of course it had absolutely nothing to do with buck fever or the fact that you were literally shaking or the fact that you flinched when you shot. That is near impossible. The fact is, of course, whether the excuse is legitimate or not, you have nothing to show for it. And, isn't it interesting that those that get away are always the biggest ones too.

Then, too, are those times when the hunt is successful. The patient waiting is rewarded. The countless trips to scout out the area, plan your hunt, and bring home a trophy finally pay off. Well, not really pay off, as I seriously doubt that anyone does it for profit. In fact, discussing the price per pound is actually off limits. That isn't why we hunt and we certainly don't want to be burdened with that information. By pay off, I really mean that we have accomplished what we set out to do. We beat the odds while at the same time providing some nourishment for the family. Hopefully they will enjoy it and want us to go back out for some more the following year. That way we have good reason to go, and we won't need to think up any excuses.

So what is it that lures hunters into the big woods anyway? What is it that keeps them hanging out on the side of a tree for hours and why would they give up a day's wages? Why they put themselves through all the agony and pain is somewhat of a mystery and only if you're a hunter would you understand. If you're not a hunter, it is no use trying to explain.

—M. Gingrich

The Problem Is Inside

A story is told of Thomas K. Beecher, who could not bear deceit in any form. Finding a clock that was too fast or too slow, he hung a placard on the wall above it which read: "Don't blame my hands—the trouble lies deeper." That is where the trouble lies with us when our hands do wrong or our feet or our lips or even our thoughts. The trouble lives so deep that only God's miracle power can deal with it. Sin indeed goes deep; but Christ goes deeper.

The Rat, The Chicken, & The Farmer

A rat looked through a crack in the wall to see the farmer and his wife opening a package. What food might it contain? He was aghast to discover that it was a rat trap. Retreating to the farmyard the rat proclaimed the warning; "There is a rat trap in the house, a rat trap in the house!"

The chicken clucked and scratched, raised her head and said, "Excuse me, Mr. Rat, I can tell this is a grave concern to you, but it is of no consequence to me. I cannot be bothered by it." The rat turned to the pig and told him, "There is a rat trap in the house, a rat trap in the house!"

"I am so very sorry, Mr. Rat," sympathized the pig, "but there's nothing I can do about it but pray. Be assured that you are in my prayers."

The rat turned to the cow. She said, "Like wow, Mr. Rat. A rat trap. I am in grave danger. Duh?"

So the rat returned to the house, head down and dejected, to face the farmer's rat trap alone. That very night a sound was heard throughout the house, like the sound of a rat trap catching its prey.

The farmer's wife rushed to see what was caught. In the darkness, she did not see that it was a venomous snake whose tail the trap had caught. The snake bit the farmer's wife. The farmer rushed her to the hospital.

She returned home with a fever. Now everyone knows you treat a fever with fresh chicken soup, so the farmer took his hatchet to the farmyard for the soup's main ingredient. His wife's sickness continued so that friends and neighbors came to sit with her around the clock. To feed them the farmer butchered the pig.

The farmer's wife did not get well. She died, and so many people came for her funeral that the farmer had the cow slaughtered to provide meat for all of them to eat. So the next time you hear that someone is facing a problem and think that it does not concern you, remember that when there is a rat trap in the house, the whole farmyard is at risk.

The Skunk Encounter

A few years ago, our neighborhood was overrun by stray cats. Cats everywhere! Something had to be done. Residents of the development used to feed them, but soon the cats became pests. Particularly disgusting was their habit of using well-groomed flower beds as litter-boxes. Since I had a few rabbit traps in my shed from a "Trap & Transfer" program, I decided to try my traps on the cats; sort of a "Trap & Transfer" program for cats. Normally, a slice of apple placed in the trap is bait for the rabbits. So here, I reasoned, some dry cat food would entice the cat into the trap to be harmlessly captured. So, I set my renovated rabbit trap on my carport, less than ten feet from my back door. Surely, I'll be able to out wit a cat. Well, one afternoon when I arrived home from work, I noticed that the back door of the trap had been tripped, indicating that I caught one.

"Good," I thought, "I can run this cat out to a farmer-friend of mine who lives less than fifteen miles away." I gently picked up the trap to look inside. And through the screen-covered end, to my surprise, two shiny black eyes were staring back at me…skunk eyes. Oh no! Now what?

Fortunately, inside the trap, the skunk could not lift his tail to spray me. (But I wasn't too sure of that at the time). So how do I get him out of the trap without getting a spray of skunk "perfume"? I gently carried the box trap a few steps onto the back yard grass. "I don't want to upset this guy," I thought. As I put it down, I rolled it over so the door would drop back open. Then I quickly backed up, out of spraying range.

After what seemed like an eternity, out waddled Mr. Skunk, looking none-the-worse for the ordeal and still "fully-loaded" for his next encounter. I felt a huge sense of relief as I watched him head away from my house!

—Robert H. Checket

The World Puzzle

A father wanted to read a magazine, but was being bothered by his little daughter, Vanessa.

Finally, he tore a sheet out of his magazine on which was printed the map of the world. Tearing it into small pieces, he gave it to Vanessa, and said, "Go into the other room and see if you can put this together." After a few minutes Vanessa returned and handed him the map correctly fitted together. The father was surprised and asked how she had finished so quickly.

"Oh," she said, "on the other side of the paper is a picture of Jesus. When I got Jesus back where He belonged, then the world came together."

Today's Math Students

Last week I purchased a burger for $1.58. I handed the cashier $2.00 and started digging for some change. I pulled out eight cents and gave it to her. She stood there with $2 and eight cents. She looked bewildered, holding the nickel and three pennies, while looking at the screen on her register.

I sensed her discomfort and tried to tell her to just give me two quarters, but she hailed the manager for help. While he tried to explain the transaction to her, she burst into tears.

The incident got me thinking about how children are learning math in school (or not).

Teaching Math in 1950: A logger sells a truckload of lumber for $100. His cost of production is 4/5ths of the price. What is his profit?

Teaching Math in 1960: A logger sells a truckload of lumber for $100. His cost of production is 4/5ths of the price, or $80. What is his profit?

Teaching Math in 1970: A logger exchanges a set "L" of lumber for a set of "M" of money. The cardinality of set "M" is one hundred. Each element is worth one

dollar. Make the cost of product a "C", which contains twenty fewer points than set "M." Represent the set "C" as a subset of set "M." Answer this question: What is the cardinality of the set "P" of profits?

Teaching Math in 1980: A logger sells a truckload of lumber for $100. His cost of production is $80 and his profit is $20. Your assignment: Underline the number twenty.

Teaching Math in 1990: By cutting down beautiful forest trees, the logger makes $20. What do you think of this way of making a living? Topic for class participation after answering the question: How did the forest birds and squirrels feel as the logger cut down the trees.

(There are no wrong answers)

Teaching Math in 2000: A logger sells a truckload of lumber for $100. His cost of production is $120. How does Arthur Anderson determine that his profit margin is $60?

Teaching Math in 2005: el hachero vende un camion carga por $100. La cuesta de production es…

Today's Taxation

Let's put tax cuts in terms everyone can understand. Suppose that every day, ten men go out for dinner. The bill for all ten comes to $100. If they paid their bill the way we pay our taxes, it would go something like this:

- The first four men (the poorest) would pay nothing.
- The fifth would pay $1.
- The sixth would pay $3.
- The seventh $7.
- The eighth $12.
- The ninth $18.
- The tenth man (the richest) would pay $59.

So, that's what they decided to do, The ten men ate dinner in the restaurant every day and seemed quite happy with the arrangement, until one day, the owner threw them a curve, "Since you are all such good customers," he said, "I'm going to reduce the cost of your daily meal by $20."

So, now dinner for the ten only cost $80. The group still wanted to pay their bill the way we pay our taxes, so, the first four men were unaffected, they would still eat for free, but what about the other six, the paying customers? How could they divvy up the $20 windfall so that everyone would get his 'fair share'? The six men realized that $20 divided by six is $3.33, But if they subtracted that from everybody's share, then the fifth man and the sixth man would each end up being 'PAID' to eat their meal. So, the restaurant owner suggested that it would be fair to reduce each man's bill by roughly the same amount, and he proceeded to work out the amounts each should pay, and so:

- The fifth man, like the first four, now paid nothing (100% savings),
- The sixth now paid $2 instead of $3 (33% savings),
- The seventh now paid $5 instead of $7 (28% savings),
- The eighth now paid $9 instead of $12 (25% savings),
- The ninth now paid $14 instead of $18 (22% savings),
- The tenth now paid $49 instead of $59 (16% savings).

Each of the six was better off than before and the first four continued to eat for free. But once outside the restaurant, the men began to compare their savings. "I only got a dollar out of the $20," declared the sixth man. He pointed to the tenth man "but he got $10!"

"Yeah, that's right," exclaimed the fifth man. "I only saved a dollar, too. It's unfair that he got ten times more than me!"

"That's true!!" shouted the seventh man. "Why should he get $10 back when I got only $2? The wealthy get all the breaks!"

"Wait a minute," yelled the first four men in unison. "We didn't get anything at all. The system exploits the poor!"

The nine men surrounded the tenth and beat him up. The next night the tenth man didn't show up for dinner, so the nine sat down and ate without him. But when it came time to pay the bill, they discovered something important. They didn't have enough money between all of them for even half of the bill!

And that, men and women, boys and girls, journalists and college professors, is how our tax system works. The people who pay the highest taxes get the most benefit from a tax reduction. Tax them too much, attack them for being wealthy, and they just may not show up at the table anymore. There are lots of good restaurants in Europe and the Caribbean.

Togetherness Warms The Heart!

I have had fellows rave about how much money they save by burning wood, but they never have a dollar figure of what expenses they incur for equipment. These include the fuel and oil for the chainsaw, the replacement chains, gas for the pickup, chiropractor services, towing charges, log splitter rental, time off from work, and liniment for massaging aching muscles. It is hard to convince some folks that those are costs that must be considered. I guess sometimes ignorance is bliss. It is almost a repeat scenario of those hard core Ford fanatics. They just don't get it. You can't reason with the woodcutters that cutting wood costs just as much as other methods of heating when you include all the costs. You can't convince a Ford diehard that Ford's are not cut out to do the job. They would rather just pay the towing charges than to admit it. Perhaps once they have time to sit next to the fire and their blood begins to thin out a bit then perhaps we can begin to reason. Until then ignorance will reign.

In reality, guys that cut wood are okay. It's just that they work a lot harder to get their years supply of fuel. It is possible that they could use the exercise. The same is true of those fellows who drive Fords. It is possible they could use the excerise and that is one way to get it. Hopefully, once you get all that wood cut, split, and stacked you'll have time to sit by the fireplace and enjoy some relaxing moments laughing over a few jokes about guys who cut wood and drive Fords.

Another source of heat that was quite popular a number of years ago was Armstrong Heaters. It didn't seem to matter how cold it was outside, as long as a girl had her Armstrong Heater, she was warm inside. Many of these heaters have since been converted over to Old Fashioned Pot-bellied Stoves. This change took place through the good cooking of the girl who was once kept warm by the Armstrong Heater. Snow on the ground and smoke curling from the chimney are signs of home sweet home. What better place to be when the winds are blowing. Play a game, put a puzzle together, read a book, or just relax with family and friends. Togetherness warms the heart.

—M. Gingrich

Unlocking The Door

The tale is told of a king who wanted to find the wisest man in his kingdom to be his prime minister. When the search had narrowed down to three finalists they were presented with a test. They were placed together in a room in the palace. On the door was a sophisticated lock. They were told that whoever was able to open the door first would be appointed to the post of honor. Immediately they set to the task. Two of them began to work out special formulas to discover the lock combination. The third man pondered for a moment then walked over to the door turned the handle and the door opened. It had been unlocked all the time.

This tale demonstrates a scenario that is often repeated in our everyday lives. We fret about unknowns, we surmise, we imagine, we jump to conclusions, and we conjure up all kinds of solutions to resolve problems that don't exist. In the process of our distractions the doors appear to be locked and so we fail to open them and walk through. A lot of time is lost dealing with the trifle and the insignificant rather than focusing on the things that need our attention. This is repeated over and over in many businesses, organizations, and even in government. It happens in their meetings, in the way they organize, and in how they service the customer.

Why does this happen? Is it perhaps an unwillingness to face up to reality? Is it a lack of vision? Is it a sign of laziness? Is it because we get in a rut and don't want to accept changes? These are all possibilities.

How many opportunities are lost due to our failure to try the door and see if it opens? I'm sure the two men who were trying to come up with a formula were astounded to witness the ease with which the third man opened the door. I'm sure they questioned themselves over and over as to why they didn't try it. But all their questioning would not change the fact that they had lost their chance. Perhaps the other two men were wiser intellectually but this tale bears out the fact that the one who put his shoulder to the wheel was the one who gained the prize. It was the one who was willing to give the door a try!

—M. Gingrich

"Up"—A Unique English Word

It's no wonder people can't master the English language! There is a two letter word that perhaps has more meanings than any other two letter word, and that is "UP."

It's easy to understand UP, meaning toward the sky or at the top of the list, but when we awaken in the morning, why do we wake UP?

At a meeting, why does a topic come UP? Why do we speak UP, and why are the officers UP for election, and why is it UP to the secretary to write UP a report? We call UP our friends, we use it to brighten UP a room, polish UP the silver, we warm UP the leftovers and clean UP the kitchen. We lock UP the house, and some guys fix UP the old car.

At other times the little word has real special meaning. People stir UP trouble, line UP for tickets, work UP an appetite, and think UP excuses. To be dressed is one thing, but to be dressed UP is special.

And this is confusing: A drain must be opened UP because it is stopped UP. We open UP a store in the morning but we close it UP at night. We seem to be pretty mixed UP about UP.

To be knowledgeable of the proper uses of UP, look UP the word in the dictionary. In a desk size dictionary, UP takes UP almost a quarter of the page and definitions add UP to about thirty. If you are UP to it, you might try building UP a list of the many ways UP is used. It will take UP a lot of your time, but if you don't give UP, you may wind UP with a hundred or more.

When it threatens to rain, we say it is clouding UP. When the sun comes out we say it is clearing UP. When it rains, it wets UP the earth. When it doesn't rain for a while, things dry UP.

One could go on and on, but I'll wrap it UP, for now my time is UP, so I'll shut UP...

Your Check Is In The Mail!

In reply to your request to send a check, I wish to inform you that the present condition of my account makes it almost impossible.

My shattered financial condition is due to the many federal laws, state laws, county laws, city laws, township laws, mother-in-laws, brother-in-laws, sister-in-laws, and also to some outlaws.

Through these laws I am compelled to pay a business tax, income tax, school tax, federal tax, state tax, real estate tax, head tax, amusement tax, gas tax, light tax, furniture tax, carpet tax, food tax, excise tax, and per capita tax. Even my brains are taxed! I am required to get a business license, car license, truck license, boat license, fishing license, hunting license, trapping license, not to mention marriage license and dog license.

I am also required to contribute to every society and organization which the genius of man is capable of bringing to life: United Way, Red Cross, Boy Scouts, Girl Scouts, 4-H Clubs, YMCA, Fresh Air, Salvation Army, rescue missions, food banks, Asthma Foundation, Alzheimer's Association, American Cancer Society, American Diabetes Association, American Heart Association, American Lung Association, Arthritis Association, Cyptic Fibrosm Foundation, Kidney Foundation, Leukemia & Lymphoma Society, March of Dimes Foundation, Multiple Sclerosis Society, Muscular Dystrophy Association, Spina Bifida Association, United Disabilities Services, to woman's relief, unemployment relief, and the gold diggers relief, also to every hospital and charitable institution within the United States of America. Simply because I refuse to donate something or other, I am boycotted, talked about, gossiped about, lied about, held up, held down, and robbed until I am almost ruined.

For my own safety I must carry fire insurance, property insurance, car insurance, truck insurance, liability insurance, unemployment insurance, burglar insurance, health insurance, dismemberment insurance, life insurance, and funeral insurance.

My business is so governed that it is no easy matter for me to find out who really owns it. I am inspected, expected, suspected, disrespected, infected, rejected, dejected, examined, cross-examined, informed, required, summoned, fined, commanded, and compelled until I provide an inexhaustible supply of money for every known need in the human race.

I tell you that except for a miracle, I can not send you any money!

P.S. The stray hound that came to my door last week just had pups under my porch. I sold the pups. Your check is in the mail!

Zucchini Anyone?

Ummm! Ummm! Corn on the cob fresh from the garden. It must be summertime for sure. Green beans, potatoes, cucumbers, tomatoes, and lest I forget, zucchini, too. Yes, yes, it is zucchini season. Lock the car doors for somebody will surely decide to share their bountiful harvest. Don't put them out by the road with a free sign either for the few you have are likely to multiply as other folks add theirs to the pile. Forget the idea of setting them on something so that people will see, for most certainly the object you set them on will meet someone's approval and thinking it is free will take it and leave you stuck with plenty of zucchini.

Grill it, fry it, cook it, bake it, steam it, and just about anything else you do in the kitchen. Zucchini can be used in so many different ways. I've eaten it in stir fry, bread, quiche, in casseroles and with mixed vegetables. Every one of them was good.

Then there are newly dug potatoes and fresh green beans. Throw in some ham or bacon and cook just right and you have a delicacy that is hard to beat. Fortunately, not everything comes at once so that when you have just about had your fill of one along comes another. Like sweet succulent corn on the cob smothered in butter and sprinkled with salt. A meal all by itself! Or delicious BLT sandwiches with red vine-ripened tomatoes.

Surely freshly grown fruits and vegetables right from the garden are one of the blessings of summertime. A bountiful harvest rewarding your minimal efforts to prepare the soil and plant the seed. A harvest so plentiful that it allows us to share it with neighbors and friends and fill our freezers and pantries for the months ahead. Yes, so plentiful we finally decide we have enough and since we can hardly give it away we feel almost guilty of being wasteful. Especially when we think of those who don't have enough to eat. Yes, we are blessed indeed.

We are given the responsibility to prepare the soil, plant the seed, water it, and then harvest the promised fruit. The fruit is a gift from God, produced from a tiny seed that pours the nutrients it receives into a healthy plant that in turn produces edible fruit. The texture, the taste, the appearance, and the time till it reaches maturity are unique to each species. Each one is then used in a multitude of different ways to garnish and enhance the dinner table and satisfy the hungry stomachs that gather around.

Take the opportunity a bountiful harvest brings and share it with your neighbors. Ask around and you will find somebody who can use it. If that doesn't work, every August there is National Sneak Some Zucchini Onto Your Neighbor's Porch Night. If you have some other extras I suppose you could get rid of those this way too, but please don't tell them you got the idea from *The Fishwrapper*.

Enjoy your zucchini.

—M. Gingrich

Mothers

A Little Parable For Mothers

The young mother set her foot on the path of life. "Is the way long?" she asked. And her guide said, "Yes. And the way is hard. And you will be old before you reach the end of it. But the end will be better than the beginning." But the young mother was happy, and she would not believe that anything would be better than these years. So she played with her children, and gathered flowers for them along the way, and bathed with them in the clear streams; and the sun shone on them, and life was good, and the young mother cried, "Nothing will ever be lovelier than this."

Then night came, and storm, and the path was dark, and the children shook with fear and cold, and the mother drew them close and covered them with her mantle, and the children said, "Mother, we are not afraid, for you are near, and no harm can come." And the mother said, "This is better than the brightness of day, for I have taught my children courage."

And the morning came, and there was a hill ahead, and the children climbed and grew weary, and the mother was weary, but at all times she said to the children, "A little patience, and we are there." So the children climbed, and when they reached the top they said, "Mother, we would not have done it without you." And the mother, when she lay down that night, looked up at the stars and said, "This day is a better day than the last, for my children have learned fortitude in the face of hardness. Yesterday I gave them courage. Today I have given them strength."

And the next day came strange clouds which darkened the earth; clouds of war and hate and evil, and the children groped and stumbled, and the mother said, "Look up. Lift your eyes to the light." And the children looked and saw above the clouds an Everlasting Glory, and it guided them and brought them beyond the darkness. And that night the mother said, "This is the best day of all, for I have shown my children God."

And the days went on, and the weeks and the months and the years, and the mother grew old, and she was little and bent. But her children were tall and strong, and walked with courage. And when the way was hard, they helped their mother; and when the way was rough, they lifted her; for she was as light as a feather, and at last they came to a hill, and beyond they could see a shining road and golden gates flung wide.

And the mother said, "I have reached the end of my journey. And now I know that the end is better than the beginning, for my children can walk alone, and their children after them. And the children said, "You will always walk with us, Mother, even when you have gone through the gates."

And they stood and watched her as she went on alone, and the gates closed after her. And they said, "We cannot see her, but she is with us still. A mother like ours is more than a memory. She is a living presence."

—*Temple Bailey*

Before I Was A Mom

Before I was a Mom...
I made and ate hot meals. I had unstained clothing. I had quiet conversations on the phone.

Before I was Mom...
I slept as late as I wanted and never worried about how late I got into bed. I brushed my hair and my teeth everyday.

Before I was a Mom...
I cleaned my house each day. I never tripped over toys or forgot words to lullabies.

Before I was a Mom...
I didn't worry whether or not my plants were poisonous. I never thought about immunizations.

Before I was a Mom...
I had complete control of my mind, my thoughts, my body. I slept all night.

Before I was a Mom...
I never held down a screaming child so that doctors could do tests or give shots. I never looked into teary eyes and cried. I never got gloriously happy over a simple grin.
I never sat up late hours at night watching a baby sleep.

Before I was a Mom…
I never held a sleeping baby just because I didn't want to put it down. I never felt my heart break into a million pieces when I couldn't stop the hurt. I never knew that something so small could affect my life so much. I never knew that I could love someone so much. I never knew I would love being a Mom.

Before I was a Mom…
I didn't know the feeling of having my heart outside my body. I didn't know how special it could feel to feed a hungry baby. I didn't know that bond between a mother and her child. I didn't know that something so small could make me feel so important.

Before I was a Mom…
I had never gotten up in the middle of the night every ten minutes to make sure all was okay.

Before I was a Mom…
I had never known the warmth, the joy, the love, the heartache, the wonderment, or the satisfaction of being a Mom. I didn't know I was capable of feeling so much…

—Source Unknown

Being A Mother

- Somebody said a mother is an unskilled laborer… somebody never gave a squirmy infant a bath.
- Somebody said it takes about six weeks to get back to normal after you've had a baby…somebody doesn't know that once you're a mother, "normal" is history.
- Somebody said a mother's job consists of wiping noses and changing diapers…somebody doesn't know that a child is much more than the shell he lives in.
- Somebody said you learn how to be a mother by instinct…somebody never took a three-year-old shopping.
- Somebody said being a mother is boring…somebody never rode in a car driven by a teenager with a driver's permit.
- Somebody said teachers, psychologists, and pediatricians know more about children than their mothers… somebody hasn't invested her heart in another human being.
- Somebody said if you're a "good" mother, your child will "turn out!"…somebody thinks a child is like a bag of Plaster of Paris that comes with directions, a mold, and a guarantee.
- Somebody said being a mother is what you do in your spare time…somebody doesn't know that when you're a mother, you're a mother ALL the time.
- Somebody said "good" mothers never raise their voices…somebody never came out the back door just in time to see her child wind up and hit a golf ball through the neighbor's kitchen window.
- Somebody said you don't need an education to be a mother…somebody never helped a fourth grader with his math.
- Somebody said you can't love the fifth child as much as you love the first…somebody doesn't have five children.
- Somebody said a mother can find all the answers to her child rearing questions in the books…somebody never had a child stuff beans up his nose.
- Somebody said the hardest part of being a mother is labor and delivery…somebody never watched her baby on the bus for the first day of kindergarten.
- Somebody said a mother can do her job with her eyes closed and one hand tied behind her back…somebody never organized seven giggling Brownies to sell cookies.
- Somebody said a mother can stop worrying after her child gets married…somebody doesn't know that marriage adds a new son or daughter-in-law to a mother's heartstrings.
- Somebody said a mother's job is done when her last child leaves home…somebody never had grandchildren.
- Somebody said being a mother is a side dish on the plate of life…somebody doesn't know what fills you up.
- Somebody said your mother knows you love her, so you don't need to tell her…somebody isn't a mother.

Happy Mother's Day

It's been over twenty years since my buddy Dan and I loaded his metallic blue Chevy, and headed for Florida. We were armed with pockets full of crisp new dollar bills from our week's pay. Blessed by not finding our names on the weekend duty roster, we had decided a weekend at the beach would be just the thing we needed.

As we cruised into Birmingham we decided to stop to phone our mothers and wish them a Happy Mother's Day before resuming our journey south on I-65. Reaching my mother at home, I learned she had just returned from grocery shopping. I could tell by the tone in her voice that she was disappointed I wouldn't be spending her special day with the family. "Have a nice trip and be careful. We'll miss you," she said. When I got back into the car, I could tell by Dan's face that he was suffering from the same guilty conscience that was haunting me. Then we had this brainstorm. Send flowers, of course.

Pulling into the parking lot of a southside Birmingham florist, we each scribbled a note to go with the flowers that would absolve us of the guilt of spending our free weekend on the beach rather than with dear old Mom.

We waited while the clerk assisted a little boy who was selecting a floral arrangement, obviously for his mother. Fidgeting, we were anxious to pay for our flowers and be on our way.

The little boy beamed with pride as he turned to me and held up his selection while the clerk rang up his order. "I'm sure my mama would love these," he said.

"These are carnations. Mama always loved carnations. I'm going to put them with some flowers from our yard," he added, "before I take them to the cemetery." I looked up at the clerk, who was turning away and reaching for a handkerchief. Then I looked at Dan. We watched the little boy leave the store with his prized bouquet and crawl into the back seat of his dad's car.

"Have you fellas made a selection?" asked the clerk, barely able to speak. "I guess we have," answered Dan. We dropped our notes in the trash and walked to his car in silence. "I'll pick you up Sunday evening about five," said Dan, as he pulled up in front of my parents' house. "I'll be ready," I answered, as I wrestled my duffel bag out of the back of the car. Florida would have to wait.

I'm Invisible

It all began to make sense, the blank stares, the lack of response, the way one of the children will walk into the room while I'm on the phone and ask to be taken to the store. Inside, I am thinking, "Can't you see that I'm on the phone?" Obviously not. No one can see if I'm on the phone, or cooking, or sweeping the floor, or even standing on my head in the corner, because no one can see me at all. I'm invisible.

Some days, I am only a pair of hands, nothing more. Can you fix this? Can you tie this? Can you open this?

Some days, I'm not a pair of hands. I'm not even a human being. I'm a clock to ask, "What time is it?" I'm an encyclopedia, answering a host of intriguing inquiries. I'm a car to order, "Pick me up around 5:30 P.M., okay?"

I was certain that these were the hands that once held books and the eyes that studied history and the mind that graduated summa cum laulde—but now, they have disappeared into the peanut butter, never to be seen again. She's going, she's going...she's gone!

One night, a group of friends were having dinner, celebrating the return of a friend from England. Janice had just gotten back from a fabulous trip, and she was going on and on about the hotel she stayed in. I was sitting there, looking around at the others all put together so well. It was hard not to compare and feel sorry for myself as I looked down at my out-of-style clothing, as it was the only thing I could find that was clean. My unwashed hair was pulled up in a hair clip and I was afraid I could actually smell peanut butter in it. I was feeling pretty pathetic, when Janice turned to me with a beautifully wrapped package, and said "I brought you this."

It was a book on the great cathedrals of Europe. I wasn't exactly sure why she'd given this to me, until I read her inscription: "To Charlotte: with admiration for the greatness of what you are building when no one sees."

In the days ahead, I would read—no—devour this book. I would discover what would become for me, four life-changing truths, after which I could pattern my work. No one can say who built the great cathedrals—we have no records of their names. These builders gave their whole lives for a work that they would never see finished. They made great sacrifices and expected no credit. The passion of their building was fueled by their faith that the eyes of God saw everything.

A legendary story in the book told of a rich man who came to visit the cathedral while it was being built, and he saw a workman carving a tiny bird on the inside of a beam. He was puzzled and asked the man, "Why are you spending so much time carving that bird into a beam that will be covered by the roof? No one will ever see it."

And the workman replied, "Because God sees." I closed the book, feeling the missing piece fall into place. It was almost as if I heard God whispering to me, "I see you. I see the sacrifices you make every day, even when no one around you does. No act of kindness you've done, no sequin you've sewn on, no cupcake you've baked, is too small for me to notice and smile. You are building a great cathedral, but you can't see right now what it will become." At times, my invisibility feels like an affliction. But it is not a disease that is erasing my life. It is the cure for the disease of my own self-centeredness. It is the antidote to my strong, stubborn pride.

I keep the right perspective when I see myself as a great builder. As one of the people who show up at a job that they will never see finished, to work on something that their name will never be on. The writer of the book went so far as to say that no cathedrals could ever be built in our lifetime because there are so few people willing to sacrifice to that degree.

When I really think about it, I don't want my son to tell the friend he's bringing home from school for thanksgiving, "My mom gets up at 4 A.M. in the morning and bakes homemade pies, and then she hand bastes a turkey for three hours and presses all the linens for the table." That would mean I had built a shrine or a monument to myself. I just want him to come home. And then, if there is anything more to say to his friend, I hope he says, "You're gonna love it here."

As mothers, we are building great cathedrals. We cannot see if we're doing it right. And one day, it is very possible that the world will marvel, not only at what we have built, but at the beauty that has been added to the world by the many sacrifices of all the invisible women.

Mama's Mama

Mama's mama, on a winter's day,
Milked the cows and fed them hay,
Slopped the hogs, saddled the mule,
And got the children off to school.

Did washing, mopped the floors,
Washed the windows, and did some chores.
Cooked a dish of home-dried fruit,
Pressed her husband's Sunday suit.

Swept the parlor, made the bed,
Baked a dozen loaves of bread.
Split some wood and lugged it in,
Enough to fill the kitchen bin,

Cleaned the lamps and put in oil,
Stewed some apples she thought might spoil,
Churned the butter, baked a cake,

Then exclaimed, "For goodness sake!
"The calves have got out of the pen!"
Went out and chased them in again.
Gathered the eggs and locked the stable,
Returned to the house and set the table.

Cooked supper that was delicious,
And afterward washed all the dishes,
Fed the cat, sprinkled the clothes,
Mended a basket full of hose.

Then opened the organ
And began to play,
"When You Come
to the end
Of a Perfect Day."

Mothers

The human baby is probably the most helpless of all living creatures. While babies in the animal world begin to walk or swim within a few days of birth, a human baby is largely dependent upon its mother for 1-2 years. At first it can't even hold its head upright. It must be fed, clothed, and nurtured. Most babies only learn to walk between 9-15 months. It is during these formative years that mother and child bond. Mother is naturally protective and caring of the delicate form that she holds. She sees in her child a physical likeness of herself. She often sacrifices her own plans and desires to respond to the cries of her newborn baby. There are times a mother may struggle to understand the meaning of those cries. Is the child hungry? Is something wrong? Is he or she tired? Sometimes the frustration level builds when everything she tries fails to satisfy.

As a child grows those cries may at times become cries of self will and determination. Parents must be observant and patient as they endeavor to teach, train, and meet the needs of a child. Sleep deprivation and time consuming tasks of child care, can wear down the tolerance level. In those times of frustration, anger and resentment need to be kept in check. Taking care of a newborn is a lot of work. It takes a lot of commitment. A mother's love looks beyond the moment and focuses on the times of joy, peace, and contentment that she experiences with her child. A mother has a special gentleness and kindness that meets the need of a child like no one else can. She is concerned that her child is growing and becomes alarmed if it isn't. She disciplines in a way that the child learns to obey and finds contentment because it knows the boundary line where it is safe. The child may not realize those boundaries are for his or her well-being and may even resent them at times. A loving and caring mother will remain firm and resolute because she knows what is best for her child.

Being a mother ranks higher than any executive position in the business world. It takes more patience, more wisdom, more work, and more love than any other occupation. A mother's influence upon a child can reach down through multiple generations. Hers is a daunting task to say the least, but it is also a task punctuated with special blessings and joys. A child that is well trained when it is young, will be a blessing to its parents, society, and the world. Someone has said, "The hand that rocks the cradle is the hand that rules the world." To all the mothers who have sensed their greatest calling, and have loved, cared, and prayed for their children, may God bless you abundantly with joy untold for your dedication and commitment.

—M. Gingrich

Paid In Full

A little boy came up to his mother in the kitchen one evening while she was fixing supper, and he handed her a piece of paper that he had been writing on. After his Mom dried her hands on an apron, she read it, and this is what it said:

- For cutting the grass: $5.00
- For cleaning up my room this week: $1.00
- For going to the store for you: $.50
- Babysitting my brother while you went shopping: $.25
- Taking out the garbage: $1.00
- For getting a good report card: $5.00
- For cleaning up and raking the yard: $2.00
- Total owed**:** **$14.75**

Well, his mother looked at him standing there, and the boy could see the memories flashing through her mind. She picked up the pen, turned over the paper he'd written on, and this is what she wrote:

- For all the nights that I've sat up with you, doctored, and prayed for you: No Charge.
- For all the trying times, and all the tears that you've caused through the years: No Charge.
- For all the nights that were filled with dread, and for the worries I knew were ahead: No Charge.
- For the toys, food, clothes, and even wiping your nose: No Charge.
- Son, when you add it, the cost of my love is**:** No Charge.

When the boy finished reading what his mother had written, there were big tears in his eyes, and he looked straight at his mother and said, "Mom, I sure do love you".

And then he took the pen and in great big letters he wrote: "PAID IN FULL".

—Author Unknown

Parenting

When my wife quit work to take care of our new baby daughter, countless hours of peekaboo and other games slowly took their toll. One evening she smacked her bare toes on the corner of a dresser and, grabbing her foot, sank to the floor.

I rushed to her side and asked where it hurt. She looked at me through tear-filled eyes and managed to moan, "It's the piggy that ate roast beef."

Talking About Others

A young mother was riding the bus with her four-year-old boy when he suddenly blurted out so that everyone in the bus could hear: "Look, Mom, see that man's nose? It looks soooo funny!"

The mother was quite embarrassed and scolded her son. Then she whispered to him that if he wanted to say something about someone, then he had to wait until they got home or at least where nobody could hear them, so that nobody would be sad.

A moment later, the boy blurted out in the same loud voice: "Look, Mom, we've got to talk about that big fat lady when we get home!"

The Images Of Mother

- 4 Years of age—My mommy can do anything!
- 8 Years of age—My mom knows a lot! A whole lot!

- 12 Years of age—My mother doesn't really know quite everything.
- 14 Years of age—Naturally, mom doesn't know that, either.
- 16 Years of age—Mom? She's hopelessly old-fashioned.
- 18 Years of age—She's way out of date!
- 25 Years of age—Well, she might know a little bit about it.
- 35 Years of age—Before we decide, let's get my mother's opinion.
- 45 Years of age—Wonder what mom would have thought about it?
- 65 Years of age—Wish I could talk it over with my mom.

Things Moms Don't Want To Hear

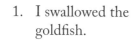

1. I swallowed the goldfish.
2. Does grape juice leave a stain?
3. The principal called…
4. What's it cost to fix a window?
5. Has anyone seen my earthworms?
6. I painted your shoes pretty, huh Mommy?

Time For School, Son

Early one morning, a mother went in to wake up her son. "Wake up, son. It's time to go to school!"

"But why, Mom? I don't want to go."

"Give me two reasons why you do not want to go."

"Well, the students hate me for one, and the teachers hate me too!"

"Oh, that's no reason not to go to school. Come on now and get ready."

"Give me two reasons why I should go to school."

"Well, for one, you're fifty-two years old. And for another, you're the principal!"

What Mother Said

- Paul Revere's mother: "I don't care where you think you have to go, young man. Midnight is past your curfew!"
- Mary, Mary, Quite Contrary's mother: "I don't mind you having a garden, Mary, but does it have to be growing under your bed?"
- Humpty Dumpty's mother: "Humpty, if I've told you once, I've told you a hundred times not to sit on that wall. But would you listen to me? Noooo!"
- Columbus' mother: "I don't care what you've discovered, Christopher. You still could have written me a letter!"
- Babe Ruth's mother: "Babe, how many times have I told you—quit playing ball in the house! That's the third broken window this week!"
- Michelangelo's mother: "Mike, can't you paint on walls like other children? Do you have any idea how hard it is to get that stuff off the ceiling?"
- Abraham Lincoln's mother: "Again with the stovepipe hat, Abe? Can't you just wear a baseball cap like the other children?"
- Mary's mother: "I'm not upset that your lamb followed you to school, Mary, but I would like to know how he got a better grade than you."
- Goldilocks' mother: "I've got a bill here for a busted chair from the bear family. You know anything about this, Goldie?"
- Little Miss Muffet's mother: "Well, all I've got to say is if you don't get off your tuffet and start cleaning your room, there'll be a lot more spiders around here!"
- Albert Einstein's mother: "But, Albert, it's your senior picture. Can't you do something about your hair? Styling gel, mousse, something…?"
- George Washington's mother: "The next time I catch you throwing money across the Potomac, you can kiss your allowance goodbye!"
- Thomas Edison's mother: "Of course I'm proud that you invented the electric light bulb, Thomas. Now turn off that light and get to bed!"

Prayer

A Child's Prayer

Dear God, are you still awake?
Have you got a minute or two?
You're pretty good at understanding,
And I really need to talk to you.

You see, mommy came to tuck me in,
Like she does every night.
I was trying to play a trick on her,
Since she can't see without the light.

I was going to close my eyes
And pretend to be asleep.
But when I heard her crying,
I didn't dare let out a peep.

She started talking to you, God.
Did you hear the things she said?
Could you hear what she was saying
As she stood beside my bed?

Why would mommy be so sad?
I wondered just what I had done,
And then I began to remember it all
As she named them one by one…

This morning we worked in the garden,
But, honest, I really didn't know
That if I picked all those little yellow blooms
The tomatoes wouldn't grow!

Charlie and I were trying to be helpers,
'Cause I know that's what mommy needs,
But I don't think she was too happy with us
When we pulled up carrots instead of weeds.

Mommy said we should stop for the day,
She decided we had helped quite enough.
I sure had worked up an appetite…
I didn't know gardening was so tough!

We had peanut-butter and jelly for lunch
And I shared too
much, I guess…
But I didn't realize
until I was done
That Charlie had
made such a mess.

Mommy said she
needed a nap,
She had one of
her headaches today.
She told me to keep an eye on my sister
And find something quiet to play.

We sat and watched poor old Albert,
I just knew he must be so bored
Goin' round and round in the same place all day,
Wouldn't you think so, Lord?

I didn't think it would hurt to let him out for a while.
I mean, mice need exercise, too.
By the way, have you seen Albert lately?
He's been sort of missing since two.

Mommy sent us outside for the rest of the day.
She said we needed fresh air.
But when daddy came home she told him
She was trying to get something out of her hair.

We thought mommy needed cheering up,
So we decided to brighten her day.
But, God, did you see the look on her face
When we gave her that pretty bouquet?

We had gotten a little bit dirty,
So mommy said to get in the tub.
"Use soap this time," she reminded,
"And please don't forget to scrub."

Charlie didn't like the water too much,
But I lathered up real good.
I knew mommy would be so proud of me
For cleaning up like I should.

I went downstairs to the table,
But during dinner it started to rain,
I'd forgotten to turn off the water, it seems,
And I hadn't unplugged the drain!

I decided right then it was just about time
To start getting ready for bed,
When mommy said, "It's sure been a long day,"
And her face began turning all red.

I lay there listening to mommy
As she told you about our day.
I thought about all of the things I had done
And I wondered what I should say.

I was just about to tell her
That I'd been awake all along,
And ask her to please forgive me
For all of those things I'd done wrong.

When suddenly, I heard her whisper,
"God, forgive me for today,
For not being more understanding
When those problems came my way.

"For not handling situations in the way
You wanted me to, for getting angry
And losing my temper,
Things I know you don't want me to do.

"And, God, please give me more patience,
Help me make it through another day,
I'll do better tomorrow, I promise,
In Jesus' name I pray."

Wiping her eyes, she kissed me
And knelt here beside my bed.
She stroked my hair for a little while,
"I love you, precious," mommy said.

She left the room without ever knowing
That I'd been awake all the time.
And God, could we make it our little secret?
You know, just yours and mine?

I'm sorry I was so much trouble today,
I really didn't mean to be, Daddy says
It's tough being a child sometimes,
But I think it's harder on mommy than me.

Well, goodnight, God. Thanks for listening.
It's sure nice to know you're there.
I feel so much better when I talk to you
'Cause you always hear my prayer.

And I'll do better tomorrow, I promise,
Just you wait and see!
I'll try not to be so much trouble again,
But, God, please give more patience to mommy
...Just in case! Amen.

—Anonymous

A Man's Prayer

Teach me that 60 minutes make an hour, 16 ounces a pound, and 100 cents a dollar. Help me to live so that I can lie down at night with a clear conscience and unhaunted by the face of those to whom I may have brought pain. Grant that I may earn my meal ticket on the square, and in earning it I may do unto others as I would have them do unto me. Deafen me to the tingle of tainted money. Blind me to the faults of other fellows and to reveal to me my own. Guide me so that each night when I look across the table at my wife, who has been a blessing to me, I will have nothing to conceal. Keep me young to laugh with little children and sympathetic so as to be considerate of old age. And comes the day of darkening shades make the ceremony short and the epitaph simple: "Here lies a man."

A Prayer As I Grow Older

"O Lord, you know I am growing older! Keep me from closing my eyes to the fact. Keep me from becoming a pest, a self-appointed sage with the annoying habit of thinking I must say something on every subject and on every occasion. Keep my mind free from the repetition of past experiences and endless details. Seal my lips about my aches and pains. I do not ask for improved memory, but for less cockiness about the memory of others. Teach me to admit that sometimes I am mistaken. Make me sweeter and mellower as my age progresses. Let me never grow old, only older. May it be said of me, 'though our outward man is perishing, yet the inward man is being renewed day by day' (2 Cor. 4:16)."

A Prayer For The New Year

Our dear God of love and care,
Another year of our lives has passed.
Please take from our hearts the burden we bear
Of the "luggage" we held so fast.

Resentment, envy, self-pity, and pride,
Help us forget all our fear.
Help us to put away things that abide
To hinder the joys of this year.

May we put behind us all of the old
To make room for the new ahead.
The new year is filled with days of gold,
If we look for the good instead.

No more of the luggage of the past;
A new year beckons us on.
Please help us to make it a better one
Than the old year that is gone.

We pray for your guidance and care
In all that we undertake.
Please help us to follow you everywhere
Through this bright new year, for Christ's sake.

—Lucille Calhoun Stewart

Choosing Sides

At a White House dinner, a churchman offered a benediction and closed with the pious affirmation: "The Lord is on our side."

When President Lincoln did not respond to this sentiment, someone asked him, "Don't you believe, Mr. President, that the Lord is always on the side of the right?"

"I am not concerned about that," was Lincoln's answer, "for we know that the Lord is always on the side of the right. My concern is that I and this nation should be on the Lord's side."

Dear Lord…

"Dear Lord, so far today, I am doing all right. I've not gossiped, lost my temper, been greedy, grumpy, nasty, selfish, or self indulgent. I have not whined, complained, or eaten any chocolate. I've charged nothing on my credit card.

But I will be getting out of bed in a minute, and I think that I will really need your help then."

Favorite Meditation

Now Lord, you've known me a long time. You know me better than I know myself. You know that each passing day I am growing older and someday may even be very old, so meanwhile please keep me from the habits of thinking I must say something on every subject and on every occasion.

Release me from trying to straighten out everyone's affairs. Make me thoughtful, but not moody, helpful but not overbearing. I've a certain amount of knowledge to share, still it would be very nice to have a few friends who, at the end, recognized and forgave the knowledge I lacked.

Keep my tongue free from the recital of endless details. Seal my lips on my aches and pains. They increase daily and the need to speak of them becomes almost a compulsion. I ask for grace enough to listen to the retelling of others' afflictions and to be helped to endure them with patience.

I would like to have improved memory, but I'll settle for growing humility and an ability to capitulate when my memory clashes with the memory of others. Teach me the glorious lesson that on some occasions, I may be mistaken.

Keep me reasonably kind; I've never aspired to be perfect. One who does must be rather difficult to live with. Yet on the other hand, an embittered old person is a constant burden.

Please give me the ability to see good in unlikely places and talents in unexpected people. And give me the grace to tell them so, dear Lord.

Independence Or Dependence

The 4th of July stirs thoughts of what transpired in America in the year 1776. The suppression of over zealous authoritarian rule, burdensome taxes, and a feeling that their voice was not being heard fostered a spirit of discontentment in the hearts of the people. The people reasoned that the government was not respecting their individual rights and they felt increasingly isolated as England tightened its control. Finally the colonists had had enough and the writing of the "Declaration of Independence" was a first step in notifying England of their intentions.

Ironically, however, woven into the fabric of the constitution are numerous references that exemplify dependence as well. It is a dependence upon God. "We hold these truths to be self-evident, that all men are created equal, that they are endowed by their Creator," leaves no doubt as to their belief in a greater power. The concluding statement, "And for the support of this Declaration, with a firm reliance on the protection of Divine Providence, we mutually pledge to each other our lives, our fortunes, and our sacred honor," further solidifies that the writers of the declaration recognized a greater power than they.

Their pursuit of freedom from the oppressive yoke of authoritarian rule was undertaken with the acknowledgement that freedom is only possible if God's laws are followed. This was the premise upon which the Declaration of Independence was written. In America today, there is another wave of independence sweeping the land. It is however uniquely different. It is a spirit of independence that says, "I will do as I please. I want what I want, when I want it." It does not recognize a sovereign God. In fact, it tries to remove any reference to God. It is different in that the tenor of it is selfish and arrogant. Secondly, it is divisive. It is a spirit fed by individual feelings and personal interests without regard for God or fellow man. This spirit is evidenced by a huge increase in personal lawsuits and anti-protests. It can also be seen in America's spending habits, namely the huge credit card debt. It is a spirit that can never be completely satisfied. Whenever it is fed a little bit it always wants more.

Some time ago I made this statement. "God said it, I believe it, and that settles it." Another individual challenged me regarding the correctness of that statement, and rightly so. You see, because God said it the issue is settled regardless of whether I choose to believe it or not. Therein lies the difference between the independent spirit felt today compared to 1776. The founding fathers of America believed God and found peace in His sovereignty whereas many today want to deny the existence of God and go to extreme ends to annihilate Him from their thinking. The end result is chaos and confusion.

One of the comments of Benjamin Franklin at the signing of the Declaration was, "We must all hang together, or we shall be hanged separately," indicating the need for unity and a concerted effort. The longevity of America's standing as a country is largely a result of a unified obedience to God's principles. That kind of unity is being severely tested in political chambers, in the courts, in the schools, in the churches, and all across America. Regardless of man's efforts to avoid God and circumvent Him, it cannot be done without consequences. America's independence as a nation is contingent upon, recognizing her dependence upon God, obedience to His laws, and reverence for His sovereignty. In the shadow of that dependence she will find rest, unity, and peace.

—M. Gingrich

Let's Use It

I read about an old man who had electricity installed in his backwoods cabin. When the meter inspector made his first call and found that very little current had been used, he asked, "Don't you ever use the lights?"

"Sure," said the old man.

"How long at a time?" the inspector asked.

"Just long enough to see to light the oil lamp," was the answer.

Electricity is like prayer. It only works if you use it.

Lord, Give Me Strength

Dear God, give me strength to do what I must
And to remember that it's You who I must trust.
Let me be kind in my words today
Despite my pain, I'll have nice things to say.

Show me Your wisdom found deep in Your Word
Perhaps there's a message I have not yet heard.
When I want to give up, keep me close to You
So I know You are with me no matter what I go through.

Those times when I stumble and fall right on my face
Remind me it's because I stepped out of my place.
You are my healer and time is Your key
Someday soon there will be a miracle for me.

Waiting on You God, is a great step of faith
But knowing You're faithful keeps me in my place.
This illness can't last forever, so in You I rest
Trusting always in the One who knows best.

—Kenneth C. Showalter

More Than We Ask

Missionary Hudson Taylor went to China on a sailing ship. As it neared a channel someone knocked urgently on his stateroom door. Opening it he saw the captain of the ship.

"Mr. Taylor," he said, "we have no wind. We are drifting toward an island where the people are heathen and I hear they are cannibals."

"What can I do?" asked Taylor.

"I understand that you believe in God. I want you to pray for wind."

"All right, captain, I will, but you must set the sail."

"Why, that's ridiculous! There is not even the slightest breeze. Besides, the sailors will think I'm crazy."

But Taylor insisted and the captain finally agreed. He returned later and the missionary was still on his knees. "You can stop praying now," said the captain. "We've got more wind than we know what to do with!"

Doesn't God often give us more than we ask?

Prayer Blessings

Prayer brings the blessings of deep peace;
There is tranquility in the soul.
You can almost hear a star moving
Almost hear a rose unfold.

There is peace that passes understanding
In thoughts, emotion, and heart;
The soul rises in rapture, and this
Blessing shall never depart.

Prayer Of Faith

An amazing true story recorded years ago in Ida Tarbell's Teacher's Guide told of a little boy in London, England, who lived with his mother in great proverty. They prayed daily for help.

When the boy's Sunday school teacher told of Jesus sending Peter to get money out of the mouth of a fish, hope arose in the child's heart. If he could just buy a fish, he too would get money. He was determined to save whatever he could earn.

He took his savings to the market and ordered a fish. When the man asked him how much money he had the man said that it was not enough. "But I only need the head," he explained. "Oh, I can sell you a head," the man answered. And he wrapped the fish head in a newspaper.

The lad hurried home and placed it on the kitchen table. "Mother, come quickly," he called. "I have money for us."

The mother came and unwrapped the package. Alas, there was no money. The little boy ran to his room crying. The mother began reading the paper.

She rubbed her eye. It can't be! But there was her name! The lawyer's ad said she had inherited money and if she could come to his office she could claim it.

Oh, I can see a mother and a little boy, mingling their tears of joy, kneeling at a kitchen chair thanking God for answered prayer.

School Teachers' Manual

What a difference it would make in our world today if these prayers were prayed on the lips of our children and on the lips of all society. The following was taken from an actual teacher's manual, entitled "Prayers to Assist Public School Teachers in Religious Exercises."

I believe they are worthy of our consideration.

The Prayers, Talks, and Observations that follow are intended for the use of the teacher as sources of information and inspiration. They may be used as a whole or in part, or they may be adapted as occasion requires.

In addition to this material, short selections from the Bible may be read with profit; and it is a good plan to occasionally have the whole school join in unison with the Lord's Prayer, the Apostles' Creed, or the Twenty-third Psalm. Teachers who give attention to the proper spiritual development of the children seldom have trouble in discipline. The Prayers and Talks which follow are suggestive. They may be used as they are or they may be revised to meet the needs of any occasion.

Prayers for the Rural School

Prayer for the First Morning of the School Year

Lord, we thank Thee for this beautiful world; for its fields and its fruits; for its trees and rivers. We thank Thee for its animals and its flowers. We thank Thee for its people everywhere. Especially do we thank Thee for friends who love us and whom we love. We are glad of those who came here in early times and whose work makes this day possible. Now be with us as we open the school year. Make us obedient, attentive, industrious, and thoughtful. Direct those who teach and help us all to work together with a glad sense of our opportunity. Amen.

Prayer for Monday Morning

Lord, we thank Thee for a new week. May we enter and continue in the work of this day with hopefulness and energy. May we do our tasks without dishonor to ourselves and with good to others. Whatever may be our deficiencies, may they not discourage us. Help us to cast away that which is evil and to cleave to that which is good. Amen.

Prayer for Tuesday Morning

The day returns and brings us another round of duties. May they not weary us because they are common. Teach us to do our part of the day's work manfully and with cheerfulness. Take us in Thy care to give us bravery of thought as well as deed. May we follow the light of Thy Spirit all through the days. We thank Thee for Thy care of children everywhere, and we pray that we may have the clean, ready mind of children so that wherever Thy call may lead us we may follow with gladness and may ever learn of Thee. Amen.

Prayer for Wednesday

We come before Thee, O Lord, midway in the week to thank Thee for all Thy good mercies.

Give us courage to do all our tasks as they should be done. Teach us the folly of indifferent effort and the uselessness of dishonest work. May we be brave to look every duty in the countenance and may no task frighten us.

Give us joy in our school work. May we do it in the pleasant spirit which helps everybody. Amen.

Prayer for Thursday

For our friends, we thank Thee, Lord, and may we be worthy of their friendship. Grant that we may not cause them pain or give them the need to apologize for our pettiness or for our indifference to those things which count. Help us to learn how to show true friendship; to look less upon our hurts and disappointments than upon those of others. And for the joys and successes which come to our friends we thank Thee, O Lord. And for the success that may be ours today we thank Thee. Amen.

Prayer for Friday

As we close the week's work, we beseech Thee, Lord, to behold us with favor. Whatever may have disappointed or grieved Thee during these days, we humbly pray Thy goodness to forgive and Thy wisdom to over-rule. Keep us free from sin, and if it be possible, from all harm. May we cast out the spirit of fear, going bravely into each day with cheery faces and brave hearts. Grant us to meet again and to take up anew with joy the tasks which fall to our common lot. Amen.

"Prayers for the Town or City School"

Prayer for the First Morning of the School Year

Lord, look with favor upon our coming together in this new school year. We are from many homes, and we have many interests, but we thank Thee that we are to work together in this our common school-home. Make us attentive, receptive and responsive, May what we learn prove to be a blessing unto us and unto others.

We thank Thee for the kindness and the care of our parents and the willingness of our teachers. Give Thy help, Lord, that we may all gladly work together in making this a fruitful year.

And we thank Thee for the city streets, for the companionship of many people together; for the alert industry that will teach us many things. Help us to hide these things in our hearts, and to use them for the good of all. Amen.

Prayer for Monday

We thank Thee for another week of chance. Whatever may have been our failures, help us to forget them and to press on with cheerful faces and grateful hearts.

Keep us, Lord, from being narrow or mean or selfish. May we look about us with a glad spirit, ready to help people who may not be as fortunate as we. Order the events of this day so that we may be helped at its close by the knowledge that we have tried to do well.

Let us be humble in our minds and brave in our hearts. Amen.

Prayer for Tuesday

Aid us to look ahead this day with expectation of good.

Although our ways may be divided, grant that our purposes may unite in the one resolve to make the utmost of our privileges. To this end, be with us and our teachers. Give us all the seeing eye and the hearing ear. Above all else, grant unto us the heart faithful to duty and responsive to opportunity. And if we have injured any, give unto us the spirit of decency that we may strive to righten what we have done amiss. Amen.

Prayer for Wednesday

Lord, receive our prayer for our school, our homes, and our city. Help us to enter this new day looking forward, and help us to keep hopefully going on. In what we may have thought, of evil, break down our plans and grant that we may have the grace to do good for evil. Make us brave with bravery of a clean conscience. Help us to be ashamed of selfishness and of all mean ambitions. May we have the grace to forget wrongs done to us and to remember benefits. Amen.

Prayer for Thursday

Lord, we know that all good gifts come from Thee.

Teach us that the best gifts are not the fine pleasures of sense which we so much enjoy; not houses and the comforts which go with a happy home-life. For such we thank Thee, but help us to thank Thee more for our minds and our hearts and for the training which our school gives. Now hearten us for this day's work. Let us see ourselves as we are. Forbid that we try to deceive ourselves or others. And wherein we have failed, help us to do better. Amen.

Prayer for Friday

Grant Thy presence with us in this closing day of the week's school. May we come to our tasks with bravery and do them with zeal. Help us to know that we are but learners. Be patient with our slowness. Overlook our follies. We bless Thee for all the good things we enjoy. Help us to use them aright that we may enjoy them the more. Today, we will separate from one another awhile. Some of us will seek pleasure, some toil and others rest. Follow us, Lord, with Thy love and Thy care. Grant that we may come together again for other days of learning and of companionship. And in all that we do, help us to fit into Thy great plan of life for us. Amen.

In Part I at the introduction it was noted that teachers who give attention to the proper spiritual development of the children seldom have trouble in discipline. We would do well to motto these prayers in our own lives, Lord, help us work together, show true friendship and have the grace to forget wrongs done to us. Keep us from being narrow and selfish. Forbid that we try to deceive ourselves or others. Thank you for your loving care in all we do. Help us to find our place in Thy great plan of life. Amen.

—Merle Gingrich

Shipwreck

A Fable

A voyaging ship was wrecked during a storm at sea and only two of the men on it were able to swim to a small, desert like island. The two survivors, not knowing what else to do, agree that they had no other recourse but to pray to God. However, to find out whose prayer was more powerful, they agreed to divide the territory between them and stay on opposite sides of the island. They first prayed for food.

The next morning, the first man saw a fruit-bearing tree on his side of the island, and he was able to eat its fruit. The other man's parcel of land remained barren.

After a week, the first man was lonely and he decided to pray for a wife. The next day, another ship was wrecked, and the only survivor was a woman who swam to his side of the island. On the other side of the island, there was nothing. Soon the first man prayed for a house, clothes, and more food.

The next day all of these were given to him. However, the second man still had nothing. Finally, the first man prayed for a ship, so that he and his wife could leave the island. In the morning, he found a ship docked at his side of the island. The first man boarded the ship with his wife and decided to leave the second man on the island. He considered the other man unworthy to receive God's blessings, since none of his prayers had been answered.

As the ship was about to leave, the first man heard a voice, "Why are you leaving your companion on the island?"

"My blessings are mine alone, since I was the one who prayed for them," the first man answered. "His prayers were all unanswered and so he does not deserve anything."

"You are mistaken!" the voice rebuked him. "He had only one prayer, which I answered. If not for that, you would not have received any of my blessings."

"Tell me," the first man asked the voice, "what did he pray for, that I should owe him anything?"

"He prayed that all your prayers be answered."

For all we know, our blessings are not the fruits of our prayers alone, but those of another praying for us.

Taxation

Income Taxes, Real Estate Taxes, Sales Taxes! Taxes, taxes and more taxes! Sometimes it seems like there is nothing left when we finally get done paying all the taxes. Matthew 22:21 says, "Render therefore unto Caesar the things which are Caesar's and unto God the things that are God's. Taxes imposed by government are nothing new. Civilization's of old have taxed their respective citizens as a means of providing security, law enforcement, and various other public services. It is a means of providing a service, that is otherwise unattainable, by pooling of resources and sharing the cost. The government or oversight of a civilization has certain duties and responsibilities bestowed to them. Taxation is a means of funding to see that those responsibilities are carried out.

One major difference lies in the rendering to God versus the rendering to Caesar. God is righteous and Holy, and He gives us more than we will ever be able to give Him. He is always worthy of everything we give Him. Government is subject to fraud, arrogance, and corruption. The integrity and honesty of government is only as good as the individuals who serve. A man corrupt in personal matters is likely to be the same in public matters. Unlike God, man has a sinful nature which can cause him to make some unwise and careless choices. These choices are often brought about by greed, pride, and selfish motives. Government, therefore, may not always be worthy of the rendering they require. Lack of integrity, however, on the part of government does not grant automatic permission to its citizens to withhold their taxes. A system of checks and balances provides safety for government and its citizens.

Every taxpayer should consider it a privilege and an honor to pay taxes. History, however, shows us what happens when taxes become too burdensome. The people grow weary, especially when they see waste and corruption as the cause. Government was designed and instituted to serve the people under its jurisdiction. When greed and selfishness find root and those entrusted with oversight responsibilities begin filling their pockets, then respect and trust are undermined. A healthy relationship between government and its citizens is cultivated when there is a system of checks and balances. Runaway spending results in runaway taxation to balance the budget. This taxation then becomes a burden on the economy and the citizens and becomes a point of contention.

God outlined some basic precepts by which man should live. Love, truth, and honesty are core ingredients of those principles. When these principles are grossly disregarded in our society, should we expect that government would become more frugal and concerned about their spending of taxpayer dollars? Local school boards, municipalities, and all public entities should have checks and balances so that over spending and over taxation do not occur.

Unfortunately, that has not always been the case and many property owners are paying the price. Real estate taxes have far exceeded the rate of inflation and in some cases folks who own a home can ill afford to live in it because of taxes. Something is amiss.

People thought the Titanic was unsinkable, but it sank, and the loss was great. Unless the ship of taxation is righted it will sink America and its economy. Unless men turn their hearts toward God and his principles the ship will eventually sink. Love of God and fellow man rather than love of self, followed by truthfulness, honesty, and integrity are key steps to righting the ship. When they become a priority than tax relief is sure to follow.

P.S. Everybody should pay his income tax with a smile. I tried it, but they wanted cash.

—M. Gingrich

What Prayer Has Done?

Prayer has divided the seas, quenched the flames of fire, muzzled lions, disarmed vipers, marshaled the stars against the wicked, and stopped the course of the moon. Prayer has burst open iron gates, it has raised the dead, bridled raging passions of man, and destroyed vast armies of atheists. Prayer has brought one man from the bottom of the sea, and carried another in a chariot of fire into heaven. What hasn't prayer done?

—Source Unknown

Puzzlers

Animal Love Notes

Zachary the zoologist wants to write a love letter to his beloved. Just to be clever, he's decided to use animal names in place of real words. Fill in the blanks as Zachary would in order to complete his letter.

1. You are ________ to my heart.
2. You'll never know how much I miss ________ .
3. I treasure every ________ on your head.
4. I can't ________ to be away from you.
5. You'll never catch me ________ to you.
6. Loving you will never ________ me.
7. Losing you would be a ________ moment in my life.
8. I'd scream out my love for you, but it would make me ________.
9. Your love makes me feel rich, even though I'm low in ________ .

Answers:

1. Deer
2. Ewe
3. Hare
4. Bear
5. Lion
6. Boar
7. Fowl
8. Horse
9. Doe

A Quiz For People That Know Everything

1. There's one sport in which neither the spectators nor the participants know the score or the leader until the contest ends. What is it?
2. What famous North American landmark is constantly moving backward?
3. Of all vegetables, only two can live to produce on their own for several growing seasons. All other vegetables must be replanted every year. What are the only two perennial vegetables?
4. At noon and midnight the hour and minute hands are exactly coincident with each other. How many other times between noon and midnight do the hour and minute hands cross?
5. What is the only sport in which the ball is always in the possession of the team on defense, and the offensive team can score without touching the ball?
6. What fruit has its seeds on the outside?
7. Only three words in standard English begin with the letters "dw." They are all common. Name two of them.
8. There are fourteen punctuation marks in English grammar. Can you name half of them?
9. Where are the lakes that are referred to in the "Los Angeles Lakers?"
10. There are seven ways a baseball player can legally reach first base without getting a hit. Taking a base on balls —a walk—is one way. Name the other six.
11. It's the only vegetable or fruit that is never sold frozen, canned, processed, cooked, or in any other form but fresh. What is it?
12. How is it possible for a pitcher to make four or more strikeouts in one inning?
13. Name six or more things that you can wear on your feet, that begin with the letter "s."

Answers:

1. Boxing.
2. Niagara Falls. The rim is worn down about 2 and a half feet each year because of the millions of gallons of water that rush over it every minute.
3. Asparagus and rhubarb.
4. Ten times (not eleven, as most people seem to think, if you do not believe it, try it with your watch, it is only 10 times).
5. Baseball.
6. Strawberry.
7. Dwarf, dwell, and dwindle.
8. Period, comma, colon, semicolon, dash, hyphen, apostrophe, question mark, exclamation point, quotation marks, brackets, parenthesis, braces, and ellipses.
9. In Minnesota. The team was originally known as the Minneapolis Lakers, and kept the name when they moved west.
10. Batter hit by a pitch; passed ball; catcher interference; catcher drops third strike; fielder's choice; and being designated as a pinch runner.
11. Lettuce.
12. If the catcher drops a called third strike, and doesn't throw the batter out at first base, the runner is safe.
13. Shoes, socks, sandals, sneakers, slippers, skis, snowshoes, stockings, and so on.

Brain Teasers

1. How can you arrange for two people to stand on the same piece of newspaper and yet be unable to touch each other without stepping off the newspaper?
2. How many 3-cent stamps are there in a dozen?
3. A rope ladder hangs over the side of a ship. The rungs are one foot apart and the ladder is 12 feet long. The tide is rising at four inches an hour. How long will it take before the first four rungs of the ladder are underwater?
4. Which would you rather have, a trunk full of nickels or a trunk half full of dimes?
5. Steve has three piles of sand and Mike has four piles of sand. If they put them all together, how many do they have?
6. In which sport are the shoes made entirely of metal?
7. If the Vice President of the United States should die, who would be President?
8. How can you throw a golf ball with all your might and without hitting a wall or any other obstruction have the ball stop and come right back to you?
9. Find the English word that can be formed from all these letters: PNLLEEEESSSSS.

Answers:
1. Slide the newspaper half way under a closed door and ask the two people to stand on the bit of newspaper on their side of the door.
2. There are twelve (not four).
3. Actually, the ladder will rise with the ship!
4. Dimes are smaller than nickels, SO choose the dimes!
5. If they put them all together, there will be one pile.
6. Horse racing.
7. The President.
8. Throw the ball straight up.
9. Sleeplessness.

How Smart Are You?

Here is a very simple little test comprised of four questions to determine the level of your intellect. Your replies must be spontaneous and immediate, with no deliberating or wasting time. And no cheating.

1. Q: You are competing in a race, and overtake the runner in second place. In which position are you now?

   A: If you answered that you're now first, then you're completely wrong. You overtook the second runner and took their place, therefore you're second. For the next question try not to be so dim.

2. Q: If you overtake the last runner, what position are you now in?

   A: If you answered second-last, once again you're completely wrong. Think about it…How can you over take the person coming last? If you're behind them then they can't be last. The answer is impossible!! It would appear that thinking is not one of your strong points.

Anyway, here's another to try, don't take any notes or use a calculator, and remember your replies must be instantaneous. Take heart! (That was the dictionary's suggestion)

3. Q: Take 1000.
   Add 40.
   Add another 1000.
   Add 30.
   Add 1000
   again.
   Plus 20.
   Plus 1000.
   And plus 10.
   What is the total?

   A: 5000??? Wrong again! The correct answer is 4100 Try again with a good calculator. Today is clearly not your day! Although you should manage to get the last question right…

4. Q: Marie's father has five daughters:

   1. Chache
   2. Cheche
   3. Chichi
   4. Chocho
   5. ???

   What is the fifth daughter's name? Think quickly …You'll find the answer below…

   A: Chuchu??? Wrong!! It's obviously Marie!! Read the question properly!!

Mental Test

Q: What do you put in a toaster?
A: The answer is bread. If you said "toast," then give up

now and go do something else before you hurt yourself. If you said "bread," go to the next question.

Q: Say "silk" five times. Now, spell "silk." What do cows drink?
A: Cows drink water. If you said "milk," please do not attempt the next question. Your brain is obviously overstressed and may even overheat. It may be that you need to content yourself with reading something more appropriate such as "Children's World." If you said "water," then proceed to the next question.

Q: If a red house is made with red bricks, a blue house is made with blue bricks, a pink house is made with pink bricks, a black house is made with black bricks, what is a greenhouse made with?
A: Greenhouses are made from glass. If you said "green bricks," wrong again! If you said "glass," then go on to the next question.

Q: A plane was flying at 20,000 feet over Germany. Germany at the time was politically divided into West Germany and East Germany. During the flight, two of the engines failed. The pilot, realizing that the last remaining engine was also failing, decided on a crash landing. Unfortunately, the engine failed before he had time and the plane crashed smack in the middle of "no-man's land" between East Germany and West Germany. Where should the survivors be buried—East Germany or West Germany or in "no-man's land"?
A: You don't, of course, bury the survivors. If you said anything else, you must never try to rescue anyone from a plane crash. Your efforts would not be appreciated. If you said, "Don't bury the survivors" then proceed to the next question.

Q: If the hour hand on a clock moves 1/60th of a degree every minute, then how many degrees will the hour hand move in one hour?
A: One degree. If you said "360 degrees" or anything else other than "one degree," you are to be congratulated. Proceed to the final question.

Q: Without using a calculator—You are driving a bus from London to Milford Haven in Wales. In London, 17 people get on the bus. In Reading, six people get off the bus and nine people get on. In Swindon, two people get off and four get on. In Cardiff, 11 people get off and 16 people get on. In Swansea, three people get off and five people get on. In Carmathen, six people get off and three get on. You then arrive at Milford Haven. Now, what was the name of the bus driver?
A: Oh, come on now...It was you!

Questions

The average person only gets seven right.

This is based on U.S. and Canadian info, so use all lobes of your brain. This can be more difficult than it looks—it just shows how little most of us really see! Here are twenty-three questions about things we see every day or have known about all our lives. How many can you get right? These little simple questions are harder then you think. It just shows you how little we pay attention to the commonplace things of life. Put your thinking caps on. No cheating! No looking around! No getting out of your chair! No using anything on or in your desk or computer!

1. On a standard traffic light, is the green on the top or bottom?
2. How many states are there in the USA? (Don't laugh, some people don't know)
3. In which hand is the Statue of Liberty's torch?
4. What six colors are on the classic Campbell's® soup label?
5. What two numbers on the telephone dial don't have letters by them?
6. When you walk does your left arm swing with your right or left leg?
7. How many matches are in a standard pack?
8. On the United States flag is the top stripe red or white?
9. Which way does water go down the drain, counter or clockwise?
10. Which way does a "no smoking" sign's slash run?
11. On which side of a women's blouse are the buttons?
12. Which way do fans rotate?
13. What is on the back of a Canadian dime?
14. How many sides does a stop sign have?
15. Do books have even-numbered pages on the right or left side?
16. How many lug nuts are on a standard car wheel?
17. How many sides are there on a standard pencil?
18. How many ho buns are in a standard package?
19. On which side of a Venetian blind is the cord that adjusts the opening between the slats?

20. On the back of a Canadian $1 coin, what is in the center?
21. There are 12 buttons on a touch tone phone. What 2 symbols bear no digits?
22. How many curves are there in the standard paper clip?
23. Does a merry-go-round turn counter or clockwise?

Answers:

1. Bottom
2. 50
3. Right
4. Blue, red, white, yellow, black, & gold
5. 1,0
6. Right
7. 20
8. Red
9. Clockwise (north of the equator)
10. Towards bottom right
11. Left
12. Clockwise as you look at it
13. The Bluenose
14. 8
15. Left
16. 5
17. 6
18. 8
19. Left
20. Loon
21. *, #
22. 3
23. Counter

Short Quiz

The following short quiz consists of four questions and will tell you whether you are qualified to be a professional.

1. How do you put a giraffe into a refrigerator? The correct answer is: Open the refrigerator put in the giraffe and close the door. This question tests whether you tend to do simple things in an overly complicated way.
2. How do you put an elephant into a refrigerator? Open the refrigerator put in the elephant and close the refrigerator. Wrong answer! Correct Answer: Open the refrigerator, take out the giraffe, put in the elephant and close the door. This tests your ability to think through the repercussions of your previous actions.
3. The Lion King is hosting an animal conference. All the animals attend except one. Which animal does not attend? Correct Answer: The Elephant. The elephant is in the refrigerator. This tests your memory. Okay, even if you did not answer the first three questions correctly, you still have one more chance to show your true abilities.
4. There is a river you must cross, but it is inhabited by crocodiles. How do you manage it? Correct Answer: You swim across. All the crocodiles are attending the animal meeting. This tests whether you learn quickly from your mistakes. According to Anderson Consulting Worldwide, around 90% of the professionals they tested got all the questions wrong. But many preschoolers got several correct answers. Anderson Consulting says this conclusively disproves the theory that most professionals have the brains of a four year old.

Unusual Paragraph

How quickly can you find out what is so unusual about this paragraph. It looks so ordinary that you would think that nothing was wrong with it at all and, in fact, nothing is. But it is unusual. Why? If you study it and think about it you may find out, but I am not going to assist you in any way. You must do it without coaching. No doubt, if you work at it for long, it will dawn on you. Who knows? Go to work and try your skill.

Answer: Although the letter "e" is the most used letter in the English language here is a paragraph without a single "e."

Words In Common

Give this plenty of thought, and don't cheat! I am only sending this to my smart friends and relatives. I couldn't figure it out till I saw the answers, so see if you can figure out what these words have in common…??

Are you peeking or have you already given up?

Give it another try…

You'll kick yourself when you discover the answer. Go back and look at them again; think hard.

Ok…Here you go.. Hope you didn't cheat. This is neat!!

- Banana
- Dresser
- Grammar
- Potato
- Revive
- Uneven
- Assess

Answer….

In all of the words listed, if you take the first letter, place it at the end of the word, and then spell the word backwards, it will be the same word!!! Told ya it was neat!

Quotations

A Christian is a living sermon whether or not he preaches a word.

A Christian is a person who makes you think of Jesus.

A Christian is one who does not have to consult his bank balance to see how wealthy he is.

A senior adult was filling in an application to attend a Senior Adult Retreat. When filling out the address, he came to "ZIP"—he filled in, "Not as much as I once had."

A beautiful heart seems to transform the homeliest face.

A best friend is like a four leaf clover, hard to find and lucky to have.

A boy was watching his father, a pastor, write a sermon. "How do you know what to say?" he asked. "Why, God tells me." "Oh, then why do you keep crossing things out?"

A day of worry is more exhausting than a week of work.

Adult: A person who has stopped growing at both ends and is now growing in the middle.

A farmer called his pig "Ball Point." Well, it wasn't its real name, just a pen name.

A father holds his children's hands for awhile, but he holds their hearts forever.

A fine is a tax for doing wrong. A tax is a fine for doing well.

A friend is never known until he is needed.

A happy home is more than a roof over your head—it's a foundation under your feet.

A heart of praise and love shows others just what Jesus can do in the lives of men.

A home is a house with a heart inside.

A humble talent that is used is worth more than one of a genius that is idle.

A husband is someone who takes out the trash and tries to give the impression that he just cleaned the whole house.

A lady got a new cell phone from her husband. The next day she went to ® and her phone rang, so she answered. It was her husband. He said, "How's the new cell phone?" She replied, "Great…but how did you know I was at Walmart®?"

A little girl was diligently pounding away on her father's word processor. She told him she was writing a story. "What's it about?" he asked. "I don't know," she replied. "I can't read."

A livestock truck overturned in my town. A reporter was doing the broadcast and stated, "Two cows, Black and Gus, escaped into the nearby woods." After the commercial break, the reporter corrected himself, "About the overturned truck, make those Black Angus cattle."

A living Christ in a living man is a living sermon.

Alone we can do so little; together we can do so much.

Always remember that you are unique; just like everyone else.

A man may go to heaven without health, without wealth, without fame, without a great name, without learning, without culture, without friends, without ten thousand other things. But he can never go to heaven without Christ.

A man put his fifty cents in a vending machine and watched helplessly while the cup failed to appear and a nozzle sent coffee down the drain while another poured cream after it. "Now that's automation!" he exclaimed. "It even drinks it for you!"

A man's body is so sensitive that when you pat him on the back, his head swells.

America is the only country where it takes more brains to complete the income tax return than it does to make the income.

A mother asked her six-year-old what lovingkindness meant. "Well," he said, "when I ask you for a piece of bread and butter and you give it to me, that' s kindness, but when you put jam on it, that's lovingkindness."

A napkin is for what you got on you that should have gotten in you.

A new Chinese diet—eat all you can with only one chopstick. Try it—you might like it!!!

An important part of praying is a willingness to be a part of the answer.

An intelligence test sometimes shows you how smart you would have been not to have taken it.

Anything that matters more to you than God is an idol.

A person cannot be a peacemaker until first he finds peace for himself.

A person who takes time for prayer will find time for all the other things needing his attention.

A photographer was hired to take pictures at a lawyers' convention. When he lined up his subjects he got them to look their best by shouting, "Okay everyone, say fees!"

A right attitude toward God fosters the right attitudes toward your family and others.

As he saw his father leaving for work one morning, the child posed a question. "Dad," the youngster asked, "can you bring home a rat from the race today?"

A small step of obedience is a giant step to blessing.

A smile is a powerful weapon. You can even break ice with it.

A smile is a very inexpensive way to improve your looks.

A smile is the lighting system of the face and the heating system of the heart.

A spider web strung across a garden path was the inspiration for the suspension bridge.

A supermarket is where you spend a half-hour looking for instant coffee.

As you get old there are three things to remember. Memory, and the other two I can't remember.

A true friend is someone who reaches for your hand and touches your heart.

A visitor from India came to America, and after weeks of travel he was asked to give his number one impression. His reply, "The size of the American garbage cans."

A wife asked her husband for a mink. He said, "You may have a mink if you're willing to clean its cage and feed it every day."

A word of encouragement can mean the difference between giving up or going on.

A young cowboy asked his father, "Do you think I can make a good living riding wild horses in a rodeo?" His dad replied, "You should get a couple of bucks out of it."

Because God never sleeps, we can sleep in peace.

Before God exalts a person, he humbles him.

Before you criticize someone, you should walk a mile in their shoes. That way, when you criticize them, you're a mile away and you have their shoes.

Before you give somebody a piece of your mind, be sure you can get by with what you have left.

Be sure to concentrate on your blessings—not your distresses.

Be the change you want to see in the world.

Bills travel through the mail at twice the speed of checks.

Blessed are they who can laugh at themselves, for they shall never cease to be amused. —***Anonymous***

Christ died to save us—He now lives to keep us.

Christ gave Himself for us that we might give ourselves for others.

Christ has replaced the dark door of death with the shining gate of life.

Christians show what they are by what they do with what they have.

Christ offers a crown only to those who take up His cross.

Christ was born here below that we might be born from above.

Christ's forbearance and long-suffering transformed Peter. It can change us, too.

Christ's friendship prevails when human friendship fails.

Christ's sacrifice was exactly what God desired and we required.

Compassion is the capacity to put love into action.

Counting time is not as important as making time count.

Customer: "Hey, this lumber has holes in it!"
Clerk: "Those are knot holes."
Customer: "Well, if they're not holes, what are they?"

Dad: "What's this low mark on your report card?"
Junior: "Maybe it's the temperature of the schoolroom."

Daylight savings time—why are they saving it and where do they keep it?

Did you know that dolphins are so intelligent that within only a few weeks of captivity, they can train people to stand at the very edge of the pool and throw them fish?

Don't be afraid of opposition—a kite rises best against the wind.

Don't knock the weather. Nine-tenths of the people couldn't start a conversation if it didn't change once in a while. —*Kin Hubbard*

Don't let the best you have ever done, be the standard for the rest of your life.

Don't miss the world around you. Always look at the world as though you just came out of a tunnel.

Don't pray for an easy life; pray to be stronger men.

Don't put a question mark where God put a period.
Don't put people down, unless it is on your prayer list.

Do that good deed now; you never know how soon it will be too late.

Eat a live toad first thing in the morning, and nothing worse can happen to you the rest of the day!

Employment application blanks always ask who is to be notified in case of emergency. I think you should write… A Good Doctor!

Evangelism is the responsibility of every Christian.

Ever notice when you blow in a dog's face he gets mad at you, but when you take him in a car he sticks his head out the window?

Every Christian is a missionary—if only in the supermarket.

Every day is a free gift from God.

Every heart without Christ is a mission field—every heart with Christ is a missionary.

Everyone can afford to give away a smile.

Everyone has a photographic memory. Some just don't have film.

Everyone seems normal until you get to know them.

Everything should be made as simple as possible, but no simpler.

Everywhere is walking distance if you have the time.

Experience is a wonderful thing. It enables you to recognize a mistake when you make it again.

Experience is something you don't get until just after you need it.

Faith honors God—God honors faith!

Faith is more than waiting upon God—it's expecting an answer.

Faith is not believing that He can—it's knowing that He will.

Faith is the simple confidence that God is and that He will do what He has promised.

Faith looks beyond the darkness of earth to the brightness of heaven.

Families are like fudge…mostly sweet with a few nuts.

Flashlight: A case for holding dead batteries.

Folks who think they'd be happy if they lived someplace else probably wouldn't be—but their neighbors might!

For every cloud in life, God gives a rainbow.

Friendship doubles our joy and divides our grief.

Friendship is born at the moment when one person says to another, "What! You too? I thought I was the only one!"

Friendship is the cement that holds the world together.

Frogs have it easy; they can eat whatever bugs them.

Frustration is trying to find your glasses without your glasses.

General Store: "I went to a general store, but they wouldn't let me buy anything specific."

Gentle words fall lightly, but they have great weight.

Give to God what's right—not what's left.

Giving your best today is the best recipe for a better tomorrow.

God can take the place of anything, but nothing can take the place of God.

God does not ask how many talents one has; He asks for faithfulness.

God doesn't call the qualified, He qualifies the called.

God gives His best to those who leave the choice with Him.

God give us faces; we create our own expressions.

God has included you in His plans; have you included Him in your plans?

God judges us, not by what others say, but by what we do.

God may not shield us from all life's storms, but He shelters us in life's storms.

God often uses life's reverses to move us forward.

God often uses our difficulties to help develop our character.

God often uses people to solve problems and make peace.

God promises us daily bread—not flour for a year in advance.

God sends us the storms to prove that He is the only shelter.

God wants us to cast upon Him all that burdens us.

God will accept a broken heart, but He must have all the pieces.

God without man is still God—man without God is nothing!

God's Word tells us of His love; our words show Him of our love.

God's best gifts are not things, but opportunities.

God's promises are always greater than our needs.

God's promises are always greater than our problems.

God's work in us isn't over when we receive Christ—it has just begun.

Good character is like soup—it's homemade.

Good friends are like stars…you don't always see them, but you know they are always there.

Good judgment comes from bad experience, and a lot of that comes from bad judgment.

Go to church to worship, not to whisper—to commune, not to criticize.

Gratitude is the interest we owe God for the life He has given us.

Greatness lies not in trying to be somebody, but in trying to help somebody.

Grocery clerks make you pick paper or plastic because baggers can't be choosers.

Half of Americans live within 50 miles of their birthplace.

Happiness is not having what you want—but wanting what you have.

Happiness multiplies as we divide it with others.

Happy people don't always have the best of everything—they make the best of everything.

Have courage for the great sorrows of life and patience for the small ones; and when you have laboriously accomplished your daily task, go to sleep in peace. God is awake. —*Victor Hugo*

Help others today and God will help you tomorrow.

He pleases God best who trusts Him most.

He who cannot pray when the sun shines will not know how to pray when the clouds come.

He who cares will share.

He who is on the road to heaven will not be content to go there alone.

He who lives like Christ wins men to Christ.

He who waits on the Lord will not be crushed by the weight of adversity.

Hold God's hand; He will do the holding if you do the trusting.

Hospitality: Making your guests feel at home, even if you wish they were.

How can a two pound box of candy make you gain five pounds?

How come wrong numbers are never busy?

How do they get the "Do not walk on the grass" signs way out in the middle of the lawn?

How do those dead bugs get into those closed fixtures?

How do you get off a non-stop flight?

How is it one careless match can start a forest fire, but it takes a whole box to start a campfire?

Husband to wife: "How do you expect me to remember your birthday when you never look any older?"

I am an old man who has had many troubles; most of which never happened. —*From Silas Marner*

I am only one, but still I am one. I cannot do everything, but I can do something and because I cannot do everything, I will not refuse to do the something I can do.
—*Edward Everett Hale*

I cleaned my house yesterday. Sure wish you could have seen it.

If God writes opportunity on one side of the door, he writes responsibility on the other.

If a care is too small to be made into a prayer, it is too small to be made into a burden.

If cats and dogs didn't have fur would we still pet them?

If it doesn't affect your hands, feet, and thinking, it isn't Christianity.

If it were not for the hot water, the teakettle would not sing.

If money doesn't grow on trees, then why do banks have branches?

If someone didn't win you to Christ, where would you be today?

If the grass is greener on the other side of the fence, you can bet the water bill is higher.

If there is smiling in your heart, your face will show it.

If we pause to think, we'll have cause to thank.

If we pray in times of victory, we will not need to plead in times of defeat.

If we trust, we don't worry—if we worry, we don't trust.

If you adore Christ as your Saviour, you won't ignore Him as your Lord.

If you cannot think of any nice things to say about your friends, then you have the wrong friends.

If you fear someone will find out, don't do it.

If you have a bunch of odds and ends and get rid of all but one of them, what do you call it?

If you have the faith—God has the power.

If you look like your passport picture, you probably need the trip.

If you never undertake more than you can possibly do, you will never do more than you can possibly do.

If you share another's burden, both of you will walk straighter.

If you want to be happy for a day, go fishing.
If you want to be happy for a lifetime, serve others.
If you want to be happy for a month, get married.
If you want to be happy for an hour, take a nap.
If you want to be happy for a year, inherit money.
If you want to know how rich you are, find out what would be left of you tomorrow if you should lose every dollar tonight. —***Beak & Quill***

If you're too open minded, your brains will fall out.

I got a package envelope in the mail the other day that had written on the front, "Photographs: Do Not Bend." Underneath the mailman wrote, "Oh, yes they do."

I have held many things in my hands and I have lost them all; but whatever I have placed in God's hands, that I still possess. —***Martin Luther***

I just let my mind wander, and it didn't come back.

In Shakespeare's time, mattresses were secured on bed frames by ropes. When you pulled on the ropes the mattress tightened, making the bed firmer to sleep on. Hence the phrase "Goodnight, sleep tight."

In five minutes a woman will clean up a man's room in such a way that it will take him five minutes to find out where she put things.

In prayer it is more essential to have a heart without words than words without heart.

Instead of giving people a piece of your mind, give them a piece of your heart.

In the straight and narrow way the traffic is always one way.

I signed up for an exercise class and was told to wear loose fitting clothing. If I had any loose fitting clothing I wouldn't have signed up in the first place!

Is what you are living for worth dying for?

It is Christmas in the heart that puts Christmas in the air.

It is a great responsibility to own a Bible.

It is easy to sing when we walk with the King.

It is good to mark your Bible, but it is better to let your Bible mark you.

It is impossible to travel in the wrong direction and reach the right destination.

It is not the hours you put in, but what you put in the hours.

It takes more time to hide's one's talent than it does to use it for God.

It's easier to have patience with others when we remember God's patience toward us.

It's nice to be important—but it's more important to be nice.

It's not what you gain but what you give, that measures the worth of the life you live.

It's so simple to be wise. Just think of something stupid to say and then don't say it.

I went out to buy some goose feather pillows, but I found they were so expensive I couldn't even afford the down payment.

I'm very pleased with each advancing year. It stems back to when I was 40. I was a bit upset about reaching that milestone, but an older friend consoled me. "Don't complain about growing old—many people do not have that privilege." —*Chief Justice Earl Warren*

Jesus Christ is the light that knows no power failure.

Jim was asked by the school teacher, "Give me Lincoln's Gettysburg Address." Jim scratched his head and responded, "I didn't know he lived in Gettysburg."

John: "What did the judge say when a skunk wandered into the courtroom?"
Larry: "I give up, what?"
John: "He banged his gavel and said, 'Odor in the courtroom!'"

Junk is something you've kept for years and throw away three weeks before you need it.

Keep your light shining—God will place it where it will do the most good.

Kindness is the oil that takes the friction out of life.

Kind words are short to speak, but their echoes are endless.

Know how to prevent sagging? Just eat till the wrinkles fill out!

Last summer we had a family reunion. Who do you think showed up? Five cousins, four grandparents, six uncles, and about two thousand ants.

Let us remember that the Christmas heart is a giving heart, a wide open heart that thinks of others first.
—*George Matthew Adams*

Life is like a mirror—we get the best results when we smile at it.

Life is like a well—the deeper you go in God, the more living you will find.

Life is only boring when it has no purposes or goals.

Lighthouses don't make noise—they just shine.

Little Johnny asked his grandma how old she was. Grandma answered, "39 and holding." Johnny thought for a moment, and then said, "And how old would you be if you let go?"

Live as if Christ died yesterday, arose today, and is coming tomorow.

Live so that if people get to know you, they will get to know Christ better.

Live today as you will wish you had lived when you stand before God.

Living on earth is expensive, but it does include a free trip around the sun every year.

Long before man discovered the power in the atom, God put it there.

Lord, do in me what You need to do, so You can do through me, what You have to do.

Love cannot be forced, it must be spontaneous. It cannot be faked, it must be demonstrated. It cannot be proffered, it must be possessive.

Love increases as we give it away.

Love is giving someone your undivided attention.

Love is made visible by work.

Love isn't like a resevoir. You'll never drain it dry. It's much like a natural spring. The longer and farther it flows, the stronger, deeper, and cleaner it becomes. *—Cantor*

Love is patient, love is kind. It does not envy, it does not boast, it is not proud. It is not rude, it is not self-seeking, it is not easily angered, it keeps no record of wrongs. Love does not delight in evil but rejoices with the truth. It always protects, always trusts, always hopes, always perseveres (1 Corinthians 13).

Love is the fountain from which all goodness flows.

Love is the thing that enables a woman to sing while she mops up the floor after her husband has walked across it in his barn boots. *—Hoosier Farmer*

Love is what makes two people sit in the middle of the bench when there is plenty of room at both ends.

Make friendship a habit and you will always have friends.

Make the least of the worst and the most of the best.

Man weighs the deeds, but God weighs the intentions.

Many people will walk in and out of your life. But only true friends will leave footprints in your heart.

Man's way leads to a hopeless end; God's way leads to an endless hope.

May peace be your gift at Christmas and your blessing all year through!

Money: A lot of money is tainted—'Taint yours and it 'taint mine.

Money can't buy happiness—unless you spend it on somebody else.

More important than the length of life is how we spend each day.

My grandson was visiting one day when he asked, "Grandpa, do you know how you and God are alike?" I mentally polished my halo while I asked, "No, how are we alike?" "You're both old," he replied.

My neighbor's driving is amazing. No matter what happens he is always innocent. Like last week, a building backed into him.

My wife has a way of saving money—she uses mine.

My wife recently came home from shopping with an escalator. She'll buy anything marked down!

My wife says I never listen to her. At least I think that's what she said.

Never wrestle with a pig; the pig enjoys it and all you do is get dirty.

No God, No Peace; Know God, Know Peace.

No man ever injured his eyesight by looking on the bright side of things.

Nothing lies outside the reach of prayer except that which is outside of the will of God.

No weakness is beyond God's strength, no sorrow is beyond God's comfort, no worry is beyond God's assurance, and no question is beyond God's answer. No problem is beyond God's solution, no sin is beyond God's forgiveness, no anxiety is beyond God's peace, no sickness is beyond God's healing even in death and then it's eternal. No need is beyond God's grace. Settle it therefore in your heart.

No wonder people talk to their animals and plants—they listen.

Obeying God is the best prescription for spiritual health.

Old telephone books make ideal personal address books. Simply cross out the names and addresses of people you don't know.

One hundred years from now it will not matter what kind of house we live in, how much money we had, nor what our clothes were like. But the world will be a little better, because I was important in a child's life.

One plus God is a majority.

One thing you cannot recycle is wasted time!

One way to pay less tax—earn less.

Only as we go God's way can we know God's will.

On the first day of school, a first grader handed his teacher a note from his mother. The note read, "The opinions expressed by this child are not necessarily those of his parents."

Open minded or empty-headed…it depends on whether you're defining yourself or someone else.

Our language is funny—a fat chance and a slim chance mean the same thing.

Our love for Christ is only as real as our love for our neighbor.

Our present choices determine our future rewards.

Power of cooperation: one snowflake may seem harmless, but when millions cooperate, it can mean a snowstorm. This applies to one drop of water, too. When millions cooperate, it can mean a river, or an ocean!

People usually describe their circumstances in two ways. "I'm high as a kite," or "I'm down in the dumps." Too many, including Christians, live upon feelings alone. Christians cannot always live on the mountain. Time must be spent in the valley. There must be a proper balance. As a bird needing both wings to fly, so we need both, the mountain and the valley.

Physiology: The study of carbonated drinks.

Positive thinking is the only way to produce positive results.

Praise, like sunlight, helps all things grow.

Prayer is a time of exposure of the soul to God.

Prayer is measured by its depth, not its length.

Prayer is not a way of getting what we want, but the way to become what God wants us to be.

Prayer must mean something to us if it is to mean anything to God.

Prayer need not be long when faith is strong.

Pride is a funny thing—it makes fools out of some people, but prevents others from making fools of themselves.

Retirement—It is time to retire when your "get up and go" has gone and went.

Real love is helping someone for Jesus' sake who can never return the favor.

Salvation is not something we achieve but something we receive.

Share your joy—it takes two to be glad.

Small deeds done are better than great deeds planned.

Smile a while and give your frown a rest.

Smiles never go up in price nor down in value.

Some don't know what happiness is until it's gone.

Some of my best words are those I never spoke.

Some people want to check government spending and others want to spend government checks.

Sometimes storms of life come to teach us that God is in control—that we must lean on Him and learn to be thankful for the riches of His blessings to us.

Student to teacher: "I can't get that report card back for you—you gave me an 'A' in something and they're still mailing it to relatives."

Take a lesson from the clock. It passes the time by keeping its hands busy.

Take time to laugh—it is the music of the soul.

Temper often causes a man to speak his mind when he ought to be minding his speech.

Thankfulness is the soil in which joy thrives.

The Bible is most helpful when open.

The Christian's heart is Christ's home.

The Lord wants our precious time—not our spare time.

The Son of God became the Son of Man, that He might change the sons of men into sons of God.

The average American is a guy who was born in the country, worked hard so he could live in the city, then worked even harder to get back to the country.

The bathtub was invented in 1850 and the telephone in 1875. Stop and think for a moment…people could take a bath for 25 years without hearing the phone ring.

The best way to double your money is fold it in half and stick it in your pocket!

The best way to forget your own problems is to help someone else solve his.

The birth of Christ brought God to man, but it took the cross of Christ to bring man to God.

The boy in the Bible, who gave up his loaves and fishes, didn't have to go hungry.

The branches that bear the most fruit hang the lowest.

The bumper sticker said, "Humpty Dumpty didn't fall—he was pushed." It's so easy to blame our faults and failures on others, yet we don't credit our success to others helping us.

The church can preach, the school can teach, but the home must convert sermons and lessons into the way of life.

The door of heaven is open to everyone whose heart is open to God.

The easiest way to find something lost around the house is to buy a replacement.

The family that prays together, stays together.

The first step to wisdom is silence—the second is listening.

The good we do today becomes the happiness of tomorrow.

The gospel breaks hard hearts and heals broken hearts.

The ground at the foot of the cross is level—all may come.

The happiest marriages are those in which both partners think they got the best of the deal.

The hardness of butter is directly proportional to the softness of the bread.

The heart is like a treasure chest that's filled with souvenirs. It's there we keep the memories we gather through the years.

The light of God's Son in your heart will put His sunshine on your face.

The man was asked how it felt being 102 years old. His response, "I have no peer pressure."

The man who worked in the gum factory fell in a vat of bubblegum! His boss had to chew him out.

The more closely we live to God, the more sensitive we will be to His voice.

The most powerful position is on your knees.

The most valuable gift you can give others is example.

The mystery of love is that the more you give, the more remains in your heart.

The nice thing about a gift of money for Christmas is that it's so easy to exchange.

The one good thing about the gas prices is, it doesn't take me nearly as long to put in my $10 worth.

The only limits to God's grace are the limits we put on it.

The only place success comes before sweat is in the dictionary.

The other day, I was standing in the park wondering why Frisbees get bigger and bigger the closer they get. Then it hit me!

The pessimist says, "It can't be done." The optimist says, "I just did it."

There are more stars in the universe than grains of sand on all the beaches in the world.

There are three kinds of people: Those who can count and those who can't.

There are three kinds of people—those that make things happen, those that watch things happen, and those who have no idea what happened.

There are three types of memory—good, bad, convenient.

There will be no peace as long as God remains unseated at the conference table. ***—Unknown***

There's a new Pasta diet—Just walk pasta bakery without stopping, walk pasta candy store without stopping, walk pasta ice cream store without stopping.

There's a sign above the scale in my doctor's office that says, "Pretend it's your IQ."

There's no limit to what God can do, if He can find the right person to work through.

The right road may be rough and steep, but the vision from the summit is well worth all the effort.

The shin bone is a device for finding furniture in the dark.

The task ahead of us is never as great as the power behind us.

The trials on earth are nothing compared to the triumphs of heaven.

The ultimate measure of a man is not where he stands in moments of comfort and convenience, but where he stands in moments of challenge and controversy.
—Martin Luther King, Jr.

The ultimate miracle of love is this—that love is given to us to give to one another.

The way to heaven is too straight for the man who wants to walk crooked.

The way we treat our neighbor is the way we treat God.

The wonderful thing about patience is that it goes a long way, and yet the more you use it, the more you have.

The words we speak, the songs we sing, the doctrines that we teach…will have their greatest meaning when we practice what we preach.

The word "aerobics" came about when the gym instructors got together and said: "If we're going to charge $10 an hour, we can't call it 'jumping up and down.'"

Those who see God's hand in everything, can best leave everything in God's hand.

Those who think lightly of sin, think lightly of God.

Time is a little chunk of eternity that God has given us.

Time spent with children is never wasted.

To show others what Christ will do for them, show them what Christ has done for you.

To show your love for God, live for God.

To the world you may be one person, but to one person you may be the world.

To touch the heart of another, use your heart.

To walk with God, we must make it a practice to talk with God.

To win the respect of intelligent people and the affection of children, to earn the appreciation of honest critics and endure the betrayal of false friends, to appreciate beauty, to find the best in others, and to know even one life has breathed easier because you lived.
This is to have succeeded.

Treat your friends as you do your pictures—always show them in their best light.

True charity, is the desire to be useful to others without the thought of recompense.

True happiness lives in satisfaction.

True love is willing to help people even if it hurts them.

Trusting God's promises doesn't demand explanations.

Ulcers are not caused by what you eat, rather by "what's eating you."

We all get heavier as we get older because there is a lot more information in our heads.

We cannot change the direction of the wind…but we can adjust our sails.

We could learn a lot from crayons: some are sharp, some are pretty, some are dull, some have weird names, and all are different colors…but they all have to learn to live in the same box.

We do not really pray to God until we are absolutely honest with God.

We flatter those we scarcely know, we please the fleeting guest, and deal full many a thoughtless blow to those we love the best!

We have freedom of choice—not freedom from the consequences of our choice.

We may give without loving, but we can't love without giving.

We must be in tune with Christ to be in harmony with one another.

We serve a God who is greater than any problems, and bigger than any of our needs.

We're in a fast-moving, fast-paced society. We need to build bridges between our hearts and those people we see who need a friend, and allow Jesus to cross that bridge of friendship and walk into their hearts.

"Was Grandpa mad when they went through his luggage at the airport?" "Not in the least," said Grandma. "They found his glasses that he'd lost two weeks earlier."

What God gives by promise we must accept by faith.

What would a chair look like if your knees bent the other way?

What would some people talk about if they didn't have troubles?

What you are is always more important than what you do!

What you think of God determines what you think of others.

What you will be tomorrow, you are becoming today.

When God allows extraordinary trials, he gives extraordinary comfort.

When I got home last night, my wife demanded that I take her out to someplace expensive…So I took her to a gas station!

When dog food is "new and improved tasting", who tests it?

Whenever someone gets something without earning it, another person has to earn something without getting it.

When in doubt, tell the truth.

When it hurts to look back, and you're scared to look ahead, you can look beside you and your best friend will be there.

When one door of happiness closes, another opens; but often we look so long at the closed door that we don't see the one which has opened for us.

When someone asks you, "A penny for your thoughts" and you put your two cents in…what happens to the other penny? —***Helen Keller***

When troubles call on you, call God.

When we know that God is for us, it doesn't really matter who is against us!

When we put our cares in God's hands, he puts his peace in our hearts.

When you come to the end of your rope, tie a prayer-knot and hang on.

When you pray for God's will and guidance, don't complain if His will is different than what our plans or desires are.

When your wife says, "What do you think?" she is not asking for your opinion. She is asking for her opinion, from your mouth.

When you see a dirty face in the mirror, wash the face, not the mirror.

When you turn your back on God, you can't see His face, nor His hand directing you in the way He would have you go.

While I was getting my hair cut at a neighborhood shop, I asked the barber when would be the best time to bring in my two-year-old son? Without hesitation, the barber answered, "When he's four."

Why Grouchy People are Always Tired. It takes 43 face muscles to frown and only 15 to smile. Give your face a rest and smile!

Why are there three interstate highways in Hawaii?

Why do croutons come in airtight packages? Aren't they just stale bread?

Why does Christmas always come just when the stores are so crowded?

Why does a slight tax increase cost two hundred dollars and a substantial tax cut save you thirty cents?

Why isn't the number 11 pronounced "onety one"?

Why is "abbreviations" such a long word?

Why worry when you can pray?

Women work all the time. When men work, they put up a sign, "Men Working."

Work isn't work if you enjoy it.

Worry gives small things big shadows.

Worry is as useless as saving sawdust.

Worry is like a rocking chair: It gives you something to do, but doesn't get you anywhere.

You may be a genius: A teakettle singing on the stove suggested the building of the steam engine.

Yesterday is a canceled check. Tomorrow is a promissory note. Today is ready cash. Use it!

Yesterday is gone, tomorrow isn't here yet, so all that is available is today.

You are a senior citizen when your actions squeak louder than your words.

You are only poor when you want more than you have.

You can lose weight by giving up three things—your fork, knife, and spoon.

You cannot do a kindness too soon because you never know how soon it will be too late.

You cannot have the peace of God until you know the God of peace.

You cannot kindle a fire in another's heart until it is burning in your own.

You can often tell a wise man by the things he does not say.

You can't change the past, but you can ruin the present by worrying about the future.

You can't have a good day with a bad attitude and you can't have a bad day with a good attitude.

You can't have everything. Where would you put it?

You can't make someone love you. All you can do is be someone who can be loved. The rest is up to the person to realize your worth.

You can't really give away kindness, because it always has a way of returning.

You get the most out of your life when you give your life to Christ.

You have given no gift to God if you have not given yourself.

You have the rest of your life to be miserable, so enjoy today.

You must be willing to follow if you expect God to lead.

Your life is God's gift to you; what you do with it is your gift to God.

Your promises to God should be as binding as your signature on the mortgage.

You will be happier if you try to give people a bit of your heart, rather than a piece of your mind.

You will never find time for anything—you must take time.

You will never stub your toe standing still. The faster you go, the more chance of stubbing your toe, and the more chance of getting somewhere. —***Charles F. Kettering***

Time

A.A.A.D.D.

Age Activated Attention Deficit Disorder

This is how it manifests: I decide to water my lawn.

As I turn on the hose in the driveway, I look over at my car and decide my car needs washing.

As I start toward the garage, I notice that there is mail on the porch that I brought from the mail box earlier.

I decide to go through the mail before I wash the car.

I lay my car keys on the table, put the junk mail in the garbage can under the table, and notice that the can is full.

So, I decide to put the bills back on the table and take out the garbage first.

But then I think, since I'm going to be near the mailbox when I take out the garbage anyway, I may as well pay the bills first.

I take my checkbook off the table, and see that there is only one check left.

My extra checks are in my desk in the study, so I go to my desk where I find the can of Coke that I had been drinking.

I'm going to look for my checks, but first I need to push the Coke aside so that I don't accidentally knock it over.

I see that the Coke is getting warm, and I decide I should put it in the refrigerator to keep it cold.

As I head toward the kitchen with the Coke, a vase of flowers catches my eye—they need to be watered.

I set the Coke down on the counter, and I discover my reading glasses that I've been searching for all morning.

I decide I better put them back on my desk, but first I'm going to water the flowers.

I set the glasses back down on the counter, fill a container with water and suddenly I spot the stereo remote. Someone left it on the kitchen table. I realize that the next time I want to listen to something, I will be looking for the remote, but I won't remember that it's on the kitchen table, so I decide to put it back in the living room where it belongs, but first I'll water the flowers.

I pour some water in the flowers, but quite a bit of it spills on the floor. So, I set the remote back down on the table, get some towels and wipe up the spill.

Then I head down the hall trying to remember what I was planning to do.

At the end of the day: the lawn isn't watered, the car isn't washed, the bills aren't paid, there is a warm can of Coke sitting on the counter, the flowers don't have enough water, there is still only one check in my checkbook, I can't find the remote, I can't find my glasses, I don't remember what I did with the car keys, and my neighbor called to tell me he turned off the hose that was flooding the driveway.

Then when I try to figure out why nothing got done today, I'm really baffled for I know I was busy all day long, and I'm really tired. I realize this is a serious problem, and I'll try to get some help for it, but first I'll check my e-mail.

A Little Mixed Up

Just a line to say I'm living,
That I'm not among the dead;
Though I'm getting more forgetful
And more mixed-up in the head.

For, sometimes, I can't remember
Standing at the bottom of the stair,
If I must go up for something,
Or if I've just come down from there.

And before the fridge, so often
My poor mind is filled with doubt,
Have I just put food away or
Have I come to take some out?

And there's times when it is dark out,
With my nightcap on my head,
I don't know if I'm retiring
Or just getting out of bed.

So if it's my turn to write you,
There's no need in getting sore,
I may think that I have written
And don't want to be a bore.

So remember—I do love you
And I wish that you were here,
But now it's nearly mail time,
So I must say, "Good-bye, dear."

There I stood beside the mailbox
With a face so very red—
Instead of mailing you my letter,
I opened it instead.

A Speed Driven Society

We live in a society that is speed driven. How quickly can you get it done? What is the quickest way to get there? Overnight delivery! Airborne Express! Express Lane checkouts! Online banking! Faster computers! Megabytes to Gigabytes! Fast Food drive-ups! Etc., Etc.

Drive down the interstate where the posted speed limit is 65 mph and watch people pass you doing 75 mph and 85 mph. Will fast ever be fast enough? Probably not. If we step back in time to the early part of the 19th century, speed was little more than the pace of a man. In fact, as late as 1896, England had a law prohibiting any power driven vehicle from traveling over 4 miles per hour on the public highways. I doubt that we would be content for very long at those speeds.

Companies are continually trying to do the same amount of work in less time to stay ahead of the competition. They invest in more modern and faster machinery. The more work they can turn out in less time, the better their production rate, and the lower the price for the consumer. Obviously, the company that can produce more work with less man power, is going to have a competitive edge.

Is speed always the answer? Did the pace in 1896 allow more time to smell the flowers and to observe the beauty of the earth? Was there a bit more time to enjoy a good laugh over a cup of coffee or to wave while passing on the street? It appears, that in our quest for speed, we may have left behind some intangible values. How do you put a price tag on friendships or acquaintances? Relationships aren't built on speed, they are built on togetherness. Perhaps, just perhaps that is part of the reason so many relationships are falling apart. Our quest for speed has allowed important associations to be strewn by the wayside. We don't have time to stop. We'll be late. We have so much to do and too little time to do it. Let us not forget that an opportunity missed is an opportunity lost. If we go too fast we may miss those opportunities.

—M. Gingrich

Clotheslines

A clothesline was a news forecast,
To neighbors passing by.
There were no secrets you could keep,
When clothes were hung to dry.

It also was a friendly link,
For neighbors always knew,
If company had stopped on by
To spend a night or two,

For then you'd see the fancy sheets,
And towels upon the line;
You'd see the company tablecloths
With intricate design,

The line announced a baby's birth,
To folks who lived inside,
As brand new infant clothes were hung
So carefully with pride,

The ages of the children could
So readily be known.
By watching how the sizes changed,
You'd know how much they'd grown.

It also told when illness struck,
As extra sheets were hung;
Then nightclothes, and a bathrobe, too,
Haphazardly, were strung.

It said, "Gone on vacation now,"
When lines hung limp and bare.
It told, "We're back!" when full lines sagged,
With not an inch to spare.

New folks in town were scorned upon,
If wash was dingy gray,
As neighbors raised their brows,
And looked disgustedly away.

But clotheslines now are of the past,
For dryers make work less.
Now what goes on inside a home,
Is anybody's guess.

I really miss that way of life,
It was a friendly sign,
When neighbors knew each other best,
By what hung on the line!

Comments In 1957

The following were some comments made in the year 1957:

- "I'll tell you one thing, if things keep going the way they are, its going to be impossible to buy a weeks groceries for $20.00."
- "Have you seen the new cars coming out next year? It won't be long when $5,000 will only buy a used one."
- "Did you hear the post office is thinking about charging a dime just to mail a letter?"
- "If they raise the minimum wage to $1.00, nobody will be able to hire outside help at the store."
- "When I first started driving, who would have thought gas would someday cost 29 cents a gallon. Guess we'd be better off leaving the car in the garage."
- "I read the other day where some scientist thinks it's possible to put a man on the moon by the end of the century. They even have some fellows they call astronauts preparing for it down in Texas."
- "Did you see where some baseball player just signed a contract for $75,000 a year just to play ball? It wouldn't surprise me if someday they will be making more than the President."
- "I never thought I'd see the day all our kitchen appliances would be electric. They are even making electric typewriters now."
- "I'm just afraid the Volkswagen car is going to open the door to a whole lot of foreign business."
- "Fortunately, I won't live to see the day when the government takes half our income in taxes. I sometimes wonder if we are electing the best people to Congress."
- "The drive-in restaurant is convenient in nice weather, but I seriously doubt they will ever catch on."
- "I guess taking a vacation is out of the question these days. It costs nearly $15.00 a night to stay in a hotel."
- "No one can afford to be sick any more; $35.00 a day in the hospital is too rich for my blood."
- "35 cents for a haircut? Cut it all off!"

Do You Remember These Days?

"Hey Dad," one of my children asked the other day, "what was your favorite fast food when you were growing up?"

"We didn't have fast food when I was growing up," I informed him. "All the food was slow."

"C'mon, seriously. Where did you eat?"

"It was a place called 'at home'," I explained. "Grandma cooked every day and when Grandpa got home from work, we sat down together at the dining room table, and if I didn't like what she put on my plate I was allowed to sit there until I did like it."

By this time, my son was laughing so hard I was afraid he was going to suffer serious internal damage, so I didn't tell him the part about how I had to have permission to leave the table. But, here are some other things I would have told him about my childhood, if I figured his system could have handled it. Many folks never owned a car. They didn't wear Levi's. They never traveled out of the country. A credit card didn't even exist. In their later years some had something called a revolving charge card. The card was good only at Sears Roebuck.

My parents never drove me to soccer practice. This was mostly because we had never heard of soccer. I had a bicycle that weighed probably fifty pounds, and only had one speed (slow).

I was thirteen before I tasted my first pizza; it was called "pizza pie". When I bit into it, it burned the roof of my mouth and the cheese slid off, swung down, plastered itself against my chin and burned that, too. It's still the best pizza I ever had.

We didn't have a car until I was fifteen. Before that, the only car in our family was my grandfather's Ford. He called it a "machine".

I never had a telephone in my room. The only phone in the house was in the living room and it was on a party line. Before you could dial, you had to listen and make sure some people you didn't know weren't already using the line.

Pizzas were not delivered to our home, but milk and bread were.

All newspapers were delivered by boys and all boys delivered newspapers. I delivered a newspaper, six days a week. It cost seven cents a paper, of which I got to keep two cents. I had to get up at 4 A.M. every morning. On Saturday, I had to collect the forty-two cents from my customers. My favorite customers were the ones who gave me fifty cents and told me to keep the change. My least favorite customers were the ones who seemed to never be home on collection day.

I grew up in a generation before there was fast food. I wouldn't trade it. Growing up just isn't what is used to be.

Do You Remember When?

If you are old enough...take a stroll with me...close your eyes...and go back...way back!

I'm talkin' bout "Hide-and-go-seek" at dusk, Sittin' on the porch, "Simon Says", "Kick the Tin Can", "Red Light—Green Light". Lunch boxes with a thermos, chocolate milk, going home for lunch, penny candy from the store, hopscotch, butterscotch, skates with keys, jacks, and "Mother May I?" Hula hoops and sunflower seeds, "Whist" and "Old Maid" and "Crazy Eights", Mary Janes, saddle shoes, and Coke bottles with the names of cities on the bottom.

When around the corner seemed far away, and going downtown seemed like going somewhere. Bedtime, climbing trees, making forts...backyard shows, lemonade stands, Cops and Robbers, Cowboys and Indians, sittin' on the curb, staring at clouds, jumping down the steps, jumping on the bed, pillow fights, "getting company", walking to church, being tickled to death, running till you were out of breath, laughing so hard that your stomach hurt, being tired from playin'...Remember that?

Not steppin' on a crack or you'll "break your mother's back"...paper chains at Christmas, silhouettes of Lincoln and Washington. Remember when there were two types of sneakers for girls and boys (Keds & PF Flyer) and the only time you wore them at school was for gym class. When nearly everyone's mom was at home when the children got home from school. When a quarter was a decent allowance, and another quarter, a huge bonus. When you'd reach into a muddy gutter for a penny.

When you got your windshield cleaned, oil checked, and gas pumped, without asking—all for free, every time. And, you didn't pay for air. And, you got trading stamps to boot! When laundry detergent had free glasses, dishes, or towels hidden inside the box. When any parent could discipline somebody else's child or feed him or use him to carry groceries, and nobody, not even the child, thought a thing of it. When it was considered a great privilege to be taken out to dinner at a real restaurant with your parents. When they threatened to keep children back a grade if they failed.

No one ever asked where the car keys were because they were always in the car, in the ignition, and the doors were never locked. And you got in big trouble if you accidentally locked the doors at home, since no one ever had a key. Remember lying on your back in the grass with your friends and saying things like, "That cloud looks like a...?" And playing baseball with no adults to help children with the rules of the game. Back then, baseball was not a psychological group learning experience—it was a game. Remember when stuff from the store came without safety caps and hermetic seals because no one had yet tried to poison a perfect stranger.

And, with all our progress don't you just wish, just once, that you could slip back in time and savor the slower pace...and share it with the children of today?

Remember the sound of a hand-pushed, reel mower on a Saturday morning, and summers filled with bike rides, playing in cowboy land, baseball games, and swimming and eating Kool-Aid® powder with sugar. When being sent to the principal's office was nothing compared to the fate that awaited a misbehaving student at home.

We were in fear for our lives, because of our parents and grandparents discipline. But we all survived because their love was greater than any punishment they gave and life was enjoyable because we knew if we obeyed there was nothing to fear.

Fender Skirts

What a great blast from the past! I haven't thought about "fender skirts" in years. When I was a child, I considered it such a funny term—made me think of a car in a dress.

Thinking about "fender skirts" started me thinking about other words that quietly disappear from our language with hardly a notice. Like "curb feelers" and "steering knobs". Since I'd been thinking of cars, my mind naturally went that direction first. You will probably have to find some elderly person over fifty to explain one of these terms.

Remember "Continental kits"? They were rear bumper extenders and spare tire covers that were supposed to make any car as cool as a Lincoln Continental. When did we quit calling them "emergency brakes"? At some point "parking brake" became the proper term, but I miss the hint of drama that went with "emergency brake".

I'm sad, too, that almost all the old folks are gone who would call the accelerator the "foot feed". Didn't you ever wait at the street for your daddy to come home, so you could ride the "running board" up to the house?

Here's a phrase I heard all the time in my youth but never anymore—"store-bought". Of course, just about everything is store bought these days, but once it was bragging material to have a store bought dress or a store-bought bag of candy.

"Coast to coast" is a phrase that once held all sorts of excitement and now means almost nothing. Now, we take the term "worldwide" for granted.

On a smaller scale, "wall-to-wall" was once a magical term in our homes. In the '50s everyone covered his or her hardwood floors with, wow, wall-to-wall carpeting! Today, everyone replaces their wall-to-wall carpeting with hardwood floors. Go figure.

Here's a word I miss—"percolator". That was just a fun word to say. And what was it replaced with? "Coffeemaker." How dull! Mr. Coffee, I blame you for this. I miss those made-up marketing words that were meant to sound so modern but now sound so retro. Words like "DynaFlow" and "ElectraLuxe".

Food for thought—Was there a telethon that wiped out lumbago? Nobody complains of that anymore. Maybe that's what castor oil cured, because I never hear mothers threatening their children with castor oil anymore.

Some words aren't gone, but are definitely on the endangered list. The one that grieves me most, "supper." Now everybody says "dinner". Save a great word—invite someone to supper. Discuss fender skirts.

Going For A Drive!

A drive through the country is a favorite pastime for folks of all ages whether it's just the two of you or the whole family. No need to hurry, no agenda, no need for special gear or skills, and everyone participates. All you need is a set of wheels including the steering wheel, of course, a tank full of gas, roll down windows, and a bit of time on your hands and you're all set. So where do we go?

Shall we try a right, left, right, left, right, left deal and see where we end up or is that too much planning? This is supposed to be relaxing, you know. Well off we go with the windows open and our hair blowing in the breeze, to check out the progress in that new development or drive by the old home place and see how it has fared. The development has a lot more houses than when we were here last time. It is filling up fast. The old homestead, now, that stirs up some memories to be sure and the stories begin—when I was a little boy or girl—and you know the rest of the story. The old barn is showing its age but it sure holds a lot of memories of neighbor children playing together in its mammoth enclosure. What fun it was to jump and play in the hay and straw. Hide and seek took on new meaning with all the nooks and crannies. And one can't forget the smell of fresh hay in the mow and the cattle down below contentedly chewing their cud. Sorry, we got off the road!

We mosey on down the back road stopping briefly on the bridge by the old swimming hole. Again, it's story time. Jumping off the bridge, daring each other, the tree swing, and just having the time of our lives. We drive on through the old neighborhood and wonder how Fred and Kathy and George and Mildred are doing, and speculate on where they are and how they may look by now, etc.

Turning back onto the four lane highway we are quickly reminded that these drivers aren't in tourism or reminiscent mode. Why, years ago this was just a two lane highway and these hills posed quite a challenge for the old Ford. Going so slow, we could really enjoy the scenery. Pulling into the driveway back home everyone jumps out tired and ready to stretch their legs! So was the drive worth it? Did the scenery and the memories of bygone years and the wind in your face have a rejuvenating effect? I have confidence it did and I hope you enjoyed the drive!

—M. Gingrich

Grandmother's Receet

Years ago when my mother was a bride, my Kentucky grandmother gave her a "receet for washing clothes". This treasured bit of writing now hangs above my gleaming automatic washer.

1. Build fire in backyard to heat kettle of rain water.
2. Set tubs so smoke won't blow in eyes if wind is peart.
3. Shave one whole cake lye soap in boiling water.
4. Sort things: make three piles—one pile white, one pile colored, one pile work briches and rags.
5. Stir flour in cold water to smooth, then thin down with boiling water.
6. Rub dirty spots on board, scrub hard, and then bile. Rub color but don't bile—just rench and starch.
7. Shake white things out of kettle with broomstick handle, then rench, blow, and starch.
8. Spread tee towels on grass.

9. Hang old rags on fence.
10. Pour rench water in flower bed.
11. Scrub porch with hot soapy water.
12. Turn tubs upside down.
13. Go put on cleen dress—smooth hair with side combs.
14. Brew cup of tee.
15. Set and rest and rock a spell.
16. Count blessings.

How Did We Survive?

Looking back, it's hard to believe that we have lived as long as we have. As children, we would ride in cars with no seat belts or air bags. Riding in the back of a pickup truck on a warm day was always a special treat.

Our baby cribs were painted with bright colored lead based paint. We often chewed on the crib, ingesting the paint. We had no childproof lids on medicine bottles, doors, or cabinets, and when we rode our bikes we had no helmets.

We drank water from the garden hose and not from a bottle.

We would spend hours building our go-carts out of scraps and then ride down the hill, only to find out we forgot the brakes. After running into the bushes a few times we learned how to solve the problem. We would leave home in the morning and play all day, as long as we were back when the streetlights came on. No one was able to reach us all day.

We played dodgeball and sometimes the ball would really hurt. We ate cupcakes, bread and butter, and drank sugar soda, but we were never overweight; we were always outside playing.

Little League had tryouts and not everyone made the team. Those who didn't had to learn to deal with disappointment. Some students weren't as smart as others so they failed a grade and were held back to repeat the same grade.

That generation produced some of the greatest risk-takers and problem solvers. We had the freedom, failure, success, and responsibility, and we learned how to deal with it all.

If Noah Built The Ark Today

Suppose it is the 21st century and Noah lived in the United States. Would he need to get a permit for construction and comply with the codes?

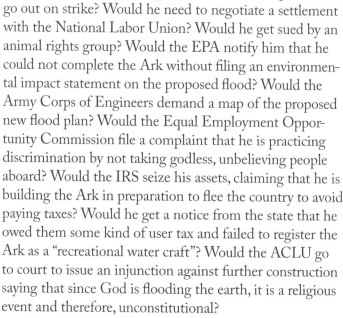

Would he need an engineering firm to redraw the plans? Would he get into a fight with OSHA over whether or not the Ark needed a fire sprinkler system and flotation devices? Would his neighbors object and claim he is violating zoning ordinances by building the Ark in his front yard? Would he have to get a variance from the city planning commission? Would he have problems getting enough wood for the Ark, because there was a ban on cutting trees to protect the Spotted Owl? Would he have to convince the U.S. Forest Service that he needed the wood to save the owls? Would the carpenters go out on strike? Would he need to negotiate a settlement with the National Labor Union? Would he get sued by an animal rights group? Would the EPA notify him that he could not complete the Ark without filing an environmental impact statement on the proposed flood? Would the Army Corps of Engineers demand a map of the proposed new flood plan? Would the Equal Employment Opportunity Commission file a complaint that he is practicing discrimination by not taking godless, unbelieving people aboard? Would the IRS seize his assets, claiming that he is building the Ark in preparation to flee the country to avoid paying taxes? Would he get a notice from the state that he owed them some kind of user tax and failed to register the Ark as a "recreational water craft"? Would the ACLU go to court to issue an injunction against further construction saying that since God is flooding the earth, it is a religious event and therefore, unconstitutional?

Yes, if Noah were to build an Ark today those things would appear as obstacles, but God is not limited like man. If he wanted Noah to build an Ark in the 21st century, there is no obstacle sufficient to stop him.

It Gets Better With Age

Age 5—I learned that our dog doesn't want to eat my broccoli either.

Age 7—I learned that when I wave to people in the country, they stop what they are doing and wave back.

Age 9—I learned that just when I get my room the way I like it, Mom makes me clean it up again.

Age 12—I learned that if you want to cheer yourself up, you should try cheering someone else up.

Age 14—I learned that although it's hard to admit it, I'm secretly glad my parents are strict with me.

Age 15—I learned that silent company is often more healing than words of advice.

Age 24—I learned that brushing my child's hair is one of life's great pleasures.

Age 26—I learned that wherever I go, the world's worst drivers have followed me there.

Age 29—I learned that if someone says something unkind about me, I must live so that no one will believe it.

Age 30—I learned that there are people who love you dearly but just don't know how to show it.

Age 42—I learned that you can make someone's day by simply sending them a little note.

Age 44—I learned that the greater a person's sense of guilt, the greater his or her need to cast blame on others.

Age 46—I learned that children and grandparents are natural allies.

Age 47—I learned that no matter what happens, or how bad it seems today, life does go on, and it will be better tomorrow.

Age 48—I learned that singing "Amazing Grace" can lift my spirits for hours.

Age 49—I learned that motel mattresses are better on the side away from the phone.

Age 50—I learned that you can tell a lot about a man by the way he handles these three things: a rainy day, lost luggage, and a tangled cord.

Age 51—I learned that keeping a vegetable garden is worth a medicine cabinet full of pills.

Age 52—I learned that regardless of your relationship with your parents, you miss them terribly after they die.

Age 53—I learned that making a living is not the same thing as making a life.

Age 61—I learned that life sometimes gives you a second chance.

Age 62—I learned that you shouldn't go through life with a catchers mitt on both hands. You need to be able to throw something back.

Age 64—I learned that if you pursue happiness, it will elude you. But if you focus on your family, the needs of others, your work, meeting new people, and doing the very best you can, happiness will find you.

Age 65—I learned that whenever I decide something with kindness, I usually make the right decision.

Age 66—I learned that everyone can use a prayer.

Age 72—I learned that even when I have pains, I don't have to be one.

Age 82—I learned that every day you should reach out and touch someone. People love that human touch-holding hands, a warm hug, or just a friendly pat on the back.

Age 90—I learned that I still have a lot to learn.

Age 92—I learned that you should always try to do something to make others smile.

Medical News

Thought I'd let my doctor check me
Cause I didn't feel quite right,
All those aches and pains annoyed me
And I couldn't sleep at night.

He could find no real disorder
But he wouldn't let it rest
What with Medicare and Blue Cross,
We would do a couple tests.

To the hospital he sent me
Though I didn't feel that bad,
He arranged for them to give me
Every test that could be had.

I was fluoroscoped and cystoscoped,
My aging frame surveyed;
Laid on an ice cold table,
While my gizzards were x-rayed.

I was checked for worms and parasites,
For fungus and the crud,
While they pierced me with long needles
Taking samples of my blood.

Doctors came to check me over,
Probed and pushed and poked around,
And to make sure I was living
They then wired me up for sound.

They have finally concluded
(Their results have filled a page)
What I have will someday kill me;
My affliction is old age.

—Author Unknown

Memories

My dad was cleaning out my grandmother's house after she died, and he brought me an old Royal Crown Cola bottle. In the bottle top was a stopper with a bunch of holes in it. I knew immediately what it was, but my daughter had no idea. She thought they had tried to make it a salt shaker or something. I knew it as the bottle that sat on the end of the ironing board to "sprinkle" clothes with because we didn't have steam irons. Man, I am old.

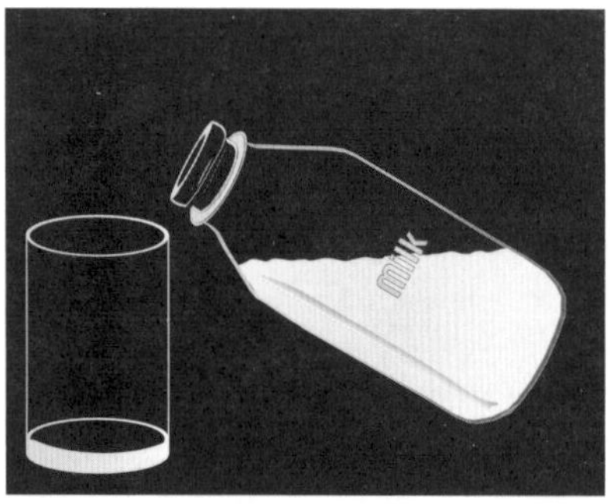

Multi-Tasking

The ability to multi-task is a coveted attribute in our fast paced modern day society. Multi-tasking has become the buzzword of the workplace. With the computer we have greater ability to perform more than one task at a time. Competition and high labor rates have motivated us to implement methods so one person can accomplish more work in less time. Mankind has always sought better and more efficient ways to accomplish his work. Modern day technology and equipment is a testimony to that fact. Our forefathers worked extremely hard to accomplish similar tasks that we now accomplish in less time and with far less effort. The reason is not because we work harder or faster (in fact most times it is the opposite), but because we have found better methods and invented machinery to help do the work.

The printing business, in which I myself am involved, is one that has seen tremendous strides in technology. Entire departments have been eliminated or replaced. Dark room and paste up work is now completed by graphic designers sitting at a computer rather than working in a dimly lit dark room or bent over a light table. Press plates are generated directly from the computer so everything is completely in register, thereby reducing setup time on the press and at the same time producing a higher quality end product. It takes persistent effort to stay abreast of the changes taking place, but it is essential to staying in business and being competitive.

With all the advances in technology we should be finished with our day by noon time and have the afternoon off. Why not? Same amount of work in less time should leave more hours for personal time. Right? Not so! Every time there is an improvement you have a pay off for research and development, but eventually the standard of expectation follows suit and more is required as an accepted norm. Improved performance raises the bar so what was once considered okay is no longer acceptable. The end result is this; we still need to work a minium of eight hours a day, forty hours a week to feed the family and provide for our basic needs.

Multi-tasking sounds neat and certainly has its benefits, but sometimes I question if we are any better off than our forefathers, who worked hard all day in the field, but still found time to sit on the porch in the evening and visit with the neighbors. Perhaps the ease with which our work is accomplished leaves us with too much energy at days end that we aren't ready to sit down and relax. Or, perhaps our focus and values have changed. Maybe multi-tasking doesn't leave time in our schedules for rest and relaxation. Maybe it has caused us to become more self-centered rather than people centered. Perhaps we have become victims of greed. Just perhaps we have gotten caught in the rat race and didn't even take notice. Why not? We were too busy multi-tasking!

—M. Gingrich

My Forgetter

My forgetter's getting better
But my rememberer is broke,
To you that may seem funny
But, to me, that is no joke.

For when I'm "here" I'm wondering
If I really should be "there"
And, when I try to think it through,
I haven't got a prayer!

Oft times I walk into a room,
Say "What am I here for?"
I wrack my brain, but all in vain
A zero, is my score.

At times I put something away
Where it is safe, but, see!
The person it is safest from
Is, generally, me!

When shopping I may see someone,
Say "Hi" and have a chat,
Then, when the person walks away
I ask myself, "Who was that?"

Yes, my forgetter's getting better
While my rememberer is broke,
And it's driving me plumb crazy
And that isn't any joke.

No Time For God

You've time to build houses, and in them dwell
And time to do business—to buy and to sell;
But none for repentance, or deep earnest prayer;
To seek your salvation you've no time to spare.

You've time for earth's pleasures, for frolic and fun,
For her glittering treasures, how quickly you run;
But care not to seek that fair mansion above,
The favor of God or the gift of His love.

You've time to take voyages over the sea,
And time to take in the world's jubilee;
But soon your bright hopes will be lost in the gloom
Of the cold, dark river of death, and the tomb.

You've time to resort to the mountain and glen,
And time to gain knowledge from books and from men;
Yet no time to search for the wisdom of God,
But what of your soul when you're under the sod?

For time will not linger when helpless you lie,
Staring death in the face you will take time to die.
Than what of your judgement—pause, think, I implore
For time will be lost on eternity's shore.

—*Author Unknown*

Now Is The Time

Where have all the flowers gone—a long time growing?

Those were the words to an old song. They come to mind often, usually when a friend or acquaintance passes. As I reflect on those moments, I imagine our lives as flowers, growing from seeds to full bloom then fading into time. During that time my thoughts wander, between the affect my friends had on my life, and I on theirs, from the time we first met to this day of reminiscing.

This reflection brought many questions, such as, was I always kind, was I rude or impatient to them, did I take the time to show an interest in their lives? Were they lonely or in need of companionship? Could I have communicated in some other way, other than the usual, "How are you?" There can be many questions. Some could be answered in a confident way, other answers were left unsure, and some were even regretful.

As I thought about these questions, it caused me to examine my conscience, and my life, and even it's purpose. It seemed like when we were young, time dragged to the point of boredom. There were almost always parents, siblings, and friends filling in the time of our days as a child. Then came schooling and training, and we became interested in all there was to learn. We expanded out into the world and grew with it. Marriage, new friends, and acquaintances, were added into our daily living as we matured. We were occupied with a myriad of things, family, work, daily problems, and other activities. Experiencing everyday life became challenging. Naturally, there were ups and downs but we found we could learn to cope and so we settled into living, rushing through each day and on to the next. Time in days and years quickly and unexpectedly flew by.

Now retirement years are upon us, and we move into smaller homes or a new neighborhood. In some ways we are back at the beginning. We face new challenges with less support than we had in past years. It's like we all aged, suddenly. We are often heard to say, "My friends have moved or passed on; my family has their own lives; I don't know what to with myself; my health is not good, or I'm bored." In self criticism we state, "Sure, I'm set in my ways or I'm afraid of change in my life or maybe I'll just settle in and wait." Our time is filled with trying to find the peace that is our due. Yet still another question arises. How does one go about realizing their peace? Just what do I do with this "now" in my life, this day and the next?

It is important that we make an extra effort to become involved in something that gives us a sense of belonging, even a purpose. By this time we've learned that friends are important, and we need people in our lives to stimulate us, even if we live alone. Becoming active, reaching out, or having some expectations can make life more enjoyable.

Senior citizens always have a wealth of talent and know-how. Just because we've reached retirement age doesn't mean we should give up on life. Imagine all the new encounters still ahead of us. Someone once said, "Our time is like a jewel, it is valuable to others as well as to us." Some of us respond to the environment or the outdoors for activity. Others want social and community activity. Sharing a small part of our time with someone else can compensate us in many ways.

Communities and local organizations need seniors to be advocates for change. After all, we are becoming quite a large majority in our nation. We've got the years of trials and errors behind us, and coupled with that, the wisdom to bring about improvements where needed. Volunteer opportunities are all around for the choosing. Our enthusiasm is an important part in moving forward in spirited living and being thankful for the memories.

—Avanell Pyle

Our Childhood

My mom used to cut chicken, chop eggs, and spread mayo on the same cutting board…with the same knife and no bleach…but we didn't seem to get food poisoning.

My mom used to defrost hamburger on the counter, and I used to eat it raw sometimes too, but I can't remember getting E-coli.

Almost all of us would have rather gone swimming in the lake instead of a pristine pool. (Talk about boring!)

The term cell phone would have conjured up a phone in a jail cell, and a pager was the school PA system.

We all took gym, not P.E. and risked permanent injury with a pair of high top Ked's (only worn in gym) instead of having cross training athletic shoes with air cushion soles and built-in light reflectors. I can't recall any injuries, but they must have happened because they tell us how much safer we are now.

Flunking gym was not an option! I guess P.E. must be much harder than gym.

Every year someone taught the whole school a lesson by running in the halls with leather soles on linoleum tile and hitting the wet spot. How much better off would we be today if we only knew we could have sued the school system?

Speaking of school…we all said prayers, and staying in detention after school caught all sorts of negative attention.

I just can't recall how bored we were without computers and cell phones, etc.

I must be repressing that memory as I try to rationalize through the denial of the dangers that could have befallen us as we trekked off each day about a mile down the road…to some guy's vacant twenty, built forts out of branches and pieces of plywood, made trails, and fought over who got to be the Lone Ranger.

What was that property owner thinking letting us play on that lot? He should have been locked up for not putting up a fence around the property, complete with a self closing gate and an infrared intruder alarm.

Oh yeah…and where was the Benadryl and the sterilization kit when I got that bee sting? I could have been killed!

We played King of the Hill on piles of gravel left on vacant construction sites and when we got hurt, mom pulled out the 48¢ bottle of mercurochrome and then we got a spanking. Now it's a trip to the emergency room, followed by a one-day dose of a $49 bottle of antibiotics and then mom calls the attorney to sue the contractor for leaving a horribly vicious pile of gravel where it was such a threat.

We didn't act up at the neighbor's house either because if we did, we got spanked there too…(physical abuse) and then we got spanked again when we got home.

Mom invited the door-to-door salesman inside for coffee, and children choked down the dust from the gravel driveway while playing with Tonka trucks. (Remember why Tonka trucks were made tough? It wasn't so that they could take the rough Berber carpet in the family room!).

Our music had to be left inside when we went out to play, and I am sure that I nearly exhausted my imagination a couple of times when we went on two week vacations. I should probably sue the folks now for the danger they put us in when we all slept in campgrounds in the family tent.

Summers were spent behind the push lawn mower, and I didn't even know that mowers came with motors until I was thirteen, and we got one without an automatic blade stop or an auto-drive.

I recall Donny from next door coming over and doing his tricks on the front stoop just until he fell off. Little did his mom know that she could have owned our house. Instead she picked him up and spanked him for being such a goof.

Not a single person I knew had ever been told that they were from a dysfunctional family. How could we possibly have known that? We needed to get into group therapy and anger management classes! We were obviously duped by so many societal ills, that we didn't even notice that the entire country wasn't taking Prozac!

How did we survive??

Remember When…

- A 57 Chevy was everyone's dream car?
- Spinning around, getting dizzy, and falling down was cause for giggles?
- The worst embarrassment was being picked last for the team?
- Baseball cards on the spokes transformed any bike into a motorcycle?
- Decisions were made by going "eeny-meeny-miney-moe"?
- Mistakes were corrected by simply exclaiming, "Do Over!"?
- Catching fireflies could happily occupy an entire evening?
- It wasn't odd to have two or three "Best Friends"?
- A foot of snow was a dream come true?
- Water balloons were the ultimate weapon?

Do These Sound Familiar, Too…?

- Mimoegraph paper
- Roller-skate keys
- Home milk delivery in glass bottles with cardboard stoppers
- Wax Coke-shaped bottles with colored sugar water inside
- Cork pop guns
- Studebakers
- Washtub ringers
- The Fuller Brush Man
- Reel-To-Reel tape recorders
- Tinkertoys
- Erector Sets
- Lincoln Logs
- 15¢ McDonald's® hamburgers
- 5¢ packs of baseball cards with that awful pink slab of bubblegum
- Penny candy
- 35¢ a gallon gasoline
- Jiffy Pop popcorn
- Soda pop machines that dispensed glass bottles
- Blackjack, Clove and Teaberry chewing gum
- Party lines
- P.F. Fliers
- Telephone numbers with a word prefix…(Raymond 4-601
- Peashooters
- 45 RPM records
- Metal ice cube trays with levers
- Headlight dimmer switches on the floor
- Ignition switches on the dashboard
- Heaters mounted on the inside of the fire wall
- Real ice boxes
- Pant leg clips for bicycles without chain guards
- Soldering irons you heat on a gas burner
- Using hand signals for cars without turn signals
- Party phone lines
- S&H Green Stamps
- Blue flashbulb

If you can remember most or all of these, then you have lived!!!! With all our progress don't you wish, just once, you could slip back in time and savor the slower pace and share it with the children of today?

Signs Of Aging

You know you're getting older if:

1. You and your teeth don't sleep together.
2. You try to straighten out the wrinkles in your socks and discover you aren't wearing any.
3. At the breakfast table you hear snap, crackle, pop; and you're not eating cereal.
4. Your back goes out, but you stay home.
5. You wake up looking like your driver's license picture.
6. It takes two tries to get up from the couch.
7. Your idea of a night out is sitting on the patio.
8. The happiest hour of the day is naptime.
9. You're on vacation, and your energy runs out before your money does.
10. You say something to your children, your mother used to say to you, and you always hated it.

The Calendar

I am the calendar:

- I have two missions: one of utility, one of sentiment.
- I am the symbol of time: combining the past, the present, and the future.
- As the clock records the seconds, minutes, and hours, I record the days, weeks, and years.
- All the world looks at me, talks about me, and regulates its social life by me.
- No letter is ever written, no check is ever signed, no book is ever published, no money ever coined that does not bear my imprint. I am the one thing in addition to the clock that the world must constantly consult.
- I ask for and get display space in the home, office, and public places. In return, I am both useful and decorative.
- In the space alloted me I work constantly, for those I represent, telling folks who they are, where they are, and what they have to sell.
- I am an omnipresent salesperson, impressing people favorably, reminding them tactfully on each day of the year, that my employers value their business.
- But I am more—I am an ambassador of good will entrusted with a special mission: to remind all men and women of the value that is placed upon the greatest asset my employers own—the friendship of those they serve.

—I am the calendar.

The Days That Used to Be

It's when our thoughts turn to the past,
That we, of age, can see;
The ways of life, we knew back then,
Are now, just "Used to be".

When the milkman and the baker,
Delivered to our door;
Most households items could be bought,
At the nearby general store.

When the doctor still made house calls,
With his satchel and his pills;
And usually was effective,
In conquering our ills.

The front porch, was a place of rest,
A social center, too;
A place where neighbors, met and talked,
Of issues, old and new.

Now, the milkman and the baker,
Have both changed their routine;
The general stores, that we once knew,
No longer, grace the scene.

The doctor has a clinic now,
We go to him for care;
The front porch has lost its status,
The chairs stand empty there.

The ways of life, are temporal,
For people change their ways;
And man will see them, come and go,
All of his earthly days.

—Robert K. Phillips

The Perks Of Being Over The Hill

1. Kidnappers are not very interested in you.
2. In a hostage situation you are likely to be released first.
3. No one expects you to run anywhere.
4. People call at 9 P.M. and ask, "Did I wake you?"
5. There is nothing left to learn the hard way.
6. Things you buy now, won't wear out.
7. You can eat dinner at 4 P.M.
8. You enjoy hearing about other peoples' operations.

9. You get into heated arguments about pension plans.
10. You have a party and the neighbors don't even realize it.
11. You no longer think of speed limits as a challenge.
12. You quit trying to hold your stomach in, no matter who walks into the room.
13. You sing along with elevator music.
14. Your eyes won't get much worse.
15. Your investment in health insurance is finally beginning to payoff.
16. Your joints are more accurate meteorologists than the National Weather Service.
17. Your secrets are safe with your friends because they can't remember them either.
18. Your supply of brain cells is finally down to manageable size.

Time Is A Gift

As I sit and think of words,
To set this poem to rhyme,
I think of years we do our part,
The years of marking time,

I think of time spent together,
The time of doing one's best,
But time has a way of moving on,
And we think of our time to rest.

There's nothing as great as friendship
Or love for our fellow man,
But the time of rest is waiting,
And all great things must end.

I am the most sensible,
When I think of these words,
No man is indispensable,
Truer words were never heard.

The years have moved very swift,
And I have aged with them,
But tho' I was given a gift,
I learned to grow with them.

During our lifetime we all face some sorrow
To give us strength to carry on,
So we can face our tomorrows,
With the stamina to be strong.

Yes, life is very precious,
As we face each newborn day.
But there's always God's hand to guide us
And God's love to show us the way.

Timed Precision

People glance at their watches as they hurry down the street hoping they are on time for their scheduled appointment. Meetings, schedules, appointments are all planned around that one element we call time. Some schedules and events are planned years ahead, others just a few weeks or days. All of them are planned knowing, that as long as time continues, eventually, that meeting or event will take place. News reports have just announced the death of former President Gerald Ford. Events like this are a reminder of the passing of time. No one is able to stop it, slow it down, or speed it up. Its pace is set, and we simply need to plan around its schedule.

We can plan events because of the precise manner in which time operates. Imagine for a moment if suddenly the moon stopped, or the sun stood still, or the planets began orbiting rapidly, or if time suddenly decided to double the length of a second. NASA would be in a heap of trouble. Doctors would need to recalculate their instruments. Speed limit signs would need to be changed. Wages would need to be realigned. Clocks would need to be replaced. Airlines would need to make up new schedules. Cookbook recipes would need to be reformulated. Textbooks would need to be rewritten. Vary the length of a second at different intervals and you will have utter confusion. Planning an appointment or meeting would be an effort in futility. It would become impossible to monitor heart and pulse rates. Calendars would become inaccurate and obsolete. Everything would be chaos.

Time equals 60 seconds in a minute, 60 minutes in an hour, 24 hours in a day, 7 days in a week, 52 weeks in a year, 10 years in a decade, 100 years in a century. Because of its preciseness man has traveled to the moon and back. He can calculate the day, the hour, and the minute when the sun will rise and set in any given place upon the earth, years in advance of its occurring. Meetings can be planned and held with everyone in attendance. The parameters of time help us to be productive and profitable. They are in place for our good and well being.

We commemorate the birth of Christ. It was an event that was foretold many years prior to its happening but at just the precise moment it took place. Christ's return to earth, is another event that will take place. No man knows the day nor the hour except for God who is the controller of time. While no one knows the exact time there are signs that give us warning. One thing we know is that God is never late. He is always right on time! It is possible that these events will take place at any moment, but even if they don't we must always remember that we live on borrowed time. Time is not our own. It is a gift from the giver of life, God himself. If we use the time He gives us for His service then we can look with joy to the future when time will be no more!

By the way if you check out your Bible you will find there was a day when the sun actually did stand still.

—M. Gingrich

Timely Seating

Because they had no reservations at a busy restaurant, my elderly neighbor and his wife were told there would be a 45-minute wait for a table.

"Young man, we're both 90 years old," the husband said. "We may not have 45 minutes."

They were seated immediately.

What Time Is

Time is money...we have no right to waste it. Time is power... we have no right to dissipate it. Time is influence...we have no right to throw it away. Time is life...we must value it greatly. Time is God's...He gives it to us for a purpose. Time is a sacred trust...we must answer for every moment. Time is wisdom...we have no right to be ignorant. Time is preparation for eternity...we must redeem it.

Trivia

Automotive Gift Suggestions

If you have an "Automotive Minded" person in your life, these gift suggestions should be considered.

1. Tire Air Change Kit. This kit comes with everything you need to change the air in your tires. This highly recommended, but often overlooked maintenance item, is much easier now. Remember to change your air every 3000 miles or twice a year. $25
2. Blinker Fluid. You knew it existed but, wow, is this stuff hard to find. 4 oz. bottle. $12
3. Synthetic Blinker Fluid. Better yet! 4 oz. bottle. $24
4. Light Bulb Filaments. Why throw away a perfectly good turn signal or stop light bulb when you can just install a new filament? Premium Filaments, made in the USA! $1
5. Manifold Heat. Yes, your exhaust manifold should be hot. If it's not, you may need this item. Sold by the pound. $3.50
6. Steering Wheel Gaskets. All sizes available! Email for specific application. From $9.99
7. Alternator Batteries. (4 required, replace them all!) From $2.99
8. Fan Belt Buckles. Specify brass or chrome. Gold available special order. $14.99
9. Muffler Bearing Manual. Print version. $59.95
10. Muffler Bearing Manual. CD version. $49.99
11. Universal Muffler Bearing Tool Kit. $105.59
12. Muffler Bearing Hi Temp Synthetic Lube (the only kind we sell!) $40.24
13. Muffler Bearings. From $19.95
14. Muffler Bearing Gasket Kits. From $9.99
15. Momentum (required for tackling some off road obstacles). Sold by the lb-ft/sec. $0.50
16. Microsoft Windows Eliminator. If your car or truck begins to run poorly, (long time to start, frequent crashes, etc.), it's computer, (ECM, ECU, black box, etc.), may have become infected with this nasty computer virus. This product will safely remove the virus. $199
17. Mirror Image Flipper Film. Did you know that the image you see in your rear-view mirrors is reversed! This is a manufacturing flaw that the auto companies have kept secret for years as the recall would cost billions! This film can be cut and placed over any mirror to correct the image. Now you'll be able to read signs in the rear view mirror! $5 per square ft.

Average Adult

If you are an adult, about average weight, here's what you do every 24 hours.

- Your heart beats 103,689 times; it pumps your blood through your body for 168 million miles!
- You breathe 23,040 times; take in 438 cubic feet of air—enough air to fill a box 7 feet by 9 feet!
- You eat 3¼ pounds of food; drink a ½ gallon of liquids. You excrete 7.8 pounds of wastes.
- You perspire 1½ pints of liquid.
- Your body gives off 85.6 degrees of heat.
- You turn in your sleep 25 to 30 times.
- You speak 48,000 words!
- You move 750 major muscles!
- Your fingernails and toenails grow .000046 of an inch!
- Your hair grows .01717 of an inch!
- You exercise 7 million brain cells (Did you know you had that many?)

Bounce This Around!

The U.S. Postal Service sent out a message to all letter carriers to put a sheet of Bounce in their uniform pockets to keep yellow jackets away. The yellow jackets just veer around you. And all this time you've just been putting Bounce in the dryer!

Here are some other great things that you can use Bounce sheets for...

- It will chase ants away when you lay a sheet near them.
- It also repels mice. Spread them around foundation areas, or in trailers and cars that are sitting, and it keeps mice from entering your vehicle.

- It takes the odor out of books and photo albums that don't get opened very often.
- Repels mosquitoes. Tie a sheet of Bounce through a belt loop when outdoors during mosquito season.
- Eliminates static electricity from your computer screen. Wipe your screen with a used sheet of Bounce to keep dust from resettling.
- Dissolve soap scum from shower doors. Clean with a sheet of Bounce.
- Freshen the air in your home. Place an individual sheet of Bounce in a drawer or hang in the closet.
- Put a Bounce sheet in vacuum cleaner.
- Prevent thread from tangling. Run a threaded needle through a sheet of Bounce before beginning to sew.
- Prevent musty suitcases. Place an individual sheet of Bounce inside empty luggage before storing.
- Freshen the air in your car. Place a sheet of Bounce under the front seat.
- Clean baked-on foods from a cooking pan. Put a sheet in a pan, fill with water, let sit overnight, and sponge clean. The antistatic agent apparently weakens the bond between the food and pan.
- Eliminate odors in wastebaskets. Place a sheet of Bounce at the bottom of the wastebasket.
- Collect cat hair. Rubbing the area with a sheet of Bounce will magnetically attract all the loose hairs.
- Eliminate static electricity from Venetian blinds. Wipe the blinds with a sheet of Bounce to prevent dust from resettling.
- Wipe up sawdust from drilling or sand papering. A used sheet of Bounce will collect sawdust like a tack cloth.
- Eliminate odors in dirty laundry. Place a sheet of Bounce at the bottom of a laundry bag or hamper.
- Deodorize shoes or sneakers. Place a sheet of Bounce in your shoes or sneakers over night.
- Golfers put a Bounce sheet in their back pocket to keep the bees away.
- Put a Bounce sheet in your sleeping bag and tent before folding and storing them. It keeps them smelling fresh.

Did You Know...?

- A crocodile can't stick its tongue out.
- A shrimp's heart is in its head.
- In a study of 200,000 ostriches over a period of 80 years, no one reported a single case where an ostrich buried its head in the sand.
- It is physically impossible for pigs to look up in the sky.
- Horses can't vomit.
- The "sixth sick sheik's sixth sheep's sick" is said to be the toughest tongue twister in the English language.
- If you sneeze too hard, you can fracture a rib. If you try to suppress a sneeze, you can rupture a blood vessel in your head or neck and die. If you keep your eyes open by force, they can pop out.
- Rats multiply so quickly that in 18 months, two rats could have over a million descendants.
- Wearing headphones for just an hour will increase the bacteria in your ear by 700 times.
- Most lipstick contains fish scales.
- Like fingerprints, everyone's tongue print is different.
- No building in Washington, D.C., may be taller than 13 floors. This is so that no matter where in the city you are, you can see the Washington Monument.
- Theodore Roosevelt was the first U.S. president to ride in an airplane. He flew for four minutes in a plane built by the Wright brothers on October 11, 1910.
- All of the U.S. presidents have had a sibling.
- The Baby Ruth candy bar was named after Grover Cleveland's baby daughter, Ruth.
- More U.S. presidents have been born in Virginia than any other state. Washington, Jefferson, Madison, Monroe, William Henry Harrison, Tyler, and Wilson.
- Ronald Reagan's favorite Christmas Carol was "Silent Night".
- George Washington had to borrow money to go to his own inauguration.
- John Quincy Adams kept silkworms as pets.
- Bill Clinton is the first left-handed U.S. president to serve two terms.
- When Gerald Ford proposed to his wife, he was wearing one brown and one black shoe.
- Lyndon B. Johnson loved the soda Fresca® so much that he had a fountain installed in the Oval Office.

Did You Know...M&M's®?

A conveyor printing press is used to print the tiny white M's on each M&M's® candy. Because the peanut sizes vary, the press must be always adjusted to prevent smashing the peanuts in peanut

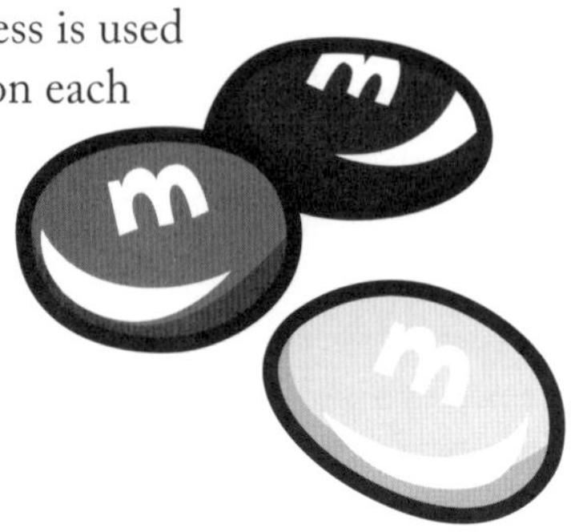

M&M's®. Regular M&M's®, all the same size, are much easier to send through the printer.

Dividing The Lunch Check

Dividing the lunch check by four people means confusion. When a fellow eats out a thousand times a year, nothing that happens in a restaurant is surprising. I thought I'd seen it all, the day I watched my Michigan friend, Nancy, trying to eat hush puppies with a knife and fork. Not so. That was topped last month as I dined on barbecued ribs in a restaurant near Atlanta. The hostess seated me next to a table occupied by four women who had been shopping. Shortly after ordering, I heard the beginning of what would develop into a complicated conversation when their check arrived. It went some thing like this:

I can't help it, Ethel, they don't give separate checks here, and calling it an exclusive dump won't help... What's that, Lois? Ask the waiter again? All right. Waiter! Yoo-hoo, Number seventeen! Antonio! Sev-unntee-un! Could you come back here, please?...Thank you, Antonio. Could you please go back and make out separate checks for us?...Oh, I see. You haven't the slightest idea who had what. You say we changed our minds so many times that you got confused? What's that, Anne? Howard Johnson's the next time? Now look, Anne, that doesn't help us not one whit right now and...What? I have no idea what a whit is, Lois. What's that Ethel? Split it down the middle? But that only gives us two checks in quarters?

Beg pardon, Lois?...Right, I know you're on a diet and didn't eat as much as we did, but you had the lobster saute and that's more than the broiled trout...What's that, Anne?.. You say Lois had extra dessert? Well, I don't think it was extra. It just cost extra because of the whipped cream. What's that Antonio?.. Just be patient and we'll figure it out. You're a waiter, so wait. Very well, girls, let's start over. And you help us, Antonio. Okay, Lois had the onion soup, the lobster saute, hold the fries, June peas. What, Lois?.. You say you had no June peas? Well, Antonio says you had them. Anyway, they're free, they come with the lobster. How much is that all, Antonio? What's that Antonio? You say she had a chocolate fudge sundae with extra walnuts? Hah! Some diet, Lois. All right, so you didn't have the regular dinner. It was à la carte. So what's that, Antonio?.. Seven dollars even.

Okay, now then, Ethel had the special: corned beef,cabbage, rolls, tomato juice, and mince pie. Right, Antonio? What's that? Yes, Ethel is the one with glasses and the feathers in her hat...Well, I wouldn't call her the chubby one, Antonio, but you're entitled to your own opinion. Although such a statement certainly won't help your cause any. So how much is Ethel's special, Antonio?.. $5.75. Okay, wait a minute, I have to write this down. What's that Ethel?.. Well, what about the mince pie? You gave it to Anne because it came with the dinner. But Anne says she gave you her butterscotch pudding. Which is worth more, Antonio? Antonio, you are not listening. What's that? You say you have a headache? Well, if you think you have a headache, what about me?

Wait a minute, what's this for, Ethel? Thirty-five cents toward the tip? Wait, Anne...all right, you can make change for your tip later. Right now, let's get on with the check. Hmmmm, Anne had a dessert worth twenty-five cents more than Lois's. I don't see how it could be worth more when both came with the dinner... Oh, I see it now. One dinner was worth more.

Ethel, Lois, please don't get the change mixed up. We'll work out a ratio for the tip later. Isn't that the best way, waiter?.. What? You couldn't care less? Well, I don't consider that cooperation at all.

Now, Anne had the regular dinner: two pork chops, mashed potatoes, broccoli, onion soup, and all that...what was that, Antonio? Oh, the onion soup is $1.75? But she had it on the dinner. Anne, I beg you, don't flare up. Everything will be straightened out. This is worse than the United Nations trying to admit another country. What, Antonio? Much worse? You see, Anne, dear, it says, "Choice of soup or appetizer", not both. Can't you make a small concession here, Antonio? It might get confusing otherwise. Most places, my friends claim, give you both on the regular dinner.

What's that, Antonio?.. I know you have other customers. But, for your information, young man, I have to decide today whether or not to buy a pair of the most beautiful shoes you ever laid eyes on, and they're on sale at Rich's at 50% off.

Okay, let's add this up. Let's see, two and two is four, eight and eight is fifteen and one to carry, two, nineteen...Hmmm, I get $19.55...You don't get that, Antonio? I probably added it up wrong...Yes, I know there was an extra coffee. I don't know who had the extra coffee. You don't charge for extra coffee, do you?.. Well, most places...I know you don't get coffee for nothing, Antonio. But there is a vast surplus of the stuff in Brazil. I just read that last week.

Now, Antonio, shall we be calm and mature about this and go over it once more just to be sure? Anne had the lobster saute which is worth…

Antonio! Don't tear it up, Antonio! You don't need to…

Well, wasn't that nice of him. He just tore up the check and said forget it…what, dear?…What is it, Lois?.. A tip? Yes, of course. He certainly deserves a tip. Let's figure it out. Anne had the regular dinner plus $1.75 for the extra soup…What's that, Anne? You won't tip on the extra soup? But at 15% it's only 23¢.

I'll tell you what. Next week let's come on Tuesday. According to the menu they have a shopper's special for $2.75, and let's ask for Antonio. He'll like that, don't you think?

—Bo Whaley
All I Ever Wanted was a Piece of Cornbread and a Cadillac

Enough Facts Already?

- Your stomach has to produce a new layer of mucus every two weeks otherwise it will digest itself.
- The dot over the letter 'i' is called a tittle.
- A male emperor moth can smell a female emperor moth up to 7 miles away.
- Some insects can live up to a year without their heads.
- A giraffe can clean its ears with its 21-inch tongue.
- John Wilkes Booth's brother once saved the life of Abraham Lincoln's son.
- Chocolate kills dogs! True, chocolate affects the dog's heart and nervous system; a few ounces are enough to kill a small dog.
- Daniel Boone detested coonskin caps.
- Money isn't made out of paper, it's made out of cotton; before the 1950's it was made from hemp.
- Ketchup was sold in the 1830's as medicine.
- Leonardo da Vinci could write with one hand and draw with the other at the same time.
- The number of possible ways of playing the first four moves per side in a game of chess is 318,979,564,000.
- Upper and lowercase letters are named "upper" and "lower" because back when all type was set in individual letters, the upper case letters were stored above the case (drawer) that stored the smaller, lower case letters.

Every Day In America

- One hundred and eight thousand of us move to a different home, and 18,000 move to another state. In the process, the national "center of population" creeps 72 feet to the southwest.
- The U.S. Government issues 50 more pages of regulations.
- 40 Americans turn 100, about 5,800 become 65, and 8,000 try to forget their 40th birthdays.
- 167 businesses go bankrupt, while 689 new ones start up—and 105 Americans become millionaires.
- The Smithsonian adds 2,500 things to its collections.

- Americans purchase 45,000 new automobiles and trucks, and smash up 87,000.
- 20,000 people write letters to the president.
- More than 6,300 people get divorced, while 13,000 get married.
- Dogs bite 11,000 citizens, including 20 mail carriers.
- We eat 75 acres of pizza, 53 million hot dogs, 167 million eggs, 3 million gallons of ice cream, and 3,000 tons of candy. We also jog 17 million miles and burn 1.7 billion calories while we're at it.

Expensive Gas?

Try buying some of these things by the gallon. Think a gallon of gas is expensive? This puts things in perspective.

- Diet Snapple®, 16 oz. $1.29.............$10.32 per gallon
- Lipton Ice Tea®, 16 oz. $1.19.............$9.52 per gallon
- Ocean Spray®, 16 oz. $1.25...............$10.00 per gallon
- Brake Fluid, 12 oz. $3.15...................$33.60 per gallon
- Vick's Nyquil®, 6 oz. $8.35.............$178.13 per gallon
- Pepto Bismol®, 4 oz. $3.85.............$123.20 per gallon
- Whiteout, 7 oz. $1.39........................$25.42 per gallon
- Scope®, 1.5 oz. $0.99.........................$84.48 per gallon

And this is the REAL KICKER…

- Evian Water®, 9 oz. $1.49.................$21.19 per gallon —FOR WATER, and the buyer doesn't even know the source.

So, next time you're at the pump, be glad your car doesn't run on water, Scope® or whiteout or Pepto Bismol® or Nyquil®. Just a little humor to help ease the pain of your next trip to the pump.

Fast Facts

- It takes 4,000 grains of sugar to fill a teaspoon.
- The Sears Tower contains enough phone wire to wrap around the earth 1.75 times and enough electrical wiring to run a power line from Chicago to Los Angeles.
- On average, people spend more than five years of their lives dreaming.
- About 3% of pet owners give Valentine's Day gifts to their pets.
- Because it is continually losing body heat, the shrew must keep moving to stay warm. If inactive for more than a few hours, the animal will lose enough body heat to freeze to death.
- Rats can swim for a ½ mile without resting, and they can tread water for 3 days straight.
- It would require an average of 18 hummingbirds to weigh in at 1 ounce.
- The armor of the armadillo is not as tough as it appears. It is very pliable like a human fingernail.
- You burn 3½ calories each time you laugh.
- When you blush, the lining of your stomach also turns red.
- There are five types of simple machines: the lever, the pulley, the inclined plane, the screw, and the wheel.
- It would take 11 Empire State Buildings, stacked one on top of the other, to measure the Gulf of Mexico at its deepest point.
- Bulb thermometers rely on the simple principle that a liquid changes its volume relative to its temperature. Liquids take up less space when they are cold and more space when they are warm.

For Lexophiles (Lovers Of Words)

- A bicycle can't stand alone; it's two tired.
- A will is a dead giveaway.
- Time flies like an arrow; fruit flies like a banana.
- In a democracy it's your vote that counts; in feudalism, it's your count that votes.
- A chicken crossing the road is poultry in motion.
- When she got married she got a new name and a dress.
- When a clock is hungry it goes back four seconds.
- The guy who fell onto an upholstery machine was fully recovered.
- You are stuck with your debt if you can't budge it.
- He broke into song because he couldn't find the key.
- Local Area Network in Australia: The LAN down under.
- A calendar's days are numbered.
- When she saw her first strands of gray hair, she thought she'd dye.
- Bakers trade bread recipes on a knead to know basis.
- Acupuncture: a jab well done.
- Marathon runners with bad shoes suffer the agony of defeat.

For Those Who Mow

Things to ponder when mowing the grass…

"Jim, you know all about gardens and nature. What is going on? What happened to the dandelions, violets, thistles, and stuff? It was a perfect, no-maintenance garden. Those plants would grow in any type of soil, withstand drought, and multiply with abandon. The nectar from the long lasting blossoms attracted butterflies, honey bees, and flocks of songbirds. Now instead of a vast garden of colors, all I see are these green rectangles."

Jim replied, "Oh, that's The Suburbanites. They started calling flowers 'weeds' and went to great extent to kill them and replace them with grass."

"Grass? But it's so boring. It's not colorful. It doesn't attract butterflies, birds, and bees, only grubs and sad worms. It's temperamental with temperatures. Do these Suburbanites really want all that grass growing there?"

"Apparently so. They go to great pains to grow it and keep it green. They begin each spring by fertilizing grass and poisoning any other plant that crops up in the lawn."

"The spring rains and cool weather probably make grass grow really fast. That must make The Suburbanites happy."

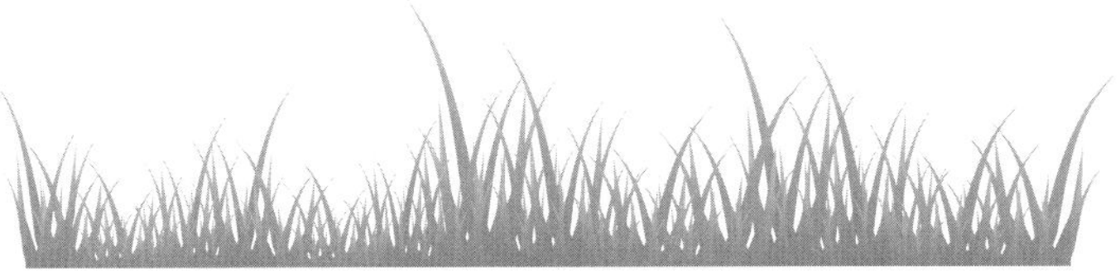

"Apparently not. As soon as it grows a little, they cut it—sometimes twice a week."

"They cut it? Do they then bale it like hay?"

"Not exactly. Most of them rake it up and put it in bags."

"They bag it? Why? Is it a cash crop? Do they sell it?"

"No, sir. Just the opposite. They pay to throw it away."

"Now let me get this straight. They fertilize grass so it will grow. And when it does grow, they cut it off and pay to throw it away?"

"Yes, sir."

"These Suburbanites must be relieved in the summer when it doesn't rain and the heat dries things up. That surely slows the growth and saves them a lot of work."

"You aren't going to believe this, sir. When the grass stops growing so fast, they drag out hoses and pay more money to water it so they can continue to mow it and pay to get rid of it."

"What nonsense! At least they kept some of the trees. That was a sheer stroke of genius, if I do say so myself. The trees grow leaves in the spring to provide beauty and shade in the summer. In the autumn they fall to the ground and form a natural blanket to keep moisture in the soil and protect the trees and bushes. Plus, as they rot, the leaves form compost to enhance the soil. It's a natural circle of life."

"You better sit down. The Suburbanites have drawn a new circle. As soon as the leaves fall, they rake them into great piles and have them hauled away."

"No! What do they do to protect the shrub and tree roots in the winter and keep the soil moist and loose?"

"After throwing away your leaves, they go out and buy something they call mulch. They haul it home and spread it around in place of the leaves."

"And where do they get this mulch?"

"They cut down trees and grind them up."

"Enough! I don't want to think about this anymore."

Intelligence Test

1. Some months have thirty days, some months have thirty-one days. How many months have twenty-eight days?
2. If a doctor gives you three pills and tells you to take one pill every half hour, how long would it be before all the pills had been taken?
3. I went to bed at eight o'clock in the evening and wound up my clock and set the alarm to sound at nine o'clock in the morning. How many hours sleep would I get before being awoken by the alarm?
4. Divide thirty by half and add ten. What do you get?
5. A farmer had seventeen sheep. All but nine died. How many live sheep were left?
6. If you had only one match and entered a cold and dark room, where there was an oil heater, an oil lamp and a candle, which would you light first?
7. A man builds a house with four sides of rectangular construction, each side having a southern exposure. A big bear comes along. What color is the bear?
8. Take two apples from three apples. What do you have?
9. How many animals of each species did Moses take with him in the Ark?
10. If you drove a bus with forty-three people on board from Chicago and stopped at Pittsburgh to pick up seven more people and drop off five passengers and at Cleveland to drop off eight passengers and pick up four more and eventually arrive at Philadelphia twenty hours later, what's the name of the driver?

Answers:

1. All of them. Every month has at least twenty-eight days.
2. One hour. If you take a pill at one o'clock, then another at one thirty and the last at two o'clock, they will be taken in one hour.
3. One hour. It is a wind up alarm clock which cannot discriminate between a.m. and p.m.
4. Seventy. Dividing by half is the same as multiplying by two.
5. Nine live sheep.
6. The match.
7. White. If all walls face south, the house must be on the North Pole.
8. Two apples.
9. None. It was Noah, not Moses.
10. *You* are the driver.

Interesting Geography

Alaska

More than half of the coastline of the entire United States is in Alaska.

Amazon

The Amazon Rainforest produces more than 20% of the world's oxygen supply. The Amazon River pushes so much water into the Atlantic Ocean, that more than one hundred miles at sea off the mouth of the river, one can still dip fresh water out of the ocean. The volume of water in the Amazon River is greater than the next eight largest rivers in the world combined and three times the flow of all rivers in the United States.

Antarctica

Antarctica is the only land on our planet that is not owned by any country. Ninety percent of the world's ice covers Antarctica. This ice also represents seventy percent of all the fresh water in the world. As strange as it sounds, however, Antarctica is essentially a desert. The average yearly total precipitation is about two inches. Although covered with ice (all but 0.4% of it), Antarctica is the driest place on the planet, with an absolute humidity lower than the Gobi Desert.

Brazil

Brazil got its name from the nut, not the other way around.

Canada

Canada has more lakes than the rest of the world combined. Canada is an Indian word meaning "Big village".

Detroit

Woodward Avenue in Detroit, Michigan, carries the designation M-1, so named because it was the first paved road anywhere.

Istanbul, Turkey

Istanbul, Turkey, is the only city in the world located on two continents.

New York City

The term "The Big Apple" was coined by touring jazz musicians of the 1930's who used the slang expression "Apple" for any town or city. Therefore, to play New York City is to play the big time—the big apple.

There are more Irish in New York City than in Dublin, Ireland; more Italians in New York City than in Rome, Italy; and more Jews in New York City than in Tel Aviv, Israel.

Ohio

There are no natural lakes in the state of Ohio, every one is man-made.

Rome

The first city to reach a population of 1 million people was Rome, Italy, in 133 B.C. There is a city called Rome on every continent.

Siberia

Siberia contains more than 25% of the world's forests.

Sahara Desert

In the Sahara Desert, there is a town named Tidikelt, which did not receive a drop of rain for ten years. Technically though, the driest place on earth is in the valleys of the Antarctic near Ross Island. There has been no rainfall there for many years.

Spain

Spain literally means "The land of rabbits".

St. Paul, Minnesota

St. Paul, Minnesota, was originally called Pig's Eye after a man named Pierre "Pig's Eye" Parrant who set up the first business there.

Roads

Chances that a road is unpaved in the U.S.A.—1%. In Canada—75%.

Texas

The deepest hole ever made in the world is in Texas. It is as deep as 20 Empire State Buildings but only 3 inches wide.

United States

The Eisenhower Interstate System requires that one-mile in every five must be straight. These straight sections are usable as airstrips in times of war or other emergencies.

Waterfalls

The water of Angel Falls (the world's highest) in Venezuela drops 3,212 feet (979 meters). It is 15 times higher than Niagara Falls.

I have always said you should learn something new every day. Unfortunately, many of us are at that age where what we learn today, we forget tomorrow. But, give it a shot anyway!...

Interesting Stuff

1. If you are right handed, you will tend to chew your food on your right side. If you are left-handed, you will tend to chew your food on your left side.
2. If you stop getting thirsty, you need to drink more water. When the human body is dehydrated, its thirst mechanism shuts off.
3. Your tongue is germ free only if it is pink. If it is white there is a thin film of bacteria on it.
4. The Titanic was the first ship to use the SOS signal.
5. The pupil of the eye expands as much as 45 percent when a person looks at something pleasing.
6. The average person who stops smoking requires one hour less sleep a night.
7. Laughing lowers levels of stress hormones and strengthens the immune system. Six-year-olds laugh an average of 300 times a day. Adults only laugh 15 to 100 times a days.
8. The roar that we hear when we place a seashell next to our ear is not the ocean, but rather the sound of blood surging through the veins in the ear.
9. Dalmatians are born without spots.
10. The owl is the only bird to drop its upper eyelid to wink. All other birds raise their lower eyelids.
11. Roosters cannot crow if they cannot extend their necks.
12. Every time you sneeze some of your brain cells die.
13. When hippos are upset, their sweat turns red.
14. Google is actually the common name for a number with a million zeros.
15. Switching letters is called spoonerism. For example, saying jag of Flapan, instead of flag of Japan.
16. It cost $7 million to build the Titanic and $200 million to make a film about it.
17. The attachment of the human skin to muscles is what causes dimples.
18. The sound you hear when you crack your knuckles is actually the sound of nitrogen gas bubbles bursting.

19. It takes about 20 seconds for a red blood cell to circle the whole body.
20. Most soccer players run seven miles in a game.
21. The only part of the body that has no blood supply is the cornea in the eye. It takes in oxygen directly from the air.
22. In most watch advertisements the time displayed on the watch is 10:10 because then the arms frame the brand of the watch (and make it look like it is smiling).
23. Colgate faced a big obstacle marketing toothpaste in Spanish speaking countries. Colgate translates into the command "Go hang yourself".
24. The only two animals that can see behind themselves without turning their head are the rabbit and the parrot.
25. Intelligent people have more zinc and copper in their hair.
26. Women blink nearly twice as much as men.
27. German Shepherds bite humans more than any other breed of dog.
28. Large kangaroos cover more than 30 feet with each jump.
29. A whip makes a cracking sound because its tip moves faster than the speed of sound.

Miracle of the Sun

The sun's temperature is 10,000 degrees Fahrenheit at the surface and 27 million degrees Fahrenheit at the center. Nuclear fusion takes place in its core, which proceeds to its surface, and then radiates out into space as heat and light.

Remarkably, the sun is the perfect size, distance, temperature, and brightness for life to exist on earth.

The sun is 93 million miles from the earth, which is the perfect distance to heat our land, oceans, and air. If the earth's diameter were 10% larger or smaller, life would either be burned up or frozen.

Not only does the sun produce heat and light, it also affects the earth's atmospheric conditions, which produce wind and rain. The sun's gravitational pull keeps earth in orbit at the exact distance to sustain life, and produces enough light for plants to photosynthesize.

Is this by coincidence, or was it designed by an Sovereign Creator?

Now You Know Everything

Thought you knew it all? Did you know the following?

1. Rubber bands last longer when refrigerated.
2. Peanuts are one of the ingredients of dynamite.
3. There are 293 ways to make change for a dollar.
4. The average person's left hand does 56% of the typing.
5. A shark is the only fish that can blink with both eyes.
6. There are more chickens than people in the world.
7. Two-thirds of the world's eggplant is grown in New Jersey.
8. The longest one syllable word in the English language is "screeched".
9. No word in the English language rhymes with month, orange, silver, or purple.
10. "Dreamt" is the only English word that ends in the letters "mt".
11. All 50 states are listed across the top of the Lincoln Memorial on the back of the $5 bill.
12. Almonds are a member of the peach family.
13. Maine is the only state with just one syllable.
14. There are only four words in the English language which end in "dous": tremendous, horrendous, stupendous, and hazardous.
15. A cat has 32 muscles in each ear.
16. An ostrich's eye is bigger than it's brain.
17. A dragonfly has a life span of 24 hours.
18. A goldfish has a memory span of three seconds.
19. A dime has 118 ridges around the edge.
20. It's impossible to sneeze with your eyes open.
21. The giant squid has the largest eyes in the world.
22. In England, the Speaker of the House is not allowed to speak.
23. The average person falls asleep in seven minutes.
24. On a Canadian $2 bill, the flag flying over the Parliament Building is an American Flag.
25. "Stewardesses" is the longest word that is typed with only the left hand.

Now, you know…everything!!!

Oddities In Geography

We are all familiar with strange and interesting facts regarding geography.

- Reno, Nevada is actually 100 miles farther west than Los Angeles, California.
- Atlanta, Georgia is closer to Detroit, Michigan, Chicago, Illinois, and Keokuk, Iowa than it is to Miami, Florida.
- The whole of Chesapeake Bay is north of Cairo, Illinois.
- If you went due north from Rome, Georgia, do you know in which Great Lake you would enter Canada? (The answer is Lake Superior, the westernmost of the Great Lakes.)
- The western tip of Virginia is 25 miles west of Detroit, Michigan.
- The entire state of Connecticut is south of the northern part of Pennsylvania—a Middle Atlantic State.
- The southernmost part of Canada is within 35 miles of the Mason & Dixon line.
- Virtually the entire continent of South America is east of Savannah, Georgia.
- All of Cape Cod, Massachusetts, is south of Northern Pennsylvania.
- The northern tip of Virginia is 25 miles north of Atlantic City.
- Most of New Hampshire and Vermont, 110 miles of New York, and practically all of Maine, are north of Cape Sable, Nova Scotia.
- The Atlantic Ocean end of the Panama Canal is west of the Pacific Ocean end, and the canal is due south of Charleston, South Carolina.
- Pennsylvania is opposite of southern Spain and the Mediterranean Sea and just north of Algiers, Africa.
- And if you are a Boston traveler—beware! You won't know which end is up, and a compass won't help either. South Boston is east of downtown and north of more than half the city. East Boston is north of downtown, and the south end is far north of West Roxbury, which itself is almost at the southern end of the bottom. It's been known of a visitor who had to use a map of the city, to find his way out of a telephone booth!

Orange Trivia

- The orange is technically a hesperidum, a type of berry.
- In Queen Victoria's day, oranges were given as Christmas gifts in England.
- Almost 40% of the orange crop in the U.S. goes to make frozen concentrate.
- Florida produces about 70% of the total U.S. crop, and 90% of its production goes to make juice.
- Brazil produces more oranges than any country.

- A popular demonstration at the 1922 Los Angeles Fair was how to make toothpaste from orange by-products.
- Oranges were introduced to Hawaii in 1792.
- The most valuable fruit crops in the United States are, in order: grapes, apples, oranges, and strawberries.

Oreo® Eaters Personality Guide

Psychologists have discovered that the manner in which people eat Oreo® cookies provides great insight into their personalities. Choose which method best describes your favorite method of eating Oreos®:

1. The whole thing all at once.
2. One bite at a time.
3. Slow and methodical nibbles, examining the results of each bite afterwards.
4. In little feverous nibbles.
5. Dunked in some liquid (milk, coffee…).
6. Twisted apart, the inside, then the cookie.
7. Twisted apart, the inside, and toss the cookie.
8. Just the cookie, not the inside.
9. Just lick them, not eat them.
10. No favorite way. Do not like Oreos®.

Your Personality:

1. The whole thing. This means you consume life with abandon, you are fun to be with, exciting, and carefree with some hint of recklessness. You are totally irresponsible. No one should trust you with their children.
2. One bite at a time. You are lucky to be one of the 5.4 billion other people who eat their Oreos® this very same way. Just like them, you lack imagination, but that's okay, not to worry, you're normal.
3. Slow and Methodical. You follow the rules. You're very tidy and orderly. You're very meticulous in every detail with everything you do, to the point of being analytical, retentive, and irritating to others. Stay out of the fast lane if you're only going to go the speed limit.
4. Feverous Nibbles. Your boss likes you because you get your work done quickly. You always have a million things to do and never enough time to do them. Ritalin may do you good.
5. Dunked. Everyone likes you because you are always upbeat. You like to sugar coat unpleasant experiences and rationalize bad situations into good ones.
6. Twisted apart, the inside, and then the cookie. You have a highly curious nature. You take pleasure in breaking things apart to find out how they work, though you are not always able to put them back together, so you destroy all the evidence of your activities. You deny your involvement when things go wrong.
7. Twisted apart, the inside, and then toss the cookie. You are good at business and take risks that payoff. You take what you want and throw the rest away. You are greedy, selfish, mean, and lack feelings for others. You should be ashamed of yourself. But that's ok, you don't care, you got yours.
8. Just the cookie, not the inside. You enjoy pain.
9. Just lick them, not eat them. Stay away from small furry animals and seek professional medical help—immediately.
10. No favorite way. You do not like Oreo® cookies. You probably come from a rich family, like to wear nice things, and go to upscale restaurants. You are particular and fussy about the things you buy, own, and wear. Things have to be just right. You like to be pampered. There's just no pleasing you.

Some Stuff You May Not Know

- The liquid inside young coconuts can be used as substitute for blood plasma.
- Donkeys kill more people annually than plane crashes.
- Oak trees do not produce acorns until they are fifty years of age or older.
- The first product to have a barcode was Wrigley's Gum.
- A Boeing 747's wingspan is longer than the Wright brother's first flight.
- Venus is the only planet that rotates clockwise.
- The plastic things on the end of shoelaces are called aglets.
- Pearls melt in vinegar.
- It is possible to lead a cow upstairs…but not downstairs.
- All U.S. presidents have worn glasses. Some just didn't like being seen wearing them in public.
- George H.W. Bush was the first and only U.S. president to publicly refuse to eat broccoli.
- John F. Kennedy was the first U.S. president to also be a Boy Scout.

- Thomas Jefferson was the first U.S. president to have a grandchild born in the White House.
- James Buchanan was said to have the neatest handwriting of all the U.S. presidents.
- Abraham Lincoln was the tallest U.S. president. He was six feet, four inches tall.

State Facts & Trivia

Alabama Facts and Trivia

- Alabama introduced the Mardi Gras to the western world. The celebration is held on Shrove Tuesday, the day before Lent begins.
- Alabama workers built the first rocket to put humans on the moon.
- The world's first Electric Trolley System was introduced in Montgomery in 1886.
- Alabama is the only state with all major natural resources needed to make iron and steel. It is also the largest supplier of cast-iron and steel pipe products.

Carolina Facts and Trivia

- Campbell's Covered Bridge built in 1909, is the only remaining covered bridge in South Carolina, located off Hwy 14 near Gowensville.
- The salamander was given the honor of official state amphibian.
- The walls of the American Fort on Sullivan Island, in Charleston Harbor, were made of spongy Palmetto logs. This was helpful in protecting the fort because the British cannonballs bounced off the logs.

Florida Facts and Trivia

- Greater Miami is the only metropolitan area in the United States whose borders encompass two national parks. You can hike through pristine Everglades National Park or ride on glass-bottom boats across Biscayne National Park.
- Saint Augustine is the oldest European settlement in North America.
- The name Punta Gorda means "fat point" when translated from Spanish. The moniker was given to the city because a broad part of the land in Punta Gorda juts into Charlotte Harbor. The harbor itself is somewhat unique, as it is the point where the Peace River meets the ocean.
- Orlando attracts more visitors than any other amusement park destination in the United States.

Mississippi Facts and Trivia

- In 1963, the University of Mississippi Medical Center accomplished the world's first human lung transplant and, on January 23, 1964, Dr. James D. Hardy performed the first heart transplant surgery.

New Jersey Facts and Trivia

- "I'm From New Jersey" is the only state song that is adaptable to any municipality with a two or three syllable name.
- New Jersey has the highest population density in the U.S. An average 1,030 people per sq. mi., which is 13 times the national average.
- New Jersey has the highest percent urban population in the U.S. with about 90% of the people living in an urban area.
- In November of 1914, the New York Tribune, cooperating with Mr. Bertram Chapman Mayo (founder of Beachwood), issued an "Extra" announcing: Subscribe to the New York Tribune and secure a lot at beautiful Beachwood. Act at once, secure your lot in this summer paradise now! This was the greatest premium offered by a newspaper—nothing equal to it was ever attempted in the United States.

New York Facts and Trivia

- The first American chess tournament was held in New York in 1843.
- The 641 mile transportation network known as the Governor Thomas E. Dewey Thruway is the longest toll road in the United States.
- In 1979, Vassar students were the first from a private college to be granted permission to study in the People's Republic of China.
- The Fashion Institute of Technology in Manhattan is the only school in the world offering a Bachelor of Science Degree with a Major in Cosmetics and Fragrance Marketing.
- Borden's Milk was first canned in Liberty, NY.
- In 1902, while on a hunting expedition in Sharkey County, President Theodore (Teddy) Roosevelt refused to shoot a captured bear. This act resulted in the creation of the world-famous teddy bear.
- The world's largest shrimp is on display at the Old Spanish Fort Museum in Pascagoula.

Strange & Unusual Facts

- People do not get sick from cold weather; it's from being indoors a lot more.
- When you sneeze, all bodily functions stop…even your heart.
- Only 7% of the population are lefties.

- Forty people are sent to the hospital for dog bites every minute.
- The toothbrush was invented in 1498.
- The average housefly lives for one month.
- A coat hanger is 44 inches long when straightened.
- The average computer user blinks seven times a minute.
- Your feet are bigger in the afternoon than the rest of the day.
- Prince Charles and Prince William NEVER travel on the same airplane just in case there is a crash.
- The first Harley Davidson motorcycle, built in 1903, used a tomato can for a carburetor.
- If coloring weren't added to Coca-Cola®, it would be green.

The Right Way Versus My Way

- **The Right Way #1:** Stuff a miniature marshmallow in the bottom of a sugar cone to prevent ice cream drips.
- **My Way:** Just suck the ice cream out of the bottom of the cone since you are probably lying on the couch with your feet up eating it anyway.

- **The Right Way #2:** Use a meat baster to "squeeze" your pancake batter onto the hot griddle and you'll get perfectly shaped pancakes every time.
- **My Way:** Buy the precooked kind you nuke in the microwave for 30 seconds. The hard part is getting them out of the plastic bag.

- The Right Way **#3:** To keep potatoes from budding, place an apple in the bag with the potatoes.
- **My Way:** Buy Hungry Jack mashed potato mix and keep it in the pantry for up to a year.

- **The Right Way #4:** To prevent eggshells from cracking, add a pinch of salt to the water before hard boiling.
- **My Way:** Who cares if they crack, aren't you going to take the shells off anyway?

- **The Right Way #5:** To get the most juice out of fresh lemons, bring them to room temperature and roll them under your palm against the kitchen counter before squeezing.
- **My Way:** Sleep with the lemons in between the mattress and box springs.

- **The Right Way #6:** To easily remove burnt-on food from your skillet, simply add a drop or two of dish soap and enough water to cover the bottom of the pan, and bring to a boil on the stovetop.
- **My Way:** Eat at Chili's® every night and avoid cooking.

- **The Right Way #7:** Spray your Tupperware with nonstick cooking spray before pouring in tomato based sauces and there won't be any stains.
- **My Way:** Feed your garbage disposal and there won't be any leftovers.

- **The Right Way #8:** When a cake recipe calls for flouring the baking pan, use a bit of the dry cake mix instead and there won't be any white mess on the outside of the cake.
- **My Way:** Go to the bakery. They'll even decorate it for you.

- **The Right Way #9:** If you accidentally over salt a dish, while it's still cooking drop in a peeled potato and it will absorb the excess salt for an instant "fix me up".
- **My Way:** If you over salt a dish while you are cooking, that's too bad. My motto: I made it and you will eat it no matter how bad it tastes.

- **The Right Way #10:** Wrap celery in aluminum foil when putting in the refrigerator and it will keep for weeks.
- **My Way:** Celery? Never heard of the stuff.

- **The Right Way #11:** Brush some beaten egg white over pie crust before baking to yield a beautiful glossy finish.
- **My Way:** The Mrs. Smith frozen pie directions do not include brushing egg whites over the crust, so I don't do it.

- **The Right Way #12:** Place a slice of apple in hardened brown sugar to soften it.
- **My Way:** Brown sugar is supposed to be "soft"?

- **The Right Way #13:** When boiling corn on the cob, add a pinch of sugar to help bring out the corn's natural sweetness.
- **My Way:** The only kind of corn I buy comes in a can.

- **The Right Way #14:** To determine whether an egg is fresh, immerse it in a pan of cool, salted water. If it sinks, it is fresh, but if it rises to the surface, throw it away.
- **My Way:** Eat, cook, or use the egg anyway. If you feel bad later, you will know it wasn't fresh.

- **The Right Way #15:** Cure for headaches: Take a lime, cut it in half and rub it on your forehead. The throbbing will go away.
- **My Way:** The only reason this works is because you can't rub a lime on your forehead without getting lime juice in your eye, and then the problem isn't the headache anymore, it is because you are now blind.

- **The Right Way #16:** Potatoes will take food stains off your fingers. Just slice and rub raw potato on the stains and rinse with water.
- **My Way:** Mashed potatoes will now be replacing the anti-bacterial soap in the handy dispenser next to my sink.

The Tomb Of The Unknown Soldier

Do you know…?

- How many steps does the guard take during his walk across the Tomb of the Unknown Soldier and why? Twenty-one steps. It alludes to the twenty-one gun salute, which is the highest honor given any military or foreign dignitary.
- How long does he hesitate after his about face to begin his return walk and why? Twenty-one seconds for the same reason as the first answer.
- Why are his gloves wet? His gloves are moistened to prevent his losing his grip on the rifle.
- Does he carry his rifle on the same shoulder all the time, and if not, why not? He carries the rifle on the shoulder away from the tomb. After his march across the path, he executes an about face, and moves the rifle to the outside shoulder.
- How often are the guards changed? Guards are changed every thirty minutes, twenty-four hours a day, 365 days a year.
- What are the physical traits of the guard limited to? For a person to apply for guard duty at the tomb, he must be between 5' 10" and 6' 2" tall and his waist size cannot exceed 30".

Other requirements of the Guard:

1. They must commit two years of life to guard the tomb, live in a barracks under the tomb, and cannot drink any alcohol on or off duty for the rest of their lives. They cannot swear in public for the rest of their lives and cannot disgrace the uniform {fighting} or the tomb in any way. After two years, the guard is given a wreath pin that is worn on their lapel signifying they served as guard of the tomb. There are only 400 presently worn. The guard must obey these rules for the rest of their lives or give up the wreath pin.
2. The shoes are specially made with very thick soles to keep the heat and cold from their feet. There are metal heel plates that extend to the top of the shoe in order to make the loud click as they come to a halt. There are no wrinkles, folds, or lint on the uniform. Guards dress for duty in front of a full-length mirror.
3. The first six months of duty a guard cannot talk to anyone, nor watch TV. All off duty time is spent studying the 175 notable people laid to rest in Arlington National Cemetery. A guard must memorize who they are and where they are interred. Among the notables are: President Taft, Joe E. Lewis, and Medal of Honor winner Audie Murphy, the most decorated soldier of WWII of Hollywood fame.
4. Every guard spends five hours a day getting his uniforms ready for guard duty.
5. When Hurricane Isabelle approached Washington D.C., the military members assigned the duty of guarding the Tomb of the Unknown Soldier were given permission to suspend the assignment. They respectfully declined the offer, "No way, Sir!" Soaked to the skin, marching in the pelting rain of a tropical storm, they said that guarding the Tomb was not just an assignment, it was the highest honor that can be afforded to a service person. The tomb has been patrolled continuously, 24/7, since 1930.

Weird Facts

- Betsy Ross, Daniel Boone, and Paul Revere are the only real people to ever have been the head on a Pez dispenser.
- The citrus soda 7UP® was created in 1929; "7" was selected because the original containers were 7 ounces. "UP" indicated the direction of the bubbles.
- The albatross drinks sea water. It has a special desalinization apparatus that strains out and excretes all excess salt.
- In Clarendon, Texas, there is reportedly a law on the books that lawyers must accept eggs, chickens, or other produce, as well as money, as payment of legal fees.
- A dragonfly flaps its wings 20 to 40 times a second, bees and house flies 200 times, some mosquitoes 600 times, and a tiny gnat 1,000 times.
- Blueberry Jelly Bellies were created especially for Ronald Reagan.
- All porcupines float in water.
- Non-dairy creamer is flammable.
- When opossums are playing "possum", they are not "playing". They actually pass out from sheer terror.

What Is A Billion?

We're not sure if this list is accurate, but the next time you hear a politician use the word "billion" casually, think about whether you want that politician spending your tax money. A billion is a difficult number to comprehend, but one advertising agency did a good job of putting that figure into perspective in one of its releases:

- A billion seconds ago, it was 1959
- A billion minutes ago, Jesus was alive.
- A billion hours ago, our ancestors were living in the Stone Age.
- A billion dollars ago was only 8 hours and 20 minutes, at the rate Washington spends it.

Who Knew

1. If Jell-O® is hooked up to an EEG, it registers movements virtually identical to the brain waves of a healthy adult.
2. The original Twinkies® filling was banana; it was replaced by vanilla-flavored cream during WWII, when the U.S. experienced a banana shortage.
3. On average, a Twinkie® will explode in a microwave in 45 seconds.
4. The squiggle atop every Hostess cupcake has 7 loops.
5. There are 1,218 peanuts in a single 28 oz. jar of peanut butter.
6. Peanut butter's high protein content draws moisture from your mouth—which is why, in the end, it always sticks to the roof of your mouth.One hundred shares of McDonald's® stock purchased for $2,250 when first offered in 1965, was worth more than $1.4 million in 1995.
7. The largest McDonald's® is in Beijing, China. It measures more then 28,000 square feet, seats 700, and has two kitchens and twenty-nine cash registers.

Your Job

Wherever you're working—in office or shop
And however far you may be from the top —
And though you may think you're just treading the mill,
Don't ever belittle the job that you fill.

For, however little your job may appear,
You're just as important as some little gear
That meshes with others in some big machine,
That helps keep it going—tho' never is seen.

They could do without you—we'll have to admit—
But business keeps on when the big fellows quit!
And always remember, my son, if you can,
The job's more important—oh, yes—than the man!

So if it's your hope to stay off the shelf,
Think more of your job than you do of yourself.
Your job is important—don't think it is not,
So try hard to give it the best you've got.

And don't ever think you're of little account
Remember—you're part of the total amount,
If they didn't need you, you wouldn't be there
So, always, my son, keep your chin up in the air!

A digger of ditches, mechanic or clerk—
Think well of your company, yourself, and your work.

Values

A Cup Or Coffee

What's more important—the coffee or the cup it's in?

A group of alumni, highly established in their careers, got together to visit their old university professor. Conversation soon turned into complaints about stress in work and life.

Offering his guests coffee, the professor went to the kitchen and returned with a large pot of coffee and an assortment of cups—porcelain, plastic, glass, crystal, some plain looking, some expensive, some exquisite—telling them to help themselves to the coffee. When all the students had a cup of coffee in hand, the professor said: "If you noticed, all the nice looking expensive cups were taken up, leaving behind the plain and cheap ones. While it is but normal for you to want only the best for yourselves, that is the source of your problems and stress. Be assured that the cup itself, adds no quality to the coffee, in most cases, it is just more expensive and in some cases even hides what we drink. What all of you really wanted was coffee, not the cup, but you consciously went for the best cups…and then began eyeing each other's cups.

Where is your focus? Jobs, money, and position in society are cups that we use everyday. They sustain life. When we focus on the cups we have a tendency to become discontent, envious, and jealous. The real blessings in life: joy, peace, happiness, and friendship, are largely a result of our attitudes and our goals in life. When we redirect our focus, the type of cup in which those blessings are received, loses its importance. When we resort to meeting the needs of others rather than becoming selfish, we can enjoy life even if it is served in a styrofoam cup.

Bread & Butter

Man's thinking is often influenced by the person or persons who "butter their bread." There is probably no place this is more evident than in the arena of politics. It would seem a most difficult task to try and please, the constituents he or she represents, when the wishes and the mentality of the people is so varied. The politician is forced in a sense, to walk a tight rope and perform a balancing act that is neither too far to the right nor too far to the left, so that he will win the majority of votes in his constituency to be reelected. He must also vote on legislation that often includes multiple issues, some to which he may agree, and others to which he may disagree. To make matters even more complicated is a media that is hungry for any story that will sell. They look for any little flaw or mistake that is made, and then blow it out of proportion or slant it, in such a fashion as to bring the reader to their side of the story. Needless to say their task is a difficult one.

But what about your thinking and my thinking? Is it influenced by who "butters our bread"? Are we swayed by popularity or the desire to be accepted? Are we brainwashed by the media and others so that we no longer think for ourselves? In the world of automation so many things are accomplished without the need to think. All we need to know is which button to push and technology takes over. Perhaps our thinking caps have become wrinkled and ragged. Are we more concerned about who "butters our bread" than we are about speaking the truth? Do we stand on principles, or do we cave in when the pressure is on? That is the real question that we must answer. It is easy to point a finger at others when things go against our way of thinking. Perhaps the butter has become too thick and the bread too thin.

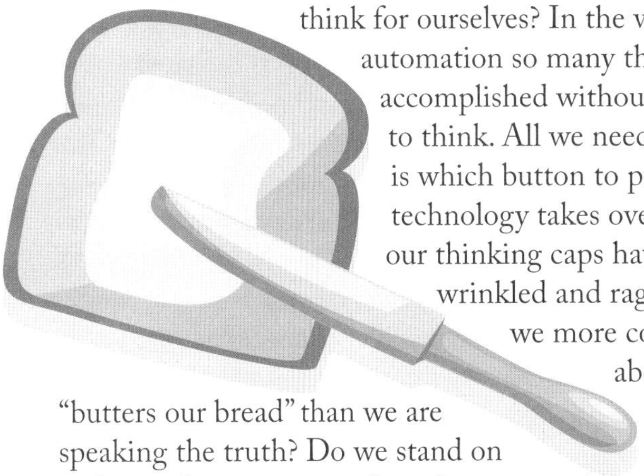

What is the basis for our thinking? Why are the thought patterns of people so different, and yet each one is determined that theirs is the right one? Thought patterns are based on values and principles. Those values and principles are taught, developed, and encouraged by parents, teachers, friends, the media, books, and whatever else we allow our minds to feed on. It is of vital importance that we have a system of values and principles in place, so that we don't become so narrow minded as to refuse to consider any idea other than ours. Neither is it good to become so broad in our thinking that there is no identifying pattern of values.

Thinking is the ability to take the knowledge we acquire and to process it so that our decisions reflect wisdom, integrity, and values. Thinking is arriving at a conclusion on our own rather than having others always "buttering our bread".

—M. Gingrich

Choices

It is a cool fall morning, and as I look out the window I see the sun beginning to warm the earth. Steam rises from the wet grass giving a mist in low lying areas and leaving a telltale sign of cool nights and warm days. There is hardly a cloud in the sky, a welcome reprieve from the showers and wind of the past several days. I am reminded to be thankful that I have the opportunity to see this day, a beautiful day indeed. I'm reminded to be thankful that I can see, hear, smell, feel, and express with my lips the beauty of this day. I have the privilege to enjoy this day to its fullest.

This day will present many opportunities to make choices. I can choose to sing. I can choose to complain. I can choose to show love. I can choose to show hatred. I can choose to be a willing worker, or I can choose to be irresponsible. I can choose to make the most of my circumstances, or I can hide behind a curtain of bitterness. I can choose to compliment those around me, or I can choose to brag about my own accomplishments. I can choose to make friends, or I can choose to isolate myself. I can choose to learn from my past mistakes, or I can choose to wallow in the mire by refusing to own up. I can choose to be humble and serving, or I can choose to be arrogant, boastful, and proud. I can choose to be selfish, or I can choose to give a helping hand.

Each new day brings with it the opportunity to make choices. Choices, that will not only impact our lives but the lives of others. Some of those choices will need to be made in a split second, while others will allow ample time for consideration. What will be the criteria for deciding my choices? How will I determine which choice is the right choice? It begins with my system of values. If I care about me, myself, and I, my choices will be based on how I can benefit. If I value family and friends, my choices will be based on how it will affect my relationships. If I value God, I will seek to determine His will before I choose.

My choices will affect my self esteem. Wrong choices make us feel miserable and discouraged. Right choices bring satisfaction and happiness. It doesn't matter how perfect we are, there will still be times when we make a wrong choice. When that happens we still have opportunity to correct our mistake and suffer limited consequence, or we can choose to suffer the ultimate consequences by refusing to acknowledge any mistake.

Choices are inevitable. We choose our friends, our place of employment, our spouse, our lifestyle, etc. Choices build character and establish long term values. The choices you make have an impact today, tomorrow, and for eternity. Today and tomorrow will quickly pass but eternity is forever. Make your choice based on eternal values. Choose wisely and you will not be disappointed! —*M. Gingrich*

Count Your Blessings

Counting our blessings is good practice.

1. It makes us get along with people better.
2. It makes us focus on others instead of ourselves.
3. It makes us more considerate and sympathetic.
4. It causes us to live for others, not ourselves.
5. It makes us a blessing instead of a burden.
6. It corrects our perspective of life.
7. It strengthens our inner resources of faith and hope.
8. It increases our confidence for living.
9. It increases our awareness of God.

Don't Forget To Give Thanks

I once had the daunting task of proofreading a cookbook. Proofreading is a task that you simply have to train yourself to stick at and get done whether you enjoy it or not. Computers and spell check programs have made the task somewhat less cumbersome but there are still some quirks that only get discovered by manually checking the typed copy. It doesn't catch mistakes like substituting 114 for 1/4 or baking soda for flour which could cause some major problems. Thankfully, we don't need to mix up each recipe and try it out. We let that for the cooks.

While proofreading I became more puzzled than ever how somebody can sit down and read through a cookbook, recipe after recipe and find it enjoyable. I will admit that reading some recipes makes your mouth water, and you can almost smell the aroma coming from the kitchen, but there are some recipes such as Rosy Rhubarb Puff and Dandelion Flower Fritters that really make you wonder. I have concluded that there are possibly a few things that really weren't meant to be eaten by people.

Another thing I came across was a special section where they take out all the good things like "calories". Let me ask you, for instance, would "Diet Pumpkin Cake" go over at your house for Thanksgiving Dinner? Doesn't that take the enjoyment out of eating. My version of "Diet Pumpkin Cake" is eating a little less of the real thing.

I have often wondered what folks did years ago when they didn't have cookbooks. How did they ever arrive at the conclusion that 1/2 teaspoon or 1 cup or a tablespoon or a pinch is just the right amount of each ingredient. How did they discover that certain ingredients mixed together make bread while a few different ones make a cake? I suppose there must have been a lot of trial and error.

The compilation of recipes is yet another indication of our rich heritage. It is a heritage that continues to build as new products come on the market, and as people experiment with new ideas. The selection and variety of food that is available today is overwhelming. We certainly are living in a land of plenty.

Good food has its place but the satisfaction from a meal is short lived. Far more rewarding is the fellowship of family and friends.

When you pull up to a table full of food remember to say thanks. It is but a small token of appreciation for the bountiful harvest and the blessings that are ours. Give thanks for the provision of food. Give thanks for family and friends. Give thanks to God for the opportunity to see another day. Give Thanks! It is a great recipe, that has all the ingredients to make your every day most enjoyable! You may not find this recipe in the index of a cookbook but you will find it in the book of books, the Bible itself. The Bible is full of tried and proven recipes for every situation we face. One of those recipes is thanksgiving. It is woven through its entire volume and blessings are pronounced on those who are grateful. History records when people forgot to be thankful they eventually lost the blessing. Happiness is found, not in the abundance of things, but in being thankful for what we have. May we never forget to give thanks!

—M. Gingrich

In Teamwork Everyone Counts

Xvxn though my typxwritxr is an old modxl, it works quitx wxll xcxpt for onx of thx kxys. I'vx wishxd many timxs it workxd pxrfxctly. It is trux thxrx arx forty-onx kxys that work wxll xnough,

but just onx kxy not working makxs all thx diffxrxncx. Somxtimxs it sxxms to mx that an organization is somxwhat likx my typxwritxr…not all thx pxoplx arx working propxrly. You must say to yoursxlf; "Wxll, I'm thx only pxrson. I won't makx or brxak thx organization." But it doxs makx a diffxrxncx, bxcausx for any group to bx xffxctivx, it nxxds thx activx participation of xvxry mxmbxr.

So, thx nxxt timx you think you arx only onx pxrson and that your xfforts arx not nxxdxd, rxmxmbxr my typxwritxr and say to yousxlf; "I'm a kxy pxrson in my organization and I am nxxdxd vxry much!!!!!"

Politics As Usual?

In America every four years there is a presidential election. The media is saturated with political advertisements promoting the candidates. The winner will assume the highest office in the Unites States government. He will wield tremendous authority in legislative decisions. He will represent the United States in meeting with other world leaders. The burden of responsibility for foreign affairs, economic conditions, and the safety of the American people will rest on his shoulders. It is an office of great importance to the American people and one that requires a high degree of integrity and fortitude. When the economy is bad who gets the blame? The president. When unemployment is high, who gets the blame? The president. He is the one who must give an answer for the actions of all those under his jurisdiction, as well as the general economic conditions. It is a daunting task to say the least.

Listen to a few talk show hosts, a few news commentators and read the editorial columns and you will quickly conclude that there are varying opinions of who should serve, who is qualified, and who is not. That is what elections are all about. We are all free to form our own opinions. Those opinions, however, can be influenced by the information we get. That is where politics comes in. One of the definitions for politics according to Webster is: political methods, tactics, sometimes crafty or unprincipled methods. Right or wrong, every election has its fair share of mud-slinging propaganda. The danger in all of this is that in an effort to win at all costs, principles of integrity, honesty, human dignity, and a host of other virtues are often compromised. Statements are taken out of context. Skeletons of the past are put out for public viewing. Much effort is taken to expose the weaknesses in the other candidates. Comments and view points are exaggerated and manipulated or altered to get the results the media wants. It is a "no man's" land. For example, if a public official visits a disaster area he is wasting public money. If he fails to show up he just isn't interested. It is a "no win" situation.

This article is an endorsement for integrity and truth. It is an endorsement of values that are important to everyone. There is a level of trust in society that runs from top to bottom. When that level is warped by unscrupulous actions and antagonistic remarks, there is trouble on the horizon. We hear concerns registered about sports heroes and the impression they have on our children, and rightly so. Is that not also true of the one who will hold the highest office in the land? It is an office that commands respect and dignity. Pray that God will help each one of us to live above "politics as usual". Pray that we might conduct our affairs with honesty and unquestionable integrity. Pray that the president may provide leadership that we can admire and trust, a leader who values and reflects integrity, honesty, and truth.

—M. Gingrich

Thanks For Your Time

It had been some time since Jack had seen the old man. College, girls, career, and life itself got in the way. In fact, Jack moved clear across the country in pursuit of his dreams. There, in the rush of his busy life, Jack had little time to think about the past and often no time to spend with his wife and son. He was working on his future, and nothing could stop him.

Over the phone, his mother told him, "Mr. Belser died last night. The funeral is Wednesday." Memories flashed through his mind like an old newsreel as he sat quietly remembering his childhood days.

"Jack, did you hear me?"

"Oh, sorry, mom. Yes, I heard you. It's been so long since I thought of him. I'm sorry, but I honestly thought he died years ago," Jack said.

"Well, he didn't forget you. Every time I saw him he'd ask how you were doing. He'd reminisce about the many days you spent over 'his side of the fence' as he put it," mom told him.

"I loved that old house he lived in," Jack said.

"You know, Jack, after your father died, Mr. Belser stepped in to make sure you had a man's influence in your life," she said.

"He's the one who taught me carpentry. I wouldn't be in this business if it weren't for him. He spent a lot of time teaching me things he thought were important. Mom, I'll be there for the funeral," Jack said.

As busy as he was, he kept his word. Jack caught the next flight to his hometown. Mr. Belser's funeral was small and uneventful. He had no children of his own, and most of his relatives had passed away.

The night before he had to return home, Jack and his mom stopped by to see the old house next door one more time.

Standing in the doorway, Jack paused for a moment. It was like crossing over into another dimension, a leap through space and time. The house was exactly as he remembered. Every step held memories. Every picture, every piece of furniture...Jack stopped suddenly.

"What's wrong, Jack?" his mom asked.

"The box is gone," he said.

"What box?" Mom asked.

"There was a small gold box that he kept locked on top of his desk. I must have asked him a thousand times what was inside. All he'd ever tell me was 'the thing I value most'," Jack said.

It was gone. Everything about the house was exactly how Jack remembered it, except for the box. He figured someone from the Belser family had taken it.

"Now I'll never know what was so valuable to him," Jack said. "I better get some sleep. I have an early flight home, mom."

It had been about two weeks since Mr. Belser died. Returning home from work one day, Jack discovered a note in his mailbox. "Signature required on a package. No one at home. Please stop by the main post office within the next three days," the note read.

Early the next day Jack retrieved the package. The small box was old and looked like it had been mailed a hundred years ago. The handwriting was difficult to read, but the return address caught his attention, "Mr. Harold Belser" it read. Jack took the box out to his car and ripped open the package. There inside was the gold box and an envelope. Jack's hands shook as he read the note inside.

"Upon my death, please forward this box and its contents to Jack Bennett. It's the thing I valued most in my life." A small key was taped to the letter. His heart racing, as tears filled his eyes, Jack carefully unlocked the box. There inside he found a beautiful gold pocket watch.

Running his fingers slowly over the finely etched casing, he unlatched the cover. Inside he found these words engraved:

"Jack, thanks for your time! —Harold Belser."

"The thing he valued most...was...my time."

Jack held the watch for a few minutes, then called his office and cleared his appointments for the next two days. "Why?" Janet, his assistant asked.

"I need some time to spend with my son," he said.

"Oh, by the way, Janet...thanks for your time!"

Thanksgiving A To Z

"In all things give thanks" (I Thess.5: 17)

A...America, Affliction, Adversity
B...Bible, Blessing, Books
C...Church, Children, Compassion
D...Doctors, Dentists
E...Education, Enjoyment, Eyes, Eating

F...Faith, Family, Friends
G...God, Grace, Goodness
H...Home, Heaven, Happiness, Health
I...Information, Intelligence, Ideas
J...Jesus, Joy, Job, Justice
K...Kindness, Knowledge
L...Life, Law, Liberty, Laughter
M...Mind, Memory, Mercy, Minister
N...Nurses, Nature
O...Opportunity, Options
P...Parents, Prayer, Patience, Peace
Q...Quietness, Questions
R...Rest, Reading, Recreation
S...Salvation, Savior
T...Teachers, Talent, Truth, Trials
U...Understanding, Unity
V...Victory, Vision
W...Work, Wisdom, Water
X...X-rays, Xerox
Y...Youth, Yielding
Z...Zest, Zippers

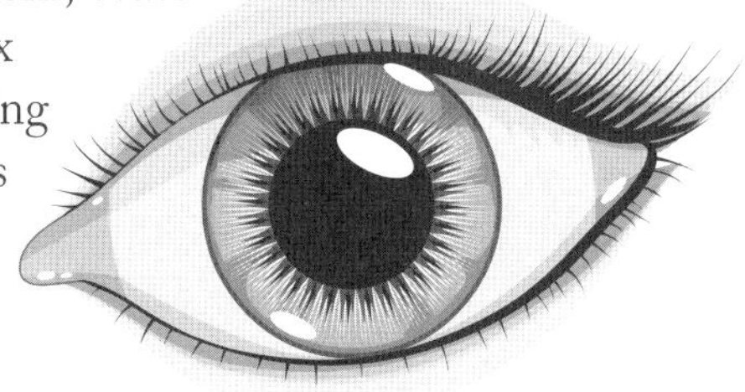

The Mayonnaise Jar & Coffee

When things in your life seem almost too much to handle, when 24 hours in a day are not enough, remember the mayonnaise jar and the coffee.

A professor stood before his philosophy class and had some items in front of him. When the class began, wordlessly, he picked up a very large and empty mayonnaise jar and proceeded to fill it with golf balls. He then asked the students if the jar was full. They agreed that it was.

The professor then picked up a box of pebbles and poured them into the jar. He shook the jar lightly. The pebbles rolled into the open areas between the golf balls. He then asked the students again if the jar was full. They agreed it was.

The professor next picked up a box of sand and poured it into the jar. Of course, the sand filled up everything else. He asked once more if the jar was full. The students responded with a unanimous "Yes."

The professor then produced two cups of coffee from under the table and poured the entire contents into the jar, effectively filling the empty space between the sand.

The students laughed. "Now," said the professor, as the laughter subsided, "I want you to recognize that this jar represents your life. The golf balls are the important things. Your family, your children, your faith, your health, your friends, and your favorite passions. Things that if everything else was lost and only they remained, your life would still be full. The pebbles are the other things that matter. Your job, your house, and your car. The sand is everything else. The small stuff. If you put the sand into the jar first," he continued, "there is no room for the pebbles or the golf balls. The same goes for life. If you spend all your time and energy on the small stuff, you will never have room for the things that are important to you. Pay attention to the things that are critical to your happiness. Play with your children. Take time to get medical checkups. Take your partner out to dinner. There will always be time to clean the house and fix the disposal. Take care of the golf balls first, the things that really matter. Set your priorities. The rest is just sand."

One of the students raised her hand and inquired as to what the coffee represented.

The professor smiled. "I'm glad you asked. It just goes to show you that no matter how full your life may seem, there's always room for a couple of cups of coffee with a friend."

Visibility

During a corn harvest I was reminded of how much visibility is limited by the standing corn. When the corn is harvested you see things that were hidden from view. This obscurity comes on gradual. As the corn grows we hardly realize how much our visibility is reduced. Then when it is eventually removed we are surprised by how much farther we can see again.

A similar thing happens with a cataract. Visibility is decreased in slow increments so that the person hardly notices what is happening. When the cataract is removed the person can hardly believe how much they were missing. It is the huge contrast from poor visibility to excellent visibility that makes a notable difference. When it is a slow progression it is not as easily recognized, and the condition may actually be much worse than we realize.

Visibility is important when we drive. We scrape the ice and snow off the windshield and run the defroster so we can see better. Sometimes objects such as signs or trees obscure our vision. I personally, prefer driving a vehicle where you sit up higher rather than a car for the simple reason that you have better visibility.

Businesses and manufacturers are always concerned about visibility. They want customers to think of them and call them for their services and products. To make themselves more visible they use a variety of methods.

They put an attractive sign in front of their place of business. They advertise their products and services in various media. They put their name on calendars and promotional products. The more they put their name in front of the consumer, the more visible they become. They want the consumer to perceive them as a good place to do business. It's all about perception and making themselves known.

How society in general views things has changed over the years. Things that were unacceptable are now accepted. Things that were not tolerated because they were considered indecent and immoral, are now met with a shrug of indifference. It is obvious by the trends we see in our society, that core values of morality, honesty, and integrity have lost ground in their rank of importance. Is it possible that, were we to show the contrast in one simple step, we would be appalled? Have dishonesty and immorality become cornfields and cataracts that obscure our vision of where society is headed? Has the gradual shift failed to set off alarms?

While society in general may have changed their view, God has not. Those core values are still as important as they always were. They were prescribed by God for the well being of society. The failure of men to hold them in high esteem does not change their level of importance. The good news is our visibility can be restored if we allow the master surgeon, God himself, to remove our cataracts. If we turn to Him, He will restore our vision. The fog and haze of a corrupt society will lift and our perception of honesty, integrity, and morality will become visibly different than the general view of society.

—M. Gingrich

What Will My Reward Be?

One day a fisherman was lying on a beautiful beach with his fishing pole propped up in the sand and his solitary line cast out into the sparkling blue surf. He was enjoying the warmth of the afternoon sun and the prospect of catching a fish.

About that time, a businessman came walking down the beach, trying to relieve some of the stress of his workday. He noticed the fisherman sitting on the beach and decided to find out why this fisherman was fishing instead of working hard to make a living for himself and his family. "You aren't going to catch many fish that way," said the businessman to the fisherman. "You should be working rather than lying on the beach!"

The fisherman looked up at the businessman, smiled and replied, "And what will my reward be?"

"Well, you could get bigger nets and catch more fish!" was the businessman's answer.

"And then what will my reward be?" asked the fisherman, still smiling.

The businessman replied, "You will make money and you'll be able to buy a boat, which will then result in larger catches of fish!"

"And then what will my reward be?" asked the fisherman again.

The businessman was beginning to get a little irritated with the fisherman's questions. "You can buy a bigger boat, and hire some people to work for you!" he said.

"And then what will my reward be?" repeated the fisherman.

The businessman was getting angry. "Don't you understand? You can build up a fleet of fishing boats, sail all over the world, and let all your employees catch fish for you!"

Once again the fisherman asked, "And then what will my reward be?"

The businessman was red with rage and shouted at the fisherman, "Don't you understand that you can become so rich that you will never have to work for your living again! You can spend all the rest of your days sitting on this beach, looking at the sunset. You won't have a care in the world!"

The fisherman, still smiling, looked up and said, "And what do you think I'm doing right now?"

So easy it is, to get caught up in going further and further and doing more and more, in the hopes of obtaining the ultimate reward in the end. The truth is…if you live every day to it's fullest with what you have, and do it from right where you are, every day can be rewarding!

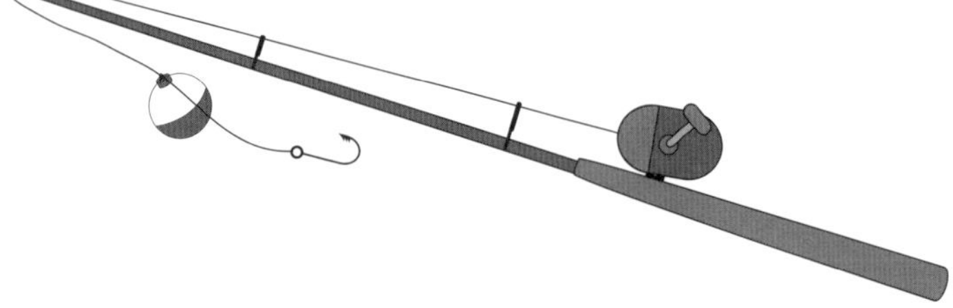

Index